Novell's Guide to Troubleshooting eDirectory™

Peter Kuo and Jim Henderson

Novell
PRESS™

Novell®

800 East 96th Street, Indianapolis, Indiana 46240 USA

Novell's Guide to Troubleshooting eDirectory

International Standard Book Number: 0-7897-3146-0

Library of Congress Catalog Card Number: 2003114715

Printed in the United States of America

First Printing: July 2004

07   06   05   04   4   3   2   1

Trademarks

All terms mentioned in this book that are known to be trademarks or service marks have been appropriately capitalized. Pearson cannot attest to the accuracy of this information. Use of a term in this book should not be regarded as affecting the validity of any trademark or service mark.

Warning and Disclaimer

Every effort has been made to make this book as complete and as accurate as possible, but no warranty or fitness is implied. The information provided is on an "as is" basis.

Bulk Sales

Pearson offers excellent discounts on this book when ordered in quantity for bulk purchases or special sales. For more information, please contact

U.S. Corporate and Government Sales

1-800-382-3419

corpsales@pearsontechgroup.com

For sales outside of the U.S., please contact

International Sales

1-317-428-3341

international@pearsontechgroup.com

Acquisitions Editor
Jenny L. Watson

Development Editor
Emmett Dulaney

Managing Editor
Charlotte Clapp

Project Editor
George E. Nedeff

Copy Editor
Kitty Jarrett

Indexer
Chris Barrick

Proofreader
Paula Lowell

Technical Editor
Warren Wyrostek

Publishing Coordinator
Vanessa Evans

Multimedia Developer
Dan Scherf

Book Designer
Gary Adair

Page Layout
Kelly Maish
Eric S. Miller

Contents At a Glance

Table of Contents

Part III Troubleshooting and Resolving Problems

Chapter 7 Diagnostic and Repair Tools 229

Chapter 8 eDirectory Data Recovery Tools 323

Chapter 9 Diagnosis and Recovery Techniques   391

Chapter 10 Programming for eDirectory   417

Chapter 11 Examples from the Real World   443

Part IV   Managing eDirectory to Prevent Problems

Chapter 12 eDirectory Management Tools   507

Chapter 13 eDirectory Health Checks   573

About the Authors

Peter Kuo is a Novell Master CNI, Master CNE, NCIP, CNS, and one of the very first CDEs. He co-authored the first edition of *Novell's Guide to Troubleshooting NDS* and has authored and co-authored more than a dozen NetWare, Unix, and other networking-related titles. Peter has been working with NetWare since the early 1980s and with NDS since NetWare 4.0 was still in beta. The information presented in this book is based on his hands-on experience in assisting many companies around the world implement NDS and eDirectory trees of various sizes. Peter has helped users from around the world in the capacity as a volunteer sysop for both the Novell Product Support Forums and Novell Developer Support Forums. Peter has also presented a number of NDS/eDirectory troubleshooting sessions at Novell BrainShare over the years.

Jim Henderson has worked for companies ranging from small corporations to Fortune 500 companies in IT capacities ranging from end user support to directory architecture, design, and implementation. Jim has been working with NDS and eDirectory since the release of NetWare 4.0, has co-authored two books on troubleshooting and resolving NDS/eDirectory issues, and is a 10-year veteran of the Novell Support Forums. Currently, Jim is employed as a technical instructor in the NSure practice of the Advanced Technical Training group at Novell, and he teaches courses across the United States on eDirectory design, implementation, and troubleshooting.

Dedication

This book is dedicated to all the service, assistance, and working dogs, including the seldom-mentioned military dogs, in the world. Thank you for making our lives better.

Acknowledgements

Writing a book about troubleshooting Novell eDirectory requires not only knowing the current information that needs to be put into print but also knowing the people who can either provide or nudge us in the direction of the correct information. Without the people behind the NDS/eDirectory codes and our backline support contacts at Novell Product Support Forums and Novell Developer Support Forums, much of the information in this book would not have come to light.

We appreciate the backing we received from the various groups at Novell. In particular, we thank Paul Reiner (who told us NDS was a "slam-dunk" so many years ago), DeAnne Higley, Gary Hein, and especially David Smith, for their insights into the inner workings of the earlier versions of NDS. Giant hugs go to Pam Robello and Jenn Bitondo, our backline contacts at Novell Product Support Forums, for having *much* patience in answering many of our stupid questions ("can't we just FDISK it instead of doing it the long way using DSRepair?") and being sympathetic when listening to all our whining ("why does this stupid thing do that?!").

We're grateful that Kim Groneman (Chief Grasshopper Herder, Novell Product Support Forums) and John Cox (Chief Grasshopper Herder, Novell Developer Support Forums) tolerated our disappearance from the forums for days at a time when we were busy meeting the book schedule. Deep appreciation goes to our fellow sysops, both in the Novell Product Support and Developer Support Forums, for putting up with our lack of appearance and picking up the slack during this project.

The folks at Novell Press who were involved with this project provided much-needed guidance throughout the project. Emmett Dulaney, our development editor, did an outstanding job in providing the much-needed prodding, shaping, and formatting of the book. Additional thanks to George Nedeff and Kitty Jarrett for keeping the project moving and on track for us. It has been a number of years since the first edition of *Novell's Guide to Troubleshooting NDS* was written. However, this second edition, which contains updated information about eDirectory and cross-platform coverage, would never have gotten off the ground if not for our acquisitions editor, Jenny Watson, for recognizing the need for this book and for finding Warren Wyrostek as our technical editor. If it weren't for Warren's careful combing through the manuscript for errors and scrawling detailed comments and helpful suggestions, the technical content of this book would resemble Swiss cheese!

Peter would like to thank to his dad and mom for stocking the fridge with brain food and Coke for his late-night (or early-morning, depending on your time zone) writing marathons and not just sliding pieces of cold pizza under the office door! He also thanks SAB for not calling him a "glutton for punishment" this time around because he didn't (forgot to?) tell her about writing this book until it's done. Finally, Peter appreciates Tasha (`www.unionvilledogs.ca/tasha.htm`), his beloved Golden Retriever, for tagging along for long walks in the knee-deep snow when he needed to do some thinking and tirelessly listening to all his complaints about book deadlines. (Here's a cookie, Tash!)

We Want to Hear from You

As the reader of this book, *you* are our most important critic and commentator. We value your opinion and want to know what we're doing right, what we could do better, what areas you'd like to see us publish in, and any other words of wisdom you're willing to pass our way.

You can email or write me directly to let me know what you did or didn't like about this book—as well as what we can do to make our books stronger.

Please note that I cannot help you with technical problems related to the topic of this book, and that due to the high volume of mail I receive, I might not be able to reply to every message.

When you write, please be sure to include this book's title and author as well as your name and phone or email address. I will carefully review your comments and share them with the author and editors who worked on the book.

Email: feedback@novellpress.com

Mail: Mark Taber
            Associate Publisher
            Novell Press/Pearson Education
            800 East 96th Street
            Indianapolis, IN 46240 USA

Reader Services

For more information about this book or others from Novell Press, visit our Web site at **www.novellpress.com**. Type the ISBN (excluding hyphens) or the title of the book in the Search box to find the book you're looking for.

Introduction

In 1993 Novell became the first company to integrate directory services—NetWare Directory Services (NDS), later renamed Novell Directory Services because of its cross-platform support, and now known as eDirectory—with its NetWare server operating system. Since then, NDS has been ported to the major enterprise server platforms, and today eDirectory remains a dominant leader as a general-purpose enterprise directory in the LAN market, deployed worldwide in 80% of Fortune 500 companies, such as CNN, Yahoo!, and Lufthansa Airlines.

Novell eDirectory is a multiple-platform, distributed database that stores information about the hardware and software resources available on your network. It provides network users, administrators, and application developers seamless, global access to all network resources. eDirectory also provides a flexible directory database schema, unmatched network security, and a consistent cross-platform development environment.

eDirectory uses objects to represent all network resources and maintains them in a hierarchical directory tree. By pointing, clicking, and dragging, you can make changes to directory trees without downing network servers. You can easily manage multiple trees, maintain and repair the networkwide directory from a client workstation, and automatically update distributed eDirectory replicas on all supported operating system platforms, including NetWare, Windows, Solaris, Linux, AIX, and HP/UX.

NDS/eDirectory is the core of NetWare-based networks and is also widely used in Lightweight Directory Access Protocol (LDAP) directory implementations for identity management on both NetWare and non-NetWare server platforms. No matter what your purpose is, if you implement NDS/eDirectory in your networking environment, you need to have a firm handle on how it works and know what actions to take in the event of a problem. What's more, good network administrators take proactive actions to prevent trouble from developing in the first place. This book is a comprehensive troubleshooting guide for Novell eDirectory.

You'll find this book to be a rich and definitive source of information for eDirectory troubleshooting methodologies. No matter the size of your NDS tree, you'll find this book to be indispensable. Topics covered in this book range from the fundamentals of

Novell eDirectory and its new features, to troubleshooting, to proactively managing the internal operations of eDirectory. The information presented in this book will help you maintain and troubleshoot all aspects of Novell eDirectory.

Who This Book Is For

This book is written for all LAN administrators, system administrators, consultants, resellers, and any others who design, implement, and support NDS/eDirectory networks.

Using this book, you will learn basic to complex concepts and techniques for diagnosing and repairing eDirectory problems. Whether your interest lies solely in understanding how NDS background processes function or in knowing how to deal with specific NDS problems, this book is the definitive source. All versions of NDS, up to and including eDirectory 8.7.3 (which is the latest at the time of this writing), are covered.

How This Book Is Organized

This book is organized into four logical parts:

- ▶ Part I, "eDirectory Fundamentals," includes an overview of Novell eDirectory basics, such as objects, partitions, and time synchronization. Part I also provides a comprehensive look at Novell Directory Services classes and how these classes are used to build objects in the directory tree. Having an understanding of NDS objects is a prerequisite to utilizing the full potential of NDS/eDirectory and the information in the rest of this book.

- ▶ Part II, "Understanding the Error Codes and eDirectory Processes," describes in great details the internal operations of eDirectory and associated error codes.

- ▶ Part III, "Troubleshooting and Resolving Problems," provides a thorough discussion of troubleshooting Novell eDirectory using various tools and utilities included with NetWare/eDirectory and available from third-party vendors. This part covers how to use the DSRepair, DSTrace, NDS iMonitor, and other utilities during troubleshooting operations.

  In addition, this part covers NDS/eDirectory data recovery procedures and techniques, including the combination of various tools to diagnose, troubleshoot, and resolve problems. This section concludes by applying the tools and techniques discussed to real-world examples.

▶ Part IV, "Managing eDirectory to Prevent Problems," rounds out the many day-to-day aspects of NDS that you need to know about in order to proactively prevent problems. Topics include eDirectory health checking, performance tuning, and providing a comprehensive eDirectory security plan for your network. By proactively managing your NDS tree, you can prevent many problems; this part shows you how.

The four appendixes in this book include valuable information that you can use as a handy reference:

▶ Appendix A, "eDirectory Error Codes," provides an exhaustive listing of all the NDS/eDirectory error codes and their explanations. This list of error codes helps you identify problems and determine resolution steps.

▶ Appendix B, "DS Verbs," provides information on the NDS verbs used by DSTrace.

▶ Appendix C, "eDirectory Classes, Objects, and Attributes," contains eDirectory schema information on *all* the object classes and attribute definitions found in eDirectory 8.7.3.

▶ Appendix D, "eDirectory Resources," lists resources used during the development of this book—third-party software products, good NDS resources found on the Internet, and other publications that cover related subject matter.

Special Features in This Book

All the information and techniques presented in this book have been gathered from hands-on, real-world experiences learned from working with customers from around the world. Being SysOps for the Novell Product Support Forums (`http://support.novell.com/forums`) and Novell Developer Support Forums (`http://developer.novell.com/ndk/devforums.htm`) exposed us to a wide range of NDS/eDirectory implementations and issues. In this book, we share with you a selected number of the most frequently encountered DS problems and steps toward troubleshooting and fixing them.

eDirectory Fundamentals

The Four Basics of eDirectory Troubleshooting

The purpose of network troubleshooting is the timely restoration of essential services. Troubleshooting is part science, part art, and part pure luck. Many attempts have been made to reduce troubleshooting to a set of procedures and flowcharts; however, given the diversity of problems, no one has yet come up with a procedure or flowchart that covers every possible situation.

The key to any successful troubleshooting is to develop the ability to break down a problem ("it doesn't work") into its elemental parts ("it works when I do this but doesn't when I do that"). This ability is the cumulation of personal experience and knowledge gained by exchanging war stories with others who have "been there, done that, and gotten the T-shirt." A combination of knowledge and experience (and some dumb luck doesn't hurt either) helps you to develop an efficient on-the-spot strategy to tackle each problem. You can apply this divide-and-conquer technique to troubleshooting eDirectory problems.

REAL WORLD

The Troubleshooting Process

A typical troubleshooting model consists of these five steps:

1. Gather information.
2. Develop a plan of attack.
3. Execute the plan.
4. Evaluate the results; go back to step 1 if necessary.
5. Document the solution.

The material presented in this book focuses on the first three steps of the troubleshooting process: Gather information, develop a plan of attack, and execute the plan.

In order to be able to break down an eDirectory error into its elemental parts, it is necessary to have an understanding of how eDirectory functions. Regardless of the nature and cause of an eDirectory issue, there are four rules you can follow to make your eDirectory troubleshooting efforts much easier. This chapter briefly outlines and explains each of the four rules. The rest of this book covers in detail the various information and tools that you need to troubleshoot and resolve eDirectory errors. Chapter 11, "Examples from the Real World," in particular, illustrates how you can use the knowledge presented in this book to solve a number of real-world eDirectory issues.

TIP

The four basics outlined here are not specific to troubleshooting eDirectory issues. You can easily modify them to resolve other problems, such as NetWare operating system ABENDs or a network communication problem.

A solid understanding and reasonable application of the following four eDirectory troubleshooting doctrines will assist you in quickly and efficiently identifying the cause of and restore any disruptions in your eDirectory tree:

▶ Don't panic.

▶ Understand the error codes and eDirectory processes.

▶ Troubleshoot and resolve the problem.

▶ Proactively manage eDirectory to prevent problems.

NOTE

eDirectory is the current name of the directory services (DS) product from Novell, Inc. In the past, the product was generally referred to as NDS (which stood for NetWare Directory Services, and later on, Novell Directory Services, when it was made available for operating system platforms other than NetWare). The concepts and much of the information presented in this book are applicable to both eDirectory and previous versions of NDS. However, some of the information (such as filtered replica) and tools (such as iManager) discussed in this book apply only with eDirectory. Where that is the case, every attempt is made to note this.

Don't Panic

When an essential network service is down, you are generally under pressure to restore it—quickly. When the service is eDirectory, the pressure is much higher because it can potentially affect all your users; however, the first rule of dealing with eDirectory issues is to be patient and *don't panic*.

Often, the eDirectory errors you encounter are transitional, and eDirectory self-heals; furthermore, sometimes the eDirectory error condition is a secondary result of other network-related problems. For example, a -625 (unable to communicate) error is not a true eDirectory error but a by-product of a network communication problem. So, without first trying to understand the cause of the eDirectory error, if you start performing eDirectory-related "corrections," such as running DSRepair needlessly, you could *cause* eDirectory errors where there weren't really any to start with.

Many current administrators have worked with NetWare since the days of the NetWare 3 bindery. Certain actions could be easily performed with the bindery, but you can't and shouldn't treat eDirectory the same way. You need to keep in mind that eDirectory is implemented as a *globally distributed, replicated, loosely consistent, hierarchical* database. The primary challenge in maintaining a globally distributed database is keeping all the information up-to-date when changes are made. For example, when you create a new user in a container, the change must be propagated to all servers that hold a replica of that container; however, the loose-consistency nature of eDirectory means that the eDirectory database is not necessarily in strict synchronization all the time.

Because of the loosely consistent nature of eDirectory, when major changes are made, such as moving a Server object or splitting a partition, it can take some time for the changes to propagate to all replicas. Therefore, there can be periods of time during which the information in one replica is different from that in another replica. But the information held by the replicas *does* eventually converge to an identical state, making eDirectory consistent once again. Because eDirectory is replicated, you shouldn't perform any partition-related operations when any of the servers holding a replica of the affected partition(s) are not available. If you do, you'll get eDirectory into a *stuck state,* where it is unable to complete the operation because it can't communicate the change to some servers.

As the old sayings go, "haste makes waste" and "patience is a virtue." You should *always* allow eDirectory sufficient time to perform what it is designed to do: replicate data without flooding the network with eDirectory traffic.

Understanding the Error Codes and eDirectory Processes

Frequently, in order to keep an application's file size (and thus, memory and disk space requirements) down, the programmer opts to substitute comprehensive error and debugging messages with cryptic error codes. For example, instead of telling you, "The eDirectory object you're searching for doesn't exist in the current context," an error code of -601 is displayed. If you don't have ready access to these error codes, your effort in determining the cause of the eDirectory error can be greatly hampered.

In addition to knowing the meanings of the various error codes, you also need to understand the eDirectory processes that are involved when an error code is generated. Some could be due to *legal* error conditions ("false-positives"), suggesting that there is not an actual error, while others indicate real error conditions. For instance, if you have enabled DSTrace at the server console with the **+ERR** flag, you may see a -601 error when an application is searching for an object in multiple containers. In such a case, they are legal errors that are to be expected. On the other hand, if you receive a -618 (eDirectory database inconsistent) error, it could mean real trouble; therefore, it is essential to know what the various error codes mean and to understand the processes that generate them.

NOTE   You can find some of the most commonly encountered eDirectory error codes and eDirectory processes discussed, respectively, in Chapters 5, "eDirectory/NDS Error Codes Explained," and 6, "Understanding Common eDirectory Processes." A list of all published eDirectory error codes and their explanations is presented in Appendix A, "eDirectory Error Codes."

An important side benefit of developing this understanding is your ability to determine whether a problem is indeed eDirectory related or whether it's caused by other sources, such as network communication faults. This ability can save you from going on a wild goose chase.

Troubleshoot and Resolve the Problem

After you've determined the cause of eDirectory trouble and formulated an attack plan, it's time to select your weapons. eDirectory ships with a wide range of utilities, such as DSRepair, iManager, and DSTrace, which you can use to troubleshoot and fix your eDirectory tree. Also, there are a number of third-party tools that help fill the gap in areas that Novell-supplied utilities don't cover. You need to know the capabilities of these tools, however, and know when to use the one best suited for the task. This is discussed in more detail in Chapters 7, "Diagnostic and Repair Tools," and 8, "eDirectory Data Recovery Tools."

Proactively Manage eDirectory to Prevent Problems

As you probably know, troubleshooting is a *reactive network management* process: You're on the defensive and are trying to stop the bleeding. Seasoned network managers tell you that the best network management tactic is a proactive one: You should take actions to actively and properly manage your eDirectory so that problems don't occur in the first place. Treat the health of your eDirectory tree as you would your family's health: *Prevention is better than cure*.

Refer to Chapters 12, "eDirectory Management Tools," 13, "eDirectory Health Checks," and 14, "eDirectory Management Techniques," for details on proactive eDirectory management tips and information. Of particular interest to security-conscious network administrators is Chapter 15, "Effectively Setting Up eDirectory Security;" that chapter covers various techniques used to detect intruders and minimize eDirectory security risks.

Summary

This chapter introduces four eDirectory troubleshooting doctrines that can assist you in quickly and efficiently identifying the cause of and restore any disruptions in your eDirectory tree:

- ▶ Don't panic.

- ▶ Understand the error codes and eDirectory processes.

- ▶ Troubleshoot and resolve the problem.

- ▶ Proactively manage eDirectory to prevent problems.

You'll find in-depth discussion of these topics in the remainder of this book. Before we go into them, however, Chapter 2, "eDirectory Basics," provides a quick review of eDirectory terminology and basics that you should know and be familiar with before proceeding with the rest of this book.

eDirectory Basics

Troubleshooting and managing eDirectory can be difficult if you do not have a good grasp on how eDirectory works. In preparation for the advanced information presented in this book, you need to have a baseline understanding of certain terms and concepts. This chapter provides that baseline, including information on the following:

- ▶ A brief history of NDS/eDirectory and its versioning

- ▶ The eDirectory database structure

- ▶ Partition and replica types

- ▶ Bindery services

- ▶ Time synchronization

- ▶ DHost

- ▶ Service Advertising Protocol (SAP) and Service Location Protocol (SLP)

- ▶ Object attribute names versus schema attribute names

As more and more applications are starting to include Lightweight Directory Access Protocol (LDAP) as an option to access directory services (DS), it is essential to also include LDAP terminology in your knowledge repertoire. Also discussed in this chapter is the integration of NDS and LDAP, and some of the new LDAP server features introduced for eDirectory versions 8.5 and higher.

> **NOTE** Much of the information presented in this chapter is also applicable to versions of NDS prior to eDirectory 8.5. Version-specific features are noted where applicable.

A Brief History of NDS/ eDirectory and Its Versioning

The meaning of the acronym NDS has changed a number of times since it was first introduced with NetWare 4.0. When Novell initially introduced NDS as a component of NetWare 4.0 in 1993, NDS stood for *NetWare Directory Service* because at that time NDS was available *only* on NetWare. Working with third-party vendors such as IBM, Hewlett-Packard (HP), Microsoft, and Sun, in 1999 Novell made NDS available for a number of different platforms:

- ▶ NDS for Windows NT
- ▶ NetWare Services for UnixWare 7
- ▶ NDS for Solaris
- ▶ NetWare 4.1 Services for HP 9000
- ▶ Novell Network Services for AIX
- ▶ Novell Network Services for OS/390

Accordingly, in 1999 the meaning for the NDS acronym was changed to *Novell Directory Services*. Later in the same year, Novell introduced the next generation of NDS, NDS 8 for NetWare 5 servers. Shortly after that, Novell split NDS off from NetWare into a separate standalone product, with a new name—eDirectory (which essentially is a rebranding of NDS 8).

eDirectory versions 8.5 and higher are platform independent and exist for a number of operating systems, such as Solaris, Linux, Tru64, Windows NT/2000, and, of course, NetWare. NetWare 6.0 shipped with eDirectory 8.6, and NetWare 6.5 shipped with eDirectory 8.7.1.

> **NOTE** During the 2002–2003 time frame, Novell consolidated the code base for eDirectory 8.7 so that the same version runs on NetWare, Linux, Solaris, Windows NT/2000, AIX, and HP/UX. Support for Tru64 was dropped starting in eDirectory 8.6.

Confused about the naming? The confusion between NDS 8, eDirectory, and eDirectory 8.x stems from the fact that eDirectory 8.5 was conceived long before eDirectory (NDS 8.x) ever reached a patch level of 8.73 (or higher). Despite these versioning conflicts, eDirectory 8.x is a new product and is an extension of the feature set originally released in 1999 with eDirectory (NDS 8.x). So how do you determine if you have NDS 8, or eDirectory, or eDirectory 8.5/8.6/8.7? One way is to look at the version numbering of the NDS module.

When NDS was introduced, Novell Engineering used the industry-standard version-numbering convention, such as "version 2.96," in version-stamping the DS module files. At the same time, it used a variant of standard version numbering (296 for version 2.96, 489 for version 4.89, and so on) to refer to the same version in print or in conversation. For instance, `DS.NLM` for NetWare 4.10 would report "version 4.89," but when you were communicating with Novell or looking at the Novell Support Knowledge Base, it would be referred to as "DS 489." By the time NetWare 5.0 was released, NDS was up to the "700 series," while NetWare 4.11 and 4.2 continued with the "600 series" of version numbering. Next came NDS 8/eDirectory. They were given the "800 series" numbering. But Novell broke the mold when eDirectory 8.5 was released; its numbering is not the "850 series" as you might expect, but 85.xx! What is more annoying is that eDirectory 8.6 on NetWare 6.0 reports a version number in the form 10110.20!

REAL
WORLD

Versions of Novell eDirectory

Because of the versioning confusion, Novell eDirectory Development and Marketing have finally agreed to have two different version strings for their modules, and eDirectory 8.6 is the first product to use this new versioning process. For eDirectory 8.6, the Marketing version string will be "eDirectory 8.6.0," and the Development version string will be "10110.20." Both of these version strings are displayed when you type MODULES DS.NLM at the server console prompt.

The Marketing string is pretty easy to understand: *product major_rev.minor_rev.update.* **The Development version string, however, is a bit more complicated. The breakdown is as follows:** *release_number_(1-4293)subrelease number_(01-99)release source_(1-4=Product or 5-9=CPR).build_number_(001-999)build_source_(0, 5, 6-26)].*

So the Development string 10110.20 indicates release number 1 (Dove), the first subrelease (01), released by the Product group (1), build number 2, built by Engineering (0).

Although this is still a little confusing, in the long run, the new versioning will be able to provide more definitive information as to what DS version you are running and where you got it.

PART I eDirectory Foundations

The seemingly inconsistent numbering system is a major source of confusion for network administrators when they're trying to figure out whether they are running NDS 8/eDirectory or eDirectory 8.x. For instance, NDS 8/eDirectory reports (via `NDIR DS.NLM /VER` or `MODULES DS`, for example) the version of `DS.NLM` as 8.77 when you are running NDS 8. Common logic would suggest that because `DS.NLM` v8.77 is numerically higher than eDirectory 8.5, you are running "the latest." Unfortunately, this is not the case.

NOTE Novell is now using the terms *NDS 8.xx* to refer to the original eDirectory product, *NDS* to refer to the non-cross-platform versions of NDS, and *eDirectory 8.x* to refer to the newer product.

NOTE The term *NDS* is also used to refer to Novell's DS technology in general. The context in which NDS is used should not cause any confusion if reference is made to the technology or to legacy versions of DS.NLM.

Table 2.1 lists the version number associated with each different version of NDS to help you determine what version of NDS/eDirectory you are running.

TABLE 2.1 **NDS and eDirectory Version Numbering**

YEAR RELEASED	MARKETING NAME	DS MODULE VERSION	OPERATING SYSTEM SUPPORTED
1993	NetWare Directory Services	v2.xx–v5.xx	NetWare 4.0x–4.10
1999	Novell Directory Services	v6.xx (NDS 6)	NetWare 4.11 and 4.2, HP 9000, S/390, AIX, Solaris, UnixWare, and Windows NT
1999	Novell Directory Services	v7.xx (NDS 7)	NetWare 5.0 and 5.1
1999	NDS 8	v8.1x (NDS 8)	NetWare 5.0 and 5.1
1999	eDirectory or eDirectory 8	v8.3x (NDS 8)	NetWare 5.0 and 5.1, Solaris, Windows NT, and Linux
2000	eDirectory 8.5.*x*	v85.xx	NetWare 5.0 and 5.1, Solaris, Windows NT/2000, Tru64, and Linux

Table 2.1   Continued

YEAR RELEASED	MARKETING NAME	DS MODULE VERSION	OPERATING SYSTEM SUPPORTED
2001	eDirectory 8.6.*x*	v10110.xx	NetWare 5.1 and 6.x, Solaris, Windows NT/2000, and Linux
2002	eDirectory 8.7.0	v10410.xx	NetWare 5.1 and 6.x, Solaris, Windows NT/2000, AIX, and Linux
2003	eDirectory 8.7.1	v10510.xx (for instance, NetWare and Linux report 1051.64 but Windows reports 10510.65)	NetWare 5.1 and 6.x, Solaris, Windows NT/2000, AIX, and Linux
2003	eDirectory 8.7.2	v10512.19 (version not publicly released but was used in Novell Nterprise Linux Services [NNLS] beta)	NetWare 5.1 and 6.x, Solaris, Windows NT/2000, HP/UX, AIX, and Linux
2003	eDirectory 8.7.3	v10550.98	NetWare 5.1 and 6.x, Solaris, Windows NT/2000, HP/UX, AIX, and Linux

---

TIP

A list of specific version numbers assigned to eDirectory 8.6 and above (including patches) can be found in Novell Technical Information Document (TID) #10066623.

The most accurate way to determine the version of NDS you are currently running is to query the DS module when it is running. For a NetWare server, you can use the console commands **VERSION** or **MODULE DS**. The following is an example of output from the **MODULE** command:

```
NETWARE61_SERVER: module ds
DS.NLM
  Loaded from [SYS:\SYSTEM\]
  (Address Space = OS)
  Novell eDirectory Version 8.7.1 SMP
```

```
Version 10510.64 July 11, 2003
Copyright 1993-2003, Novell, Inc.  All Rights Reserved.
  ➥Patents Pending.
```

Alternatively, you can use `DSREPAIR.NLM`. It reports the version of DS at the top of the screen (using the Development string). `NDIR.EXE` run from a workstation could report inconclusive version information. For instance, the following is the output from scanning `DS.NLM` for NetWare 6.5:

```
F:\>ndir \system\ds.nlm /ver
NETWARE_65_A/SYS:SYSTEM


    DS.NLM:
    Version Novell eDirectory Version 8.7.1 SMP
    Copyright 1993-2003 Novell, Inc.  All rights reserved.
      ➥Patents Pending.
    Checksum is BA00 F7C1 2553 3F47 9F4F 43C2
```

Notice that the Development version string is not displayed in this output. If you examine the file using Windows Explorer, however, both the Marketing and Development strings are reported.

On non-NetWare platforms (such as Windows 2000 or Solaris), you will likely already be running at least NDS 8/eDirectory, if not eDirectory 8.5 or higher. On Windows NT/2000, you can either launch `dsrepair.dlm` or look at the Agent tab of `ds.dlm`'s configuration screen, as shown in Figure 2.1. On Unix/Linux, you use the `ndsstat` command to determine the exact version number:

```
[RH8-VM root]# ndsstat
Tree Name: RH9-NDSTREE
Server Name: .CN=RH9-VM.O=Testing.T=RH8-NDSTREE.
Binary Version: 10510.64
Root Most Entry Depth: 0
Product Version: NDS/Unix - NDS eDirectory v8.7.1 [DS]
```

FIGURE 2.1
Checking the version of eDirectory running on Windows 2000.

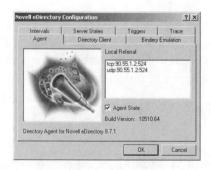

The eDirectory Database Structure

This section discusses the components that make up the eDirectory database structure. For any kind of database, there exists a set of rules that govern the type of information the database can contain and possible relationships between the different data items contained within. This set of rules is known as the database *schema*.

In simple terms, eDirectory's schema is a set of rules that stipulate the type of objects that can exist in an eDirectory tree, the possible locations of those objects in the tree, and the information that can and must be maintained about the object. Each object belongs to an *object class* that specifies which *attributes* (that is, types of information) can be associated with the object. Every attribute is based on a set of attribute types that are, in turn, based on a standard set of attribute *syntaxes*.

Base Schema and Operational Schema

REAL WORLD

The term *base schema* refers to the built-in set of classes and attributes shipped with the eDirectory product itself (that is, it does not include extensions added by other Novell products, such as DirXML or BorderManager). Depending on the situation, the base schema may be extended to include new classes and new attributes for objects. These new definitions, however, must be defined in terms of the existing syntaxes; defining new syntaxes is not allowed. The user-added classes may be removed when they are no longer used, but base classes cannot be removed or modified.

The term *operational schema* refers to the set of schema rules that are *required* to be present for NDS/eDirectory to function correctly. If any of the operational schema definitions are deleted or otherwise damaged, DS will fail to function properly.

The eDirectory schema controls not only the structure of individual objects but also the relationship among objects within the DS tree. The schema rules allow some objects to contain other subordinate objects. Thus the schema gives structure to the DS tree. Furthermore, eDirectory implements an object-oriented structure made up of objects that can receive attributes from other objects; this idea is referred to as *inheritance* in object-oriented paradigms.

Classes

A *class* in eDirectory is a definition for an object type. Classes you are likely to be most familiar with are the `User` class, `Print Queue` class, and the `NCP Server` class. Each class definition contains a list of properties (known as *attributes*) that are used to describe the class. In essence, the class definition is a blueprint or set of rules for how to make an object of a specified class.

There are three categories of classes: the effective class, the non-effective class, and the auxiliary class.

An *effective class* is a class that can be used to make objects that actually show up in the eDirectory tree. `User`, `Print Queue`, and `NCP Server` are examples of effective classes; if you search the eDirectory tree using NetWare Administrator or ConsoleOne, you can find objects that are of these types.

A *non-effective class* is a class whose objects do not appear in the eDirectory tree but is used to build other non-effective and effective classes. This allows classes to simply inherit the class information from the non-effective superclass rather than repetitively define it. Examples of non-effective classes are the `Person`, `Queue`, and `Server` classes, as illustrated in Figure 2.2.

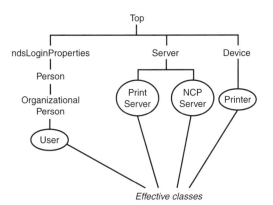

FIGURE 2.2
An example
of the NDS/
eDirectory class
hierarchy.

You can use NDS Snoop to manage and examine your schema. You can download a copy of Snoop from www.novell.com/coolsolutions/nds/features/a_ndssnoop_nds.html. Because NDS Snoop can modify the schema and NDS objects, you need to be careful when using it. Figure 2.3 shows the class hierarchy of the User class, as viewed in NDS Snoop.

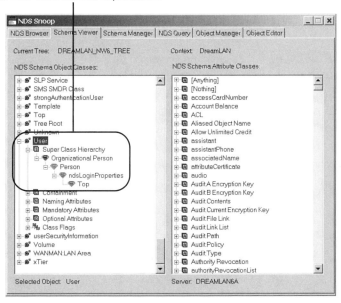

FIGURE 2.3
Viewing class
hierarchy by
using NDS
Snoop.

NOTE

In essence, a non-effective class can be considered a placeholder for a group of attributes. A non-effective class cannot be used to create objects but can be specified as a class from which other classes can inherit attributes.

All objects of a given effective class carry the same set of properties associated with the effective class and its parent classes (which are referred to as *superclasses*). There are, however, circumstances in which a set of attributes needs to be added to only a subset of objects of a given class rather than to all the objects of that class. This is where auxiliary classes come in.

> **NOTE**
>
> **The base schema defines the following non-effective classes:**
> - ndsLoginProperties
> - Partition
> - Resource
> - Server
>
> **Although Top is flagged as an effective class, no object can be created by using the Top class.**

> **NOTE**
>
> **Starting with NetWare 5, the schema class Tree Root (T=) is used to indicate the top of the tree. Previously, this was referred to as [Root]. Therefore, you will find documentation and utilities still making references to [Root], especially when discussing NDS partitioning and related concepts.**

An *auxiliary class* is a class whose set of attributes can be added to particular eDirectory object instances rather than to an entire class of objects. For example, a network monitoring application could extend the schema of your eDirectory tree to include an On-Call Pager auxiliary class. You could then extend individual User objects with the attributes of the On-Call Pager class as needed by adding the auxiliary class to the Object Class attribute of the User object. When the auxiliary class is added, the object inherits all the attributes of the auxiliary class while retaining all its own attributes. When the auxiliary class is removed from the object, the auxiliary class attributes are removed from the object, and the object no longer has access to those attributes.

The following are some rules for using auxiliary classes:

- The Object class flag should only set the Auxiliary class flag.
- Auxiliary classes cannot have the Container flag set.
- Auxiliary classes cannot have the Effective class flag set.
- Creation fails if rules are not followed.
- Auxiliary classes can have mandatory attributes, optional attributes, or both. (DS will not add an auxiliary class to an object without values for all mandatory attributes.)

▸ Auxiliary classes are not required to have superclasses but may contain superclasses.

▸ Auxiliary classes should not contain Top as a superclass or define containment.

▸ Auxiliary classes and superclasses are combined.

▸ Attributes of an auxiliary class and a superclass are deleted if the auxiliary class is removed.

▸ Auxiliary classes can define naming attributes. (If an auxiliary class attribute is used to name an object, the object must be renamed to use a non-auxiliary class attribute before the auxiliary class can be removed.)

WARNING

When additional attributes are added to class definitions shipped with eDirectory (which are known as *base* classes), these extensions *cannot* be removed. On the other hand, you can remove an auxiliary class definition from the schema when you no longer need it. For instance, if you added an On-Call Pager attribute directly to the User class, you *cannot* remove this attribute at a later time. If you have defined an auxiliary class that contains this On-Call Pager attribute and associated this auxiliary class to existing User objects, however, you can later delete the auxiliary class when no more User objects are using it.

NOTE

Auxiliary classes are supported only by NDS 8 and higher. That is to say, NetWare 4.x (which runs NDS 6) and NetWare 5.x servers running NDS 7 do *not* support auxiliary classes. Objects containing auxiliary classes will be displayed as Unknown objects (but they are still known on the servers running NDS 8 or higher).

TIP

If you have a mixed-NDS-version environment that includes NDS 6 and 7, you need to ensure that you are using the latest DS.NLM updates. You can also refer to TID #10083622 for more information.

Every class in eDirectory has at least one superclass (as illustrated in Figure 2.2), with the exception of the Top class. Top is where all classes start their inheritance. This means all classes in eDirectory contain some attributes that are common to all—those defined in the Top class. Some of these common attributes are ACL, Back Link, CA Private Key, CA Public Key, Equivalent to Me, GUID, and Revision.

NOTE   Appendix C, "eDirectory Classes, Objects, and Attributes," lists some of the most commonly encountered object class and base attribute definitions found in an NDS/eDirectory tree.

The following are some of the schema changes made since NDS/eDirectory 8:

▶ ndsLoginProperties is a new non-effective class. It contains all the attributes required for an object to authenticate to the DS tree.

▶ The Person and Organizational Person classes are now effective classes, and because they now inherit the required login attributes, Person and Organizational Person objects can log in to the DS tree.

▶ The ability for Country, Locality, Organization, and Organizational Unit class objects to contain domain objects comes with the installation of NDS 8 and higher. The domain (not to be confused with Windows NT or Active Directory domain) and dcObject classes and the dc attribute were introduced to support RFC 2247, "Using Domains in LDAP/X.500 Distinguished Names."

domain objects can contain all the leaf objects in the operational schema. The ability for domain objects to contain container objects such as Country, Locality, Organization, or Organizational Unit, however, does not come automatically. This functionality must be added to the schema by running the Optional Schema Enhancement option (see Figure 2.4) in DSRepair, which is for eDirectory 8.5 or higher.

FIGURE 2.4
Extending schema containment functionality.

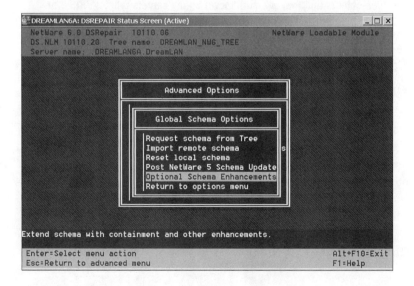

Attributes

Attributes are used to define the various aspects of an object. Examples of attributes associated with a `User` class object are be `Surname`, `Full Name`, and `Network Address`. Each of these holds a piece of information relevant to the `User` class object in question.

Novell documentation and utilities use the terms *property* and *attribute* interchangeably to mean the same thing.

It is important to understand other aspects of attributes. The first of these aspects is the idea of a mandatory attribute. A *mandatory attribute* is an attribute that is required in order for the object to be created; if a mandatory attribute is missing, the object cannot be created. The `Surname` attribute, for example, is required when creating a user. That is to say, if you do not provide the user's surname, you will be unable to create the `User` object.

With many of the DS-aware utilities, when one or more of the mandatory attribute values have not been supplied, the Create or OK button is grayed out, preventing you from creating the object.

TIP

Loss of a mandatory attribute after creation of the object causes the object's class attribute to be changed to `Unknown`. Figure 2.5 shows ConsoleOne with several `Unknown` objects in the tree. The circles with the question marks in the figure are yellow, making the `Unknown` class objects easy to spot.

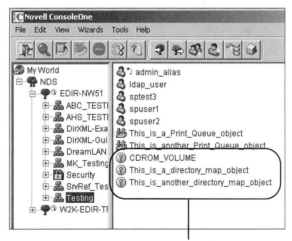

These are objects of the Unknown class

FIGURE 2.5
An example of Unknown class objects in ConsoleOne.

There is a second type of object seen in NetWare Administrator, ConsoleOne, and other management utilities that many people mistake for an Unknown class object. This type of object appears either as a white square with a black question mark inside it in NetWare Administrator (see Figure 2.6), a cube with a black question mark beside it (see Figure 2.7), or a white dog-eared rectangle with a black question mark inside it in NDS iMonitor (see Figure 2.8). This particular type of object is *not* of the Unknown class but means that the necessary snap-in component for NetWare Administrator, ConsoleOne, or NDS iMonitor/iManager is not available, and consequently the object cannot be administered with the tools. Such objects are referred to as *unmanaged* or *unmanageable* objects.

FIGURE 2.6

An example of unmanageable objects in NetWare Administrator.

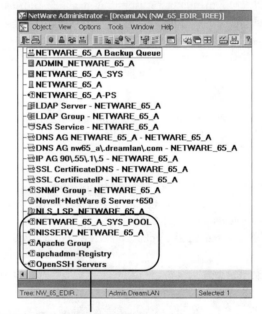

Icons indicating these are unmanageable
objects—not Unknowns

Icons indicating these are unmanageable objects—not Unknowns

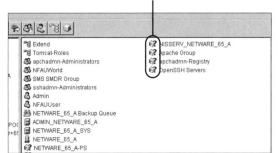

FIGURE 2.7
An example of
unmanageable
objects in
ConsoleOne.

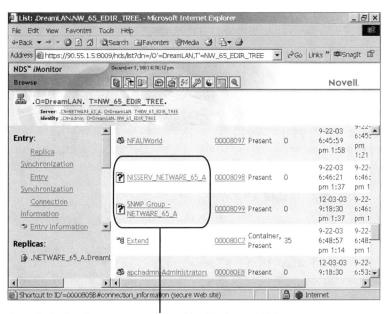

FIGURE 2.8
An example of
unmanageable
objects in NDS
iMonitor.

Icons indicating these are unmanageable objects—not Unknowns

The opposite of a mandatory attribute is an *optional attribute*. As the name implies, this is an attribute that is not necessary to create the object in question. The `Full Name` attribute of the `User` class is an example of an optional attribute. It can be present in the object that has been created, or it can be omitted.

Attributes can also be single valued or multivalued. A single-valued attribute, such as the `Surname` attribute, can contain only one value. If you change that value, the old value is replaced with the new one.

A multivalued attribute is an attribute that can contain a number of entries. The `Network Address` attribute is such an attribute. It can contain one entry for every workstation a user has logged in to, and when you look at the list in management tools such as NetWare Administrator or ConsoleOne, you may see multiple values listed, one for each station the user is logged in to.

REAL WORLD

Operational Attributes

In NDS/eDirectory, not all information about an object is kept in attributes. For example, an object's base class name, last modified time, and creation time are not stored as standard attributes but are stored in *operational attributes*. These attributes are related with the operational status of an object. The following is a list of operational attributes:

▶ `createTimeStamp`—Shows when the object was created. (This is also a standard LDAP attribute.)

▶ `creatorsName`—Shows the distinguished name (DN) of the user that created the object. (This is also a standard LDAP attribute.)

▶ `entryFlags`—Indicates the object's state, such as whether the object is an alias, a container, or a partition. (This is a DS-specific attribute.)

▶ `federationBoundary`—Shows where the federation boundary begins for a Domain Name Service (DNS)-root tree. (This is a DS-specific attribute.)

▶ `localEntryID`—Shows the object ID or record number for the object in the server's local database. (This is a DS-specific attribute.)

▶ `modifiersName`—Shows the DN of the last user that modified the object. (This is also a standard LDAP attribute.)

▶ `modifyTimeStamp`—Shows when the object was last modified. (This is also a standard LDAP attribute.)

▶ `structuralObjectClass`—Shows the base class of the object. (This is also a standard LDAP attribute.)

▶ `subordinateCount`—Shows the number of objects immediately subordinate to this object. (This is a DS-specific attribute.)

▶ `subschemaSubentry`—Shows the LDAP name for the schema location. For eDirectory, it is `cn=schema`. (This is also a standard LDAP attribute.)

An object's information is read-only by the clients and maintained by DS. Figure 2.9 shows some of these operational attributes, as they appear in the DSBrowse NetWare Loadable Module (NLM).

Each class has one or more attributes designated as *naming attributes* (referred to with *Named By* in the schema definition) used to name the actual objects. These attributes can be either mandatory or optional, but you must give at least one of them a value when creating an object of that class. If the only naming attribute is declared as optional, it is, in effect, considered to be mandatory.

localEntryID

subordinateCount

structuralObjectClass   createTimeStamp

modifyTimeStamp

FIGURE 2.9

Examining operational attributes by using DSBrowse.

Naming attributes can be multivalued; in other words, more than one name (value) can be added to the naming attribute. For example, a `User` object can have both `Tasha` and `Chelsea` as values for the `CN` attribute. (Additional `CN` entries are associated with the `Other Name` field found in tools such as ConsoleOne and NetWare Administrator.)

Some object class definitions specify multiple naming attributes. For example, the NetWare server license container object is of the `NLS:Product Container` object class and is named by three attributes `NLS:Publisher`, `NLS:Product`, and `NLS:Version`. An example of a typeless relative distinguish name (RDN) for such an object is

```
Novell+NetWare 6 Server+600
```

where plus signs (+) are used to indicate where the additional attributes' values begin.

A naming attribute does not necessarily reflect the class an object belongs to. Many classes, such as `Computer`, `User`, and `Server`, are named by their `CN` (`Common Name`) attribute. In such names, the naming attribute itself does not indicate which class the object belongs to, but the value of the naming attribute might suggest the nature of the object. For instance, the `Security` container found in eDirectory trees uses `CN` as its naming attribute. However, some naming attributes are closely tied to specific classes. For example, the `C` (`Country Name`) attribute is used to name only `Country` objects.

It is a common misconception that all leaf objects in a DS tree have `CN` in their typeful partial name (for example, `CN=objectname`). Because there is no (schema) rule stating that one must use `CN` as the naming attribute for a leaf object, not all leaf objects have `CN` in their typeful partial names. The `License Certificate` object is an example of such an object (see Figure 2.10). It uses `NLS:License ID` as the naming attribute.

This leaf object does not use CN for its naming attribute

FIGURE 2.10

License
Certificate
objects do not
use CN for their
naming attribute.

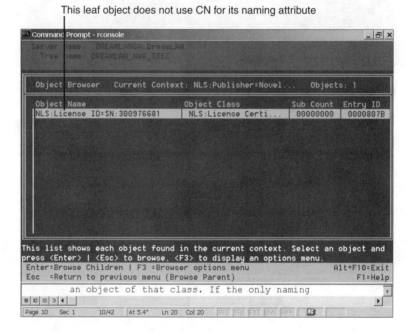

Attribute data can be represented in many different forms in the eDirectory database. In defining an attribute, you also need to define the format used to store the data. This format is called the *syntax*.

Syntaxes

Another important piece of the database structure to be aware of is *syntax*— a definition for what format an attribute's data is in, such as "this is a text string" or "this is to be interpreted as a network address." Table 2.2 lists all 28 syntaxes employed in every NDS/eDirectory tree. The syntax names are given in standard C-code format. Also listed in the table is the minimum DS version needed for accessing those syntaxes via LDAP.

eDirectory Attribute Syntaxes

TABLE 2.2

SYNTAX ID	SYNTAX ID VALUE (DECIMAL)	LDAP NAME	DESCRIPTION	MATCHING RULES	ATTRIBUTE EXAMPLE	MINIMUM DS VERSION FOR LDAP
SYN_BACK_LINK	23	taggedName	Used by DS for the Back Link attribute.	Equality Approximate (not supported through LDAP)	Back Link	eDirectory 8.5
SYN_BOOLEAN	7	boolean	Represents a true/yes (1) or false/no (0) value.	Equality	Password Required	NDS 7
SYN_CE_STRING	2	IA5String	A text string for which the case (upper- or lowercase) is significant when performing comparisons. (CE stands for "case exact.")	Equality Substring (that is, may use * as a wildcard match pattern)	NDSCat:Attributes	NDS 7
SYN_CI_LIST	6	caseIgnorelist	An ordered sequence of text strings for which the case (upper- or lowercase) is not significant when performing comparisons. (CI stands for "case insensitive.")	Equality Approximate	Language	NDS 7

Table 2.2 Continued

SYNTAX ID	SYNTAX ID VALUE (DECIMAL)	LDAP NAME	DESCRIPTION	MATCHING RULES	ATTRIBUTE EXAMPLE	MINIMUM DS VERSION FOR LDAP
SYN_CI_STRING	3	directory String	A text string for which the case (upper- or lowercase) is not significant when performing comparisons	Equality Substring	Full Name	NDS 7
SYN_CLASS_NAME	20	oid	A text string representing object class names.	Equality	Object Class	NDS 7
SYN_COUNTER	22	counter	A signed (32-bit) integer value. (The value range of a signed integer is ± 2147483648.)	Equality Ordering (such as less than, equal to, and greater than)	Grace Login Remaining	eDirectory 8.5
SYN_DIST_NAME	1	dn	A text string that denotes the DN of an NDS object. (The value is not case sensitive.)	Equality	Dn	NDS 7
SYN_EMAIL_ADDRESS	14	taggedString	A value that represents an email address and its type (such as GroupWise or Internet).	Equality	Email Address	eDirectory 8.5
SYN_FAX_NUMBER	11	faxNumber	A text string that complies with the internationally agreed format for showing international telephone	Equality	Facsimile Telephone Number	NDS 7

Table 2.2 Continued

SYNTAX ID	SYNTAX ID VALUE (DECIMAL)	LDAP NAME	DESCRIPTION	MATCHING RULES	ATTRIBUTE EXAMPLE	MINIMUM DS VERSION FOR LDAP
			numbers, E.123, and an optional bit string formatted according to Recommendation T.30.			
SYN_HOLD	26	N/A	A value that is composed of a server name and a signed integer number. (NetWare Accounting uses this. Each time a server is about to perform an action that will be charged against a user's account, the server makes sure the account has a sufficient balance. To do this, the server places a hold (via the Server Holds attribute) against an object's balance, which is an estimate of what the final charge will be. If the hold is successful, sufficient balance remains and the action is	Equality Approximate (not supported through LDAP)	Server Holds	Unsupported

Table 2.2   Continued

SYNTAX ID	SYNTAX ID VALUE (DECIMAL)	LDAP NAME	DESCRIPTION	MATCHING RULES	ATTRIBUTE EXAMPLE	MINIMUM DS VERSION FOR LDAP
			performed. When the action is completed, the hold is cancelled, and a true charge for the actual amount is made against the object's balance. When a hold is pending, this attribute contains the name of the server requesting the hold and the total hold amount. LDAP does not currently support the Hold syntax; therefore, LDAP clients cannot access this attribute.)			
SYN_INTEGER	8	integer	A signed integer value.	Equality Ordering	Login Maximum Simultaneous	NDS 7
SYN_INTERVAL	27	integer	A signed integer value that presents the amount of time in seconds.	Equality Ordering	Intruder Lockout Reset Interval	NDS 7
SYN_NETWORK_ ADDRESS	12	taggedData	A value that repre-.sents a network address. It consists of the address and its	Equality	Network Address	eDirectory 8

Table 2.2 Continued

SYNTAX ID	SYNTAX ID VALUE (DECIMAL)	LDAP NAME	DESCRIPTION	MATCHING RULES	ATTRIBUTE EXAMPLE	MINIMUM DS VERSION FOR LDAP
			type (such as Internet Protocol [IP] or Internetwork Packet Exchange [IPX])			
SYN_NU_STRING	5	numericString	A numeric value that is a text string format, as defined in CCITT X.208.	Equality Substring	International iSDNNumber	NDS 7
SYN_OBJECT_ACL	17	ndsAcl	A value representing the access control list (ACL) entries of an object.	Equality Approximate	Inherited ACL	eDirectory 8
SYN_OCTET_LIST	13	octectList	An ordered sequence of octet strings.	Equality (must match on the size of the list and for each string in the list) Approximate (only one string in the list needs to match)	WANMAN:WAN Policy	eDirectory 8.5
SYN_OCTET_STRING	9	octetString	A list of byte strings used to represent information in a proprietary format. (DS does not interpret the information.)	Equality Ordering	CA Public Key	NDS 7

Table 2.2 Continued

SYNTAX ID	SYNTAX ID VALUE (DECIMAL)	LDAP NAME	DESCRIPTION	MATCHING RULES	ATTRIBUTE EXAMPLE	MINIMUM DS VERSION FOR LDAP
SYN_PATH	15	taggedName AndString	A value representing a file system path. (The information includes namespace, volume, and path.)	Equality Substrings Approximate (not supported through LDAP)	Home Directory	eDirectory 8
SYN_PO_ADDRESS	18	postalAddress	A text string containing postal address information. The case (upper- or lowercase) is not significant when comparing strings.	Equality	Postal Address	NDS 7
SYN_PR_STRING	4	printable String	A string of characters that represents a printable string, as defined in CCITT X.208. The case (upper- or lowercase) is significant when performing comparisons.	Equality Substrings	Serial Number	NDS 7
SYN_REPLICA _POINTER	16	ndsReplica Pointer	A value composing of five parts: complete name of the server holding the replica, replica type (for example, Master), replica state (for	Equality Approximate (not supported through LDAP)	Replica	eDirectory 8.5

Table 2.2 Continued

SYNTAX ID	SYNTAX ID VALUE (DECIMAL)	LDAP NAME	DESCRIPTION	MATCHING RULES	ATTRIBUTE EXAMPLE	MINIMUM DS VERSION FOR LDAP
			example, On), replica ID, and referral information. (Matching is based on server name only and is case insensitive.)			
SYN_STREAM	21	binary	Used for login script, print job configuration information, and other stream-based data.	None (Streams are files of information. The data stored in a stream file has no syntax enforcement of any kind. It is purely arbitrary data, defined by the application that created and uses it. Therefore, no matching is possible.)	Login Script	NDS 7
SYN_TEL_NUMBER	10	telephone Number	A text string that complies with the internationally agreed format for showing international telephone numbers, E.123,	Equality Substrings	Telephone Number	NDS 7

Table 2.2 Continued

SYNTAX ID	SYNTAX ID VALUE (DECIMAL)	LDAP NAME	DESCRIPTION	MATCHING RULES	ATTRIBUTE EXAMPLE	MINIMUM DS VERSION FOR LDAP
			and an optional bit string formatted according to Recommendation T.30.			
SYN_TIME	24	generalized Time	A signed integer number representing the number of seconds since midnight, January 1, 1970, UTC. The LDAP server converts the DS time to the LDAP format specified by X.208, which includes the year, month, day, hour, minute, optionally seconds, and time zone (GMT is recommended by X.208 for the time zone and uses Z as its symbol). An attribute with an LDAP time syntax would have a value similar to the following: 200412241032Z or 20041224103200Z.	Equality Ordering	Login Expiration Time	NDS 7

Table 2.2 Continued

SYNTAX ID	SYNTAX ID VALUE (DECIMAL)	LDAP NAME	DESCRIPTION	MATCHING RULES	ATTRIBUTE EXAMPLE	MINIMUM DS VERSION FOR LDAP
SYN_TIMESTAMP	19	ndsTimestamp	A value that marks the time when a particular event occurred or will occur. It has three components: the number of seconds since midnight, January 1, 1970, UTC; the replica number identifying the server that created the timestamp; and an event ID that orders events occurring within the same whole-second interval (the event number restarts at one for each new second).	Equality Ordering	Synchronized Up To	eDirectory 8.5
SYN_TYPED_NAME	25	typedName	A value representing a level (indicating the priority) and an interval (indicating the frequency of reference) associated with an object.	Equality Approximate (not supported through LDAP)	Notify	eDirectory 8.5
SYN_UNKNOWN	0	unknown	Used for attributes whose attribute definition was deleted from the schema.	Equality Ordering	Auxiliary Class Flag	NDS 7

NOTE   Attribute type definitions are built on attribute syntaxes. For example, the On-Call Pager **attribute is of the type** SYN_TEL_NUMBER. **Software developers extending the schema can create new attribute types by using these predefined syntaxes, but they cannot create any new syntax definitions.**

NOTE   The nwdsdefs.h **C header file of the Novell Developer Kit (NDK) also shows a** SYNTAX_COUNT **(decimal value 28) definition. It is not a syntax type, but it shows the number of syntaxes defined.**

Matching rules indicate the characteristics that are significant when comparing two values of the same syntax. The approximate comparison rule is used in searches and comparisons on syntaxes with lists of strings, and it can also be used with syntaxes that have multiple fields and an ID field:

▶ **Strings**—The approximate rule determines whether a string is present in a syntax with a string list.

▶ **IDs**—The approximate rule determines whether an ID matches the ID in a corresponding field while ignoring the other fields in the syntax. Although most of the application programming interface (API) structures for syntaxes require an object name, NDS replaces these names with IDs in the comparison and search operations.

Bear in mind that this NDS approximate matching rule is quite different from the LDAP approximate matching rule. In LDAP, approximate matching (known as soundAlikeMatch) means that the names sound similar. NDS does not support this type of matching; implementation of approximate matching rules is *not* a must for LDAP servers, as per RFC 2252.

Default ACL Templates

Every object in the DS tree has an (optional) ACL attribute so you can control and protect the object and its attribute values from being modified. The ACL holds information about which trustees have access to the object itself (entry rights) and which trustees have access to the attributes for the object. This information is stored in sets of information that contain the following:

▶ The trustee name (full DN [FDN])

▶ The attribute in question: [Entry Rights], [All Attributes Rights], or a specific attribute

▶ The privileges (such as Browse or Write)

Default ACL templates are defined for specific classes in the base schema and provide a minimum amount of access security for newly created objects. This permits ACL values to be assigned automatically when the object is created, without manual intervention. The `Top` class defines a default ACL template:

Object Name	Default Rights	Affected Attributes
`[Creator]`	Supervisor	`[Entry Rights]`

This allows the object that creates another object to have full control (Supervisor rights) over the created object. Because of class inheritance, all object classes get this default ACL template. As a result, all objects created have at least one ACL assignment made upon their creation. The purpose of this ACL is to ensure that every object added to the DS tree is manageable, unless manually changed later.

NOTE

At some companies, the DS administrator sets up some help desk users that have Create (but not Delete) rights in certain containers in the tree so the help desk can, for instance, create users and groups when necessary but not allow them to delete anything. Because of this default ACL template from the `Top` class, however, these help desk users will be able to delete the objects they created, thus defeating the intention, unless extra steps are taken. See Chapter 15, "Effectively Setting Up eDirectory Security," for details on how to best set up help desk rights.

Because an object inherits the default ACL templates that are defined for the object class and its superclasses, the overall ACL template is the sum total of all default ACL templates of its superclasses plus any defined for that object class. For example, the `NCP Server` object inherits default ACL templates from `Top` and `Server` and then defines one for itself, as follows:

Object Name	Default Rights	Affected Attributes	Class Defined For
`[Creator]`	Supervisor	`[Entry Rights]`	Top
`[Self]`	Supervisor	`[Entry Rights]`	Server
`[Public]`	Read	Network Address	Server
`[Public]`	Read	Messaging Server	NCP Server

The net effect is that the user who creates an `NCP Server` object in the tree and the server itself are granted Supervisor rights to this `NCP Server` object, and the other objects in the tree (through `[Public]`) have Read access to the server's `Network Address` and `Messaging Server` attributes.

There are two situations in which the default ACL template values are not applied:

▶ The code that creates the object overrides the default values.

▶ The creator of the object has effective rights comparable to those in the default template. In this case, the rights are not granted explicitly.

NOTE Only base schema objects can have default ACL templates. Software developers extending the schema cannot create any default ACL templates for new objects. When an object is created in the tree, however, the creation process can set the object's ACLs to any value, including one that changes a value that comes from a default ACL template.

Naming Rules and Restrictions

If you are considering extending your schema, using either standard classes or auxiliary classes, you should be aware of the naming rules and restrictions of class and attribute names. For a new class name or attribute name to be a valid NDS name, it must fit two criteria:

▶ The name cannot exceed 32 characters. Spaces are allowed but are counted as part of the 32-character limit. Spaces are not recommended because they are not allowed in LDAP schema names.

▶ The name must be unique in its level of hierarchy in the NDS tree. Names are case-insensitive, although case can be used for easier visual discrimination.

For example, NDS considers `Accounting` and `accounting` to be the same and will not allow two class names or two attribute names different only in capitalization to be created. However, NDS *does* allow the same name to be used for a class name and an attribute name. Thus `Accounting` could be the name of a class and `accounting` the name of an attribute. For example, NDS has defined a number of classes and attributes with the same name: `User` (class) and `User` (attribute), `Queue` (class) and `Queue` (attribute), and `Resource` (class) and `Resource` (attribute).

If you want an application to also work with LDAP applications, your schema extensions should conform to the LDAP naming conventions, which are more restrictive than NDS schema naming conventions. When creating an LDAP schema name, you must conform to the following rules:

▶ Use alphanumeric characters. LDAP allows one hyphen in a name. The hyphen is the only non-alpha-numeric character allowed, and it cannot start the name. It is recommended that a name contain only alphanumeric characters, without a hyphen.

▶ Start with an alphabetic character. Numeric characters cannot start a name, nor can a hyphen.

▶ Do not include spaces.

▶ Create a unique name for the type (class or attribute). Note that like NDS, LDAP names are not case-sensitive.

▶ Do not create a name with more than 32 characters. This is actually an NDS restriction. LDAP allows longer names, but NDS does not currently support names longer than 32 characters. (At the time of this writing, there is no RFC that specifies any size limits for the various LDAP entities, such as class names or DNs.)

The restriction on alphanumeric characters and one hyphen in the name applies only when dealing with the LDAP schema. Objects in an LDAP-compliant directory may contain multiple hyphens as well as metacharacters such as + and ;. If one of the following characters appears in the name, it must be escaped using the backslash character (\):

▶ **A space or # character occurring at the beginning of the string**

▶ **A space character occurring at the end of the string**

▶ **One of these characters: , + " \ < > ;**

NOTE

A typical LDAP convention is to lowercase the first word in the name and then capitalize the initial letter of other words that make up the attribute's or class's descriptive name. If the name is composed of a single word, it is generally used as all lowercase. Here are some examples:

```
chair

leatherChair

importedSofaBed
```

For more information about LDAP and NDS integration, refer to the section "The LDAP Server for NDS," later in this chapter.

NOTE

The following is a brief review of some of the NDS object naming rules and conventions:

▶ NDS treats underscores the same as spaces. Therefore, `name has spaces` is the same as `name_has_spaces`. Consequently, if a DS object is called `name_has_spaces`, Novell's LDAP server would return that object as the result for a search query for `name has spaces`.

▶ The *RDN* or partial name is the name of the object itself and does not include names of its parent objects (for example, `CN=Tasha`).

▶ The *DN* or *FDN* is the full name of an object, which includes the names of its parent objects. It is referred to as the complete name in some cases. An example is `CN=Tasha.OU=Customer_Service.O=Company`.

▶ The NDS *context* identifies an object's location within the NDS tree. It is a list of *all* the container objects leading from the object toward the top of the tree, called `[Root]`. Each NDS client (which may be a workstation, a workstation-based utility, or a server-based application) maintains a name context. When an RDN is used, the name is expanded with the addition of the name context to the name, thus forming an FDN, before being passed to DS.

NOTE An object is exactly, and uniquely, identified by its DN. No two objects can have the same FDN. Furthermore, no two objects can have the same RDN if they both exist in the same context, even if they are of different object classes. For example, NDS will not allow you to create a user called `Tasha Golden` and a group called `Tasha_golden` in the same container because names are case-insensitive and underscores are the same as spaces.

▶ A *typeful* object name uses attribute type abbreviations (based on the naming attributes) to distinguish between the different container types and leaf objects in an object's DN or RDN.

If you do not provide a typeful object name, NDS uses the following guidelines, known as the default typing rule, for the attribute types for each object:

  ▶ The leftmost object is assumed to be `CN=`.

  ▶ The rightmost object is assumed to be `O=`.

  ▶ All intermediate objects are assumed to be `OU=`.

NDS, however, is smart enough to automatically determine whether the leftmost object is a leaf or container object and derive a proper type for it.

A typeful FDN is also known as a *canonical name*: a name that includes a full naming path with a type specification for each naming component. DS operates on canonical names only.

The default typing rule is only applied to untyped portions of a name; typed objects are not touched. For example, the default naming rule will expand the typeless name `Kim.Webservices.L=Novell.Company` **to** `CN=Kim.OU=Webservices.L=Novell.O=Company`.

WARNING

The fact that the default typing rule always assumes that the *rightmost* object is an `Organization` **object (**`O=`**)** and the leftmost object is an object named by `CN=` poses a problem to applications if the object's topmost container is not an `Organization` object or if its naming attribute is not `CN` (as is the case for the `License Certificate` object). For example, if you have a `Country` object at the top of your tree and try to use a typeless name similar to `Kim.Webservices.L=Novell.Company.C=US`, you might expect the converted name to be `CN=Kim.OU=Webservices.L=Novell.O=Company.C=US`. Unfortunately, what you get is `CN=Kim.OU=Webservices.L=Novell.OU=Company.C=US`. This is because the rightmost object is already typed, and the default typing rule says that all intermediate objects are assumed to be `OU=` (unless they're already typed.

> ▶ A typeless name does not include any of the object attribute types. For example, the typeless FDN for `CN=Tasha.OU=Customer_Service.O=Company` is `Tasha.Customer_Service.Company`.

NOTE

There is no published guideline that a DS-aware application needs to support typeful or typeless naming. Therefore, it is all up to the developer. A "well-written" utility will accept an object name in either format. However, some accept only typeful names. In most cases, unless specified, you should try the typeless name first—it is easier to type. But if the object is located in a tree branch that contains `Country, Locality,` **or** `domain` objects, you need to use the typeful name.

You should also be familiar with the significance of periods in DS object names. NDS uses periods as delimiters between object names in the context. This means you should *not* use periods when naming objects. If there is a need, however, you can use periods; ConsoleOne allows you to create an object that has embedded periods. With other tools, however, you must escape the period by using a backslash (for example, enter the name as *firstname\.lastname*). Note that ConsoleOne permits the creation of such an object without having to escape the period and shows the object as *firstname.lastname* (see Figure 2.11), but other tools do not (see Figure 2.12).

FIGURE 2.11
ConsoleOne, showing a User object containing a period in its name.

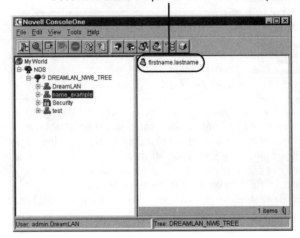

Does not indicate the period needs to be "escaped"

FIGURE 2.12
NetWare Administrator, showing a back-slash in an object name.

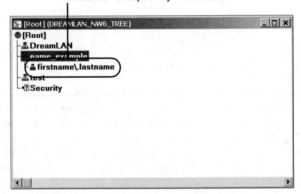

If a period must be part of an object name, it must be "escaped" by a backslash

An LDAP query of an NDS object that has embedded periods in its name will result in the name without the periods being escaped. That is, the object will appear as *firstname.lastname* and not *firstname\.lastname*, as shown in Figure 2.13.

NOTE   To log in as a user that has embedded periods in the name, you must escape each period when entering the name, unless the application you use takes care of that for you.

LDAP doesn't show the escaped periods.

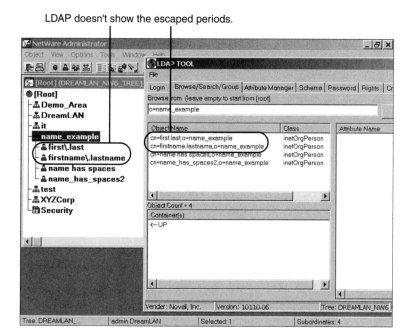

FIGURE 2.13
LDAP, not showing escaped periods in object names.

We have all become familiar with using a leading period in an object name to mean that the name is to be treated as an FDN and that the name context information should not be added to it. However, there is also a *trailing period rule* that not everyone is aware of. Each trailing period in a name tells DS to remove one object name from the *left* side of the name context before appending the remaining names to the RDN. For example, say your current name context is `OU=Department1.O=Company` and you specified the following RDN:

`CN=Admin.`

DS will remove *one* name (`OU=Department1`) from the left side of the name context and append the remaining name to the RDN (`CN=Admin`), producing the following FDN:

`CN=Admin.O=Company`

Multiple trailing periods can be used to move up multiple levels in the tree; some utilities (such as `CX.EXE`) will return an error if you specify too many trailing periods, taking you past the `[Root]` level in the tree.

You cannot use the leading period rule in conjunction with the trailing period rule. An entry such as `.CN=admin.` **would result in an error.**   **NOTE**

TIP

The trailing period rule can come in handy when your current name context is set to Container A (for example, *containerA.department.company*) but you need to specify an object name from Container B (whose context is *containerB.department.company*). Instead of changing your current context or having to enter a long FDN such as *objectname.containerB.department.company*, you can simply type *objectname.containerB..*

The RDN of a DS object is limited to 128 characters, and the FDN can be a maximum of 256 characters. However, the total number of intermediate containers you can specify in a typeful FDN is less than in its typeless variant, due to the overheads in typeful naming. Table 2.3 summarizes the maximum number of characters allowed in the various categories of names.

TABLE 2.3   **NDS Object Naming Restrictions**

NAME CATEGORY	MAXIMUM NUMBER OF CHARACTERS
NDS RDN	128
NDS DN	256
NDS schema class name	32
NDS schema attribute name	32
Tree name	32
SAP service name	47

NOTE Bear in mind that although the maximum number of characters allowed for an RDN is 128, *most* of the DS objects' RDNs are actually restricted to 64 characters. This is because they use CN as the naming attribute, and CN is defined to be a 64-byte case-ignored string. This limitation is causing some headaches in situations where long Internet domain names are used and NetWare 6.5's certificate service (Novell Modular Authentication Service [NMAS]) is unable to create key material objects (KMOs)—digital certificates—because a KMO object name includes the server name plus domain name. As a result, you cannot use secure Web services on these servers. Novell is aware of this shortcoming, and a longer CN limit may be introduced in a future release of eDirectory.

Partition and Replica Types

Now that you have an understanding of what makes up the eDirectory database, let's look at how the database is distributed.

The eDirectory database is a loosely consistent, partitioned, hierarchical database. This means that the data can be divided into many different logical pieces, called *partitions*, and you can put a copy, or *replica*, of any user-created partition on a number of servers. The DS module will keep the information in different replicas synchronized, but bear in mind that at any given point in time, the information in one replica may not fully match the information in another replica. The DS module handles the discrepancy between copies by maintaining information about which copy has the most current changes and propagating, or *replicating*, that information to the servers that have older information. It is important to note that the eDirectory database is continually converging to a consistent state. When it completes synchronization on a partition, the partition is consistent until the next time data is changed.

When you first installed your server, the system created a number of special partitions in the eDirectory database:

- ▶ The System partition
- ▶ The Schema partition
- ▶ The External Reference partition
- ▶ The Bindery partition

The partitions discussed here are logical partitions that exist within the eDirectory database (see Figure 2.14). They are not physical partitions on a hard disk.

System-created partitions

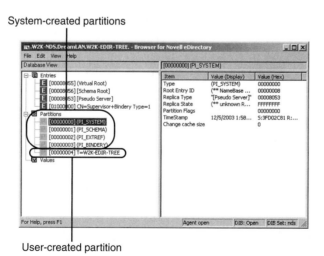

FIGURE 2.14
eDirectory partitions.

User-created partition

In addition, a user-defined partition may have been automatically added if the server is one of the first three servers installed in the partition.

The System Partition

The *System partition* keeps track of information specific to the local server. This information is *not* synchronized with other servers in the tree. This is the partition that the Limber process operates on. See Chapter 6, "Understanding Common eDirectory Processes," for more information on the Limber process.

Information contained in the System partition includes the following:

▶ Information on where the server is located in the eDirectory tree, including its typeful FDN (for example, `CN=RH9-VM.O=Testing`).

▶ eDirectory indexes defined on the server. (See Chapter 16, "Tuning eDirectory," for information about the use of indexes.)

▶ The state of background processes (including errors), if the server is running NDS 5.95 or later (for NetWare 4.11 and NetWare 4.2) or any version of NDS/eDirectory on NetWare 5.x and higher.

The partition ID of the System partition is *always* 0.

The Schema Partition

The *Schema partition* keeps track of all the object class and attribute definition information for the server. This information is synchronized between servers, using a process called *Schema Skulk* or *Schema Sync,* and it means that each server has a *complete* copy of the schema. The Schema Sync process starts with the server that contains the Master replica of the `[Root]` partition and propagates to the other servers with a copy of `[Root]`. Then it continues with the servers in the child partitions, until all servers have received a copy of the schema.

The partition ID of the Schema partition is *always* 1.

The External Reference Partition

The *External Reference* partition (commonly referred to as the ExRef partition) contains information about objects that don't exist in a partition on the local server. For instance, when a user logs in to the network, NDS looks up the user information by performing a *name resolution process* (discussed in the

"NDS Name Resolution and Tree Walking" section in Chapter 6). The client software navigates the different partitions in the NDS tree until it finds the User object. If this process is repeated, however, every time the user logs in or the object is referenced, efficiency suffers. To avoid having to repeat the process, NDS builds an external reference (a pointer, essentially) to that object and stores it in the ExRef partition on the server from which the User object is making the request. The next time this user authenticates to the network, the external reference (exref) is used to quickly locate the object within NDS. Such exrefs are deleted if not used for an extended period of time.

In addition to providing tree connectivity (that is, tree-walking) and speeding up object authentication, exrefs are also used to keep track of nonlocal objects when an object is added as a file system or local object trustee, or when an object is added as a member of a group.

NOTE

When NDS creates an exref, a `Back Link` **attribute is added to the referenced object to keep track of the server on which the exref was created. This becomes inefficient as the number of exrefs increases. Back links require a server to communicate with every server that contains a Read/Write replica of the partition the back link resides on. eDirectory 8.7 and higher uses the** `Distributed Reference Link (DRL)` **attribute instead of the** `Back Link` **attribute. Distributed reference links have the advantage of referencing a partition rather than a specific server. When information is needed about a** `DRL`**, any server with a replica of the partition can supply the information.**

TIP

Although the ExRef partition exists on every server, only servers with exrefs populate it. Like the System partition, the ExRef partition is not synchronized with other servers. The partition ID of the ExRef partition is *always* 2.

Objects stored in the ExRef partition are called, appropriately, *external reference objects*. These objects are simply placeholders (but are not pointers, like `Alias` **objects) that are simply representations of the real objects existing in the tree. An exref object is not a copy of the object because it does not contain any of the attributes that the real object has.**

NOTE

The Bindery Partition

All servers that have IPX enabled keep track of services learned from SAP traffic; SLP services are stored in the DS database. Each of these services is stored as a bindery SAP object, and these services are classified as dynamic bindery objects because they are automatically deleted when the server is shut down or when the offered service is no longer available. To provide backward compatibility with NetWare 2.x and NetWare 3.x and bindery-based applications, every server has a **SUPERVISOR** (pseudo) bindery user and maintains a bindery NetWare Core Protocol (NCP) file server's Type 4 SAP object. These two bindery objects are static in nature and cannot be removed. All this information is maintained in the server's *Bindery partition*.

Like the System and ExRef partitions, the Bindery partition is not replicated to all servers. Rather, it is kept specific to the server in question. The partition ID of the Bindery partition is *always* 3.

User-Defined Partitions

The last type of partition is the *user-defined* (or *user-created*) *partition*. This is the most common type of partition, and it is likely the type you are already familiar with. Any DS server may hold a copy of a user-defined replica. Changes to a user-defined partition must be distributed to other servers that hold a copy of the same user-defined partition. When these changes occur, they are replicated under the control of the Synchronization process.

A *replica* is a copy of a user-defined partition that is placed on an NDS server. There is no limit to how many replicas a server can hold, subject to disk space availability. Only one replica of the same user-defined partition can exist on a server. There are six replica types:

- ▶ Master
- ▶ Read/Write
- ▶ Read-Only
- ▶ Subordinate Reference
- ▶ Filtered Read/Write (eDirectory 8.5 and higher)
- ▶ Filtered Read-Only (eDirectory 8.5 and higher)

Table 2.4 shows a summary of the capabilities of the various replica types. Each replica type is discussed in detail in the following sections.

Replica Types and Their Capabilities — TABLE 2.4

CHARACTERISTIC	MASTER	READ/ WRITE	READ- ONLY	SUBORDINATE REFERENCE	FILTERED READ/WRITE	FILTERED READ-ONLY
Maintains a list of all other replicas	×	×	×	×	×	×
Contains a complete copy of all object information of the partition	×	×	×			
Controls partition boundary changes (merging, splitting, moving, creating, deleting, and repairing)	×					
Controls object changes (creating, moving, deleting, and modifying objects and object property values)	×	×			×	
Supports authentication	×	×			×	
Supports viewing of objects and their information	×	×	×		×	×
Can have multiple replicas per partition		×	×	×	×	×
Can be changed into a master replica		×	×	(see the "SubRef" section, later in this chapter)		
Can be changed into a Read/Write replica	×		×			×

Table 2.4   Continued

CHARACTERISTIC	MASTER	READ/ WRITE	READ- ONLY	SUBORDINATE REFERENCE	FILTERED READ/WRITE	FILTERED READ-ONLY
Can be used on a server where bindery services are required	×	×			×	
Only contains the partition root object				×		
Is automatically removed if you add a replica of that child partition to the server				×		
Can be created by the network administrator	×	×	×		×	×
Cannot be created by the network administrator (created automatically by the system)				×		
Controls background processes	×					

The partition ID of a user-defined partition is always 4 or higher.

NOTE   Typically, the Master replica of [Root] will have a partition ID of 4 because that is the first user-defined partition that gets created. This may not always be the case, however, because another (Read/Write or Read-Only) replica may be designated as the Master replica at a later time and thus will have a different partition ID.

Master Replicas

The Master replica is the *first* copy of a new partition. When you install a new server into a new tree, that server automatically receives a Master replica of the [Root] partition. If you then create a new partition by using NDS

Manager or ConsoleOne, the already-installed server receives the Master copy of that partition as well because it has the Master replica of the parent partition.

As discussed in Chapter 6, the Master replica must be available for certain partition operations, such as a partition join, a partition split, or an object/partition move. The Master replica can also be used to perform NDS operations such as object authentication, object addition, deletion, and modification.

A Master replica may be used to provide bindery emulation services because it is a writable replica type.

Read/Write Replicas

Similar to Master replicas, a Read/Write (R/W) replica is a writable replica type that can be used to effect object changes. Unlike Master replicas, however, Read/Write replicas are not directly involved in replica operations. The NDS server installation process will ensure that there exists one Master replica and two "full" replicas. (Filtered replicas do not count, as discussed later in this chapter.) When you install an NDS server into a partition that has only two replicas (one Master and one Read/Write replica, for instance), a third replica (Read/Write) will automatically be added to the new server. You normally create additional Read/Write replicas of a given partition to provide fault tolerance and to provide faster access to eDirectory data across WAN links.

TIP

If a Master replica is lost or damaged, a Read/Write replica can be promoted to become the new Master replica. See Chapter 11, "Examples from the Real World," for some examples of this.

A Read/Write replica may be used to provide bindery emulation services because it is a writable replica type.

Read-Only Replicas

The Read-Only (R/O) replica type is seldom—if ever—used. It was added because Novell built NDS based on the X.500 directory standard, which specified Read-Only replicas.

Use of R/O replicas is strongly discouraged. They do not provide any advantages with regard to traffic management because they can actually generate more traffic than a Read/Write replica due to referral and redirection.

Any change directed at a server that holds an R/O replica of a partition would end up being redirected by the server to a server with a Read/Write or Master replica. The change would then be synchronized back to the server holding the R/O replica, through the normal synchronization process.

R/O replicas have been used to provide NDS data lookup, as in the case of an address book application. However, Filtered replicas (discussed later in this chapter) are better suited for these types of applications.

Read-Only replicas cannot be used to provide bindery emulation services because they are not writable.

Subordinate Reference Replicas

The Subordinate Reference (SubRef) replica type is the only user-defined replica type that is not actually placed manually. Rather, its creation and deletion are managed automatically by NDS. SubRef replicas are used primarily to provide tree connectivity. In simplest terms, a subordinate reference (subref) is a (downward) pointer to the child partitions. It links a parent partition to a child partition. A SubRef replica contains a complete copy of the partition root object of the child partition. It does not, however, contain any other data for the child partition. A SubRef replica has a complete copy of the partition root object, and it has a `Replica` attribute that contains the following information:

- ▶ A list of servers where replicas of the child partition are stored
- ▶ The servers' network addresses (both IPX and IP)
- ▶ Replica types stored on these servers
- ▶ Other NDS partition information, such as an ACL summarizing all the effective rights at this point in the tree

In essence, a SubRef replica can be considered the glue that binds parts of the NDS tree together.

SubRef replicas cannot be used to provide bindery emulation services because they are not writable. Also, they cannot be used for fault tolerance purposes because they do not contain all the objects of a partition.

WARNING It is possible to promote a SubRef replica to a Master replica as a last resort. However, because a SubRef replica does not contain any objects in the partition, you will lose all data in that partition. Refer to the "Server and Data Recovery" section in Chapter 11 for more details.

Filtered Replicas

eDirectory 8.5 introduced two new replica types: Filtered Read/Write and Filtered Read-Only replicas. A Filtered replica is essentially a Read/Write or Read-Only replica that holds only a subset of the objects or attributes found in a normal Read/Write or Read-Only replica. Filter replicas are used to specify which schema classes and attributes will be allowed to pass during synchronization. A Filtered replica ignores changes made to objects outside the filter.

Filtered replicas can be sparse or fractional replicas. A *sparse filtered* replica contains only objects of selected object classes. All other objects are filtered and not placed in the local database. A *fractional Filtered* replica contains only attributes of selected attribute types. All other attributes are filtered and not placed in the local database. A typical Filtered replica is both sparse *and* fractional because it filters both object classes and attribute types.

NOTE

An eDirectory sparse or fractional Filtered replica is also known as a *virtual replica*.

Filtered replicas are useful in the following situations:

- ▶ To control the size of the eDirectory Directory Information Base (DIB) on a server
- ▶ To improve search efficiency on specific object classes by storing just those object types and attributes in the replica
- ▶ To reduce eDirectory synchronization traffic directed at specific servers by eliminating unneeded objects and attributes from the synchronization process

To create a Filtered replica, you must first create a replication filter on the server that will host the Filtered replica. This replication filter determines which objects and attributes are allowed in the Filtered replicas that reside on the server. You create the replication filter via ConsoleOne.

NOTE

Each eDirectory server can hold only *one* replication filter. Consequently, all Filtered replicas stored on a server must use the same replication filter. It is possible to have a mixture of filtered replicas and unfiltered replicas on the same server.

WARNING   After a replication filter is modified, all filtered replicas that use it will be placed in the New replica state until they are refreshed with up-to-date data from the unfiltered replicas. This ensures that the information in the Filtered replicas is consistent and complete with respect to their unfiltered counterparts.

In addition to the desired classes and attributes stored in a Filtered replica, eDirectory must always synchronize attributes that are critical to the operation of eDirectory. The following schema flags cause the affected object classes and attributes to be included in a Filtered replica:

▶ **SF_SPARSE_REQUIRED**—Object classes and attributes designated with this flag will always pass through the replication filter, regardless of the filter settings. The ACL attribute is an example (see Figure 2.15).

▶ **SF_SPARSE_DESIRED**—This flag allows desired classes and their required attributes to pass through the replication filter.

▶ **SF_SPARSE_OPERATIONAL**—This flag identifies classes and attributes that *must* be cached on Filtered replicas (because they are part of the operational schema). Setting this flag on an object class or attribute type definition guarantees that the class or attribute is created as a reference object if it is not in the replication filter. The DS Revision attribute is an example of this.

This attribute will be unaffected by the filter of a Filtered replica

FIGURE 2.15

The SF_SPARSE_ REQUIRED schema flag, which causes the ACL attribute to pass through a Filtered replica filter.

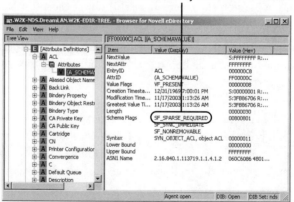

eDirectory will also allow any objects referenced by an allowed attribute to pass through the filter in a reference state. For example, say a replication filter allows the object class User and attribute Group Membership but filters the object class Group. The Filtered replica will create the Group object and flag it as a reference object. The Group object is required to ensure database consistency, and the reference tag is used to ensure that the incomplete `Group` object does not synchronize to other servers.

Container objects in an eDirectory database are also allowed to pass through to any filtered replica. This ensures that all objects beneath the container can be created, if the filter allows them through. Container objects created in this manner are also flagged as reference objects. The `Unknown` object class is flagged as a container. This causes all objects with an object class type `Unknown` to also be created as reference objects in a Filtered replica.

NOTE

The eDirectory replica synchronization process takes advantage of Filtered replica types. If the outbounding server is running eDirectory 8.5 or higher, the destination server's replication filter is read, and only the required data is sent. Network traffic is significantly reduced during these types of replica synchronizations. If the outbounding server is not running eDirectory 8.5 or higher, the standard replica synchronization process takes place (that is, sending *all* changed data), but the inbounding server accepts only the data that is allowed through the replication filter.

Filtered Read/Write replicas can make modifications to objects and attributes that pass through the replication filter. These changes will be passed to all other servers in the replica ring. However, a Filtered Read/Write replica is not allowed to fully participate in the transitive synchronization process (see the section "The Synchronization Process" in Chapter 6) and will not send changes that did not originate in the local database. This is necessary to ensure database consistency for all changes.

NOTE

Because Filtered Read/Write replicas do not contain complete information about objects, you should avoid using them to provide bindery emulation services. Filtered Read-Only replicas cannot be used to provide bindery emulation services. Furthermore, Filtered replicas do not provide fault tolerance because they do not contain complete information about the objects in a replica.

Like their Read-Only replica cousins, Filtered R/O replicas cannot make modifications to objects and attributes that pass through the replication filter. Filtered Read-Only replicas can be used for data lookup only.

Because data in a Filtered replica is incomplete, an LDAP search could produce constrained or incomplete results. Therefore, by default, an LDAP search request does not examine filtered replicas. While you're performing a Filtered replica search, the search may not return the results as per the replica filter due to either chaining or referral (see the "LDAP Name Resolution Models" section, later in this chapter). If you are certain that a Filtered replica holds the data you need, you can configure the LDAP server to search Filtered replicas (through the Filtered Replica Usage tab in the LDAP server object properties).

Parent/Child Relationships

Each server that contains a replica of the parent partition also contains a Subordinate Reference replica of every child partition that is not physically located on that server. Consider the sample NDS tree shown in Figure 2.16. This tree contains four partitions: Root, A, B, and C. Three file servers— FS1, FS2, and FS3—are installed in this tree, one server in each of the o= containers. Each server holds the only copy of the partition (Master replica) in which the server is contained; the [Root] partition is stored on FS1.

FIGURE 2.16
A sample NDS tree with four partitions.

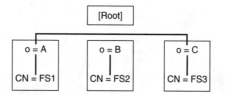

Table 2.5 shows the replica structure in this tree.

TABLE 2.5

Replica Structure of a Sample NDS Tree

SERVER	[ROOT]	PARTITION A	PARTITION B	PARTITION C
FS1	Master	Master	Subordinate Reference	Subordinate Reference
FS2			Master	
FS3				Master

FS1 contains Subordinate Reference replicas because the parent of Partitions B and C, Partition [Root], resides on the server, but Partitions B and C do not. Neither FS2 nor FS3 needs a SubRef replica because neither Partition B nor Partition C has a child partition. If the Master partition of [Root] were placed on FS2 rather than FS1, FS2 would contain Subordinate Reference replicas for Partitions A and C.

As a rule of thumb for determining where a subordinate reference partition is going to be placed, remember that a SubRef replica will be placed everywhere the parent partition is but the child partition is not.

NOTE

Bindery Services

Bindery services, also referred to occasionally as *bindery emulation mode* or *bindery emulation services*, are used to provide backward compatibility with NetWare 2.x and NetWare 3.x services and legacy bindery-only applications. These are the most common uses for bindery services:

▶ To support software that requires a login as the `SUPERVISOR` object in order to install it or to use it. (This situation is very rare these days, but there are still legacy applications being used.)

▶ To support legacy NetWare clients for Mac computers.

▶ To support older printing devices, such as HP JetDirect cards, manufactured before NDS was released. These devices typically work on a bindery print queue. (On rare occasions, perhaps because of a bug in a device's firmware, the bindery mode works better than the NDS mode. As a result, bindery emulation is required.)

Bindery services are enabled as follows:

▶ On NetWare servers, using the `SET BINDERY CONTEXT=` console command

▶ On Windows, via the Bindery Emulation tab in the eDirectory configuration dialog (see Figure 2.17)

▶ On Unix/Linux, by setting a value for the variable `n4u.nds.bindery-context` in the `/etc/nds.conf` file

In order to enable bindery services, you must have a Master or Read/Write replica of the partition that will hold the bindery objects created by the service. Failure to do this will result in bindery services not being enabled for that container and the following error message being displayed (in the case of NetWare):

```
Bindery context OU=WEST.O=XYZCORP set,
     ➥illegal replica type.
Error: The Bindery context container must be set to a
       location that is present in a replica on this server.
       Bindery context NOT set.
Bindery Context is set to: O=XYZCORP
```

FIGURE 2.17

Configuring
Windows for
bindery emula-
tion.

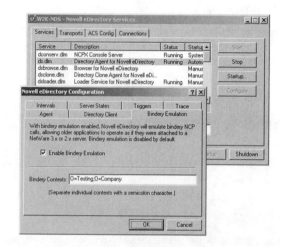

Bindery services allows you to set up to 16 (or to a combined length of 255
characters) NDS contexts as an NDS server's virtual bindery. The context
you set is called the server's *bindery context*.

The following are some important facts about bindery services:

▶ To use bindery services, you must set a bindery context for the NDS
server.

▶ The bindery context boundary is a single container that does not
include any subordinate containers. For example, say that a replica
has `OU=Department` as its partition root, and it contains two subordinate OUs, called Sales and Support. Setting the bindery context to
`OU=Department` does not make any of the objects in `OU=Sales` and
`OU=Support` available to the bindery clients. To do that, you need to
also include them in the bindery context specification, as in the following example:

```
SET BINDERY CONTEXT=OU=Department;OU=Sales.OU=Department;
    ➥OU=Support.OU=Department
```

▶ Not all objects map to bindery objects. Many objects, such as `Alias`
objects, do not have bindery equivalents. Only `Users`, `Group`, `Queue`,
`Print Server`, and `Bindery` objects benefit from the use of bindery
emulation.

▶ Each NDS server with a bindery context must hold a Master or
Read/Write replica (that is, a writable replica) of the partition that
includes the bindery context.

> **WARNING**
>
> A bindery service process is single threaded, whereas NDS is multithreaded. Therefore, if the server is servicing many bindery requests, you may experience high server CPU utilization and a slowdown of other network services provided by this server.

Time Synchronization

Although it is not a service provided by NDS, time synchronization is a very important part of maintaining the integrity of the NDS tree. Every time a change is made to an object, the change is timestamped in order to allow the change to be made on all servers holding a copy of that object, in the proper sequence. Without time synchronization, it would be possible to set up two servers with different times but holding copies of the same objects. In that case, you could change a user's password on one server and that change might not be propagated to the second server properly, and the user would be forced to log in with his or her old password.

> **NOTE**
>
> It is important to realize that NDS requires that the DS servers within a network all agree on a common time. This doesn't necessarily have to be the correct time, but everyone's time has to be in synchronization with each other.

There are four time server types:

- ▶ Single Reference
- ▶ Reference
- ▶ Primary
- ▶ Secondary

The Single Reference, Reference, and Primary time servers are referred to as *time providers*, and they establish the network time. Secondary time servers determine the correct time by polling a time provider. Table 2.6 shows a summary of the legal provider/client combinations. No matter what role the time server plays within the network time synchronization, all the combinations shown in Table 2.6 provide time information to workstations (clients).

TABLE 2.6　**Legal Time Provider/Client Combinations**

TIME SOURCE TYPE	CLIENT
Single Reference	Secondary and Workstation
Reference	Primary, Secondary, Workstation, and Reference
Primary	Primary, Secondary, and Workstation
Secondary	Workstation and Secondary

NOTE　The time server types discussed in the following sections really apply only to NetWare servers (but work over both IPX and IP). Non-NetWare DS servers always report a time server type of Secondary. Furthermore, because Novell does not provide a `TimeSync` module for non-NetWare platforms, you need to separately set up time synchronization by using a Network Time Protocol (NTP) application of your choosing (discussed later in this chapter).

Single Reference Time Servers

The Single Reference time server type is typically used in a small network, where one server holds the definitive time for the entire network. If you need to change the time for some reason (perhaps because the network time drifted), the Single Reference server is the one where you would change the time.

NOTE　It is generally recommended that if the time on the network needs to be changed, it should be changed with the `SET TIMESYNC TIME ADJUSTMENT` console command. You should not use the `SET TIME` console command because it does not perform the change in as orderly a manner.

A Single Reference time server is intended to be the only time source provider within a network. All other servers must receive time from this Single Reference time server and cannot in turn provide time to other servers (including back to the Single Reference time server). Consequently, a Single Reference time server is only useful in a network environment where there are no more than 30 DS servers because it is a potential single point of failure.

An *external* time source, such as an atomic clock located on the Internet, can be used to set the local time on a Single Reference time server. However, the Single Reference time server will not receive time information from other DS servers on the network. Consequently, the Single Reference server decides unilaterally what time it is and tells the rest of the servers on the network that it is correct. Because of this, a Single Reference time server is incompatible with other time source provider types.

Because a Single Reference time server is the authoritative time source on an NDS network, its time is always considered to be synchronized to the network, regardless of the time on any other server.

See TID #10011518 and #10050215 for details on configuring TIMESYNC.NLM **to obtain time from external time sources.**

Reference Time Servers

A Reference time server does not adjust its time to match the time obtained from the other time-provider servers. In addition, a Reference server has more voting weight than other time-provider servers in the polling process (16 versus 1). The result is that the Primary time servers adjust their time to (rather quickly) converge on the time specified by the Reference time server. The Reference time server is also part of that process, however, and if the polling servers determine that the time on the Reference server is too far off, they will disregard the time change and maintain correct time.

Like Single Reference time servers, Reference time servers can use an external time source to set their local time in order to maintain accurate time. One Reference time server is allowed per NDS tree, and it can coexist with Primary time servers (but not with a Single Reference time server).

NOTE

To utilize a Reference time server, you need at least one other time-provider server, such as a Primary time server, to complement the operation of the Reference time server—so the time servers have polling partners. You cannot use a Single Reference time server in this case because it does not allow itself to be polled. It is possible to have more than one Reference time server in the same network. But because Reference servers do not adjust their internal clocks, multiple Reference servers never synchronize with each other, even though they poll each other for time information. If you need to use two or more Reference servers, you should use a common external time source to synchronize them.

NOTE

In implementations where a Reference time server is used, it is strongly recommended that you have at least *two* Primary time servers as well. This way, if one of the three time-provider servers becomes unavailable, the remaining two servers can still poll each other to exchange time information. If you have a Reference time server and only one Primary and one of these becomes unavailable, the remaining time server has no one to poll with and thus will lead to out-of-time synchronization with the network.

Reference time servers are generally used in medium- to large-size networks consisting of more than 30 DS servers.

Primary Time Servers

Primary time servers are used in the polling process with a Reference time server. Typically, more than one Primary time server is used in conjunction with a Reference time server. Primary time servers are best used when positioned geographically to allow time synchronization to continue with other servers, even if a link to the Reference time server is down.

A Primary time server polls another Primary time server or Reference time server to determine whether that server's time matches its time. If the difference is less than the value of the **SET TIMESYNC Synchronization Radius** parameter, the Primary time server indicates that its time is synchronized. If the difference is greater than the value of the **SET TIMESYNC Synchronization Radius** parameter, the Primary time server adjusts its local time by 50% of the difference. This allows the Primary time servers to (slowly) converge on a correct network time instead of causing a sudden (big) jump in time change.

Secondary Time Servers

A Secondary time server receives its time from another server on the network—whether from a Single Reference, Reference, or Primary time server. Secondary time servers do not participate in polling in the sense that their time contributes nothing to the network time. They are essentially slaves to the time synchronization process. If the difference between the network time and a Secondary time server's local time is less than the value of the **SET TIMESYNC Synchronization Radius** parameter, the Secondary time server indicates that its time is synchronized. Otherwise, it adjusts its local time *totally* (that is, by 100% of the difference) to match the network time (instead of 50% at a time, like Primary time servers).

Secondary time servers are *time consumers* because they receive time from a time source such as a Single Reference or Primary time server. However, Secondary time servers act as time providers to clients such as workstations. Although not normally done nor generally recommended, it is indeed possible to configure a Secondary time server to obtain time information from another Secondary time server.

Cross-Platform Time Synchronization Using NTP

The TimeSync protocol is a Novell-proprietary time synchronization protocol, first introduced with NetWare 4.0. The protocol was implemented using IPX via `TIMESYNC.NLM`. With the release of NetWare 5, Novell enhanced its time synchronization service to also function over IP natively and to interoperate directly with Internet standards–based NTP time sources. `TIMESYNC.NLM` can now handle both IP- and IPX-related communication and provides Novell TimeSync protocol, NTP client, and NTP server capability.

Instead of time server *types* (such as Single Reference) used by Novell, NTP uses the term *stratum* to indicate the accuracy of a time source. The stratum ranges from 1 to 16. 1 stands for the time source itself, 2 stands for the first server referencing that time source, 3 stands for the server referencing stratum 2, and so on. An NTP server at stratum $n+1$ is one that accepts time from an NTP server at stratum n. Thus a server at a lower stratum is accepted as a server that is more accurate than one at a higher stratum.

Internet time sources are typically public-domain NTP time sources that are at Stratum 1 or 2.   **NOTE**

NTP is very strict in considering a time source. If a time source is more than 1,000 seconds (17 minutes) away from the local clock, NTP rejects the time source and labels it as *insane*. Because of its refusal to accept insane time sources, NTP time sources are usually very reliable. You can find more information about NTP at www.ntp.org.

When NTP is activated on a NetWare server, the server can serve as a NTP time server for all IP-capable servers on the network. An NTP time source can be used for IPX networks if the Reference time server (running on NetWare 5 or higher) has both IP and IPX bound to its network boards or if the Reference time server is running a Compatibility Mode Driver (CMD). The IPX-based servers must be set to act as Secondary time servers.

At the time of this writing, NTP version 3 is the Internet Draft standard, formalized in RFC 1305. NetWare 6.5 supports NTP v3, but you need to use `XNTPD.NLM` **instead of** `TIMESYNC.NLM` **for full NTP compatibility (see TID #10084753).**   **NOTE**

NTP version 4, a significant revision of the NTP standard, is the current development version but has not yet been formalized in an RFC.

eDirectory Foundations

Depending on your environment, you first need to make a decision about whether to use TimeSync or NTP. You can use either method in a pure NetWare environment; however, if you have non-NetWare servers on the network, such as Unix servers, you should implement NTP. When implementing eDirectory on a mixture of NetWare and non-NetWare platforms, such as Solaris and Linux, you have no other option but to use NTP because it is the most common cross-platform time synchronization protocol.

> **NOTE** Although Novell does not provide applications to ensure that network time is synchronized for non-NetWare platforms, time synchronization across the network is still critical and must exist for eDirectory to function properly.

Server platforms such as Solaris and Linux provide for time synchronization via NTP as part of their core operating systems. See your operating system's documentation for information on configuring time synchronization on those platforms. Windows NT and higher does not provide this functionality out-of-the-box, so you need a third-party application to synchronize time with this server platform. Several third-party applications exist for this function. You can find information regarding such applications at `www.ntp.org/links.html`.

> **NOTE** Simple NTP (SNTP) is an adaptation of NTP. SNTP can be used when the ultimate performance of the full NTP implementation described in RFC 1305 is not needed or justified. Therefore, you can use an SNTP application or the NET TIME facility in a Windows environment, for instance, to provide time synchronization services that eDirectory requires. (On Windows 2000 and higher, you type NET TIME /HELP at a command prompt for more information.) At the time of this writing, SNTP version 4 is the current standard; it is described in RFC 2030.

DHost

Starting with eDirectory 8.5, the eDirectory software for all supported platforms, such as Windows NT/2000 and higher, Solaris, Linux, AIX, and HP-UX, has been built on the same core code as eDirectory for NetWare. This ensures maximum compatibility between platforms and makes it easier to make the same version of software available on multiple platforms. In order for eDirectory for Windows and Unix to properly interact with the NetWare-based eDirectory and previous versions of NDS, eDirectory for non-NetWare supports a subset of NCP services. A program called *DHost* manages these services.

NOTE

Although DHost was first introduced with NDS for Windows NT, the cross-platform base-code consolidation did not occur until eDirectory 8.5. It was not until eDirectory 8.7.1 that a Novell Client (generally referred to as Client32) was no longer required for the Windows version of eDirectory.

DHost sits underneath eDirectory and provides the following functionality on non-NetWare platforms that the NetWare operating system provides naturally:

▶ **NCP Engine**—The NCP engine implements a packet-based protocol that enables a client to send requests (over IP or IPX) to and receive replies from a NetWare server or a non-NetWare server that also has an NCP engine. This allows, for instance, the DSRepair NLM to check and report on the time synchronization status of all servers in the tree, even if some of them are non-NetWare DS servers.

▶ **Watchdog service**—The watchdog service involves packets used to make sure workstations are still connected to the (NetWare) server. When a workstation is logged in to a server but has not transmitted a packet for some period of time (the default is 5 minutes), the server sends a watchdog query packet to the workstation. If the workstation does not send back a watchdog response packet after 5 minutes, the server sends additional queries at specified intervals, until 15 minutes have elapsed. If the workstation still has not replied, the server terminates the connection.

▶ **Connection table management**—NetWare assigns a unique number to any process, print server, application, workstation, or other entity that is attached to the server. The number can be different each time an attachment is made. Connection numbers are used in implementing network security and for network accounting. They reflect the objects' places in the file server's connection table. In addition, they provide an easy way to identify and obtain information about the objects logged in on the network.

▶ **Event system**—The event system provides a way for applications to monitor the activity of an individual server. You can configure eDirectory 8.7 and later to send Simple Network Management Protocol (SNMP) traps when certain DS event takes place. eDirectory 8.7.3 defined 119 traps in the Management Information Base (MIB). Out of these, 117 traps map to eDirectory events such as object creation, object move, and password change events. The other two traps, `dsServerStart` and `ndsServerStop`, are directly generated by the SNMP subagent, based on the state of the eDirectory server.

▶ **Thread pool management**—eDirectory is multithreaded for perform-ance reasons. The way multithreading works is that when the system is busy, more threads are created to handle the load. Otherwise, threads are killed to avoid the extra overhead. However, it is inefficient and costly (CPU cycle-wise) to frequently create and destroy threads. Therefore, instead of a given process spinning up new threads or destroying idle threads as necessary, a number of threads are started and placed in a pool. The system then allocates the threads from the thread pool to various processes as needed, thus increasing perform-ance.

▶ **NCP extensions**—The fundamental NetWare services are provided by a set of functions implemented by the NCP engine. Each routine is referred to as an NCP. NetWare allows you to register the services of an NLM as an NCP extension, allowing you to extend the services provided by the NetWare operating system while maintaining the advantages associated with NCPs. Under DHost, this feature allows eDirectory processes to register NCP extensions on non-NetWare plat-forms.

▶ **Message digest**—A message digest is a data string distilled from the contents of a text message, created using a one-way hash function. Encrypting a message digest with a private key creates a digital signa-ture, which is an electronic means of authentication. This function supports NMAS, which is used to manage the various security policies and login methods, such as Simple password.

You can determine the status of the modules managed by DHost by using the DHost iConsole Manager (see Figure 2.18), which is accessed through NDS iMonitor. You can also use the Modules page in the DHost iConsole Manager to start and stop (load or unload) these services. However, not all modules can be stopped; system modules, such as the NCP extensions, can-not be stopped. Clicking the icon located to the right of the description tog-gles the status of nonsystem modules such as LDAP Server (called LDAP Agent for eDirectory), SNMP Trap Server, and HTTP Protocol Stack.

You can also use DHost iConsole Manager as a diagnostic and debugging tool. It allows you to access the HTTP server when the eDirectory server is not functioning correctly. (See Chapter 7, "Diagnostic and Repair Tools," for more information on this.)

Click to start process

Click to stop process

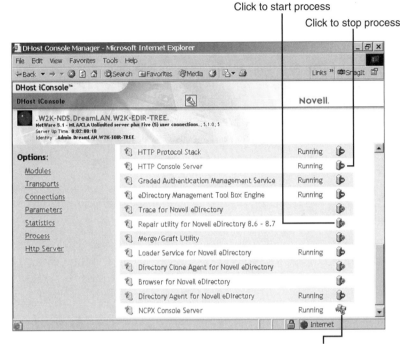

FIGURE 2.18
The Modules
page of DHost
iConsole.

Indicates it's a system module
that cannot be stopped

SAP and SLP

NetWare has traditionally used SAP, a Novell-proprietary protocol, to discover and advertise various services on an IPX network. NetWare 4 uses SAP to discover and advertise NDS tree names, for instance. With NetWare 5 and higher, servers running IP use SLP instead of SAP. This is also the case when in environments that include non-NetWare-based DS servers.

Given that more and more networks are using IP as their main networking protocol (even in pure NetWare environments), SAP will eventually disappear and be completely replaced by SLP. Furthermore, in a mixed operating system environment, SLP must be used. Information about SAP has been widely available for quite some time; therefore, it is not discussed here any further. However, the following sections provide a brief review of SLP terms and concepts.

TIP

The following Novell TIDs provide information on implementing and configuring SLP:

- ▶ #10025313—Frequently Asked Questions about SLP
- ▶ #10014396—SLP Terms and Configuration Reference
- ▶ #10014467—Configuring a LAN/WAN Infrastructure for SLP
- ▶ #10059981—Configuring SLP with a SCOPED directory agent (DA)
- ▶ #10014466—Configuring SLP for a NetWare Client
- ▶ #10027163—Configuring SLP for a NetWare Server
- ▶ #10062474—SLP Design and Implementation Guidelines

SLP Agents

SLP supports a framework in which client applications are modeled as user agents (UAs), and service agents (SAs) advertise services. A third entity, called a directory agent (DA), provides scalability to the protocol. These agents are used to register, maintain, and locate services on a network:

- ▶ **SAs**—An SA runs on every server that is running SLP. Applications on this server register with the SA, and that information is stored in local cache memory. The SA also listens for service requests. If a request is received that matches a service that is registered, the SA will respond to that request.

- ▶ **UAs**—A UA makes requests for service information. A UA is most likely to be a client that is looking for a service. The client can be a server application. For example, NDS makes requests for SLP service information when the server is brought up.

- ▶ **DAs**—A DA stores and disseminates service information for the network. In Novell's implementation of SLP, the DA uses NDS as the data store for this information. An SA registers its services with a DA, and a UA requests service information from the DA. The SA registers its services for a specific period of time, called the *service lifetime*. If the SA does not re-register, or refresh, the service before this lifetime expires, the service is purged.

NOTE

DAs are optional in an SLP implementation, but UAs and SAs are not.

The SLP framework allows the UA to directly issue requests to SAs. In such a case, the request is multicast (because the UA does not know, initially, where the service is located). SAs receiving a request for a service that they advertise unicast a reply containing the service's location (see Figure 2.19). The multicast address that a UA sends to is 224.0.1.22. Note that this multicast packet is sent to *every* network and router that has multicasting enabled. Therefore, the UA may receive more than one response because every SA that receives this packet responds with service information if it has what the UA is asking for.

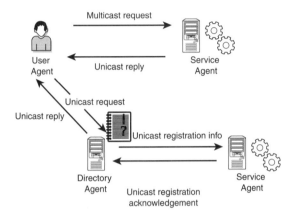

FIGURE 2.19
Communication methods between a UA, a DA, and SAs.

In larger networks, one or more DAs are generally used in order to reduce the amount of SLP-related multicast traffic attributed to service location queries. The DA functions as a central repository, or cache in this environment. SAs send register messages containing all the services they advertise to DAs and receive acknowledgements in reply. UAs unicast requests to DAs instead of to SAs if any DAs are known.

UAs and SAs discover DAs two ways. First, they issue a multicast service request (to address 224.0.1.35), looking for the DA service when they start up. Second, the DA multicasts an unsolicited advertisement periodically (but infrequently), which the UAs and SAs listen for. In either case, the agents receive a DA advertisement, thus learning the whereabouts of DAs.

NOTE

SLP uses the following two multicast addresses:
- ► **224.0.1.22 for service location general multicast**
- ► **224.0.1.35 for DA discovery multicast**

DAs listen on both UDP and TCP port number 427 for multicast traffic addressed to it.

SLP Services

SLP services are applications that run on a host (server or client) that other hosts on the network can access. Common examples of services include NDS, `RCONAG6.NLM`, and `TIMESYNC.NLM` running on a NetWare 6 server. When a NetWare 6 server starts up, these services (applications) register themselves with SLP and make themselves available to the network. From a high-level viewpoint, the information that SLP maintains about a service is the service name and the IP address or DNS name of the host (normally a server) that is running this service.

Each service on the network has a unique uniform resource locator (URL). This URL contains the details of the service, such as the IP address (or the DNS name or both) and port of the server on which this service is running and the version of SLP that this server is running. Table 2.7 lists some of the common NetWare 6.5 URL name prefixes and what they represent.

TABLE 2.7   **Common NetWare 6.5 SLP Service URL Prefixes and Their SAP Equivalents**

SLP SERVICE URL	SAP EQUIVALENT (HEX)	WHAT IT REPRESENTS
bindery.novell	0004	NetWare server.
ldap.novell	N/A	LDAP service.
ndap.novell	0278	DS on a server—one entry for *each* NDS partition on a server.
nlsmeter.novell	N/A	Software-usage-metering database manager.
nwserver.novell	N/A	A special server-centric service. This SLP service was designed to list any service that might potentially be available and eliminate the need for a separate service entry (and thus DS object) for every service the server offers. For example, the rcon-sole.novell, bindery.novell, srs.novell, rms.novell, and other third-party services would all be detectable from this single SLP service. At the time of this writing, however, no applications have been rewritten to take advantage of this,

Table 2.7   Continued

SLP SERVICE URL	SAP EQUIVALENT (HEX)	WHAT IT REPRESENTS
		and only the NetWare server itself registers with this service.
portal.novell	N/A	iManager service.
rconsole.novell	N/A	RCONAG6 running on a server (for RconsoleJ).
rms.novell	8202	NDPS Resource Management Service (RMS).
sapsrv.novell	N/A	IPX services on a NetWare 5 or higher server, available via the SCMD driver. IPX services from NetWare 4 are not registered.
securerconsole. novell	N/A	Secure RCONAG6 service (NetWare 6 and higher).
smdr.novell	023F	Storage Management Data Requester (SMDR).
srs.novell	0282	NDPS Service Registry Services (SRS); NDPS Broker NLM.
timesync.novell	026B	TimeSync service.

The following is sample output of a DISPLAY SLP SERVICES console command on a NetWare 6.5 server:

```
DISPLAY SLP SERVICES
   Usage: display slp services [<service type>/<scope>/
         ➥<predicate query>]/
     Example 1: 'display slp services'
     Example 2: 'display slp services bindery.novell//
                 ➥(svcname-ws==abc*)/'

Searching Network . . .
   service:nwserver.novell:///NETWARE6A
   service:nwserver.novell:///NETWARE_51
   service:portal.novell://10.6.6.1:8008/NETWARE6A
   service:securerconsole.novell:///10.6.6.1:2036;
    ➥NETWARE6A.XYZCorp.com
   service:rconsole.novell:///10.6.6.1:2034;
    ➥NETWARE6A.XYZCorp.com
   service:rconsole.novell:///10.55.66.77:2034;netware_51
```

```
service:timesync.novell://10.6.6.1
service:timesync.novell://10.55.66.77
service:smdr.novell://10.6.6.1:413/NETWARE6A
service:ldap.novell:///10.6.6.1:389
service:bindery.novell:///NETWARE6A
service:bindery.novell:///NETWARE_51
service:ndap.novell:///EDIR-NW51.
service:ndap.novell:///
  ➥eDir-to-eDir.DirXML-Guide-NW.EDIR-NW51.
service:nlsmeter.novell://10.6.6.1:21571/NETWARE6A

Displayed 15 URL's.
```

SLP Scopes

When more than one DA is used, services (and SAs) advertised by the several DAs are collected together into logical groupings called *scopes*. The scope names are simply text strings assigned by the network administrator. A scope could indicate a location, an administrative grouping, or proximity in a network topology or some other category.

A UA is normally assigned a scope name (in which case the UA will only be able to discover that particular grouping of services). This allows a network administrator to provision services to users. Alternatively, the UA may be configured with no scope at all (that is, it is unscoped). In that case, it will discover *all* available scopes and allow the client application to issue requests for any service available on the network. SAs and DAs are always assigned scope names.

In Novell's implementation, a scope is simply a container within NDS for SLP services that have been registered with a DA. The SLP `Scope Unit` container object is the actual storage container for SLP service information. Each `Scope Unit` container holds all the SLP service objects for a specific scope. It is possible to replicate this container into other partitions within the tree or within federated trees. Associated with the `Scope Unit` container is the attribute `Scope Name`. The SA and UA use `Scope Name` to define what scopes they are to work with.

SLP scopes are either scoped or unscoped:

▶ An *unscoped scope* is a general default scope. It is a grouping of all service URL information that is not tied to a particular scope. In SLP version 1, the default scope is called the *unscoped scope*. In SLP version 2, it is called the *default scope*.

▶ A *scoped scope* is a `Scope Unit` container that has been defined with a specific `Scope Name` attribute value.

NOTE

NetWare 5 implements SLP v1, as defined in RFC 2165. The latest support pack updates the SLP support to SLP v2, as defined in RFC 2608. NetWare 6 and later versions support SLP v2 out of the box. The related module names are `SLP.NLM` and `SLPTCP.NLM`.

For non-NetWare platforms, such as Unix or Linux, the eDirectory installation process installs OpenSLP, an open-source implementation of SLP (see `www.openslp.org`). This application is called slpuasa and is found in the NDSslp package. On Windows, the program is `slpd.exe`, and it is installed in the `%WINDIR%\system32\Novell\eDir\OpenSLP` folder.

NOTE

If a network requires more than one scope and you want to set up a default scope container, create a scope called `Default Scope`. Do not use the unscoped scope in this configuration. This will make the transition to SLP version 2 easier.

If you are using SLP v1 on a network that has many services, you need to set up multiple scopes. This is due to the 64KB limit of SLP reply packet and service information.

When a UA requests information about a specific service from a DA, it sends an SLP service type request, asking for all services of the same type (such as `bindery.novell`). The DA responds with a *single* UDP reply packet. If there are so many `bindery.novell` services registered in SLP that they do not all fit within one UDP packet, the DA sets an overflow bit. The UA then opens a TCP connection with the DA and asks for all the `bindery.novell` services again.

64KB of data is all the DA can send to the client via a TCP connection. This is because in SLP version 1.0, the Length field in the SLP response packet header is only 16 bits, allowing for up to 64KB of service data. If there is more than 64KB of a certain service type, the list is truncated. The workaround is to implement multiple scopes serviced by different DAs. A better solution, however, is to upgrade to SLP v2, where the length field has been expanded to 24 bits, thus allowing for up to 16MB of response data. For more information about the SLP packet structure, see `www.networksorcery.com/enp/protocol/slp.htm`.

> **NOTE**
>
> The following is a list of how many of the common service types will fit into a 64KB response packet:
>
> | Service | Number per response packet |
> |---|---|
> | bindery.novell | 700–1,100, depending on the size of partition and tree names. |
> | ndap.novell | Around 1,200, depending on the size of partition names. |
> | saprrv.novell | Around 550 IPX services. |

The LDAP Server for NDS

LDAP is an Internet communications protocol standard that lets client applications access directory information. It is based on the X.500 Directory Access Protocol (DAP) but is much less complex (thus "Lightweight") than a traditional DAP client and can be used with any other directory service that follows the X.500 standard.

To provide LDAP connectivity to NDS/eDirectory, Novell has been shipping LDAP Services for Novell NDS since NetWare 4.10. This server application lets LDAP clients access information stored in NDS/eDirectory. The current version is LDAP v3 compliant.

> **NOTE**
>
> LDAP servers are specific to the back-end database they support. For instance, you cannot use the Novell LDAP server for Windows (included with eDirectory for Windows) to access Active Directory, even when both are running on the same Windows server. The LDAP server basically serves as the translator between the (Internet standard) LDAP client and the (proprietary) directory service database; this is very similar to the concept of using Open Database Connectivity (ODBC) drivers to access databases.
>
> In Novell documentation, the LDAP server for NDS/eDirectory is sometimes referred to as the LDAP agent for eDirectory because it acts on your behalf to access information from eDirectory.

> **NOTE**
>
> The LDAP server modules shipped with eDirectory are NLDAP.NLM for NetWare; nldap.dlm for Windows 2000/NT; libnldap.so for Linux, Solaris, and AIX systems; and libnldap.sl for HP-UX systems. Except on the NetWare platform, the LDAP server for eDirectory runs as a task under DHost. Therefore, you will not find a process called nldap.dlm in Task Manager on Windows servers, for instance. (DHost is discussed earlier in this chapter, in the section "DHost.")

The following LDAP tools are included with LDAP Services to help you manage the LDAP server:

> **On Unix/Linux, the LDAP tools are stored in** /usr/ldaptools/bin **(except** ice,
> **which is stored in** /usr/bin)**. On Windows all but** ndsindex **are found in the**
> \Novell\ConsoleOne\1.2\bin **directory (**ndsindex **is located in**
> \Novell\NDS **instead). On NetWare, all but** ndsindex **are in the**
> SYS:PUBLIC\mgmt\ConsoleOne\1.2\bin **directory;** ndsindex **is implemented**
> **as** NINDEX.NLM **and is located in** SYS:SYSTEM.

- ▶ **ice**—Imports entries from a file to an LDAP directory, modifies the entries in a directory from a file, exports the entries to a file, and adds attribute and class definitions from a file.

- ▶ **ldapadd**—Adds new entries to an LDAP directory.

- ▶ **ldapdelete**—Deletes entries from an LDAP directory server. The **ldapdelete** tool opens a connection to an LDAP server and binds and deletes one or more entries.

- ▶ **ldapmodify**—Opens a connection to an LDAP server and binds and modifies or adds entries.

- ▶ **ldapmodrdn**—Modifies the RDNs of entries in an LDAP directory server. Opens a connection to an LDAP server and binds and modifies the RDNs of entries.

- ▶ **ldapsearch**—Searches entries in an LDAP directory server. Opens a connection to an LDAP server and binds and performs a search, using the specified filter. The filter should conform to the string representation for LDAP filters, as defined in RFC 2254.

- ▶ **ndsindex**—Creates, lists, suspends, resumes, or deletes indexes for NDS servers. This tool is useful in performance tuning (see Chapter 16).

Table 2.8 summarizes the availability of features in various releases of the LDAP server for NDS. The various features are discussed in the sections that follow.

TABLE 2.8 **LDAP Server for NDS Feature Comparison**

LDAP FEATURE	EDIRECTORY 8.7	EDIRECTORY 8.6	EDIRECTORY 8.5	EDIRECTORY 8	NDS 8	NDS 7
Support for LDAP v2	×	×	×	×	×	×
Support for LDAP v3	×	×	×	×	×	
Authentication (anonymous, clear-text, and Secure Sockets Layer [SSL]/ Transport Layer Security [TLS])	×	×	×	×	×	×
Mutual authentication	×	×	×			
Simple Authentication and Security Layer (SASL) authentication	×	× (using X.509 certificates)				
Digest-MD5 bind	×					
NMAS_LOGIN bind	×					
Configuration of port for secure bind	×	×	×			
Enforcement of NDS-based connection management policies (for example, concurrent connections and time restrictions)	×	×	×			

Table 2.8   Continued

LDAP FEATURE	EDIRECTORY 8.7	EDIRECTORY 8.6	EDIRECTORY 8.5	EDIRECTORY 8	NDS 8	NDS 7
Enforcement of NDS-based password restrictions (for example, password length, grace logins, expiration, and uniqueness)	×	×	×			
Entry management (search, modify, compare, rename, add, delete)	×	×	×	×	×	×
User self-password management	×	×	×	×	×	Must be changed by administrator
NDS partition and replica management	×	×	×			
Setting of (NDS) indexes for faster searching	×	×	×			
LDAP controls (query root DSE for supported controls)	×	×	×	×	×	
Support for LDAP extensions		×	×	×	×	
Referrals and traversals	×	×	×	×	×	With restrictions
Readable root DSE (to determine supported features)	×	×	×	×	×	×

Table 2.8   Continued

LDAP FEATURE	EDIRECTORY 8.7	EDIRECTORY 8.6	EDIRECTORY 8.5	EDIRECTORY 8	NDS 8	NDS 7
Reading and writing of schema (that is, writable root DSE)	×	×	×	×	Read only	
Modification of existing schema definitions	×	×	×			
Auxiliary class support	×	×	×	×	×	
Valid LDAP names requiring no mapping	×	×	×	×		
Generated LDAP name for each NDS name that is not mapped or that is not valid	×	×	×			
Access to NDS compound syntaxes	×	×	×	Selected		
LDAP and NDS operational attributes	×	×	×			
Support for NDS dynamic groups	×	×				
Persistent search	×	×				
Refreshing of LDAP server from LDAP	×	×	×	Must use NCP calls		
Superior referrals	×					
Referrals for non-search operations	×					
TLS (SSL) encryption	×	×	×	×	×	

Table 2.8   Continued

LDAP FEATURE	EDIRECTORY 8.7	EDIRECTORY 8.6	EDIRECTORY 8.5	EDIRECTORY 8	NDS 8	NDS 7
Start/stop TLS	×					
Extensible match search filters	×					
NDS events notification	×					

LDAP server features are server-centric. Therefore, for an application to use a particular LDAP feature, the application must attach to an LDAP server running a version of NDS or eDirectory that supports the feature. For example, the client cannot bind to an LDAP server for eDirectory 8.6 to receive DS event notification.

LDAP and NDS/eDirectory Terminology

When combining two technologies, there is often conflict between the meanings of the terms used. This is true in the case of integrating LDAP with NDS/eDirectory. In LDAP documentation, an *entry* consistently means a record in the directory database. On the other hand, in DS documentation, such a record is fairly consistently called an *object*. Because the term *object* becomes ambiguous when describing object-oriented programming languages, DS developer documentation is beginning to use the LDAP term—*entries*—but not completely. Some functions, attribute names, and class names still use the term *object*. Novell product documentation for DS utilities and applications continues to use the DS term, *objects*.

In most DS documentation, *attributes* refers to the fields of a record. LDAP and X.500 conform to this standard. However, a lot of LDAP documentation also uses the word *attribute* to refer to the attribute's value; NDS/eDirectory programming documentation, for example, uses *attribute*. However, Novell product documentation for NDS/eDirectory utilities and applications uses the term *properties* to describe fields in a record.

In DS, a *partition* is a branch of the DS tree with only one parent that is hosted on a server. In LDAP parlance, this is called a *naming context*. Figure 2.20 illustrates a simple hierarchical tree with four naming contexts:

- ▶ O=Universal_Export

- ▶ OU=Customer_Service, O=Universal_Export

- ▶ OU=Gadgets, O=Universal_Export

- ▶ OU=M, OU=Gadgets, O=Universal_Export

Just as with DS partitions, LDAP's naming context is named by the DN of the root container. The exception is the [Root] naming context. LDAP's root object is called a *DSA-specific Entry (DSE)*, or *root DSE*, and is not part of any naming context. Each LDAP server can have different attribute values in the root DSE. (Directory system agent [DSA] is an X.500 term for the directory server.)

FIGURE 2.20
LDAP naming
context example.

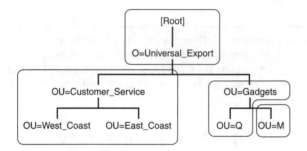

REAL WORLD

Root DSE Explained

Root DSE is a pseudo, unnamed, entry at the root of the directory tree. Because it is not a named entry in the tree, an LDAP server does not return root DSE to the client as part of any normal search operation.

Root DSE holds information that is specific to the server that you are connected to. The following is some of the information you can obtain by querying root DSE:

- ▶ **namingContexts**—Naming contexts held in the server.

- ▶ **subschemaSubentry**—Subschema entries (or subentries)—classes and attributes—known by this server.

- ▶ **altServer**—Alternative servers in case this one is later unavailable.

- ▶ **supportedExtension**—List of supported extended operations.

- ▶ **supportedControl**—List of supported controls.

- ▶ **supportedSASLMechanisms**—List of supported SASL security features.

- ▶ **supportedLDAPVersion**—LDAP versions implemented by the server.

Additional information about root DSE and schema attribute definitions can be found in RFCs 2251 and 2252, respectively.

LDAP and eDirectory Integration

The LDAP server included with eDirectory supports the following features:

▶ Authentication support. Standard LDAP authentication methods
include anonymous binds, clear-text binds, SSL and SASL (RFC 2222)
binds. From DS's perspective, these LDAP authentication methods
mean the following:

    ▶ An anonymous bind is an unauthenticated connection with pub-
lic access to the directory.

    ▶ A clear-text bind is an authentication over an unencrypted chan-
nel. The client sends a username and a clear-text password. The
LDAP server must be configured to accept unencrypted passwords.

    ▶ An SSL bind is an authentication over an encrypted channel
(secured by an SSL certificate). All data, including the password,
is encrypted. DS clients have access to SSL binds only through
LDAP.

▶ Adding, modifying, and deleting of entries and attributes in the directory.

▶ Reading, sorting, and searching of entries and attributes in the directory.

▶ Reading, adding, and deleting of schema definitions (object classes
and attributes). The LDAP server for eDirectory 8.5 and higher supports the modification of class definitions and attribute definitions as
long as the modifications increase functionality rather than restrict it.

LDAP Extensions and Controls

The standard LDAP protocol specification does not yet support access to
replication, partition, and synchronization services. However, these services
are available through (Novell-specific) LDAP extensions that are available for
eDirectory 8.5 and higher.

NOTE

**LDAP v3 provides a method for extending its functionality through LDAP controls
and extensions. For example, RFC 2891 defines two LDAP v3 controls for server-
side sorting of results; this instructs the LDAP server to sort the search results
before sending them back to the client. An LDAP control is a command sequence
that contains a predefined object ID (OID) that the LDAP server understands as an
extension, and instructions specific for the requested action.**

**Keep in mind that some LDAP controls and extensions are vendor specific, and
controls that are common among some vendors may not be implemented alike.**

Tables 2.9, 2.10, and 2.11 show controls and extensions supported by eDirectory 8.5 and higher that allow LDAP clients to perform the following request:

- ▶ Naming contexts: split, join, return number of entries, abort operation
- ▶ Replicas: add, remove, change type, enumerate number of replicas on a server, retrieve replica information
- ▶ Replica synchronization: to a specified server, to all replicas, at a specified time
- ▶ Synchronize schemas
- ▶ Get effective NDS rights for attributes
- ▶ Get DN of logged in caller
- ▶ Restart the LDAP server
- ▶ Change Simple passwords via LDAP
- ▶ Monitor events (some extensions require eDirectory 8.7 and higher)

TABLE 2.9   **LDAP Extensions Supported by eDirectory**

OID	EXTENSION NAME
1.3.6.1.4.1.1466.20037	startTLS (eDirectory 8.7 and higher)
2.16.840.1.113719.1.27.100.1	ndsToLdapResponse
2.16.840.1.113719.1.27.100.2	ndsToLdapRequest
2.16.840.1.113719.1.27.100.3	createNamingContextRequest (also known as SplitPartitionRequest)
2.16.840.1.113719.1.27.100.4	createNamingContextResponse (also known as SplitPartitionResponse)
2.16.840.1.113719.1.27.100.5	mergeNamingContextRequest (also known as MergePartitionRequest)
2.16.840.1.113719.1.27.100.6	mergeNamingContextResponse (also known as MergePartitionResponse)
2.16.840.1.113719.1.27.100.7	addReplicaRequest
2.16.840.1.113719.1.27.100.8	addReplicaResponse
2.16.840.1.113719.1.27.100.9	refreshLDAPServerRequest
2.16.840.1.113719.1.27.100.10	refreshLDAPServerResponse
2.16.840.1.113719.1.27.100.11	removeReplicaRequest
2.16.840.1.113719.1.27.100.12	removeReplicaResponse

Table 2.9 Continued

OID	EXTENSION NAME
2.16.840.1.113719.1.27.100.13	namingContextEntryCountRequest (also known as PatitionEntryCountRequest)
2.16.840.1.113719.1.27.100.14	namingContextEntryCountResponse (also known as PartitionEntryCountResponse)
2.16.840.1.113719.1.27.100.15	changeReplicaTypeRequest
2.16.840.1.113719.1.27.100.16	changeReplicaTypeResponse
2.16.840.1.113719.1.27.100.17	getReplicaInfoRequest
2.16.840.1.113719.1.27.100.18	getReplicaInfoResponse
2.16.840.1.113719.1.27.100.19	listReplicaRequest
2.16.840.1.113719.1.27.100.20	listReplicaResponse
2.16.840.1.113719.1.27.100.21	receiveAllUpdatesRequest
2.16.840.1.113719.1.27.100.22	receiveAllUpdatesResponse
2.16.840.1.113719.1.27.100.23	sendAllUpdatesRequest
2.16.840.1.113719.1.27.100.24	sendAllUpdatesResponse
2.16.840.1.113719.1.27.100.25	requestNamingContextSyncRequest (also known as RequestPartitionSyncRequest)
2.16.840.1.113719.1.27.100.26	requestNamingContextSyncResponse (also known as RequestPartitionSyncRequest)
2.16.840.1.113719.1.27.100.27	requestSchemaSyncRequest
2.16.840.1.113719.1.27.100.28	requestSchemaSyncResponse
2.16.840.1.113719.1.27.100.29	abortNamingContextOperation Request (also known as AbortPartitionOperationRequest)
2.16.840.1.113719.1.27.100.30	abortNamingContextOperation Response (also known as AbortPartitionOperationRequest)
2.16.840.1.113719.1.27.100.31	getContextIdentityNameRequest (also known as GetBindDNRequest)
2.16.840.1.113719.1.27.100.32	getContextIdentityNameResponse (also known as GetBindDNResponse)
2.16.840.1.113719.1.27.100.33	getEffectivePrivilegesRequest

Table 2.9 Continued

OID	EXTENSION NAME
2.16.840.1.113719.1.27.100.34	getEffectivePrivilegesResponse
2.16.840.1.113719.1.27.100.35	setReplicationFilterRequest
2.16.840.1.113719.1.27.100.36	setReplicationFilterResponse
2.16.840.1.113719.1.27.100.37	getReplicationFilterRequest
2.16.840.1.113719.1.27.100.38	getReplicationFilterResponse
2.16.840.1.113719.1.27.100.39	CreateOrphanPartitionRequest
2.16.840.1.113719.1.27.100.40	CreateOrphanPartitionResponse
2.16.840.1.113719.1.27.100.41	RemoveOrphanPartitionRequest (also known as splitOrphanPartitionRequest)
2.16.840.1.113719.1.27.100.42	RemoveOrphanPartitionResponse (also known as splitOrphanPartitionResponse)
2.16.840.1.113719.1.27.100.43	triggerBackLinkerRequest
2.16.840.1.113719.1.27.100.44	triggerBackLinkerResponse
2.16.840.1.113719.1.27.100.45	triggerDRLProcessRequest
2.16.840.1.113719.1.27.100.46	triggerDRLProcessResponse
2.16.840.1.113719.1.27.100.47	triggerJanitorRequest
2.16.840.1.113719.1.27.100.48	triggerJanitorResponse
2.16.840.1.113719.1.27.100.49	triggerLimberRequest
2.16.840.1.113719.1.27.100.50	triggerLimberResponse
2.16.840.1.113719.1.27.100.51	triggerSkulkerRequest
2.16.840.1.113719.1.27.100.52	triggerSkulkerResponse
2.16.840.1.113719.1.27.100.53	triggerSchemaSyncRequest
2.16.840.1.113719.1.27.100.54	triggerSchemaSyncResponse
2.16.840.1.113719.1.27.100.55	triggerPartitionPurgeRequest
2.16.840.1.113719.1.27.100.56	triggerPartitionPurgeResponse
2.16.840.1.113719.1.27.100.79	MonitorEventRequest (eDirectory 8.7 and higher)
2.16.840.1.113719.1.27.100.80	MonitorEventResponse (eDirectory 8.7 and higher)
2.16.840.1.113719.1.27.100.81	FilteredMonitorEventRequest

Table 2.9   Continued

OID	EXTENSION NAME
2.16.840.1.113719.1.27.100.84	Undocumented (eDirectory 8.7 and higher)
2.16.840.1.113719. 1.27.103.1	CreateGroupingRequest
2.16.840.1.113719.1.27.103.2	EndGroupingRequest
2.16.840.1.113719.1.39.42.100.1 through 2.16.840.1.113719.1.39.42.100.12	Undocumented (eDirectory 8.7 and higher)
2.16.840.1.113719.1.39.42.100.13 through 2.16.840.1.113719.1.39.42.100.22	Undocumented (eDirectory 8.7.3 and higher)

Table 2.10 lists the extensions used by the Novell Import Convert Export (ICE) utility. They are not general extensions designed for developer use but are designed to support the LDAP Bulk Update Replication Protocol (LBURP).

ICE-Specific LDAP Extensions for eDirectory 8.5 and Higher   **TABLE 2.10**

OID	EXTENSION NAME
2.16.840.1.113719.1.142.100.1	StartFramedProtocolRequest (also known as startLburpRequest)
2.16.840.1.113719.1.142.100.2	StartFramedProtocolResponse (also known as startLburpResponse)
2.16.840.1.113719.1.142.100.4	EndFramedProtocolRequest (also known as endLburpRequest)
2.16.840.1.113719.1.142.100.5	EndFramedProtocolResponse (also known as endLburpResponse)
2.16.840.1.113719.1.142.100.6	LburpOperationRequest (also known as lburpOperation)
2.16.840.1.113719.1.142.100.7	LburpOperationResponse (also known as lburpOperationDone)

TABLE 2.11 | **LDAP Controls Supported by eDirectory**

OID	DESCRIPTION
1.2.840.113556.1.4.473	Server-side sort control request. Returns results from a search operation in sorted order. This can be used to offload processing from the client or if you cannot sort the results on the client. (NDS 8 and higher.)
1.2.840.113556.1.4.474	Server-side sort control response. (NDS 8 and higher.)
2.16.840.1.113719.1.27.101.5	NMAS simple password request.
2.16.840.1.113719.1.27.101.6	Create forward reference request. (When an entry is going to be created before its parent exists, a placeholder called a *forward reference* is created for the entry's parent to allow the entry to be successfully created. If a later operation creates the parent, the forward reference is changed into a normal entry.)
2.16.840.1.113719.1.27.103.7	Server-side grouping control that provides a general mechanism for grouping related LDAP operations. Grouping of operations can be used to support replication, proxies, and high-level operations such as transactions. This is currently an Internet Draft: `www.ietf.org/internet-drafts/ draft-zeilenga-ldap-grouping- 06.txt`. (eDirectory 8.7 and higher.)
2.16.840.1.113730.3.4.2	`ManageDsaIT` control request. This causes directory-specific entries, regardless of type, to be treated as normal entries. See RFC 3296 for details. (eDirectory 8.7 and higher.)
2.16.840.1.113730.3.4.3	Persistent search request. Performs continuous search operations. (eDirectory 8.6 and higher.)
2.16.840.1.113730.3.4.7	Entry change notification. It is a response to a persistent search request. (eDirectory 8.7 and higher.)

Persistent search is an LDAP v3 extension that enables applications to maintain a connection to an LDAP-compliant directory even after that directory has returned the results of a search request. For example, say that an LDAP application searches for all entries in the tree for which the CN attribute has a value beginning with the letter *A*, and 500 hits are expected. However, this application supports increments of only 10 search results. Using persistent search, this application could receive search results for this request in increments of 10 CN attributes without having to establish a new connection to the directory for each increment. Otherwise, this application would have to establish a new connection and issue a new search request for each increment.

WARNING

Two LDAP controls, 2.16.840.1.113730.3.4.9 (Virtual List View [VLV] request) and 2.16.840.1.113730.3.4.10 (VLV response), working in conjunction with the server-side sort control to provide a dynamic view of a scrolling list, are not fully supported by eDirectory. Refer to TID #10084069 for details on the limitations.

If you are unsure what extensions and controls are supported by the version of the LDAP server for eDirectory that you have, you can query its root DSE by using an LDAP search tool. For example, this is the syntax for using ldapsearch:

```
ldapsearch -h host -b "" -s base -D cn=admin,o=org
   ➥-w password objectclass=*
   ➥supportedcontrol supportedextension
```

The following is an example of some of the output from this command, showing just the supported extensions and controls, from a Windows 2000 server running eDirectory 8.7.3:

```
dn:
supportedExtension: 2.16.840.1.113719.1.142.100.1
supportedExtension: 2.16.840.1.113719.1.142.100.2
supportedExtension: 2.16.840.1.113719.1.142.100.4
supportedExtension: 2.16.840.1.113719.1.142.100.5
supportedExtension: 2.16.840.1.113719.1.142.100.6
supportedExtension: 2.16.840.1.113719.1.142.100.7
supportedExtension: 2.16.840.1.113719.1.27.100.1
supportedExtension: 2.16.840.1.113719.1.27.100.2
supportedExtension: 2.16.840.1.113719.1.27.100.3
supportedExtension: 2.16.840.1.113719.1.27.100.4
supportedExtension: 2.16.840.1.113719.1.27.100.5
supportedExtension: 2.16.840.1.113719.1.27.100.6
supportedExtension: 2.16.840.1.113719.1.27.100.7
supportedExtension: 2.16.840.1.113719.1.27.100.8
```

```
supportedExtension: 2.16.840.1.113719.1.27.100.11
supportedExtension: 2.16.840.1.113719.1.27.100.12
supportedExtension: 2.16.840.1.113719.1.27.100.13
supportedExtension: 2.16.840.1.113719.1.27.100.14
supportedExtension: 2.16.840.1.113719.1.27.100.15
supportedExtension: 2.16.840.1.113719.1.27.100.16
supportedExtension: 2.16.840.1.113719.1.27.100.17
supportedExtension: 2.16.840.1.113719.1.27.100.18
supportedExtension: 2.16.840.1.113719.1.27.100.19
supportedExtension: 2.16.840.1.113719.1.27.100.20
supportedExtension: 2.16.840.1.113719.1.27.100.21
supportedExtension: 2.16.840.1.113719.1.27.100.22
supportedExtension: 2.16.840.1.113719.1.27.100.23
supportedExtension: 2.16.840.1.113719.1.27.100.24
supportedExtension: 2.16.840.1.113719.1.27.100.25
supportedExtension: 2.16.840.1.113719.1.27.100.26
supportedExtension: 2.16.840.1.113719.1.27.100.27
supportedExtension: 2.16.840.1.113719.1.27.100.28
supportedExtension: 2.16.840.1.113719.1.27.100.29
supportedExtension: 2.16.840.1.113719.1.27.100.30
supportedExtension: 2.16.840.1.113719.1.27.100.31
supportedExtension: 2.16.840.1.113719.1.27.100.32
supportedExtension: 2.16.840.1.113719.1.27.100.33
supportedExtension: 2.16.840.1.113719.1.27.100.34
supportedExtension: 2.16.840.1.113719.1.27.100.35
supportedExtension: 2.16.840.1.113719.1.27.100.36
supportedExtension: 2.16.840.1.113719.1.27.100.37
supportedExtension: 2.16.840.1.113719.1.27.100.38
supportedExtension: 2.16.840.1.113719.1.27.100.39
supportedExtension: 2.16.840.1.113719.1.27.100.40
supportedExtension: 2.16.840.1.113719.1.27.100.41
supportedExtension: 2.16.840.1.113719.1.27.100.42
supportedExtension: 2.16.840.1.113719.1.39.42.100.1
supportedExtension: 2.16.840.1.113719.1.39.42.100.2
supportedExtension: 2.16.840.1.113719.1.39.42.100.3
supportedExtension: 2.16.840.1.113719.1.39.42.100.4
supportedExtension: 2.16.840.1.113719.1.39.42.100.5
supportedExtension: 2.16.840.1.113719.1.39.42.100.6
supportedExtension: 2.16.840.1.113719.1.39.42.100.7
supportedExtension: 2.16.840.1.113719.1.39.42.100.8
supportedExtension: 2.16.840.1.113719.1.39.42.100.9
supportedExtension: 2.16.840.1.113719.1.39.42.100.10
supportedExtension: 2.16.840.1.113719.1.39.42.100.11
supportedExtension: 2.16.840.1.113719.1.39.42.100.12
supportedExtension: 2.16.840.1.113719.1.39.42.100.13
```

```
supportedExtension: 2.16.840.1.113719.1.39.42.100.14
supportedExtension: 2.16.840.1.113719.1.39.42.100.15
supportedExtension: 2.16.840.1.113719.1.39.42.100.16
supportedExtension: 2.16.840.1.113719.1.39.42.100.17
supportedExtension: 2.16.840.1.113719.1.39.42.100.18
supportedExtension: 2.16.840.1.113719.1.39.42.100.19
supportedExtension: 2.16.840.1.113719.1.39.42.100.20
supportedExtension: 2.16.840.1.113719.1.39.42.100.21
supportedExtension: 2.16.840.1.113719.1.39.42.100.22
supportedExtension: 2.16.840.1.113719.1.27.100.9
supportedExtension: 2.16.840.1.113719.1.27.100.10
supportedExtension: 2.16.840.1.113719.1.27.100.43
supportedExtension: 2.16.840.1.113719.1.27.100.44
supportedExtension: 2.16.840.1.113719.1.27.100.45
supportedExtension: 2.16.840.1.113719.1.27.100.46
supportedExtension: 2.16.840.1.113719.1.27.100.47
supportedExtension: 2.16.840.1.113719.1.27.100.48
supportedExtension: 2.16.840.1.113719.1.27.100.49
supportedExtension: 2.16.840.1.113719.1.27.100.50
supportedExtension: 2.16.840.1.113719.1.27.100.51
supportedExtension: 2.16.840.1.113719.1.27.100.52
supportedExtension: 2.16.840.1.113719.1.27.100.53
supportedExtension: 2.16.840.1.113719.1.27.100.54
supportedExtension: 2.16.840.1.113719.1.27.100.55
supportedExtension: 2.16.840.1.113719.1.27.100.56
supportedExtension: 1.3.6.1.4.1.1466.20037
supportedExtension: 2.16.840.1.113719.1.27.100.79
supportedExtension: 2.16.840.1.113719.1.27.100.80
supportedExtension: 2.16.840.1.113719.1.27.100.84
supportedExtension: 2.16.840.1.113719.1.27.100.80
supportedExtension: 2.16.840.1.113719.1.27.103.1
supportedExtension: 2.16.840.1.113719.1.27.103.2
supportedControl: 2.16.840.1.113719.1.27.101.6
supportedControl: 2.16.840.1.113719.1.27.101.5
supportedControl: 2.16.840.1.113730.3.4.3
supportedControl: 2.16.840.1.113730.3.4.7
supportedControl: 2.16.840.1.113730.3.4.2
supportedControl: 2.16.840.1.113719.1.27.103.7
```

The LDAP `Server` object has a multivalued attribute called `extensionInfo`, which contains the list of supported controls and extensions supported by that server, as shown in Figure 2.21. To access this screen, you select the LDAP `Server` object in ConsoleOne and then right-click and select the Properties option from the context menu. Next, you select the Other tab,

PART I   eDirectory Foundations

open the `extensionInfo` listing, and click the Extended Editor button, which is denoted by an ellipsis (…).

You can deselect an extension from being supported by the server by deleting the attribute value that corresponds to the extension in question. However, because the attribute value is an octet string (`SYN_OCTET_STRING`), it could be cumbersome to put it back at a later time. (Note that this is not supported by Novell.) Alternatively, you can edit the value and change the starting *E* to a *D* (or basically anything other than *E*). This deselects the extension. Then you restart the LDAP server for the change to take effect. To reselect the extension at a later time, you change the *D* back to an *E* and restart the LDAP server.

FIGURE 2.21
The
`extensionInfo`
attribute of the
LDAP Server
object.

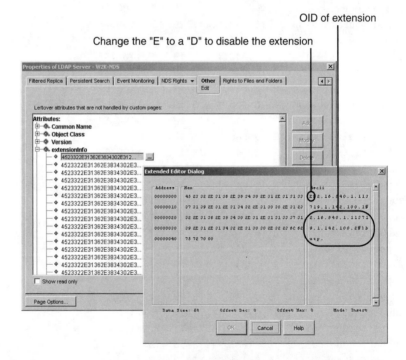

OID of extension

Change the "E" to a "D" to disable the extension

> **NOTE**   The server-side sort controls (1.2.840.113556.1.4.473 and 1.2.840.113556.1.4.474) are supported by the eDirectory LDAP server. However, they do not show up in the `supportedControl` listing shown earlier in this section.

LDAP Bind Methods

LDAP requires a client to employ a two-step process to connect with and authenticate to its back-end directory service. You first need to establish a connection to the LDAP server. This can be either an insecure, clear-text connection (with the default port 389) or a secured, encrypted connection (with the default port 636). Then the client has to perform a *bind*, the LDAP term for sending user information and password for the purpose of authentication, with the LDAP server. In the case of eDirectory, the supplied user credential is used for authentication against eDirectory, and the level of access is subject to eDirectory security (this includes user-level restrictions such as login time restriction and account lockout due to intrusion detection).

TIP

eDirectory's LDAP server uses the following attributes, not just the userPassword **attribute (which is essentially mapped to the public/private key pair), to control access to an account:**

- ▶ Locked By Intruder
- ▶ Login Allowed Time Map **(this is the login time restriction)**
- ▶ Login Disabled
- ▶ Login Expiration Time
- ▶ Login Maximum Simultaneous
- ▶ Password Expiration Interval
- ▶ Password Required

If a user is having difficulty accessing eDirectory via LDAP and the password is verified as being valid, you should check these attributes to help determine why the client cannot access the account.

LDAP supports a number of bind methods involving just the use of usernames and passwords. The bind methods defined in RFC 2829, "Authentication Methods for LDAP," are as follows:

- ▶ In an *anonymous bind*, the client sends empty strings for the DN/password pair. The eDirectory LDAP server establishes the client as [Public] or as the proxy user that you have configured. (The proxy user must not have a password.)

NOTE

If the LDAP connection was made by anonymous bind, the ldap_get_context_ identity_name **API function returns an empty string rather than** [Public].

- ▶ In a *simple bind*, the client sends non-null strings for the DN/password pair. However, the data is sent as clear text across the wire when using port 389. The eDirectory LDAP server establishes the client as the supplied DN. This method is called *simple bind* because using identity/ password pairs is simple (that is, not complicated compared to using X.509 security certificates, for instance).

> **NOTE** Because clear-text passwords can be easily captured off the wire with network traffic sniffer software that is easy to obtain these days, the eDirectory LDAP server accepts only TLS/SSL encrypted passwords by default. You need to specifically enable the clear-text support by *unchecking* the Require TLS for Simple Binds with Passwords check box either during the LDAP server installation process or in the General Information Properties tab of the LDAP Group object in ConsoleOne or iManager.

▶ In a *secure bind*, the DN/password pair is sent over TLS/SSL using port 636. This method is often considered a bind method, but technically, the TLS/SSL encryption sitting on top of the LDAP simple bind is securing the data; the heart of the operation is still a simple bind.

> **NOTE** If you have *not* disabled TLS/SSL for simple bind, your LDAP application may report an "ldap_bind: Confidentiality required" error. If you look in DSTrace with the +LDAP filter enabled, you will see something like this:
>
> ```
> Error: "Rejecting unencrypted bind on cleartext port in
>             nds_back_bind, err[equal]13"
> ```
>
> This is because the application is not using TLS/SSL when the LDAP server expects it.

> **NOTE** SSL 3.1 was released through Netscape. However, the Internet Engineering Task Force (IETF) took ownership for that standard by implementing TLS 1.0. As a result, Novell documentation often uses the two terms interchangeably or together: TLS/SSL.

▶ *SASL bind* uses the SASL specification as defined in RFC 2222. SASL is really a method for adding authentication support to connection-based protocols, and it does not dictate the mechanism to be used. The SASL protocol includes a command for identifying and authenticating a user to a server and for optionally negotiating a security layer for subsequent protocol interactions. The command has a required argument that identifies a SASL mechanism. (SASL mechanisms are named by text strings, ranging from 1 to 20 characters in length, consisting of uppercase letters, digits, hyphens, and/or underscores. SASL mechanism names must be registered with the Internet Assigned Numbers Authority [IANA].) Therefore, SASL binds are implementation specific.

The LDAP server for eDirectory 8.7.1 and higher supports Digest-MD5 (RFC 2831) and NMAS_LOGIN as SASL bind methods; NMAS_LOGIN provides support for the biometrics capability in

NMAS. eDirectory 8.5/8.6 supports the EXTERNAL SASL mechanism, in which the client presents an X.509 user certificate to the server, and the server checks that the certificate is signed by the eDirectory tree's Certificate Authority (CA).

NOTE

Digest-MD5 is a required authentication method defined for LDAP v3 (RFC 2829). The LDAP servers for eDirectory prior to 8.7 did not support Digest-MD5, nor did they support extensible match search filters (discussed in the following section). Therefore, they are not *fully* LDAP v3 compliant; however, because most installations use SSL/TLS anyway, instead of SASL, this is not a major issue.

Every LDAP operation requires the client to be bound before the operation is attempted. After the completion of the operation (be it successful or failed), the connection is automatically terminated. Therefore, to perform an add entry operation and then a modify entry operation, you must bind twice. The exception to this rule is if you are using persistent search, where you need to bind only once to retrieve all the search results.

Access Control

Another feature introduced in LDAP v3 is the ability to apply access control. Access control determines who has rights to entry information in a directory. In an NDS tree, every entry has an ACL attribute, which contains the explicit trustee assignments that have been made to the entry and its attributes. In addition, NDS allows rights to be inherited, so that an assignment in a parent container can allow additional trustees to have access to an entry. Functions that calculate effective rights gather information from these parent containers as well as from the ACL attribute. When an LDAP client queries for effective rights, the result returned by an eDirectory LDAP server is based on the explicit assignments *as well as* the inherited rights. Directories that do not allow the inheritance of rights implement the functions to return only explicit trustee assignments.

The LDAP server for eDirectory 8.7 also implements support for extensible match search filtering, as defined in RFC 2251. An *extensible match* allows an LDAP client to specify multiple match rules for the same type of data and to include dn attribute elements in the search criteria. For example, the following extensible match filter searches for all User objects in containers that have OU=Grade5 as part of their DNs:

```
(&(ou:dn:=Grade5)(objectClass=user))
```

As you can imagine, this feature allows applications to perform complex searches much more easily. Without it, the client itself has to provide more processing in order to filter out the desired data.

LDAP Event Services

Perhaps the most useful feature of the LDAP Server is LDAP Event Services, which was added to the Novell LDAP server for eDirectory 8.7. LDAP Event Services provides a way, via the standard LDAP extension mechanism, for applications to monitor the activity of eDirectory on an individual server.

LDAP Event Services supports more than 200 events that are divided into the following event types or categories:

- ▸ **Bindery events**—These events indicate the occurrence of bindery object creation or deletion operations.

- ▸ **Change server address events**—These events indicate the detection of a server address change.

- ▸ **Connection change events**—These events indicate that the state of a connection has changed (perhaps from unauthenticated to authenticated).

- ▸ **Dataless events**—This classification includes all events that do not have associated data (for instance, a bindery context was set on a server).

- ▸ **Debug events**—These events indicate the occurrence of debugging messages sent by various NDS background processes, such as Limber.

- ▸ **Entry events**—These events indicate the occurrence of individual entry operations such as creating or deleting an object.

- ▸ **General DS events**—These are general events used to indicate a wide variety of DS operations, such as a partition join operation or a user login.

- ▸ **Module state events**—These events indicate the change of state (from active to inactive, for example) of a DHost module.

- ▸ **Network address events**—These events indicate a possible communication problem. It is triggered if DS reports a remote server down or an NCP retry timed out.

- ▸ **Security Equivalence events**—These events indicate that an entry's security equivalence vector (SEV) is being checked.

- ▸ **Value events**—These events indicate the occurrence of attribute value operations such as deleting or adding a value.

The event system extension allows a client to specify the events for which it wants to receive notification. This information is sent in the extension request. If the extension request specifies valid events, the LDAP server keeps the connection open (through the use of the persistent search feature) and uses the intermediate extended response to notify the client when events occur. Any data associated with an event is also sent in the response. This feature provides an easy mechanism for network management applications to include eDirectory in their list of managed services.

NOTE

Although any LDAP client can register to monitor any event, access restrictions are enforced at the time of event notification. If the authenticated client does not have sufficient access rights to view all the information in the event (such as Browse rights to attributes of interest), the event will not be sent. The one exception to this rule is the perpetrator DN: If the client does not have rights to the perpetrator object, the object will be sent as a zero-length string and represented as a NULL pointer value at the client. The event notification, however, will still be sent.

Schema Mapping Between LDAP and eDirectory

The LDAP server for eDirectory automatically maps the DS attributes and classes that are defined in RFC 2256 to their LDAP-equivalent names. Alas, not all DS names can be mapped to LDAP names due to naming convention incompatibility, as discussed earlier in this chapter, in the section "Naming Rules and Restrictions." If LDAP clients need access to DS classes and attributes that have incompatible names, you need to manually map them to LDAP-compatible names by using ConsoleOne. Even if a name is compatible with LDAP conventions, an LDAP client may still not be able to access a certain attribute because the LDAP server does not support that attribute's syntax.

eDirectory 8.5 and higher map `inetOrgPerson` to the DS object class `User` by default. LDAP clients can access this class by using the LDAP names `inetOrgPerson` or `user`. In NDS 7 and NDS 8, by default, the `User` class definition does not contain all the standard attributes for `inetOrgPerson`. To add these attributes to the `User` class definition, you must update the schema by using a schema file (`nov_inet.sch`), available from Novell. With eDirectory 8.5 and later, however, this is all done automatically for you.

The LDAP server allows LDAP access to DS attributes if the DS attribute uses LDAP-compatible syntax. For example, any DS attribute that uses the case ignore string syntax (`SYN_CI_STRING`) is available through LDAP because LDAP supports this syntax (which is called `directoryString` in LDAP). DS attributes that use a compound syntax (such as the timestamp syntax, SYN_TIMESTAMP, with its fields for time, replica number, and event identifier) are not automatically accessible through LDAP. Instead, the LDAP server converts such a syntax to case ignore strings, using dollar ($) signs to separate fields of the same data type and (#) signs to separate fields of different data types. For example, the ACL is represented as follows:

```
acl: 2#subtree#cn=admin,o=testing#[All Attributes Rights]
```

where the first field is the trustee rights value (2 = Read), the next field indicates that it applies to the whole object (subtree), the next field is the object that has been granted the rights (cn=admin,o=testing), and the last field is the attribute name ([All Attributes Rights]). Postal Address is an example of an attribute that uses $ as data field delimiters (because all its data fields are of the type CI string):

```
postalAddress: CN$Street$Post Office Box$City$State$Zip Code
```

REAL WORLD

Base-64 Encoding of Attribute Values

The LDAP server encodes the values of attributes that use either SYN_STREAM or SYN_NET_ADDRESS, using the Base-64 Content-Transfer-Encoding mechanism (RFC 3548) before sending them to the client. Base-64 encoding is designed to represent arbitrary sequences of octet data streams in a printable (ASCII) format. base-64 uses a 64-character subset of US-ASCII (hence the name base 64) such that the characters are represented identically in all versions of ISO 646, including US-ASCII. All characters in the subset are also represented identically in all versions of EBCDIC. A 65th character, =, is used for padding and appears only at the end of the encoded output data stream, if ever.

When you query eDirectory for a login script, you get back something that looks like this:

```
loginScript:: d3JpdGUgIkhlbGxvIHdvcmxkISIN
```

When you run that through a Base-64 decoder (there are many available on the Internet), the preceding (without the loginScript:: part) translates to this:

```
write "Hello world!"
```

It gets a little more complicated when you're deciphering the networkAddress attribute. Typical output looks like this:

```
networkAddress:: MSNaBAQE
```

Decoding this produces 6 bytes of data, 3 bytes of which are none-printable characters. You need to actually look at the decoded information in hexadecimal format:

```
31 23 5A 04 04 04
```

> **The first byte represents the transport type. 0x31 is ASCII character 1, so the transport type is 1, or TCP/IP. The next byte is the # delimiter used by the LDAP server to separate fields of different data types. The last four bytes are the IP address 90.4.4.4.**

The LDAP server converts the DS time information (which uses the SYN_TIME syntax) to the LDAP format specified by X.208, which includes the year, month, day, hour, minute, optionally seconds, and time zone (GMT is recommended by X.208 for the time zone and uses Z as its symbol). The Login Time attribute would have a value similar to the following:

loginTime: 20031217051015Z

> **NOTE**
>
> The SYN_HOLD syntax is not supported through LDAP and is being phased out from use in NDS/eDirectory.

If you need to look up the attribute and class mapping between LDAP and NDS, from ConsoleOne you open the LDAP Group object, and from its Properties page, you check the Attribute Mappings (see Figure 2.22) and Class Mappings (see Figure 2.23) tabs, respectively. You can also use these tabs to add, delete, or modify the mapping assignments.

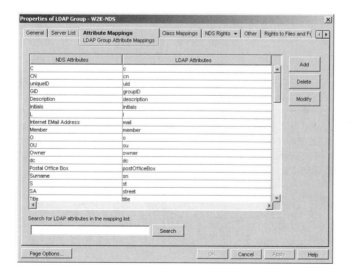

FIGURE 2.22
The Attributes Mappings tab of the LDAP Group object.

FIGURE 2.23

The Class
Mappings tab of
the LDAP Group
object.

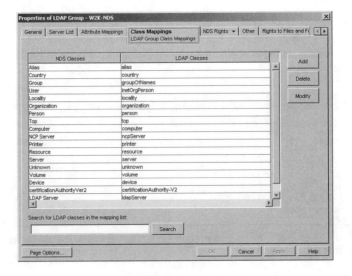

LDAP Name Resolution Models

Almost every LDAP operation takes a DN identifying a target entry as a
parameter. The first step in performing an LDAP operation is to find a copy
of the target entry somewhere in the eDirectory tree. LDAP v3 supports two
basic name resolution models—chaining and referral—that are discussed in
the following sections. Also discussed in the following sections is how the
eDirectory LDAP server uses eDirectory knowledge references for name resolution.

NOTE   DS maintains certain information in the replica rings of each partition root object
(by using the `Replica` attribute) and keeps track of subordinate references to
partition roots. This information includes the server's ID, address, and transport
type (such as IP or IPX), and the replica type that is stored on that server. This
information is termed *NDS knowledge references.*

Chaining

Sometimes when an LDAP client issues a request to an LDAP server, the
server may not contain the target entry of the operation in its local database.
However, the server can use the NDS knowledge references that it has about
partitions and other servers in the eDirectory tree to contact another LDAP
server that knows more about the DN. This process is called *chaining*, and it
is a server-based form of name resolution. If necessary, the chaining process
continues until the first server contacts a server that holds a replica of the
entry. eDirectory then handles all the details to complete the operation. The

LDAP server performs all this on behalf of the client. Therefore, unaware of the server-to-server operations, the client assumes that the first server completed the request.

Earlier versions of the NDS LDAP server used the term *traversal* instead of *chaining* in the NWAdmin and ConsoleOne snap-ins. The current implementation consistently uses *chaining* in both the administration tools and documentation.

NOTE ■

Through chaining, an LDAP server provides the following advantages:

- ▶ It hides all name-resolution/tree-walking details from the client.
- ▶ It automatically takes care of remote authentication to other LDAP servers, using the same identity with which the LDAP client is bound.
- ▶ It acts as a proxy for the client and requests the remote server to complete the operation. Then it reports the result to the client as though the entry were stored locally.
- ▶ It works seamlessly, even when some servers in the eDirectory tree don't support LDAP services.

Chaining has disadvantages as well as advantages. For instance, the client might have to wait for some time without any feedback from the server while the server chains to resolve the name. If the operation requires the LDAP server to send many entries across a WAN link, the operation might be very time-consuming. If several servers are equally capable of processing the operation, different servers might process two requests to operate on the same entry. In 99% of the cases, this is not an issue. However, depending on the type of operation, the client may receive an erroneous indication that the requested operation—say, deletion of an entry—failed (due to duplicate processing).

Chaining can be bandwidth-intensive for large LDAP search operations. This is because in the chaining mode, the first LDAP server acts as the proxy to the client, where it receives the search results from another LDAP server and then passes the results back to the client; the data is transmitted on the network twice.

---

eDirectory attempts to sort the servers by the cost associated with contacting them (such as hop count). For load balancing, when there is more than one server available, eDirectory randomly selects among the servers with the lowest cost.

NOTE ■

In a way, LDAP chaining is similar to NDS's tree-walking mechanism. However, there is a difference between the two in terms of performance. LDAP chaining requires a bind every time a server is chained to. If the chained-to server does not have the required entry, the overhead spent on the bind operation is wasted, and another bind has to be made to the next server. (The way around this is for the client to first do an anonymous bind to search for the target entry before binding to perform the operation. This does not always work, however, because the anonymous user may not have the necessary browse rights to the target entry, and the client application will have to be smart.) NDS tree-walking, on the other hand, does not require authentication. Only when the target object is located is an authenticated connection made to that server.

TIP

In an NDS tree where not all servers are running the LDAP service and the LDAP servers do not have partitions of the whole tree, the chaining method works better than tree-walking because the LDAP server can access the whole tree on behalf of the clients.

Referrals

Referrals are a client-based name resolution method in which the client decides what to do if the target LDAP server does not have a local copy of the target entry. In this model, whenever a server cannot find the requested DN within its local database, it uses the knowledge reference it has to generate a referral to another server that does have the desired information or knows more about the target DN. The client then makes a new request to the referred server and retries the operation. If the second LDAP server has the target DN for the operation, it performs the request; otherwise, it also sends a referral back to the client. This continues until the client contacts a server that has the entry and can perform the desired operation or until an LDAP server returns an error that the entry cannot be found. The client can also decide to not connect to the next referred server and return an error instead or prompt the user before contacting the referred server.

The main advantage of the referrals-based method is that the client has total control. When the server returns a referral to the client, the referral contains information for each of these other servers. To continue the operations, the client can be smart about which server it picks from the list, or it can prompt the user for a selection. Another advantage is that when the client knows where an entry is located, it can go directly to the server that has the entry for additional operation requests, thus increasing efficiency and reducing network traffic.

The main downside of the referral method is that the client has to be smart and know how to handle and then follow referrals. The other drawback is that an LDAP server must service every partition in the NDS tree. Otherwise, some entries will not be accessible by LDAP clients because no referrals can be generated for data in the partitions that are not serviced by an LDAP server.

NOTE

LDAP v2 does not support referrals. If the LDAP server cannot find the requested information in its local data store, it fails the search and returns an error. The University of Michigan created an extension to LDAP that allows LDAP v2 to return referrals to clients as error messages. This adds complexity to the client because it must follow the referrals, but the server retains simplicity.

LDAP v3 introduced a new type of referral call *superior referrals*. Superior referrals enable an eDirectory tree to refer directory requests to other directories (such as a separate eDirectory tree or one hosted on a Netscape directory server). This capability enables eDirectory to function as part of a larger directory tree that comprises two or more separate directory trees. In other words, this feature can help companies federate two or more directory trees to function as a single directory tree. For example, suppose your company acquired a subsidiary that is using eDirectory. Your company is not using eDirectory but is using an LDAP v3–compliant directory. Your company wants to add the subsidiary's directory tree as a branch of its corporate tree. By using superior referrals, you can configure eDirectory to consult your company's corporate directory to fulfill requests for information that resides in that directory. Superior referrals are supported by eDirectory 8.7 and higher.

LDAP Objects in NDS/eDirectory

When LDAP Services for eDirectory is installed, it creates two objects in the tree: an **LDAP Group** object and an **LDAP Server** object in the same container as the **NCP Server** object. These objects initially contain the default configuration for LDAP Services:

▶ The **LDAP Server** object (called **LDAP Server - *servername***) represents server-specific configuration data, such as the port numbers to be used for clear-text and TLS/SSL bind, and whether the server supports anonymous binds from LDAP clients.

▶ The **LDAP Group** object (called **LDAP Group - *servername***) provides common configuration data for a group of LDAP servers, such as the proxy user to be used for an anonymous bind.

You can associate multiple LDAP Server objects with one LDAP Group object. All the associated LDAP servers then get their server-specific configuration from their LDAP Server object but get common or shared information from the LDAP Group object.

The LDAP Services installation program creates these objects by default. Later, you can associate multiple LDAP Server objects with a single LDAP Group object (and perhaps rename the LDAP Group object to something more meaningful that does not contain the server name). You can modify the default configuration by using either the ConsoleOne LDAP snap-in or the LDAP Management task in Novell iManager. On Unix/Linux, you can also use the ldapconfig utility.

NOTE

With iManager 2.x, there is also an LDAPManagement **object under the** Extend **container (see Figure 2.24). However, this object does not contain configuration information for LDAP Services.**

FIGURE 2.24
The Extend container created by iManager 2.x.

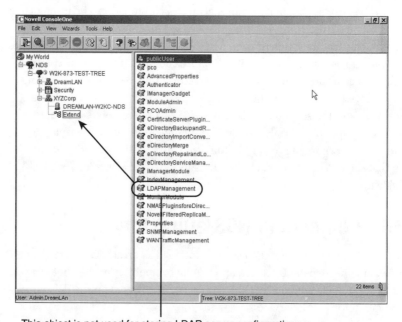

This object is not used for storing LDAP server configurations

WARNING

Although it is possible to associate newer versions of an LDAP Server **object with older versions of** LDAP Group **objects, Novell does not recommend that you mix versions due to the fact that certain feature sets are only available to newer versions of LDAP Services. For example, you should avoid associating an** LDAP Group **object for eDirectory 8.5 with an** LDAP Server **object for eDirectory 8.7.**

However, it is okay to include eDirectory 8.7.0 and 8.7.1 LDAP Server **objects with the same eDirectory 8.7.1** LDAP Group **object.**

Object Attribute Names Versus Schema Attribute Names

As mentioned earlier in this chapter, many of the LDAP attribute names are either the same as or derived from the NDS schema names. For instance, `Account Balance` in NDS is `accountBalance` in LDAP—you simply run the words together. Note that schema names are not case-sensitive. Therefore, the use of case in the name is just to help make the name more readily recognizable.

Frequently, schema names do not reflect their true meaning to a casual user because (mostly) programmers design them. Therefore, you often find that the attribute names used in Novell or third-party DS-aware utilities do not match those used in the schema. This makes troubleshooting using tools such as DSBrowse a little challenging because it's difficult to locate the correct name. Table 2.12 shows some of the most commonly used `User` object attribute names and descriptions, as used by ConsoleOne, and their corresponding NDS and LDAP schema names.

Attribute Names Used in ConsoleOne Versus Schema Names **TABLE 2.12**

CONSOLEONE DESCRIPTION	NDS SCHEMA NAME	LDAP SCHEMA NAME
Account balance	Account Balance	accountBalance
Allow unlimited credit	Allow Unlimited Credit	allowUnlimitedCredit
Other name	CN	cn
Description	Description	description
Fax Number	Facsimile Telephone Number	facsimileTelephone Number
Full name	Full Name	fullName
Qualifier	Generational Qualifier	generationQualifier

Table 2.12   Continued

CONSOLEONE DESCRIPTION	NDS SCHEMA NAME	LDAP SCHEMA NAME
Given name	Given Name	givenName
Middle Initial	Initials	initials
E-Mail Address	Internet Email Address	mail
Location	L	l
Language	Language	Language
Account disabled	Login Disabled	loginDisabled
Expiration date and time (under Account has expiration time)	Login Expiration Time	loginExpirationTime
Grace logins allowed	Login Grace Limit	loginGraceLimit
Remaining grace logins	Login Grace Remaining	loginGraceRemaining
Maximum connections	Login Maximum Simultaneous	loginMaximum Simultaneous
Low balance limit	Minimum Account Balance	minimumAccountBalance
Department	OU	ou
Allow user to change password	Password Allow Change	passwordAllowChange
Days between forced changes	Password Expiration Interval	passwordExpiration Interval
Date and time password expires	Password Expiration Time	passwordExpirationTime
Minimum password length	Password Minimum Length	passwordMinimumLength
Require a password	Password Required	passwordRequired
Require unique passwords	Password Unique Required	passwordUniqueRequired
City	Physical Delivery Office Name	physicalDelivery Office Name

Table 2.12 Continued

CONSOLEONE DESCRIPTION	NDS SCHEMA NAME	LDAP SCHEMA NAME
Mailing label information (found under the Postal Address option under the General tab)	Postal Address	postalAddress
Zip Code	Postal Code	postalCode
Post Office Box	Postal Office Box	postOfficeBox
Last name	Surname	sn
State	S	st
Street	SA	street
Telephone	Telephone Number	telephoneNumber
Title	Title	title
Testuser	uniqueID	uid

NOTE

Bear in mind that the default attribute mapping used by the LDAP server is to map DS's Generational Qualifier attribute (which is an eight-character CI string) to the LDAP attribute generationQualifier. There is also a DS attribute called generationQualifier (which is a 32KB CI string) that is *not* mapped to an LDAP attribute.

TIP

Chapter 7 contains a table similar to Table 2.12 that compares the ACL attribute names used by Novell utilities with their schema names.

Summary

This chapter establishes a base of information necessary to begin looking at eDirectory tree design and troubleshooting. Starting with a look at how NDS and eDirectory version numbering work, followed by a study of classes, attributes, and syntaxes, this chapter examines how the database is structured and then moves into a discussion of the partitioning and replication features of eDirectory. This chapter also looks at why time synchronization is important to the eDirectory database. This chapter also includes a discussion about how network services are located using SAP and SLP, the functions and role of DHost in non-Netware platforms. The chapter ends with a review of LDAP support and LDAP features that are included with eDirectory.

Chapter 3, "The Directory Information Base," examines the data store used by eDirectory—the DIB.

The Directory Information Base

Just as you don't really need to know how a combustion engine works in order to drive a car, it is not necessary for you to have an intricate knowledge of the directory services (DS) database file structure in order to use, manage, and troubleshoot eDirectory. On the other hand, knowing that the eDirectory database is made up of a number of files and knowing what components make up the eDirectory database can make troubleshooting easier. Although this chapter is by no means an in-depth technical view of the DS database files, it gives you an idea of what the files are named, where they are located, and what the purpose of each is.

The set of DS database files is officially known as the *Directory Information Base* (DIB). Oftentimes, these files are simply referred to as *NDS files*; however, in a number of Novell utilities, such as DSRepair, the term *DIB* is used.

Because there are still many NetWare 4 and NetWare 5 servers being used around the world, this chapter covers the DIB sets used in NDS 6, 7, and NDS 8/eDirectory.

The NDS 6 DIB

The main DIB set used by NDS 6 is composed of four files:

- ▶ PARTITIO.NDS
- ▶ ENTRY.NDS
- ▶ VALUE.NDS
- ▶ BLOCK.NDS

Each of these files is examined individually in the sections that follow.

PARTITIO.NDS

The `PARTITIO.NDS` file contains information specific to partitions that are stored on the file's server. This data is server-centric because it has no correlation with the data in the `PARTITIO.NDS` file on another server. The file contains the following fields to help DS replicate and synchronize data between servers:

▶ **Partition ID**—This is the hexadecimal number assigned to a replica (by NetWare) when it is created. This number is used to associate an object with its partition. It is also referred to as the replica ID in DSRepair and the root entry ID in DSBrowse.

▶ **Partition root object**—This is the hexadecimal object ID number of the object that is the root of the partition. This is also known as the replica root object.

▶ **Replica type**—This is the type of replica (such as Master or Read/Write).

▶ **Replica state**—This is the state of the replica (such as On or Split).

▶ **Replica flags**—The replica flags are used by the NDS synchronization processes. They are also referred to as partition flags.

▶ **Next timestamp**—This is the minimum value of the next timestamp the server issues to an object in the partition.

You can look up this information by using `DSREPAIR.NLM` in the following way: From the main menu, select Advanced Options, Replica and Partition Operations. Then you select any one of the partitions from the displayed list and choose Display Replica Information. The resulting log file shows the data from the `PARTITIO.NDS` file in a readable format, as shown in Figure 3.1. You can obtain similar information by using DSBrowse, as illustrated in Figure 3.2.

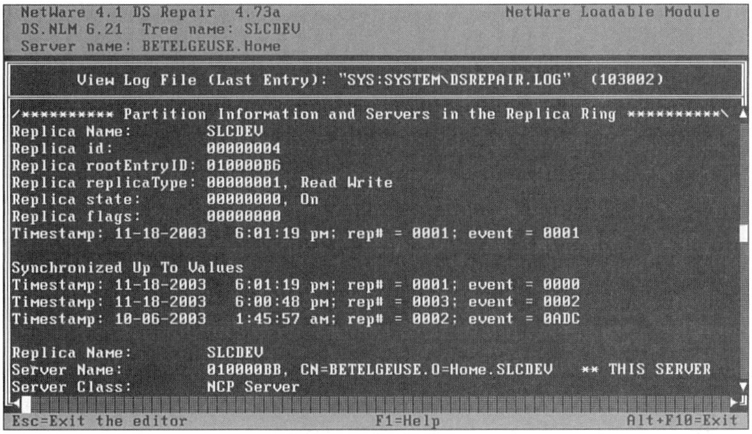

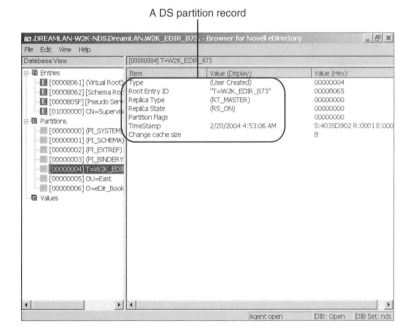

FIGURE 3.1
A sample
DSREPAIR.NLM log
file, showing
information
about the SLCDEV
partition.

A DS partition record

FIGURE 3.2
DSBrowse, show-
ing information
about a partition.

ENTRY.NDS

All objects stored on the server are located within the ENTRY.NDS file. Each
object has a record entry in the file, and each record contains the following
fields:

▶ **Object Name**—This is the typed relative distinguished name of the object (for example, `CN=Tasha`).

▶ **Partition ID**—This is the hexadecimal ID of the partition in which the object exists. This corresponds to the records in the `PARTITIO.NDS` file.

▶ **Base Object Class**—This is a pointer to the record within the `ENTRY.NDS` file that contains the schema definition (such as User), which is used as the object's base object class.

▶ **Creation Time**—This is the timestamp of when the object was created.

▶ **Parent Object**—This is a pointer to the record within the `ENTRY.NDS` file that contains the object that is the parent of the current object. For example, if the current object's full name is `CN=Tasha.OU=North_America.O=Testing`, this field points to `OU=North_America.O=Testing`, which is the parent of the `CN=Tasha` object.

▶ **Sibling Object**—This is a pointer to the record within the `ENTRY.NDS` file for the object that is a sibling object.

> **NOTE**
>
> A *sibling object* is an object that has the same parent object (or name context) as another object. For example, `CN=Tasha.OU=North_America.O=Testing` is a sibling object to `CN=Chelsea.OU=North_America.O=Testing` because both objects have the same parent object, `OU=North_America.O=Testing`.

▶ **First Child Object**—This is a pointer to the record within the `ENTRY.NDS` file for the object that is the first child object. If the current object is a leaf object, such as a user, then there is no child object.

▶ **Last Child Object**—This is a pointer to the record within the `ENTRY.NDS` file for the object that is the last child object. If the current object is a leaf object, such as a user, then there is no child object.

▶ **First NDS Attribute**—This is a pointer to the record within the `VALUE.NDS` file that contains the object's first attribute.

▶ **Subordinate Count**—This is the number of records that are subordinate to (that is, reference) the current object. In essence, this is the number of child objects the object has. For example, if the current object is a container and has four `User` objects and two organizational units (OUs), the subordinate count is six.

▶ **Object Flags**—This is a set of flags that identifies the characteristics of the object. The following are the possible flag values:

- ▶ `Alias` indicates that the object is an alias to another object.

- ▶ `Backlinked` indicates that the object is an external reference that has established a backlink.

NOTE

An *external reference* is a placeholder used to store information about an object that is not contained in a partition held by the server. See Chapter 6, "Understanding Common eDirectory Processes," for more information about external references and backlinks.

- ▶ `Partition` or `Partition Root` indicates that the object is a partition root object.

- ▶ `Present` indicates that the object is present in the DS tree.

- ▶ `Not Present` indicates that the object is no longer considered by DS to exist within the tree, but its record still exists in the DIB because the Janitor process hasn't purged it yet. See the "Delete Object" and "Obituaries" sections in Chapter 6 for more information about the Janitor process.

Figure 3.3 shows a sample entry record for the `User` object `Tasha`, located in `OU=North_America.O=Testing`.

A DS entry record

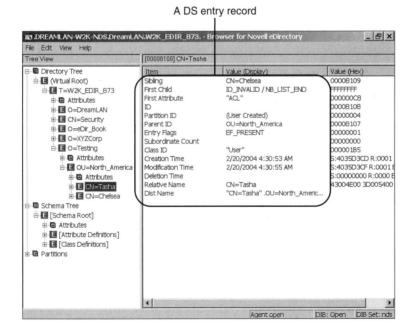

FIGURE 3.3
Viewing DS entry record information by using DSBrowse.

VALUE.NDS

The VALUE.NDS file contains attribute values associated with records in the ENTRY.NDS file. The structure of the VALUE.NDS file is similar to that of ENTRY.NDS. The following fields are stored in the VALUE.NDS file:

- ▶ **Object Name**—This is a pointer to the object record in the ENTRY.NDS file to which this attribute is associated.

- ▶ **Attribute**—This is a pointer to the record within the ENTRY.NDS file that contains the schema attribute definition (such as Surname) for this attribute.

- ▶ **Next Value**—This is a pointer to the record within the VALUE.NDS file that contains the attribute's next value if the attribute is multivalued.

- ▶ **Next Attribute**—This is a pointer to the record within the VALUE.NDS file that contains the next attribute assigned to the object.

- ▶ **First Block**—Each VALUE.NDS record can hold up to 16 bytes of data (such as the number of days before a password expires). If the data for an attribute's value doesn't fit in a single VALUE.NDS record, the extra data is stored in a record in the BLOCK.NDS file. The First Block field is a pointer to a record in this file that holds the first block of overflow data.

- ▶ **Modification Time stamp**—This field contains the time stamp when the attribute value was created or last modified.

- ▶ **Attribute Value**—This is the data associated with the attribute. If the attribute's data type or syntax is stream (SYN_STREAM), the filename containing the stream data is recorded instead.

NOTE

All stream data, such as login scripts, is stored in individual files, where the filename is an eight-digit hexadecimal number and the file extension is .000. The hexadecimal number in the filename has no direct relationship to the hexadecimal object ID of the DS object to which the file is associated. For example, the container login script for OU=North_America (whose object ID is 0x01000124) is stored in a stream file named 0004B3C0.000, and the print job configuration information associated with the same container is stored in a stream file called 0031B000.000. You can look up the filenames by using DSBrowse, as illustrated in Figure 3.4. DSBrowse on NetWare does not provide that information. However, you can use MONITOR to see the filename that is opened when you are editing the login script and print job configuration.

Name of stream file containing the login script

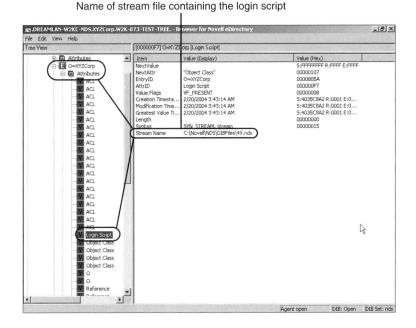

FIGURE 3.4
Looking up the name of a stream file for the login script.

▶ **Attribute Flags**—This is a set of flags that identify the characteristics of the attribute. The following are the possible flag values:

  ▶ `Base Object Class` indicates that the value in the record is the value used as the base object class for the object that this attribute is associated with.

  ▶ `Naming` indicates that the value in the record is used as the relative distinguished name of the object that this attribute is associated with.

  ▶ `Present` indicates that the object is present in the DS tree.

  ▶ `Not Present` indicates that the object is no longer considered by NDS to exist within the tree, but its record still exists in the DIB because the Janitor process hasn't purged it yet. See the "Delete Object" and "Obituaries" sections in Chapter 6 for more information.

BLOCK.NDS

The `BLOCK.NDS` file is used to store the value of an object's attribute that exceeds 16 bytes in size. Each record in `BLOCK.NDS` consists of the following fields:

▶ **Attribute Name**—This is a pointer to the attribute record in the
VALUE.NDS file to which this data block is associated.

▶ **Value**—This is the value or data for the attribute. Each record in
BLOCK.NDS can hold up to 108 bytes of data.

▶ **Next Block**—If the data is larger than 124 bytes (16 bytes in the
VALUE.NDS file and 108 bytes in the first block of BLOCK.NDS), additional records in the BLOCK.NDS file are used for the excess data. The
next block points to the next record within the BLOCK.NDS file that
contains data for the attribute.

NDS and Transaction Tracking System

If you are familiar with database structures, you'll readily recognize that the
DIB set is implemented as a set of linked lists. The link generally starts in
the ENTRY.NDS file and is then linked to VALUE.NDS and then to BLOCK.NDS.
By using linked lists, NDS can easily insert data into the DIB by simply
adjusting the pointers accordingly. Any nodes (that is, elements in the list)
that are deleted can be easily reused; therefore, there is generally no need to
repack the DIB unless you have deleted a large number of objects. Even
then, you might not see much of a size reduction of the DIB because only
empty nodes at the end of the lists are deleted.

To reduce the chance of pointer corruption and data integrity, DS transactions are protected by NetWare Transaction Tracking System (TTS); therefore, if for some reason the server's TTS mechanism is disabled, DS.NLM
automatically shuts down the DIB. Because TTS uses disk space on the SYS:
volume to create transaction log files, it is essential that you ensure that the
SYS: volume always has sufficient free disk space; otherwise, you risk shutting down NDS.

NOTE   eDirectory does not depend on TTS because it is a cross-platform product and TTS
is available only on NetWare. However, eDirectory also keeps its roll-forward log
(RFL) files on the same disk on which the DIB is installed. Therefore, it is also
essential that you ensure that sufficient free disk space is available; otherwise,
you risk eDirectory shutting down unexpectedly.

On NetWare 4 servers, you can easily look up the object and attribute information by using Novell's DSView NetWare Loadable Module (NLM). This
NLM is not included with NetWare but can generally be found included
with the DS.NLM updates. For NetWare 5 and higher, the corresponding

utility is the DSBrowse NLM that is included with NetWare; a DSBrowse module is included for the other platforms that eDirectory runs on. The DSView screen in Figure 3.5 shows the information related to the `Login Intruder Limit` attribute, such as timestamp and syntax.

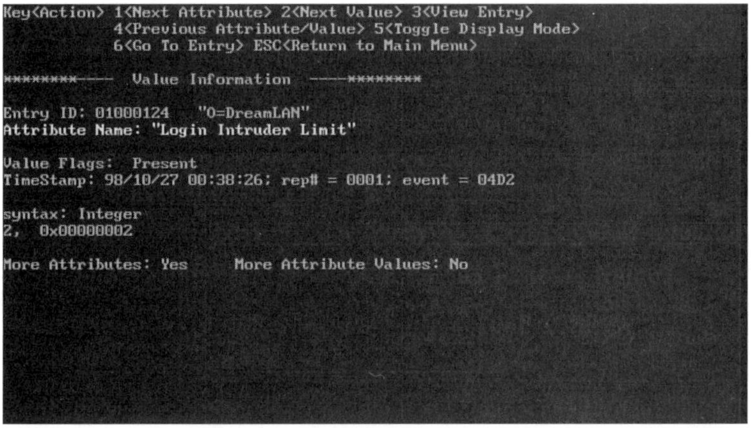

```
Key<Action> 1<Next Attribute> 2<Next Value> 3<View Entry>
         4<Previous Attribute/Value> 5<Toggle Display Mode>
         6<Go To Entry> ESC<Return to Main Menu>

********----- Value Information -----********

Entry ID: 01000124   "O=DreamLAN"
Attribute Name: "Login Intruder Limit"

Value Flags:  Present
TimeStamp: 98/10/27 00:38:26; rep# = 0001; event = 04D2

syntax: Integer
2,  0x00000002

More Attributes: Yes     More Attribute Values: No
```

FIGURE 3.5
Examining the NDS 6 DIB by using DSView on a NetWare 4 server.

NOTE

By default, DSRepair saves the old DIB files after a repair operation. The four files in the main DIB set used by DS 6 are renamed with a `.OLD` extension. Because of the backup DIB files, you essentially double your DIB size after you run DSRepair. Keep this in mind if you're low on disk space on the `SYS:` volume.

NDS 7 DIB

The names of the four core NDS files are changed in NetWare 5 (because of NDS 7), but their functions remain the same as their cousins in NetWare 4. Also, two new DS-related files are also included with NetWare 5. The NDS 7 DIB is composed of the following files:

- ▶ **0.DSD**—This file contains the same type of data as and performs the same function as the `ENTRY.NDS` file in NetWare 4.
- ▶ **1.DSD**—This file contains the same type of data as and performs the same function as the `VALUE.NDS` file in NetWare 4.
- ▶ **2.DSD**—This file contains the same type of data as and performs the same function as the `BLOCK.NDS` file in NetWare 4.
- ▶ **3.DSD**—This file contains the same type of data as and performs the same function as the `PARTITIO.NDS` file in NetWare 4.
- ▶ **0.DSB**—This is a lookup table that holds the names of the `.DSD` files to facilitate faster server start.

> **NOTE**
>
> The Ø.DSB file is 28 bytes in size, and if it's missing or corrupted, the NetWare 5 server (if running DS 7) displays a -723 or -736 error on bootup. You can copy this file from another server or download ØDSB.EXE (which contains a copy of Ø.DSB) from Novell's support Web site, at support.novell.com.

▶ **NLSLIST.DAT**—This file contains NetWare 5 licensing (both server and connection) data used by Novell Licensing Services (NLS).

In NetWare 4, DSRepair renames old DIB files with the .OLD extension. Under NetWare 5, however, DSRepair renames the old DIB .DSD files to files with the .DOD extension, and it renames the Ø.DSB file Ø.DOB.

NDS 8 and eDirectory DIB

Versions of NDS prior to NDS 8 use a database engine called Recman, which, as the name suggests, is a record-based database management engine. NDS 8 and eDirectory uses a database engine called FLAIM, which stands for *Flexible and Adaptable Information Manager*. It is a database engine that is optimized for search and retrieval for a large number of small interrelated objects. (Novell's GroupWise email system also uses the FLAIM engine for its database.)

> **REAL WORLD**
>
> ## What Is FLAIM?
>
> The initial idea for what later became FLAIM came from the genealogy world. Genealogical databases can be huge. When you consider that there are now more than 6 billion people on the planet, and a genealogical database stores information about the ancestors of these people, the sheer size of the data store and the complex relationships between arbitrarily structured data items challenges conventional database techniques. FLAIM was designed to handle databases of this scale and to have the very desirable attribute of handling information whose interrelationships (and hence the database schema) may not be known in advance of adding data to the database.
>
> WordPerfect Corporation acquired the initial idea for FLAIM and developed it for use in the WordPerfect product. Over time, the database came to be known as FLAIM. With Novell's merger with WordPerfect in 1994, FLAIM became the property of Novell. At that time, NDS was just being introduced to the world and already had its own database. However, a few years later, when looking to make the next generation of NDS more scalable and more efficient, Novell investigated several databases as potential candidates but then realized that a high-performance, expandable, and quick database had already been developed

in-house. To make a long story short, Novell eventually investigated **FLAIM** and decided to use it for **NDS 8**. The **FLAIM** development team joined the NDS development team, and the result was a much more robust directory.

As an impressive demonstration of the increased capabilities of eDirectory due to FLAIM, Novell has publicly showcased, several times since 2000, eDirectory running on a single server with 1.5 billion objects in the database!

A FLAIM database file is divided into logical files called *containers*. A FLAIM database can have multiple containers, including custom containers. Each FLAIM database must have at least a Default Data, a Local Dictionary, and a Tracker container. Data in one container can reference data in another container, by using the data record number (DRN) of the data being referenced. Table 3.1 lists the containers used in DS 8 and eDirectory databases.

FLAIM Container Descriptions   **TABLE 3.1**

FLAIM CONTAINER	DESCRIPTION
Default Data	Actual data records (entries, values, schema definitions, and so on)
Local Dictionary	Container and field definitions
Tracker	A tracker for record changes
Partition_Cont	Partition records
AttrInfo_Cont	Attribute syntax information
Stream_Cont	Stream records
PCC0_Cont	The change cache for system-created Partition 0 (System)
PCC1_Cont	The change cache for system-created Partition 1 (Schema)
PCC2_Cont	The change cache for system-created Partition 2 (External Reference)
PCC3_Cont	The change cache for system-created Partition 3 (Bindery)
PCC4_Cont	The change cache for user-created Partition 4; this is the first user-created partition, and other containers will be created for each new partition
Attr_246_Cont	The Member container
Attr_277_Cont	The Private Key container

Table 3.1   Continued

`Attr_281_Cont`	The Public Key container
`Attr_286_Cont`	The Reference container
`Attr_361_Cont`	The Equivalent to Me container
`Attr_431_Cont`	The `NLS:Common_Certificate` container
`Attr_455_Cont`	The `NLS:List_Of_Handles` container
`Attr_518_Cont`	The `NDSPKI:Key_File` container
`Attr_468_Cont`	The `NLS:Cert_Peak_Used_Pool`

These logical files may be stored in one or more physical files. eDirectory's implementation is that each physical file can grow to 2GB in size for NDS 8/eDirectory 8.5 and to 4GB in size for eDirectory 8.6 and higher; then the content is "spilled" over to another file. Therefore, depending on the size of your DS database, you will at least have a file called **NDS.01**, and when it reaches the maximum allowed size, an **NDS.02** file is created, and when that file reaches the maximum allowed size, an **NDS.03** file is created, and so on.

TIP

The FLAIM database can be compressed to remove blank or deleted records. Therefore, one of the options in DSRepair for DS 8 and eDirectory is to reclaim unused space. In Figure 3.6 later in this section, you can see the option about halfway down the list.

The following is a list of files employed by eDirectory 8.5 and higher:

▶ **NDS.xx**—These are the main eDirectory database files, where **xx** is **01**, **02**, and so on. These files contain several types of records (such as partition and schema records) and also any eDirectory attribute indexes (such as **CN** and **Surname**, which can be used to speed up DS and Lightweight Directory Access Protocol queries) defined on the server.

▶ **NDS.RFL\xxxxxxxx.LOG**—These are the RFL files, where **xxxxxxxx** ranges from **00000001** to **FFFFFFFF**. In order to protect against loss of data from a catastrophic failure such as a server crash, eDirectory uses an RFL to track all changes made to the database. Hence, if necessary, eDirectory can recommit lost data to the database by examining the **xxxxxxxx.LOG** files when the server is restarted.

As records are modified in the eDirectory database, but before they are committed to the disk, a copy of the changes is stored in the RFL file. These entries are completed transactions that had not been written to disk. Upon server failure, the records committed to the disk may be lost, but the changes are maintained in the RFL file. This process is handled by the checkpoint thread on the server, and the size of the RFL file should decrease in time as transactions are written to disk.

TIP

The RFLs are typically stored in the NDS.RFL **directory under the main DIB folder (for example, for NetWare, it is** SYS:_NETWARE\NDS.RFL**). With eDirectory 8.7 and higher, you can store this file in a different location. To ensure database integrity, it is recommended that you do place the RFLs on a disk other than the one that holds the eDirectory database. You accomplish this by using the eDirectory Backup eMTool utility. It is possible to delete this directory, but it is _not_ recommended because it involves the possibility of corrupting the eDirectory database.**

▶ **NDS.DB**—This is the roll-back log file. Because changes to the eDirectory database can include operations that require many data packets' worth of information to be sent to the server, eDirectory commits each packet to the database as it is being received—even though the entire transaction may not yet be complete. To safeguard against communication failure, eDirectory writes these transactions to a roll-back log. If an incomplete operation is encountered, eDirectory can use the roll-back log to undo incomplete transactions. (This is why TTS is not required for eDirectory to function.)

▶ **NDS.LCK**—This is the NDS lock file. During database maintenance, sometimes the eDirectory database needs to be closed or locked for modifications. The **NDS.LCK** file is used to designate this locked condition. For eDirectory 8.5 and higher, this file shows as a 0 byte file. When the database is locked, attributes are changed on this file to signify that condition, and the file still shows as a 0 byte file. The timestamp of the file is updated whenever the database is locked or unlocked.

▶ **_NDSDB.INI**—This is the database cache configuration file. When an eDirectory tuning parameter, such as the hard limit of the database cache size, is statically assigned, the setting is stored in the **_NDSDB.INI** file.

> **NOTE**
>
> See Chapter 16, "Tuning eDirectory," for information about eDirectory tuning.

> ▶ ***.FRS**—These are the temporary FLAIM record set files used by FLAIM.
>
> ▶ **NDT.DB**—This is a DSRepair temporary database file for **NDS.DB**.
>
> ▶ **NDT.xx**—These are DSRepair temporary database files for **NDS.xx**.
>
> ▶ **NDT.RFL\xxxxxxxx.LOG**—These are DSRepair temporary database files, where *xxxxxxxx* ranges from **00000001** to **FFFFFFFF**.

When you're running DSRepair to repair the local database, one option (see Figure 3.6) is to use a temporary DS database during the repair. This allows the repair operation to be done on a copy of the database (using the **NDT.*** files) and not the live database.

FIGURE 3.6
Select Use Temporary NDS Database During Repair? if you do not want to work on a live data-base.

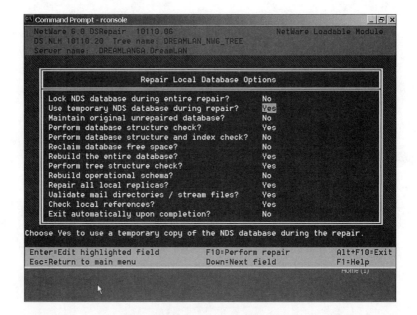

Table 3.2 gives the names of the database files used by the various versions of NDS/eDirectory and summarizes their purposes. It also shows the location of each of these files.

Summary of DS File Functions

TABLE 3.2

NDS 6 AND PRIOR	NDS 7 (RECMAN)	NDS 8 AND ABOVE (FLAIM)
Located in SYS:_NETWARE	Located in SYS:_NETWARE	Located in SYS:_NETWARE on NetWare servers, [drive:]\Novell\NDS\DIBFiles on Windows, and /var/nds/dib on Unix servers
ENTRY.NDS—Object information	0.DSD—Entry information	NDS.01—Entry, attribute, schema, and partition information; rolls over to NDS.02 and so on when file size reaches 2GB or 4GB
VALUE.NDS—Attribute information	1.DSD—Attribute information	N/A
BLOCK.NDS—Attribute (more than 16 bytes) overflow	2.DSD—Attribute overflow	N/A
PARTITO.NDS—Partition information	3.DSD—Partition information	N/A
N/A	0.DSB—[Lookup table of names of .DSD files (only 28 bytes in size!)	N/A
Stream files (*.000)—Login scripts and so on	Stream files (*.000)—Login scripts and so on	Stream files (0-9, A-F.NDS)—Login scripts, and so on (for example, 1.NDS, 4F.NDS)
N/A	N/A	NDS.DB—Control file containing rollback information for aborted transactions
N/A	N/A	NDS.RFL*.LOG—RFL file to reapply transactions that have been completed but not written to disk
N/A	N/A	_NDSDB.INI—File that keeps cache information
N/A	N/A	NDS.LCK—File that prevents access to database when open

Locating the DIB

You can find the DIB files in the following locations on Windows and Unix systems:

▶ Windows: [*drive*:]\Novell\NDS\DIBFiles

▶ Unix: /var/nds/dib

WARNING   Because access to the DIB files on non-NetWare servers is readily available to standard utilities, such as Explorer, you need to take care when accessing the folder that is holding the DIB files.

However, many administrators often wonder where NetWare stores the DIB files. NetWare hides its DIB files in the **SYS:_NETWARE** directory. This is a system-protected directory that can't be accessed using standard utilities such as FILER. However, you can easily view the contents of this directory by using RConsole (which requires the Internet Packet Exchange [IPX] protocol to be enabled at the server and your workstation) as follows:

1. Use RConsole to connect to your server.

2. Press Alt+F1 to bring up the Available Options menu.

3. Select Directory Scan and enter **SYS:_NETWARE** as the name for the directory to scan. A list of DIB and stream files is displayed.

NOTE   You cannot use RConsoleJ to view the contents of the SYS:_NETWARE **directory because it does not have the Alt+F1 hotkey feature.**

Figure 3.4 shows the contents of the **SYS:_NETWARE** directory on a NetWare 5 server running NDS 7. On a NetWare 5 server running eDirectory or a NetWare 4 server running NDS 6, the output is similar, but the filenames are different, as noted earlier in this chapter.

TIP   From a NetWare server, you can access the SYS:_NETWARE **directory by using NetBasic (included with NetWare 5.x and 6.0) or Novell Script for NetWare (shipped with NetWare 6.5):**

NetWare 5.*x* and 6.0	NetWare 6.5
load netbasic	load nsninit
shell	nsnshell
cd _netware	cd _netware

Because these utilities allow you to delete files, you need to be careful with them, or you could damage your DS database.

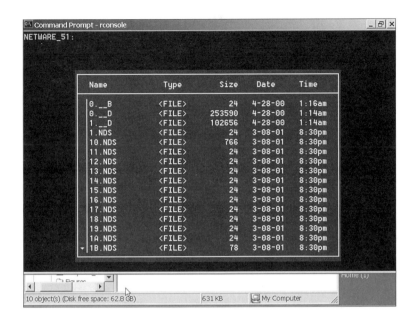

FIGURE 3.7

A sample directory list of SYS:_NETWARE from a NetWare 5 server running NDS 7.

TIP

After you upgrade a previous version of NDS on your NetWare server to the latest version of eDirectory, the old database files are left in the SYS:_NETWARE directory. If you have any *.41x files, the server was upgraded from NetWare 4.1x (thus NDS 6) to the current version; *.__B and *.__D files are a result of upgrading from NDS 7; and *.OLD, *.DOB, and *.DOB files are DSRepair backup files (from NDS 6 and NDS7, respectively). If you are short on disk space or want to clean house, you should consider deleting the old database files only after a successful upgrade.

Backing Up the DIB

In a single-server environment, it is possible to back up your DS by making a copy of the DIB files. This is analogous to backing up the bindery in the old NetWare 2 and NetWare 3 environments because all the data is located on a single server. It is *not* a good idea at all, however, to consider backing up your DS by simply copying the DIB files if you have a multiserver environment. Because the DS database is often in a loosely synchronized, loosely consistent state, you can't guarantee that the DIB on a given server has full data integrity at the time you make a copy of the files.

In a multiserver configuration, it is best to use a Storage Management Service (SMS)–compliant backup application to back up the DS via proper application programming interface calls. eDirectory 8.7 introduced a new backup and restore utility called eDirectory Backup eMTool to back up the eDirectory database on individual servers. You can learn more about SMS, eDirectory Backup eMTool, and other tools that back up and restore DS in Chapter 8, "eDirectory Data Recovery Tools."

Summary

This chapter presents a high-level look at the file structure of NDS/eDirectory databases. It identifies the filename differences between the NDS and eDirectory and shows you how you can view—using DSRepair, DSBrowse, and DSView—some of the information recorded and used by DS that is not displayed by conventional utilities such as NetWare Administrator and ConsoleOne.

Don't Panic

In the world of networking and when dealing with critical problems, the absolutely worst thing you can do is panic. This is especially true when you're working with eDirectory. In traditional network troubleshooting, changes that are made are typically easy to undo. For example, if you are working on a routing problem, you can change a setting in the router that disables packet forwarding on a particular interface and observe the change in the environment; if the change does not affect the problem the way you thought it would, you can (easily) change the setting back.

However, when you're working with eDirectory, certain changes are easy to make but are extremely difficult to undo. As you will read in later chapters, it takes a thorough understanding of how eDirectory works combined with a full understanding of what the problem actually is to determine a proper course of corrective action.

It is not uncommon for a network administrator to run into a situation that demands immediate attention. Critical eDirectory problems tend to have fairly high visibility—either because the problem affects users' ability to log in and do the work that makes the company run or because a major piece of network functionality is affected. For example, printing might be offline. Users may be able to work on documents but unable to print out the sales reports that upper management needs to see every day by 10:00 a.m.

In this sort of high-visibility (not to mention high-stress) environment, it is very easy to fall into the trap of doing *something* for the sake of just doing something. Compounding this, upper management often does not under-stand the intricacies of what makes the network tick, but they certainly can identify when the person who is responsible for fixing the problem is not doing anything about it.

Or so they believe.

Doing something for the sake of doing something is almost always counter-productive. It is easy to make a change at the server and then when upper management wants to know what you are doing about the problem, you can say "I changed this, this, and this." This is an easy out but can actually make the problem resolution process take much longer because of new factors introduced to the problem that have actually made the situation worse.

This book is about the technical aspects of working with and fixing eDirectory problems, but we want to diverge for a second and talk about how to deal with the difficult situation of working with people and stress. If not handled properly, they can have a very negative impact on your ability to deal with the eDirectory problems effectively.

Dealing with People

The vast majority of technical people in the IT industry prefer working with machines over working with people. This statement is based largely on many discussions we have had with administrators, engineers, and consultants working in this industry.

Computers are easy to work with. They do what they are told—even if that does not equate to what you *want* them to do. They wait for you while you have lunch, and they never have a bad attitude or demand that you do something *right now*.

Conversely, people can be difficult to work with. They do not necessarily do what they are told, interrupt your lunch to have you work on a project they forgot needed to be done *right now*, and when things are not going their way, they can have a very bad attitude.

People skills are a very important part of a system administrator's job. You have to be a salesperson, a diplomat, a teacher, a student of technology, and a technical guru all at the same time. It is very difficult to do any of these things well if you have a hard time dealing with people and communicating effectively with them.

Take some time to learn how to interact with the people you work with. Learning how to communicate with them outside a crisis will help you know how to communicate with them effectively during a crisis situation. Learn the best way to tell people that they are in your way and continually interrupting your thought processes by asking when the system is going to be operational again. Let them know that this is not going to help you get things running again any time soon. Different people react differently to being told this, so it is important that you know how best to communicate this information to the people who will invariably seek you out to find out what is going on.

One invaluable skill that people working in IT should master is active listening. The ability to not only listen to what you want to hear but to reflectively respond to co-workers and management lets you get more from the person you are speaking to, making problem analysis more effective and efficient. Many system engineers consider end users and management as deterrents or problems. However, when you look at them as assets, reflectively listening to them in a crisis situation, you gain allies as opposed to combatants, thus making your job a lot easier.

Another tactic that most SEs do not call upon in a crisis—one that helps prevent a panic situation from becoming inflamed—is the knowledge that experience has provided. In a panic situation, if you can simply stop and ask "What did I do, or what did so-and-so do, when faced with a similar situation?" many insurmountable problems have a way of being addressed calmly.

NOTE

It is important to correctly manage the expectation levels of your users, especially those in upper management. Provide them with a time frame that gives you some breathing room (so you are not rushed into doing something rash), but at the same time, do *not* overexaggerate it in order to try to look like a miracle worker (as depicted in some TV shows) because the ploy almost always backfires. For instance, if you feel the problem can be resolved in 30 minutes, tell your co-workers that the system "should be back up in about an hour." This gives you some flexibility. However, do not go so far as to tell them it will "take the rest of the morning" because that could place upper management in a crisis mode and force undue stress on you and your co-workers.

TIP

If you are indeed dealing with a major problem, it would be wise to provide frequent updates to your users and management. It is not necessary to provide hourly updates, but several updates (especially when breakthroughs are made) throughout the day can prove useful.

In addition to learning to deal with people effectively, it is important to manage your own stress level in a crisis situation.

Dealing with Stress

Your own stress can be the biggest detriment to getting a problem resolved. Stress creates an environment that is not conducive to clear thinking, and being able to think clearly about what you are seeing and reason through the problem is absolutely critical to resolving a problem.

The following are some techniques you can use to clear your head and perform a type of mental "soft reset":

▶ Take a walk while DSRepair (or some other automated process) is doing its job.

▶ Close your eyes and count to 10 when you are in front of the server that is exhibiting the problem.

▶ Laugh. This one sometimes brings on strange looks from co-workers, but it really works. Laughter is one of the best stress relievers there is. (Sometimes, having a few copies of *Dilbert* books around comes in handy.)

▶ Stretch. Stretching helps work out the tension you can get in your neck and shoulders. It often helps you relax, and you can think more clearly and effectively when relaxed.

Other people use other techniques. The important thing is to find out what works for you. When in a crisis situation, it is important that the stress relief method you use is something that can be applied quickly and works quickly. Going on a five-mile jog might be a great stress reliever for you, but when in a crisis situation, this is not likely to be a viable option.

Summary

When you are calm and in control of the situation, you can begin to address the problem, starting with understanding eDirectory processes and error codes. These are discussed in the chapters that follow.

Understanding the Error Codes and eDirectory Processes

eDirectory/NDS Error Codes Explained

DS errors occur during the processing of a directory services (DS) request or the execution of a DS background process. These errors can happen as a result of a hardware or software failure, data inconsistency, or unexpected responses received; therefore, when you're troubleshooting a problem, it is essential that you know where the error originated, the condition that caused the error, and what the error code or message means. Unfortunately, computer-generated error messages are notoriously cryptic at best and frequently don't easily provide the source of the error. For example, a DS error can be generated from one of three possible sources:

- ▶ The DS service running on the server
- ▶ The client application (workstation based or server based)
- ▶ The DS agent (DSA) running on the server.

It gets even more frustrating if multiple causes can result in the same error code.

NOTE

Each DS-capable server runs both DS service (which processes DS requests locally) and the DSA service. The DSA *tree-walks* and queries other DS servers on behalf of the requesting client—which can be either a workstation or another server—if the local server doesn't have the requested information.

By examining the code number returned or associated with an error message, you can determine the most likely source (the server, the client, or the DSA) and the possible cause of the DS error. Keep in mind that the information provided here does not necessarily give remedies; this chapter provides developers' explanations of the errors. Several factors can help you to identify the root cause of an error and then eliminate or correct the error, including the following:

- ▶ An understanding of DS processes (see Chapter 6, "Understanding Common eDirectory Processes")

- ▶ An understanding of DS error code definitions and possible conditions under which they can occur (see Appendix A, "eDirectory Error Codes")

- ▶ Familiarity with the DS tree that is experiencing the error

- ▶ Familiarity with the placement of the replicas

- ▶ Familiarity with various DS diagnostic and repair tools, such as DSTrace, DSBrowse, DSRepair, and the eDirectory Maintenance Tool Box (eMBox) included with eDirectory 8.7 and higher (see Chapter 7, "Diagnostic and Repair Tools").

This chapter provides information to help you understand the most commonly encountered DS error codes. You can use this as a starting point to further determine the actual cause of a problem and then formulate a corrective action plan. An exhaustive list and explanation of all the published DS error codes is presented in Appendix A.

REAL WORLD

Lightweight Directory Accoess Protocol (LDAP)

You can access an NDS/eDirectory tree by using Lightweight Directory Access Protocol (LDAP). Because LDAP is an Internet standard, the error codes returned by the LDAP client and server applications are not those used by NDS or eDirectory, but they are a set of standardized values. Error codes from an LDAP server ranges from 0 (0x00) through 80 (0x50), and LDAP clients may return error codes between 81 (0x51) and 137 (0x89). Sometimes a Novell-supplied LDAP application shows an LDAP error as well as a DS error code, if appropriate. For instance, if an object is not found, the application may report an LDAP error of 32 (0x20), meaning the target object cannot be found, and also the DS error code -601.

You can find a list of LDAP error codes in Novell TID #10018955 and on the Internet. The following are some useful URLs:

```
http://nimbus.ocis.temple.edu/ldap/error.htm#1915315
http://help.netscape.com/kb/corporate/19970303-9.html
www.opus1.com/www/iii/SDK/errors.html
```

Types and Causes of DS Errors

The first step in dealing with DS problems is to understand the nature of the error. DS errors can be categorized into *transitory DS errors* and *recurring DS errors*. These terms refer to the conditions that cause the DS error to occur and not to the DS error code reported in response to the conditions. In addition to understanding the nature of a DS error, you need to have an understanding of the types of conditions that can cause DS errors to occur in order to narrow down the area in which to concentrate your trouble-shooting efforts.

NOTE

Not all DS errors are *bad* errors. Some errors are considered *normal* errors. A normal error—perhaps a better term is *informational error*—is one that logically happens in the DS. Examples are the collision errors and DSA common request errors you see in DSTrace. These informational errors are displayed to help you see how DS handles processes such as user logins and changes in the DS. For example, DSTrace shows a -601 error (no such object) when a user tries to log in using a wrong context; this is an error from a programmatic point of view, but it's not an error from the DS operation's point of view.

Transitory DS Errors

As mentioned previously, *transitory DS errors* are errors that occur on an intermittent basis or that occur only for a short time and do not reoccur. These errors are generally caused by conditions external to the server that report the error; however, transitory errors can also occur due to data inconsistency between different replicas of the same partition.

A commonly encountered transitory DS error is error code -625 (transport failure). It is caused by communication failure between two servers that hold replicas of the same partition. The communication fault may be due to a down WAN connection or a disruption of the LAN (such as beaconing in a Token Ring environment). Both of these error conditions are external to the servers, out of the control of DS, and can't be resolved by DS; however, when the communication link is reestablished, the DS -625 error automatically stops and does not reoccur unless the link is down again.

In a well-maintained, healthy DS tree, most of the DS errors are of the transitory type. Therefore, when you're presented with a DS error, it is best to remember not to panic and to give DS some time (say, 30 minutes to an hour; 2 to 4 hours for a large tree or a situation that involves slow WANs) to see whether the error can be autocorrected.

Recurring DS Errors

As mentioned previously, a *recurring DS error* is an error that results from a permanent error condition that can't be correctly resolved without human intervention. Errors of this type persist until the cause of the error is identified and corrected. It is important to note that not all recurring errors are attributed to DS or the DS databases.

Although most of the time error -625 is a transitory error, it can also be a recurring error. For example, if a server holding a replica of a partition is removed from the network without going through the proper procedure, the replica ring becomes inconsistent. This is a result of the fact that the other servers in the replica ring are not aware that this one server is no longer available and will continue to attempt to synchronize updates with this server. The resulting -625 error continues to be reported until the replica ring is repaired.

> **NOTE**   For the procedure on repairing replica ring inconsistency, see Chapter 11, "Examples from the Real World."

Another common recurring DS error is -601 (no such object). A DS user or an application attempting to access a nonexistent DS object causes this. For instance, say a user is trying to log in, but the context of the User object is wrong. The user will continue to receive this -601 error code after each attempt. Keep in mind, however, that this -601 error code may also be transitory, depending on the cause of the error. For example, the login process will check to see whether the `Login Script` attribute exists for a user before executing it. If the user does not have a personal login script, a -138601 error will be returned to the login process.

DS Error-Causing Conditions

DS errors can be divided into three categories: informational messages, communication-related errors, and errors due to data inconsistency. Informational messages are nonfatal errors that are returned by DS to the requesting client to inform it of one or more of the following conditions:

▶ The request cannot be processed at this time due to outstanding operation. For example, you're trying to perform a partitioning operation while a previous one is still in progress.

▶ The request cannot be processed due to insufficient DS rights. For example, if the requesting client doesn't have the Browse object right to an object, a -601 error (no such object) will be returned, even though the object does exist.

▶ The information provided in the request is invalid or is missing some mandatory fields.

▶ The request references a nonexistent object or object class.

▶ An unexpected response was received while the request was being processed. For example, the source server cannot connect to another server for tree-walking purposes (error -635).

Communication-related errors are errors that result from LAN or WAN failures. Given that DS is a distributed and replicated database, DS must be able to communicate with other servers within the same DS tree. Any failure in the underlying hardware and software to provide the capability to communicate between servers results in disruption of DS processes and operations. Fortunately, communication-related DS errors are generally transitory and are resolved when the communication capability between servers is restored. Some possible causes of communication-related DS errors are as follows:

▶ Faulty LAN drivers

▶ Faulty LAN/WAN hardware, such as cable and network cards

▶ Unreliable network infrastructure, such as slow or often congested WAN links

▶ Incorrect server (internal) network addresses contained in the DS database of a server (perhaps the server didn't receive the updated information from other servers in the replica ring due to other errors)

▶ Duplicate server internal network addresses or IP addresses

▶ Route and/or Service Advertising Protocol (SAP) filtering, or Service Location Protocol (SLP)–related problems.

NOTE

In NetWare 3 and NetWare 4, IPX INTERNAL NET **is used in the** AUTOEXEC.NCF **to specify the server's internal (Internetwork Packet Exchange [IPX]) address. In NetWare 5 and higher,** ServerID **is used instead. However, the server console command** CONFIG **still reports the value as the IPX internal network number.**

Communication errors can result in DS data inconsistency, such as a user object existing in one replica but not in another. This is due to replicas of the same partition being out of sync; however, such inconsistencies are often transitory in nature and self-correct when communication is reestablished.

On the other hand, DS data inconsistency can be of the recurring type. For example, if the schema or one of the DS database files on a server is corrupted, DS can't rectify the resulting data inconsistency automatically, and manual intervention is required.

To correctly identify the condition under which a specific DS error occurs, you need to know the meaning of the reported error code and the source of the error code. The rest of this chapter is dedicated to describing some of the most commonly encountered DS error codes and the possible conditions under which they occur. The discussions are divided into the following categories, based on the error code grouping:

- ▶ Operating system–related DS error codes (-1 through -255)

- ▶ DS client application programming interface (API) error codes (-301 through -399)

- ▶ Server-based DS client library error codes (-400 through -599)

- ▶ DSA error codes (-601 through -799, and -6001 through -6999).

NOTE Error codes used by Novell's DirXML (between -286 and -300) and SecureLogin (between -102 and -430) products overlap with the DS error codes. Therefore, you should be careful when interpreting the meaning of an error code if you have these products installed.

TIP Due to the way the search engine works, when searching for DS error codes using Novell's online support knowledge base, you enter the code using the positive version of a negative number that is reported. For instance, if you are looking for information about error code -6018, enter 6018 in the search box instead of -6018. Alternatively, you can put the negative number within quotes, such as "-6018". Otherwise, the search could result in a large number of irrelevant hits.

One set of server-based error codes, -4991 through -4999, is related to eDirectory errors, but these errors are not observed on the NetWare platform. These error codes are associated with the DHost process.

Because NDS was initially developed for the NetWare platform, NetWare Core Protocol (NCP) is used for communications between NetWare servers and between clients and the servers. In order for eDirectory running on Windows and Linux/Unix/Linux to properly communicate with the NetWare implementation, a special application, called DHost, is used. DHost sits underneath eDirectory and provides functionality on non-NetWare platforms that the NetWare operating system provides naturally. The services provided by DHost include the (small) NCP Engine to handle communications with NetWare servers, the Watchdog function to ensure that workstations running Client32 are still connected, and an event system to provide a way for applications to monitor the DS activity of the server.

DHost error codes range between -4991 (0xFFFFEC81) and -4999 (0xFFFFEC79), and NCP Engine–related errors range between -5187 (0xFFFFEBBD) and -5199 (0xFFFFEBB1).

See Chapter 6 for a detailed discussion about the DS processes that generate the errors.

Operating System-Related DS Error Codes

Error codes -1 through -255 are operating system–related errors (such as from the file system, IPX, the bindery NCP, and other operating system services) returned through DS. The operating system error codes are 1 byte in size and are mapped to -1 to -255 when returned as DS errors. For example, when an application makes a DS API call but didn't allocate a large enough buffer for the data to be returned by the server, it results in a -119 error (buffer too small).

You normally do *not* come across these operating system–related DS error codes because the applications should trap them and take appropriate action; however, if the application fails to trap the error, you may encounter these error codes.

In general, the error codes listed in this section are of more interest to programmers writing DS-aware applications than they are to network administrators.

Table 5.1 lists the operating system–related errors that you are most likely to see and what they mean. You can find a complete list of all the operating system–related errors in Appendix A.

TABLE 5.1   **Common Operating System–Related DS Error Codes**

DECIMAL	HEXADECIMAL	CONSTANT
-131	0xFFFFFF7D	DSERR_HARD_IO_ERROR
-149	0xFFFFFF6B	DSERR_FILE_DETACHED
-150	0xFFFFFF6A	DSERR_NO_ALLOC_SPACE
-188	0xFFFFFF44	DSERR_LOGIN_SIGNING_REQUIRED
-189	0xFFFFFF43	DSERR_LOGIN_ENCRYPT_REQUIRED
-190	0xFFFFFF42	DSERR_INVALID_DATA_STREAM
-191	0xFFFFFF41	DSERR_INVALID_NAME_SPACE
-192	0xFFFFFF40	DSERR_NO_ACCOUNTING_PRIVILEGES
-193	0xFFFFFF3F	DSERR_NO_ACCOUNT_BALANCE
-194	0xFFFFFF3E	DSERR_CREDIT_LIMIT_EXCEEDED
-195	0xFFFFFF3D	DSERR_TOO_MANY_HOLDS
-196	0xFFFFFF3C	DSERR_ACCOUNTING_DISABLED
-197	0xFFFFFF3B	DSERR_LOGIN_LOCKOUT
-198	0xFFFFFF3A	DSERR_NO_CONSOLE_RIGHTS
-239	0xFFFFFF11	DSERR_ILLEGAL_NAME

You should pay special attention if you encounter error -149. It is an internal auditing error that should generally *not* happen in the first place unless there's internal system corruption. If you encounter it, you need to contact Novell to resolve this error. Error -150 is important because it suggests that the server doesn't have sufficient dynamic memory to process the current auditing request; this error could be due to RAM shortage or memory fragmentation on the server. If you encounter a -239 error, it means the server received a request made with an object or a property name containing illegal characters, such as a control character, a comma, a colon, a semicolon, a slash, a backslash, a question mark, an asterisk, or a tilde. This error may also be due to the fact that the DS module can't map the supplied object or attribute name to its Unicode representation and could be a result of missing or corrupted Unicode files in the `SYS:LOGIN\NLS` directory on a NetWare server (`\winnt\system32\nls` on Windows or `/usr/share/nwlocale` on Unix/Linux).

Some of these operating system–related error codes (such as -254 and -255) have multiple meanings. And because -001 to -255 are mostly server operating system error codes reported as DS errors, you need to be aware of the context under which the error code is returned in order to correctly interpret the cause of the error.

NOTE

Some of the error codes in the range of –001 through –255 may be caused by Secure Authentication Services (SAS), the Authentication Tool Box (ATB) library (on a NetWare server), or even the Novell SecureLogin product. Therefore, knowing the condition under which the error occurred will help you to correctly interpret the error code, thus helping you find the proper fix to the problem.

NOTE

Interestingly, error code –25 is used by a number of applications (including eMBox), but its use is not clearly documented.

DS Client API Library Error Codes

Error codes -301 through -399 are errors returned by DS client API library functions. For example, when an application makes a call to an API function using an invalid object name (such as CN=Test.O=ABC.O=TopLevel) a -314 error (invalid object name) will be returned because one Organization object is inside another Organization object, which is not allowed by the schema containment rules.

As with the DS operating system errors, you normally do *not* come across these client API DS error codes because the applications should have trapped them and taken appropriate action; however, if the application fails to trap the error, you might encounter these error codes. Sometimes, the error code is shown as part of the error message displayed by the application. For example, the NetWare Administrator application (nwadmn32.exe) displays error messages as shown in Figure 5.1.

Unique id number

Error message text

Error code number

FIGURE 5.1

A sample NetWare Administrator error dialog box.

In Figure 5.1, the ID number (945) is the index of the text message in the System Message Help file, and the number following the error code (35327) is a reference number that is strictly for Novell's internal use.

> **NOTE**
>
> **In general, the error codes listed in this section are of more interest to programmers writing DS-aware applications than they are to network administrators.**

Table 5.2 lists some common DS client API library error codes. You can find a complete list of all the DS client API library errors in Appendix A.

TABLE 5.2   **Common DS Client API Library Error Codes**

DECIMAL	HEXIDECIMAL	CONSTANT
-301	0xFFFFFED3	ERR_NOT_ENOUGH_MEMORY
-302	0xFFFFFED2	ERR_BAD_KEY
-318	0xFFFFFEC2	ERR_COUNTRY_NAME_TOO_LONG
-319	0xFFFFFEC1	ERR_SYSTEM_ERROR
-320	0xFFFFFEC0	ERR_CANT_ADD_ROOT
-321	0xFFFFFEBF	ERR_UNABLE_TO_ATTACH
-338	0xFFFFFEAE	ERR_INVALID_PASSWORD_CHARS
-339	0xFFFFFEAD	ERR_FAILED_SERVER_AUTHENT
-345	0xFFFFFEA7	ERR_INVALID_DS_VERSION
-346	0xFFFFFEA6	ERR_UNICODE_TRANSLATION
-347	0xFFFFFEA5	ERR_SCHEMA_NAME_TOO_LONG
-348	0xFFFFFEA4	ERR_UNICODE_FILE_NOT_FOUND

Error -301 means the application is unable to allocate memory. This suggests that the client (workstation) may be low on memory or that the application has repeatedly allocated buffers and failed to release them (memory leak). Therefore, if you still receive this error code after closing all other applications running on the client, there's a good chance the application has a memory leak and you need to contact the vendor for an update.

Error -348 means the application can't locate the required Unicode file or files. This error can be due to one of two reasons. The first reason is that, because DS stores all characters using Unicode representation, DS-aware applications need access to country-code and code-page specific Unicode files. Often, a programmer may hard-code the country-code information into the software (typically country code 001 and code page 437, for the

United States). When you try to run such an application on a workstation that's configured for, say, German, it may fail with error -348 because the necessary Unicode files may not have been installed. In North America, these are a workstation's default country settings:

▶ Country code = 001 (United States)

▶ Code page = 437 (United States)

These Unicode files are needed:

```
UNI_437.001
UNI_COL.001
UNI_MON.001
437_UNI.001
```

If you set the code page to 850 instead of 437 (the default), these required Unicode files are needed:

```
UNI_850.001
UNI_COL.001
UNI_MON.001
850_UNI.001
```

Sometimes even when the programmer retrieves the country information during runtime, you may still encounter the -348 error. It is important to realize that different operating system platforms use different code pages, even if the country code is the same. For example, the default DOS country setting in North America is country code 001 and code page 850; however, the default Windows NT/2000 North America country setting (for the Windows 32-bit GUI environment) is country code 001 and code page 1252. As a result, if you try to run a DOS-based DS-aware application in the command prompt box on Windows NT/2000, you might receive the -348 error because the Unicode files for code page 850 are not found.

The second reason that error code -348 might occur is that DS-aware applications search for Unicode files in the following locations, in the order listed:

1. The directory in which the DS-aware application is located

2. The NLS directory directly under the directory in which the DS-aware application resides (This is why you have NLS directories in **LOGIN** and **PUBLIC** on the NetWare server.)

3. Your search drives or paths

For example, if the application is installed on a NetWare server in SYS:NDSAPP, the application looks, in the following order, at SYS:NDSAPPS, SYS:NDSAPPS\NLS, and your search drives. Therefore, you have to ensure that the Unicode files can be found in one of these locations.

DS Server-Based Client Library Error Codes

Error codes -400 through -599 are errors returned by DS server-based client API library functions. They are typically generated by the DS module and other related modules, such as DSRepair. However, certain DS processes require the functionality from server modules such as the Unicode module. If one of these supporting modules encounters an error, the error may be passed back to DS, and the DS module will then report the error.

You generally do not encounter these error codes because they are mostly trapped and handled by the modules. But in case you do encounter these error codes, they are included here for your reference.

NOTE   In general, the error codes listed in this section are of more interest to program-mers writing DS-aware applications than they are to network administrators.

Table 5.3 shows common DS client API library error codes specific to server-based applications. You can find a complete list of all the DS client API library error codes specific to server-based applications in Appendix A.

TABLE 5.3   Common DS Client API Library Error Codes Specific to Server-Based Modules

DECIMAL	HEXADECIMAL	CONSTANT
-400	0xFFFFFE70	ERR_BAD_SERVICE_CONNECTION
-401	0xFFFFFE6F	ERR_BAD_NETWORK
-403	0xFFFFFE6D	ERR_SLOT_ALLOCATION
-405	0xFFFFFE6B	ERR_BAD_SERVER_NAME
-406	0xFFFFFE6A	ERR_BAD_USER_NAME
-408	0xFFFFFE68	ERR_NO_MEMORY
-412	0xFFFFFE64	ERR_CONNECTION_ABORTED

Table 5.3   Continued

DECIMAL	HEXADECIMAL	CONSTANT
-413	0xFFFFFE63	ERR_TIMEOUT
-414	0xFFFFFE62	ERR_CHECKSUM

Many server-based API functions require the application to first be attached to *and* authenticated to the target server (thus receiving a valid server handle). If the application failed to first obtain a valid server handle before making the API call, error -400 is returned.

> **NOTE**
>
> **The -400 error could also indicate that the target server is not available. Therefore, before you jump to the conclusion that there is a bug in the application, check that the target server is reachable.**

The other most commonly encountered errors in this category are -405 and -406. These error codes result when one or more illegal characters are found in the server name and usernames, respectively. For example, depending on the API in question, the specified server name may just be the CN portion of the object name (such as TEST_SERVER1) rather than the full object name (such as TEST_SERVER1.Org_Unit.Org); the dots in the name would be considered illegal characters.

> **NOTE**
>
> **As discussed in Chapter 2, "eDirectory Basics," although a DS object name may be up to 255 characters in length, including context information, the CN portion of the object name is limited to 64 characters.**

DSA Error Codes

Error codes -601 through -799 and -6001 through -6999 are errors returned by the DSA that is running on the DS server. The DSA errors are what you generally see in the DSTrace screen and reported by various DS utilities, such as NetWare Administrator and ConsoleOne; therefore, you should be well versed in these error codes.

Table 5.4 shows some of the common error codes returned by the DSA. You can find a complete list of all the DSA error codes in Appendix A.

TABLE 5.4   **Common DSA Error Codes**

DECIMAL	HEXADECIMAL	CONSTANT
-601	0xFFFFFDA7	ERR_NO_SUCH_ENTRY
-602	0xFFFFFDA6	ERR_NO_SUCH_VALUE
-603	0xFFFFFDA5	ERR_NO_SUCH_ATTRIBUTE
-624	0xFFFFFD90	ERR_REPLICA_ALREADY_EXISTS
-625	0xFFFFFD8F	ERR_TRANSPORT_FAILURE
-626	0xFFFFFD8E	ERR_ALL_REFERRALS_FAILED
-654	0xFFFFFD72	ERR_PARTITION_BUSY
-659	0xFFFFFD6D	ERR_TIME_NOT_SYNCHRONIZED
-666	0xFFFFFD66	ERR_INCOMPATIBLE_DS_VERSION
-672	0xFFFFFD60	ERR_NO_ACCESS
-698	0xFFFFFD46	ERR_REPLICA_IN_SKULK
-715	0xFFFFFD35	ERR_CHECKSUM_FAILURE
-782	0xFFFFFCF2	ERR_ROOT_UNREACHABLE
-785	0xFFFFFCEF	ERR_DIB_ERROR
-6018	0xFFFFE87E	ERR_SERIAL_NUM_MISMATCH
-6024	0xFFFFE878	ERR_RFL_FILE_NOT_FOUND

The -601 error is perhaps the most common DS error code that you will encounter. This error refers to the fact that the specified object is not found on the server replying to the request. The specified object context could be wrong, or the client might not have sufficient DS rights (such as Browse) to the object. If you see this error code in a DSTrace screen, it simply means the server handling the request doesn't have the information and will have to perform a tree-walk; therefore, in most cases, a -601 error is an informational error.

Errors -602 and -603 mean the requested attribute value and attribute, respectively, are not found on the server replying to the request. The client may not have sufficient DS rights to the data. Unlike with the -601 error, however, with -602 and -603, no tree-walking will be performed to look for the information elsewhere.

Next to the -601 error, -625 is probably the second most commonly reported DSA error. Error -625 means the reporting server is unable to communicate with the target server. This is generally a result of the target server being down, a LAN/WAN outage, or some sort of routing problem.

The -698 error code is another nonfatal error. It means an attempt was made to start the NDS replica synchronization process with a target server, but the target server was busy synchronizing with another server. This is a transitory error, and the NDS replica synchronization process will reschedule. You are likely to see this error on partitions that have a large replica ring (say, 10 or more servers) or have slow or busy servers in the replica ring.

NOTE

To prevent data conflicts, a DS server will only receive inbound DS replica synchronization traffic from other servers, in the replica ring, one at a time. When two servers in the same replica ring try to synchronize to the same DS server before one of them completes the synchronization, the second server reports error –698 and retries at a later time.

A routing problem could result in a misleading -715 error code, which means the NDS checksum in the request packet is invalid. We have encountered one instance where a duplicate IPX network address on the network caused DS to erroneously report a -715 error. After removing the duplicate route, DS resolved the -715 error without further intervention, such as the need to run DSRepair.

If you don't have sufficient privileges to modify an object's attribute values, error -672 occurs. Similarly, when a server-based application authenticates to only the local server and not the DS tree, the application also results in a -672 error if the object it tries to modify does not exist in a replica held on that server. Incidentally, performing a send all operation by using eMBox may also result in a -672 error, although it works fine if you use the DSRepair module instead. In this situation, the error is due to the fact that eMBox does not have all the necessary information to perform the task. You must enter two data fields when you send all objects to every replica in the ring by using eMBox:

1. You must select the partition you want to perform the send all operation on. Make sure the radio button is *not* selected for the partition ID but is on the partition DN.

2. You must select the server object you want to send from (using the Server DN option). It must be a server that holds at least a read/write replica of the partition in question.

If you do not enter the correct information (as illustrated in Figure 5.2) into either of these two fields, you will most likely get a -672 error as a result.

Ensure these 2 fields are filled in

FIGURE 5.2
Using eMBox to
perform a send
all operation.

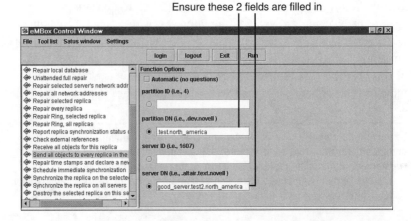

> **WARNING**
>
> **Remember that there is no way to do a send all to just one specific server in the replica ring. A send all will send all objects to *all* other servers in the replica ring. Therefore, with a large replica ring, it could take some time to complete, and a large volume of DS traffic could be generated.**

Many of the -6001 through -6999 series of error codes were introduced for eDirectory 8.7 and higher. These error codes are mostly related to the operation of eDirectory Backup eMTool (called eMTool for short) and the roll-forward log (RFL) files. For instance, if RFL files from another server were used when restoring the eDirectory database via eMTool, error -6018 will be reported. If one or more of the required RFL files required for an eDirectory database restoration is missing, eMTool will report a -6024 error.

> **TIP**
>
> **There is an interesting bug in the eMBox version 10410.68 (shipped with eDirectory 8.7.1) that occurs when you set the RFL directory name. If the name of the RFL directory is longer than eight characters, the eMBox client reports a –785 error, saying that it was unable to update the backup configuration information. This is misleading because -785 means an internal Directory Information Base error, but there isn't one. The error is due to that the fact that although the eMBox client supports long directory names, the FLAIM engine is rejecting the long name (for some unknown reason). Therefore, the workaround is to use a directory name that is eight or fewer characters.**
>
> **Also be aware that if the specified directory does not already exist, eMBox will return a -25 error, indicating an invalid directory.**

Summary

This chapter presents a discussion of the various error types and some possible sources. The errors are broken into following categories: errors returned by the DS service running on the server, errors returned by the client application (workstation based or server based), and errors returned by the DSA running on the server.

Chapter 6 provides an in-depth look at the common DS processes and helps explain the causes of the errors.

CHAPTER 6

Understanding Common eDirectory Processes

Chapter 1, "The Four Basics of eDirectory Troubleshooting," defines Novell's directory services (DS) implementation as a loosely consistent distributed database. Several autonomous background processes ensure the integrity of the data in the DS database and must run smoothly to provide consistent operation. There are also several processes you initiate with administration tools such as ConsoleOne and NDS iMonitor when managing objects, partitions, and replicas.

This chapter looks at the most common of these processes, to help you develop a better understanding of how they work. A thorough understanding of how they work makes it easier to determine a proper course of action to take to resolve DS problems.

NOTE

The various DS processes discussed in this chapter exist in all versions of NDS, including eDirectory. There are some subtle differences in how the processes function internally (such as the frequency at which a process runs) depending on the version of DS in question. These differences are highlighted in this chapter as applicable.

TIP

This chapter goes into some detail about the DS processes themselves. For step-by-step detail of the operation of a specific process, refer to Novell's CD-ROMs LogicSource II for NDS and LogicSource for eDirectory. These CD-ROMs were once available for purchase as part of the LogicSource offering, but now are offered as part of the Novell Professional Resource Suite and as part of the Novell Product Toolkits. For more information about Novell Technical Subscriptions, visit `http://support.novell.com/subscriptions`.

Before we talk about the background processes, we need to discuss DS name resolution, tree-walking, and obituaries, which DS uses to locate information in the tree and to keep track of the state of some of the operations, respectively.

NDS Name Resolution and Tree-Walking

NDS name resolution is the process of DS navigating through the different partitions in the tree—using tree-walking—until it finds the requested object. When DS finds the object, it retrieves the object ID and returns it to the caller. All DS information requests can be broken down into one or more names that identify the objects. In pursuing each name component in a request, DS searches for a partition that contains some part of the name path associated with the request. When a partition is found, the search moves from that partition to the partition that actually contains the object. Until a relevant partition is found, the search proceeds *upward* toward [Root]; any request can be pursued successfully by beginning at [Root] and working downward.

Consider the sample tree shown in Figure 6.1. Let's assume that your currently context is at O=East_Coast. In order to locate the User object Dilbert, looking down the current tree branch does not find him. By moving upward to [Root], you have two additional tree branches (O=West_Coast and O=Central) from which to pursue the object.

FIGURE 6.1
An example of a DS tree structure.

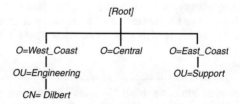

Tree-walking is the process of a NetWare Core Protocol (NCP) client, commonly referred to as the DS agent (DSA), walking through the NDS tree to locate a server hosting the partition that has a particular object. Each DS server (be it a NetWare server or Linux system running eDirectory) has a built-in client agent to facilitate DS name resolution and tree-walking.

NOTE

The name resolution process is initiated by the DS DSAResolveName **"verb." (DS verbs are predefined functions within the DS engine. Refer to Appendix B, "DS Verbs," for a complete list of DS verbs.)**

An application may disable the tree-walking component of the name resolution process by setting the DCV_DISALLOW_REFERRALS **flag to** TRUE **and calling the** NWDSSetContext **API. This is useful if the application wants to search only the database local to the server it is communicating with. When you set the** DCV_DISALLOW_REFERRALS **flag to** TRUE**, the DSA returns a failure (-601 error [object not found]) if the object being sought is not located in the local database.**

The tree-walking process relies on Subordinate Reference (SubRef) partitions to connect the tree. If a server can provide no other DS information, the least it can offer is a reference to another server higher in the tree that has a partition with information about objects. When walking the tree, a server is given the object name of interest. Based on the name, the server decides whether it needs to move upward toward [Root] or downward away from [Root] in order to access the next partition in its efforts to locate the object.

NOTE

Tree-walking can go up *or* down a DS tree, depending on the location of the partition that holds the desired object.

NOTE

eDirectory 8.5 introduced a new feature called *referral hints* to help make tree-walking more efficient. Prior to eDirectory 8.5, NDS may have had to walk through a large portion of the tree, which could span slow WAN links, before locating the server holding a real replica of the desired object. This could consume a lot of time and overhead. With referral hints, the network addresses of servers that "should" have a real copy of the partition are kept on the External Reference (ExRef) partition root object. eDirectory simply walks to the partition root object and uses the referrals listed on that object to contact the servers directly and see whether they have real copies of the partition of interest. If this fails, the old way of walking the tree is then used to try to locate the desired partition.

The act of the workstation locating the server that holds the partition with the desired object constitutes half the name-resolution process. Up to this halfway point, the tree-walking process is solely carried out by the server on behalf of the workstation. The second half of name resolution is complete when the client retrieves the object ID from the server containing the partition. There are three ways in which this second half of the process is accomplished, depending on the DSA's request setting (NWC_DS_PREFER_ONLY_REFERRALS, NWC_DS_PREFER_REFERRALS, or not set).

If the DSA has the resolve name request flag set to
NWC_DS_PREFER_ONLY_REFERRALS (0x00004000) and the requested distinguished name (DN) is not in the local database, the agent returns to the
caller a list of referrals of servers that will have real copies of the DN in
question. If the DSA has the resolve name request flag set to NWC_DS_
PREFER_REFERRALS (0x00002000) instead, the agent returns only one referral (the first entry in the list) instead of the entire list.

> **NOTE**
>
> When the resolve name request flag is set, the behavior of the DSAResolveName
> process is very similar to the LDAP referral process: The client is given a list of
> referrals, and it is up to the caller to decide what to do with that information.

When the referral information is returned to the call, it is up to the caller to
make a new request to the new servers. If the caller (such as the Novell
Client for Windows on a workstation) did not previously have a connection
to the referred server, an authenticated-but-not-licensed connection is created in order to retrieve the (server-centric) object ID from the server.

> **NOTE**
>
> One of the steps in the DSAResolveName process in eDirectory 8.5 and higher
> checks whether the object has a global unique identifier (GUID). If a GUID value is
> not found, one will be created. eDirectory 8.7 requires that every object have a
> GUID. Therefore, DSAResolveName is a process that ensures that the objects have
> GUIDs because this routine is used often.
>
> Many processes (such as file system trustee assignments on Novell Storage
> Service [NSS] version 3 volumes on NetWare 6 servers) are starting to use GUIDs
> instead of the server-centric IDs of the objects. To maintain backward compatibili-
> ty with previous versions of NDS, however, the server-centric IDs are still being
> maintained and used.

If the DSA request flag did not specify referrals, a temporary external reference will be created on the local server (the one the workstation sent the
initial request to), and its object ID will be returned to the caller. (If the
server no longer needs an ExRef, background processes will have it removed
after 192 hours [eight days]. See the section "The Backlink Process," later in
this chapter.)

> **NOTE**
>
> If the object ID of the real object is desired, the calling application should set the
> request flags for one of the two referral options discussed previously.

The name resolution and tree-walking processes are best illustrated by the following login example. In this example, three different partitions in the DS tree are located on three separate servers (see Figure 6.2), and the replica placement is as follows:

	ACME_Inc Partition	OU_2 Partition	Testing Partition
Server FS1	—	—	Master
Server FS2	—	Master	SubRef
Server FS3	Master	SubRef	—

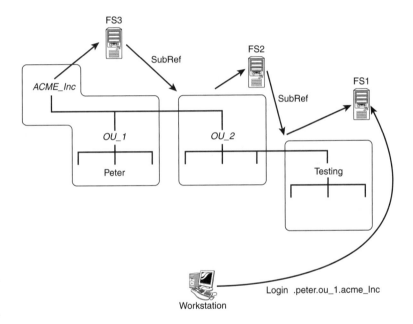

FIGURE 6.2
A tree-walking example with three partitions.

Suppose the workstation is initially attached to FS1. The user logs in as `.peter.ou_1.acme_inc`. Server FS1 does not contain information for this `User` object, nor does it have information about `OU_1` or `ACME_Inc`. Rather than immediately returning an error message (indicating that the object is not found) to the workstation, however, FS1 passes the query up the tree—using its internal DS client agent—to FS2. (It knows FS2 is closer to `[Root]` because of the SubRef pointer.)

If FS2 does not contain information for the object (which it does not in this example), it passes the name of the server containing a parent partition of itself—in this case, FS3—back to FS1. Then FS1 queries FS3 for the desired information; FS1 has "walked" up the DS tree structure, toward `[Root]`. In this instance, FS3 holds the partition that contains the User object. Therefore, FS1 redirects the workstation (transparently to the user) to query server FS3 directly; if the workstation did not previously have a connection to FS3, an authenticated-but-not-licensed connection will be created in order to retrieve the information from the server. (The redirection here is a function of the Novell Client, and the behavior is hard-coded and cannot be changed.)

Tree-walking gives a DS client the ability to log in or authenticate without having to attach to the specific server holding the partition (or replica of the partition) that contains the User object. Tree-walking is also used to locate services—such as servers and print queues—anywhere within a DS tree. You might have noticed the similarities between DS's tree-walking and LDAP's chaining process. The main difference between the two is the DS's tree-walking does not require the requesting server to authenticate to the target server every time it connects, whereas LDAP's chaining process does.

> **NOTE**
>
> In an NDS/eDirectory environment, after a client is authenticated to a DS tree, that client can locate any (DS-aware) service within the tree without the use of a SAP packet or an SLP packet. NetWare 2 and NetWare 3 services, such as print servers and database servers, must broadcast the services' availability (over IPX) on a regular basis (the default is 60 seconds) so clients that can locate these services.
>
> This feature is especially beneficial for networks that have many services. The use of DS to locate services significantly reduces the amount of network broadcast or multicast traffic due to SAP or SLP. This reduction in network traffic is also of importance to companies that have WAN links. It is one of the many reasons NDS/eDirectory works well in large networks where other DS failed to deliver the expected performance.

Obituaries

Some of the most common problems in NDS/eDirectory are caused by obituaries (commonly referred to as *obits*) not being processed properly. Any number of reasons can cause obituaries to not be processed (resulting in what is known as *stuck obits*), ranging from a down server or communication link to an invalid backlink list in an object. If you understand the background processes and how certain processes use obituaries, you may find it easier to determine the best course of action for correcting a problem.

NOTE

Many of the most common DS problems are caused by problems with obituaries purging, but they initially appear to be caused by something else.

Obituaries are operational attributes (that is, not attributes that can be controlled by the user) that DS uses to ensure referential integrity between objects during certain operations—such as object and partition move operations, object deletions, and object restorations. DS uses the obit attribute internally, with the syntax type `SYN_OCTET_STRING`. The attribute has the `DS_READ_ONLY_ATTR` constraint flag that restricts its access to only the DS servers.

There are three obituary type classes: primary, secondary, and tracking. A *primary obituary* indicates an action on an object. A *secondary obituary* indicates the servers that must be contacted and informed of the primary obituary's action. A *tracking obituary* is an informational obituary that is associated with certain primary obituaries. A tracking obit does not go through the same process as the primary and secondary obits.

Table 6.1 shows the different obituary types and when DS generates them.

Obituary Types and Classes **TABLE 6.1**

OBITUARY TYPE	TYPE VALUE	CONSTANT NAME	OBITUARY CLASS	DESCRIPTION
Restored	0x0000	OBT_RESTORED	Primary	Created when an object is restored from a backup.
Dead	0x0001	OBT_DEAD	Primary	Created when an object is deleted.
Moved	0x0002	OBT_MOVED	Primary	Created when an object is moved from one container to another. This obituary is created for the object's original location.

Table 6.1   Continued

OBITUARY TYPE	TYPE VALUE	CONSTANT NAME	OBITUARY CLASS	DESCRIPTION
Inhibit Move	0x0003	OBT_INHIBIT _MOVE	Tracking	Created when an object is moved from one container to another. This obituary is created for the object's destination location. This obituary prevents the object from being moved again until the previous move has completed.
OLD_RDN	0x0004	OBT_OLD_RDN	Tracking	Created when an object is renamed. This obituary is created for the old object name.
NEW_RDN	0x0005	OBT_NEW_RDN	Primary	Created when an object is renamed. This obituary is created for the new object name.
BackLink	0x0006	OBT_BACKLINK	Secondary	Represents the object on another server's database that must be notified when the object is modified (such as when it is deleted, renamed, or moved). This is a secondary obituary. BackLink

Table 6.1   Continued

OBITUARY TYPE	TYPE VALUE	CONSTANT NAME	OBITUARY CLASS	DESCRIPTION
				obituaries may represent real copies of the object as found on a Read/Write replica or any server with an external refer- ence to the object.
Tree_OLD_RDN	0x0007	OBT_TREE_ OLD_RDN	Tracking	Created when a partition root object (and *not* an NDS tree name) is renamed. This is a special case of the OLD_RDN obituary type.
Tree_NEW_RDN	0x0008	OBT_TREE_ NEW_RDN	Primary	Created when a partition root object (and *not* an NDS tree name) is renamed. This is a special case of the NEW_RDN obituary type.
Purge All	0x0009	OBT_PURGE_ ALL	Primary	Created internally by NDS to identi- fy an object whose attribute values need to be purged (so that only an object husk remains).

Table 6.1   Continued

OBITUARY TYPE	TYPE VALUE	CONSTANT NAME	OBITUARY CLASS	DESCRIPTION
Move Subtree	0x000A	OBT_MOVE_ALL	Secondary	Created when a partition root object is moved from one container to another.
Moved From	0x000B	OBT_MOVED_ FROM	Secondary	Created when an object is moved from one container to another.
Used By	0x000C	OBT_USED_BY	Secondary	Contains a list of partitions that have an interest in this object and need to be notified of changes to the modified object. The creation time of the primary obituary is stored on the Used By obituary value.

NOTE   **Some Novell documentation and TIDs refers to the** Used By **obit as the** Type C **obit because of its value.**

In addition to the obituary types and classes, obituaries move through four distinct states or stages. These states are always executed in the same order to ensure that the servers process obituaries properly and then purge them from the system. Obituary advancement through the four states occurs during the synchronization process. By observing the synchronization process, you can see the obituaries actually being purged. Listing 6.1 shows where obituaries appear in the synchronization process. Notice that the object User1.West.XYZCorp has two obituary entries: one of Type 2 (Moved) and one of Type 6 (BackLink). The obituary stage is shown in the flags= field.

Listing 6.1 Obituary State Advancement

```
SYNC: Start sync of partition <[Root]> state:[0] type:[0]
 SYNC: Start outbound sync with (#=2, state=0, type=1)
       ➥[010000C3] <RIGEL.West.XYZCorp>
 SYNC: Using version 5 on server <CN=RIGEL>
   SENDING TO ------> CN=RIGEL
  SYNC: sending updates to server <CN=RIGEL>
   SYNC:[010000B8][(22:20:00),2,1] ORION.East.XYZCorp
       ➥(NCP Server)
   SYNC:[010002A4][(19:49:49),2,1] JimH.West.XYZCorp(User)
   SYNC:[010000C3][(08:31:47),1,1] RIGEL.West.XYZCorp
       ➥(NCP Server)
   SYNC: [150002E4] obituary for User1.West.XYZCorp
     valueTime=36905EB9,1,20 type=2, flags=0,
➥oldCTS=36905E6F,1,1
     valueTime=36905EB9,1,21 type=6, flags=0,
➥oldCTS=36905E6F,1,1
   SYNC:[150002E4][(00:04:05),1,1] User1.West.XYZCorp (User)
   SYNC: [0E0002BC] obituary for User1.East.XYZCorp
     valueTime=36905EB9,1,17 type=3, flags=0,
➥oldCTS=36905EB9,1,1
   SYNC:[0E0002BC][(23:24:57),1,1] User1.East.XYZCorp (User)
  SYNC: Objects: 7, total changes: 74, sent to server
➥<CN=RIGEL>
 SYNC: update to server <CN=RIGEL> successfully completed
 Merged transitive vector for [010000C3] <RIGEL.West.XYZCorp>
  succeeded
SYNC: SkulkPartition for <[Root]> succeeded
SYNC: End sync of partition <[Root]> All processed = YES.
```

The stages that an obituary passes through before it is deleted are shown in
Table 6.2. The four stages are always followed in the order presented. When
an obituary is marked `Flags=0004` (`Purgeable`), it is then up to each server
to purge it from its local database.

Obituary Processing Stage Definitions

TABLE 6.2

OBITUARY STAGE	FLAG VALUE	DESCRIPTION
Issued	0	This is the initial stage, in which an obit has been created and is ready for processing.

Table 6.2   Continued

OBITUARY STAGE	FLAG VALUE	DESCRIPTION
Notified	1	This stage indicates that the obituary is at the Notified stage, which means that the servers identified in the BackLink or Tree Move obituaries have been contacted and notified of the operation or action on an object.
Ok_to_Purge	2	At this stage, the obituary is being cleaned up on the local database of each server identified in the BackLink or Tree Move obituaries. This cleanup includes resolving all objects that reference the object with the obituary and informing them of the change (such as a deletion or a move).
Purgeable	4	At this stage, all servers are ready to purge the value or object from their local databases. The purge process essentially recovers the value to the free chain and enables it to be reused.

You might notice a couple weird things about the information in Table 6.2. The first oddity is the flag values—the progression is 0, 1, 2, 4. This field is referred to as a *bit field*. The software checks specific bits rather than looking for specific integer values.

The second thing that may appear strange is the Issued (flags=0) and Ok_to_Purge (flags=2) states; these states indicate the beginning or end of another stage rather than their own processing procedure. Stage 0 is initially set when an obituary is set; this change is then replicated to all servers. When the replication cycle is complete, DS knows that all servers are at Stage 0, and it can go ahead and start the notification process (Stage 1). A change in the obituary is made, and that information is replicated to the other servers that need to be notified. After all servers have been notified, the obituary is set to Stage 2, meaning that Stage 1 (notification) has completed. When all servers have received a flag indicating that it is okay to purge (flags=2), the servers mark the obituaries as purgeable (flags=4), and that change is replicated to all the servers. At this point, the individual servers process the actual purge process, but because all servers have to know that the obituary is now purgeable, no additional notification needs to be done after the obituaries have actually been purged.

NOTE

The four obituary processing stages actually describe a multiserver transaction processing system. You can think of the processing of obituaries as a synchronized transaction that takes place nearly simultaneously on multiple servers.

Before an obituary (regardless of its class) can move to the next state, the current state must have been synchronized to all replicas of the real object. In order to determine whether all replicas in the replica ring have seen a given obituary state, a time is computed from the `Transitive Vector` attribute of the partition that contains the obituary. If the modification timestamp (MTS) on the obituary is *older* than this time, the server responsible for that obituary can advance it to the next state.

NOTE

eDirectory 8.5 and previous versions of NDS use the `Purge Vector` attribute's time as the time to indicate when an obituary's state should be advanced. (`Purge Vector` is a nonsynchronizing, single-valued attribute of the partition root object whose value, according to the `Transitive Vector` attribute (NetWare 5 and higher) or the `Synchronized Up To` attribute (NetWare 4) of this partition represents the oldest state in time that has been seen by each DSA in the replica ring. `Purge Vector` is updated only if the partition has a successful sync cycle. On the other hand, eDirectory 8.6 and higher use the `Obituary Time Vector` attribute— a value stored in server memory that is recalculated each time the Janitor process runs (every two minutes, by default).

Primary obituaries can be advanced in their states only after *all* associated secondary obituaries have advanced through all their states. After the primary obituary reaches its last state and that state synchronizes to all servers in the replica ring, all that remains is the object "husk," which is an object without attributes—an object that can subsequently be purged from the database by the `Purge` process. Tracking obituaries are removed after the primary obituary is ready to be removed or, in the case of `OBT_INHIBIT_MOVE`, the tracking obituary is removed after the primary obituary has moved to the `flags=1` (`Notified`) state on the Master replica.

For a secondary obituary of type `BackLink`, the server that holds the Master replica of the object with the obituary is responsible for advancing the states. For a secondary obituary of type `Used By`, the server that created it is responsible for advancing the obituary states as long as that replica still exists. If it does not still exist, the server holding the Master of that partition takes over advancing the obituary states for the `Used By` obituary. For a `Move Subtree` obituary, the Master replica of the parent partition is responsible for advancing the states.

> **NOTE**
>
> **The Obituary process is scheduled on a per-partition basis, after the partition finishes a successful inbound sync. If only one replica (the Master) of a partition exists, the Heartbeat interval still schedules an Outbound Replication process, which in turns kicks off the Obituary process.**
>
> **The type of the obituary determines the replica responsible for processing the obits (the sender). With the exception of `OBT_USED_BY`, the Master replica is responsible for starting the background process. The processing of a `Used By` obit is started by the replica that actually modified the object. If this replica no longer exists, the Master replica then kicks off the background process.**

The steps involved in obituary processing are complicated. However, the basic concept can be illustrated by using a somewhat simplified example. eDirectory performs the following operations when an object is deleted:

1. eDirectory adds a primary obituary of type `Dead` to the "deleted" object and sets the flag to `Issued`. This takes place on the Master replica.

2. eDirectory creates a secondary obit of the type `BackLink` and sets the stage flag to `Issued` for every server that has an external reference to this object; the server DNs are listed in the `BackLink` attribute of the object. Store the creation time of the `Dead` obit as part of this secondary obit.

3. eDirectory creates a secondary obit of type `BackLink` and sets the stage flag to `Issued` for every server that holds a real replica of the object—not an external reference. Store the creation time of the `Dead` obit as part of this secondary obit.

4. eDirectory creates a secondary obit of type `Used By` and sets the stage flag to `Issued` for every DN listed in the `Used By` attribute of the deleted object. The `Used By` attribute contains a list of *partitions* (not servers) that have an interest in this object and need to be notified of changes to this entry. Store the creation time of the `Dead` obit as part of this secondary obit.

5. eDirectory removes all attributes except the obituaries, which results in an object husk. The flag on the entry's `Object Class` attribute is set to `Non Present`, making the object "invisible" in most of the standard management tools, such as ConsoleOne (but not in DSBrowse or NDS iMonitor).

6. The Outbound Replication process synchronizes the deletion of attributes to all other servers in the replica ring.

7. After the next successful inbound synchronization of this partition, the Obituary process is started.

The Obituary process does the following:

▶ Computes a time vector that is equivalent to the minimum `Transitive Vector` attribute, referred to as the `Purge Vector` attribute. eDirectory 8.6 and higher compute a second minimum vector, called the `Obituary Time Vector` attribute, which does not include timestamp values from Subordinate Reference replicas.

▶ Categorizes each obituary in this partition and takes appropriate action:

  ▶ If the obituary is a `Used By` obit and this server is the server where the deletion occurred (determined by comparing the replica number in the obituary's MTS to the replica number), this server is responsible for processing this obituary. Therefore, the main server notifies the other servers about this obit and sets the stage flag to `Notified`. The next time the Obituary process runs, this state flag is advanced to the next stage, until it reaches `Purgeable` (that is, after all partitions in the `Used By` attribute have been notified), and then it is purged.

  ▶ If the obituary is a `BackLink` obit and this server has the Master replica, this server is responsible for processing this obituary. Therefore, the *xxx* notifies the other servers about this obit and sets the stage flag to `Notified`. The next time the Obituary process runs, this state flag is advanced to the next stage, until it reaches `Purgeable` (that is, after all servers in the `BackLink` attribute have been notified), and then it is purged.

  ▶ If the obituary is a primary obituary (such as a `Dead` obit, in this example), there are no secondary obituaries outstanding for this primary obit, and the attribute's MTS on the obituary is older than the `Purge Vector/Obit Time Vector` attribute, the obit's flag value can be set to `Purgeable` because all servers have seen the change.

  ▶ When the obit value flag on the primary obit is set to `Purgeable`, the Purger process, also known as the Flat Cleaner process, removes the object's record (which is no longer flagged as `Present`) from the database and completes the deletion action.

Because stuck obits—that is, servers not clearing out obits from their local databases, thus preventing certain operations from being performed—are the source of many NDS/eDirectory problems, your having a good grasp of obituaries' dependency of other DS processes is important to understanding DS background processes, which are discussed next.

Background Processes

The DS module maintains the database through several background processes running on each server. These processes run automatically and generally do not need to be manually invoked. There are cases in which there is benefit in forcing a process to run, but as a general rule, you should not force them to run unless necessary. As discussed in Chapter 4, "Don't Panic," doing something just for the sake of doing it is frequently not a good idea.

The Synchronization Process

The Synchronization process, sometimes referred to as the *Skulker process*, keeps the information in multiple replicas of the DS database current on all servers. The process is event driven, meaning it is kicked off after an object has been modified. Listing 6.2 shows a sample of the Sync process in the DSTrace screen.

> **NOTE**
>
> The exact format of DSTrace output varies, depending on the version of NDS/eDirectory (thus, the version of the utilities), flag settings, and sometimes the operating system platform. Therefore, the DSTrace, DSRepair, and other listings shown in this and other chapters in this book may not exactly match what you find on your systems, but they serve as a guide to the correct information.

Listing 6.2   A Sample Synchronization Process

```
SYNC: Start sync of partition <[Root]> state:[0] type:[0]
 SYNC: Start outbound sync with (#=2, state=0, type=1)
        [010000C3]<RIGEL.West.XYZCorp>
(21:11:57) SYNC: failed to communicate with server
                <CN=RIGEL> ERROR: -625
SYNC: SkulkPartition for <[Root]> succeeded
SYNC: End sync of partition <[Root]> All processed = NO.
```

Listing 6.2 demonstrates a failed synchronization condition. The local server is attempting to contact the server named CN=Rigel.OU=West.O=XYZCorp but is unable to complete the Synchronization process. The error -625 indicates a transport failure—also known as a communications failure. To correct this problem, the easiest way to proceed is to verify that the target server is up and that the communications links between the two servers are working properly.

A successful synchronization cycle of the [Root] partition between the two servers is shown in Listing 6.3.

Listing 6.3   A Successful Synchronization

```
SYNC: Start sync of partition <[Root]> state:[0] type:[0]
 SYNC: Start outbound sync with (#=2, state=0, type=1)
      [010000C3]<RIGEL.West.XYZCorp>
 SYNC: Using version 5 on server <CN=RIGEL>
  SENDING TO ------> CN=RIGEL
 SYNC: sending updates to server <CN=RIGEL>
   SYNC:[010000B7][(20:02:16),1,3] XYZCorp (Organization)
   SYNC:[010000B8][(22:20:00),2,1] ORION.East.XYZCorp
       ↪(NCP Server)
   SYNC:[0100029A][(20:02:50),2,1] Jim.East.XYZCorp (User)
   SYNC:[0100029B][(19:50:43),2,1] Amy.East.XYZCorp (User)
   SYNC:[010002A4][(19:49:49),2,1] Kenny.East.XYZCorp (User)
   SYNC:[010002A8][(19:58:46),2,1] WINNT.Scripts.East.XYZCorp
       ↪(Profile)
   SYNC:[100002E1][(02:36:26),1,1] WIN98.Scripts.East.XYZCorp
       ↪(Profile)
  SYNC: Objects: 7, total changes: 25, sent to server
       <CN=RIGEL>
 SYNC: update to server <CN=RIGEL> successfully completed
 Merged transitive vector for [010000C3]<RIGEL.West.XYZCorp>
 succeeded
SYNC: SkulkPartition for <[Root]> succeeded
SYNC: End sync of partition <[Root]> All processed = YES.
```

This time the servers are talking to each other, and there are a few updates that need to be sent from one server to the other.

Unlike many other DS implementations, NDS/eDirectory sends only the changed attribute values (the *deltas*) of a given object, even if they are part of a multivalued attribute.   ■ **NOTE**

The frequency at which the Sync process runs depends on the object attribute being changed. Each attribute has a flag called that determines whether it is "high convergence." This flag has one of two possible values:

▶ **Sync Immediate (DS_SYNC_IMMEDIATE_ATTR)**—With this flag, the attribute value is scheduled for immediate synchronization (with a 10-second holding time after the first event is detected so that if there are subsequent events within this time window, they can be processed at the same time). This is required on some attributes, such as the **Password Required** attribute of a **User** object, to either maintain proper data integrity or security.

▶ **Sync Never (DS_SCHEDULE_SYNC_NEVER)**—The name of this flag is a little misleading. This flag indicates that a change to the attribute's value does not trigger synchronization (immediately). The attribute can wait to propagate the change until the next regularly scheduled synchronization cycle (30 minutes for NetWare 4 servers and 60 minutes for NetWare 5 servers and higher, including eDirectory servers) or some other event triggers synchronization.

NOTE

If the **Sync Immediate** flag is not specified for an attribute, DS automatically assumes the attribute to be **Sync Never**.

A **Per Replica (DS_PER_REPLICA)** flag also exists and can be defined for attributes. When an attribute is defined as **Per Replica**, the information of the attribute is not synchronized with other servers in the replica ring. Most of the DirXML-related attributes are defined with this flag.

TIP

Appendix C, "eDirectory Classes, Objects, and Attributes," lists all the attributes defined for eDirectory 8.7.3, along with synchronization flag information.

Nontransitive Synchronization in NetWare 4

In NetWare 4.x any server that holds a replica of an NDS partition has to communicate with all the other servers that hold a replica of that partition. Figure 6.3 shows the type of communication that has to take place in order for synchronization to be completely successful on all NetWare 4.x servers.

As you can guess, the number of synchronization processes (or *vectors*, as they are sometimes called) that must complete grows exponentially as replicas are added. The amount of traffic generated can be tremendous. In fact, the number of communications vectors is $n \times (n-1)$, where n represents the number of replicas in the replica ring. Thus, at 27 replicas, a total of 27 × 26, or 702, communications vectors exist.

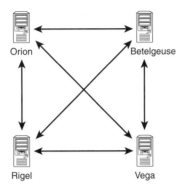

Orion
Betelgeuse
Rigel
Vega

FIGURE 6.3
Nontransitive replica synchronization between four NetWare 4.x servers.

Transitive Synchronization in NetWare 5 and Higher

In NetWare 5 Novell introduced the idea of transitive synchronization. Transitive synchronization is a synchronization methodology wherein a server doesn't have to contact every other server in the replica list. It can enable other servers to ensure that synchronization is complete, as demonstrated in Figure 6.4.

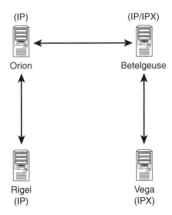

(IP)
(IP/IPX)
Orion
Betelgeuse
Rigel
(IP)
Vega
(IPX)

FIGURE 6.4
Transitive replica synchronization between four NetWare 5 and higher servers.

The reduction in traffic in a transitive synchronization environment is very significant, and the completion of the entire synchronization cycle is reduced. Ideally, this would create a scenario in which the vector count would simply equal $n-1$, so with 27 replicas, only 26 communications vectors would be needed. Table 6.3 shows the difference in vectors between transitive and nontransitive synchronization.

TABLE 6.3   **The Number of Communications Vectors with Transitive and Nontransitive Synchronization**

NUMBER OF SERVERS IN REPLICA RING	NUMBER OF NONTRANSITIVE VECTORS	NUMBER OF TRANSITIVE VECTORS
2	2	1
3	6	2
4	12	3
5	20	4
6	30	5
7	42	6
8	56	7
9	72	8
10	90	9

This discussion represents the ideal number of synchronization vectors when using transitive synchronization. As you can see in Table 6.3, the number of communications vectors with transitive synchronization is significantly smaller than the number with nontransitive synchronization, although it is possible that the number of vectors could increase, depending on the network design and availability of services. The actual number of synchronization vectors with transitive synchronization could be larger but will always be smaller than without transitive synchronization.

NOTE   In a way, you can consider transitive synchronization a feature of NDS 7 and higher. Therefore, you do not need to have NetWare servers to take advantage of it because the non-NetWare DS servers will be running eDirectory, which supports transitive synchronization.

Transitive synchronization also addresses mixed transport protocols used on different DS servers. Consider the example presented in Figure 6.4. Without transitive synchronization support, the servers Rigel and Orion will not be able to synchronize with the server Vega because they do not share a common transport protocol. With transitive synchronization, however, there is no problem because the server Betelgeuse acts as a gateway or a mediator.

One side effect of replica rings with mixed transport protocols is that the servers Rigel and Orion in this example will attempt to talk directly to Vega (and vice versa). They will report "Unable to communicate with server *x* " errors. However, this does not indicate a problem with your DS. It's just that DS has detected a situation that is really not a problem.

To understand how transitive synchronization works, you must first be familiar with transitive vectors. NDS uses a time vector—also called a *time array*—to keep track of changes to a given partition. This time vector holds timestamps for all the replicas in the replica ring from a given server's perspective. (For instance, if there are two replicas for this partition, two timestamps will be found in the time vector, as illustrated in Figure 6.5.) Each server holds a copy of its own time vector as well as copies of time vectors from the other servers in the ring. This group of time vectors is collectively known as the *transitive vector*. The `Transitive Vector` attribute is multivalued and associated with the partition root object, so NDS/eDirectory can manage the synchronization process and determine what needs to be sent to other replicas. Each replica has its own transitive vector; there is only one transitive vector for each replica, and it is synchronized between all servers within the replica ring.

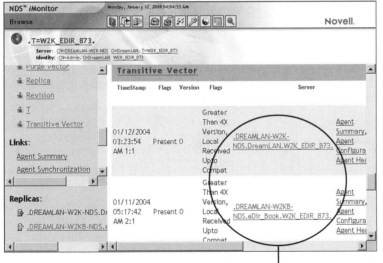

One time vector per server in the replica ring

FIGURE 6.5
NDS iMonitor showing the time vector values of a transitive vector.

To see the transitive vector values in NDS iMonitor, as shown in Figure 6.5, from Agent Summary, you click the Partition Replica link and then click the Partition link, followed by Attributes. Finally, you click the Transitive Vector link.

> **NOTE** In NDS 6 and earlier, the single-valued attribute Synchronized Up To is used to determine when the latest changes were made. The value of this attribute is unique for each replica and is *not* synchronized to the other servers in the replica ring.

When you synchronize the transitive vector values, all the replicas can synchronize without needing to have every replica communicate with every other replica. Each time the replica synchronization process begins its scheduled run, it first checks the entries in the transitive vector to determine which other servers hold replicas that need to be synchronized. The check compares the timestamps of the time vectors of the source server that received the update with those of the destination server. If a timestamp is greater for the source server, replica updates are transferred. The source server updates its own time vector within the transitive vector and sends the updated transitive vector to the target server. At the end of the replica update process, the target server updates its own time vector within the transitive vector and sends that updated transitive vector back to the source server. Now the two servers know they are both up-to-date, and the target server will not try to sync with the source server with the same update.

> **NOTE** Under the transitive synchronization scenario, the source server does not request the target server's timestamps because they are already present in the transitive vector that is stored on the source server.

Multithreaded Synchronization

One of the most significant performance-enhancement features in eDirectory is the introduction of multithreaded replica synchronization, starting with eDirectory 8.6. In previous versions of eDirectory and NDS, all inbound and outbound synchronization was performed using a single thread. Partitions were synchronized in a serial manner—changes in one partition could not be synchronized until the previous partition had been completely processed. However, this is not very efficient for trees where there may be many partitions.

Starting with eDirectory 8.6, outbound synchronization is now multithreaded. Partitions stored on one server can be synchronized out in a parallel manner, allowing replicas to be synchronized in a much more efficient manner.

Inbound synchronization is still single threaded. An eDirectory server can receive inbound synchronization for only one partition at a time.

Multithreaded synchronization takes place using one of two synchronization methods (see Figure 6.6):

▶ **By partition**—This method causes eDirectory to send out one partition to multiple recipient servers at a time.

▶ **By server**—This method causes eDirectory to send out multiple partitions to multiple unique servers at one time.

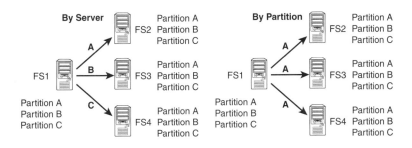

FIGURE 6.6
Multithreaded synchronization methods.

When eDirectory starts up, it analyzes all partitions and corresponding replica rings stored on the server. This analysis procedure results in a list of all servers involved in replica synchronization and all partitions stored on those servers. If the number of partitions stored on the local server is equal to or greater than the number of unique servers minus one (the local server), eDirectory will automatically synchronize using the by-partition method. Otherwise, eDirectory uses the by-server method. By default, the synchronization method is dynamically adjusted (that is, selected by eDirectory upon startup). But you can also manually select a preferred method via NDS iMonitor (see Figure 6.7).

The number of threads used for synchronization determines how multi-threaded synchronization behaves. For example, if only one thread is configured for synchronization, multithreaded synchronization is effectively disabled. By default, eDirectory allows a maximum of eight threads for multithreaded synchronization.

eDirectory automatically determines the number of threads to use in multi-threaded synchronization by determining whether the number of partitions is less than or equal to two times the number of unique servers in those partitions' replica rings. If the number of partitions is less than or equal to two times the number of unique servers in those partitions' replica rings, eDirectory will set its maximum thread usage to the number of partitions stored on the local server. Otherwise, the number of threads is set to half the number of unique servers in shared replica rings. This allocatable thread count is used only if it does not exceed the configured maximum thread count. If this count is exceeded, the number of allocatable threads will be set to the configured maximum thread count.

FIGURE 6.7
Use the Agent Synchronization link under Agent Configuration in NDS iMonitor to view and manage multithreaded synchronization.

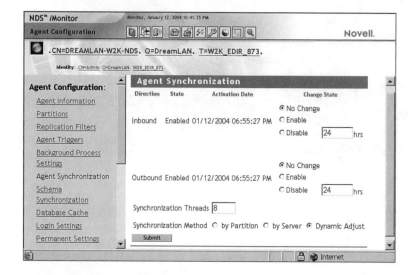

Incremental Replication

Perhaps the most problematic issue you're likely to encounter with database synchronization is designing correct methods for protecting against data loss or preventing unnecessary duplication of synchronization work due to communication failures. Prior to eDirectory 8.6, any type of communication failure during the replica synchronization process would cause the entire process to be restarted when communication was reestablished. With large partitions containing millions of objects, this could prove to be a very costly restart, especially if slow WAN links are involved.

eDirectory 8.6 addressed this problem by implementing incremental replication. *Incremental replication* allows for the replica synchronization process to be interrupted and later resume from the point of failure. To understand the how the incremental replication process works, you need to first understand the following related key terms and concepts:

▶ **Window vector**—The *window vector*, stored in the `SyncWindowVector` attribute (of type `SYNC_OCTET_STRING`) on the partition root object of the *receiving* server, is the point in time to which the source replica is attempting to move the destination replica. For example, if the latest modification timestamp in the source replica is 2/14/2004 2:35 p.m. and the destination replica has a timestamp of 2/14/2004 1:10 p.m., the window vector in use for the synchronization process would be 2/14/2004 2:35 p.m.

Generally speaking, the window vector is equal to the source replica's transitive vector, unless the destination replica is more than 30 days behind the source replica. In that situation, the window vector is divided into 30-day intervals.

▶ **Window pane**—A *window pane* is a discrete unit of work. In the case of replica synchronization, a window pane represents a complete synchronization cycle. This would be the difference between the current transitive vector of the destination server and the transitive vector of the source server. In other words, the window vector represents the final point in the synchronization cycle, and the window pane represents the entire amount of work—the number of objects and attributes values that need to be sent—necessary to meet that window vector.

▶ **Distributed consistent ordering of objects**—To allow incremental replication, the object synchronization process must be able to stop and then pick up again at the point where it was stopped. For fault tolerance and performance, the synchronization process must also be able to be resumed by any other server in the replica ring. This is possible only if all servers in the replica ring are synchronizing objects in the same order as every other server. Because objects can be added to any replica at any time, all servers in the replica ring must use a consistent index of objects, based on some unique value for all objects, within a partition. eDirectory uses the object creation timestamp because all creation timestamps are unique.

▶ **Synchronization point**—The *synchronization point* is a collection of information that can be used to determine how far the synchronization process has progressed. This collection of information consists of the following types of data:

  ▶ **An object producer**—The *object producer* is one of several sources or background processes that evaluate objects as candidates for the synchronization process. Examples of these producers are the Partition Send All, Change Cache, and Obituary processes.

> ▶ **An ordering of objects**—The ordering of objects that have been produced by the object producer is based on the creation time-stamps of the objects being produced.

> ▶ **A key**—The *key* is the value used to determine the current synchronization location within the ordering of objects. This key is typically the creation timestamp of the objects being synchronized.

The synchronization point is stored as the `SyncPanePoint` attribute (of type `SYN_OCTET_STRING`) on the partition root object of the *receiving* server.

REAL WORLD

Object Producers

Object producers are DS internal processes that are responsible for providing (that is, *producing*) entries based on different criteria. The following are the producers for the synchronization process and a brief description of the purpose of each:

▶ **ChangeCache**—The `ChangeCache` producer is responsible for synchronizing all entries that exist in the local server's change cache for the current partition. (Entries are added to the change cache when they are modified in any way on the local server.)

▶ **EntrySendAll**—The `EntrySendAll` producer is used when a Send All for a replica has been performed or a Send All has been performed on an individual entry.

▶ **Obituary**—The `Obituary` producer is responsible for synchronizing all entries in an obituary state.

▶ **PartitionBoundary**—The `PartitionBoundary` producer is responsible for sending information about the current partition's boundaries.

▶ **PartitionIndex**—The `PartitionIndex` producer is used to walk through any partition on the server and is used by background processes such as the Janitor, Backlinker, and other processes.

▶ **PartitionIndexSync**—The `PartitionIndexSync` producer is used to walk through the partition being synchronized. It also provides keys used in the synchronization process to establish synchronization points.

▶ **PartitionRoot**—The partition root object is always synchronized first during all partition synchronization processes. The `PartitionRoot` producer is responsible for sending this object at the beginning of every synchronization cycle.

Now that you are familiar with the elements of incremental replication, let's discuss the incremental replication process. The following is an overview of the incremental replication portion of the replica synchronization process:

1. **The Replica Synchronization process begins**. The transitive vector has been checked, and a replica synchronization process has been started.

2. **The replication process checks for the existence of the `SyncPanePoint` attribute on the target server**. If the `SyncPanePoint` attribute is found, it indicates that the receiving server was in the middle of a replica synchronization process and was interrupted. When a `SyncPanePoint` attribute is located, the source server reads in the value of the `SyncPanePoint` attribute and determines the window vector, object producer, and key for the interrupted synchronization. Using that information, the source server resumes the synchronization process that was interrupted.

   If no `SyncPanePoint` attribute is located, the source server calculates and establishes a new window vector for the synchronization process.

If the window vector of the interrupted synchronization is newer than the transitive vector of the source server, the source server reestablishes a window vector equal to the source server's local transitive vector.

NOTE

3. **The replication process sends updates from the source server to the target server**. Updates are sent as data packets across the wire. An individual packet can contain one or more object changes that need to be synchronized. To minimize data loss in the event of communication failure, each packet begins with a new `SyncPanePoint` attribute. The `SyncPanePoint` data contains the key, which indicates the present position in the synchronization process. This key provides a pointer for the last packet sent from the source server.

4. **The receiving server updates its `SyncPanePoint` attribute for each data packet received**. In the event that communication is interrupted, all data received before the last `SyncPanePoint` attribute will be preserved. At most, two data packets' worth of information would be lost.

5. **The receiving server removes the `SyncPanePoint` attribute at the end of a successful sync**. When the replica update process is completed, the `SyncPanePoint` attribute is removed from the receiving server's partition root object. This allows subsequent synchronization cycles to establish new window vectors.

As mentioned previously, incremental replication is available only in eDirectory 8.6 and higher. Safeguards are in place to prevent loss of data where DS servers running pre-eDirectory 8.6 are unable to synchronize replicas with `SyncPanePoint` attributes. When these servers with the older DS attempt to synchronize with an eDirectory 8.6 or higher server, they encounter error -698 (`ERR_REPLICA_IN_SKULK`), indicating that the target server is currently in the middle of a replica synchronization process. The purpose of the -698 error is to allow time for another eDirectory 8.6 or higher server to synchronize with the server reporting the -698 error. When another eDirectory server that is capable of incremental replication encounters the `SyncPanePoint` attribute, the synchronization process will be able to pick up at the point of failure (as indicated by the window vector), and no data will be lost.

TIP

The *infrequent* occurrence of the -698 error is an example of when an error is not indicative of a real error. However, if its frequency is high, it can indicate a communication issue lurking in the background.

To ensure that an eDirectory server capable of incremental replication is not a requirement for future synchronization (because of the presence of the `SyncPanePoint` attribute after an aborted sync), the `SyncPanePoint` attribute is automatically purged after a two-hour timeout. After the timeout period has passed, the `SyncPanePoint` attribute is purged, and any data received during the incomplete synchronization cycle is lost. At that point, *any* DS server can begin a new replica synchronization cycle with this server because there is no more `SyncPanePoint` attribute present to cause a -698 error.

NOTE

Although multithreading and incremental replication make the eDirectory synchronization process much more efficient, they also make LAN trace analysis and reading of DSTrace results more challenging.

Auxiliary Class Object Handling

NDS versions prior to NDS 8 do not understand or know how to handle auxiliary classes. Consequently, NDS 8 and higher servers only send auxiliary class and auxiliary attribute information to servers running NDS 8 and above. When synchronizing to servers running previous versions, eDirectory must send the auxiliary class information in a manner that is compatible with the previous releases. Because an auxiliary class adds attributes to an object that previous versions of NDS consider illegal, NDS 8 and eDirectory servers make the following modifications to the objects with auxiliary classes before they are sent to servers with previous versions of NDS:

- ▶ The `AuxClass Object Class Backup` attribute (of type `SYNC_CLASS_NAME`) is added to the object, and all the information from the object's `Object Class` attribute is stored in the attribute. This attribute is stored only on the pre-NDS 8 servers.

- ▶ The object's class is changed to `Unknown`.

- ▶ The `auxClassCompatibility` attribute (of type `SYNC_CLASS_NAME`) is added to the object on all replicas and is used to maintain timestamps for the object.

Table 6.4 demonstrates how eDirectory modifies an object's `Object Class`, `AuxClass Object Class Backup`, and `auxClassCompatibility` attributes as it synchronizes to an NDS 7 or older server when an auxiliary class is present for the object.

TABLE 6.4

Auxiliary Class and Attribute Information, as Seen on Servers Running Different DS Versions

EDIRECTORY SERVER	NDS 7.X OR OLDER SERVER	NDS 8 SERVER
Object Class attribute value: User, Organizational Person, Person, ndsLoginProperties, Top	Object Class attribute value: Unknown, Top	Object Class attribute value: User, Organizational Person, Person, ndsLoginProperties, Top
—	AuxClass Object Class Backup attribute value: User, Organizational Person, Person, ndsLoginProperties, Top	—
auxClass Compatibility attribute value: Unknown, Top	auxClass Compatibility attribute value: Unknown, Top	auxClass Compatibility attribute value: Unknown, Top

When an NDS 8/eDirectory server receives an `Unknown` object, it checks whether the object has an `auxClassCompatibility` attribute. If there is such an attribute, NDS 8/eDirectory replaces the `Unknown` class with information from the `AuxClass Object Class Backup` attribute and restores the object to normal. The `auxClassCompatibility` attribute is maintained on all servers in the replica ring as long as at least one NDS 7.x or older server is in the ring. When all NDS 7.x and older servers are removed from the replica ring, the attribute is removed from the object. This information is often referred to as the "Aux Class Lie."

> **NOTE**   Because many existing applications that read NDS/eDirectory class definitions do not necessarily understand auxiliary classes, Novell modified the read class definition APIs to provide backward compatibility. All the new routines do is intercept the client responses and substitute the class information located in the `Object Class` attribute with the information located in the `AuxClass Object Class Backup` attribute. As a result, if you look at the object in DSBrowse or NDS iMonitor, the object will still show up with an `Unknown` class, but NetWare Administrator and ConsoleOne will now show up as known objects. You should be able to administer such objects with NetWare Administrator or ConsoleOne as if they were normal objects. Only applications that have been updated to be compatible with NDS 8 and higher can display auxiliary class definitions with an auxiliary object class flag.

> **NOTE**   You need `DS.NLM` 6.19/7.62 and higher to take advantage of the updated APIs.

The Schema Synchronization Process

You can modify the NDS schema by adding or deleting attribute definitions and object class definitions. Such changes need to be replicated among all the servers within the same tree that contain replicas. This synchronization is done through the Schema Synchronization process. This process is started within 10 seconds following completion of the schema modification operations; the 10-second delay enables several modifications to be synchronized at the same time.

> **NOTE**   Although the Schema Sync process targets only servers hosting replicas, servers without replicas still receive schema information through the Janitor process (which is discussed later in this chapter).

Keep in mind that base schema definitions cannot be modified. When a new attribute is added to a base class object definition, it cannot be removed.

The updates to the schema are propagated from one server to another; this is similar to the Replica Synchronization process. However, the Schema Synchronization process does *not* use a replica ring to determine which servers to send the schema updates to. Schema updates are sent to servers that contain either replicas of a given partition or Child partitions of the given partition.

Because schema modifications must occur on the server that is hosting the Master replica of **[Root]**, the modifications flow from the **[Root]** partition down to the extreme branches of the tree.

The actual Schema Synchronization process is made up of several different processes:

- ▶ **Schema process**—This process, which runs every four hours by default, is the main process. It schedules the execution of the following subprocesses (in the order listed). (DSTrace displays the message "Begin schema sync…" at the start of the sync and either an "All Processed = Yes" or an "All Processed = No" message at the end. If processing is successful, the next Schema process is scheduled to run again after **HeartBeatSchemaInterval**, which is four hours by default; otherwise, the next Schema process is scheduled to run after **SchemaUpdateInterval** [60 seconds] plus 1 second.)

- ▶ **Skulk Schema process**—This process determines which servers the local server needs to synchronize to (by maintaining a server-centric schema sync list in server memory) and in what order to synchronize to them. It also ensures that the local server is in a state to successfully synchronize the schema. If the process detects that a schema epoch is in progress, DSTrace reports a -654 error ("partition busy"). A -657 error ("schema sync in progress") will be reported if a schema reset is detected.

- ▶ **Send Schema Updates process**—This process is the workhorse in the Schema Synchronization process. It is responsible for sending the schema changes—all deleted classes and deleted attributes—as well as the present attributes and present classes. eDirectory makes several passes through this process to ensure that all these changes are synchronized correctly. (During this phase, DSTrace reports "Sending *<present or deleted> <Attributes or classes>*".)

▶ **Schema Purger process**—This process is responsible for cleaning up any entry or value records that are no longer needed. (During the cleanup, DSTrace reports "Purger purged *<class or attribute>*; entries purged *<number of values>*."

▶ **DSA Start Update Schema process**—This process is the process that the receiving server goes through while another server is sending schema to it. When a server receives a request to send schema, it goes through the next two processes. (DSTrace reports "* Start inbound sync from server *<senderID>* version *<protocol number>*, epoch *<epoch in seconds>*:*<epoch replica number>*.")

TIP

Although the Schema Synchronization process never sends schema to itself, a check is made to ensure that the sender is never the receiver. In the unlikely event that the sender is the receiver, DSTrace displays "Warning - Rejecting DSAStartUpdateSchema Client *<serverID>*" and reports the error –699 ("fatal").

▶ **DSA Update Schema process**—This process details what the receiving server does with each update it receives. This process is looped through over and over, as long as the sending server continues to send updates. (During this phase, DSTrace reports "DSAUpdateSchema: Processing inbound packet one at a time because of…" or "DSAUpdateSchema: Packet with *<number of updates>* updates," depending on the information found inside the data packets.)

▶ **DSA End Update Schema process**—This process signals the end of the update. The receiving server goes through the DSA End Update Schema process when it receives a `DSAEndUpdateSchema` request from the sending server. (Upon completion of the cycle, DSTrace reports "* End inbound sync from server *<serverID>*, Version *<version>*, Epoch *<epoch in seconds>*:*<epoch replica number>*.")

The detailed operation of the Schema Synchronization process is rather involved. The following simple example serves to illustrate how the Schema Synchronization process works from a high-level point of view. Figure 6.8 depicts a small tree with five servers and three partitions.

A schema change is made to Betelgeuse because it holds the Master replica of the [Root] partition. After this server has been updated, this server sends the schema changes out to the other servers that hold copies of [Root]: Rigel and Andromeda. After all servers in the [Root] partition have received the updates, DS sends the updates to the other servers in the tree. It does this by looking at the servers that hold copies of [Root] and reading the replica list information to find out what other replicas are out there; then it builds a schema sync list. Each server's schema sync list may be different, depending on what replicas it hosts.

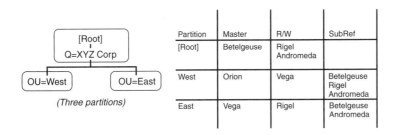

FIGURE 6.8
A Schema Synchronization process example.

Partition	Master	R/W	SubRef
[Root]	Betelgeuse	Rigel Andromeda	
West	Orion	Vega	Betelgeuse Rigel Andromeda
East	Vega	Rigel	Betelgeuse Andromeda

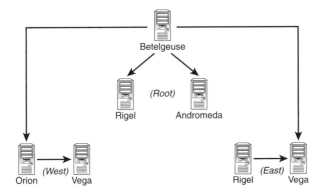

You can look up a server's schema sync list by using either DSTrace or NDS iMonitor. It is easiest to use NDS iMonitor, as shown in Figure 6.9; it is found under Service List under the Schema link.

To use DSTrace, you first enable the DSTrace filter with the **+SCHEMA** flag on NetWare or the **+SCMA** flag on Unix, and then you use the **set dstrace=*ssl** DSTrace option. The output looks similar to this:

```
SchemaSyncList:
--->>> [000080a3] <.DREAMLAN-W2KB-NDS.eDir_Book.W2K_EDIR_873.>
        Flags: 0001  Lists: 0005  Expiration: 2004/01/12
              ➥6:11:21
        List(s): [0005] Replica   Service
Inbound schema synchronization lock status: Released
resetSuccessfulSync = 0 in GetServersInSchemaSyncList
```

On Windows, you need to enable DSTrace's Schema Details from the DSTrace Edit menu and then trigger the Schema Sync process from the Trace tab of the DSA window.

Server Schema Sync List

FIGURE 6.9
A server's
schema sync list.

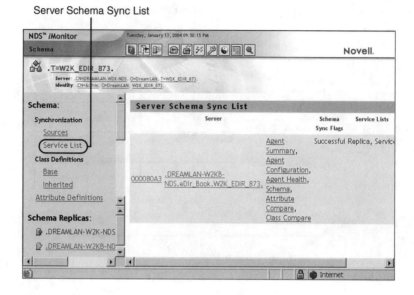

By looking at the replica list on Rigel, for example, DS can determine that there are two child partitions—OU=West.O=XYZCorp and OU=East.O=XYZCorp. The replica list on Rigel also indicates what other servers are in the tree. DS determines that the servers Vega and Orion also need to be updated. During this determination, note that Vega and Rigel are listed twice because of the replication scheme in this tree; even though Rigel receives an update in the first round of schema synchronization, after Vega receives the updates to the schema, Rigel is again checked to see whether its schema is current. If the schema is not current, it is updated.

TIP

Schema updates are normally not something to be concerned about unless the change is being made because of an update in the DS module. In cases where Novell has introduced a schema change in a new version of the DS module, you should first update the module on the server that holds the Master replica of [Root]—because that is where schema modification takes place—and then update the rest of your servers after the schema update has completed.

As discussed earlier in this chapter, schema changes are synchronized from the root of the DS tree down to its branches. Because a tree can have NDS 8 servers near the root, with NetWare 6 or 4.2 servers in the middle, and an eDirectory 8.7 server below them, eDirectory must be able to send schema information about auxiliary classes in a manner that is compatible with lega-cy versions of NDS. It must do so with sufficient clues that an eDirectory server can re-create an auxiliary class from the information. To accomplish this, when synchronizing schema with a server running NDS 7 or older, eDirectory makes the following changes to the three auxiliary class characteristics to make them compatible with previous versions of NDS:

- ▶ **Auxiliary class flag**—NDS 8 introduced this object class flag to indicate which classes are auxiliary classes. Because pre-NDS 8 versions do not recognize this flag, eDirectory servers send auxiliary class definitions as standard class definitions with one additional attribute, the `Auxiliary Class Flag` attribute, which contains the auxiliary class flag information. When an eDirectory server receives a class definition with this attribute, it removes the attribute from the class definition and re-creates an auxiliary class from the class definition.

- ▶ **Superclasses**—Prior to NDS 8, NDS required every class to have a superclass. To make auxiliary classes compatible with these rules, NDS 8 and higher servers send `Top` as the superclass of any auxiliary class that has declared no superclass. When an eDirectory server receives a class definition with the `Auxiliary Class Flag` attribute and with `Top` as its superclass, the server removes `Top` as its superclass.

- ▶ **`Object Class` Attribute**—In versions of NDS prior to NDS 8, the `Object Class` attribute is a Read-Only attribute. When NDS 8 or higher servers send the definition of this attribute to servers with previous versions of NDS, the source servers include the Read-Only constraint. When eDirectory servers receive the definition for this attribute from a server with previous versions of NDS, the Read-Only constraint is removed from the definition.

The Janitor Process

The NDS Janitor process is responsible for a number of different tasks, including the following:

- ▶ Scheduling the Flat Cleaner process.

- ▶ Issuing console messages when synthetic time is issued (on NetWare servers only).

- ▶ Optimizing the local DS database.

- ▶ Checking whether the partition root object has been renamed.

- ▶ Updating and verifying the `Inherited ACL` attributes of partition root objects.

- ▶ Updating the `Status` attribute in the DS database for the local server.

▶ Ensuring that the local server is registered with another server to receive schema updates if there is no local replica.

▶ Validating the partition nearest [Root] on the server and the replica depth of that partition.

The Janitor process has responsibility for some fairly critical tasks. By default, the Janitor process runs every two minutes, although it doesn't perform every task in its list each time it runs. (For example, it schedules the Flat Cleaner process only once every 60 minutes.)

DS uses synthetic time to manage situations where the current timestamp on an object is later than the current time. The Janitor process checks the timestamps on the objects in the server and when a new timestamp is needed for an object. If an object in the server's replicas has a timestamp greater than the current server time, the Janitor process notifies the operating system, and a message is generated on NetWare's system console:

```
1-02-2004   6:33:58 pm:    DS-8.99-12
Synthetic Time is being issued on partition "NW7TEST."
```

Timestamps and Synthetic Time

Chapter 2, "eDirectory Basics," discusses the importance of time synchronization in regard to event timestamping. The timestamp itself is not discussed in detail in Chapter 2. A timestamp consists of three fields: the time and date when the timestamp was issued (more specifically, the number of seconds since midnight January 1, 1970), the replica number, and an event counter. The event counter is incremented every time a timestamp is issued until one second has advanced or 65,535 (64KB minus 1) events have been issued. The following sample timestamp indicates that the server holding Replica 2 issued this timestamp on October 10, 2004, at 04:23:18, and it was for the 34th event within that second:

```
10/10/2004 04:23:18  2;34
```

DS uses two types of timestamps to keep track of changes in the database:

▶ **Creation timestamp**—This timestamp is issued when an object is created. A creation timestamp is used to identify an object; therefore, no two sibling objects (that is, objects in the same context) can have the same creation timestamp.

▶ **Modification timestamp**—This timestamp is issued whenever an attribute is added to, modified, or removed from an object. Every attribute has a modification timestamp that denotes the date and time the attribute was created or last modified (but not when the attribute was removed).

When a timestamp (either a creation or modification timestamp) is issued, the Next Timestamp field (also known as the Partition Timestamp field) in the partition record representing the partition in which this modified object resides is updated. The value placed in the Next Timestamp field is equivalent to the timestamp just issued, but the event counter is incremented by one. This allows DS to identify the minimum value for the next timestamp to be issued.

When a new timestamp is needed, the server obtains the next timestamp based on the partition timestamp of the partition in which the object is being modified. The server also obtains the current time from the operating system. The server then performs one of the following tasks:

▶ If the time obtained from the operating system is higher than the Next Timestamp value (that is, if it is later in time), the server resets the event counter back to 1 and issues a new timestamp, using the time provided by the operating system, its replica number, and the new event counter.

▶ If the time obtained from the operating system is equal to the Next Timestamp value, the server uses the value from the Next Timestamp field.

▶ If the time obtained from the operating system is less than the Next Timestamp value (that is, if the Next Timestamp value is in the future compared to the operating system's time), the server uses the Next Timestamp value and displays on the operating system console that it is using "synthetic time."

When synthetic time is used, the partition timestamp is frozen, and the only thing that changes is the event count portion of the timestamp. Because every change that occurs requires a unique timestamp, the event counter is incremented from 1 to 65,535 as the server issues timestamps. When the event counter reaches its maximum allowed value, the counter is reset to 1, the next second is used, and the process repeats until the partition timestamp catches up with the current system time.

Synthetic time being issued is *not* always a critical problem. If a server's time is set back from within a few hours to within a few days, it is not necessary to correct the problem. This situation is a case where waiting is a better solution than doing something. Using DSRepair to repair timestamps is a serious step to take in that the fix actually destroys replicas on all servers except the server with the Master replica. When all non-Master replicas are destroyed, the replicas are re-created. See Chapter 12, "eDirectory Management Tools," for information about resolving synthetic time errors.

Janitor Process Optimization

One of the Janitor process optimization steps is the rehashing of the database information to enable the server to perform lookups more quickly.

If the Janitor process detects that the name of the partition root object has changed, it notifies all servers holding external references of this object of the new name.

Updating the `Inherited ACL` attribute values starts with the first partition in the partition database. After the Janitor process has located the partition, it validates that the parent object is not an external reference and looks at the ACL to determine whether any of the attribute values have been modified. If they have, it validates whether the attribute is inheritable, and if it is, it recalculates the `Inherited ACL` attribute values. The Janitor process performs this process for all the partitions on the server.

REAL WORLD

Inherited ACL **Explained**

`Inherited ACL` is an attribute that is assigned to and found only on a partition root object. It is used to identify effective rights that are inherited by trustees on the partition root object and that were assigned at a container higher up in the tree.

The `Inherited ACL` attribute provides a way for NDS to determine each object's effective rights, without having to walk past that object's partition boundary (that is, upward in the tree).

The NDS Janitor process calculates the `Inherited ACL` attribute by starting at the partition root object of a partition (if there are multiple partitions, beginning with the one closest to [Root]) and performing the following tasks:

1. The Janitor process searches each of the subordinate containers for rights assignments.

2. The Janitor process replaces the rights assignment found on a subordinate container with the one found on a superior container object whenever it encounters a duplicate privilege assignment for a trustee.

3. The Janitor process searches for and applies any inherited rights filter (IRF) found on a subordinate container object to all trustee rights assignments inherited by that subordinate container.

After the NDS Janitor process has reached the lower boundary of the partition, the process adds the `Inherited ACL` values gathered up to that point to the child partition's partition root object; the child partitions could be Master, Read/Write, Read-Only, or SubRef partitions. The process then repeats itself, proceeding through the same steps with each child partition until all partitions on the server have been processed and no additional partitions exist.

The `Inherited ACL` attributes are synchronized to the other servers in each partition's replica ring. In the process, the servers that hold child partitions—but not the parent partition—are able to calculate the proper rights for objects without having to communicate with other servers.

Updating the `Status` attribute involves validating that the DS attribute `Status` of the `NCP Server` object is set to `Up`. Because the server that performs the validation is up and running, this server always checks for an `Up` value. If it is set to `Down`, the Janitor process updates the attribute. Figure 6.10 shows where in NDS iMonitor you can see the result of this operation. To reach this screen, you select Agent Summary, Known Servers; click the server of interest; and select Status.

Determined by the Janitor process

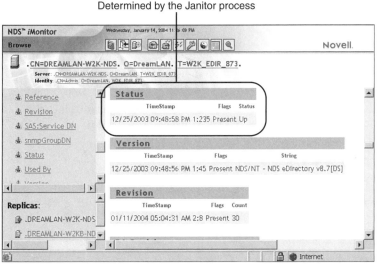

FIGURE 6.10
A server status value shown in NDS iMonitor.

When an `NCP Server` object's `Status` attribute is set to `Down`, the synchronization processes does not attempt to communicate with that server. Sometimes when a server is brought back online, its `Status` attribute value of `Up` might not be noticed by the other servers in the replica ring right way. You can manually force the status to `Up` by using NDS iMonitor as shown in Figure 6.11 by clicking the Agent Configuration link and then selecting the Agent Triggers link.

FIGURE 6.11
Manually forcing
server status
to **Up**.

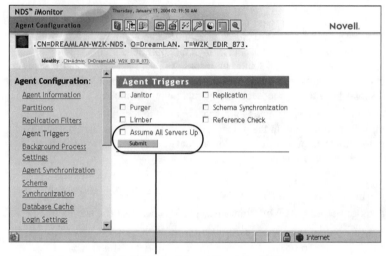

Check the option and click Submit to set the status to Up

The Janitor process's role in ensuring that the server can receive schema updates if it holds no replicas is particularly important. Even if a server has no local replicas, it still receives information for external references (such as those used to grant rights in the file system). In order to handle this properly, the server needs to know about all the different class definitions in case an extended class object receives rights to the file system. Equally important is the need for the schema partition to be maintained in case a new replica is added to the server later. If the server does not have current information about the schema and a replica is added to the server, many objects will change to **Unknown** objects in the local database, which can cause problems with object administration if those copies of the objects are read by the various management tools.

Finally, the Janitor process is also responsible for updating the **Revision** attribute of external references when the attribute value on the referenced object is changed.

The Flat Cleaner Process

The Flat Cleaner process is scheduled by the Janitor process and runs
192every 60 minutes by default. Responsibilities of the Flat Cleaner process include the following:

▶ Purging unused objects and attributes stored in the bindery partition or external reference partition

▶ Purging obituaries that have reached the **Purgeable** state

▸ Revalidating the **Status** and **Version** attributes of servers in all partitions of which the server has the Master replica

▸ Verifying that all objects in the user-defined partitions on the server have valid public keys and Certificate Authority (CA) public keys.

Because the Flat Cleaner process performs much of the purging of deleted records, it is also known as the *Replica Purger process* or simply the *Purger process*.

As described in Chapter 2, the bindery partition is the partition that is used to store information about the bindery user **Supervisor**. This partition also stores the SAP information that is received from IPX networks connected to the server. If a service is removed from the network, the SAP table in the server needs to be updated; this is one of the tasks the Flat Cleaner process is responsible for.

Obituaries that have reached the **Purgeable** stage need to be removed from the database, and the Flat Cleaner takes care of this. Essentially, the Flat Cleaner process removes any object or attribute flagged as **Non Present**.

Deletion of External Referenced Objects

REAL WORLD

When an entry is deleted, the Janitor and Flat Cleaner processes are the main processes responsible for cleaning up any associated external references. The Janitor process notifies the server holding an external reference of an object deleted from the tree. That server then marks the external referenced object as Non Present. **The Flat Cleaner process then deletes the database record for this now non-present object.**

The Flat Cleaner process is also responsible for validating the **Up** state of all servers that hold Master replicas. As discussed earlier in this chapter, the Janitor process is responsible for setting the server **Status** attribute to **Up**. The Flat Cleaner process is responsible for setting the **Status** attribute to **Down** as necessary if it finds that it cannot communicate with the server.

To understand the process better, let's consider a simple example where there are two servers, Orion and Rigel. Orion holds the Master copy of **[Root]**, the only partition in the tree. If Rigel is offline when Orion's Flat Cleaner process runs, Orion sets the **Status** attribute for Rigel to **Down**. When Rigel is brought back online, it runs its Janitor process, checks the **Status** attribute, and sees that it is set to **Down**. Because the server is no longer down, Rigel changes the **Status** attribute to **Up**.

The Flat Cleaner process also performs checks to validate all `Public Key` and `CA Public Key` attributes for objects the server holds. If it finds an invalid or missing key, it attempts to create new keys for the object. DS uses the `Public Key` and `CA Public Key` attribute values during the authentication process; if these keys are not valid on `User` objects, the user (or an administrator) has to change his or her password to fix the problem. If, however, these keys are corrupted on an `NCP Server` object, server-to-server authentication is disrupted, and synchronization does not occur.

The Backlink Process

The Backlink process, or *Backlinker process*, as it is called in some Novell documentation, checks on the validity of external references by verifying whether the original entry still exists and whether the reason for its existence is still valid. If the external reference is no longer needed or used after a given time period, the Backlink process removes it.

NOTE

The `BackLink` attribute consists of two fields: the DN of each remote server holding the external reference and the object ID of each of these servers (known as the remote ID). The Backlink process periodically verifies the DNs and remote IDs to ensure that they are valid.

The Backlink process also helps clean up external references. If the server holding the external reference no longer requires it or if the ExRef partition's life span has expired after not being used for a certain amount of time (the default is 192 hours [that is, 8 days]), the external reference of the object is deleted when the Backlink process has conformed *each* of the following conditions *seven* times:

▶ The object represented by the exref has no file system rights assignments to a volume on the server.

▶ The object represented by the exref is not listed on the connection table of the server.

▶ The object represented by the exref is not required to complete the fully qualified DNs (FQDNs)—that is, FDNs using typeful naming rules—of any subordinate objects.

▶ The object represented by the exref is not used as a local reference by an attribute stored in the attribute database.

The Backlink process is also responsible for ensuring that every external reference has a copy of the actual object's GUID attribute. This is necessary for file system rights for NSS volumes in NetWare 6 and higher.

By default, this process runs every 13 hours (that is, 780 minutes). You can modify the default value with via either DSTrace or NDS iMonitor (see Figure 6.12).

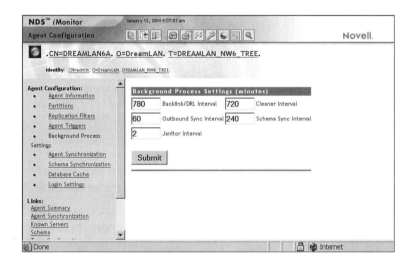

FIGURE 6.12
DSA background process settings in NDS iMonitor.

Because the Backlink process works with external references, it is also known as the External Reference Check process.

NetWare 5 introduced distributed reference links (DRLs) to replace backlinks. DRLs have the advantage of referencing a partition rather than a specific server. Consequently, the Backlink process has since been updated to work with both backlinks and DRLs.

The Limber Process

The last of the automated background processes is the Limber process. Primary responsibilities of the Limber process include the following:

▶ Verifying the network address for the server in all partitions of which the server holds a replica

▶ Validating that the relative DN (RDN) for the server is correct on the server that holds the Master partition of the replica in which the server exists

▶ Updating and maintaining the `Version` attribute for the server in the NDS database

▶ Locating the entry closest to `[Root]` by pinging each server in the replica ring list, in order, and selecting the responding server whose entry closest to `[Root]` is closest to the tree root

▶ Starting the Predicate Statistics collection (see Chapter 16, "Tuning eDirectory," for more information about Predicate Statistics)

▶ Verifying that the network address for the server is correct in the server's DS object.

TIP

These operations perform verifications on the replica list information and server network addresses. If a replica list is inconsistent, forcing the Limber process to run by using NDS iMonitor (refer to Figure 6.11) on the server that appears to have the problem may correct the problem.

If a server name or address changes, the Limber process is responsible for ensuring that the modifications are made to each replica pointer table in the partition ring. If the changes occur on the server that holds the Master replica, the Limber process changes its local address in the replica pointer table. If the changes occur on a server that holds a non-Master replica, the Limber process tells the Master replica about the changes. The Limber process can initiate the Backlink process, which does part of the checking (on exref objects) for the Limber process.

TIP

After changing the server name or its network address (such as the IP address) of a server in a replica ring, you should force the Limber process to run to ensure that all other servers in the replica ring detect the change.

CAUTION

Never change the server name *and* its network address at the same time. If you do so, eDirectory will lose track of which server this is. You should follow these steps:

1. **Change the server name.**
2. **Restart the server.**
3. **Force the Limber process to run (for example, by using NDS iMonitor).**
4. **Verify that the new object name has been synchronized throughout the ring and that the other servers in the replica ring see the new server name.**
5. **Change the network address.**
6. **Restart the server.**
7. **Force the Limber process to run (for example, by using NDS iMonitor).**

8. **Verify that the new network address has been synchronized throughout the ring and that the other servers in the replica ring see the new network address.**

9. **If other servers in the replica ring also need their names or network addresses changed, repeat steps 1–8 on each server, one at a time.**

As mentioned in Chapter 2, some of the information maintained by the Limber process is stored in part in the local System partition. The following tasks are considered to be secondary functions of the Limber process but are nonetheless important:

- ▶ Verifying that the directory tree name stored in the server's System partition is correct

- ▶ If the server does not hold a writable replica of the partition its own DS object is in, verifying that the external reference for this object is valid and checking that the `BackLink` attribute is valid on a server that holds a writable copy of the server object

- ▶ Checking to ensure that the server's public/private key credentials are correct.

The Limber process is one of the background processes that cannot have its schedule interval changed. If the Limber process's primary operations complete successfully, the process reschedules itself to run again in three hours. If the primary operations have not completed successfully, the Limber process reschedules itself to run again in five minutes.

Manual Object-Related Processes

Now that we have reviewed the major background processes, the following sections examine the processes you invoke by using the administrative utilities. The first set of such processes is object-related processes. The following sections examine the creation, renaming, deletion, and movement of objects in the NDS tree.

Creating Objects

Object creation is a fairly straightforward process. In ConsoleOne, for instance, you select the context where you want the new object to be placed and either click Insert or right-click the container you want to create the object in and then select Create from the menu. ConsoleOne asks you for the object class, and after you select that, you are presented with an appropriate dialog box to enter the mandatory attributes of the object.

From the server's perspective, object creation is also a simple process. The client API generates the DSA request verb DSV_ADD_ENTRY (decimal value 7) and submits it to the server. Listing 6.4 shows the DSA Add Entry request for User object PKuo.

> **NOTE**
>
> **You can find a list of DS verbs and their values, along with explanations of their functions, in Appendix B.**

Listing 6.4   A DSA Add Entry Request Shown on a Server Processing a Client Request

```
DSA: DSACommonRequest(7) conn:3 for client <JIM>
DSA REQUEST BUFFER:
02 00 00 00 00 00 00 00 FF FF FF FF E3 02 00 12
➡...............
0A 00 00 00 50 00 4B 00 75 00 6F 00 00 00 00 00
➡....P.K.u.o.....
02 00 00 00 10 00 00 00 53 00 75 00 72 00 6E 00
........S.u.r.n.
61 00 6D 00 65 00 00 00 01 00 00 00 08 00 00 00
➡a.m.e..........
4B 00 75 00 6F 00 00 00 1A 00 00 00 4F 00 62 00
➡K.u.o.......O.b.
6A 00 65 00 63 00 74 00 20 00 43 00 6C 00 61 00
➡j.e.c.t...C.l.a.
73 00 73 00 00 00 00 00 01 00 00 00 0A 00 00 00
➡s.s............
55 00 53 00 45 00 52 00 00 00                        U.S.E.R...
```

The request buffer is filled with the information entered in the Create Object dialog box. In the listings in this section, this information is seen on the server processing the client request by enabling the +DSA and +BUFFERS (+CBUF on Unix) flags in DSTrace.

> **NOTE**
>
> **Offset counting always starts with zero.**

The information shown in the request buffer is in Unicode format, which is a 2-byte character format. For English-language objects, Unicode fills the first byte with 00. In Listings 6.4 and 6.5, you can see the object name starting at offset 19, followed by the mandatory attribute Surname (offset 39) and its value (offset 63). Finally, you can see the `Object` class attribute and the value `USER`. This is the minimum information needed to create a `User` object and is passed directly to the DSA from ConsoleOne.

If the object already exists, the server's reply is shown right after the request, as shown in Listing 6.5.

Listing 6.5   A DSA Add Entry Request with Failure

```
DSA: DSACommonRequest(7) conn:3 for client <JIM>
DSA REQUEST BUFFER:
02 00 00 00 00 00 00 00 FF FF FF FF E3 02 00 12
➡..............
0A 00 00 00 50 00 4B 00 75 00 6F 00 00 00 00 00
➡....P.K.u.o.....
02 00 00 00 10 00 00 00 53 00 75 00 72 00 6E 00
➡........S.u.r.n.
61 00 6D 00 65 00 00 00 01 00 00 00 08 00 00 00
➡a.m.e...........
4B 00 75 00 6F 00 00 00 1A 00 00 00 4F 00 62 00
➡K.u.o.......O.b.
6A 00 65 00 63 00 74 00 20 00 43 00 6C 00 61 00
➡j.e.c.t...C.l.a.
73 00 73 00 00 00 00 00 01 00 00 00 0A 00 00 00
➡s.s............
55 00 53 00 45 00 52 00 00 00                    U.S.E.R...
DSA REPLY BUFFER:
DSA: DSACommonRequest(7): returning ERROR -606
```

The error code -606 is defined as `ERR_ENTRY_ALREADY_EXISTS`. This makes sense because in this example, the object does in fact already exist in the specified context.

Object creation can take place on any writable replica. When a create request is completed on the server that the workstation contacts, the object is queued up for the next synchronization cycle and sent out to the other servers in the replica ring. As discussed in the section "The Synchronization Process," this synchronization cycle is either transitive or nontransitive, depending on the version of NetWare and NDS/eDirectory running on the servers in the replica ring.

Renaming Objects

Renaming an object is a fairly simple process. The request is actually broken into two parts—a Resolve Name request (DSV_RESOLVE_NAME, decimal value 1), as shown in Listing 6.6, and the actual Rename operation, as shown in Listing 6.7. This example renames the object PKuo as JimH. This operation requires that the client be able to contact a server holding a writable copy of the object being renamed.

Listing 6.6   An Object Resolve Name Request Issued During an Object Renaming Operation

```
DSA: DSACommonRequest(1) conn:3 for client <JIM>
DSA REQUEST BUFFER:
00 00 00 00 24 20 00 00 00 00 00 00 30 00 00 00
➥............0...
50 00 4B 00 75 00 6F 00 2E 00 4F 00 55 00 3D 00
➥P.K.u.o...O.U...
45 00 61 00 73 00 74 00 2E 00 4F 00 3D 00 58 00
➥E.a.s.t...O...X.
59 00 5A 00 43 00 6F 00 72 00 70 00 00 00 00 00
➥Y.Z.C.o.r.p.....
02 00 00 00 00 00 00 00 08 00 00 00 02 00 00 00
➥................
00 00 00 00 08 00 00 00                              ........
DSA REPLY BUFFER:
01 00 00 00 BC 02 00 0E 01 00 00 00 00 00 00 00
➥................
0C 00 00 00 84 12 30 01 00 00 00 00 00 01 04 51
➥......0........Q
```

Listing 6.7   An Object Rename Request

```
DSA: DSACommonRequest(10) conn:3 for client <JIM>
DSA REQUEST BUFFER:
00 00 00 00 BC 02 00 0E 01 00 00 00 0A 00 00 00   ..............
4A 00 69 00 6D 00 48 00 00 00 6F 00               J.i.m.H...o.
DSA REPLY BUFFER:
```

The reply sent to the Resolve Name request returns the object ID of the object being renamed, starting at offset 4 in reverse-byte order, as shown in bold in Listing 6.6. In this example, the entry being renamed has an entry ID of 0E0002BC. The server responding also includes its network address in the reply buffer. In this example, the (IPX) address is shown starting at offset 20. Unlike the entry ID, the address value is *not* in reverse-byte order, and it includes the network, the node, and the socket address. In this example, the address is 84123001:000000000001:0451.

When the requested information is returned, the client sends the Rename request (`DSV_MODIFY_RDN`, decimal value 10) to the server that replied to the Read request. The request buffer for the Rename request does not include the old object name; rather, it uses the object's ID, retrieved from the Resolve Name request that occurred at the start of the rename operation. This object ID is again put at offset 4, in reverse-byte order. In Listing 6.7, this is 0E0002BC, shown in bold, the same object ID returned by the Resolve Name request. In a rename operation, the object ID in the Rename request always matches the ID read in the initial Resolve Name request. This is how the client knows which object is being renamed.

NOTE

When an object is renamed, only its RDN is changed; thus, the verb is `DSV_MODIFY_RDN`.

In a multiserver environment, the rename operation sets in motion a series of events to ensure that the rename operation is synchronized properly. The old object ID has an `OLD_RDN` obituary issued for it in order to start processing the purge of the old name from the DS database. At the same time, a `NEW_RDN` obituary is issued for the new object name.

If one of the servers in the replica ring is unavailable, you can see the obituaries that have been issued for the rename operation. By running DSRepair (with the `-A` command-line parameter), you can view the current obituaries and their states on the server by performing an external reference check. Listing 6.8 shows the information written to the `DSREPAIR.LOG` file about the two obituaries that have been created by renaming the object `PKuo` as `JimH`.

Listing 6.8   A DSRepair Log File, Showing Obituaries Created by a Rename Operation

```
/***************************************************************/
Directory Services Repair 10550.61, DS 10550.98
Log file for server ".VEGA.DreamLAN.W2K_EDIR_873." in tree
 "W2K_EDIR_873"
External Reference Check
Start:  01/16/2004 10:37:16 PM Local Time
```

continues

Listing 6.8   Continued

```
(1) Found obituary for: EID: 0e0002bc,
      DN: CN=JimH.OU=East.O=XYZCorp.T=W2K_EDIR_873
-Value CTS : 01/16/2004 10:36:42 PM  R = 0001  E = 0003
-Value MTS = 01/16/2004 10:36:42 PM  R = 0001  E = 0003,
 Type = 0005 NEW_RDN,
-Flags = 0000
-RDN: CN=JimH


(2) Found obituary for: EID: 0e0002bc,
      DN: CN=JimH.OU=East.O=XYZCorp.T=W2K_EDIR_873
-Value CTS : 01/16/2004 10:36:42 PM  R = 0001  E = 0004
-Value MTS = 01/16/2004 10:36:42 PM  R = 0001  E = 0004,
 Type = 0006 BACKLINK,
-Flags = 0000
-Backlink: Type = 00000005 NEW_RDN, RemoteID = ffffffff,
 ServerID = 000080a3, CN=RIGEL.O=eDir_Book.T=W2K_EDIR_873


Checked 0 external references
Found: 2 total obituaries in this dib,
       2 Unprocessed obits, 0 Purgeable obits,
       0 OK_To_Purge obits, 0 Notified obits


*** END ***
```

From the section "Obituaries," you know that a Backlink obituary was created because the server Rigel contains either a real copy or an exref of the
object. The obituaries that are issued do not prevent you from performing
other operations on the object. In fact, after an object is renamed, it is possible to create a new object by using the original object's name.

TIP

Because the OLD_RDN and NEW_RDN obituary types do not hold up other opera-
tions, these obituaries can hang around for a very long time and not be detected.
Periodically checking the state of obituaries by using DSRepair helps ensure that
Flat Cleaner process is properly advancing and purging the obituaries.

Deleting Objects

Deleting an object from the tree is similar to renaming an object in the tree.
As with the rename operation, the delete operation requires that the client
be able to communicate with any server that holds a writable copy of the
object.

First, a Resolve Name request is sent; it is similar to the one that appears before the rename operation in Listing 6.6. As with the rename object operation, the reply buffer includes both the object ID of the object being deleted and the network address of the server that responded to the request. When this information is returned, the client requests the actual deletion of the object by using DSA verb `DSV_REMOVE_ENTRY` (decimal value 8). This request is shown in Listing 6.9.

Listing 6.9   A DSA Remove Entry Request

```
DSA: DSACommonRequest(8) conn:3 for client <JIM>
DSA REQUEST BUFFER:
00 00 00 00 BA 02 00 10                          ........
DSA REPLY BUFFER:
```

You again see the object ID passed into the request starting at offset 4, in reverse-byte order. This request is for object ID 010002BA to be deleted. The object ID requested again corresponds to the object ID returned by the Resolve Name request at offset 4.

Object deletion creates an obituary of class `Dead`. Again, by using DSRepair with the `-A` switch and checking external references, you can see the obituaries created by deleting the object. Listing 6.10 shows the log file entries that result from this operation.

Listing 6.10   A DSRepair Log, Showing Obituaries Created by a Deletion

```
/*****************************************************************/
Directory Services Repair 10550.61, DS 10550.98
Log file for server ".BETELGEUSE.DreamLAN.W2K_EDIR_873."
 in tree "W2K_EDIR_873"
External Reference Check
Start:  01/16/2004 11:00:50 PM Local Time

(1) Found obituary for: EID: 010002ba,
    DN: CN=JimH.OU=East.O=XYZCorp.T=W2K_EDIR_873
-Value CTS : 01/16/2004 11:00:32 PM  R = 0001  E = 0001
-Value MTS = 01/16/2004 11:00:32 PM  R = 0001  E = 0001,
 Type = 0001 DEAD,
-Flags = 0000

(2) Found obituary for: EID: 010002ba,
```

continues

Listing 6.10   Continued

```
    DN: CN=JimH.OU=East.O=XYZCorp.T=W2K_EDIR_873
-Value CTS : 01/16/2004 11:00:32 PM   R = 0001   E = 0002
-Value MTS = 01/16/2004 11:00:32 PM   R = 0001   E = 0002,
 Type = 0006 BACKLINK,
-Flags = 0000
-Backlink: Type = 00000001 DEAD, RemoteID = ffffffff,
 ServerID = 000080a3,
 CN=DREAMLAN-W2KB-NDS.O=eDir_Book.T=W2K_EDIR_873

(3) Found obituary for: EID: 010002ba,
    DN: CN=JimH.OU=East.O=XYZCorp.T=W2K_EDIR_873
-Value CTS : 01/16/2004 11:00:32 PM   R = 0001   E = 0003
-Value MTS = 01/16/2004 11:00:32 PM   R = 0001   E = 0003,
 Type = 000c USED_BY,
-Flags = 0002  OK_TO_PURGE
-Used by: Resource type = 00000000, Event type = 00000003,
 Resource ID = 00008065, T=W2K_EDIR_873

Checked 0 external references
Found: 3 total obituaries in this dib,
    3 Unprocessed obits, 0 Purgeable obits,
    1 OK_To_Purge obits, 0 Notified obits

*** END ***
```

As with a Rename request, a `Backlink` obituary is generated in addition to the `Dead` obituary; a `Used By` obit is also generated. And as with the rename operation, these obituaries do not cause any delay in creating an object with the same name.

Moving Objects

The final object-level operation to examine is the move object operation. This operation is more complex than the other object-level operations and differs slightly from them because of the added complexity.

The first difference between moving an object and performing any other object-level operation is that a Move request requires communication with the server that holds the Master replica of the object. If an object is moved across a partition boundary, communication with the servers that hold the Master replicas of both partitions is required. In addition, those servers must be able to communicate with each other in order for an object's data to be moved from one partition to the other.

For simplicity, let's examine an object move within a partition (**User** object **PKuo** from **East.XYZCorp** to **West.XYZCorp**) because this operation does not vary much between a single server operation and a multiserver operation.

In Listing 6.11, you start by reading object information, using DS verb **DSV_READ_ENTRY_INFO** (decimal value 2), for the source organizational unit (OU) and destination OU. The request made for the objects is by ID, and the reply buffers contain information about the object: the container class and the full DN of the container in question.

Listing 6.11   DSA Read Entry Information Requests for the Source and Destination Containers in Preparation for an Object Move

```
DSA: DSACommonRequest(2) conn:3 for client <JIM>
DSA REQUEST BUFFER:
02 00 00 00 01 00 00 00 1D 28 00 00 E3 02 00 12
➡...............
DSA REPLY BUFFER:
1D 28 00 00 04 00 00 00 01 00 00 00 4F E3 8F 36
➡...........O..6
28 00 00 00 4F 00 72 00 67 00 61 00 6E 00 69 00
➡....O.r.g.a.n.i.
7A 00 61 00 74 00 69 00 6F 00 6E 00 61 00 6C 00
➡z.a.t.i.o.n.a.l.
20 00 55 00 6E 00 69 00 74 00 00 00 1A 00 00 00
➡..U.n.i.t.......
45 00 61 00 73 00 74 00 2E 00 58 00 59 00 5A 00
➡E.a.s.t...X.Y.Z.
43 00 6F 00 72 00 70 00 00 00                      C.o.r.p...


DSA: DSACommonRequest(2) conn:3 for client <JIM>
DSA REQUEST BUFFER:
02 00 00 00 00 00 00 00 1D 28 02 00 E2 02 00 12
➡...............
DSA REPLY BUFFER:
1D 28 02 00 04 00 00 00 01 00 00 00 5B E3 8F 36
➡..............6
28 00 00 00 4F 00 72 00 67 00 61 00 6E 00 69 00
➡....O.r.g.a.n.i.
7A 00 61 00 74 00 69 00 6F 00 6E 00 61 00 6C 00
➡z.a.t.i.o.n.a.l.
20 00 55 00 6E 00 69 00 74 00 00 00 24 00 00 00
➡..U.n.i.t.......
```

continues

Listing 6.11 Continued

```
4F 00 55 00 3D 00 57 00 65 00 73 00 74 00 2E 00
➥O.U...W.e.s.t...
4F 00 3D 00 58 00 59 00 5A 00 43 00 6F 00 72 00
➥O...X.Y.Z.C.o.r.
70 00 00 00 28 00 00 00 4F 00 72 00 67 00 61 00
➥p.......O.r.g.a.
6E 00 69 00 7A 00 61 00 74 00 69 00 6F 00 6E 00
➥n.i.z.a.t.i.o.n.
61 00 6C 00 20 00 55 00 6E 00 69 00 74 00 00 00
➥a.l...U.n.i.t...
```

These requests validate that the source and target containers are known to the client, and they ensure that the client is communicating with the server that holds the Master copy of the object and the server that will hold the Master copy of the object. Next, you see a Read request to obtain information about the actual object being moved. This is shown in Listing 6.12.

Listing 6.12 DSA Read Entry Information for an Object Being Moved

```
DSA: DSACommonRequest(2) conn:3 for client <JIM>
DSA REQUEST BUFFER:
02 00 00 00 00 00 00 00 1D 28 02 00 BC 02 00 0E
➥................
DSA REPLY BUFFER:
1D 28 02 00 00 00 00 00 00 00 00 00 6F 5E 90 36
➥............o..6
0A 00 00 00 55 00 73 00 65 00 72 00 00 00 00 00
➥....U.s.e.r.....
34 00 00 00 43 00 4E 00 3D 00 50 00 4B 00 75 00
➥4...C.N...P.K.u.
6F 00 2E 00 4F 00 55 00 3D 00 45 00 61 00 73 00
➥o...O.U...E.a.s.
74 00 2E 00 4F 00 3D 00 58 00 59 00 5A 00 43 00
➥t...O...X.Y.Z.C.
6F 00 72 00 70 00 00 00 0A 00 00 00 55 00 73 00
➥o.r.p.......U.s.
65 00 72 00 00 00                               e.r...
```

The next step in the move process is to issue a start move operation (DS verb DSV_BEGIN_MOVE_ENTRY, decimal value 42). This request, shown in Listing 6.13, involves the name of the object and the server involved in the communications. Starting at offset 16, you can see the object name, and at offset 32, the FQDN of the server.

Listing 6.13   A DSA Start Move Operation

```
DSA: DSACommonRequest(42) conn:3 for client <JIM>
DSA REQUEST BUFFER:
00 00 00 00 00 00 00 00 E3 02 00 12 0A 00 00 00
➥...............
50 00 4B 00 75 00 6F 00 00 00 0C 01 2A 00 00 00
➥P.K.u.o........
43 00 4E 00 3D 00 42 00 45 00 54 00 45 00 4C 00
➥C.N...B.E.T.E.L.
47 00 45 00 55 00 53 00 45 00 2E 00 4F 00 55 00
➥G.E.U.S.E...O.U.
3D 00 6F 00 6D 00 65 00 45 00 61 00 73 00 3D 00
➥..E.a.s.t...O...
58 00 59 00 5A 00 43 00 6F 00 72 00 70 00 00 00
➥X.Y.Z.C.o.r.p...
C8 00                                         ..
DSA REPLY BUFFER:
```

At this point, the obituaries are issued for the moved object as well as for
the object in its new location. Listing 6.14 shows the DSRepair log after an
exref check is performed.

Listing 6.14   Obituaries Issued Due to a Move Operation

```
/****************************************************************/
Directory Services Repair 10550.61, DS 10550.98
Log file for server ".BETELGEUSE.DreamLAN.W2K_EDIR_873."
 in tree "W2K_EDIR_873"
External Reference Check
Start:  01/17/2004 03:11:07 AM Local Time

(1) Found obituary for: EID: 0e0002bd,
    DN: CN=PKuo.OU=East.O=XYZCorp.T=W2K_EDIR_873
-Value CTS : 01/17/2004 03:10:43 AM  R = 0001  E = 0026
-Value MTS = 01/17/2004 03:10:43 AM  R = 0001  E = 0026,
 Type = 0002 MOVED,
-Flags = 0000
-MoveObit: destID = 0e0002bc,
 CN= PKuo.OU=West.O=XYZCorp.T=W2K_EDIR_873

(2) Found obituary for: EID: 0e0002bd,
    DN: CN=PKuo.OU=East.O=XYZCorp.T=W2K_EDIR_873
-Value CTS : 01/17/2004 03:10:43 AM  R = 0001  E = 0028
-Value MTS = 01/17/2004 03:10:43 AM  R = 0001  E = 0028,
```

continues

Listing 6.14   Continued

```
Type = 0006 BACKLINK,
-Flags = 0000
-Backlink: Type = 00000002 MOVED, RemoteID = ffffffff,
 ServerID = 000080a3, CN=RIGEL.O=eDir_Book.T=W2K_EDIR_873

(3) Found obituary for: EID: 0e0002bd,
    DN: CN=PKuo.OU=East.O=XYZCorp.T=W2K_EDIR_873
-Value CTS : 01/17/2004 03:10:43 AM  R = 0001  E = 002a
-Value MTS = 01/17/2004 03:10:43 AM  R = 0001  E = 002a,
 Type = 000c USED_BY,
-Flags = 0002  OK_TO_PURGE
-Used by: Resource type = 00000000, Event type = 00000001,
 Resource ID = 00008065, T=W2K_EDIR_873

(4) Found obituary for: EID: 0e0002bc,
    DN: CN=PKuo.OU=West.O=XYZCorp.T=W2K_EDIR_873
-Value CTS : 01/17/2004 03:10:43 AM  R = 0001  E = 0021
-Value MTS = 01/17/2004 03:10:43 AM  R = 0001  E = 0021,
 Type = 0003 INHIBIT_MOVE,
-Flags = 0000

Checked 0 external references
Found: 4 total obituaries in this dib,
    3 Unprocessed obits, 0 Purgeable obits,
    1 OK_To_Purge obits, 0 Notified obits

*** END ***
```

NOTE

When an object is moved, it is essentially deleted from its original context and re-created in the target context. However, the entry ID is preserved. You accomplish this by first changing the entry ID of the object in the source context (refer to obits 1 and 4 in Listing 6.14) and then assigning the original entry ID to the object in the new context.

Now you see more differences between the move operation and the previously described object operations. The Inhibit Move obituary issued for the new object (Obit 4 in Listing 6.14) blocks further operations (except modify) on the object, including renames, deletions, and moves until the move operation is completed. It is possible to change the attributes of the object, but all other requests receive a -637 error "previous move in progress"). This is one of the most common error messages received while performing administrative tasks. If you understand how the move process operates, you can understand what a -637 error means and know what needs to be done to resolve the situation.

Although the target object can only be manipulated in a minimal number of ways because of the Move Inhibit **obituary, a new object with the same name can be created in the original location. The** Moved **obituary type does not prevent object creation.**

As with the previous object operations, with this operation, you also have a Backlink obituary created.

When the move is complete, DS requests that the move be finished by issuing DS verb DSV_FINISH_MOVE_ENTRY (decimal value 43). This initiates the purge process for the Move Inhibit and Moved obituaries. Listing 6.15 shows this request.

Listing 6.15 A DSA Finish Move Operation

```
DSA: DSACommonRequest(43) conn:3 for client <JIM>
DSA REQUEST BUFFER:
00 00 00 00 01 00 00 00 BC 02 00 0E E3 02 00 12
➥...............
0A 00 00 00 50 00 4B 00 75 00 6F 00 00 00 6F 00
➥....P.K.u.o...o.
2A 00 00 00 43 00 4E 00 3D 00 42 00 45 00 54 00
➥....C.N...B.E.T.
45 00 4C 00 47 00 45 00 55 00 53 00 45 00 2E 00
➥E.L.G.E.U.S.E...
4F 00 55 00 3D 00 6F 00 6D 00 65 00 45 00 61 00
➥O.U...E.a.s.t...
73 00 3D 00 58 00 59 00 5A 00 43 00 6F 00 72 00
➥O...X.Y.Z.C.o.r.
70 00 00 00 65 00                          p...e.
```

The finish move operation completes, and the obituary purge process begins. When the obituaries are purged, you can proceed with other move operations, and you can rename the object or delete it. However, if you try to delete an object that was just moved without waiting for its associated obits to be purged, you will get a response similar to that shown in Listing 6.16.

Listing 6.16   A Delete Request on an Object with a Previous Move in Progress

```
DSA: DSACommonRequest(8) conn:16 for client <JIM>
DSA REQUEST BUFFER:
00 00 00 00 BC 02 00 0E                              ........
DSA REPLY BUFFER:
DSA: DSACommonRequest(8): returning ERROR -637
```

The error message in the reply buffer is expected in this case: -637 error ("previous move in progress"). This error occurs because the obituaries created for the Move request have not yet purged, even though the finish move operation has executed successfully. You can retry in a short while and succeed. However, if the error is not cleared after some time (say, 10 minutes), you should check server-to-server communications and determine why the obits are not being purged.

Manual Partition and Replication Processes

Partitioning and replication operations all require communications with the server that holds the Master replica or replicas. The following sections examine the common operations used in manipulating partitions and replicas.

WARNING
Although many of these operations function even if some of the servers in the replica ring are unavailable, it is not at all recommended that they be performed until connectivity can be restored and verified. Even though the impact to users is not noticeable if everything proceeds normally, any partition-related operations (including adding or removing a replica) should be considered to be major changes to the tree.

Prior to initiating a partition or replica operation, it is always a good idea to perform a basic health check to verify communication to all the servers that will be involved in the operation. You can easily do this by using NDS iMonitor. NDS iMonitor has a couple different options that are useful in this situation—the Agent Synchronization option, shown in Figure 6.13, and the partition Continuity option, shown in Figure 6.14.

NOTE
You can find detailed NDS/eDirectory health check recommendations in Chapter 13, "eDirectory Health Checks."

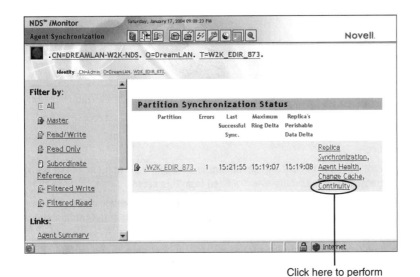

FIGURE 6.13
The NDS
iMonitor Agent
Synchronization
status screen.

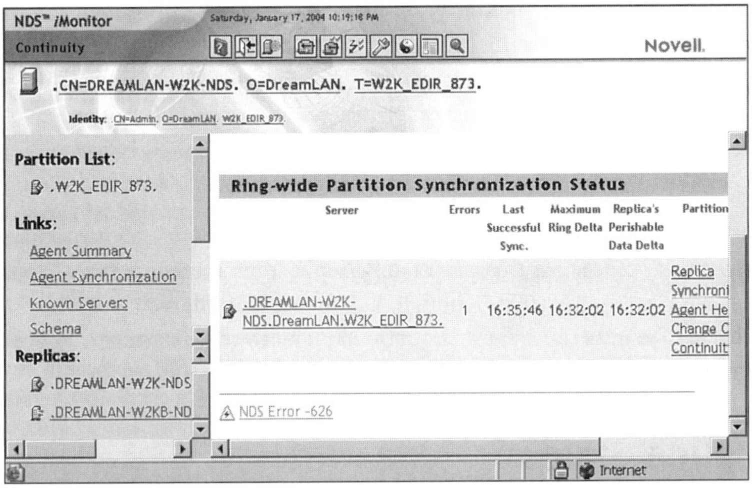

Click here to perform
Partition Continuity check

FIGURE 6.14
The NDS
iMonitor partition
Continuity status
screen.

WARNING

Do not confuse the Agent Synchronization link under the Links listing with the Agent Synchronization link found on the Agent Configuration page. The latter is used to change synchronization-related settings.

As you can see in Figure 6.13, the Agent Synchronization screen shows a quick overview of synchronization status. This status is obtained by reading a single server and seeing the status that the server recorded for the last synchronization. If the last synchronization status was `All Processed=YES`, the synchronization is determined to have been successful and the errors count is zero. If the status was `All Processed=NO`, the synchronization failed and the errors count shows the number of errors.

NOTE   The following information is shown on the Agent Synchronization status screen:

▶ Partition—The names of the partitions located on this server.

▶ Errors—The number of errors encountered during the last synchronization cycle.

▶ Last Successful Sync.—The amount of time since all replicas of the partition were successfully synchronized from this server.

▶ Maximum Ring Delta—The oldest send delta of any server in the replica ring. This value is the same as the highest send delta in the replica status list.

▶ Replica's Perishable Data Delta—The amount of data on the partition that has not yet been successfully replicated since the server last synchronized that partition.

This basic check shows high-level problems in synchronization, but in order to really determine the status, you should check each server in the replica ring. The Partition Continuity screen (refer to Figure 6.14) provides this information. Synchronization errors between one server and another are apparent here. If there is a synchronization problem reported between servers, errors are reported at the end of the page.

After you have verified that the involved replicas are properly synchronized, you can then proceed with a partitioning/replication operation. Before looking at the various operations, though, let's first review the states in which a replica can be in because they can help you determine what stage you are at during a partitioning or replication operation.

Replica States

When working with partitions and replicas, you need to be familiar with the various states they can be in. Table 6.5 lists the possible states that a partition or replica can go through and their values (in both hexadecimal and decimal).

Replica States

TABLE 6.5

REPLICA STATE	DECIMAL VALUE	HEXA-DECIMAL VALUE	DESCRIPTION	CAN BE ABORTED?
On	0	0	Replica is on	N/A
New Replica	1	1	Replica is new	No
Dying Replica	2	2	Replica is dying (that is, being removed)	No
Partition Locked	3	3	Replica is locked in preparation for a move	No
Change Replica Type	4	4	Replica is currently having its type changed	Yes
—	5	5	Replica is almost finished changing types	No
Transition On	6	6	Replica is changing to the On state	No
Transition Move	7	7	Replica is changing to the Move state	Yes
Transition Split	8	8	Replica is changing to the Split state	Yes
Create	32	20	Replica is being created	Yes
	33	21	Replica is almost created	No
Split	48	30	Replica is preparing to split	Yes
	49	31	Replica is almost finished splitting	No

Table 6.5   Continued

REPLICA STATE	DECIMAL VALUE	HEXA-DECIMAL VALUE	DESCRIPTION	CAN BE ABORTED?
Join	64	40	Replica is preparing to join, or merge	Yes
	65	41	Replica is almost finished joining, or merging	No
Move	80	50	Replica is preparing to move a container	Yes
	81	51	Replica is almost finished moving a container	No

The values that appear in some DSRepair log files and DSTrace screens can provide insight into the current state of operations. A detailed explanation of some of the states follows:

▶ **On**—Indicates the normal state of a replica.

▶ **New Replica**—Indicates that the replica is in the process of forming. This state should last no more than a few minutes.

▶ **Dying Replica**—Indicates that the replica is in the process of being deleted. This replica should disappear completely in a few hours.

▶ **Transition On**—Indicates that the replica is in the process of going on but is currently in transition. This state is typical during a replica installation. The replica is not fully on until the installation is complete.

▶ **Transition Move**—Indicates that the replica is in the process of going to the Move state but is currently in transition. This state is typical during a Move Partition operation.

▶ **Transition Split**—Indicates that the replica is in the process of going to the Split state but is currently in transition. This state is typical during a Split Partition operation.

The two important states to watch for are whether the replica is on or successfully deleted. If the replica is stuck in a split, join, or move state, the value itself is not necessarily important, except as an indication that the operation is not yet complete. You should then determine the reason for the operation's incompletion. It could be due to communication failure between servers.

NetWare 4.1 and higher enable you to abort a partition operation that is in progress. A pending partitioning or replication operation can be aborted through DSRepair, as shown in Figure 6.15.

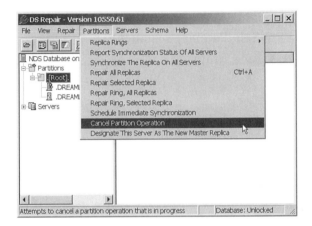

FIGURE 6.15
Using DSRepair to abort an in-progress partition operation.

Not all partition operations can be canceled successfully (refer to Table 6.5). DSRepair might judge that a given operation couldn't be canceled due to potential damage to the tree. In such cases, the operation continues as scheduled.

Now that you have a good grounding in the replica states, the following sections examine the various partitioning/replication operations, starting with the Split Partition operation.

The Split Partition Operation

The Split Partition operation is the process that is used to create a new (child) partition. When you install the first DS server in a tree, the [Root] partition is created automatically; any other partitions created are split off the [Root] partition.

The information reported by the DSTrace screen is fairly minimal. Watching the operation entails enabling the Partition DSTrace flag (+PART in NetWare and Unix). This enables the trace information for all partitioning operations. Listing 6.17 shows the information presented during a Split Partition operation.

Listing 6.17   A Split Partition Operation

```
SPLITTING -- BEGIN STATE 0
(20:28:39)
*** DSALowLevelSplit <[Root]> and <XYZCorp> ***

Successfully split all partitions in ring.
ADDED 010000B6 and 0C0000BC to partition busy list.
SPLITTING -- END STATE 0
*CNTL: This server is the new master for [0C0000BC]<XYZCorp>
*CNTL: SetNewMaster for [0C0000BC]<XYZCorp> succeeded.
Turning replicas on after changing replica type.
```

While a Split Partition operation is being performed, further partitioning and replication operations for that partition are suspended. Further operations will result in an error -654 (ERR_PARTITION_BUSY) until the replicas are turned on (that is, become usable). This operation is indicated in the last line of Listing 6.17.

TIP

Although you can perform operations on multiple partitions concurrently, it is best to work on them one at a time, especially if the partitions share common servers.

Notice that lines 7 and 8 in Listing 6.17 (which appear in boldface) indicate that the server the trace was done on became the Master replica for the new partition. This is to be expected because this server holds the Master replica of the parent partition. When you perform a Split Partition operation, the servers that end up with replicas are the same as the ones that hold replicas of the parent partition. After the replicas are turned on, you can further manipulate the replicas by adding, removing, or changing the replica types.

The Merge Partition Operation

Merging a partition—also referred to as *joining* a partition—is the reverse of splitting a partition. The Merge Partition operation merges parent and child partitions into a single partition. As Listing 6.18 shows, two operations actually take place during a join—a *join up* operation and a *join down* operation. The join up operation is the process of joining of the child partition with the parent; the join down operation is the process of the parent joining with the child partition.

Listing 6.18   DSTrace Messages from a Join Operation

```
(20:28:08)*** DSAStartJoin <XYZCorp> to <[Root]> ***

JOINING DOWN -- BEGIN STATE 0
JOINING DOWN -- END STATE 0
JOINING UP -- BEGIN STATE 0
JOINING UP -- END STATE 0
JOINING DOWN -- BEGIN STATE 1
PARENT REPORTING CHILD IS STILL IN STATE 1
JOINING UP -- BEGIN STATE 1
JOINING UP -- END STATE 1
JOINING DOWN -- BEGIN STATE 1
JOIN: Reassigning unowned replica changes for [010000B6]
 <[Root]> succeeded, total values reassigned 1
 (20:28:12)
*** DSALowLevelJoin <[Root]> and <XYZCorp> ***

ADDED 010000B6 to partition busy list.
JOINING DOWN -- END STATE 1
```

The Merge Partition operation results in a single partition where there were two; however, the replicas for each of the old partitions have to be dealt with in such a way that bindery services on all servers are not disrupted. When you're merging partitions together, it is very important to determine where the new partition's replicas are going to be. For example, if you have eight servers involved in the Merge Partition operation, you will end up with eight replicas of the new partition. This might not be desirable, so you will want to examine where these new replicas will be and what services would be affected on each server if you were to remove the replica from this server.

The Move Partition Operation

Moving a partition is similar to moving an object—in fact, the operation uses the same code within the DS module to perform the operation. The biggest difference is that the Move Partition operation also generates Create Replica operations, which in turn result in object Synchronization operations. The Move Partition operation is a fairly complex operation— more so than the other operations discussed in this chapter. Before you commence, you must make sure you have *no* synchronization problems in the partitions involved.

> **WARNING**
>
> **A total of three existing partitions can be affected by a move operation: two parent partitions and the partition being moved. It is important that you verify the synchronization status of all three partitions before initiating a Move Partition operation.**

There are two rules to remember when moving partitions:

▶ Moving a partition cannot violate containment rules for the partition root object.

▶ The partition being moved must not have any child partitions.

Figure 6.16 shows an example of a violation of the first rule. This Move Partition operation is invalid because containment rules are violated: `O=XYZCorp` cannot be moved to under `O=DIV1` because an organization cannot contain another organization.

FIGURE 6.16
Illegal partition moves.

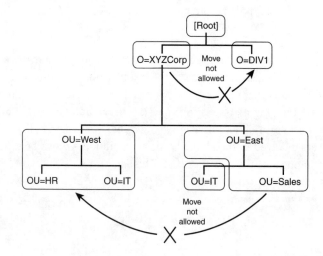

By extension of the second rule, it is not possible to move a partition so that it becomes subordinate to a child partition. As Figure 6.16 shows, it is also not permissible to move the `East.XYZCorp` partition under the `OU=West.O=XYZCorp` partition because there exists a child partition, `OU=IT.OU=East.O=XYZCorp`, under `OU=East.O=XYZCorp`.

The following sections focus on some things you need to watch out for when moving a partition.

Important Considerations for Partition Moves

NetWare 5 and higher introduce several objects into the tree at the time of installation, depending on which additional services are installed on the server. In addition, other Novell products (including eDirectory) or third-party products may also create dependencies on a server's context in the tree. When you're moving a partition, it is useful to determine which objects will be affected by a server's move if the server should be in the partition being moved. References to objects within the partition being moved may not be changed. In this section we'll look at a few NetWare-specific examples.

NetWare 6 installs Secure Authentication Services (SAS), used for security services such as Secure Sockets Layer (SSL) communication, as part of the basic core component. This add-on creates an object in the tree (named SAS Service – *servername*) and references the server that hosts the service. When a partition containing this service is moved, you need to re-create the object by unloading the `SAS.NLM` module, loading `SASI.NLM` (the SAS installation utility), and logging in with sufficient rights to re-create the SAS object in the tree.

TIP

Refer to TID 10063314 for information on how to create the SAS Service object manually on different operating system platforms.

The Novell Distributed Print Services (NDPS) broker service also has dependencies on the server location: A `Broker` object is created in the tree in the server's context. When the server object is moved, shut down, and brought back up in the new location, the broker service will not start properly.

Of particular significance is NetWare's license service. If you relocate a partition that contains license information for NetWare 5 servers, you will need to reassign the license files to the servers. This requires reinstalling the license service on the server or servers that have moved as a result of the Move Partition operation. NetWare 6, on the other hand, does not suffer from this problem because its licensing model changed to be user based.

Many other add-on services can be affected by the Move Partition operation. The best thing to do is check all your non-User objects and see which of them reference servers. Moving a server object—and a partition, by extension—is not a trivial operation and has widespread impact in most production environments.

The Process Involved in the Move Partition Operation

The Move Partition operation consists of two parts: the Move Partition request and the Finish Partition Move request. The Move Partition request is sent by the client to schedule the move. This process performs several verification operations, including the following:

▶ Ensuring that the user has Create object rights to the destination container to which the partition is being moved.

▶ Verifying that there is not an object in the destination container that has the same name as the partition root object being moved.

▶ Verifying that the affected replicas are all available to perform partition operations.

▶ Ensuring that the Transaction Tracking Service (TTS) is available and enabled on all NetWare servers that are running pre-NDS 8 and are involved in the Move Partition operation. NDS operations are dependent on TTS, and if TTS is not available, NDS cannot function. (eDirectory, on the other hand, does not have this limitation because of the FLAIM database it uses.)

When the preceding tasks are completed, the servers handle the Finish Partition Move request. This process has two functions:

▶ Moving the partition root object and all subordinate objects from one context to another valid context

▶ Notifying the server that holds the Master replica of the partition that the partition has moved

This process also performs several verification operations, including verifying that the partition root object being moved and all subordinate objects do not have an `Inhibit Move` obituary on them. If there is such an obituary within the partition, the process aborts with a -637 error (`ERR_PREVIOUS_MOVE_IN_PROGRESS`).

A second verification process involves testing to see whether the partition root object to be moved is the `[Root]` object for the tree. It is not possible to move the `[Root]` object, and attempting to do so will result in a -641 error (`ERR_INVALID_REQUEST`).

NOTE

The Finish Partition Move process also tests to see whether you are attempting to move an object that is not a partition root. If you are, you get a -641 error. The standard Novell-supplied administration utilities do not allow such as move, but the check is there to prevent third-party utilities from attempting such an illegal move due to inadequate safeguards.

A further test is done to verify that the servers involved in the move are running at least NDS 4.63; there is no reason you should still be running NDS 4.63 or an older version, but the DS code needs to perform this check as a precaution. Novell made changes to the DS code that are involved in partition moves, and using versions older than NDS 4.63 with versions newer than NDS 4.63 causes a move to fail. Mixing versions in this manner causes a -666 error (`ERR_INCOMPATABLE_DS_VERSION`) to be reported.

NOTE

The DS engine on the Master replica of the partition being moved generates a list of the servers that need to be informed about the Move Partition operation. This list includes the servers containing real copies of the partition root object as well as all the servers listed in the `BackLink` attribute for the partition root object (that is, servers holding external references of the partition root object). Each server object is then checked to see whether there is a `DS Revision` attribute. The value of this attribute is then checked to see whether it meets the minimal version requirement for the operation, which is 463.

If a server in the list happens to be an `Unknown` object or an external reference object that is not backlinked, there is a good possibility that no `DS Revision` attribute exists. In that case, the `DS Revision` value is 0. This value does not meet the minimal version requirement, and the operation fails with a -666 error.

Next, DS checks to verify that the containment rules are not being violated by the move. The DSA finds a server with a copy of `[Root]` and asks for the class definition for the destination parent object's class; if the partition root object being moved is in the containment list of the destination, the move is allowed to proceed. Otherwise, a -611 error (`ERR_ILLEGAL_CONTAINMENT`) is generated, and the process aborts.

Another verification is done to ensure that the partition root object's DN and the DNs of all subordinate objects do not exceed the maximum length of 256 Unicode characters (512 bytes). If any of the objects affected has a DN that exceeds this length, a -610 error (`ERR_ILLEGAL_DS_NAME`) is returned.

> **NOTE** In the check of the objects that are subordinate to the partition root object, the actual returned code may be a -353 error (`ERR_DN_TOO_LONG`). This error code means the same thing as -610 but is reported by the client library instead of the server.

A further step in the Move Partition process is the submission of a third process to the destination server: an NDS Start Tree Move request. This request actually performs the move operation and is responsible for moving both the partition root object and all the child objects to the new context.

When the move is complete and the partition root object being moved has been locked to prevent other partition operations from occurring, the Replica Synchronization and Backlinker processes are scheduled. When they are successfully scheduled, the partition root object is unlocked.

Moving a partition also causes the creation and deletion of SubRef replicas, which are needed to provide connectivity between partitions, as discussed in Chapter 2. The old SubRef replicas will be deleted from the servers that hold them, and new SubRef replicas will be created as necessary to provide connectivity to the new context.

The Rename Partition Operation

The Rename Partition operation is very similar to the Rename Object operation, except that the obituaries issued are different—rather than the `OLD_RDN` and `NEW_RDN` obituaries being issued, the obituaries issued are `Tree_OLD_RDN` and `Tree_NEW_RDN`. Renaming a partition is really a special case of the Object Rename operation because the only object directly affected is the partition root object.

The Rename Partition operation is one operation that can hold up any other type of partition or replication operation. NDS/eDirectory checks for this condition before attempting the Add Replica, Delete Replica, Split Partition, Join Partition, and Change Partition Type operations.

The Create Replica Operation

Creating a replica, also known as an Add Replica request, requires communication with each server in the replica ring for the partition being affected. An inability to communicate with a server in the replica ring results in a -625 error (`ERR_TRANSPORT_FAILURE`) or a -636 error (`ERR_UNREACHABLE_SERVER`).

If a server has a SubRef replica and you want to promote it to be a real replica on the server, the operation you need to use is the Create Replica operation, not the Change Replica Type operation. This is because a SubRef replica is not a real copy of the partition; rather, it contains just enough information for NDS operations such as tree-walking. Therefore, the only way to change its type is to place a copy of the real replica on that server.

You should *never* change a SubRef replica type except in a DS disaster recovery scenario, and you should do that only as a very last resort. Refer to the section "Replica Ring Inconsistency" in Chapter 11, "Examples from the Real World" for more information about this process.

Creating a replica of a partition involves making changes to the local partition database and then performing a synchronization of all objects in the partition to the server receiving the new replica. Problems can occur for two reasons:

▶ Communication cannot be established or maintained with a server in the replica ring.

▶ If the server being examined to determine the location of the Master replica does not have a replica attribute, error -602 (`ERR_NO_SUCH_VALUE`) is returned, and the operation is aborted.

The Delete Replica Operation

The Delete Replica operation is similar in requirements to the Create Replica operation. The Delete Replica operation requires all servers in the replica ring be reachable. The server holding the Master replica of the partition processes the request.

The verification routines ensure that the replica being removed is a Read/Write or Read-Only replica. If the replica in question is the Master replica, a -656 error (`ERR_CRUCIAL_REPLICA`) is returned.

> **NOTE**
>
> Some utilities give you the option of making another replica the Master replica before you delete the current one, instead of returning the –656 error and aborting the operation.

A lock is placed on the partition during the operation. Unlike in other operations, this lock is left in place for a number of steps, including an immediate synchronization that is scheduled to ensure that all objects in the replica being moved have been synchronized. This ensures that information in the objects stored in the replica being deleted does not get lost if it is newer than the information in other replicas.

The Change Replica Type Operation

Compared to the other operations we have looked at in this chapter, the Change Replica Type operation is relatively simple. This operation is easiest to perform from the ConsoleOne utility. Figure 6.17 shows the ConsoleOne dialog box, Change Replica Type, that is used during this operation.

FIGURE 6.17
The Change
Replica Type
dialog box.

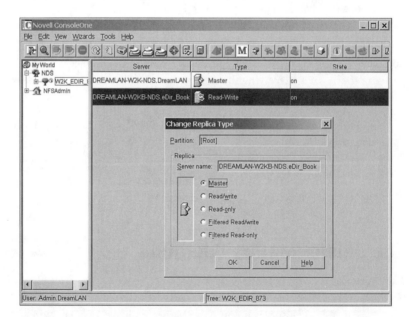

> **NOTE**
>
> As discussed earlier in this chapter, changing a SubRef replica to a Master, Read/Write, or Read-Only replica is treated as a Create Replica operation. You should not confuse it with the "force promotion" process discussed in Chapter 11 that is used for DS disaster recovery. ConsoleOne does not present you with a Change Replica Type option if the selected replica is a SubRef or Master replica.

In Figure 6.17 you can see the replica types available for changing the selected server's replica type. Because the selected server currently holds a Read/Write replica of the partition, you have a number of options to choose from.

NOTE

Even though you have an option to change the replica type to a Read/Write replica, if you select that option, the OK button is disabled because the replica is already a Read/Write replica.

Changing a Read/Write or Read-Only replica to a Master replica actually causes two changes to be made. First, the Master replica is changed to a Read/Write replica. Second, the Read/Write or Read-Only replica becomes the Master replica; this is done because there cannot be two Master replicas for a given partition—and it is done for you automatically.

NOTE

When running eDirectory 8.5 and higher, you can also change a replica's type to either Filtered Read/Write or Filtered Read-Only. However, note that before you set up any replication filters, which are server-specific, only the following objects (if they exist within the partition) will be placed in a Filtered replica:

- ▶ **Container objects (and their subordinate container objects), such as organizations and organizational units**
- ▶ **NCP Server objects and their SAS objects, but not their other associated objects, such as the SSL objects**
- ▶ **The Security container and its (leaf and container) subordinate objects**
- ▶ **The Admin User object if it exists in the partition in question, but not other User objects**

These objects allow you to authenticate to the target server as Admin and set up replication filters at a later time.

The Change Replica Type operation generally occurs very quickly because no replicas need to be created or deleted in order to change the replica. The replica ring is updated on all servers that hold replicas (including SubRef replicas), and the server or servers affected have a change made in their partition entry tables to reflect the change in replica type.

TIP

If you receive a -637 error ("move in progress") during a Change Replica Type operation, you should check for possible stuck obits in that partition.

Summary

This chapter examines NDS/eDirectory's use of obituaries and the major NDS/eDirectory background processes. The following is a summary of the time intervals at which the various processes run:

NDS Background Process	Default Time Interval
Backlink/DRL	780 minutes (that is, 13 hours)
External reference life-span	192 hours (that is, 8 days)
Flat Cleaner	720 minutes
Heartbeat—data	60 minutes
Heartbeat—schema	240 minutes (4 hours)
Janitor	2 minutes
Limber	3 hours; 5 minutes if processing was unsuccessful
Server state Up threshold	30 minutes
Schema update interval	60 seconds
Schema synchronization interval	If processing was successful, schedule to run after next schema heartbeat (which is 4 hours); otherwise, schedule to run after schema update interval plus one second
Synchronization interval for attributes flagged as Sync Immediate	10 seconds
Synchronization interval for attributes flagged as Sync Never	30 minutes for NetWare 4; 60 minutes for NetWare 5 and higher and eDirectory servers

This chapter also examines several object-related and partitioning replication–related operations to show how DS actually performs these operations. Understanding how these processes operate lays a foundation for understanding how to effectively troubleshoot and resolve problems. The next two parts of this book examine how to use this information to troubleshoot and resolve issues with NDS/eDirectory, using the different tools available. The following chapters also examine ways to combine tools using different techniques in order to streamline the troubleshooting-resolution process.

Troubleshooting and Resolving Problems

Diagnostic and Repair Tools

Regardless of the type of troubleshooting you need to perform, having the right tools is essential. You can't troubleshoot effectively if you can't see what and where the error is. This chapter introduces you to the various NDS/eDirectory server- and workstation-based diagnostic tools and utilities included with the NetWare 4, 5, and 6 operating systems, those included with eDirectory for non-NetWare platforms, and additional tools available from Novell sources.

Server Tools

It is important to keep in mind that NDS/eDirectory is a global, distributed name service whose database exists as a set of files stored on one or more DS servers. These servers continually exchange updates and other time-sensitive information. If a server's local copy of the DS information is corrupted, it can prevent the rest of the servers in the same DS tree from communicating changes. Therefore, NetWare and eDirectory for non-NetWare platforms ship with a number of server-centric diagnostic and repair tools that can help you determine whether the local DS database has problems and repair those errors automatically if possible.

Oftentimes, the same tool that provides diagnostic information is also the tool to use to rectify the detected problem(s). The features of these utilities are discussed in the following sections; specific applications of the tools can be found in later chapters.

> **NOTE**
>
> You will find that much of the discussion about server-based tools concentrates on the nonbrowser-based products, such as DSRepair and DSTrace. There are two reasons for this: The first is that nonbrowser-based tools do not depend on a working HTTP stack, a functional Web server, or other components on the target server (as is the case of iManager). You simply run the module on the server console and they interact with the local DIB directly. Secondly, nonbrowser-based tools tend to have a less intuitive user interface, thus a little more explanation is generally required.

Over time, you will find that you rely more on server-based tools than workstation-based ones because the server utilities can provide much more information. This is due to their capability to access the DIB directly, bypassing much of the DS security. Because of that, much of the material presented in this chapter centers more on the server tools than their workstation counterparts.

> **NOTE**
>
> All server-based eDirectory tools (such as DSRepair and DSTrace) and related modules (such as the Directory Agent for Novell eDirectory, ds.dlm) for the Windows platform are accessed through the NDSCons utility (*drive*:\Novell\ NDS\NDSCons.exe). **NDSCons** is installed as a Control Panel applet (labeled as Novell eDirectory Services). It is recommended that you create a shortcut on the desktop to access it more easily.

DSRepair

The most commonly used DS diagnostic utility is probably DSRepair. It is provided with NetWare 4 and higher operating systems and is included with eDirectory for non-NetWare platforms. DSRepair allows you to check for and correct problems in the DS database on a server-centric basis.

> **NOTE**
>
> The DSRepair utility is frequently updated to include new functionalities and bug fixes. Generally, new versions of DSRepair are included with new versions of DS.NLM or eDirectory releases, and you should use the latest version whenever possible. Check support.novell.com/filefinder/ for information about newer releases of DSRepair.

Depending on the operating system and the version of DSRepair, the opening screen of DSRepair can look different. Figure 7.1 shows the opening screen for DSRepair NLM on a NetWare 6 server that offers seven options:

- ▸ Single Object Repair

- ▸ Unattended Full Repair

- ▸ Time Synchronization

- ▸ Report Synchronization Status

- ▸ View Repair Log File

- ▸ Advanced Options Menu

- ▸ Exit

The version of DSRepair, along with the name of the current NDS tree and server name, is always shown at the top of the menu.

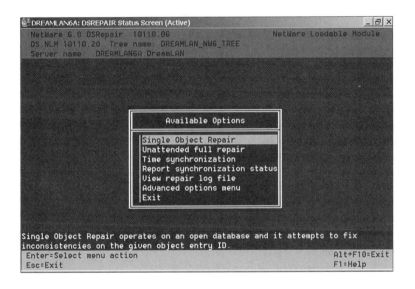

FIGURE 7.1
DSRepair NLM
opening screen.

On Windows servers, DSRepair is started from NDSCons by highlighting dsrepair.dlm **and clicking Start. On Linux/Unix servers, the executable for DSRepair is called** ndsrepair.

Due to the GUI nature of the Windows platform, the various menu options you see in the NLM version of DSRepair are accessed via the various pull-down menus in **dsrepair.dlm**, as shown in Figure 7.2. Depending on whether a partition, replica, or server is selected, menu options not related to the selected object might not be active for a selection.

FIGURE 7.2
DSRepair for
Windows.

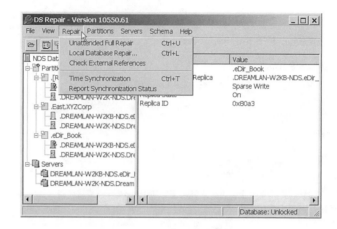

On the other hand, `ndsrepair` on Linux/Unix is a command-line-based
application that requires you to specify options to select the various repair
features. To display a list of supported options, type **ndsrepair -?** (or
ndsrepair --help) at a terminal window. The output looks similar to the
following:

```
The locale is en_US.UTF-8
Repair utility for Novell eDirectory 8.6 - 8.7.1 v10510.53


ndsrepair - corrects problems in the NDS database
Usage: ndsrepair { -U ¦ -E ¦ -C ¦ -P [-Ad] ¦ -S [-Ad] ¦ -N  ¦
➥ -T ¦ -J <entry_id> ¦ --version} [-F filename]
➥ [-A <yes/no>] [-O <yes/no>]
-U Unattended Full Repair option
-R Repair Local Database option
-E Report Synchronization Status option
-C Check External References option
-P Replica and Partition Operations option
-S Global Schema operations
-N Servers Known to this Database
-T Time Synchronization option
-J Repair Single Object
--version Print DSRepair Version Information


-A Append to the existing Log File
-O Log Output to file
-F Log Output to file 'fileName'


By default -A and -O options are set
Press ENTER to continue...
```

```
The default file name is /var/nds/ndsrepair.log
Log file size = 426 bytes.


The -R option has the following sub options:
ndsrepair -R [-l <yes/no>] [-u <yes/no>] [-m <yes/no>]
➡ [-i <yes/no>] [-f <yes/no>][-d <yes/no>]
➡ [-t <yes/no>] [-o <yes/no>][-r <yes/no>]
➡ [-v <yes/no>] [-c <yes/no>] [-F filename]
➡ [-A <yes/no>] [-O <yes/no>]
-l lock nds database during entire repair
-u use temporary nds database during repair
-m maintain original unrepaired database
-i perform database structure and Index check
-f reclaim database free space
-d rebuild entire database
-t perform Tree structure check
-o rebuild Operational schema
-r repair all local replicas
-v validate stream files
-c check local references
By default -i, -d, -t, -r, -v and -c options are set.
```

Keep in mind that the command-line options for ndsrepair **are case sensitive.
Notice that all first-level options, such as** -T **for the time synchronization check,
are in uppercase.**

NOTE

To make ndsrepair a little more user-friendly and to look more like its
NetWare counterpart, Novell has developed a "menu wrapper" using a shell
script. The wrapper provides a text-based menu that has the look-and-feel
of DSREPAIR.NLM (see Figure 7.3). Refer to TID #2964755 for more information about the wrapper and to download it.

The Single Object Repair selection allows you to repair a specific object on
an open database, based on the object ID you provide. It is a useful option if
you know which particular object is inconsistent and the operation is performed quickly.

The Unattended Full Repair option automatically performs all the possible
repair operations that don't require user input. You can select the items to
be checked or repaired using the Repair Local Database option in the
Advanced Repair Options menu. A log file (called DSREPAIR.LOG) located in
the SYS:SYSTEM directory on NetWare records all actions during the repair
operation so you can later determine what was done; on Windows servers,

the file is located in *drive*:\Novell\NDS\DIBFiles, and on Linux/Unix servers the file is in /var/nds and is called ndsrepair.log.

FIGURE 7.3
Menu wrapper for ndsrepair.

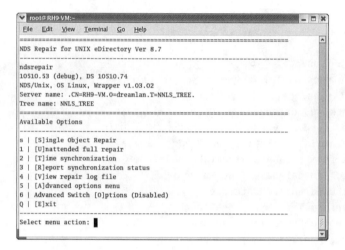

> **NOTE**
>
> During the repair of the local database, the DS database (on the server running DSRepair only) might be locked, making it inaccessible to the client or any other use until the repair is completed. That means new users are not able to authenticate to this server while users already logged in are able to continue to access other (non-DS) resources on this server. NDS 8 and later allows you to repair a database without locking it.

The unattended full repair goes through the following four major diagnostic and repair procedures:

- Local DS data (database can be locked during this phase)
- Validation of all network addresses (database is not locked)
- Validation of remote server IDs (database is not locked)
- Consistency check of replica rings (database is not locked)

A status menu is displayed during the repair operation (see Figure 7.4). The same information shown is also recorded in the log file. When the repair operations are completed, the log file is automatically displayed for your viewing so you can determine which repairs were done and which state of the database is following the repair operation.

FIGURE 7.4
DSRepair status
screen.

You can initiate an unattended repair option from the command line by loading DSRepair with the -U **option switch. The NLM unloads itself when the operation is completed. The** -U **switch has the same effect on Windows and Linux/Unix servers.**

The Time Synchronization check procedure contacts *every* server known to this server's local database and looks up information about DS (such as the version of DS.NLM), time synchronization status, and server status. The retrieved data is displayed on the screen (see Figure 7.5) and recorded to the log file as a table.

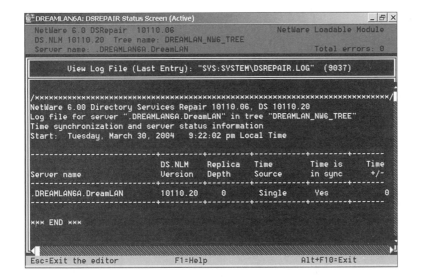

FIGURE 7.5
Sample time syn-
chronization
check report.

TIP

When performing a time synchronization check, it should be from a server that holds a copy of [Root] because that server knows of all servers in the tree and the check contacts only servers known to the local server.

The table shows the following information:

- **Server name**—This field shows the *absolute* distinguished name of the server responding to the query. For NetWare 5 and higher, including non-NetWare eDirectory servers, DSRepair reports the server names with a leading period (for example, .DREAMLAN6A.DreamLAN), whereas NetWare 4's shows the server names without the leading period.

- **DS.NLM version (DS Version on non-NetWare servers)**—This field lists the version of DS that's running on the reporting server. This is useful in determining, at a glance, the versions of DS you have running on your tree.

- **Replica depth**—This entry shows a -1 if the reporting server holds no replica. A 0 indicates the server contains a replica of the [Root] partition (as is the case for server DREAMLAN6A), and a positive integer indicates how many "levels" away from [Root] the first replica is on the reporting server.

NOTE

DSRepair for eDirectory 8.7.1 and 8.7.2 has a cosmetic bug in reporting the correct replica depth on all platforms. For servers holding the Master of [Root], it reports a depth of 5, whereas servers holding a Read/Write of [Root] show a replica depth of 2. This has been fixed in eDirectory 8.7.3.

- **Time source**—The name of this field is misleading. What this field shows is *not* the time source, but rather the time server *type* of the queried server (such as Single Reference, Primary, and so on). The information provided in this field can be useful in determining whether time synchronization has been configured properly. Non-NetWare servers *always* report a time source of Secondary.

- **Time is in sync**—A Yes here indicates the reporting server's time is in synchronization with the network time. A No status means either the reporting server can't communicate with the target server or that the reporting server's time is not in agreement with the network time.

NOTE

If a server reports time not in sync for a short period of time (perhaps 24 hours), there's nothing to worry about because the server's internal clock generally does not drift significantly. You should, however, determine and resolve this problem at your earliest convenience. All servers in the tree must be time-synchronized because DS can't otherwise resolve synchronization collisions properly, which can lead to DS data inconsistency.

▶ **Time +/-** —This field reports the time difference between the server running DSRepair and the queried server. With time sync working correctly and no network communication errors, all servers should be, by default, within 2 seconds of each other. (This threshold is determined by the NetWare `SET Timesync Synchronization Radius server` console command whose default value is 2000 milliseconds; this setting can be increased if you have slow WAN links, such as satellite hops.) This field reports up to 999 minutes and 59 seconds, or approximately 16.5 hours, in the form *MINUTES:SECONDS*. If the time difference is greater than that, the maximum value is displayed as `999:59`.

TIP

If you have non-NetWare eDirectory servers in the tree, you should periodically check the operation and status of your NTP server using a utility such as ntpq (`www.eecis.udel.edu/~mills/ntp/html/ntpq.html`). For more information, visit `www.eecis.udel.edu/~mills/ntp/html/debug.html`.

The Report Synchronization Status process checks the synchronization status by examining the Sync Up to attribute of the partition root object of all partitions that have a replica stored on the local server. Each server in the replica ring is queried and any errors found are displayed (see Figure 7.6) and logged to the DSRepair log file.

In the log file, each partition has its own section. The section starts with the name of the partition and ends with `All servers synchronized up to time`. This is the time stamp according to the Master replica of that partition and is not an average of all reported sync-up-to times for that replica ring. The sample in Figure 7.6 shows two partitions, `[Root]` and `name_example`. Below each partition name, each replica known to the local server is identified by a server name. The key thing to note here is that a synchronization status is available only for the servers that hold replicas according to this local database.

FIGURE 7.6
Sample replica
synchronization
status report.

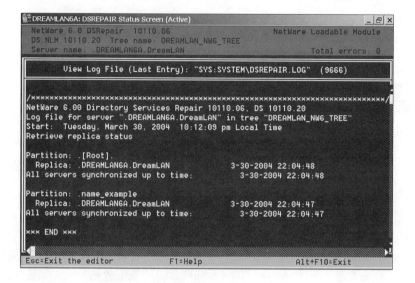

```
DREAMLAN6A: DSREPAIR Status Screen (Active)                    _ 🗗 ✕
NetWare 6.0 DSRepair   10110.06                NetWare Loadable Module
DS.NLM 10110.20  Tree name: DREAMLAN_NW6_TREE
Server name: .DREAMLAN6A.DreamLAN                      Total errors: 0

        View Log File (Last Entry): "SYS:SYSTEM\DSREPAIR.LOG"   (9666)

/*********************************************************************/
NetWare 6.00 Directory Services Repair 10110.06, DS 10110.20
Log file for server ".DREAMLAN6A.DreamLAN" in tree "DREAMLAN_NW6_TREE"
Start: Tuesday, March 30, 2004  10:12:09 pm Local Time
Retrieve replica status

Partition: .[Root].
  Replica: .DREAMLAN6A.DreamLAN            3-30-2004 22:04:48
All servers synchronized up to time:       3-30-2004 22:04:48

Partition: .name_example
  Replica: .DREAMLAN6A.DreamLAN            3-30-2004 22:04:47
All servers synchronized up to time:       3-30-2004 22:04:47

*** END ***

Esc=Exit the editor         F1=Help              Alt+F10=Exit
```

TIP

By comparing the status reports of all servers within the replica ring, you can easily determine the consistency of the ring. For example, each server in the replica ring should report the same number of replicas (regardless of the replica type, including SubRefs) for a particular partition.

To the right of each replica entry, one of the two following is displayed:

▶ The date and time of the last successful synchronization

▶ The date and time of the last successful synchronization with an error code (such as -625) and a designation of whether the error was local or remote to the server in question

The following is an example of a replica synchronization report that contains some errors:

```
Partition: .O=XYZCorp.
  Replica: CN=NETWARE6-D.OU=Consulting.OU=Toro...
➡ 2-09-2004 22:18:46
  Replica: CN=NW65B.OU=Consulting.O=North_...
➡ ******** ********  -625
  Replica: CN=NETWARE51-C.OU=Toronto.O=North_...
➡ 2-09-2004 22:17:41
    Server: CN=NW65B.OU=Consulting.O=North...
➡ 2-09-2004 22:10:05  -621 Remote

All servers synchronized up to time:      2-09-2004
➡22:17:41
```

In this example, three servers are in the replica ring: NW65B, NETWARE51-C, and NETWARE6-D. The first error suggests that the local server isn't able to obtain a replica synchronization status from the NW65B server and an error (-625) is returned. Error -625 indicates some kind of communication error. The second error means that server NETWARE51-C last successfully synchronized at 22:17:41 and failed to synchronize at 22:10:05 with the replica stored on server NW65B due to error -621. Error -621 means TTS is disabled. This could be a result of the SYS volume being out of disk space or SYS volume being dismounted. Combined with the -625 error when the synchronization check is performed, chances are good that there was a problem with NW65B's SYS volume and the server has been taken down, thus the -625 error.

Use the View Report Log File option to examine the DSRepair log file without having to first exit DSRepair. Through the Log file and login configuration option in the Advanced options menu, you can disable the logging, enable the logging, delete the log file, change the name of the log file, or change the location in which the log file is to be stored. When viewing the log file using this option, you start with the beginning of the file; when an operation—such as a time synchronization check—is completed, the most recent entry (which contains information from the operation that was just performed) of the log file is displayed instead.

NOTE

Whenever any DSRepair operation is performed, new information is appended to the log file. You should keep track of the size of this log file because it can quickly grow in size to many megabytes. The size of the file is displayed in parenthesis at the end of the log file title line.

TIP

On NetWare, you can use the -L command-line switch to specify an alternative directory path and filename for the log file (for example, -L SYS:LOGFILES\ DS.LOG). The specified path can be any NetWare volume or DOS drive. You can also use --RL in place of -L to cause the existing file to be overwritten instead of new data being appended.

For Linux/Unix, use the -F option to specify an alternative output filename.

For Windows, select File, Log File Options to change the name and location of the log file.

The Advanced Options menu should be selected when you need to perform specific repair or diagnostic operations. This menu option allows you to manually control a number of individual repair operations and global repair functions in the DS tree. Also available from this choice is diagnostic information about the local DS database and the overall status of your DS tree. The Advanced Options menu in NetWare 5 and above versions of DSRepair provides the following additional selections (see Figure 7.7):

- ▶ **Log File and Login Configuration**—Configure options for the DSRepair log file (such as enabling or disabling logging and setting the log file's size limit). Also you can use this option to log in to the Directory Services tree that is required by some operations (the login is valid only for the duration when DSRepair is running; the login name and password are not stored for later use).

- ▶ **Repair Local DS Database**—Repairs the Directory Services database files stored on this server.

- ▶ **Servers Known to This Database**—Performs verification operations on servers that are known to this database: time synchronization, network addresses, and server status check.

- ▶ **Replica and Partition Operations**—This selection provides functions to repair replicas, replica rings, and server objects. It also dynamically displays each server's last synchronization time.

- ▶ **Check Volume Objects and Trustees**—Performs checks on all mounted volumes for valid Volume objects and valid trustees on the volumes.

- ▶ **Check External References**—Checks for illegal external references or stuck obituaries.

- ▶ **Security Equivalence Synchronization**—Allows you to synchronize security equivalence attributes throughout the global tree. (This option is available only on servers running NDS v6 or NDS v7.)

- ▶ **Global Schema Operations**—Provides functions to update the schema in the tree.

- ▶ **View Repair Log File**—Views the log file that is optionally created when repair operations are performed.

- ▶ **NDS Archive Options**—This option copies the Directory Services database files into a single file in a compressed format that is to be used for offline repairs and diagnostics by Novell Technical Support. *This option is not meant to be a backup method for your DS database.*

We'll briefly discuss each of these functions and highlight some of their more salient features. You'll find examples of their application in later chapters.

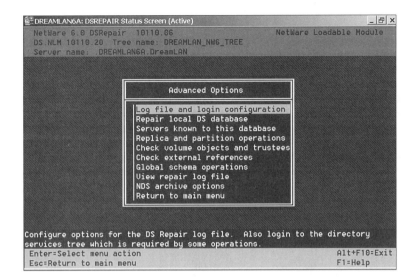

FIGURE 7.7
DSRepair's
Advanced
Options menu.

The Repair Local Database function (see Figure 7.8) works with the DS files stored on the local server and is analogous to running Bindfix in the NetWare 3 environment. You can control the following repair options:

▶ **Validate Mail Directories and Stream Files**—Select Yes to check the mail directories on volume **SYS** for users who no longer exist and deletes those directories. The option also verifies that the stream files are associated with valid DS objects and delete those that are not. (A *stream file* is a file containing a series of data bytes. An example of a stream file is the login script associated with a User object.) The default is Yes.

▶ **Check Local References**—Select Yes to check local reference properties to ensure they are valid and to check for duplicate time stamps. Using this option slows down the repair process. The default is Yes.

▶ **Rebuild Operational Schema**—Select Yes to check the schema for valid object class and attribute definitions. DSRepair rebuilds any invalid classes or attributes found in the predefined (base) schema on this server. You generally need not enable this option unless your server's schema is corrupted; it has no effect on extended schema definitions. The default is No.

▶ **Maintain Original Unrepaired Database**—Select Yes to the backup files before the repair. These files can help recover a damaged database, but they take up disk space. The default is No.

> **NOTE**
>
> All repairs are performed on a temporary copy of the DS database files, which are renamed at the end when you commit to save the database on which repairs have been made. With the Maintain Original Unrepaired Database option enabled, when DSRepair saves the changed database, it renames the previous database files to a `.OLD` extension and the temporary files (which have a `.TMP` extension) are renamed to the appropriate names. See Chapter 3, "The Directory Information Base," for naming conventions for a given version of NDS/eDirectory. One important note is that the `.OLD` files are not preserved if a `.OLD` file set exists that is less than 72 hours old. This is to provide some reference point to go back to if you run into trouble while running multiple DSRepairs within 72 hours.

> ► **Exit Automatically upon Completion**—Select Yes to immediately exit DSRepair and open the local Directory Services database files after completing the repairs. The default is No.

FIGURE 7.8
Repair local database options.

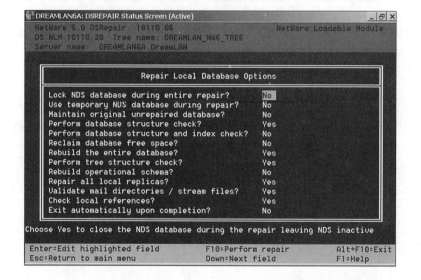

If the server is running NDS 8 or eDirectory, additional options are available. Some of these extra options deal with DIB size management and database integrity checks. The one nice feature of NDS 8 and above is that you can leave the DS database open during a repair operation to avoid preventing users from authenticating to the server.

> **NOTE**
>
> Due to the architectural differences in the DS database between NDS 6/7 and NDS 8/eDirectory, you need to be running the correct version of DSRepair for the version of DS running on the server. Otherwise, DSRepair reports an `API version mismatch` error and exits.

During the repair operation, DSRepair performs an extensive analysis of the database. It checks for invalid partitions and partition roots and fixes any errors found. For each partition, it checks all objects in the partition for valid containment and consistency with the schema. All illegal attributes are removed. DSRepair changes any object that is missing a mandatory attribute (such as a User object missing the Last Name attribute) to Unknown. It checks all attribute syntaxes for consistency and also checks for invalid checksum and links in the database records.

Like running VRepair, you should continue running DSRepair until it reports no   **TIP**
more errors. You might need to run DSRepair multiple times until you get zero
errors.

From our experience, a typical DSRepair operation for a Pentium P-4 2GHz server,   **NOTE**
with a moderately fast SCSI drive (not RAID-5) and 10,000 objects in the local
replicas, takes less than 5 minutes to perform a local database repair.

The Unattended Full Repair option in the main DSRepair menu executes all the previously mentioned checks and repairs using the default parameter settings.

The Servers Known to This Database option lists all the servers known to the local DS database. The server names are obtained from the NCP Server objects found in the replicas stored on the server, and they are *not* learned through Service Advertising Protocol (SAP) or Service Locator Protocol (SLP). If this server holds a replica of [Root], this list most likely contains all the servers in the tree. If, however, the server doesn't contain a replica of [Root], the list is a subset of the servers in the DS tree.

On Linux/Unix, type ndsrepair -N to get a list of servers known to this database.   **TIP**

The Servers Known to This Database shows the Local Status and Local ID for each server in the list (see Figure 7.9). The Local Status field reports the state of the listed server as known to this server. If the state is Up, it is active; if it is Down, some sort of communication problem has recently occurred. Upon selecting a server from the list, several options become available:

▶ **Time Synchronization and Server Status**—This option performs the same task as the Time Synchronization option found in the main DSRepair menu.

▶ **Repair All Network Addresses**—For each of the listed servers, DSRepair compares the server's network address found in the SAP table with that found in the local DS database. If they are different, the entries in the DS database are updated with the value from the SAP table. If DSRepair can't find the server in the SAP table, no repair is made.

▶ **Repair Selected Server's Network Address**—This operation is identical to the Repair All Network Addresses function, except that only the selected server's network address is checked and repaired.

▶ **View Entire Server Name**—The DSRepair log file and status screen shows only the first 35 characters in a server name. Use this option to verify the entire distinguished name, which can be as long as 256 bytes.

FIGURE 7.9
List of servers known to the local database.

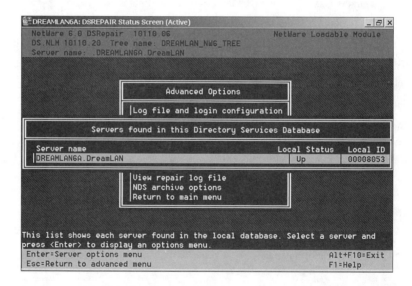

The Replica and Partition Operation function is probably the most powerful of all DSRepair options because you can "kill off" (destroy) a replica just as easily as you can repair one. The initial opening screen of this option displays a list of all replicas stored on the local server. A table shows each replica along with its replica type (Master, Read/Write, Read-Only, and so on) and replica state (On or Off) as it is stored on this server. After selecting a replica to work with, a list of replica-related functions is displayed (see Figure 7.10). Chapter 11, "Examples from the Real World," discusses the uses of these functions.

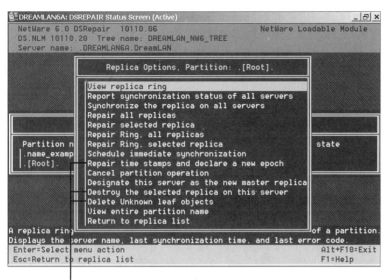

FIGURE 7.10
Replica and
Partition Options
menu.

These options are activated only when you load
DSRepair with the -A command-line switch

TIP

To protect you from inadvertently exercising some of the more destructive options in DSRepair, such as editing a replica ring or repairing time stamps and declaring a new time epoch, these options are not automatically listed in the Advanced Options menu. You need to start DSRepair with the -A switch to toggle these special options on for selection. On Windows servers, put the --A option in the Startup Parameters edit box before starting `dsrepair.dlm`. On Linux/Unix servers, use `ndsrepair -P -Ad`; or if you are using the wrapper, select Option #6 on the main menu to toggle the options on or off.

The Check Volume Objects and Trustees option (not included on Windows and Linux/Unix versions) checks the association of all mounted volumes (including CD-ROM volumes and those mounted through NFS) on the current server with volume objects in the tree. If DSRepair doesn't find a matching volume object for a given mounted volume, one is created. After the associations between the volumes and its objects are verified, file system trustee assignments for that volume are verified.

The Check External References option validates all entries found in the External Reference partition and attempts to locate a backlink for each entry. This operation also displays obituary information for all obituaries contained in the local database (if the -A startup option was used). You'll learn in Chapter 11 how to apply this information for troubleshooting obituary problems.

The functionality of global schema operations changed somewhat between NetWare 4's and later versions of DSRepair. In the NetWare 4 versions, this option can update the operational (base) schema on all servers within the tree or on only the root server—the *root* server is the server that contains the master of [Root]. You can also use this option to import schema definitions (including extensions) from a remote tree so that the schemas for both trees are identical prior to a tree merge. If the -A switch was used to start the utility, you have the additional option to update the schemas on all NetWare 4.0x servers within the current tree as well as to declare a new epoch on the schema.

WARNING   Declaring a new schema epoch causes the server holding the master of [Root] to time stamp the schema and resend it to all servers in the tree. You should use extreme caution when using this option. If the schema is bad and you force it to be sent, you will corrupt the tree. This can also generate a lot of traffic on the wire. Furthermore, if the receiving server contains a schema that was not in the new epoch, objects and attributes that use the schema are changed to the Unknown object class or attribute.

The Global Schema Operations option in post-NetWare 4's version of DSRepair performs the following tasks (see Figure 7.11):

▶ **Request Schema from Tree**—Update this server's schema by synchronizing once from the server holding the master of [Root].

▶ **Import Remote Schema**—Import schema from a remote tree. This is a helpful process when trying to merge trees.

▶ **Declare a New Epoch**—This option is available only when the -A option is specified. See the previous warning for more information about this option.

▶ **Reset Local Schema**—Resets the local schema by requesting a complete copy of the schema from the server holding the master of [Root]. After the local server receives the schema updates, it removes any additional schema it has that did not get updated. As a result, any objects and attributes that used the old schema are changed to the Unknown object class or attribute.

▶ **Post NetWare 5 Schema Update**—This option extends and modifies the schema for compatibility with Post NetWare 5 DS changes. This option requires that the local server contain a replica of the [Root] partition and that the state of the replica be in the On state.

▶ **Optional Schema Enhancements**—This option extends and modifies the schema to provide the ability for domain (dc) objects to contain container objects such as Country, Locality, Organization, or Organizational Unit. This option requires that the local server contain a replica of the [Root] partition and that the state of the replica be in the On state.

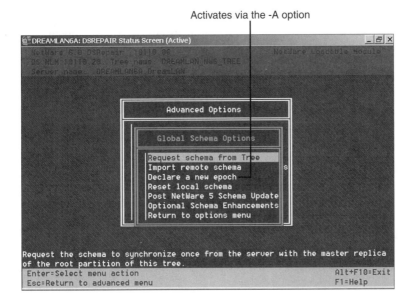

Activates via the -A option

FIGURE 7.11
Global schema options.

The NDS Archive options allow you to take a snapshot copy of the server's DIB set. The snapshot stores the data in a compressed format that can be used by Novell Technical Support for offline diagnostics and repair purposes. You should, however, not use this option as a means to back up your DS because DSRepair doesn't have an option to restore the component files of this dump file. See Chapter 8, "eDirectory Data Recovery Tools," for DS backup and restore options.

Table 7.1 is a summary of documented (meaning they are listed in DSREPAIR.NLM -?) DSRepair command-line switches and some more commonly known and used undocumented switches. Because some of these switches are undocumented, Novell might change their availability and functions without any notice. Not all switches available for DSREPAIR.NLM are supported on the Windows or Linux/Unix versions of DSRepair.

TABLE 7.1   DSRepair Command-Line Switches

Switch	Documented	Description
NetWare: -A Windows: -A Linux/Unix: -P -Ad or -S -Ad	No	Enables the advanced mode for DSRepair.
NetWare: -CV### Windows: N/A Linux/Unix: N/A	No	Reports entries whose attribute has more than ### values. Useful for tracking down the possible cause of DS high utilization. (For NDS 7 only; for NDS 8 and eDirectory, use DSBrowse instead.) See the "DSBrowse" section later in this chapter for more details about this option.
NetWare: -D <DIB extension> Windows: N/A Linux/Unix: N/A	No	Repair the DIB with extension <DIB extension>. Defaults to .NDS if not specified. The .NDS DIB is always closed and locked regardless of the DIB being repaired. Need to perform a local database repair.
NetWare: -L <filename> Windows: File > Log File Options Linux/Unix: -F <filename> -A yes	Yes	Specifies an alternative directory path and filename for the log file (for example, -L SYS:LOGFILES\DS.LOG). The path can be any NetWare volume or DOS drive, but the path and filename must be in DOS 8.3 format.
NetWare: -M Windows: N/A Linux/Unix: N/A	No	Report Move Inhibit obituaries. This is used to discover whether a move has completed or whether a partition is reported as busy because Move Inhibit obituaries are in a replica that have either not completed processing or are broken. A better way of finding obituaries is to use DSRepair -A, Advanced Menu, Check External References.

Table 7.1   Continued

Switch	Documented	Description
NetWare: -N <integer> Windows: N/A Linux/Unix: N/A	No	Specifies the number of days from which you want to purge the Network Address attribute values on a User class object (for example, -N 4 for four days). The default is 60. Need to perform a local database repair.
NetWare: -NLC Windows: N/A Linux/Unix: N/A	No	Purges all values in the NLS:Cert Peak Used Pool attribute of a NLS:License ID=SN:xxxxxx object. Usage is LOAD DSREPAIR.NLM -NLC, Advance options, Repair local DS database; keep all default settings. The DSREPAIR.NLM version has to be 5.29 or above for the switch to be supported; it's not applicable to eDirectory versions.
NetWare: -OT Windows: N/A Linux/Unix: N/A	No	Re-timestamps all obituaries to help process stuck obits. Usage is LOAD DSREPAIR.NLM -OT, Advance options, Repair local DS database; keep all default settings. The details of this switch and required DSREPAIR.NLM version can be found at TID #10062149; refer to TID #10079607 for time stamping a single obit object. The -OT switch should be used only in obituary cases where obituaries have stopped processing, even after rectifying a communication issue with another server in the obituary process. Note that this switch has no effect on INHIBIT_MOVE obituaries, but they might be removed using iMonitor (see the "Novell iManager" section later in this chapter).
NetWare: -P Windows: -P Linux/Unix: N/A	No	Marks all Unknown class objects as Referenced (so they are not synchronized between replicas). Need to perform a local database repair.

Table 7.1 Continued

Switch	Documented	Description
NetWare: -RC *<filename>* Windows: RC *<filename>* Linux/Unix: N/A	No	Creates a DIB dump file followed by an optional dump file name (for example, -RC SYS:BACKUP\SAVE.DIB); the default is SYS:SYSTEM\DSREPAIR.DIB for NDS 6 and NDS 7. For NDS 8 and higher, the default is the file is located in SYS:SYSTEM\ DSR_DIB and is called *xxxxxxxx*.$DU, where *x* is a hex value for the file. The first 100MB of the DIB is copied to 00000000.$DU, the next 100MB into 00000001.$DU, and so on. Exits DSRepair when finished.
NetWare: -RD Windows: -RD Linux/Unix: -R	No	Allows for an automated repair of the local database. Exits DSRepair when finished.
NetWare: -RI Windows: -RI Linux/Unix: N/A	No	Verifies remote server IDs. Exits DSRepair when finished.
NetWare: -RL *<filename>* Windows: File > Log File Options Linux/Unix: -F *<filename>* -A no	No	Specifies an alternative directory path and filename for the log file (for example, -RL SYS:LOGFILES\DS.LOG). The path can be any NetWare volume or DOS drive, but the path and filename must be in DOS 8.3 format. Unlike the -L option, the existing file is overwritten instead of being appended to.
NetWare: -RM *<partition root ID>* Windows: -RM *<partition root ID>* Linux/Unix: N/A	No	Set this server as the master in the replica ring of the specified replica (based on the partition root ID). Exits DSRepair when finished. Must specify any leading zeroes in the ID.
NetWare: -RN Windows: -RN Linux/Unix: N/A	No	Repairs network addresses. Exits DSRepair when finished.

Table 7.1 Continued

Switch	Documented	Description
NetWare: -RR *<partition root ID>* Windows: -RR *<partition root ID>* Linux/Unix: N/A	No	Repairs the specified replica (based on the partition root ID). Exits DSRepair when finished. Must specify any leading zeroes in the ID.
NetWare: -RV Windows: N/A Linux/Unix: N/A	No	Repairs volume objects. Exits DSRepair when finished.
NetWare: -RVT Windows: N/A Linux/Unix: N/A	No	Repairs volume objects and trustees. Exits DSRepair when finished.
NetWare: -SI Windows: N/A Linux/Unix: N/A	No	Repairs replica numbers on partition objects. Exits DSRepair when finished. This option is not available for eDirectory 8.5 or below.
NetWare: -SR Windows: N/A Linux/Unix: N/A	No	Requests a local schema switch. Exits DSRepair when finished. This option is not available for eDirectory 8.5 or below; instead you can use Advanced Options Menu, Global Schema Operations, Reset Local Schema.
NetWare: -U Windows: -U Linux/Unix: -U	Yes	Performs an unattended full repair. Exits DSRepair when finished.
NetWare: -WM Windows: N/A Linux/Unix: N/A	No	Purges all values in the WM:Registered Workstation attribute of all container objects associated with ZENworks. Usage is LOAD DSREPAIR.NLM -WM, Advance options, Repair local DS database, and keep all default settings. The DSREPAIR.NLM version has to be 4.69 (NDS 6), 5.24 (NDS 7), 7.26 (NDS 8 and eDirectory) or above for the switch to be supported.

NOTE **Many of the DSRepair command-line switches (such as** -RC**) on Windows servers cause** dsrepair.dlm ***not*** **to display its dialog box after clicking Start. Instead, it just quietly performs the task and then exits.**

Other switches, known affectionately as *killer* switches (-K*x* or -XK*x*, such as -K2 or --XK2), can be used in DSRepair to fix stubborn DS issues. These switches are not listed in Table 7.1 because inappropriate use of these killer switches could result in serious damage to parts of or your entire DS tree. The one possible safe killer switch, if you can call it that, is -XK3. This switch is used to fix broken backlinks on external referenced objects. Some of the symptoms of this problem are

▶ Local DS on a server does not hold a real copy of an object and is getting errors trying to access said object.

▶ DSRepair reports a -626 error when checking external referenced object IDs.

▶ After removing a replica, users cannot log in to the server.

▶ Error -601 is reported on an object. The server reporting the error does not hold a real (master, Read/Write, and so on) replica of the object.

▶ A renamed (#_#) NCP Server object shows on servers that do not hold real copies of the NCP Server object.

▶ Previously deleted objects are showing up in the tree.

The following outlines the procedure for fixing broken backlinks using -XK3 based on your operating system:

NetWare   At the server console, type **LOAD DSREPAIR -XK3**. Select Advanced Options, Repair Local DS Database. Set Check Local References to **Yes**. Press F10 to start the repair. This goes through all the server's backlink attribute time stamps and sets them to zero. Save the repaired database and exit from DSRepair completely. Run the Backlinker process to rebuild the backlinks:

```
SET DSTRACE=ON

SET DSTRACE=NODEBUG

SET DSTRACE=+BLINK

SET DSTRACE=*B
```

Windows	From NDSCons, highlight `dsrepair.dlm`. Enter **-XK3** in the Startup Parameters field and click Start. Click Repair in the menu and select Local Database Repair. Make sure Check Local References is checked and then start the repair.
	To start the backlink process, do the following:
	From NDSCons, highlight `dstrace.dlm` and then click Start. Click Edit in the menu and select Options. Uncheck everything except the Backlinker and Backlinker Detail filters. Click OK. Go back to NDSCons and highlight `ds.dlm`; then click Configure. Go to the Triggers tab and click Backlinker.
Linux/Unix	Run `ndsrepair -R -Ad -XK3`. Then execute ndstrace and enter **set dstrace=on, set dstrace=+blnk;** then enter **set dstrace = *b.**

The `SET DSTRACE=*B` command kicks off the backlinker process that reestablishes the backlinks and updates the time stamps on those objects that are still valid. Those that are not updated are purged the next time the Janitor and Flat Cleaner processes run.

WARNING

Unless directly instructed by Novell Technical Support, avoid using the DSRepair killer switches. Additionally, the advanced maintenance options should be enabled only for specific repair tasks. Ensure time is in sync before using any of the -A **or** -XKx **options.**

NOTE

There have been varying opinions about how often to run the repair options in DSRepair (such as Unattended full repair). From our experience, you don't need to (and shouldn't, as a matter of fact) exercise the repair functions in DSRepair on a daily or even weekly basis as part of your regular network maintenance.

The repair features in DSRepair are not meant to be day-to-day management tools nor are they intended for health checking. Rather, they are to be used as precise surgical scalpels to address specific problems. Running DSRepair on a quarterly basis is more than sufficient under normal circumstances, and even then, only after a large number of changes has been made to your tree.

DSTrace

DSTrace was originally a troubleshooting aid built in to `DS.NLM` by Novell's NDS Engineering Team to help in the development and debugging processes. It has since been made known to all that such a tool is available for diagnosing DS synchronization problems, and it has been enhanced into a standard troubleshooting tool. Because of its origin as an engineering tool, DSTrace can sometimes display a lot of obscure information that is difficult to interpret.

In the NetWare 4 context, DSTrace really referred to a group of SET commands available at the server console, although DSTrace was often referred to as a *utility*. NetWare 5 and later, however, have two DSTrace utilities. One is the built-in version in DS.NLM; the other is a DSTRACE.NLM utility that provides expanded monitoring capabilities compared to its predecessor. After DSTrace is activated (either the built-in version or the NLM one), you can use it to monitor synchronization status and errors. DSTrace is primarily used to determine and track the health of DS as it communicates with other NetWare servers in the network.

The user interface of DSTrace varies a little depending on the operating system. Use one of the following methods to enable DSTrace:

▶ **NetWare 4**—At the server console, type **SET DSTRACE=ON**. This creates a new screen called Directory Services.

▶ **NetWare 5 and higher**—To enable the built-in version, at the server console, type **SET DSTRACE=ON**. This creates a new screen called Directory Services. To use the expanded version, at the server console, type **LOAD DSTRACE**. This creates a new screen called DSTrace Console.

▶ **Windows**—From NDSCons, highlight dstrace.dlm and click Start.

▶ **Linux/Unix**—At a terminal screen, type **ndstrace**. Type **exit** to shut down ndstrace.

On a NetWare 5 and higher server, after DSTrace NLM is enabled, you can type **HELP DSTRACE** to display a list of options as shown here:

```
DSTRACE - Novell Directory Services Trace Event Monitor.

  USAGE: DSTRACE {Options}

  Options:
     {taglist}            List of qualified event tags.
     ON                   Enable tracing to target device.
     OFF                  Disable tracing to target device.
     FILE                 Change command target to log file.
     SCREEN               Change command target to trace
⇒screen.
     INLINE               Display events inline.
     JOURNAL              Display events on a background
⇒thread.
     FMAX={size}          Specify maximum disk file size.
     FNAME={name}         Specify disk file name.
```

```
Examples:
   DSTRACE INLINE
   DSTRACE SCREEN ON +AL +CB -FR
   DSTRACE FMAX=10240 FNAME=DBTRACE.LOG

Notes:
   All event type tags and keywords (except DSTRACE) may be
   shortened. To display the current configuration and a
   list of event tag names, enter 'DSTRACE' with no options.
   The default tag qualifier is '+'.
```

After DSTrace NLM is loaded and you have enabled its tracing (using the **DSTRACE SCREEN ON** command), an alternative console screen is created—called DSTrace Console—where DS event information is displayed. You can specify what type of information you would like DSTrace to display. You can select a wide variety of information to view by specifying the DSTrace command followed by a filter list. The list of possible filters and their current settings is displayed by typing **DSTRACE** at the console. Figure 7.12 shows a sample of that screen.

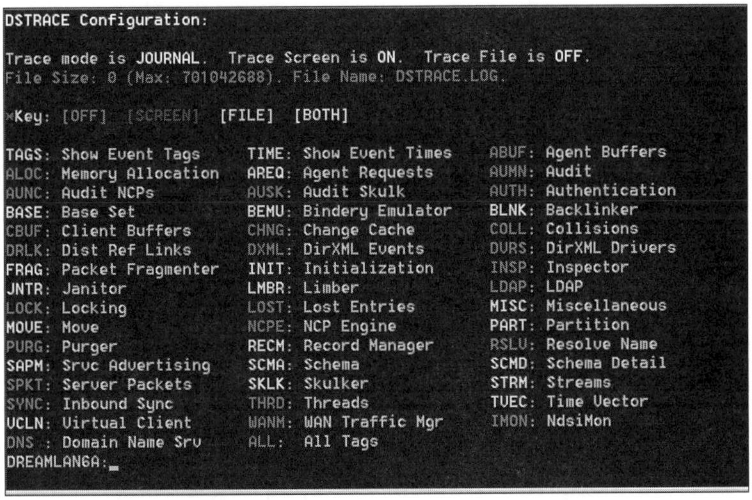

FIGURE 7.12
DSTRACE.NLM menu screen.

The status of each filter (enabled or disabled) is denoted by a different color:

- ▶ **Dimmed**—The filter is disabled.
- ▶ **Blue**—The information associated with this filter is displayed to the console screen only.

▶ **Green**—The information associated with this filter is recorded to the log file only.

▶ **Cyan**—The information associated with this filter is displayed to the console screen *and* is also recorded in the log file.

To enable a filter, you simply type **DSTRACE** at the server console followed by the filter name or item you want to view. If you specified the filter without specifying a + (to enable) or - (to disable) in front of the filter name, a + is assumed. Therefore, **DSTRACE +SYNC** is the same as **DSTRACE SYNC**. When a filter name is specified without qualifying it with either **SCREEN** or **FILE**, the action is applied to both devices. That means **DSTRACE +SYNC** enables the display of inbound synchronization information on the trace screen as well the data recorded in the log file; **DSTRACE FILE -SYNC** turns off the recording of inbound sync data to the log file.

> **TIP**
>
> **You can usually abbreviate the filter names to just the first two letters (sometimes three in order to keep it unique) of the name. For example, you can use either** DSTRACE -SKLK **or** DSTRACE -SK.

On Windows, upon `dstrace.dlm` startup, the trace status screen is displayed. To access the filter options (see Figure 7.13), select Edit, Options. The user interface for DSTrace on Linux/Unix looks similar to that on NetWare. Upon `ndstrace` startup, it automatically displays the current filter settings, as shown in Figure 7.14, in the trace status screen. Commands are entered on the last line of the screen while the rest of the screen scrolls to display new information.

If you work with NetWare 4 servers, the procedures for enabling the DSTrace screen and setting the filters are slightly different than what was described previously. In NetWare 4, you must use **SET** commands exclusively when working with DSTrace; there is no menu interface. The following commands start and stop DSTrace and its file logging function on a NetWare 4 server:

▶ **SET DSTRACE=ON**—Activates the trace screen

▶ **SET DSTRACE=OFF**—Deactivates the trace screen

▶ **SET TTF=ON**—Enables the recording of DSTrace information to the log file, SYS:SYSTEM\DSTRACE.DBG

▶ **SET TTF=OFF**—Closes the DSTrace log file so it can be viewed

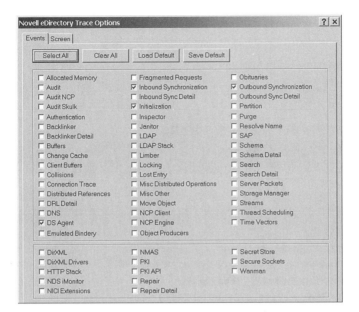

FIGURE 7.13
DSTrace option
selection on
Windows servers.

FIGURE 7.14
ndstrace screen
on Linux/Unix
servers.

NOTE

All the SET DSTRACE and SET TTF **commands also work on NetWare 5 and**
higher servers because they are built in to DS.NLM **regardless of whether it is**
NDS 6, 7, 8, or eDirectory.

WARNING

You should not leave the TTF (Trace To File) function running unattended. Due to
the amount of information DSTrace collects, the DSTRACE.DBG **file can become**
very large very quickly and could fill up your SYS **volume in a matter of hours or**
days.

In general, the DSTrace screen shows five main things about each partition that exists on the server where you run the command:

▶ The name of the partition

▶ The name of the server with which the synchronization is being performed

▶ The state and type of the partition

▶ The DS process currently taking place

▶ Whether the process completed successfully

The following is a sample of the DSTrace output, with these five items highlighted in bold:

```
[2004/02/18 22:04:01] Sync - using version 6 on server
➥ <.NETWARE65-A.East.XYZCorp.EDIR873>.
[2004/02/18 22:04:01] Sending to  ---->
➥ .NETWARE65-A.East.XYZCorp.EDIR873
[2004/02/18 22:04:01] Sync - sending updates to server
➥ <.NETWARE65-A.East.XYZCorp.EDIR873>.
[2004/02/18 22:04:01] Start outbound sync from change cache
➥ with (1) <.NETWARE65-.East.XYZCorp.EDIR873>
➥ state:0 type:1
[2004/02/18 22:04:01] Sync - [1c0000c6]
➥ <.West.XYZCorp.EDIR873.> [2003/11/29 0:22:13, 1, 1].
[2004/02/18 22:04:01] 2004/02/18 22:04:01 * SchemaPurger
➥ processing deleted classes.
[2004/02/18 22:04:01] End sync out to
➥ .NETWARE65-A.East.XYZCorp.EDIR873 from change cache,
➥ rep:1 state:0 type:1, success
[2004/02/18 22:04:01] Sync - Process: Send updates to
➥ <.NETWARE65-A.East.XYZCorp.EDIR873> succeeded.
[2004/02/18 22:04:01] 2004/02/18 22:04:01 * SchemaPurger
➥ processing deleted attributes.
[2004/02/18 22:04:01] SkulkPartition for .West.XYZCorp.EDIR873.
➥ succeeded.
[2004/02/18 22:04:01] Sync - Partition .West.XYZCorp.EDIR873.
➥ All processed = YES
[2004/02/18 22:04:01] All processed = YES.
[2004/02/18 22:04:14] Start updating inherited ACLs...
[2004/02/18 22:04:14] Update inherited ACLs succeeded.
```

The example shows that an outbound sync for partition `West.XYZCorp` occurred and is targeted at server NETWARE65-A.East.XYZCorp. The replica on NETWARE65-A is On (state 0) and has a Read/Write (type 1) replica of the partition in question. The sync process was successful.

To assist you in noticing error messages among the vast amount of data displayed on the DSTrace screen, key information and error codes are shown in color to help them stand out from the other information. For example, `DSTRACE.NLM` (and `dstrace.dlm` and `ndstrace`) displays partition and server names in blue, whereas the success and `All processed=YES` messages (actually just the word `YES`) are in green; errors are shown in red. Not all problems show up as color-coded, but in most cases the colors do help you sort through the massive amount of information.

DSTrace has a number of `SET` commands you can use to manipulate the display to show you more or less information about the various DS processes. There are also commands to initiate certain synchronization processes, such as limber, and for tuning certain DS parameters on the server. These DSTrace `SET` commands can be divided into four groups: basic functions (such as starting and stopping DSTrace), setting filters, initiating DS background processes, and tuning parameters (server-centric).

DSTrace `SET` commands are not case sensitive, even on the Linux/Unix platforms. **NOTE**

The DSTrace `SET` commands (`SET DSTRACE=command`) that control the basic functions include the following:

- ► **ON**—Starts the DS trace screen with basic trace messages.

- ► **OFF**—Disables the trace screen.

- ► **ALL**—Starts the DS trace screen with all the trace messages.

- ► **AGENT**—Starts the DS trace screen with the trace messages that are equivalent to the `ON`, `BACKLINK`, `DSAGENT`, `JANITOR`, `RESNAME`, and `VCLIENT` flags.

- ► **CHECKSUM**—Enables Transport Dependent Checksumming (TDC). This is useful in IPX networks where routers fragment and rebuild data packets. This option ensures data integrity of the reassembled packets. (This option is not supported if you're using ETHERNET_802.3 frame type.)

- ► **NOCHECKSUM**—Disables TDC.

▶ **DEBUG**—Turns on a predefined set of trace messages typically used for debugging. The flags set are ON, BACKLINK, ERRORS, EMU, FRAGGER, INIT, INSPECTOR, JANITOR, LIMBER, MISC, PART, RECMAN, REPAIR, SCHEMA, SKULKER, STREAMS, and VCLIENT.

▶ **NODEBUG**—Leaves the trace screen enabled but turns off all debugging messages previously set. It leaves the messages set to the ON command option.

WARNING   The SET DSTRACE=ON command activates the trace screen from DS.NLM (called the Directory Services screen), and the DSTRACE SCREEN ON command activates the trace screen from DSTRACE.NLM (called the DSTrace Console screen). On a NetWare 5 and higher server, you can issue both commands and can end up with *two* trace screens showing the same information—or different information if the filters are set differently.

Table 7.2 provides a list of DSTrace filters. They can be used in place of the filter list available from **DSTRACE.NLM**, with minor exceptions. For example, no corresponding DSTrace **SET** commands exist for WAN Traffic Manager. These filters are turned on by using a + (for example, SET DSTRACE=+BLINK) and off by using a - (for example, SET DSTRACE=-AUTHEN).

TABLE 7.2   **DSTrace Filters**

DSTRACE FILTER	DESCRIPTION
AUDIT	Enables messages and information related to auditing. **Caution:** In many cases, this causes the server to drop into the debugger if auditing encounters an error.
AUTHEN	Enables messages displayed while authenticating connections to the server, by workstations or servers.
BACKLINK (BLINK)	Enables messages related to the verification of backlinks and external references. The backlink process resolves external references to ensure there is a real object in DS. For real DS objects, the backlink process ensures that an external reference exists for each backlink attribute.
BUFFERS	Displays messages associated with the request and reply buffers used by the DSA.
COLLISION (COLL)	Displays messages when duplicate changes are attempted on the same object. Collisions are normal errors in DS.

Table 7.2 Continued

DSTRACE FILTER	DESCRIPTION
DSAGENT (DSA or DSWIRE)	Enables messages relating to inbound client requests and what action is requested.
EMU	Enables messages relating to Bindery Services (emulation).
ERRORS (ERR or E)	Displays error messages to show what the error was and where it came from.
FRAGGER (FRAG)	Enables messages related to the virtual client, which handles the outbound server connections needed to pass DS information.
IN	Displays messages related to inbound synchronization traffic.
INIT	Enables the showing of messages that occur during the process of initializing or opening the local DS database.
INSPECTOR (I)	Displays messages related to the inspector process, which verifies the DS name service and object integrity on the local server. The inspector is part of the janitor process. If errors are detected, it could mean that you need to run DSRepair. Be aware that messages reported by this process might not all be actual errors. For this reason, you need to understand what the messages mean.
JANITOR (J)	Enables messages related to the janitor process. The janitor controls the removal of deleted objects. It also finds the status and version of NCP servers and other miscellaneous record management data.
LIMBER	Displays messages related to the limber process, which verifies tree connectivity by maintaining the server name, address, and replicas. This involves verifying and fixing the server name and server address if it changes.
LOCKING (LOCKS)	Enables messages related to NDS database record-locking information.
MERGE	Displays messages when objects are being merged.
MIN	Enables debug messages at the minimum debug level. (To use this, first type **SET DSTRACE=NODEBUG**; then type **SET DSTRACE=+MIN**.)
MISC	Enables information from miscellaneous processes.

Table 7.2   Continued

DSTRACE FILTER	DESCRIPTION
OUT	Displays messages related to outbound synchronization traffic.
PART	Displays messages related to partitioning operations. This trace filter can be useful for tracking partition operations as they proceed.
RECMAN	Displays messages related to the record manager to track name base transactions, such as rebuilding and verifying the internal hash table and iteration state handling.
REPAIR	Enables messages from the repair process. This filter is rarely used.
RESNAME (RN)	Displays messages related to resolve name requests (tree walking). Resolves the name maps and object names to an ID on a particular server.
SAP	Enables messages related to the Service Advertising Protocol when the tree name is sent via SAP.
SCHEMA	Enables messages related to the schema being modified or synchronized across the network to the other servers.
SKULKER (SYNC or S)	Enables messages related to the synchronization process, which is responsible for synchronizing replicas on the servers with the other replicas on other servers. This is one of the most useful trace flags available.
STREAMS	Enables messages related to the stream attributes information.
TIMEVECTOR (TV)	Enables messages related to the virtual client, which handles the outbound server connections needed to pass DS information.
VCLIENT (VC)	Enables messages related to the virtual client, which handles the outbound server connections needed to pass DS information.

NOTE

Although many of the filter names listed in Table 7.2 are the same as those used in DSTRACE.NLM and ndstrace, some differences do exist. For example, the Backlinker filter for the SET command is BLINK, but for DSTRACE.NLM and ndstrace, the name is BLNK. Therefore, if your environment has NetWare 5 or higher and Linux/Unix servers, it is best to use DSTRACE.NLM on NetWare so you need to remember only one set of filter names.

Table 7.3 lists the various DS background processes (ones that have an asterisk in their names) and DS tuning parameters (ones that have an exclamation mark in their names) that can be manipulated using DSTrace `SET` commands. You can force a specific DS background process to run by using one of the `SET DSTRACE=*option` commands. For instance, to force the Schema Synchronization process to run, use `SET DSTRACE=*SS`. If you have a specific reason to change the default time intervals for an DS process, you can use the `SET DSTRACE=!parameter` command.

DS Background Processes and Tuning Parameters   **TABLE 7.3**

DSTRACE PROCESS OR PARAMETER	DEFAULT VALUE	RANGE	DESCRIPTION
*.	N/A	N/A	Unloads and reloads `DS.NLM` from the `SYS:SYSTEM` directory. The old copy of `DS.NLM` in memory is renamed to `DSOLD.NLM`; the new copy of `DS.NLM` is loaded; and then `DSOLD.NLM` is unloaded. Therefore, for a short period of time, both `DS.NLM` and `DSOLD.NLM` are loaded. This command is extremely useful when you are updating a version of `DS.NLM` and don't want to have to restart the server. You can perform this operation during normal business hours without disrupting users on that server.
*B	N/A	N/A	Forces the backlink process to begin running. Be aware that the backlink process can be traffic intensive, so you should probably wait until a slow time on the network before executing this command.

Table 7.3   Continued

DSTRACE PROCESS OR PARAMETER	DEFAULT VALUE	RANGE	DESCRIPTION
!B *time*	780	2–10,080	Sets the backlink process interval used by DS (in minutes) to check the backlink consistency. This command is the same as the SET NDS Backlink Interval command. If !B is specified without a parameter, the value defaults to 1,500 (or 25 hours).
*C	N/A	N/A	Shows connection table statistics for outbound connection caching or vclients. It's not supported on NetWare 5.
*CI	N/A	N/A	Shows connection table statistics for vclients, including idle time information. It's not supported on NetWare 5 or higher.
*CR	N/A	N/A	Shows connection table statistics for vclients, including routing table packets. It's not supported on NetWare 5.
*CT	N/A	N/A	Shows connection table statistics for vclients, including to which servers this server is connected. It's not supported on NetWare 5 or higher.
*C0 (C-zero)	N/A	N/A	Resets the display of connection table statistics for vclients. Has the same effect as reloading DS.NLM. It's not supported on NetWare 5 or higher.
!C *number*	75	26–100	Sets the maximum sockets threshold, which is the percentage of sockets to use on the server before they're recycled. If !C is specified without a parameter, the value is not changed. It's not supported on NetWare 5 or higher.

Table 7.3   Continued

DSTRACE PROCESS OR PARAMETER	DEFAULT VALUE	RANGE	DESCRIPTION
!CE *time*	135	10–1,440	Specifies the connection expiration time-out value in minutes. It's not supported on NetWare 5 or higher.
*D *rootEntry ID*	N/A	N/A	Aborts the Send All Updates or *I for a given replica (as identified by the *rootEntryID*). This command can be used only when a Send All Updates or *I can't complete and is therefore endlessly trying to send the objects to all replicas. This situation usually occurs because one of the servers is inaccessible.
!D *time*	24	2–10,080	Disables both inbound and outbound synchronization for the specified number of hours. If !D is specified without a parameter, the value defaults to 24.
!DI *time*	24	2–10,080	Disables inbound synchronization for the specified number of hours. If !DI is specified without a parameter, the value defaults to 24.
!DO *time*	24	2–10,080	Disables outbound synchronization for the specified number of hours. If !DO is specified without a parameter, the value defaults to 24.
*E	N/A	N/A	Checks the entry cache. Locks the DS database, verifies that the entry cache is okay, and then reopens the database.
!E	N/A	N/A	Enables both inbound and outbound synchronization.
!EI	N/A	N/A	Enables inbound synchronization.

Table 7.3 Continued

DSTRACE PROCESS OR PARAMETER	DEFAULT VALUE	RANGE	DESCRIPTION
!EO	N/A	N/A	Enables outbound synchronization.
*F	N/A	N/A	Forces the Flat Cleaner process, (part of the Janitor process) to run. The Flat Cleaner purges or removes the objects marked for deletion in DS.
!F *time*	60	2–10,080	Sets how often (in minutes) the Flat Cleaner process runs. The Flat Cleaner process purges or removes the deleted objects and attributes from DS. If !F is specified without a parameter, the value defaults to 240 (or 4 hours).
*G	N/A	N/A	Gives up on a server when too many requests are being processed. The process gives up on the server and sets the server status to Down.
!G *ticks*	1,000	2–19,999	Changes the amount of time (in ticks) to wait before giving up when outstanding Requests in Process are not answered.
*H	N/A	N/A	Forces the heartbeat process to start. This flag starts immediate communication to exchange time stamps with all servers in replica lists. This command is useful for force-starting the synchronization between servers so you can observe the status.
!H *time*	30 for NetWare 4; 60 for NetWare 5 and higher	2–1,440	Sets the heartbeat process interval (in minutes). This parameter changes how often the heartbeat process begins. If !H is specified without a parameter, the value defaults to 30 for NetWare 4 and 60 for NetWare 5 and higher.

Table 7.3 Continued

DSTRACE PROCESS OR PARAMETER	DEFAULT VALUE	RANGE	DESCRIPTION
*I rootEntryID	N/A	N/A	Forces the replica (as indicated by the rootEntryID) on the server where the command is issued to send a copy of all its objects to all other servers in the replica list. This command is the same as Send All Objects in DSRepair.
!I time	30	2–1,440	Sets the heartbeat interval for the base schema synchronization (in minutes). If !I is specified without a parameter, the value defaults to 30.
!J time	2	1–10,080	Sets the Janitor process interval (in minutes). This parameter changes how often the Janitor process executes. If !J is specified without a parameter, the value defaults to 2.
*L	N/A	N/A	Starts the Limber process, which checks the server name, server address, and tree connectivity of each replica.
*M hex_number	N/A	10,000–10,000,000	Sets the maximum size of the trace file in bytes. TTF must be OFF first before you can set the file size.
*P	N/A	N/A	Displays the tunable parameters and their default settings on the trace screen.
*R	N/A	N/A	Resets the SYS:SYSTEM\ DSTRACE.DBG file. This command is the same as the SET NDS Trace File Length=0 console command.

Table 7.3   Continued

DSTRACE PROCESS OR PARAMETER	DEFAULT VALUE	RANGE	DESCRIPTION
!R *number*	10	1–10,000	Sets the maximum number of times the server's disk can be accessed by DS before it yields. If !R is specified without a parameter, the value defaults to 10. However, if an invalid value is specified, the setting is changed to 20. It's not supported on NetWare 5 or higher.
*SS	N/A	N/A	Forces immediate schema synchronization.
!S *number*	1	0–1	Enables (1) or disables (0) schema synchronization.
!SI	N/A	N/A	Enables inbound schema synchronization.
!SO	N/A	N/A	Enables outbound schema synchronization.
!T *time*	30	1–720	This flag changes the server state threshold, which is the time interval (in minutes) at which the server state is checked. If !T is specified without a parameter, the value defaults to 30.
*U [*serverID*]	N/A	N/A	Forces the server state to Up and resets the communication status list. If no *serverID* (in hex) is specified, all servers in replica lists are set to Up. This command performs the same function as the SET NDS Server Status = UP console command.
!V	N/A	N/A	Lists any restricted versions of the DS. If no versions are listed in the return, there are no restrictions.

Table 7.3   Continued

DSTRACE PROCESS OR PARAMETER	DEFAULT VALUE	RANGE	DESCRIPTION
!W *ticks*	20	1–1999	Changes the IPX Request in Process delay. This is the length of time (in ticks, where 1 tick = 1/18 of a second) to wait after getting an IPX time-out before resending the request. If !W is specified without a parameter, the value defaults to 20.
!X number	3	1–49	Specifies the number of IPX retries for the DS (server-to-server) client. After the retry count has been exceeded, a DS error -625 is displayed. If !X is specified without a parameter, the value defaults to 3.
!Y *number*	2	0–529	Changes the IPX time-out scaling factor (Y) used for the estimated trip delay used in the equation: IPX Time-out = $(T \times Y) + Z$, where T is equal to the ticks required to get to the destination server and Z is specified by the !Z option. If !D is specified without a parameter, the value defaults to 2.
!Z *number*	4	0–499	Adds additional delay (Z) for the IPX time-out. To increase the time-out, change this parameter first. It is used in the equation: IPX Time-out = $(T \times Y) + Z$, where T is equal to the ticks required to get to the destination server. If !Z is specified without a parameter, the value defaults to 4.

NOTE

Some of the previously listed parameter values (such as !B) can be looked up using the SET DSTRACE=*P option. For others, you need to use NDS iMonitor. They are listed under the Agent Configuration link, such as Background Process Settings and Schema Synchronization.

Some of the tuning parameters listed in Table 7.3 can also be changed using console `SET` commands, via `SERVMAN.NLM` (NetWare 4) or `MONITOR.NLM` (NetWare 5 and higher). Many of them can also be used on Linux/Unix servers using `set dstrace=`*parameter* within `ndstrace`—for instance, `set dstrace=!b` *value*. Similarly, most of the `*` commands (such as `*H`) also work on Linux/Unix servers; the known exception is the `*.` command that does not work on Linux/Unix (but does not return an error stating such). In Windows servers, however, there is no provision to enter any set commands. Instead, the commonly used triggers (such as `*B`) are accessed by clicking the corresponding buttons in the `ds.dlm` configuration dialog box (see Figure 7.15).

FIGURE 7.15
DS background
process triggers
on Windows
servers.

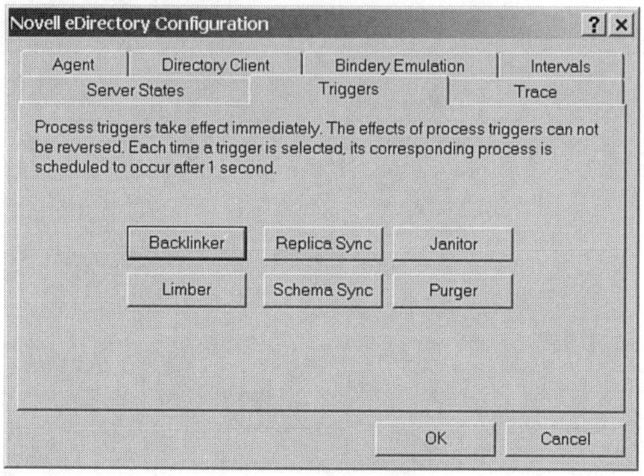

> **NOTE**   A number of Novell TIDs indicate to use `SET NDSTRACE` on Linux/Unix platforms. You can, however, also use `SET DSTRACE`. **This is especially useful when you work with both NetWare and Linux/Unix servers, because you only have to remember one syntax.**

There is a known cosmetic bug with the `SET DSTRACE=*H` command on NetWare 4.11 and above (but not for `ndstrace` on Linux/Unix). If you enter this DSTrace command twice, back-to-back, it doesn't take effect. For example, say you issue a `SET DSTRACE=*H` and follow it by another `SET DSTRACE=*H` in a few minutes because you didn't catch the displayed information and want to see it again. The server displays the message `DSTrace is ALREADY set to *H` and does nothing. For `*H` to be issued twice, you must set another (different) command after the first one and then reissue the command. For example, you could issue `SET DSTRACE=*H`, followed by `SET DSTRACE=*U`, and then `SET DSTRACE=*H` again. This does not happen with `ndstrace` on Linux/Unix.

DSBrowse

Novell has created a utility called DSBrowse that you can use to get a server-centric view of your DS data. The information you see in this utility is localized to what is in the replicas stored on the server. If the server does not hold a replica for the whole tree, you see only parts of your tree. The data shown by DSBrowse includes attribute values that standard management tools, such as ConsoleOne, can provide. DSBrowse can also show additional information, such as when an object or attribute of an object was last modified and by whom; this information is not reported by standard management utilities.

DSBrowse can display the following information categories from the main menu:

▶ **Entry Information**—Use this option to view the information about the entries themselves. In DSBrowse's vocabulary, an *entry* can be the local object ID, a base class, creation time, an attribute, an attribute's value, and so on.

▶ **Partition Information**—Displays information about DS-related partitions (such as the Schema partition and user-created partitions) located on the local server.

▶ **Attribute Definitions**—Displays the attributes defined by the schema.

▶ **Class Definitions**—Displays the classes defined by the schema.

DSBrowse navigates through the entries in the DIB using the tree model: You go from parent to child. When examining an object, you can select to view its attributes and the values or details about the object itself. Depending on the implementation of DSBrowse, a varying amount of detail is provided. For instance, when examining a container, `DSBROWSE.NLM` shows the number of subordinate objects (see Figure 7.16), but the Windows version provides a lot more information such as the object's parent object name, sibling object name, and so on (see Figure 7.17).

TIP

When browsing through the data, you'll find that `DSBROWSE.NLM` presents the entries in alphabetical order but that the Windows version does not. In most cases, the Windows version seems to present the entries according to creation time stamp, but over time you will find that there is no specific order in which the entries are listed. This is because it actually reads from the local DS data files, and the entries are listed in the order in which the entry's data records are found in the database.

FIGURE 7.16
NetWare's version
of DSBrowse.

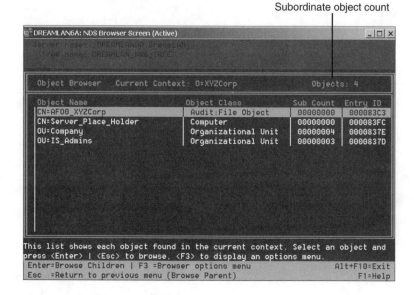

Subordinate object count

FIGURE 7.17
The Windows ver-
sion of DSBrowse
provides more
information than
NetWare's.

The value is in hex

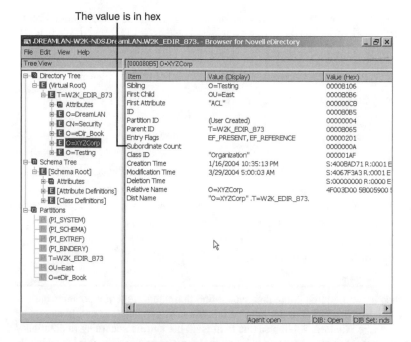

One of the most powerful features of DSBrowse is its capability to display
the attributes and attribute values of any object. One of the more useful
pieces of data provided by DSBrowse is an object's modifiersName attribute.
Starting with NDS 8, DS keeps track of the object name that last modified

an object. Using this attribute, you can see the information without having to enable auditing. modifiersName, however, is a single-valued attribute so it keeps track of only the last modifier's object name.

Because DSBrowse is a server-centric tool, you can use it to compare objects in different replicas to check for any inconsistency as a result of failed synchronization or from data corruption. In addition, DSBrowse is a powerful tool to use in learning various NDS tidbits that the standard utilities don't (and can't) provide. As such, DSBrowse can be an indispensable tool for DS-aware application programmers who need to look up attribute syntax and attribute names. The attribute names you see in NetWare Administrator, for example, do not truly reflect the names used in the schema. Therefore, if you use the attribute name listed in NetWare Administrator in your application, your program might not find that attribute.

To illustrate the point, Table 7.4 offers a comparison of ACL attribute names defined for a User object in the NetWare 4.11 schema and the ACL attribute names used in NetWare Administrator. The entries that are different are shown in italic. Due to the large number of new attributes introduced in NetWare 5 and higher and depending on the additional products installed (such as ZENworks), we have chosen to use NetWare 4.11 for simplicity.

NOTE

It is interesting that NETADMIN.EXE, the DOS version of NetWare Administrator that shipped with NetWare 4, uses the same ACL attribute names as those used to define the schema.

ACL Attribute Names   **TABLE 7.4**

USER OBJECT ACL ATTRIBUTE NAMES DEFINED IN SCHEMA	USER OBJECT ACL ATTRIBUTE NAMES USED BY NETWARE ADMINISTRATOR
[All Attributes Rights]	Property rights: All properties
[Entry Rights]	Object rights
Account Balance	Account Balance
ACL	Object Trustees (ACL)
Aliased Object Name	Aliased Object Name
Allow Unlimited Credit	Allow Unlimited Credit
App Blurb	App Blurb
App Contacts	App Contacts
App Drive Mappings	App Drive Mappings

Table 7.4   Continued

USER OBJECT ACL ATTRIBUTE NAMES DEFINED IN SCHEMA	USER OBJECT ACL ATTRIBUTE NAMES USED BY NETWARE ADMINISTRATOR
App Flags	App Flags
App Icon	App Icon
App Parameters	App Parameters
App Path	App Path
App Printer Ports	App Printer Ports
App Shutdown Script	App Shutdown Script
App Startup Script	App Startup Script
App Working Directory	App Working Directory
App:Administrator Notes	App:Administrator Notes
App:Alt Back Link	App:Alt Back Link
App:Associations	App:Associations
App:Back Link	App:Back Link
App:Caption	App:Caption
App:Contacts	App:Contacts
App:Copy Files	App:Copy Files
App:Description	App:Description
App:Drive Mappings	App:Drive Mappings
App:Error Log Path	App:Error Log Path
App:Fault Tolerance	App:Fault Tolerance
App:Flags	App:Flags
App:GUID	App:GUID
App:Icon	App:Icon
App:INI Settings	App:INI Settings
App:Inventory	App:Inventory
App:Launcher Config	App:Launcher Config
App:Load Balancing	App:Load Balancing
App:Macros	App:Macros
App:Monitor Module	App:Monitor Module
App:NLSFlags	App:NLSFlags
App:NLSProductContainer	App:NLSProductContainer

Table 7.4   Continued

USER OBJECT ACL ATTRIBUTE NAMES DEFINED IN SCHEMA	USER OBJECT ACL ATTRIBUTE NAMES USED BY NETWARE ADMINISTRATOR
App:Parameters	App:Parameters
App:Path	App:Path
App:Platform	App:Platform
App:Printer Ports	App:Printer Ports
App:Program Groups	App:Program Groups
App:Registry Settings	App:Registry Settings
App:Schedule	App:Schedule
App:Shutdown Script	App:Shutdown Script
App:Startup Script	App:Startup Script
App:Text Files	App:Text Files
App:Version String	App:Version String
App:Working Directory	App:Working Directory
Audit:A Encryption Key	Audit:A Encryption Key
Audit:B Encryption Key	Audit:B Encryption Key
Audit:Contents	Audit:Contents
Audit:Current Encryption Key	Audit:Current Encryption Key
Audit:File Link	Audit:File Link
Audit:Link List	Audit:Link List
Audit:Path	Audit:Path
Audit:Policy	Audit:Policy
Audit:Type	Audit:Type
Authority Revocation	Authority Revocation
Auto Start	Auto Start
Back Link	Back Link
Bindery Object Restriction	Bindery Object Restriction
Bindery Property	Bindery Property
Bindery Restriction Level	Bindery Restriction Level
Bindery Type	Bindery Type
C	Country Name
CA Public Key	CA Public Key

Table 7.4   Continued

USER OBJECT ACL ATTRIBUTE NAMES DEFINED IN SCHEMA	USER OBJECT ACL ATTRIBUTE NAMES USED BY NETWARE ADMINISTRATOR
Cartridge	Cartridge
Certificate Revocation	Certificate Revocation
Certificate Validity Interval	Certificate Validity Interval
CN	Name
CommonCertificate	CommonCertificate
Convergence	Convergence
Cross Certificate Pair	Default Queue
Description	Description
Desktop	Desktop
Detect Intruder	Detect Intruder
Device	Device
DS Revision	DS Revision
EMail Address	EMail Address
Equivalent To Me	Security Equal To Me
External Name	External Name
External Synchronizer	External Synchronizer
Facsimile Telephone Number	Fax Number
Full Name	Full Name
Generational Qualifier	Generational Qualifier
GID	GID
Given Name	Given Name
Group Membership	Group Membership
High Convergence Sync Interval	High Convergence Sync Interval
Higher Privileges	Higher Privileges
Home Directory	Home Directory
Home Directory Rights	Home Directory Rights
Host Device	Host Device
Host Resource Name	Volume
Host Server	Host Server
Inherited ACL	Inherited ACL

Table 7.4   Continued

USER OBJECT ACL ATTRIBUTE NAMES DEFINED IN SCHEMA	USER OBJECT ACL ATTRIBUTE NAMES USED BY NETWARE ADMINISTRATOR
Initials	Initials
Intruder Attempt Reset Interval	Intruder Attempt Reset Interval
Intruder Lockout Reset Interval	Intruder Lockout Reset Interval
L	*Location*
Language	Language
Last Login Time	Last Login Time
Last Referenced Time	Last Referenced Time
Launcher Config	Launcher Config
License Database	License Database
LicenseID	LicenseID
Locked By Intruder	*Account Locked*
Lockout After Detection	Lockout After Detection
Login Allowed Time Map	*Login Time Restrictions*
Login Disabled	*Account Disabled*
Login Expiration Time	*Account Has Expiration Date*
Login Grace Limit	*Grace Logins Allowed*
Login Grace Remaining	*Remaining Grace Logins*
Login Intruder Address	*Last Intruder Address*
Login Intruder Attempts	*Incorrect Login Attempts*
Login Intruder Limit	*Incorrect Login Count*
Login Intruder Reset Time	*Account Reset Time*
Login Maximum Simultaneous	*Maximum Connections*
Login Script	Login Script
Login Time	Login Time
Low Convergence Reset Time	Low Convergence Reset Time
Low Convergence Sync Interval	Low Convergence Sync Interval
Mailbox ID	Mailbox ID
Mailbox Location	Mailbox Location
Member	*Members*
Members Of Template	Members Of Template

Table 7.4   Continued

USER OBJECT ACL ATTRIBUTE NAMES DEFINED IN SCHEMA	USER OBJECT ACL ATTRIBUTE NAMES USED BY NETWARE ADMINISTRATOR
Memory	Memory
Message Routing Group	Message Routing Group
Message Server	*Default Server*
Messaging Database Location	*Message Database Location*
Messaging Server	Messaging Server
Messaging Server Type	Messaging Server Type
Minimum Account Balance	*Low Balance Limit*
NetWare Mobile: DIS Name	NetWare Mobile: DIS Name
NetWare Mobile: DIS Phone	NetWare Mobile: DIS Phone
NetWare Mobile: DIS Properties	NetWare Mobile: DIS Properties
NetWare Mobile: DIS Properties 2	NetWare Mobile: DIS Properties 2
NetWare Mobile: DIS Type	NetWare Mobile: DIS Type
NetWare Mobile: DIS Version	NetWare Mobile: DIS Version
NetWare Mobile: DIS Writer	NetWare Mobile: DIS Writer
Network Address	Network Address
Network Address Restriction	Network Address Restriction
New Object's DS Rights	New Object's DS Rights
New Object's FS Rights	New Object's FS Rights
New Object's Self Rights	New Object's Self Rights
NLS:Current Installed	NLS:Current Installed
NLS:Current Peak Installed	NLS:Current Peak Installed
NLS:Current Peak Used	NLS:Current Peak Used
NLS:Current Used	NLS:Current Used
NLS:Hourly Data Size	NLS:Hourly Data Size
NLS:Peak Installed Data	NLS:Peak Installed Data
NLS:Peak Used Data	NLS:Peak Used Data
NLS:Summary Update Time	NLS:Summary Update Time
NLS:Summary Version	NLS:Summary Version
NNS Domain	NNS Domain

Table 7.4 Continued

USER OBJECT ACL ATTRIBUTE NAMES DEFINED IN SCHEMA	USER OBJECT ACL ATTRIBUTE NAMES USED BY NETWARE ADMINISTRATOR
Notify	*Notification*
NRD:Registry Data	NRD: Registry Data
NRD:Registry Index	NRD:Registry Index
NWCLPROV:WIN95PNP CONTROL	NWCLPROV:WIN95PNP CONTROL
NWCLPROV:WIN95PNP DATA	NWCLPROV:WIN95PNP DATA
NWCLPROV:WINNT4PNP CONTROL V1	NWCLPROV:WINNT4PNP CONTROL V1
NWCLPROV:WINNT4PNP DATA V1	NWCLPROV:WINNT4PNP DATA V1
Object Class	Object Class
Operator	Operator
OU	Department
Owner	Owner
Page Description Language	Page Description Language
Partition Control	Partition Control
Partition Creation Time	Partition Creation Time
Partition Status	Partition Status
Password Allow Change	Allow User To Change Password
Password Expiration Interval	Days Between Forced Changes
Password Expiration Time	Date Password Expires
Password Minimum Length	Minimum Password Length
Password Required	Require a Password
Password Unique Required	Require Unique Passwords
Path	Path
Permanent Config Parms	Permanent Config Parms
Physical Delivery Office Name	City
Postal Address	Postal Address
Postal Code	Postal (Zip) Code
Postal Office Box	Postal Office Box
Postmaster	Postmaster

Table 7.4   Continued

USER OBJECT ACL ATTRIBUTE NAMES DEFINED IN SCHEMA	USER OBJECT ACL ATTRIBUTE NAMES USED BY NETWARE ADMINISTRATOR
Print Job Configuration	Print Job Configuration (Non NDPS)
Print Server	Print Server
Printer	Printer
Printer Configuration	Printer Configuration
Printer Control	Printer Control
Product	Product
Profile	Profile
Profile Membership	Profile Membership
Public Key	Public Key
Publisher	Publisher
Queue	Print Queue
Queue Directory	Queue Directory
Received Up To	Received Up To
Replica	Replica
Replica Up To	Replica Up To
Resource	Resource
Revision	Revision
Role Occupant	Occupant
Run Setup Script	Run Setup Script
S	State or Province
SA	Street
SAP Name	SAP Name
Security Equals	Security Equal To
Security Flags	Security Flags
See Also	See Also
Serial Number	Serial Number
Server	Server
Server Holds	Server Holds
Set Password After Create	Set Password After Create
Setup Script	Setup Script

Table 7.4   Continued

USER OBJECT ACL ATTRIBUTE NAMES DEFINED IN SCHEMA	USER OBJECT ACL ATTRIBUTE NAMES USED BY NETWARE ADMINISTRATOR
Status	Status
Supported Connections	Supported Connections
Supported Gateway	Supported Gateway
Supported Services	Supported Services
Supported Typefaces	Supported Typefaces
Surname	Last Name
Synchronized Up To	Synchronized Up To
Telephone Number	Telephone Number
Timezone	Timezone
Title	Title
Transaction Database	Transaction Database
Transaction Log Name	Transaction Log Name
Transaction Log Size	Transaction Log Size
Transitive Vector	Transitive Vector
Trustees Of New Object	Trustees Of New Object
Type Creator Map	Type Creator Map
UID	UID
Unknown	Unknown
Unknown Base Class	Unknown Base Class
User	Users
Version	Version
Volume Space Restrictions	Volume Space Restrictions

The Windows version of DSBrowse can also show you any deleted entries that haven't yet been removed from the DIB. These entries are shown with parentheses around their names (see Figure 7.18). As previously discussed in the "Obituaries" section of Chapter 6, "Understanding Common eDirectory Processes," when an object is deleted from the DIB, it is stripped down to its *husk*—an object with no attributes—and waits for the Purger process to remove it from the DIB. The (CN=new_user) and (CN=test_dynamic_group) are two such objects. The (CN=new_group22) is a deleted object, but it has not yet reached the All Purge state like the other two deleted objects; its obituary flag is `OBF_OK_TO_PURGE`. Next time Janitor runs, (CN=new_group22) will be turned into a husk.

FIGURE 7.18
DSBrowse showing deleted entries in the DIB.

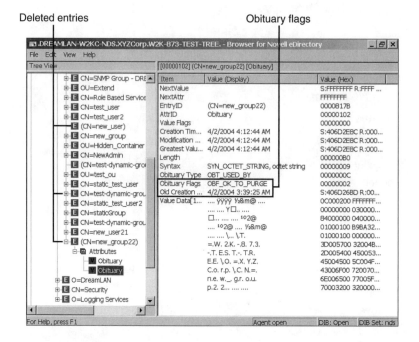

As the name implies, DSBrowse is a read-only utility. You could, however, use DSBrowse to delete an object from the DIB if necessary. On NetWare, you need to load `DSBROWSE.NLM` with the `-A` switch to enable the delete object option; on Windows, this feature is enabled by default. The delete feature is designed to remove objects from your tree that NetWare Administrator or ConsoleOne do not, but it is not a way to get around security imposed by Inherited Rights Filters (IRFs) on an object.

NOTE

Once enabled, Delete selected object is accessed via the Browsers Options menu on NetWare. On Windows, it is listed under the Edit menu. You can also select the object to be deleted and then right-click for the option in the context menu.

NetWare 5 and higher store NetWare licensing information in DS. Due to security, only the user who installed the license certificate can delete it. The NetWare Administrator snap-in checks for object ownership and gives an error about insufficient rights if a user other than the installer attempts to perform the delete. If the User object that installed the license certificates is not available, you can use the advanced mode of DSBrowse to delete the certificates.

Starting with NetWare 5 Support Pack 3, an IRF is placed on every NLS:License Certificate class object (whose name is of the form NLS:License ID=SN:*xxxxxx*; NLS:License ID is the naming attribute for the object). DSBrowse is unable to remove these objects because of the IRF.

You can use rmLicIRF (ftp.dreamlan.com/Freeware/rmLicIRF.zip), an NLM utility, to remove the IRF placed on NLS:License Certificate objects.   **TIP**

DSBROWSE -A also enables two additional features: Send Object and Receive Object. The use of these two options is discussed in the "Unknown Objects" section in Chapter 11.   **NOTE**

Sometimes when an attribute has a high number of values (for example, more than 500 members in a Group object), it can lead to synchronization problems or problems with DS high utilization. DSBROWSE.NLM has a lesser-known option that can report on attributes that have high value counts.

DSBROWSE -CV### can be used to search for objects that have attributes with a high number of values. At the server console, type **DSBROWSE --CV500** (to get a list of all the objects that have at least one attribute with more than 500 values). From the main menu, select Object Search and in the Name field enter a *; then press F10 to launch the search. This generates a list of objects matching the search criteria on the screen and creates a log file called VALCNT500.LOG in SYS:SYSTEM. The numeric value in the filename corresponds to the ### value specified in the --CV switch. The following is a sample VALCNT100.LOG file:

```
Objects with value count > 100:


[Pseudo Server]
                                         value count = 641


OU=East.O=XYZCorp.T=EDIR_873_TEST_TREE
ACL                                      value count = 1336
Inherited ACL                            value count = 257
WM:Registered Workstation                value count = 1305


CN=NETWARE65A.O=XYZCorp.T=EDIR_873_TEST_TREE
Reference                                value count = 240
```

```
CN=admin.O=XYZCorp.T=EDIR_873_TEST_TREE
Reference                                       value count = 102


CN=NETWARE65A-PS.O=XYZCorp.T=EDIR_873_TEST_TREE
ndsPredicate                                    value count = 205


CN=WebAccess_pco.OU=WebAccess.O=XYZCorp.T=EDIR_873_TEST_TREE
Reference                                       value count = 149
bhObjectList                                    value count = 131


CN=Sales_Group.OU=West.O=XYZCorp.T=EDIR_873_TEST_TREE
Member                                          value count = 1367
Equivalent To Me                                value count = 1367
```

When looking for possible causes of DS high utilization, you can safely
ignore the [Pseudo Server] object and the Reference attribute from the
previous listing. The [Pseudo Server] object refers to the (DS) System partition that is local to the server and is not synchronized with other servers.
Similarly, the Reference attribute is flagged PER_REPLICA and also is not synchronized to other servers. Therefore, these two items would not be the
cause of high DS utilization. The other attributes reported, however, are
potential sources of high DS utilization. They are as follows:

- **Sales_Group.West.XYZCorp**—This Group object has 1,367 members. This is generally not a cause of high utilization, one of the reasons being that when a member of this group logs in, it uses the
  Group Membership attribute of its object and does not search
  the 1,367 values of the Member attribute of the group. If the login script
  uses IF MEMBER OF checking, however, the high number of members in
  the group could cause slow logins because the check is done using a
  sequential search through the Member attribute values for a match.

TIP

The login performance can be further degraded if the large groups are also
global groups, meaning they contain members from different partitions and
that are located on servers separated by a slow link. You can use GGroup
(www.dreamlan.com/ggroup.htm) to check for possible global groups in your
tree.

- **ACL and Inherited ACL**—The large number of values in the ACL
  and Inherited ACL attributes of East.XYZCorp container is a potential
  cause for high utilization. The solution to this problem is explained in
  TID #10080332.

▶ **WM:Registered Workstation**—The large number of values in the WM:Registered Workstation attribute of `East.XYZCorp` container is also a point of concern. This attribute is for workstation registration entries that are invalid or old. If you are using ZENworks for Desktop version 3.0 or above, this attribute is no longer used. The solution to this problem is described in TID #10022546.

To check for attributes with high values on Windows and Linux/Unix servers, use NDS iMonitor instead (see the "Novell iManager" section later in this chapter).

NOTE

Similar to `DSREPAIR.NLM`, `DSBROWSE.NLM` is DS version-specific. Therefore, you cannot use the version of `DSBROWSE.NLM` for NDS 7 on a server that is running eDirectory, and vice versa. For NetWare 4 servers, use `DSVIEW.NLM`, a character-mode utility, instead.

Similar to DSBrowse, DSView navigates through the entries using the tree model: You go from parent to child or from sibling to sibling. When viewing the entry information, DSView displays at the bottom of the screen information telling whether the current object has any siblings (other objects at the same NDS context level). For example, the following sample DSView output shows that the entry being viewed is OU=East.O=XYZCorp in the NW411_TEST_TREE tree. OU=East.O=XYZCorp is an organizational unit (as indicated by the Class Name field) that has 26 objects within that container (Subordinate Count: 26), and it has siblings—other OUs and leaf objects at the same level (O=XYZCorp):

```
Key<Action> 1<Parent> 2<Child> 3<Sibling> 4<Goto Another Entry>
            5<Attribute list> 6<Backup To Previous Entry>
            7<View Partition Entry> 8<Find Sibling>
            9<Toggle Display Mode> ESC<Return to Main Menu>


********---- Entry Information  ----********


Entry ID: 010000B8    "OU=East".O=XYZCorp.NW411_TEST_TREE


Partition ID: 00000004
Partition Type: User Created   Name: "NW411_TEST_TREE"
Parent ID: 010000B7 "O=XYZCorp"
Class Name: "Organizational Unit"
Subordinate Count: 26
Flags:  Present
```

```
Creation TimeStamp: 04/02/09 05:16:41; rep# = 0001;
➥ event = 000B
Modification TimeStamp: 04/03/27 18:30:06; rep# = 0001;
➥ event = 0014

Siblings: Yes
```

> **NOTE**
> DSView is *not* Year 2000 compliant in that the date field shows only the last two digits of the year. Therefore, 04/03/27 is really 2004/03/27.

Instead of a menu such as the one that appears in `DSBROWSE.NLM`, you navigate DSView using the number corresponding to the desired action, such as 3 for moving to the next sibling. You can use the first letter in the action, as well. So, in this example, you can either press 3 or press the letter *S* to move to the next sibling. If more than one command has the same first letter, such as Next Attribute and Next Value, use the first letter of the second word (*A* and *V*) instead.

For speed and simplicity, DSView is not designed with a fancy user interface, nor does it have any online help. If you spend perhaps 30 minutes working with it, though, you'll find it easy to use and understand.

> **NOTE**
> At the time of this writing, no DSBrowse implementation is available for Linux/Unix platforms. Instead, you can use NDS iMonitor (discussed in the "NDS iMonitor" section).

Novell iManager

With the release of eDirectory 8.5, two Web-based eDirectory management and monitoring tools—Novell iManager and NDS iMonitor—have been included with eDirectory. They were developed as part of the effort to make management tools truly platform-independent and do not require additional software to be installed on the management workstation, as is the case with ConsoleOne, which requires a compatible Java Runtime Environment (JRE) and the Novell Client software. These two applications only require you to have a Web browser installed on the workstation and IP configured (which is a rather standard configuration for today's computers). This section looks at iManager, and the next section examines NDS iMonitor.

The current version of iManager 2.0.*x* (released with eDirectory 8.7) is a
Novell exteNd Director gadget that facilitates role-based management of
Novell eDirectory and other network resources using gadgets contained
within the iManager gadget. iManager functionality can also be extended
through other software components collectively referred to as *plug-ins.*
Figure 7.19 illustrates the iManager architecture.

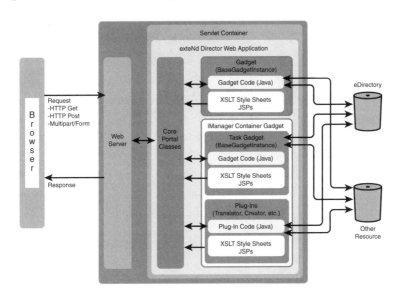

FIGURE 7.19
iManager 2
architecture.

NOTE

**iManager is designed to run on a single server within an organization and is used
to manage other network resources in the organization.**

Task gadgets consist of Java code, Extensible Stylesheet Language
Transformation (XSLT) style sheets or Java Server Pages (JSPs), configuration, and resource files that are placed in the appropriate directories within
the Novell exteNd Director servlet document root directory. Task gadgets
also take advantage of special management features of iManager, such as
role-based services.

NOTE

**iManager depends heavily on many Web-based or related technologies, such as a
functional Web server, a compatible JVM, and a working LDAP server. You have to
ensure that all these components are working correctly to take full advantage of
iManager.**

iManager uses the role-based services (RBS) technology product, which provides access to network management functions based on the user's role in an organization. RBS is a set of extensions to the eDirectory schema and defines several object classes and attributes that provide a mechanism for administrators to assign users to roles with specific tasks or responsibilities. Administrators can allow users access to only those tasks (thus, tools) that the users need to perform based on their roles.

iManager is designed to allow you to manage and maintain your eDirectory tree. The following are some of the functions provided via snap-in modules:

- ▶ Tree repair functions similar to those of DSRepair
- ▶ Tree merge functionality similar to those of DSMerge
- ▶ eDirectory backup and restore
- ▶ LDAP server configuration
- ▶ eDirectory index management
- ▶ Import Convert Export (ICE) Wizard
- ▶ DS partition management, including filtered replica support
- ▶ DS schema management
- ▶ DS object management, including dynamic groups

At the time of this writing, iManager 2.0.x is supported on the following operating system platforms:

- ▶ NetWare 6 Support Pack 3 or later
- ▶ NetWare 6.5
- ▶ Linux RedHat 8 or later, RedHat AS 2.1, SuSE SLES 8, and SuSE 8.2 or later
- ▶ Windows 2000 Pro/Server/Advanced Server
- ▶ Windows XP Pro SP1 and higher
- ▶ Solaris 8 and higher
- ▶ HP/UX 11i and higher

NOTE iManager 2 requires JVM 1.4.1 or later. Because only JVM 1.3.1 is supported on NetWare 5.x, iManager 2 is not supported on NetWare 5.x.

TIP

The iManager 2 installation is generally smooth. Installation on Windows servers, especially when Internet Information Server (IIS) is involved, can be problematic. At the time of this writing, iManager 2.0.*x* does not work with IIS6 that is shipped with Windows 2003 (but does work with Apache6). iManager installs best on Windows servers without IIS; you should let iManager install the Apache Web server instead. If you already have IIS on your Windows 2000 eDirectory server and are having trouble installing iManager, try this procedure: Uninstall eDirectory from the server, install iManager and set it to use IIS, reinstall eDirectory, and then run the exteNd Directory Configuration Wizard by accessing the URL *servername_or_IP*/nps/servlet/configure to configure iManager. For more information, see the "Configuring and Customizing iManager" section in the iManager documentation at www.novell.com/documentation/lg/imanager20.

For browsers, you can use Internet Explorer 6.0 SP1 or later, Netscape 7.1 or higher, or Mozilla 1.4 or higher. The following features are not available when using Netscape or Mozilla:

▸ ToolTips function for iManager buttons do not always work.

▸ Multiselect function does not work.

▸ Object view cannot be used.

▸ You might be unable to use the Tree button to log in to a different tree.

▸ The Repair Through iMonitor task might not work.

▸ The Install and Upgrade Plug-in task might not work.

To access iManager, point your browser to *servername_or_IP*/nps/ servlet/iManager.html. You will be required to authenticate to access iManager, and you'll have access to only those features to which your roles allow you. For full access to all iManager features, you must authenticate as a user with Supervisor rights to the tree (see Figure 7.20).

WARNING

iManager authenticates users via LDAP. Therefore, you must specify the username in LDAP format using commas to separate the context and including the object type, such as cn=*username*,ou=*ou_name*,o=*org*.

You can access iManager in Simple mode (see Figure 7.21). This is suitable for compliance with Federal accessibility guidelines. Simple mode provides the same functionality as Regular mode, but with an interface optimized for accessibility by those with disabilities (for example, expanded menus for vision-impaired users who use a screen reader). To use Simple mode, replace iManager.html with Simple.html in the iManager URL.

FIGURE 7.20
iManager 2.0.2
home page.

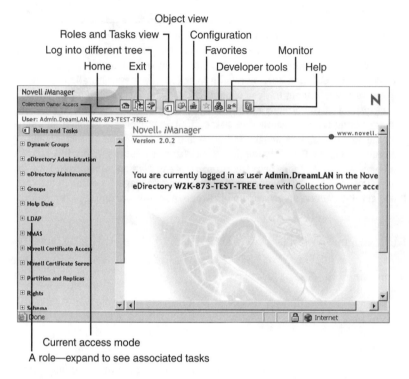

Object view
Roles and Tasks view ⌐   Configuration
Log into different tree ⌐   Favorites   Monitor
Home   Exit   Developer tools   Help

Current access mode
A role—expand to see associated tasks

FIGURE 7.21
iManager 2.0.2
home page in
Simple mode.

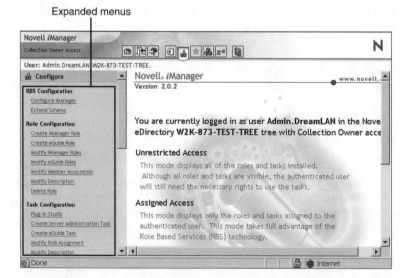

Expanded menus

Using either interface, you will have access to only those features associated with your assigned roles. The exception is when you log in to a different tree via iManager. In that case, the Unrestricted Access Mode, where all roles and tasks are visible, is used. You still need to have the necessary DS rights to perform a specific task, though.

When using iManager, be sure to use the buttons (OK, Next, and so on) within the interface. The browser's toolbar buttons (Back, Next, and so on) are not supported in iManager.

NDS iMonitor

NDS iMonitor is installed automatically as part of eDirectory 8.5 and higher. It is meant to be a Web-based alternative—and eventual replacement—for many of the console-based eDirectory management and troubleshooting tools, such as DSBrowse, DSTrace, and DSRepair. The following are some of the major features offered by iMonitor 2.3:

- ▶ **General eDirectory tasks**—This category of tasks includes searching for eDirectory objects, checking DirXML driver status, running pre-configured and customizable eDirectory health checks and reports, and online help with a list of eDirectory error codes and troubleshooting references.

- ▶ **Monitoring health of eDirectory agent**—Reports on the synchronization status, synchronization information, known eDirectory servers to the local agent, and the status of partitions and replicas stored on this server (similar to what DSRepair does).

- ▶ **Browsing eDirectory DIB**—Allows you to view objects in the local DIB and their attributes (similar to what DSBrowse does). You can browse the eDirectory schema that is known to the local agent and compare schema between two servers.

- ▶ **Configuring eDirectory agent**—Allows you to set and change replication filters, background process run intervals, agent triggers, and DIB cache settings (similar to what SET DSTRACE does).

- ▶ **Server-centric eDirectory tasks**—Includes Web-based version of DSTrace, a background process scheduler, and a simplified version of DSRepair.

To access NDS iMonitor, point your browser to *servername_or_IP*:8008. This takes you to the DHost HTTP Server URL Registration Page where you can select to access the DHost Console, DSTrace, or NDS iMonitor. After selecting a link, you might be prompted to accept a SSL certificate and then be taken to a secured page to log in to iMonitor. After authentication, you are presented with the iMonitor home page showing a summary of DSAgent information (see Figure 7.22). You can also get to the authentication screen for iMonitor directly by using *servername_or_IP*:8008/nds as the URL.

NOTE

Unlike iManager, to log in to NDS iMonitor, you use the standard dot notation for the username, such as *.username.org_unit.org*.

The ports used by iMonitor can vary depending on your operating system platform. Typically, NetWare uses ports 8008 and 8009, whereas the Windows and Linux/Unix platforms use 8008 and 8010.

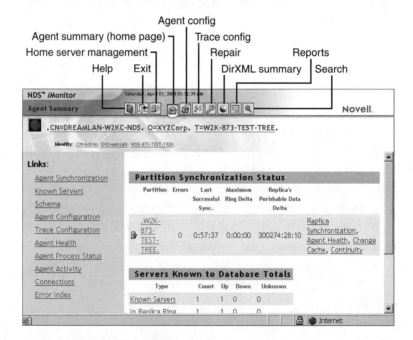

FIGURE 7.22
iMonitor 2.3 home page showing a summary of DSAgent information.

Many iMonitor pages are divided into four areas or sections (see Figure 7.23):

▶ **Navigator frame**—Located across the top of the page, this frame shows the server name where the data is being read from; your identity; and links you can click to access other screens, including online help, login, server portal, and other iMonitor pages.

▶ **Assistant frame**—Located on the left side of the page, this frame contains additional navigational aids, such as links to other pages, items that help you navigate data in the Data frame, and other items to assist you with obtaining or interpreting the data on a given page.

▶ **Data frame**—Shows the detailed information about your servers that you request by clicking one of the previously listed links. This is the only page you see if your Web browser does not support frames.

▶ **Replica frame**—Allows you to determine which replica you are currently viewing and provides links to view the same information from another replica or from another server's point of view. This frame appears only when you view pages where another replica of the requested data exists or where another replica might have a different view of the information being presented in the Data frame.

Navigator frame   Data frame

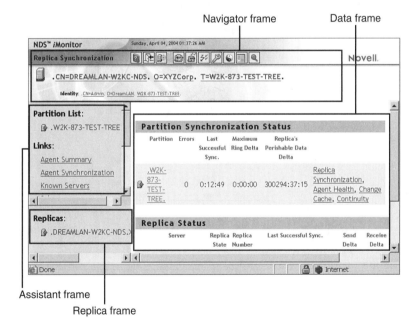

Assistant frame

Replica frame

FIGURE 7.23
Anatomy of an iMonitor page.

Similar to iManager, the amount and type of information you see in NDS iMonitor is dependent on the identity you used for authentication, as well as the version of the DSAgent with which you are currently working. As new versions of eDirectory are released, they will be updated to provide more information to iMonitor. Therefore, older versions of NDS/eDirectory, while still accessible via iMonitor, will not provide the same level of detail.

NDS iMonitor can be used in two modes of operation: Direct mode and Proxy mode, as illustrated in Figure 7.24. No configuration changes are necessary to move between these modes. iMonitor automatically moves between these modes, but you should understand them to successfully and easily navigate the eDirectory tree and properly interpret the data presented to you.

FIGURE 7.24
NDS iMonitor can operate in either Direct mode or Proxy mode.

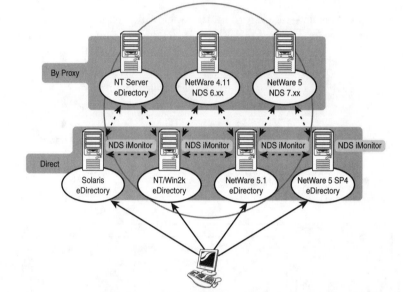

Direct mode is used when iMonitor is reading information or executing an operation on the same server from which iMonitor is running. In this mode, all iMonitor features are available on that machine, and they include the full server-centric feature set (such as DSTrace and Background Process Scheduler). Direct mode also reduces network bandwidth and provides faster access. Proxy mode is used when iMonitor is running on one machine but is gathering information or executing an operation on a different server. In this mode, iMonitor uses traditional eDirectory nonserver-centric protocols for nonserver-centric features and can access all previous versions of eDirectory beginning with NDS 6.x. This enables you to gather data from servers not running iMonitor. Server-centric features (such as DSTrace), on the other hand, use APIs that cannot be accessed remotely and thus are not available in Proxy mode.

Let's say, for example, that you are examining the Title attribute value of a
User object you suspect has not synchronized its change to other replicas.
You used iMonitor to access the server on which you made the change to
the Title attribute. iMonitor is running in Direct mode because the server
has iMonitor running. Using the links presented in the Replica frame, you've
switched to a different replica so you can check the value of the Title attribute to see whether it has synchronized to that server yet. iMonitor switches
to Proxy mode for this operation. The Repair icon in the Navigation frame
turns into a stick shift icon (see Figure 7.25). When you move the mouse
pointer over this icon, you see a link to the remote iMonitor on the remote
server. If the server on which you are gathering information by proxy is an
earlier version of NDS or eDirectory, no stick shift icon is shown (and the
Repair icon is removed). In this case, you always need to gather information
on that server by proxy until it is upgraded to a version of eDirectory that
includes iMonitor.

Click here to switch from Proxy mode to Direct mode

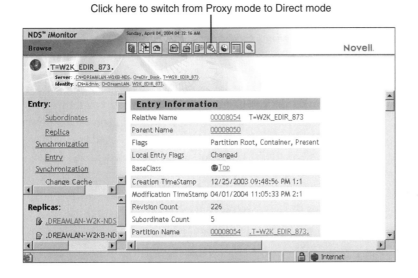

FIGURE 7.25
Switching
between Direct
mode and Proxy
mode.

The advantage of using Proxy mode is that not every server in the tree must
be running iMonitor to use most of the iMonitor features. In a tree running
pre-eDirectory 8.7 servers, only one server must be upgraded to take advantage of iMonitor, and it can access data from previous versions of
NDS/eDirectory via the Proxy mode. The main drawback, as previously discussed, is the lack of server-centric features, such as DSTrace, for troubleshooting and repair purposes.

NOTE

If you have NetWare Remote Manager (NoRM) installed on your NetWare server, iMonitor registers with NoRM (`portal.nlm`) so links to iMonitor and other eDirectory-specific information are available through the NoRM interface. These links are found under the Manage eDirectory section in the Remote Manager interface. Links to eDirectory agent health information are also found in the Diagnose Server section under Health Monitor in the eDirectory-related categories.

The default configuration of iMonitor is suitable for most environments. iMonitor offers two configuration files that allow you to customize it. The configuration files are text files containing configuration parameter tags together with their desired values. They allow you to change the general execution of iMonitor, as well as customize specific iMonitor features (such as location and maximum size of the DSTrace files).

NOTE

On NetWare 5.1 and higher servers, the trace files from iMonitor by default are stored as `SYS:SYSTEM\NDSIMON\DSTRACE\trace`x`.htm`. On Windows servers, the trace files are stored as `drive:\Novell\NDS\ndsimon\dstrace\trace`x`.htm`, and on Linux/Unix servers the trace files are stored as `\var\nds\dstrace\trace`x`.htm`.

The `ndsimon` configuration file lets you modify trace file settings, control access to the server, set the maximum number of objects to be displayed when listing a container or displaying search results, and specify the number of minutes of inactivity allowed before a connection is logged out. The `ndsimonhealth` configuration file lets you modify default settings for the Agent Health page. You can enable or disable Agent Health options, set reporting levels and ranges for options, and set server reporting levels. The names and locations of these two files are as follow:

NetWare	`SYS:\SYSTEM\NDSIMON.INI`
	`SYS:\SYSTEM\NDSIMONHEALTH.INI`
Windows	`drive:\Novell\NDS\ndsimon.ini`
	`drive:\Novell\NDS\ndsimonhealth.ini`
Linux/Unix	`/etc/ndsimon.conf`
	`/etc/ndsimonhealth.conf`

NOTE

The `ndsimonhealth` configuration file is supported only by the versions of iMonitor shipped with eDirectory 8.7 or later.

Unlike iManager, NDS iMonitor does not rely on a Web server such as IIS or Apache. Instead, iMonitor uses its own HTTP server stack. On NetWare, it uses `HTTPSTK.NLM`, which is also used by NoRM. On Windows and Linux/Unix, it uses the HTTP stack built in to DHost.

iMonitor 2.1 (shipped with eDirectory 8.7.1) and above has an advanced mode that enables extra repair features, similar to the `-A` command-line switch for DSRepair. These additional options are especially useful when troubleshooting stuck obituaries. The general steps are as follows:

1. Log in to NDS iMonitor on a server in the replica ring running eDirectory 8.7.1 or higher.

2. Enable iMonitor's Advanced Mode by clicking the NDS iMonitor logo in the upper-left corner of the browser window, and then select Enabled, Submit (see Figure 7.26). Keep in mind that when you choose to enable Advanced mode, this setting remains on the server until you disable it. Be sure to disable Advanced mode when you are finished with this process.

Click to display the About dialog

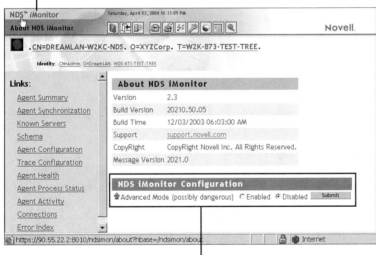

FIGURE 7.26
iMonitor's About dialog page is where you enable or disable Advanced mode.

Toggles iMonitor's advanced mode

3. Go to the Reports page and click the Report Config link on the left side of the screen.

4. Configure the Obituary Listing report to look for the desired obituary types. Take note of the Obituaries Older Than field; if the sought-after obituaries are less than 7 days old, decrease the default value of 7 to 0.

5. Run the report. You should get a listing of obituaries similar to what is shown in Figure 7.27. If Advanced mode is enabled, you see the extra options to the right of each entry specified. If no obituary shows up in the report, the iMonitor server you are logged in to might not hold a real replica of the object with the obituary or a synchronization problem might have occurred. Be sure to select a server that has Advanced mode enabled.

FIGURE 7.27
List of found obituaries.

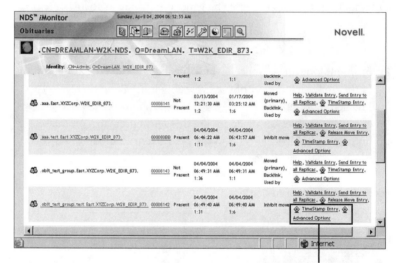

Options preceded by an
icon are advanced features

6. Select one of the listed repair options or click the Advanced Options link to see additional choices (see Figure 7.28).

7. After selecting the desired option, you are warned that the operation is irreversible. Click OK if you are sure you want to do this. You are then presented with an info message stating success or failure.

> **NOTE**
> The advanced repair options are displayed only in reports that were run *after* Advanced mode was enabled. The additional links are not added to reports run prior to activating Advanced mode.

NDS iMonitor 2.3 included with eDirectory 8.7.3 has the capability to search the server's local DIB for high values, similar to the function provided by `DSBROWSE.NLM  -CV###` as discussed previously in this chapter. Use the following URL to access the high-value report:

`https://server_address:8010/nds/valuecount?rptOption=config`

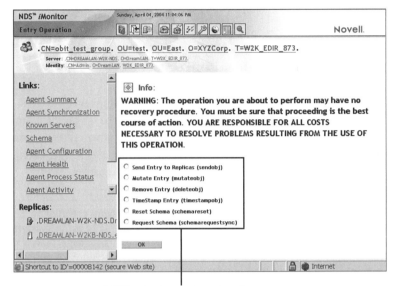

FIGURE 7.28
Additional advanced repair options.

Additional advanced repair options

You are prompted to enter the maximum value count—attributes that have more than this number in values are reported. Click the Run Report button to generate the listing. A sample report is shown in Figure 7.29.

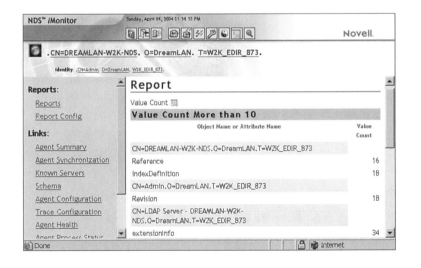

FIGURE 7.29
Sample high-value report.

For details on using the various iMonitor features and functions, refer to the "iMonitor Features" section in your eDirectory documentation.

eDirectory Management Toolbox

The Novell eDirectory Management Toolbox (eMBox) ships with eDirectory 8.7 and higher and lets you access all the eDirectory backend utilities remotely as well as on the server. eMBox works with Novell iManager to provide Web-based access to eDirectory utilities such as DSRepair, DSMerge, Backup and Restore, and the DHost/eDirectory Service Manager.

> **NOTE**
>
> eMBox requires that RBS be configured (using iManager)—more specifically, eMBox looks for the RBS collection object—for the tree that is to be administered for eMBox tasks to be run. Furthermore, for all eDirectory Management Tools (eMTools), such as Backup, DSRepair, DSMerge, Schema Operations, and eDirectory Service Manager, to run, eMBox must be loaded and running on the target eDirectory server.

All functions are accessible, either on the local server or remotely, through a command-line client. Using the eMBox Client, you can perform tasks for multiple servers from one server or workstation. Using the client's batch mode, you can automate many of your eDirectory management tasks using batch files and scripts.

The eMBox Client is a Java command-line client. It has two modes: interactive and batch. In the interactive mode, you run the eMBox commands one at a time. In the batch mode, though, you can run a group of commands unattended. The command-line client has logging service for both modes. Because the client is a Java application, you must have access to the Java Runtime Environment, Sun JVM 1.3.1 or higher, which is installed with eDirectory.

Use the following commands when running the eMBox Client in interactive mode from the eDirectory server:

- ▶ **NetWare**—At the server prompt, enter **edirutil -i**.
- ▶ **Windows**—Enter **_drive_:\Novell\nds\edirutil -i**.
- ▶ **Linux/Unix**—At the terminal prompt, enter **edirutil -i**.

The edirutil file gives you a shortcut to running the eMBox Client. It points to the Java executable and the default location where the eMBox Client is installed with eDirectory. For NetWare, it includes the necessary **-ns** option (which is a Java option on NetWare meaning "new screen").

NOTE

The -i switch starts the client in interactive mode; the -t switch starts the client in single command mode; and the -b switch puts the client in batch mode. In addition, the -g switch brings up a GUI. Although it is not officially supported by Novell, it is useful during troubleshooting because it helps to prevent issuing a wrong command.

The following is the online help of the eMBox Client in its interactive mode:

```
eMBox Client> ?
********  Novell eMBox Interactive Client Commands  **********



     Copyright 2001-2003 Novell, Inc. All rights reserved.
     Patents Pending.

login    [-s<server>] [-p<port>] [-u<user> -w<passwd>]
➥ [-m<mode>] [-n]
          Open an eMBox command line client session.
   -s  <server>    name or IP address of the eMBox server.
                   Default: 127.0.0.1.
   -p  <port>      port number of the eMBox server.
                   Default: 80.
   -u  <user>      user DN, such as admin.novell.
                   Default: anonymous.
   -w  <password>  password associated with the above user.
   -m  <mode>      login mode. Default: dclient.
   -n              do not try and make an ssl connection.

set    [-l<log file> [-o]] [-T<timeout>] [-L<languages>]
          Set the log file, response timeout and/or the language
          preferences.
   -l  <log file>  name of the log file.
   -o              overwrite the log file when opening it.
   -T  <timeout>   timeout in seconds to wait for responses
                   from the server. 0: unlimited; Default: 60.
   -L  <languages> list of comma delimited acceptable
                   languages in order of preference, such as
                   en-US,de_DE. Defaults to the client system
                   language.

setmode [-a]  Set the mode to show advanced options.
   -a              set mode to advanced.
                   no option returns to regular mode.

list    [-t<tools>] [-f] [-r]  List available services.
```

```
    -t  <tools>      comma delimited tool list. Use to list tool
                     service details.
    -f               display the command format only.
    -r               force refresh.


[<tool>.]<task> <options>  Perform a particular service.
      Run list command for details.


logout  [-m<mode>] Close the current command line client
                     session.
   -m  <mode>        login mode. Default: dclient.


exit   Exit the eMBox client.
quit   Same as exit.


version Display the eMbox client version information.


help   Display this help information.
?      Same as help.
****************************************************************
```

After starting the eMBox Client, you need to log in to the server. To do so, you must specify the server name or IP address *and* the port number—the port number must be provided because there is no default value for it—to connect to a particular server. A username and password are not needed for public logins. For example

```
login -s 10.65.123.244 -p 8008 -u admin.org -w password -n
```

After logging in to a server, you can use the **list** command to display a list of the services available on that server. The **list** command displays the following eMTools (tools within the eMBox) and their services dynamically:

```
eMBox Client> list
***************  List of Registered eMTools  ***************


Use the option -t<tool>,<tool> to list the eMTool services.
'*' is the wild card.


logger      eMBox logging utility (1.1)
backup      Novell eDirectory Backup eMTool (1.1)
dsmerge     Novell eDirectory Merge eMTool (1.1)
dsrepair    Novell eDirectory Repair eMTool (1.1)
dsschema    Novell eDirectory Schema Operations eMTool (1.1)
service     Novell eDirectory Service Manager eMTool (1.1)
```

You can use -r to force the refresh of the list, -t to list service details, and -f to list just the command format. The following shows the details of the backup service:

```
eMBox Client> list -t backup
*************** List of Registered eMTools ***************

In the format: (<tool> (<task> <format> <synopsis>
➥ <options>)+)+. If <task> is ambiguous, use the
combination <tool>.<task> as the command name.

backup       Novell eDirectory Backup eMTool (1.1)
  backup -f<file name> -l<file name> [-s<size>][-u<file name>]
    [-t][-e][-w][-b¦-i¦-c][-o][-d]
    Perform an eDirectory backup
    -f  Backup file name
    -l  Log file name
    -s  Backup file size limit (MB)
    -u  User includes file name
    -w  Overwrite backup file
    -t  Backup stream files
    -e  Include security files in backup
    -b  Perform a full backup
    -i  Perform incremental backup
    -c  Perform a cold backup
    -o  Leave database closed after cold backup
    -d  Disable database after a cold backup
  restore -f<file name> -l<file name> [-d<directory name>]
    [-r][-a][-o][-e][-u][-n][-v]
    Perform an eDirectory restore
    -f  Backup file name
    -l  Log file name
    -d  Roll forward log directory
    -e  Restore security files
    -u  Restore user included files
    -r  Restore DIB set
    -a  Activate DIB after verify
    -o  Open database when finished
  getconfig No options needed
    Retrieve backup configuration
  setconfig [-L¦-l][-T¦-t][-r <directory name>][-n <size>]
    [-m <size>][-s]
    Set backup configuration
    -L  Start keeping roll forward logs
    -l  Stop keeping roll forward logs
```

```
        -T  Start logging of stream files
        -t  Stop logging of stream files
        -r  Set roll forward log directory
        -n  Set minimum roll forward log size
        -m  Set maximum roll forward log size
        -s  Start a new roll forward log
    cancel No options needed
        Cancel running backup or restore operation
```

You can perform tasks using each of the eMTool services after you have logged in to a server. The command syntax is *servicename.taskname* [*options*]. The following is a sample command for using the backup eMTool service to perform an eDirectory full backup file called `april-1-2004.fullbackup` that includes stream and security files and generates a log file called `backup.log`:

```
backup.backup -f april-1-2004.fullbackup -l backup.log -b -t -e
```

You can perform a single eMBox task in batch mode from the command line using the `-t` switch instead of `-i`, and you can specify the desired command as part of the command-line options. For example

```
C:\>\novell\nds\edirutil -s 10.65.123.244 -p 8008 -u admin.org
➥ -w password -n -t list
Login successful.
*************** List of Registered eMTools ***************

Use the option -t<tool>,<tool> to list the eMTool services.
'*' is the wild card.

logger      eMBox logging utility (1.1)
backup      Novell eDirectory Backup eMTool (1.1)
dsmerge     Novell eDirectory Merge eMTool (1.1)
dsrepair    Novell eDirectory Repair eMTool (1.1)
dsschema    Novell eDirectory Schema Operations eMTool (1.1)
service     Novell eDirectory Service Manager eMTool (1.1)
Logout successful.
```

If you have more than one eMBox task to execute, it might be easier to create a text file containing these commands and use the batch mode of the client:

```
C:\>\novell\nds\edirutil -s 10.65.123.244 -p 8008 -u admin.org
➥ -w password -n -b myCommands.txt
```

The syntax of the text file is simple: There's one command per line and lines beginning with a # are treated as comments. Such a command file is referred to as an *eMBox internal batch file*. The following is a sample internal batch file that performs two tasks:

```
# myCommands.txt
# Updated April 01, 2004
#

# Perform a local database repair
dsrepair.rld

# before backing up the DIB.
# Will overwrite fullbackup.file if exists.
backup.backup -f fullbackup.file -l fullbackup.log -b -t -e -w
```

If you want to run the eMBox Client on a workstation other than the eDirectory server, you simply need to copy the client Java file (eMBoxClient.jar) from the server to the workstation and then set up the correct Java classpath. The .jar file can be found in one of the following locations:

NetWare	SYS:\SYSTEM\EMBOX\eMBoxClient.jar
Windows	*drive:*\novell\nds\embox\eMBoxClient.jar
Linux/Unix	/usr/lib/nds-modules/embox/eMBoxClient.jar

You can run the eMBox Client from anywhere on your machine using the following procedure:

1. Add to your path the directory where the Java executable (for example, java.exe) is located, or make sure that Java is already running. If you are on a server, this is probably already done for you. On Windows and Linux/Unix servers, the directory needs to be in your path. On NetWare, instead of adding the directory to a path, Java needs to be running. On a workstation, you might need to set it up yourself. For example, on Windows, click Start, Settings, Control Panel, System. On the Advanced tab, click Environment Variables and add the path to the Path variable.

2. Add the path to the eMBoxClient.jar file to your classpath setting:

NetWare	set ENVSET=*path*\eMBoxClient.jar
Windows	set CLASSPATH=*path*\eMBoxClient.jar
Linux/Unix	export CLASSPATH=path/eMBoxClient.jar

Alternatively, you can specify the classpath to use via the `-cp` flag for Java each time you want to run eMBox:

```
java -cp path/eMBoxClient.jar embox -i
```

For example, on Windows the command is

```
java -cp c:\jarFiles\eMBoxClient.jar embox -i
```

WARNING

To avoid ABEND on a NetWare server, you must include `-ns` **(a Java option on NetWare for "new screen") in the command line. For example**

```
java -ns -cp sys:\jarFiles\eMBoxClient.jar embox -i
```

After completing both of the previous steps, you can run the client in interactive mode from anywhere on your machine using the following command:

```
java [-ns] embox -i
```

For information on Java commands, see the Java documentation on the Sun Web site (`www.java.sun.com`).

NOTE

If you have changed the location of Java or the `eMBoxClient.jar` **file after installing eDirectory,** `edirutil` **might no longer work. In such case, you need to follow the previous procedure to set up the classpath to point to the new location of the** `.jar` **file.**

TIP

When using a non-secure connection, all the information you enter, such as usernames and passwords, is sent over the wire in clear text. To establish a secure connection using SSL, be sure you don't use the `-n` **option in your command when logging in to a server because it specifies a non-secure connection; a secure connection is the default. You need to have the following Java Secure Socket Extension (JSSE) files in your classpath:** `jsse.jar`, `jnet.jar`, **and** `jcert.jar`. **If you don't, the eMBox Client returns an error saying it cannot establish a secure connection.**

You can get these files and information about JSSE from the Sun Web site (`java.sun.com/products/jsse`**).**

As you can see, the command-line client can be difficult to use, especially its interactive mode, due to the complexity in the command syntax. Although not officially supported by Novell, the eMBox Client has a built-in GUI that can be useful (see Figure 7.30). Use `-g` as the command-line switch instead of `-i`.

Enable the Command line via the Settings menu

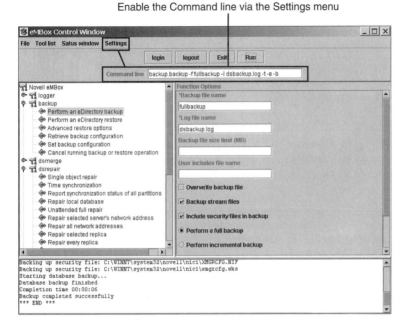

FIGURE 7.30
The GUI mode of the eMBox Client.

One of the nice features of the GUI mode is that, if you are unsure what the syntax of a specific service or task is, you can enable the command-line feature via the Settings menu. The command-line information is displayed as you select options and enter data.

As you can see, eMBox is a very powerful tool. For more information, including configuring the eMBox Logger that tracks events for all the eMTools operations, refer to the section "The eDirectory Management Toolbox" in the eDirectory documentation.

TIP

eMBox is heavily dependent on having RBS installed in the tree. If there is no RBS collection object in the tree, all eMBox utilities fail. You can log in and authenticate through eMBox without problem, but running any utilities results in a message stating Error -347156450. Ensure RBS is properly configured and make sure that the user you are authenticating as is a member of the eDirectory Maintenance Utilities Role in iManager. Regardless of the rights the user has logging in, he must be a member of this role for eMBox utilities to function properly.

Another possible cause can be having your tree name and your organization object named the same. For some reason, eMBox gets confused in certain circumstances if the tree and the organization have the same name. This seems to cause a problem only when you set the scope at the Tree level ([Root]). If you set the scope at the organization, it seems to work just fine. Unless you have multiple organization objects, you should not lose any functionality by moving the scope to the organization.

Workstation Tools

Sometimes you won't have ready access to the server console to run any of the server-based tools mentioned in the previous section. This section describes how you can use workstation-based applications to accomplish similar, if not the same, goals as those server-based utilities.

> **NOTE** The DS rights of the user you're logged in with determine the functionality you can perform as well as the number and types of objects you can see using workstation-based utilities.

> **TIP** When using workstation-based applications, the DS information is read from your current default server. For example, if you have a drive (F:) mapped to server NETWARE65-A and another drive (G:) mapped to NETWARE60-B, you'll be reading DS data from NETWARE65-A if your current drive is F:. Otherwise, the data is retrieved from NETWARE60-B. When working from the Windows desktop, such as Windows 2000, and using Novell Client, you can easily change your default server: Right-click My Network Places, select NetWare Connections from the context menu, select the server you want to be your default server, and click Set Primary.

NetWare Administrator and ConsoleOne

NetWare Administrator and ConsoleOne, which are mainly management applications, aren't often utilized as crude diagnostic tools—but they can be. When you don't have ready access to utilities such as DSBrowse and need to do a quick check on the data consistency or synchronization between servers in a replica ring, you can use NetWare Administrator or ConsoleOne. Suppose you suspect there's something wrong with the synchronization between the replicas of a given partition. You can use the following steps to see whether DS changes are being sent from one replica to another:

1. Identify the servers that have a replica of the partition in question.

2. Ensure you're only logged in to the server holding the Master replica.

3. Use NetWare Administrator or ConsoleOne to change an attribute value of one of the objects in this partition. For example, change the Location attribute of a User object.

4. At the server console of this server, issue the SET DSTRACE=*H command to force an immediate synchronization.

5. Back at the workstation, log in to each server in the replica ring separately (using LOGIN *servername/username* if logging in from DOS, or
specify the server name in the Server field in the GUI login dialog
box). Then use NetWare Administrator or ConsoleOne to check
whether the changed attribute value has been propagated correctly to
the server.

You can also use the same technique (logging in to each server in turn) and
look for Unknown objects (because of schema inconsistency or corruption) or
missing objects (perhaps due to obituaries). The key to this exercise is to log
in to only *one server at a time*, or ensure you correctly set your default server
so you know from which server you're retrieving the data.

TIP

The old NWAdmn3X has a Use Master = True INI file parameter so that, when you
create a user in NWAdmin, the Master replica is used. The same setting is available in Windows 9x and higher via the Registry key. The key that governs this
use-master situation is HKEY_CURRENT_USER\Software\NetWare\
Parameters\NetWare Administrator\UserCreation\Use Master. To
enable the feature, create the key of the type String Value (if not already there)
and set it to 1. If you know you have an inconsistent replica ring but NWAdmin
isn't showing any differences when you log in to specific servers, check whether
this setting is enabled. This also works for NetWare Administrator (NWAdmn32).

ConsoleOne 1.3.4 and higher and iManager can also be run in a mode to force the
utility to communicate with only the Master replica. Start ConsoleOne with the
-forceMaster switch. This forces ConsoleOne to read only from the Master replica. For iManager 1.5 and higher, include &forceMaster=true in the URL when
logging in.

ODBC Driver for eDirectory

With the popularity of the Open Database Connectivity (ODBC) technology,
many data applications (including spreadsheet programs such as Excel) provide an ODBC interface for connecting to an ODBC data source. And
because NDS/eDirectory is a database, you can use the Novell ODBC Driver
for eDirectory to easily query and retrieve Directory data and generate
reports either for management or diagnostic needs.

Although ConsoleOne, iManager, and NetWare Administrator provide a convenient interface for DS management, they are not the best applications
when it comes to generating reports. This eDirectory ODBC driver serves as
an independent interface for extracting and reporting specified DS information for use in the applications you use everyday. It allows you to populate

reports, import data into your custom programs, or view data within a spreadsheet. In March 2004, Novell updated the driver to include the capability to perform simple update operations such as insert, modify, and delete on eDirectory objects.

The architecture behind the Novell ODBC Driver for eDirectory consists of the application, the `ODBC.DLL` Driver Manager, the Novell `ODBCNDS.DLL` driver, the network, and eDirectory itself. The driver employs the `ODBCNDS.DLL` to abstract the directory tree into accessible relational database tables, which hides the complexity of the underlying directory syntax. Information is selected and ordered from the relational tables using standard Structured Query Language (SQL) statements embedded into the application.

Using embedded SQL statements or ODBC functions, you can set queries and sort NDS/eDirectory information. For example, you can access the account information for each user. You can also set search conditions and sort directory entries to return specified entry attributes, such as the username, user description, telephone number, address, or other user-specific information. The retrieved user data can then be viewed in a report or used in programs. Figure 7.31 shows a Visual Basic program that uses the Novell ODBC Driver for eDirectory to access DS information.

FIGURE 7.31
Access the Novell ODBC Driver for eDirectory from a sample Visual Basic program.

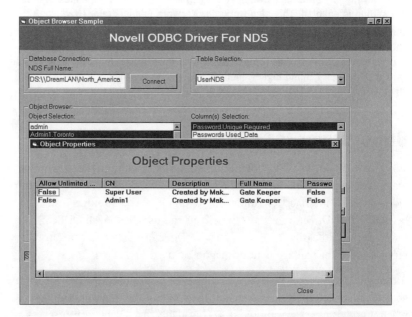

NOTE   You can download the Novell ODBC Driver for eDirectory, with read/write access, from developer.novell.com/ndk/odbcrw.htm.

Schema Manager and NDS Snoop

Schema Manager is a ConsoleOne snap-in application that allows users with Supervisor rights to a tree (the [Root] object) to customize the schema of that tree. Schema Manager is available from the Tools menu.

You can use Schema Manager to perform the following functions:

- ► View a list of all classes and attributes in the schema (see Figure 7.32). Highlight a class or attribute and then click Info to obtain additional information.

Schema extensions

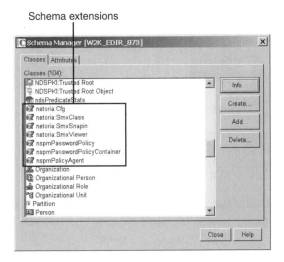

FIGURE 7.32
Viewing a tree's schema classes and attributes using Schema Manager.

- ► View an attribute's information, such as its syntax and flags.
- ► Extend the schema by adding a class or an attribute to the existing schema; you need to have Supervisor rights to [Root] for this operation.
- ► Create a new class by naming it and specifying applicable attributes, flags, containers to which it can be added, and parent classes from which it can inherit attributes. The class can be an auxiliary class if running NDS 8 or higher.
- ► Create an attribute by naming it and specifying its syntax and flags.

Any attributes added to a base class (that is, one that is part of the base schema, such as the User class), cannot be removed at a later time. **WARNING**

▶ Add an attribute to an existing class.

▶ Delete a non-base class that is not in use or that has become obsolete.

▶ Delete an attribute that is not in use or that has become obsolete.

Keep in mind that standard Novell-supplied management utilities, such as NetWare Administrator, cannot manage objects (such as create or update) that use extended schema definitions unless you have a snap-in for NetWare Administrator or custom applications that know about the extensions. Further discussions about NetWare Administrator snap-ins and a utility called ScheMax that allows you to extend the schema and create your own snap-ins can be found in Chapter 12, "eDirectory Management Tools."

An excellent Windows application called NDS Snoop is easier to use and more powerful than ConsoleOne's Schema Manager. Initially developed as an NDS developer tool by Novell Developer Support, it has since been enhanced with new features, including support for eDirectory. NDS Snoop has the following features:

▶ **NDS Browser**—It can be used to view any DS object and its corresponding attribute values. The browser allows you to browse any DS tree in your enterprise network. Continue to click the up arrow of the Containers list box until all the trees in your environment are displayed. If you select a tree to which you have not authenticated, you have `[Public]` access to that tree only.

▶ **Schema Viewer**—The Schema Viewer tool (see Figure 7.33) is used to read all the Attribute and Object class definitions from DS. Expand each definition name to see its corresponding attributes. The Object Class super class hierarchy includes its entire super class lineage all the way to Top. You can determine which attribute is derived from each super class by its icon displayed in the tree view. Matching icons indicate that those attributes were defined for the corresponding super class.

▶ **Schema Manager**—The Schema Manager tool is used to create DS schema attribute and class definitions. You must have sufficient rights to the `[Root]` of the tree to use the Schema Manager. If you do not have sufficient rights, all fields are disabled and the message `You must have Admin Equivalent rights to use the Schema Manager!` is displayed at the bottom of the view. Populate the fields with the desired values and select the desired operation for the attribute or object class definition.

▸ **NDS Query**—The NDS Query tool can be used to build complex search filters to query DS for objects that adhere to specific search criteria. For example, you could search for all User objects that have a telephone number that begins with 123. This tool is useful to determine whether you can search for an attribute value or new object you have just added to the DS tree.

▸ **Object Manager**—The Object Manager is used to create, delete, rename, or move any DS object. This tool can be used to create an object of a new custom DS Object Class schema extension you have just added. This tool automatically determines what the object's Mandatory Attributes are and allows you to add values for each.

▸ **Object Editor**—The Object Editor can be used to add values for any attribute type for all DS object classes with the exception for `SYN_STREAM` and `SYN_OCTET_STRING`. For example, you could add a value for a new attribute class definition, Student ID Number, to an existing DS object.

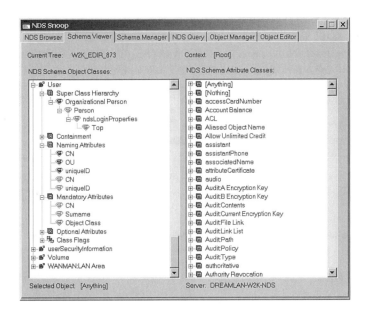

FIGURE 7.33
Viewing User class definitions using NDS Snoop.

You can download NDS Snoop from `www.novell.com/coolsolutions/tools/1005.html`.

Protocol Analyzers

What do you do when a DS-aware application worked on one DS tree but doesn't on another? When you're encountering -625 communication errors, where should you start looking? Our favorite tools for diagnosing such problems are *protocol analyzers*. A protocol analyzer is either a combination of hardware and software or pure software that can capture and analyze individual packets on your network. Some protocol analyzer manufacturers require you to use their specific hardware, but others are software-only and can be used with a variety of network cards that can operate in the promiscuous mode.

> **NOTE**
>
> *Promiscuous mode* operation is the capability of a network adapter (or network interface card [NIC]) to make a copy of the packets that are not addressed to it. Not all NICs can operate in this mode; therefore, you should check with your NIC's vendor if you're unsure.

One of the first software-only protocol analyzers is Novell's LANalyzer for Windows. It can monitor, capture, and analyze both Ethernet and Token-Ring data frames. It can decode all NetWare, AppleTalk, and TCP/IP protocol suites; for protocols it doesn't support, you're presented with the hex dump of the contents. A number of protocol analyzers are available commercially, such as Sniffer from Network Associates (`www.networkassociates.com/us/products/sniffer/home.asp`), and one of the more popular free protocol analyzers, Ethereal (`www.ethereal.com`). Although Ethereal is still technically beta software, it has a comprehensive feature set and many users have used it successfully for production use. Here is the list of features, current as of version 0.9.14, in no particular order:

- ▶ Data can be captured "off the wire" from a live network connection or read from a capture file.

- ▶ Ethereal can read capture files from tcpdump (libpcap), NAI's Sniffer (compressed and uncompressed), Sniffer Pro, NetXray, Sun snoop and atmsnoop, Shomiti/Finisar Surveyor, AIX's iptrace, Microsoft's Network Monitor, Novell's LANalyzer, RADCOM's WAN/LAN Analyzer, HP-UX nettl, i4btrace from the ISDN4BSD project, Cisco Secure IDS iplog, the pppd log (pppdump-format), the AG Group's/WildPacket's EtherPeek/TokenPeek/AiroPeek, or Visual Networks' Visual UpTime. It can also read traces made from Lucent/Ascend WAN routers and Toshiba ISDN routers, as well as the text output from VMS's TCPIPtrace utility and the DBS Etherwatch utility for VMS. Any of these files can be compressed with gzip, and Ethereal decompresses them on-the-fly.

▶ Live data can be read from Ethernet, FDDI, PPP, Token-Ring, IEEE 802.11, Classical IP over ATM, and loopback interfaces (at least on some platforms; not all those types are supported on all platforms).

▶ Captured network data can be browsed via a GUI or via the TTY-mode tethereal program.

▶ Captured files can be programmatically edited or converted via command-line switches to the editcap program.

▶ More than 500 protocols can currently be dissected, including but not limited to AARP, AIM and its related protocols, ARP/RARP, BOOTP/DHCP, BOOTPARAMS, BROWSER, DHCPv6, DNS, DNSSERVER, EIGRP, FTP, FTP-DATA, FTSERVER, H.261, H.263, H1, H225, H245, H4501, IGRP, IP, IPX, IPX MSG, IPX RIP, IPX SAP, IPX WAN, IPv6, LDAP, MySQL, NBIPX, NCP, NDPS, NETLOGON, NFS, NFSACL, NFSAUTH, NIS+, NIS+ CB, NLSP, NMAS, NNTP, NTP, NetBIOS, OSPF, PPP and its related protocols, RIP, SMB, SMB Mailslot, SMB Pipe, SMPP, SMTP, SPX, SRVLOC, SRVSVC, SSH, SSL, Syslog, TCP, TELNET, TFTP, TIME, Token-Ring, and UDP.

▶ Output can be saved or printed as plain text or PostScript.

▶ Data display can be refined using a display filter.

▶ Display filters can also be used to selectively highlight and color packet summary information.

▶ All or part of each captured network trace can be saved to disk.

To use a protocol analyzer effectively, you need to be versed in the protocols to understand what you're seeing. The analyzer tells you what it sees on the wire, but it's up to you, the user, to interpret the presented data and take appropriate action.

TIP

An excellent resource about protocol analysis is the Protocol Analysis Institute's Web site at www.packet-level.com.

Information Tools

Oftentimes, the amount of useful information provided by the various utilities we've discussed in this chapter is limited because the tools assume you know what you're looking for in the first place, which is often not the case.

Also, knowing the cause of the error or understanding the error code doesn't always automatically tell you what the solution is. Therefore, you need to combine the diagnosis of your problem with some type of knowledge base to formulate an action plan to fix your DS problem. This section introduces a number of information tools that can assist you in the task:

- ▶ LogicSource for NDS/eDirectory
- ▶ Novell's technical support knowledgebase
- ▶ Novell Internet newsgroups
- ▶ Novell's Cool Solutions for eDirectory
- ▶ Help files

LogicSource for NDS/eDirectory

In March 1998, during Novell's annual BrainShare Conference in Salt Lake City, Utah, Novell released an electronic document called "Understanding, Identifying and Resolving NDS Issues" (code named the Phoenix Document) that offered in-depth explanations of the concepts, processes, and operations of NDS. In mid-1998, the product was enhanced with more information and searching for data was made easier. The document is now known as "LogicSource for eDirectory" (see Figure 7.34) and is available as part of the Novell Professional Resource Suite (`support.novell.com/subscriptions/subscription_products/nprs16.html`) and the eDirectory Toolkit (`support.novell.com/subscriptions/subscription_products/product_toolkits17.html`).

Designed to help you manage and support all versions of NDS and eDirectory, "LogicSource for eDirectory" includes descriptions of common error codes to help you learn why they occur and how to avoid them. "LogicSource for eDirectory" contains more than 1,500 pages of detailed information (perhaps more than you ever cared to know!) about the various DS processes and steps for setting up directory trees.

The information included in "LogicSource for eDirectory" covers the following subjects:

- ▶ Understanding Novell Directory Services
- ▶ Novell Directory Services background processes
- ▶ Novell Directory Services background process requests
- ▶ Novell Directory Services partition and object operations

- ▶ Resources for supporting Novell Directory Services for different operating system platforms

- ▶ Identifying and resolving Novell Directory Services issues

- ▶ Novell Directory Services Error Codes

- ▶ Novell Client, operating system, and other error codes

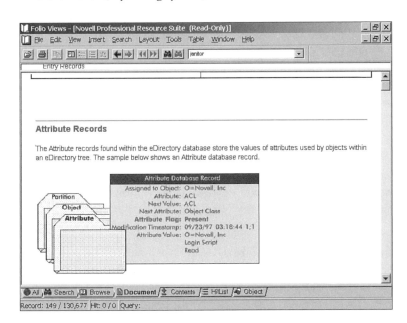

FIGURE 7.34
Sample page from "Logic-Source for eDirectory."

Novell Knowledgebase

Over the years, Novell Technical Support (NTS) has collected and published reported issues and resolutions for all Novell products, including the NetWare operating system and its components. The information is available in the form of technical information documents (TIDs). You can access these TIDs, free of charge, 24 hours a day, 7 days a week over the Internet from Novell Technical Support's Web site at `support.novell.com/search/kb_index.jsp`. The TIDs are stored in a searchable database. You can search using a single word, a phrase, or a TID number, and you can combine multiple words together using Boolean operators.

TIP

When searching for a DS error code, which is usually a negative number (such as -625), in the knowledgebase, do not enter -625 as the keyword. Instead, enter "-625" (putting quotes around the number). Without the quotes, the search engine matches on the number 625, which can appear in many TIDs.

The resulting hit list is graded by relevance. The better a TID matches your search criteria, the higher the assigned percentage. From the same Web site (`support.novell.com`), you can find and download the latest patches and file updates relevant to your problem.

The online knowledgebase is easy to use and readily available—*if* you have a reliable Internet connection. Have you ever been at a client site at 2 a.m. and needed the latest NetWare 6.5 `DS.NLM` update so you could install a NetWare 5 server into an existing NetWare 6 tree and there's no RJ-11 jack in sight? Or have you needed to download NetWare 6's Support Pack to get the new `DS.NLM` update to address an eDirectory error you have encountered, only to find your Internet connection is slower than molasses in winter because everyone is checking the Super Bowl Web site and eating up all available bandwidth? Yes, you can easily find and download these patches from the Internet, if you have a fast (T1 or better) link because the files are very large. (For example, NetWare 6.5 Support Pack 1.1 is 400MB!) But sometimes you simply can't wait an hour for a file to be downloaded. The alternative is the Novell Support Resource Library (formally Novell Support Connection CD).

Other than "LogicSource for eDirectory" (and for other products such as ZENworks), Novell also make the TIDs and patch files available on a set of CDs, known as the Novell Support Resource Library (`support.novell.com/ subscriptions/subscription_products/nsrl19.html`). The Resource Library provides fast and easy access to the specific information you need and enables you to do onsite troubleshooting, acting as an immediate first point of reference for technical information.

NOTE   The Novell Support Resource Library is usable on any Windows (and soon also on Linux) desktop. No network access is required to fully utilize the monthly updates.

The one disadvantage of Resource Library versus the online knowledgebase is that the CDs are generally a few weeks behind what's available on the Web site, due to lead time needed to produce and ship the product.

Novell Internet Newsgroups

Not all knowledge is passed on in writing; some is simply passed verbally as whispered wisdom, and some knowledge can be gained from hands-on experience. Knowledgebases are wonderful tools, but they are only as complete as the number of issues reported to Novell Technical Support. For every reported problem, there's probably five that are not reported.

To facilitate Novell customers around the world to share their experiences and tips and tricks for dealing with problems, Novell operates a set of Internet newsgroups, known as the Novell Product Support Forums (formerly Novell Support Connection forums). The main purpose of these message forums is to offer a place to discuss and obtain technical support related to released Novell products. Within these newsgroups, you're free to ask questions, respond to any forum message that interests you, or tell others about your latest adventure with your Novell product. If you can assist a fellow user, feel free to jump into the conversation because peer-to-peer support is highly encouraged.

NOTE

You might have used the Novell Product Support Forums in their previous incarnation. Prior to being on the Internet, Novell sponsored a set of messaging forums on CompuServe Information Service (CIS; now part of America Online), known as NetWire. In 1997, Novell moved off CIS and implemented the current Internet newsgroups infrastructure.

You can access the Novell Product Support Forums either via the Web interface using your favorite browser or via an NNTP newsreader, the Internet news protocol. For more information, visit `support.novell.com/forums/`.

NOTE

A number of mailing lists on the Internet are devoted to Novell products. Perhaps the most well-known one is the `NOVELL@lsv.syr.edu` mailing list. Refer to `www.nbd.dk/faq/nvfaq-b.htm` for more information.

Novell Cool Solutions for eDirectory

The Novell Cool Solutions Web site is the source of many real-world business and technology guidance and hands-on techniques for executives, managers, developers, and other professionals who must choose and use appropriate information and business technology, products, and services. Divided into a number of "communities" based on products, the Cool Solutions for eDirectory (`www.novell.com/coolsolutions/nds/`) is one of the founding communities.

From the Cool Solutions for eDirectory home page, you can access a large number of eDirectory-related articles and Q&As, as well as download tools to address any specific needs you may have in terms of eDirectory management. From time to time, you will also find announcements of new eDirectory TIDs and requests for participation in Novell's beta test program for various products.

Help Files

Other than the various knowledge sources discussed previously, many people often overlook the wealth of information available in the online help files included with many of the utilities. For example, NDS iMonitor includes context-sensitive help and can offer information about a reported DS error code (see Figure 7.35), such as possible causes and corrective actions. Also included with the NDS iMonitor help file is a list of DS and server error codes you might find useful.

FIGURE 7.35
NDS iMonitor
online help.

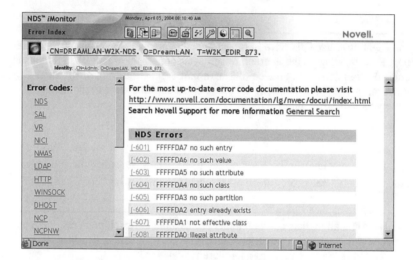

Frequently, by combining the help information offered by the utilities and the TIDs available from Novell, you'll have a good starting point for your troubleshooting efforts.

NOTE

Novell's Web site has a number of TIDs and documents that list error codes. None of them, however, are complete. Some codes are listed in one document but are missing from another. Therefore, taking all the error code documents that we can find and combining them with the information from the latest version of the Novell Development Kit results in Appendix A, "eDirectory Error Codes." We have expanded or added explanations for each of the listed error codes. At the time of this writing, the list of error codes presented in Appendix A is the most comprehensive compilation available anywhere.

Summary

This chapter introduced you to the various server- and workstation-based diagnostic tools and utilities included with the NetWare operating systems, such as DSRepair. Also covered were the new cross-platform tools included with eDirectory, such as NDS iMonitor, as well as information tools, such as LogicSource and Novell Product Support Forums newsgroup. In Chapter 8, you'll read about a number of DS data recovery tools.

CHAPTER 8

eDirectory Data
Recovery Tools

Chapter 7 discussed various utilities that can assist you in diagnosing and understanding NDS/eDirectory issues. In this chapter, you'll learn about tools that will help in protecting and recovering lost DS information. Such information may have been deleted by mistake or you may need to restore a crashed server to a working state.

Chapter 11 complements the information presented in this chapter. This chapter covers recovery tools in general and offers some one-step solutions to simple DS recovery needs, while Chapter 11 presents examples of specific DS issues in detail.

NOTE

The following topics are discussed in this chapter:

- ▶ Backing up and restoring DS with Storage Management Services (SMS) and using the eDirectory Management Tool Box (eMBox)

- ▶ NDS/eDirectory recovery using Server Specific Information (SSI) data after a server crash

- ▶ Recovering lost passwords and lost Admin user account

- ▶ Detecting and adding objects that are blocked by Inherited Rights Filters (IRFs)

SMS Backup and Restore

Storage Management Services (SMS), developed by Novell, provides a standard for data, devices, media, and storage management interfaces. With the appropriate agents, SMS can be configured to service different targets—such as NetWare, NDS/eDirectory, Unix, and so on (as long as there is an agent available for the target)—from a single backup engine. To fully understand the terminology and appreciate why you need an SMS-compliant backup solution for your NetWare network, the following sections offer a brief architectural overview of SMS and some sample SMS backup implementations.

SMS Architecture

SMS divides the storage management function into four areas of responsibility:

▶ Transparent communications interface

▶ Target-specific agent

▶ Storage engine

▶ Device interface

These are incorporated into four modules or applications, as illustrated by Figure 8.1.

FIGURE 8.1
Novell's SMS architectural overview.

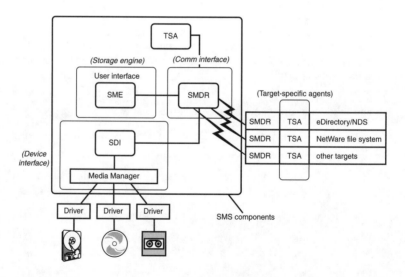

The *Storage Management Data Requester (SMDR)* provides transparent local and Remote Procedure Call (RPC) links between the SMS modules running on the storage engine and the SMS modules running on the target. When you're running an SMS-compliant tape backup software on a NetWare server that is backing up a remote NetWare server, for example, **SMDR.NLM** must be running on both servers to facilitate the communication; a Windows SMDR module (called `w32smdr.exe`) is included with eDirectory for Windows and is installed in *drive*:`\Novell\nds\sms`.

◼ **TIP**

SMDR versions prior to 5.00 depend on SPX and, thus, IPX. Starting with SMDR 5.00 (shipped with NetWare 5), it is protocol independent. For NetWare 5 and later, this requester can use TCP/IP to communicate with other SMDRs. Although SMDR 5.00 and higher can be configured to support TCP/IP and SPX/IPX, both protocols are supported by default. The SPX protocol is used with SMDR versions prior to 5.00.

The ability to back up data from a specific operation system platform is provided through the *Target Service Agent (TSA)*, which runs on the *target*. In SMS parlance, an SMS target is what you want to back up (the source of your data). The TSA is SMS's access road to a target's data. Through a set of generic Target Service APIs, SMS can read from, write to, and scan the target. All of SMS, except the TSA, treats the target's data as *"black box data"*—only the TSA knows the target's data structure. Generally, one TSA is required for each target. The following are the different TSA modules available for NetWare:

► **TSANDS.NLM**—To back up and restore tree-wide DS data.

► **TSA410.NLM**—To back up and restore the file system of a NetWare 4.1*x* or 4.2 server.

► **TSA500.NLM**—To back up and restore the file system of a NetWare 5.*x* server.

► **TSA600.NLM**—To back up and restore the file system of a NetWare 6.0 server.

► **TSAFS.NLM**—To back up and restore the file system (traditional, NSS, and cluster-enabled volumes) of a NetWare 6.5 server.

► **TSADOSP.NLM**—To back up and restore files from the DOS partition on a NetWare server. (Shipped only with NetWare 5.0 and NetWare 5.1.)

► **TSAPROXY.NLM**—To facilitate backup and restore files on Windows workstations running Novell Client software and have the Windows TSA agent running.

► **TSADOS.NLM**—To facilitate backup and restore files on DOS workstations running Novell Client software and with **TSASMS.COM** loaded.

► **GWTSA.NLM**—To back up and restore GroupWise mailboxes and related information.

TIP

TSAFS supports backup of open files on NSS volumes if the CopyOnWrite feature is enabled. Only the last closed version of the file is backed up. The Supervisor right is required to back up open files. To enable CopyOnWrite on a single NSS volume, at the server console, enter nss /FileCopyOnWrite=*volume_name*. For more information about using NSS server console commands refer to NSS documentation.

TSA500 and higher support both the traditional NetWare file system and the Novell Storage Services (NSS) released with NetWare 5 and above. The initial release of TSA500, however, does not support NSS mounted DOS FAT file systems. If you need to back up a DOS partition, use `TSADOSP.NLM` instead. To back up from or restore to the DOS FAT partition on a NetWare 6.0 and later server, load `DOSFAT.NSS` and `TSA600.NLM` (or `TSAFS.NLM` for NetWare 6.5). After loading the `DOSFAT.NSS` module, any DOS FAT partitions are dynamically made available as logical volumes. TSA600/TSAFS considers these logical volumes as resources for backup and restore.

Storage Management Engine (SME) is the heart of an SMS-compliant backup system. Its main task is to retrieve and dispense data. It is in this module where third-party vendors provide value-added features, such as maintaining a database of backed up files and management of tapes.

Instead of directly communicating with the various types of storage devices, SMS communicates with them via the *Storage Device Interface (SDI)* module. With the assistance of Media Manager, SDI provides SMS a logical view of the media and storage devices. Because of this, any applications using SDI can use all SMS-compatible devices without making any changes. In essence, SDI is a *storage device abstraction layer* within the SMS architecture, so the higher layers within SMS, such as the SME, don't need to know how to address a specific storage device for data retrieval or writing to it.

System Independent Data Format

SMS's capability to work with many different types of targets or services (such as NetWare file systems, eDirectory, Windows 2000, and so on) whose data structures are varied is due to the *System Independent Data Format (SIDF)*. SIDF specifies how a target's data is formatted, who does the formatting, how a session is placed on the media, and so on. The TSA is responsible for formatting and "deformatting" the target's data set (such as file data and name-space information) according to the specification. The SME simply writes the SIDF-formatted data to the storage media. Therefore, in concept, SMS's use of SIDF is very similar to the use of XDR (External Data Representation) in NFS (Network File System) developed by Sun

Microsystems, except the receiving side (the SME) does not deformat the data before recording it.

SMS Backup Session Example

The interactions between the various SMS modules are complex. The following example offers you a high-level look at how an SMS backup session works and gives you some insights into how and why SMS-compliant software functions the way it does. The example assumes that the SMS engine (SME, SDI, and SMDR) is running on a NetWare 6.5 server and it is backing up the SYS volume of a remote NetWare 5.1 server, which has a TSA and SMDR running (see Figure 8.2):

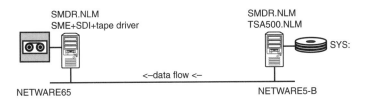

FIGURE 8.2
The SYS volume of the NETWARE5-B server is being backed up, across the wire, by NETWARE65.

1. The user selects the backup media to use. This connects the SME to SDI.

2. The user selects NETWARE5-B as the target. During this process the SMDRs on each server connect to each other; this is transparent to the user as well as the SME programmer. Through the SMDR connection, the SME running on NETWARE65 connects to the TSA running on NETWARE5-B.

If the SME is backing up local data, the SMDR is bypassed so that all communication between the SME and TSA becomes direct.

3. The SME asks the TSA to provide a list of resources or data sets the user can choose to back up. The SME presents this list to the user for selection.

4. The user selects the SYS volume and specifies that the file system trustees are to be backed up as well.

5. The SME sends the user selections back to the TSA.

6. The TSA then scans (searches) NETWARE5-B for the specified data sets (resources).

7. Upon finding a data set that matches the selection criteria, the TSA formats the data set (which includes file attributes, file names, name space information and so on) according to SIDF specifications and sends it to the SME.

8. File system trustee assignments are backed up as follows:

   a. For each given file or directory, the TSA reads the Directory Entry Table (DET) to determine whether any trustees are assigned.

   b. If a trustee assignment is found, TSA reads the trustee—this is stored as an object ID and not a DS object name.

   c. The object ID is then translated into a full DS object name.

   d. The TSA formats the data according to SIDF specifications and sends it to the SME.

9. The SME sends the received data to SDI, through Media Manager and device-specific driver, for storage on the (selected) media.

10. Steps 6 through 9 are repeated until all data sets matching the user selection criteria are found and stored.

You can use a non-SMS solution to back up your file system provided it is NetWare-aware (so file system trustee information is properly backed up). Because it doesn't make use of TSA, however, it cannot back up NDS/eDirectory; some of the DS files are kept open by `DS.NLM` and thus can't be backed up or copied by conventional means—unless it provides its own agent.

SBackup for NetWare

Included with NetWare (from NetWare 3.0 and up) is an SMS-compliant backup utility called SBackup. It is an NLM-based tape backup program. NetWare 5 and higher ship with an enhanced version of this backup engine, called SBCon. It contains all the functionality provided by earlier versions of SBackup and has the following enhancements:

▶ Autoloader support

▶ Enhanced user interface (SBCon)

▶ Windows workstation graphical interface (NWBack32)—NWBack32 is not included with NetWare 6.5

▶ Multiple and repeatable job scheduling

▸ Concurrent jobs can run on multiple devices (but not on same device)

▸ Runs on earlier versions of NetWare and is compatible with all TSAs

▸ Runs in an IP-only environment if preferred

NOTE

If multiple backup and restore jobs are submitted to run at the same time *on the same device*, the second and subsequent jobs will receive an error because the device (tape drive or other device) is busy servicing the current job. The error message does not make it sufficiently clear that the problem is simply that the device is in use. To avoid this conflict, set the execution time for subsequent jobs to run sometime after prior jobs are completed or submit concurrent jobs to different devices.

The sections that follow outline the necessary steps for backing up and restoring your NDS/eDirectory using SBCon, which is shipped with NetWare 6.5. Before learning that, however, you need to know how to correctly set up and configure SMS for your DS environment.

Configuring SMDR and QMAN

As mentioned earlier in this chapter, SMS-compliant applications make use of SMDR, and SBCon is no exception. Unlike previous versions of SMDR that use Service Advertising Protocol (SAP) to locate other SMDRs on the network, the newer SMDR uses DS and the Service Location Protocol (SLP). Older versions of SMDR advertised the server name where it was loaded using SAP type 0x23F. This mechanism worked well in small LAN environments, but did not scale well in large environments and does not work at all in a pure IP environment. In a pure IP environment, SMDR uses either DS or SLP as a service locator instead of SAPs.

NOTE

SMDR v5.04 and later can use SLP for locating other SMDRs. This enables SMDRs to locate other SMDRs running on servers belonging to different trees. Every SLP-enabled SMDR will register itself in the SMDR.Novell domain when loaded. The SLP-enabled SMDRs will query this domain for locating registered SMDRs.

NOTE

Each server that will be running SMS-compliant software needs to have its own SMDR object.

You need to install and configure SMDR and QMAN (SMS Queue Manager) before you can use any SMS applications, such as SBCon. Some third-party SMS applications may include their own queue manager instead of using QMAN. The configuration can be done during the server installation by choosing to install SMS, or you can add this service at a later time using NWConfig. If SMDR fails to load or if the SMDR object is corrupted, you can restore it to the state when the server was first installed and before it was configured. To do so, you need to delete two configuration files and two DS objects using the steps in the following procedure:

1. Log in to the server as a user that has Admin rights.

2. Make your working directory SYS:ETC\SMS.

3. There are two files within this directory, SMDR.CFG and SBACKUP.CFG (SBCON.CFG on NetWare 6.0 and later). Both of these files are text based and can be viewed with any text editor. Either delete or rename these two files. (There is also a TSA.CFG file on NetWare 6.5 servers but you don't need to delete this file.)

4. Use a management tool, such as NetWare Administrator, to locate the two SMS-related objects in the tree. Usually these two objects are generally in the container where the NCP Server object is located. If the objects are not there, look through the tree for them. Once they are found, delete them. The default names of the objects are "SMS SMDR Group" and "*server name* Backup Queue." For example, for a server named "NETWARE65," the object names are "SMS SMDR Group" and "NETWARE65 Backup Queue."

5. At the server console prompt, type **LOAD SMDR NEW**. The NEW switch brings up the SMDR Configuration Screen (see Figure 8.3), and you're asked for three pieces of information:

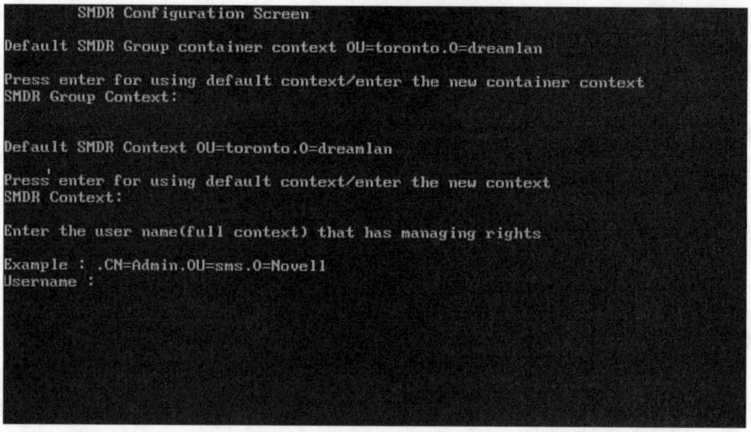

FIGURE 8.3
The SMDR configuration screen.

```
        SMDR Configuration Screen
Default SMDR Group container context OU=toronto.O=dreamlan

Press enter for using default context/enter the new container context
SMDR Group Context:


Default SMDR Context OU=toronto.O=dreamlan

Press enter for using default context/enter the new context
SMDR Context:

Enter the user name(full context) that has managing rights

Example : .CN=Admin.OU=sms.O=Novell
Username :
```

▶ The default context for the SMDR group: enter the desired context (such as `OU=Servers.O=Company`) or press Enter to use the default context.

▶ The default SMDR context: enter the desired context (such as `OU=Servers.O=Company`) or press Enter to use the default context.

▶ The name and password of the user who has managing rights to the object that will be created in the specified context: An example of a user name is given. When entering the user name, use absolute fully distinguished naming such as `.CN=Admin.OU=Servers.O=Company`.

The previous steps create a new `SYS:ETC\SMS\SMDR.CFG` configuration file that looks similar to this:

```
#This is SMDR default configuration file
#Lines beginning with # are treated as comment

SMDR Context: OU=toronto.O=dreamlan
SMDR Group Context: OU=toronto.O=dreamlan

#Both the protocols are enabled
```

4. At the server console prompt, type **LOAD QMAN NEW**. The NEW switch brings up the SMS Queue Manager Configuration Screen (see Figure 8.4). Similar to configuring SMDR, you'll be asked to specify the context and the name of the SMS Job Queue. After the job queue name is created, the name of the user who has managing rights is requested. This time, however, an example of the user name is not given. Follow the previous step's suggestion for the user naming. It is suggested that the same user be given rights to the queue object as the SMS group object.

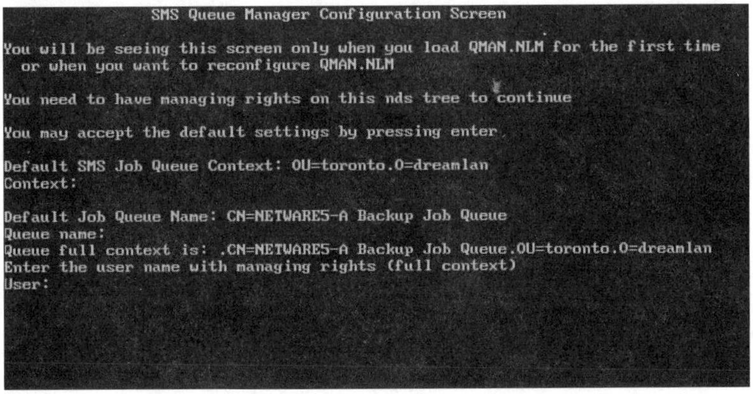

```
        SMS Queue Manager Configuration Screen
You will be seeing this screen only when you load QMAN.NLM for the first time
  or when you want to reconfigure QMAN.NLM

You need to have managing rights on this nds tree to continue

You may accept the default settings by pressing enter

Default SMS Job Queue Context: OU=toronto.O=dreamlan
Context:

Default Job Queue Name: CN=NETWARE5-A Backup Job Queue
Queue name:
Queue full context is: .CN=NETWARE5-A Backup Job Queue.OU=toronto.O=dreamlan
Enter the user name with managing rights (full context)
User:
```

FIGURE 8.4
The SMS Queue Manager configuration screen.

If everything is entered correctly, the configuration screen clears and a console message similar to the following is displayed:

```
Started service the job queue .CN=NETWARE65 Backup Job
Queue.OU=toronto.O=dreamlan
Using transfer buffer size 65536 bytes.
```

Also, this step creates a new SYS:ETC\SMS\SBACKUP.CFG (SBCON.CFG on NetWare 6.0 and later) configuration file that looks similar to this:

```
# This is QMANAGER Configuration file
# Lines beginning with # are treated as comment.
# QMAN.NLM reads the information from this file when
# loaded
Sbackup Job Queue: .CN=NETWARE65 Backup Job Queue.
➥ OU=toronto.O=dreamlan
# Default Transfer buffer size
# Transfer Buffer Size: 64000
```

Now you're ready to run SBCon.

Backing Up eDirectory

In NetWare 5 and above, the SBackup NLM has been renamed to SBCON.NLM (NetWare Storage Management Console; on NetWare 6.5 it is referred to as SMS—Backup Management Console) and has a slightly different look than previous versions of SBackup (see Figure 8.5). The main difference is in the Job Administration option, which enables you to create, submit, and administer jobs in a DS queue.

FIGURE 8.5
The version of SBackup shipped with NetWare 5 and above is now called SBCon.

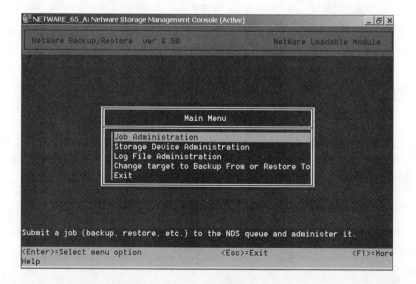

You should be aware that NDS/eDirectory partition boundary information is not backed up; therefore, you should keep a written record of your DS tree partition placement. If no partition information exists when a restore is performed (for instance, after a total loss of a DS tree), the entire tree structure is placed into one partition ([Root]). You must then manually re-create the partitions and replicas.

The following steps outline how you can use SBCon to back up your DS tree. It is assumed that you have already correctly installed and configured your tape device:

1. Load the controller and storage device driver for your tape device, if not already loaded. Load NWTAPE.CDM if required by the device driver.

2. Load TSANDS.NLM on one of your NetWare servers (SMDR will be auto-loaded if not already loaded). On NetWare 6.5 servers, you can run the SMSSTART.NCF file at the console that loads SMDR, TSAFS, and TSANDS.

You only need to load TSANDS on one server. For best performance, you should load TSANDS.NLM and SBCON.NLM on the server holding the most replicas. This reduces the amount of tree-walking required during the backing up of the whole DS tree.

If you see the "SMDR Group Context is invalid" message displayed when SMDR is loading, this means you have not completely configured the SMDR object. Refer to the earlier section, "Configuring SMDR and QMAN," to (re)configure SMDR.

3. On the server with the tape device, load QMAN.NLM and then load SBCON.NLM.

4. From the Main Menu, select Storage Device Administration.

5. From the Select a Device menu, highlight the device you want to use (see Figure 8.6). If the device is an autoloader, press Enter to display a list of loaded media.

If SBCon can't communicate with the tape drive, or if the console LIST DEVICES command shows the device in an Unbound state, ensure NWTAPE.CDM is loaded. If the LIST DEVICES console command sees the tape device properly, but SBCon does not recognize the device, it's possible that SBCon does not support the tape device. A list of SBCon-supported tape devices can be found in TID #10059850.

FIGURE 8.6
Select the back-
up device and
media using the
Select a Device
menu.

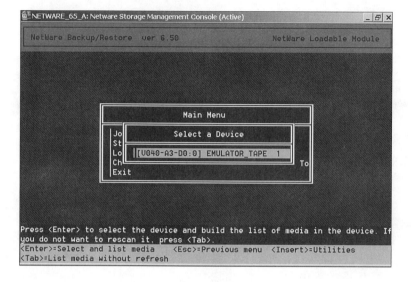

6. Highlight the media you want to use and press Enter to select it.

7. Press Esc to return to the Main Menu.

NOTE   Steps three through six are not absolutely necessary. These steps help you ascertain whether the job will be able to access the tape device or not before you submit the job.

8. Select Job Administration.

9. Select Backup from the Select Job menu.

10. Use the Target Service option of the Backup Options menu to select
the target server. If the selected target server has multiple TSAs running, such as TSANDS and TSAFS, you also need to select the appropriate service. The name of the TSANDS service is *server name*.Novell
Directory (for example, NETWARE_65_A.Novell Directory; see
Figure 8.7).

11. You're then prompted for a username and password with sufficient DS
rights to back up the tree; use the *.username.org* naming syntax. Upon
successful login, a message similar to "You are connected to the target
service *name* <Press ENTER to continue>" is displayed. In the Target
Service option, you'll now see the DS tree name listed.

12. Use the What to Back Up? option to select backing up the whole
Directory tree, the schema, objects or a branch of the tree. After selecting the option, the List Resources menu is displayed.

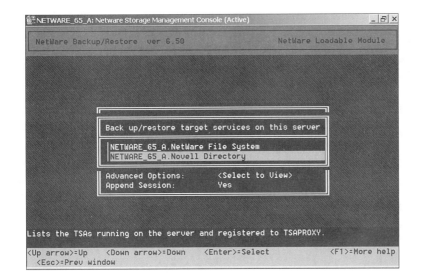

FIGURE 8.7
Select the TSANDS service for backup.

13. Press Insert to bring up a list of DS resources that you can select for backup (see Figure 8.8). To back up the schema, for example, highlight Schema in the Full Directory Backup menu, press Enter, and the Schema menu is displayed; you'll see "[..]" in the menu. Press Esc and the word Schema is now shown in the List Resources menu indicating it will be backed up.

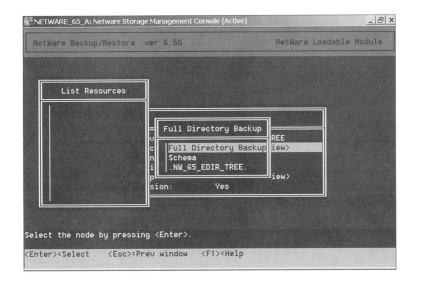

FIGURE 8.8
You can back up the whole tree, the schema, the selected objects or the selected branches of the tree.

NOTE

Selecting Full Directory Backup will back up all objects in the tree, including schema. Selecting SYS volume backup will also back up Server Specific Information (SSI) data, which is important when restoring a crashed server (see the "Server Recovery Using Server Specific Information Data" section later in this chapter for more details.)

TIP

To make it easier to back up portions of the DS tree, you can create a TSANDS.CFG file, which enables you to specify the names of containers where you want backups to begin. TSANDS.CFG is a text file listing DS contexts (one per line) located in the SYS:SYSTEM\TSA directory on the server that TSANDS.NLM is loaded on. When this file is present, SBCon lists the additional contexts as available resources that you can select for backup. Note that not all backup programs support the additional resources made available by TSANDS.CFG.

---

14. Repeat Step 13 to select any other DS resources you want to back up.

15. Enter a description (up to 23 characters), such as NETWARE 6.5 tree backup, in the Description field.

16. Use the Device/Media Name field to select the tape device that will be used.

17. Use the Advanced Options menu to schedule when the job will run (see Figure 8.9) and to designate whether it's a repeating job (see Figure 8.10).

18. Use the Append Session option to specify whether the data on the tape is to be appended or overwritten.

FIGURE 8.9
Use the Advanced Backup Options menu to further control what data to back up and to schedule the job.

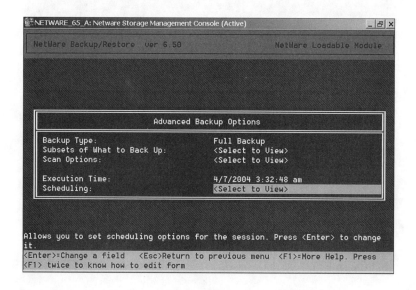

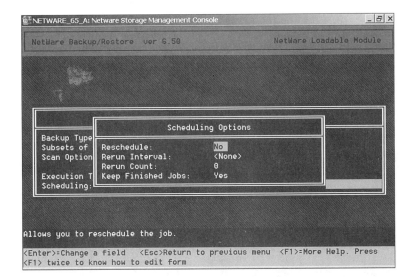

FIGURE 8.10
You can schedule the job as a run-once or as a recurring job.

19. Press Esc and select Yes in response to the Do you want to submit a job? prompt. At this point, you are returned to the Select Job menu.

The job will execute automatically at the scheduled time. You can use the Current Job List option to manage the submitted jobs: from the Main Menu, select Job Administration, Current Job List. A list of queued jobs is displayed in the Queue Job menu. Similar to managing print jobs, you can put a backup job on hold and change its execution time and scheduling (see Figure 8.11).

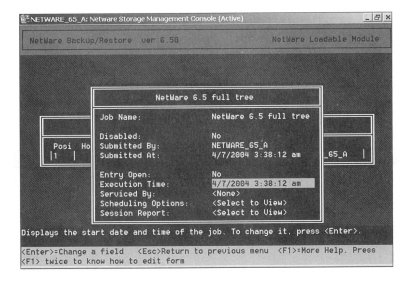

FIGURE 8.11
Use the Current Job List to manage submitted SBCon jobs.

You can monitor the runtime status of an executing job by highlighting the job in the Queue Job menu and pressing Insert. A real-time display similar to the one that existed in previous versions of SBackup is shown (see Figure 8.12). From this menu, you can delete or stop the job by pressing Delete.

FIGURE 8.12
Real-time status of a currently executing job.

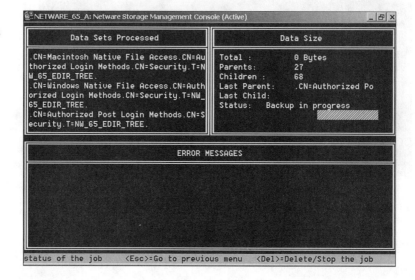

You can also check the execution status of a job using SBCon's status screen. SBCon creates two NLM screens; one is the user menu screen and the other an SMS Activity Log screen (see Figure 8.13). The information displayed in the SMS Activity Log screen is recorded in the `SYS:SYSTEM\TSA\LOG\ ACTIVITY.LOG` file and available for review at a later time. Alternatively, you can use SBCon's run logs to determine what resources were backed up and whether there were any errors. You can access the run log from the Main Menu: Log File Administration, View a log file. To access the error log, use Log File Administration, View an Error File to access the error log. By default, the SMS activity and SBCon run files are stored in the `SYS:SYSTEM\TSA\LOG` directory.

> **NOTE**
>
> `SME.NLM` **is auto-loaded when the backup job starts and is unloaded after the job finishes.**

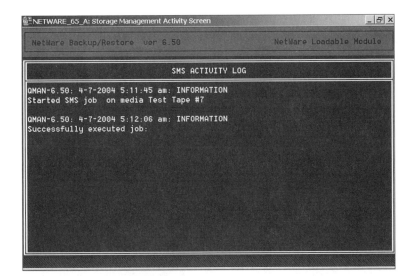

FIGURE 8.13
SBCon reports the success or failure of a given job using the SMS Activity Log screen.

Restoring eDirectory

The mechanics for restoring DS using SBCon is very similar to that of backing up DS except now your source is the tape instead of TSANDS. You can restore a single object, a branch of the tree, or the whole Directory tree. Before you restore DS data from a tape backup, you need to be aware of the following implications to your existing tree:

▶ A restore of DS from tape backup does *not* overwrite the existing database with a copy like that on the tape. Instead, the DS restore process will attempt to re-create all the objects that existed when the backup was performed.

▶ When a restore is performed under disaster recovery conditions, in which the original DS database has been destroyed and server reinstalled, the DS objects and attributes restored from the tape are added to the minimal DS tree provided by the NDS/eDirectory installation process. This results in a tree that is the same as the one saved to tape.

▶ If, however, a DS tree still exists on the server to which the restore is being performed, a restore will attempt to append to the existing tree, rather than overwrite it. In the best possible case, the restore process will have no visible effect at all. The worst possible case will result in additional, unwanted objects being added to the existing tree structure, leaving the old, corrupted structures intact, and possibly adding additional corrupt elements.

The following steps outline how to use SBCon to restore your DS (we assume that you have already correctly installed and configured your tape device):

1. Load the controller and storage device driver for your tape device, if not already loaded. Load NWTAPE.CDM if required by the device driver.

2. Load TSANDS.NLM on one of your NetWare servers. (SMDR will be auto-loaded if not already loaded.)

3. On the server with the tape device, load QMAN.NLM and then load SBCON.NLM.

4. Select Job Administration.

5. Select Restore from the Select Job menu to bring up the Restore Options menu (see Figure 8.14).

FIGURE 8.14
Configure your restore options using this menu.

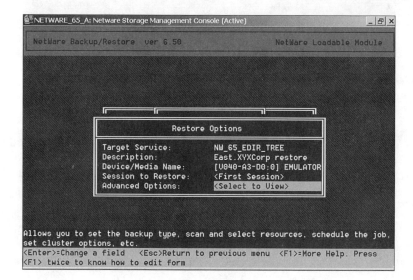

6. Select the Target Service to select the server to which you want to restore DS. Press Enter to bring up a list of servers running TSAs. If the selected server has multiple TSAs running, such as TSANDS and TSAFS, you also need to select the appropriate service. The name of the DS service is *server name*.Novell Directory (for example, NET-WARE_65_A.Novell Directory).

7. You're then prompted for a username and password with sufficient DS rights to the tree; use the *.username.org* naming syntax. Upon successful login, a message similar to "You are connected to target service *name* <Press ENTER to continue>" is displayed. In the Target Service option, you'll now see the DS tree name listed.

8. Enter a description (up to 23 characters) to identify the job in the Description field.

9. Select the device and media on which DS data is stored.

10. Select the correct session on the media containing the DS data you want to restore.

11. Use Advanced Options to set any filters desired in restoring the DS, whether any existing objects should be overwritten, and configure the execution time and run schedules (see Figure 8.15).

WARNING

Be careful when configuring the Overwrite Parent and Overwrite Child options. Any recent DS-related changes (this does not include file system trustee assignments, because they are not stored in DS) to the object, including password, will revert the values to whatever they were at the time of the backup.

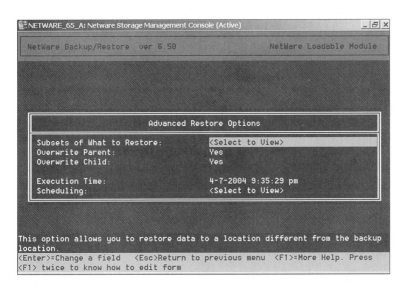

FIGURE 8.15
The Advanced Restore Options menu.

12. Press Esc and then select Yes in response to the Do you want to submit a job? prompt. You're then returned to the Select Job menu.

WARNING

Depending on the backup solution used, the trustees of [Root] might not be restored during a DS restore from tape. Admin will be the only user with full trustee rights to [Root] after a tape restore, even if other users had an explicit trustee assignment to [Root]. However, Security Equal To rights will be restored, and if a user has security equal to Admin, the user will have the same rights that admin has (which is usually full rights to the tree).

As previously mentioned in the "Backing Up eDirectory" section, your job will execute automatically at the scheduled time. You can manage and monitor your restore jobs through the Current Job List option.

Backing Up and Restoring Schema Extensions

During a DS backup, the `TSANDS.NLM` sends every object—those defined by both native (base) and extended schemas—to the backup program for backup. Versions of `TSANDS.NLM` prior to v4.14, however, do not send the extended schema definitions of the object types you have added to the DS database. Consequently, the resulting backup of DS contains information for objects defined in an extended schema, but *not* the extended schema data that defined those objects. This means that before you restore these DS objects, you have to first re-extend the schema so the definitions for extended objects exist in the tree during the restore. If this is not done, NDS/eDirectory will contain restored objects that it doesn't know how to use and will display them as Unknown objects.

The version of `TSANDS.NLM` shipped with NetWare 4.11 and higher, as well as the one included in `SMSUP6.EXE` and higher for NetWare 4.10, backs up and restores any schema extensions by default. You no longer have to re-extend the schema before DS can recognize restored objects defined by an extended schema.

Backup and Restore Services on Windows

Novell has extended the SMS architecture to include Windows NT and higher. You can use any SMS-compliant backup/restore utility to perform backup and restore operations on your eDirectory database located on your Windows eDirectory server. You can also back up the eDirectory on Windows database to a NetWare server, and vice versa. The following components facilitate the SMS-based backing up and restoring of data on Windows systems.

SMSEngn is a basic Storage Management Engine (see Figure 8.16) provided by Novell for Windows NT and higher. Unlike its NetWare cousin SBCon, SMSEngn can only back up to or restores data from a set of files—a data file (`.DAT`) and an index file (`.IDX`). A `BackupLog.log` file is either created or overwritten if it already exists. You will need to back up these files to a tape or other removable media as part of the Windows file system backup.

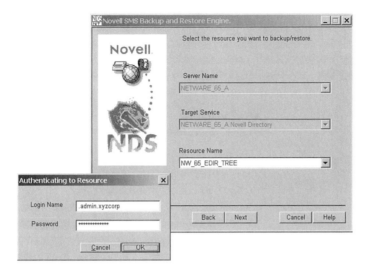

FIGURE 8.16
SMS Backup and
Restore Engine
for Windows.

When eDirectory is installed, the SMDR and TSANDS are set up by default
as a Windows service (called "W32 SMDR"). The service is always available
though it may be disabled or stopped. You can verify its status via Program
Settings, Control Panel, Administrative Tools, Services on Windows 2000
and higher, or Program Settings, Control Panel, Services for Windows NT. If
it is not listed in the Services applet, start W32SMDR.EXE located in the
drive:\Novell\NDS\SMS directory.

ndsbackup for Unix

The ndsbackup utility is a Unix command-line utility that allows you to
back up and restore eDirectory objects to and from a single file (referred to
as the *ndsbackupfile*). Like all Unix utilities, the actions of the ndsbackup
utility are controlled by command line options. The command line options
that you can give are a string of characters containing exactly one function
letter (c, r, t, s, or x) and zero or more function modifiers (letters or digits).
The string contains no space characters, and function modifier arguments
are listed on the command line in the same order as their corresponding
function modifiers appear in the string. The supported command line
options and function modifier arguments are listed in Table 8.1.

TABLE 8.1   ndsbackup **Parameters**

NDSBACKUP PARAMETER	DESCRIPTION
-a	The full (typeless) distinguished name of the user with administrator rights to the objects being archived or restored.
c	Create the *ndsbackupfile*.
f	Specifies that a file will be used. Use the *ndsbackupfile* argument as the name of the *ndsbackupfile*. If it is omitted, or if the name of the *ndsbackupfile* is -, ndsbackup writes to the standard output or reads from the input, whichever is appropriate. ndsbackup can be used as the head or tail of a pipeline.
e	Sets error handling flag. Exit immediately with an exit status if an unexpected error occurs.
-I	Use the specified include file that contains a list of eDirectory objects, one per line, and treat it as if each eDirectory object appeared separately on the command line. If an eDirectory object is specified in both the exclude file and the include file (or on the command line), it will be included. Be careful of trailing white spaces.
r	Replace existing objects in the *ndsbackupfile* file by appending the eDirectory objects to the file. Therefore, during a restore older object information in the file will be overwritten by the newer data located at the end of the file. You can consider this as a form of incremental backup.
R	Specifies a replica server name or IP address. Use the option to archive or restore eDirectory objects using a server holding the replica of the eDirectory partition. If you omit the R option, the local server is used.
s	Obtain a list of objects from the tree.
t	Obtain a list of objects from the *ndsbackupfile*.
v	Verbose mode. Outputs the name of each eDirectory object preceded by the function letter. With the t function, v provides additional information about the *ndsbackupfile* entries.

Table 8.1 Continued

NDSBACKUP PARAMETER	DESCRIPTION
w	Prompts for action. Output the action to be taken and the name of the eDirectory object, and then wait for the user's confirmation. If you enter y, the action is performed. If you enter any other key, the action is not performed. This function modifier cannot be used with the **t** function.
x	Restore objects to the tree from the *ndsbackupfile*. If a named eDirectory object matches a container whose contents have been written to the *ndsbackup-file*, this container is recursively extracted.
X	Use the exclude-file argument as a file containing a list of eDirectory objects to be excluded from the *ndsbackupfile* when using the functions **c**, **x**, **s**, or **t**. Multiple X arguments may be used, with one exclude file per argument. If an eDirectory object is specified in both the exclude file and the include file (or on the command line), it will be included. Be careful of trailing white spaces.
eDirectoryobject	The full (typeless) distinguished name of a leaf object or a container to be archived (when the **c** or **r** functions are specified), extracted (**x**) or listed (**t**). The action applies to all of the objects and (recursively) subordinate objects of that container. To archive the whole tree, specify the Tree object. You can also back up the eDirectory schema by specifying Schema as the eDirectory object. To back up the entire tree along with the schema, specify Full Directory Backup. If you do not specify the eDirectory object to be backed up, ndsbackup uses the default Full Directory Backup option.

The command syntax for ndsbackup is

```
ndsbackup function [modifier options] [option arguments]
➡ [-a admin.org] [-I include-file] [eDirectoryobject]
```

WARNING

The order of the option arguments is dependent on the order of the specified modifier options. For instance, ndsbackup fR **means the** *ndsbackupfile* **needs to be specified before the name of replica server.**

To archive, restore, or list eDirectory objects, you need to specify the fully distinguished name of a leaf object or container that is to be archived, extracted, or listed. To archive the whole tree, specify the Tree object (or leave the *eDirectoryObject* name from the command line). You can also back up the eDirectory schema by specifying Schema as the eDirectory object.

NOTE ndsbackup **is** *not* **an SMS-based application. It uses standard NDS/eDirectory APIs to access the tree, which means the target server does not need to have TSANDS running.**

The following is a partial output from **ndsbackup** when backing up the whole tree:

```
[RH9-eDir root]# ndsbackup cfRv fullbackup.april-01-2004
➥ 10.6.6.1 -a admin.xyzcorp
Password :
a .O=XYZCorp.
a .OU=IS_Admins.O=XYZCorp.
a .OU=Groups.OU=IS_Admins.O=XYZCorp.
a .CN=RootAdmins.OU=Groups.OU=IS_Admins.O=XYZCorp.
a .OU=Tree_Admins.OU=Groups.OU=IS_Admins.O=XYZCorp.
a .CN=Admin.OU=IS_Admins.O=XYZCorp.
a .OU=Scripts.OU=IS_Admins.O=XYZCorp.
a .OU=Company.O=XYZCorp.
a .OU=East.OU=Company.O=XYZCorp.
a .OU=Scripts.OU=East.OU=Company.O=XYZCorp.
a .OU=West.OU=Company.O=XYZCorp.
a .OU=Scripts.OU=West.OU=Company.O=XYZCorp.
a .CN=Admin.OU=Company.O=XYZCorp.
a .CN=LDAP_Proxy_User.OU=Company.O=XYZCorp.
[RH9-eDir root]#
```

In the previous example, the order of the function modifiers is **fR**, which means the name of the *ndsbackupfile* is **fullbackup.april-01-2004** while the address of the replica server is 10.6.6.1. An *eDirectoryObject* name is not provided, thus the backup mode defaults to full backup. Since there is no command line option to specify a password (this is for security reasons—but it also makes automating the backup process more challenging), **ndsbackup** prompts you for the password, which is not echoed (not even as a series of asterisks). If you omit the **-a** option, you will be prompted for the username.

> **NOTE**
>
> ndsbackup **will not accept input from a redirected file (*for example*,** "< *filename*"). **Thus you cannot circumvent security and send the password to** ndsbackup **that way.**

The "a" that appears in front of each object name in the **ndsbackup** output is the result of the verbose (**v**) option. It indicates that each of those objects is being archived.

You can customize the backup process of the **ndsbackup** utility by choosing specific eDirectory objects to be excluded or included in the backup session. Whether you use exclude (**X**) or include (**-I**) usually depends on the size of the data you want to back up, compared to the size you do not want to back up. As an example, to back up most of the eDirectory tree structure while omitting only a small part, use the exclude option to omit the part you do not want to back up as it is more efficient than using include and needing to specify everything else.

> **NOTE**
>
> **Everything that you do not want specifically excluded is included. After you exclude part of the structure, you cannot include objects below that container.**

Third-Party SMS-Compliant Backup Solutions

There are a number of third-party SMS-compliant backup solutions available for NetWare. Although not required, we recommend that when selecting a server-based application (such as a SMS-compliant backup solution) for your NetWare servers be certain the product has Novell's YES, Tested and Approved certification.

In order to receive a Novell YES, Tested and Approved certification, generally referred to as the YES certification, a software application must be subjected to a number of testing criteria, such as low memory conditions to see how the application handles exceptions. In the case of backup systems, testing requires that the client/server application correctly back up and restore NetWare volume (which includes NSS volumes), file, and eDirectory information.

> **NOTE**
>
> **YES certification of products that works with Novell Nterprise Linux Services and product certifications for SuSE Linux (SUSE LINUX READY Program) are also available. Visit** www.suse.com **for more information about SuSE product certifications.**

Novell Technical Support works closely with companies that test products through Novell DeveloperNet. If you call Novell for end-user or system integrator support and your network incorporates YES, Tested and Approved third-party products, Novell technicians can reference existing support documentation such as YES Bulletins and TIDs. If the error persists, technicians can duplicate the situation in one of Novell's labs or work with the product vendor, leveraging the relationship that was developed during the testing process to resolve the problem. In short, YES, Tested and Approved is Novell's first line of interoperability assurance for Novell customers.

Every YES, Tested and Approved product has a YES Bulletin that details what products were used in the testing—such as versions of Novell products, network adapters, controller devices, and supported drivers. The YES Bulletin also indicates specific product configuration, date of the testing, special network configuration information or other related information important to product interoperability in the network environment. For example, a YES Bulletin can tell you whether a particular backup solution can properly back up and restore all the various file formats supported on your network or whether a device driver handles memory over 16MB correctly. This information may be in the form of a configuration note or a line item indicating whether or not certain functionality is supported.

NOTE   **Visit the YES, Tested and Approved Bulletin Search page** (`developer.novell.com/yessearch/Search.jsp`) **to search for the latest certified products and to view existing YES Bulletins.**

The following are some of the more popular backup system choices that have received the YES certification:

▶ **VERITAS Backup Exec for NetWare Version 9.1 (YES Bulletin #70552)**—Formally developed by Seagate, VERITAS Backup Exec was the first NetWare 5–certified data protection solution. Because NetWare 5 and higher can be configured to run in a pure IP environment, Backup Exec for NetWare fully supports IP and IPX protocols, ensuring your data protection no matter how you configure the network. As a fully SMS-compliant backup application, Backup Exec protects any size Novell Storage Services (NSS) volume by utilizing Novell (or VERITAS–developed) Target Service Agents—even terabyte size volumes. In addition, Backup Exec's NDS protection includes all objects, containers, and extended schema, plus additional client network information that has been added in NetWare 5 and above. For more information about VERITAS Backup Exec for NetWare, visit `www.veritas.com`.

▶ **BrightStor ARCserve Backup for NetWare v9 (YES Bulletin #69429)**—Originally developed by Cheyenne, Computer Associates International, Inc.'s BrightStor is an enterprisewide storage management software product that enables you to back up and restore data on NetWare servers and all workstations attached to those servers. Similar to Backup Exec, BrightStor is a fully SMS-compliant backup solution that supports NSS volumes and works over both IPX and IP. For more information about BrightStor ARCserve Backup for NetWare, visit www.ca.com.

▶ **Backup Express v2.1.5 (YES Bulletin #71325)**—Originally developed by Arcadia Software, Syncsort Inc.'s Backup Express is an enterprise-class backup and restore solution designed for Unix, Linux, Windows, and NetWare environments. Backup Express supports any combination of Unix, Linux, Windows, NetWare, and Network Data Management Protocol/Network Attached Storage (NDMP/NAS) devices in a Storage Area Network (SAN) environment. It can perform backup of all data directly across the fiber or iSCSI network, dynamically share all tape drives, and control this single enterprise environment with a single catalog and easy-to-use GUI. Backup Express's distributed architecture allows it to back up to any device in the network whether it is running Unix, Linux, Windows, or NetWare, while maintaining a single central catalog for the entire enterprise. For more information about Backup Express, visit www.syncsort.com.

From our experience, the major YES certified data backup solutions players for the Intel platform are BrightStor ARCserve and VERITAS Backup Exec. Many large sites that have mainframes use a combination of BrightStor ARCserve and Backup Exec along with some form of mainframe-based backup solution (such as IBM's Tivoli Storage Management, formerly called ADSM) for their enterprisewide backup strategies.

There are a number of good, but not YES certified, backup solutions favored by customer sites. Chief among these solutions is Legato's Networker for NetWare (www.legato.com/products/networker/netware.cfm).

NOTE

When searching for a NetWare backup solution, you should not limit your selections to YES-certified products. Rather, you should evaluate a number of them and pick what works best for your particular needs and environment.

Server Recovery Using Server-Specific Information Data

With the release of NetWare 4.11, Novell introduced some enhancements to TSA modules to provide more efficient backup and restore capabilities for NDS, as well as more efficient server recovery after a failure.

In a multiple-server environment, one server can go down while the rest of the servers in its replica list remain intact. If the hard disk containing the SYS volume on one server becomes damaged, the entire server is affected. A hard disk failure involving SYS affects the entire server and halts all NetWare operating system activities. Because the eDirectory files are stored on SYS, losing this volume is equivalent to removing NetWare and eDirectory from the file server. (The same is true for Windows and Unix/Linux if the disk hosting eDirectory is down.)

WARNING

Because of the changes made in eDirectory 8.7, Server Specific Information backups created by filesystem TSAs or third-party backup tools are not supported for NetWare 5.1 and 6.0 servers running eDirectory 8.7 or 8.7.1. Instead, to restore a crashed server, you need to utilize the eDirectory Management Toolbox's Backup eMTool.

NetWare 6.0/SP3 and later running eDirectory 8.7.1 or later support the SSI information generated using file system TSA but the restoration requires using the eDirectory Backup eMTool.

Because of this, the information provided in this section is applicable to all versions of NDS and eDirectory up to and including eDirectory 8.6.*x*.

To simplify the complex recovery procedure necessary in previous versions of NetWare, enhancements that were made to the filesystem TSA module (TSA410.NLM for NetWare 4.1*x*) help facilitate server recovery in this scenario. The same improvements are carried into later versions of file system TSA for NetWare 5 and higher.

NOTE

For NetWare 4.10, you need to use TSA410.NLM dated July 23, 1996, or later (for example, v4.14 or higher) to receive the same functionality as the version of TSA410.NLM that shipped with NetWare 4.11. The updated TSA410 can be found in SMSUP6.EXE (or newer) available from the Novell Support web site at support.novell.com.

The enhanced file system TSA provides a new major SMS resource, called *Server Specific Info* (SSI), that appears in the list of Resources displayed by SMS-based backup applications along with the **SYS** volume and other mounted volumes (see Figure 8.17). The Server Specific Info resource should be backed up on a regular basis, as it plays an important role in server recovery. Selecting the Server Specific Info option stores critical server information into five files that can be used for recovery purposes:

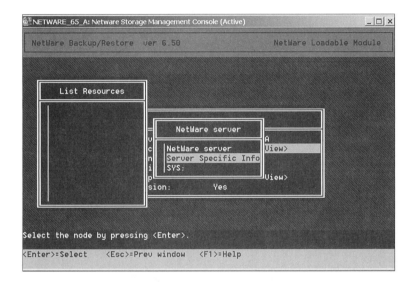

FIGURE 8.17
The Server Specific Info resource.

▶ **SERVDATA.NDS**—This (binary) file contains server-specific DS information, such as the schema information and server-centric object IDs. The information is used by Install/NWConfig to recover from a **SYS** volume drive failure. On Windows, this file is called **$svnds.bak**.

▶ **DSMISC.LOG**—This is a text file containing a list of replicas, including replica types, which the backed up server held at the time of backup. It also provides a list of the other servers that were in the failed server's replica ring. Use this information to reestablish replicas on the server. On Windows, this file is called **dsbackup.log**.

The following is an example **DSMISC.LOG** file:

```
Sunday, January 31, 2004    8:26:56 pm
Backing up server-specific NDS data
Current partition/replica list
Partition .[Root]., current replica list:
      .NETWARE65-A.XYZCorp, type master
      .NETWARE65-C.XYZCorp, type read/write
```

▶ **VOLSINFO.TXT**—This text file contains needed information about the server's volumes, including name space, compression, and data migration information, at the time of backup. Use this file as a guide to re-create the lost volumes during the recovery process. (Not applicable to Windows.)

The following is an example **VOLSINFO.TXT** file—note that the **SHARED** volume has compression enabled:

```
NETWARE65-A
Sunday, January 31, 2004     8:26:56 pm

SYS:
    Supported Name Spaces:
        DOS
        MACINTOSH
        NFS
        LONG


SHARED:
    Supported Name Spaces:
        DOS
        MACINTOSH
        NFS
        LONG
    Extended File Formats:
        Compression is enabled.
```

▶ **STARTUP.NCF**—This is a copy of the server's STARTUP.NCF file. (Not applicable to Windows.)

▶ **AUTOEXEC.NCF**—This is a copy of the server's AUTOEXEC.NCF file. (Not applicable to Windows.)

NOTE

The DSMISC.LOG file is also used by NetWare to record schema changes, and all entries to the file are done as appends. You should review the contents and size of this file periodically to ensure it is not taking up unnecessary disk space.

Conversely, the dsbackup.log on Windows is overwritten every time the local server information is backed up.

Because the backup service on Unix/Linux does not make use of SMS, no SSI data is available. To recover from a crashed Unix server, use eMBox as discussed later in this chapter.

The general steps to restore eDirectory to a single server are as follows:

1. Retrieve Server Specific Information data for the crashed server.

2. Clean up the replica ring.

3. Install the new server.

4. Add the new server to previously defined replica rings.

5. Verify eDirectory was successful restored.

To begin this operation, you need to first know how to create the SSI files so they can be retrieved when needed. This is discussed in the following section.

Creating SSI Files

There are two ways to back up SSI data using your SMS-based application. The first method is to select Server Specific Info from the list of available resources when doing a file system backup. The second way is to simply select a full file system backup of the *entire* NetWare server—the SSI data is included by default.

TIP

If you have a server crash and SSI files are not available, you can try the recovery procedure outlined in the "Recovering a Crashed SYS Volume or Server" section in Chapter 11.

NOT

If your backup software doesn't show SSI as an available resource, check with the vendor before assuming that these files are being included in a full system backup.

If your backup program doesn't support SSI, you can create the SSI files using SBCon. Use SBCon to schedule *two* jobs that execute daily (or frequently so you have up-to-date SSI files): one job that backs up and another that restores the SSI data. The restore step is necessary to create the actual SSI files on the SYS volume so your regular backup application can then back up these files to tape. Otherwise, the backup process simply creates the SSI files in server memory and then writes them to tape directly. The downside of this method is that SBCon uses the same tape as your backup software, which is sometimes not possible due to formatting requirements, unless you have two tape drives on your server.

> **NOTE**
>
> When SSI data is backed up, a copy of `SERVDATA.NDS` is created in `SYS:SYSTEM`, but not the other SSI files.

An alternative to the previous method is to use the MakeSSI utility from DreamLAN Network Consulting. This NLM is specifically designed to create the previously mentioned SSI data files (see Figure 8.18). Run the NLM just prior to your backup schedule so you can back up the SSI files to tape, ensuring you have a set of SSI files that matches the data backed up on tape. See `www.dreamlan.com/makessi.htm` for more information about the NLM.

FIGURE 8.18
Creating NetWare
SSI files using
MakeSSI.

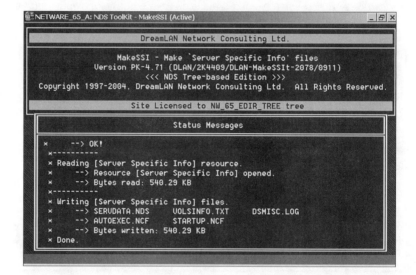

> **NOTE**
>
> Although SSI is a file system TSA resource, the actual backup and restore of SSI data is performed by the `DSBACKER.NLM`, which is auto-loaded by the file system TSA as needed.

As there is no file system TSA for Windows, the procedure to create SSI files for Windows servers is slightly different than that for NetWare. The two files that make up the SSI data on Windows are created using the `install.dlm` as follows:

1. Start `install.dlm` from NDSCons.

2. Select the Backup local server information option (see Figure 8.19) and click Next.

3. Enter a username and password that has Supervisor rights to the tree.

4. Select the directory in which the two SSI files will be created. The default is *drive*`:\Novell\NDS\DIBFiles`.

5. Click Finish to create the files.

6. The content of `dsbacklog.log` is displayed for your information. Click Done to exit.

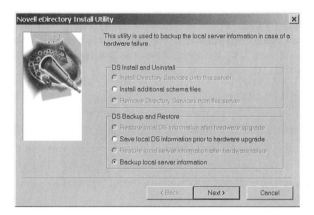

FIGURE 8.19
Creating Windows SSI files using `install.dlm`.

You should then back up `$svnds.bak` and `dsbackup.log` as part of your regular file system backup procedure.

Restoring a Failed NetWare eDirectory Server

The information presented in this section explains how to restore NDS/eDirectory (prior to eDirectory 8.7) for a specific NetWare server after you have a hardware failure that involves the SYS volume. The procedure is not applicable when you are upgrading or replacing server hardware—instead, refer to the "Upgrading/Replacing Hardware on NetWare" section in your eDirectory 8.6.x documentation.

You can also use the NetWare Migration Wizard, which can be downloaded for free from `download.novell.com`, **to upgrade or replace NetWare server hardware while maintaining the NDS/eDirectory information.**

TIP

Following are steps to restore a crashed server or a SYS volume in a multi-server tree where DS information is replicated:

> **WARNING**
>
> **These steps assume you have a current backup of the SSI data for the failed server. If you do not, you can try the procedure outlined in the "Recovering a Crashed SYS Volume or Server" section in Chapter 11, or refer to TID #10010922 entitled "Removing a Crashed Server from the NDS Tree" that covers how to recover from a server crash. However, the TID tells you to delete the Server and Volume objects, which will render all your Directory Map, Print Queue, *etc.* objects non-functional, and you'll have to manually recreate these objects after a restore. When you don't have SSI data to work with, and the procedure in Chapter 11 doesn't help you, the information in this TID may be used.**

1. *Don't panic!*

2. *Don't* delete the NCP Server or Volume objects for the failed server from the DS. Leave them intact to preserve references that other objects (such as Directory Map objects) may have to these objects as well as any DS trustee assignments made. If the NCP Server or Volume objects are deleted and you have objects that depend on them, you'll need to re-establish the relationships through a selective DS restore.

> **WARNING**
>
> **As discussed in Chapter 2 and elsewhere, when an object is missing its mandatory attributes, it will turn into an Unknown object. Because of this, you need to pay special attention when doing a partial DS restore so that any dependent object(s) are also restored, otherwise the restored object may not be functional.**

3. From your most recent tape backup of the failed server, restore the "Server Specific Information" files to another server. These SSI files, `SERVDATA.NDS`, `DSMISC.LOG`, `VOLSINFO.TXT`, `STARTUP.NCF`, and `AUTOEXEC.NCF`, will be restored to a subdirectory, named after the failed server in the DOS "8.3" naming format, under `SYS:SYSTEM`. For example, if the server was called TEST-NW6A, the SSI files will be restored to `SYS:SYSTEM\TEST-NW6.A`.

4. If the failed server held a Master replica of any partition, go to another server in the replica ring that has either a Read/Write or Read-Only replica and use DSRepair to promote that replica to a Master. (You can use the information recorded in `DSMISC.LOG` to determine what replicas were stored on the failed server and which servers are in the respective replica rings.) Repeat this step for every Master replica stored on the failed server. You then need to clean up the replica rings to remove the downed server from the lists. (Refer to the "Replica Ring Inconsistency" section in Chapter 11 for detailed steps.)

TIP

After your replica ring cleanup, you should spot-check the DSTrace output on a number of servers to see whether the replica rings are okay and verify that everything is synchronizing correctly. You *don't* want to install a server into a tree that's not fully synchronized.

NOTE

You can't use NDS Manager or ConsoleOne to perform the task in Step 4 as they require the Master replica to be up and all servers in the replica ring to be available. You *must* use DSRepair for this step.

5. If the failed server contained any non-Master replicas, you need to clean up the replica rings following the procedures given in the "Replica Ring Inconsistency" section in Chapter 11.

6. Install the new server hardware or new hard drive (if it was only the SYS volume that had failed). *Do not yet connect the new server to your network*; leave it in an isolated environment.

7. Install the NetWare operating system on the new hardware as per your standard procedure to set up the LAN and disk driver and create the volumes. (Use VOLSINFO.TXT to determine how many volumes you had on the crashed server, their names, and whether additional name spaces are required.)

   When prompted for server name and server ID (in NetWare 5 and higher; internal IPX network number in NetWare 4), enter the *same* server name and addressing information. (Use the AUTOEXEC.NCF included with the SSI for these data.)

   When you reached the point of installing DS information, create a new (temporary) tree. This allows you to complete the OS re-installation with the minimal amount of trouble.

   The reason behind creating a temporary DS tree at this point is that the GUI installation program in NetWare 5 and later doesn't have the option (that is available in NWCONFIG.NLM; and in INSTALL.NLM in NetWare 4) for you to restore DS data using SSI information. You *could*, however, not create a temporary tree by aborting out of the GUI setup when prompted for DS information and use NWConfig to restore the DS data and manually copy the server files. But it can get confusing and is a lot more extra work—something you don't need during a disaster recovery. Also, the up side of this technique is that you can build the server off-site (or have a hot standby server pre-built) and then bring it in to replace the crashed server.

8. After the server OS installation is complete, restart the server (*but keeping it off the production network*) to ensure everything is working okay. Apply any server updates, such as Support Pack, that you have previously installed and then restart the server again to ensure the updates haven't messed anything up.

WARNING   Do *not* restore file system data until after eDirectory has been restored. When file system data is restored, the process looks for the trustee objects in eDirectory. If an object that is a trustee does not exist in the eDirectory database (such as in a new installation before eDirectory has been fully restored), the rights assignments for that object will not be restored.

Log in from a workstation to test the server LAN card configuration, exercise the hard drives, and so on. After you're satisfied that the hardware is working correctly, create a directory off the root of your SYS volume and place the five SSI files there. The most important file is SERVDATA.NDS. Log out from the workstation after you've copied the files.

If your new server's hardware configuration is different from the crashed server's (such as different network card, thus different driver), make a backup copy of the new STARTUP.NCF and AUTOEXEC.NCF files as they will be overwritten when you restore the SSI data.

NOTE   If your set of SSI files is small enough, you can place them on a diskette instead.

9. At the server console, load NWCONFIG.NLM (or INSTALL.NLM in the case of NetWare 4) and use the Directory Options selection to remove DS from this new server.

10. Connect the server to your production environment. Bring up your server and load NWConfig (or Install) and select the Directory Options menu.

11. Select the Install Directory Services onto this server option. At the screen to "Select a Directory tree," press F5 (the option to Restore NDS, as indicated at the bottom right of the screen; see Figure 8.20).

TIP   *Do not select a tree by pressing Enter.* A new window comes up with two options: A: (the default) or "Press <F3> to specify a different path".

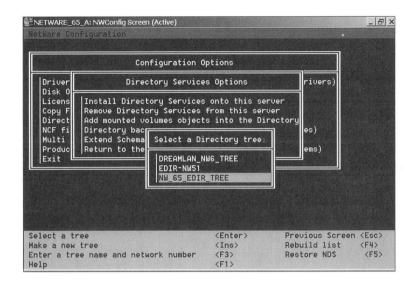

FIGURE 8.20
Restore SSI data
by pressing F5.

If your SSI files are on a diskette, insert the disk and continue with the restore. Otherwise, press F3 and specify the path to where the SSI files were copied to in Step 8.

Alternatively, you can use the Restore local server information after hardware failure option from the Directory backup and restore options menu to restore the SSI files, as shown in Figure 8.21.

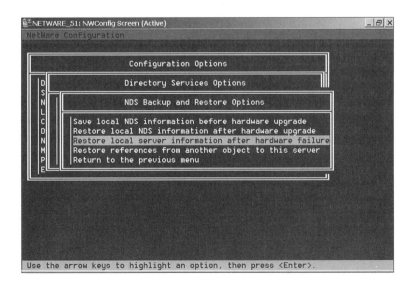

FIGURE 8.21
Restore SSI data
via the Restore
local server infor-
mation after
hardware failure
option.

After you enter the path and press Enter, the SSI files will be copied to the SYS volume. DSMISC.LOG, VOLSINFO.TXT, and AUTOEXEC.NCF are copied to the `SYS:SYSTEM` directory; `STARTUP.NCF` is copied to the DOS partition. DS information is restored at this point, using the data contained in `SERVDATA.NDS`. Unlike a traditional DS restore using SMS, `TSANDS.NLM` is not required for this. Once this is complete, DS is fully functional on the server, except that the partitions and replicas have not yet been re-established.

12. You *may* also need to re-establish licensing information. For NetWare 4, you reinstall the license(s) using `INSTALL.NLM`.

13. Prepare the restored directory for integration into the original tree by executing the following DSRepair commands in the order specified:

    1. `DSREPAIR -SI` (Repairs replica numbers on partition objects); option is not available for eDirectory 8.5 or below

    2. `DSREPAIR -RD` (Local database repair)

    3. `DSREPAIR -RN` (Repairs network addresses)

    4. `DSREPAIR -SR` (Requests local schema switch); command-line option is not available for eDirectory 8.5 or below but can instead use Advanced options menu, Global schema operations, Reset local schema.

    This is a cleanup process. It's okay to see error messages displayed during the cleanup.

14. Use DSTrace to verify that the schema has synchronized fully. From the server console, type

    ```
    SET DSTRACE = ON (Activates the NDS transactions screen)
    SET DSTRACE = +SCHEMA (Displays schema information)
    SET DSTRACE = +IN (Monitors inbound synchronization
    ➥traffic)
    ```

    Watch for the message "All processed = YES" on the trace status screen. Once the schema is synchronized, you are ready to re-establish replicas.

15. With the information recorded in the `DSMISC.LOG` file, re-establish the original replicas using NDS Manager or ConsoleOne. We recommend you place the replicas on the new server before file system restore so that any external references that might result from file system trustee assignments are minimized.

16. If the new server's hardware configuration is not identical to that of the old server's, you'll need to change the restored `AUTOEXEC.NCF` and `STARTUP.NCF` files to match the new settings, using the backup copies

you made in Step 8. After making the changes, restart the server to ensure the changes are okay.

17. At this point, you can restore the file system from your most recent backup. You should be careful when restoring the SYS volume data to ensure that you don't overwrite any new Support Pack files with older ones. If you've made modifications to your AUTOEXEC.NCF, make certain the older copy from your restore operation does not overwrite it.

Disk Space Problems

When restoring files to a volume that was nearly full before the backup, you may run into insufficient disk space issues during the operation. This is especially true when volume compression is used. Although SMS-compliant backup software can back up and restore compressed files in their compressed format, that's not the default in most backup software. Because of this, chances are good that you'll restore previously compressed files in an uncompressed format. Because compression is a background OS process, files are not compressed until the compression start time is reached.

You can, however, flag files as Immediate Compress, but that's an extra manual step. Afterward, you must remember to unflag them or else they'll always be compressed again immediately after access, causing unnecessary high server utilization.

Another volume-related issue that you can get caught with during a restore is that of suballocation. Again, because it is a background process, files are not suballocated as they are restored. Therefore, if you're restoring many (small) files, you can run out of disk space before the restore is completely finished.

To work around these two problems, it is best to either maintain at least 15–20% free disk space on each volume, or make certain the replacement drive capacity is larger.

18. After the file system restore is complete, restart the server one more time to ensure that the restore didn't overwrite any important system files. Perform a spot-check on some of the restored directories and files for trustee assignments, file ownership, and so on. Also spot-check DS objects to ensure you don't have any Unknowns. Bindery-based objects and any DS objects (such as Print Queues) that depend on object IDs should restore correctly because of the SSI information. In the event that Print Queue objects, for example, are not recovered correctly, you need to recreate them.

19. Install, if necessary, any additional server-based add-on products.

This procedure *should* work with NetWare 4.10 but we have not tested it in that environment. Also, there's a bug in TSA410.NLM for NetWare 4.10

wherein replica information is *not* recorded in the `DSMISC.LOG` file. A workaround is to use MakeSSI (discussed in the previous section) on NetWare 4.10 servers as MakeSSI creates a `PARTINFO.LST` file, which is equivalent to the `DSMISC.LOG` file, as far as recording replica information goes. Also, you need to use the most recent `TSA410.NLM` as older versions (before v4.14) don't support SSI.

Restoring a Failed Windows eDirectory Server

The information presented in this section explains how to restore eDirectory 8.5 or 8.6 (but not 8.7 or later) for a specific Windows server after you had a hardware failure that involves the disk hosting eDirectory. The procedure is not applicable when you are upgrading or replacing server hardware—instead, refer to the "Upgrading/Replacing Hardware on Windows NT/2000" section in your eDirectory 8.6.*x* documentation.

NOTE   Unlike the case with NetWare servers, you cannot use the NetWare Migration Wizard to upgrade or replace Windows server hardware as the Wizard is for NetWare-only.

The steps to restore a crashed Windows server or a damaged disk hosting eDirectory in a multiserver tree where DS information is replicated are very similar to that for NetWare outlined in the previous section. Instead of repeating the same information, we point out the differences in the procedure where applicable:

▶ The Windows SSI information consists of two files, `$svnds.bak` and `dsbackup.log`, and are located in *drive*:`\Novell\NDS\DIBFiles` by default.

▶ To remove Directory Services from a Windows server, use `install.dlm`. From NDSCons, select `install.dlm`, click Start, click Remove Directory Services, and click Finish. You will need to authenticate as a user that has Supervisor rights to the tree.

TIP   If the Remove Directory Services option is grayed out, you can remove DS as follows. First, shut down eDirectory using NDSCons, Shutdown. Then manually remove all files in *drive*:`\Novell\NDS\DIBFiles`, including subdirectories. Restart eDirectory using NDSCons, Startup.

- ▶ To restore eDirectory information using SSI files, again use `install.nlm`. From NDSCons, select `install.dlm`, click Start, click Restore Local Server Information after a Hardware Failure, click Next. Specify the path to the `$svnds.bak` and click OK.

- ▶ To prepare the restored directory for integration into the original tree, execute the following DSRepair commands:

  - ▶ From NDSCons, select `dsrepair.dlm`, enter **-si** in the Startup Parameters field, click Start to repair replica numbers on partition objects. DSRepair's GUI will not be displayed and will automatically exit when repair is completed.

  - ▶ From NDSCons, select `dsrepair.dlm`, click Start. From the Repair menu, Local Database Repair. From the Servers menu, Repair All Network Addresses. From the Schema menu, Reset Local Schema.

- ▶ To verify that the schema has synchronized fully using DSTrace, from NDSCons, select `dstrace.dlm`, click Start. Choose Edit, Options, click Clear All and mark Schema, Inbound Sync Detail, and Inbound Synchronization, then click OK. Watch for the message "All processed = YES" on the trace status screen.

When restoring file systems on the Windows server, ensure you do not overwrite the current eDirectory files with the older versions from your backup.

Changes to NetWare SSI Data

Due to some internal database structure changes in eDirectory 8.7, Server Specific Information backups created by file system TSAs or third-party backup tools are not supported for NetWare 5.1 and 6.0 servers running eDirectory 8.7 or 8.7.1. In eDirectory 8.7.3, SSI is now supported using the hot backup functionality. As in previous versions, file system TSA calls the `DSBACKER.NLM` to create the backup, but now `DSBACKER.NLM` also calls `BACKUPCR.NLM` to create a backup using the Backup eMtool functionality.

As BACKUPCR.NLM **makes use of eDirectory Backup eMTool to create SSI data, this means you need to have iManager installed and RBS configured in order to create SSI data on NetWare servers.**   **NOTE**

Table 8.2 lists recommendations for creating and restoring SSI data depending on the NetWare and eDirectory versions.

TABLE 8.2	**Recommended Backup and Restore Methods for NetWare SSI Data**		
EDIRECTORY VERSION	**NETWARE VERSION**	**BACKUP/RESTORE METHOD**	
8.6 or earlier	Any version	Refer to the "Restoring a Failed NetWare eDirectory Server" section in this chapter.	
8.7	5.1 & 6.0	Back up and restore only using the Backup eMtool. (SSI backups performed using file system TSAs cannot be successfully restored.)	
8.7.1 or later	5.1 & 6.0 with pre-SP3	Back up and restore only using the Backup eMtool. (SSI backups performed using file system TSAs cannot be successfully restored.)	
8.7.1 or later	6.0 with SP3 or later	Back up using either the Backup eMtool, file system TSA, or third-party tools. Restoration needs to be done using the Backup eMTool.	

The main differences in SSI data created by NetWare 6.0 with eDirectory 8.7.1 and later are as follows:

▶ **Larger file size**—The former method of SSI backup contained only a small portion of the database. Now, because the backup file contains all the information about all directory objects on the server, it is much bigger. It will be roughly the same size as the database.

▶ **User-defined file location**—In former versions of SSI backup, only one file, SERVDATA.NDS, was created in the SYS:SYSTEM directory. Because the file was smaller, it was not critical where the data was placed before copying off to tape. With eDirectory 8.7.1 and later you can use a file system TSA to create a full backup of the database. Instead of five files in former versions of SSI backup, only three files are involved (see Table 8.3). For one of these, SSIBACK.BAK, the file location is user definable.

▶ **Restore using Backup eMTool**—The SSI data can only be restored using the Backup eMTool.

TABLE 8.3

NetWare SSI Files for eDirectory 8.7.1 and Later

FILE NAME	DESCRIPTION	LOCATION
`SSIBACK.BAK`	This backup file is the same as the full hot backup created with the Backup eMTool.	User definable. The default is `SYS:SYSTEM`. Because of file size, were-commend it be relocated onto a volume other than the `SYS` volume.
`SSIBACK.INI`	A text file containing the path where the `SSIBACK.BAK` file is located. For example: `DATA1:/BACKUPS/ SSIBACKUP.BAK`.	`SYS:SYSTEM`
`SSIBACK.LOG`	A high-level view containing information about previous backups. The log file contains a history of all backups, records backup start time and end time, and contains information about possible errors during the backup process.	`SYS:SYSTEM`

eDirectory Backup eMTool

The eDirectory Backup eMTool allows you to back up and restore the eDirectory database and associated files on an individual server. It has the following benefits:

▶ Same tool for all platforms supported by eDirectory 8.7 and later.

▶ Provides hot continuous backup. You can back up your server without closing the eDirectory database, and you still get a complete backup.

▶ Supports a quick restore of an individual server. This is especially helpful in the event of hardware failure.

▶ Scalability. You can back up a server whose eDirectory database contains tens or hundreds of millions of objects. The speed of the backup process is limited mainly by I/O channel bandwidth.

▶ Can support a quick restore of the tree, when used with replica planning and DSMaster servers. Even without using DSMaster servers, some level of recovery for the tree should be possible.

▶ Lets you perform tasks remotely. You can perform most backup and restore tasks using iManager or the Java eMBox Client.

▶ Lets you back up related files. You can back up files on the server that are related to the database, such as Novell International Cryptographic infrastructure (NICI) security files, stream files, and any files you specify (such as `AUTOEXEC.NCF`).

▶ Can restore eDirectory to the state it was in at the moment before it went down, if you use continuous roll-forward logging.

▶ Makes hardware upgrade simpler. Doing a cold backup and then restoring the eDirectory database is an easy way to transfer the server's identity to a new machine or safeguard it while you make changes such as hardware upgrades.

▶ Works within the distributed nature of eDirectory. You can ensure that a restored server matches the synchronization state that other servers in the tree expect by turning on continuous roll-forward logging.

▶ Allows unattended backups. You can create batch files to run unattended backups through the eMBox Client.

REAL WORLD

What Is a DSMaster Server?

It is not uncommon for large sites to have one or more servers that contain a replica of every partition in the tree, so a copy of the whole tree is in the eDirectory database on just a few servers. This kind of server is often called a DSMaster server. The replicas on the DSMaster server should be Master or Read/Write replicas (generally Master, thus the name "DSMaster server").

If more than one DSMaster server is used, keep in mind that ideally each DSMaster server should have a unique set of replicas of partitions. There should be no overlap between them, to avoid inconsistencies between the replicas when restoring after a disaster. If your servers were lost in a disaster, you would not have access to the most recent roll-forward logs for restoring because roll-forward logs are saved locally on the server, so all the DSMaster servers probably could not be restored to the same moment in time. If the same replica were held on two DSMaster servers, the two copies would probably not be identical and would cause inconsistencies in the tree. So, for disaster recovery planning it's best to not have the same partition replicated on more than one DSMaster server.

Even though there are many nice features and benefits in the eDirectory Backup eMTool, it also has some drawbacks to be aware of. The main drawback is that it only deals with the database and associated files on an individual server; it does *not* support backup and restore for individual objects, branches of the tree, or the whole tree. Therefore, unless you have a single-server eDirectory tree or are making use of DSMaster servers, you will need an SMS-compliant backup solution to fully back up the tree whose partitions are distributed on more than one server. In essence, eDirectory Backup eMTool provides the same functionality as SSI data but with enhancement features.

For a Unix-only eDirectory tree, you can use ndsbackup **to back up and restore individual objects, branches of the tree, or the full tree, including schema.**

TIP

The second drawback is that eDirectory Backup eMTool must be used in conjunction with file system backups to put the eDirectory files safely on tape. Another drawback is that for a multiple-server tree, to back up a server you need to upgrade all the servers that are in the same replica ring to eDirectory 8.5 or later. This is because the restore verification process is backward compatible only with 8.5 or later.

Lastly, the eDirectory Management Tool Box (eMBox), of which eDirectory Backup eMTool is a component, depends on RBS to function. Should something unforeseen happen to the RBS configuration, you are unable to access the Backup eMTool. Although not likely if you plan your partition replication strategy properly, you might get yourself into a Catch-22 situation where you need to use Backup eMTool to restore your eDirectory DIB but the only replica containing the RBS containers is in the DIB that you are trying to restore.

It is sufficient to install iManager on just one server in the tree, launch iManager from that server, and then perform most functions on many objects in the tree. iManager makes calls to eDirectory when creating or modifying objects. eDirectory is responsible for finding the object in the tree and performing the specific function. This is independent of whether or not iManager is installed on other servers in the tree.

TIP

The only requirement when performing server-centric eMBox tool functions (such as backup, DSRepair, and so on) through iManager or the eMBox Client is that the server you are trying to perform this function on must have eDirectory 8.7 or later installed.

Overview of Backup eMTool Restore Process

When you direct the Backup eMTool to begin the restore process, either through iManager or the eMBox Client, the following steps are taken by the Backup eMTool:

1. The DS Agent is closed.

2. The current active DIB set is switched from the DIB set with filename extension `.NDS` to a new DIB set named `.RST`. (The existing DS database is left on the server; if the restore verification fails it will once again become the active DIB set.)

3. The restore is performed, restoring to the DIB set named `.RST`.

4. The DIB set is disabled by setting a Login Disabled attribute on the `[Pseudo Server]` object. This prevents the DS Agent from being able to open and using this DIB set.

5. The roll-forward log settings are reset to the default. This means that after a restore, roll-forward logging on the server is always set to Off, and the location of the roll-forward logs is reset to the default (`drive:\Novell\NDS\DIBFiles\nds.rfl`). (If you want roll-forward logging turned on for this server, you must re-create your configuration for roll-forward logging after the restore, to make sure it is turned on and the logs are being saved in a fault-tolerant location. After turning on the roll-forward logs, you must also do a new full backup.)

6. Verification of the restored `.RST` database is performed. The server attempts to verify the consistency of the data that has been restored. It does this by contacting every server that it shares a replica with and comparing the transitive vectors. The output from this verification process is printed in the log file. If the transitive vector on the remote server is ahead of the local vector, then data is missing from the restore, and the verification fails. For more information about the verification process, see the following section, "Transitive Vectors and the Restore Verification Process."

   Here is an example of the information that's recorded in the log file if verification fails for one of the replicas, showing the transitive vectors that were compared:

   ```
   Server: \T=EDIR-873-TEST-TREE\O=XYZCorp\CN=WIN2K-A
      Replica: \T=EDIR-873-TEST-TREE\O=XYZCorp
         Status: ERROR = -6034
            Local TV                    Remote TV
   ```

```
s3D35F377  r02  e002      s3D35F3C4  r02  e002
s3D35F370  r01  e001      s3D35F370  r01  e001
s3D35F363  r03  e001      s3D35F363  r03  e001
s3D35F31E  r04  e004      s3D35F372  r04  e002
s3D35F2EE  r05  e001      s3D35F2EE  r05  e001
s3D35F365  r06  e003      s3D35F365  r06  e003
```

7. If verification is successful, `.RST` is renamed to `.NDS` and the login disabled attribute is cleared so it becomes the active eDirectory database
   on the server. If verification fails, the `.RST` DIB is not renamed, and
   the active DIB set is set back to `.NDS`.

The restore verification process is backward compatible only with eDirectory
8.5 or later (due to the transitive vector requirement). If the server you are
restoring participates in a replica ring with a server running a version of
NDS earlier than eDirectory 8.5, the restore log will show a -666 error
(incompatible DS version) for that replica. This does not indicate whether
the replicas are out of sync; it merely indicates that the restore verification
was unable to compare the transitive vectors because the version of
eDirectory was earlier than 8.5. When this happens, the database will not
open (by default) because the restore verification was not completely successful. If in your best judgment, however, it is safe to open the database,
you can use the override restore option in the eMBox Client to make the
restored DIB active. Refer to the later section "Recovering the DIB if Restore
Verification Fails" on how to recover the server from a failed restore verification process.

Transitive Vectors and the Restore Verification Process

A transitive vector is a time stamp for a replica. The vector consists of the
number of seconds since midnight of January 1, 1970 (a common reference
point used by all DS-related time functions), the replica number, and the
current event number. Here's an example of a transitive vector:

`s3D35F377 r02 e002`

In the context of backup and restore, it's important because the transitive
vector is used to verify that the server restored is in sync with the replica
rings it participates in.

Servers that hold replicas of the same partition communicate with each
other to keep the replicas synchronized. Each time a server communicates

with another server in the replica ring, it keeps a record of the transitive vector the other server had when they communicated. These transitive vectors allow the servers in a replica ring to know what information needs to be sent to each replica in the ring to keep all the replicas synchronized. When a server is unavailable, it stops communicating, and the other servers don't send updates or change the transitive vector they have recorded for that server until the server starts communicating again.

When you restore eDirectory on a server, the restore verification process compares the transitive vector of the server being restored to the other servers in the replica ring. This is done to make sure the replicas being restored are in the same state the other servers expect.

If the transitive vector on the remote server is ahead of the local vector, then data is missing from the restore, and the verification fails. As an example, data might be missing because you did not turn on continuous roll-forward logging before the last full or incremental backup, you did not include the roll-forward logs in the restore, or the set of roll-forward logs you provided for the restore was not complete.

Hot Continuous Backup and Roll-Forward Logs

The eDirectory Backup eMTool provides hot continuous backup of the eDirectory database on an individual server. This feature allows you to back up eDirectory on your server *without* closing the database and still get a complete backup that is a snapshot of the moment when the backup began. This means you can create a backup at any time and eDirectory will remain accessible by your users and other clients throughout the process. Hot continuous backup is the default behavior.

The Backup eMTool also lets you turn on roll-forward logging to keep a record of transactions in the database since the last backup. This allows you to restore a server to the state it was in at the moment before it went down. In a single-server environment, roll-forward logging is not required for the restore verification process, but the log files enable you to restore eDirectory to the moment before it went down instead of just to the last backup. In a multiserver tree, however, you must turn on roll-forward logging for all servers that participate in a replica ring, so that you can restore a server to the synchronization state that the other servers expect. If you don't, then when you try to restore from your backup files you will get errors and the database will not open. Roll-forward logging is off by default.

NOTE

The concept of Backup eMTool's hot backup plus roll-forward logging is not new. It is essentially the same as that of the full data backup plus incremental backups you are accustomed to when dealing with file system backups. The difference is that roll-forward log files contain a history of changes since the last full or incremental backup.

eDirectory automatically creates a record of transactions in a log file before committing them to the database. By default, the log file for these records is reused over and over (consuming only a small amount of disk space), and the history of changes to the eDirectory database is not saved. When you turn on continuous roll-forward logging, the history of changes is saved in a set of consecutive roll-forward log files. Roll-forward logging does not reduce server performance; it simply saves the log file entries that eDirectory is already creating.

When using the continuous roll-forward logging feature, you must be aware of the following issues:

- ▶ Turn on roll-forward logging before a backup is done. This enables you to use this feature for restoring the database.

- ▶ For fault tolerance, make sure that the roll-forward logs are placed on a different storage device than eDirectory. For security, you should also restrict user rights to the logs.

- ▶ Document the location of the roll-forward logs so you can backup the log files to tape.

- ▶ Monitor the available disk space where the logs are located. If you run out of disk space and roll-forward logs cannot be created, eDirectory will stop responding—much like the situation with legacy versions of NDS when NetWare's Transaction Tracking System (TTS) shuts down.

- ▶ If the logs are turned off or lost, turn them back on, then do a new full backup to ensure that you can make a full recovery.

- ▶ If you turn on logging of stream files, the roll-forward logs use up disk space much more quickly. When logging of stream files (such as login scripts or any attribute that uses the SYN_STREAM syntax) is turned on, the *whole* stream file is copied into the roll-forward log every time there is a change. You can slow the growth of the log files by turning off roll-forward logging of stream files and, instead, back them up only when you do an incremental or full backup.

- ▶ Don't change the name of a roll-forward log file. If the filename is different than when the log was created, the log file can't be used in a restore.

Removal of eDirectory from a server also removes all the roll-forward logs. If you want to be able to use the logs for restoring in the future, copy the roll-forward logs to another location before removing eDirectory.

Configuring and Maintaining Roll-Forward Logs

The roll-forward log feature is off by default. It is easiest to use iManager for this task. Follow these steps to enable roll-forward logging on a given server:

1. Log into iManager as a user with Supervisor rights.

2. Click the Roles and Tasks button.

3. Click eDirectory Maintenance, Backup Configuration.

4. Specify the server that you want to configure and click Next.

5. If not already authenticated to the server, you will be prompted for a username and password. Enter the requested information and click Next.

6. The Backup Configuration Wizard (see Figure 8.22) is displayed showing the current setting.

FIGURE 8.22
Configuring roll-forward logging.

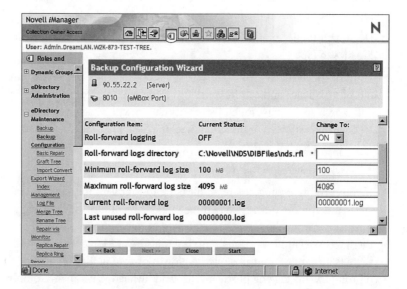

7. Change the status of Roll-forward logging to On.

8. Specify a Roll-forward logs directory. For fault-tolerance purposes, this directory should be on a separate drive or volume than where eDirectory is installed.

9. Set maximum and minimum file sizes as desired.

10. Click Start to save the new settings.

11. Document your settings.

You need to do this for every server that you want to use roll-forward logging on.

We strongly suggest that you periodically back up the log files and remove unused logs from the server to free up disk space. Use the following procedure to identify, back up, and remove roll-forward logs that are safe to remove:

1. Make a note of the name of the last unused roll-forward log. You can find out the name of the last unused roll-forward log in the following ways:

    ▶ In iManager, click eDirectory Maintenance, Backup Configuration and read the filename displayed, as shown in Figure 8.23.

    ▶ In the eMBox Client, use the backup.getconfig command in the interactive mode. If using the GUI mode, backup, Retrieve backup configuation, Run.

    The last unused roll-forward log is the most recent roll-forward log the database has completed and is no longer using to record transactions. It's called the last unused roll-forward log because the database has finished writing to it and has begun a new log file so it does not need to have this one open any more. The current roll-forward log in which the database is recording transactions is in use and is still needed by the database.

2. Do a file system backup of the roll-forward logs to put them all safely on tape.

3. Manually remove the roll-forward logs that are older than the last unused roll-forward log.

FIGURE 8.23
Determining the
name of the last
unused roll-
forward log.

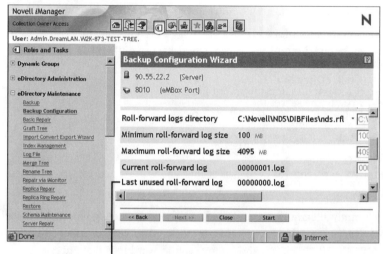

This file is no longer used

WARNING

Be cautious when removing roll-forward logs from the server. Check to ensure you have a backup copy of the log files before you delete them.

The last unused roll-forward log simply *indicates* which file the database has just completed and closed. It does *not* mean it's safe to remove that file from the server. You must make sure that you remove only files that you have a tape backup for.

Although Backup eMTool is rather easy to use and more powerful than the former SSI option, there is quite a bit of manual maintenance work in regard to the roll-forward log files.

Backing Up a Server Using Backup eMTool

The eDirectory Backup eMTool can back up data from an eDirectory database to one or more files on the server where the backup is being performed. You can do a full or incremental backup. The backup files contain information necessary to restore eDirectory to the state it was in at the time of the backup. The results of the backup process are written to the log file you specify.

Backups performed using iManager are hot continuous backups, meaning that the eDirectory database is kept open and accessible during the process, and you still get a complete backup that is a snapshot of the moment when the backup began. To perform a cold backup (a backup with the database closed) or an unattended backup, you must use the eMBox Client.

The following steps illustrate how to back up a server using iManager:

1. Log into iManager as a user with Supervisor rights.

2. Click the Roles and Tasks button.

3. Click eDirectory Maintenance, Backup.

4. Specify the server that you want to backup and click Next.

5. If not already authenticated to the server, you will be prompted for a username and password. Enter the requested information and click Next.

6. Specify the backup file options, such as full, incremental and name and location of the backup file (see Figure 8.24), optionally a maximum file size for the backup data file, and then click Next.

NOTE

When a maximum file size is specified, after the first file (whose name is what you specified) has reached the specified file size, subsequent files are created as `filename.xxxxx`, where *xxxxx* ranges from 00001 to FFFFF.

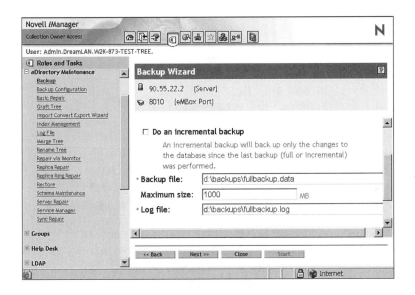

FIGURE 8.24
Server backup options.

7. Specify whether to include NICI files in the backup. Novell recommends that you *always* include NICI files.

8. Specify whether to include stream files in the backup.

9. Specify any additional files to back up via an include file. This include file is a text file that exists on the file system of the server you are backing up and contains a list of semicolon-separated files.

The filenames must not have any spaces or hard returns between each entry and the last entry *must* have a semicolon after its name; embedded spaces within a file-name is okay. For example, SYS:SYSTEM\AUTOEXEC.NCF;SYS:PUBLIC\ CUSTOM_APP.EXE;.

10. Click Start.

To make it easier to move the backup files to another storage device, you can specify the maximum size of eDirectory backup files. You can also use a third-party file compression tool (for instance, HRZIP.NLM on NetWare [www.novell.com/coolsolutions/tools/1099.html]; WinZIP on Windows; gzip on Unix) on the files after they are created. The backup files can be com-pressed by approximately 80%.

The backup log file contains a list of files that were backed up, such as the NICI files and any files you specified using an include file. The log file looks similar to the following:

```
¦==================DSBackup Log: Backup===============¦
Backup type: Full
Log file name: d:\backups\fullbackup.log
Backup started: 2004-4-11'T19:59:45
Backup file name: d:\backups\fullbackup.data
Server name: \T=W2K-873-TEST-TREE\O=XYZCorp\CN=W2KC-NDS
Current Roll Forward Log: 00000001.log
DS Version: 1055098
Backup ID: 4079DBF1
Backing up security file: C:\WIN2K\nici\NICIFK
Backing up security file: C:\WIN2K\nici\nicintacl.exe
Backing up security file: C:\WIN2K\nici\NICISDI.KEY
Backing up security file: C:\WIN2K\nici\system\Xmgrcfg.ks2
Backing up security file: C:\WIN2K\nici\system\Xmgrcfg.ks3
Backing up security file: C:\WIN2K\nici\XARCHIVE.000
Backing up security file: C:\WIN2K\nici\XMGRCFG.NIF
Backing up security file: C:\WIN2K\nici\xmgrcfg.wks
Backing up file: c:\info\backup-1.pcx
Backing up file: c:\info\backup-3.pcx
Backing up file: c:\info\backup-2 Temp.pcx
Starting database backup...
Starting new file: d:\backups\fullbackup.data.00001
Starting new file: d:\backups\fullbackup.data.00002
Starting new file: d:\backups\fullbackup.data.00003
Starting new file: d:\backups\fullbackup.data.00004
Database backup finished
```

```
Completion time 00:04:12
Backup completed successfully
```

Make sure you do a file system backup shortly after the eDirectory backup is created, to put the eDirectory backup files (*including the log file*) safely on tape since the Backup eMTool only places them on the server.

You *will* need the backup log file in order to perform a restore.   **NOTE**

To perform a cold backup (for the purpose of hardware upgrade, for example) or a scheduled unattended backup (via system batch files and scripts), you need to use the eMBox Client, and not iManager. Refer to the "eDirectory Management Toolbox" section in Chapter 7 for more information about using the eMBox Client.

Restoring a Server Using Backup eMTool

The most important part of restoring the eDirectory database is making sure it is complete. Because of the file dependencies (having the correct roll-forward logs for the specific backup and so on), you must ensure the following prerequisites have been met before restoring an eDirectory database to a server:

▶ All servers that share a replica with the server to be restored are up and communicating. This allows the restore verification process to check with servers that participate in the same replica ring.

▶ You have gathered all the backup files you need. The full backup and subsequent incremental backup files are copied to one directory on the server to be restored. And all the roll-forward logs since the last backup are in one directory on the server to be restored (so Backup eMTool can locate them), with the same filenames they had when they were created.

For procedures on how to confirm that you have the correct backup files before performing a restore or how to determine which are the correct files if names were changed, refer to the "Locating the Right Backup Files for a Restore" section in eDirectory 8.7 (or later) documentation.   **TIP**

If you do not have all the necessary backup files, you can try the procedure outlined in the "Recovering a Crashed SYS Volume or Server" section in Chapter 11. You can also refer to TID #10010922, titled "Removing a Crashed Server from the NDS Tree," which covers how to recover from a server crash.   **TIP**

▶ You have installed eDirectory, in a new temporary tree. You bring up the server in a new tree at first because you will create the server with the same name it had before the failure. Furthermore, you don't want to cause confusion in the original tree by putting the newly installed server in the tree before the restore has re-created the server's complete identity. Completing the restore process for the database will put the server back into its original tree.

▶ If any applications or objects need to find this server by its IP address, ensure the same IP address is used for the restored server.

▶ (NetWare only) Make sure the name of the server you are restoring to is the same as the name of the failed server. If the names are not the same, you might encounter errors, such as Volume objects not being correct after the restore.

▶ (NetWare only) Be sure to restore file system data only after eDirectory has been fully restored. Otherwise, you will lose file system trustee information.

During the restore process, the eDirectory Backup eMTool first restores the full backup. After this is complete, the Backup eMTool prompts you to enter the filenames of the incremental backup files. It provides you with the ID of the next file. After all incremental files are restored, the Backup eMTool moves on to the roll-forward logs.

After you have gathered all the necessary files and have placed them in the same directory, perform the restore using either iManager or the eMBox Client. The following outlines the server restore from backup files procedure using iManager:

1. Ensure that the prerequisites listed at the beginning of this section are met.

2. Log into iManager as a user with Supervisor rights.

3. Click the Roles and Tasks button.

4. Click eDirectory Maintenance, Restore.

5. Specify the server that you want to restore and click Next.

6. If not already authenticated to the server, you will be prompted for a username and password. Enter the requested information and click Next.

7. Specify the name of the backup and log files you want to use (see Figure 8.25), then click Next.

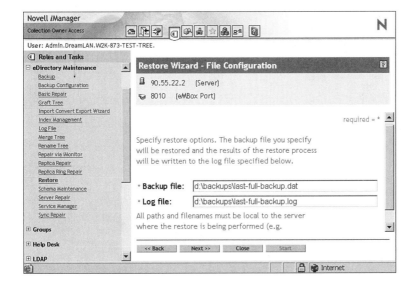

FIGURE 8.25
Specifying the backup files for restore.

8. Specify additional restore options (see Figure 8.26), then click Next. In most cases, the following check boxes should be selected for a proper restore:

   ▶ Restore database

   ▶ Activate the restored database after verification

   ▶ Open the database after completion of restore

   ▶ Restore security files (meaning NICI files)

   ▶ If you are restoring roll-forward logs, make sure you include the full path to the logs, including the directory that is automatically created by eDirectory, usually named `nds.rfl`.

   ▶ Activate the restored database after verification

9. Click Start to initiate the restore process.

10. If the restore verification fails, refer to the later section "Recovering the DIB If Restore Verification Fails."

11. If you restored NICI security files, restart the server after the eDirectory restore is complete to reinitialize NICI.

12. Verify that the server is re-introduced into the production tree correctly and check that all replicas on this server are properly synchronized.

FIGURE 8.26
Specifying additional restore options.

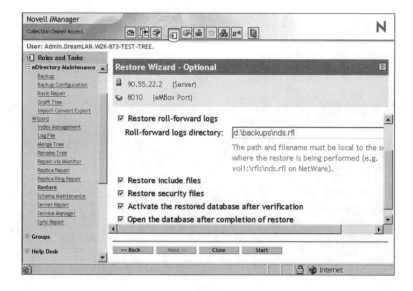

The restore process turns off roll-forward logging and resets the configuration for roll-forward logging back to the default, which is `Off`. You will need to re-enable it if the server is part of a replica ring.

You should perform a full backup soon after the server restore process is complete. The new full backup is necessary so that you are prepared for any failures that might occur before the next full backup is scheduled to take place.

Recovering the DIB If Restore Verification Fails

To ensure data consistency, the Backup eMTool restore process includes a verification step, which compares transitive vectors in the eDirectory database on the server being restored against other servers in the replica ring. If the transitive vectors do not match, the verification fails. This usually indicates that data is missing from the files you used for the restore. Data might be missing for one of the following reasons:

▶ You did not turn on roll-forward logging before the last backup was performed.

▶ You did not include the roll-forward logs in the restore.

▶ The set of roll-forward logs you provided for the restore was not complete.

Verification failure might be caused by one of the servers in the replica ring running a version of NDS earlier than eDirectory 8.5. By default the restored eDirectory database will not open after the restore if Backup eMTool determines it is inconsistent with the other replicas.

If you have all the backup files and roll-forward logs necessary for a complete restore but forget to provide all of them during the process, you can simply run the restore again with a complete set of files. If the restore is complete on a second try, the verification can succeed and the restored database will open.

If you do not have all the backup files and roll-forward logs necessary to make the restore complete so that verification will be successful, you must follow the instructions outlined later in this section to recover the server. Here is an outline of what information you can recover if verification fails:

- ▶ You can still recover the server's identity and file system rights (for a NetWare server).

- ▶ You cannot recover any replicas on this server from backup, but the server can still be used for the replicas it contained after you follow the recovery procedure in this section. You must remove the server from the replica ring and use advanced Restore options and the DSRepair Tool to bring the server to a state where it can be put back in the replica ring. Then you can re-add the desired replicas to it.

- ▶ If this server had the sole copy of any partition of the database (there were no other replicas of the partition), the partition unfortunately cannot be recovered.

If eDirectory Backup eMTool verification fails to recover the server's identity, use the following procedure to recover and re-add it to the replica ring:

1. Clean up the replica rings per the steps given in the "Replica Ring Inconsistency" section in Chapter 11.

2. Change the replica information on the server to external references, so that the server does not consider it to be part of a replica ring. After you remove the replicas from the server in this way, you can unlock the database. To accomplish this step, you need to use the advanced restore mode in the eMBox Client—you *cannot* use iManager for this step—to override the default restore behavior:

   - ▶ Launch the eMBox Client using the instructions presented in the "eDirectory Management Toolbox" section in Chapter 7. You can use either the interactive mode (-i) or the graphical mode (-g).

▶ If using the GUI mode, enable both the Show command line and Advanced mode options via the Settings menu.

▶ Log into the server you want to restore. If using the interactive mode, enter the following command:

```
backup.restadv -v -l logfilename
```

If using the GUI mode (see Figure 8.27), click Backup, Advanced restore options, mark Override restore, and click Run. This advanced restore option will rename the .RST database (the database that was restored but failed the verification) to .NDS, but keep the database locked.

FIGURE 8.27
Using the advanced restore option in eMBox Client.

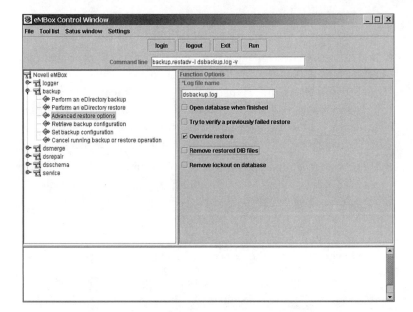

▶ At the server console, run DSRepair with the -XK2 switch to change all replica information on the server to external references:

NetWare   `DSREPAIR -XK2 -RD`

Windows   From NDSCons, select `dsrepair.dlm`, enter `-rd -xk2` in the Startup Parameters field, and click Start.

Unix   `ndsrepair -R -Ad -xk2`

`DSREPAIR.NLM` and `dsrepair.dlm` will not display their menu and will exit automatically after the repair is finished when the `-rd` switch is specified.

You can also use the DSRepair eMTool for this step (see Figure 8.28). Click dsrepair, Repair local database, uncheck all options, click Use temporary eDirectory database during repair?, click (xk2):Convert all replicas into external references, and click Run.

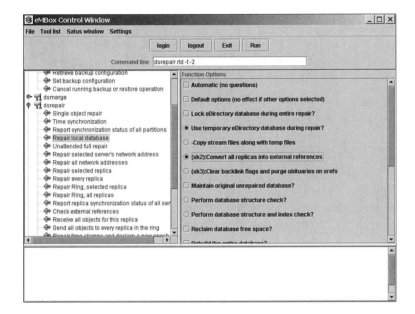

FIGURE 8.28
Using the advanced repair option to change all replica information on the server to external references.

▶ When the repair is finished, remove the lockout and open the database. If using the interactive mode, enter the following command:

`backup.restadv -o -k -l logfilename`

The `-o` opens the database and the `-k` removes the lockout.

If using the GUI mode (see Figure 8.29), click backup, Advanced restore options, mark Open database when finished, mark Remove lockout on database, and click Run.

3. You can now re-add the server into the replica rings using either ConsoleOne or iManager. When you have followed these steps and the replication process is complete, the server should function as it did before the failure (with the exception of any partitions that were not replicated and, therefore, can't be recovered).

FIGURE 8.29
Unlock and open
the database.

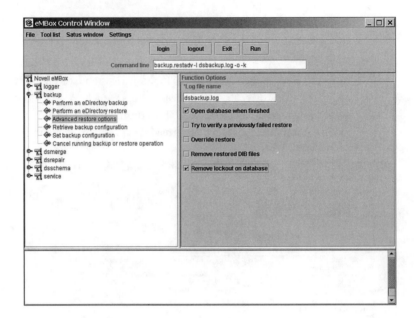

4. If you restored NICI security files, after completing the restore and replication, restart the server to reinitialize NICI.

5. If you want to use roll-forward logging on this server, you must re-create your configuration for roll-forward logging to make sure it is turned on and the logs are being saved in a fault-tolerant location. After turning on the roll-forward logs, you must also do a new full backup.

This last step is necessary because during a restore, the configuration for roll-forward logging is set back to the default, which means that roll-forward logging is turned off and the location is set back to the default. The new full backup is necessary so that you are prepared for any failures that might occur before the next full backup is scheduled to take place.

Third-Party Data Recovery Utilities

As NDS/eDirectory and DS software development tools have been available for many years, a number of third-party DS-specific utilities are available to help you manage your NDS/eDirectory trees more easily and effectively, as well as to recover lost DS data. The following introduces you to some third-party tools that can help you to recover lost DS data, and, in Chapter 12, you'll find a discussion of some third-party NDS/eDirectory management applications.

Due to the lack of documented APIs necessary to access eDirectory under a data recovery situation by Novell for non-NetWare platforms, the discussions in this section are limited to DS trees where there are NetWare servers present. Should you have a need to recover a lost Admin password or Admin user in an eDirectory tree where there is no NetWare servers hosting replicas, contact Novell for assistance: Visit support.novell.com/additional/telephone.html **for a list of telephone numbers for your region.**

Recovering a Lost Admin Password

It is not uncommon to forget a password, especially one that's considered to be a good, secure password. What can you do if the Admin password is lost, either due to human error or deliberate sabotage? If you have a backup Admin user that has Write rights to Admin's Access Control List (ACL) attribute then you can simply use it to reset Admin's password.

What if you don't have a user that can reset Admin's password? There are a few solutions that you can try.

It is generally recommended that a password should not be a common (single) word that is easily guessed; however, instead of using a meaningless word for your password, such as "435ggerpwe", combine a few meaningful (thus easily remembered) words together into a password, such as "try2guessthispassword".

The first technique is to make use of Bindery Services. If you have a server that holds a writable replica (Master or Read/Write) of the partition containing the Admin object, you can use one of the two following methods:

▶ Log in to that server using the bindery Supervisor ID, and use a bindery-based management utility, such as SYSCON, to change Admin's password. (You can download a copy of **SYSCON.EXE** from Novell's knowledgebase; see TID #1003215.)

▶ If you don't know the bindery Supervisor's password, you can use one of the NLM tools (such as SetPwd), available on the Internet, to reset the Admin password.

▶ Open an incident with Novell Technical Support. NTS can help you to reset Admin's password via remote access.

▶ DreamLAN Networking Consulting has a DSPass NLM that can reset an NDS User object password without Bindery Services, or can reset a bindery password if Bindery Services is enabled. Visit `www.dreamlan.com/dspass.htm` for more information.

> **NOTE** Although there are other NLMs easily available on the Internet that can be used to change Admin's password, DSPass is the only YES certified solution (YES Bulletin #44431) that runs on NetWare 4.10 and higher and works with all versions of NDS and eDirectory.

Because these NLMs require server console access, you should always take appropriate steps and care to secure your server console from both physical and remote (for example, RConsole) unauthorized access. Third-party utilities, such as DreamLAN Network Consulting's SSLock for NDS and Protocom Development Systems' SecureConsole can enhance your server console security. See Chapter 15 for additional information.

Recovering a Lost Admin User Account

If you administered NetWare networks prior to NetWare 4.0, you know that the user Supervisor can't be deleted (at least not by accident and not through standard management tools such as SYSCON). With NetWare 4 and higher, however, it is possible for you to (accidentally) remove the Admin user and leave yourself with an unmanageable NDS/eDirectory tree! Chapter 15 contains information on how to safeguard your administrative accounts so you'll never have an unmanageable tree. In the unpleasant event that you've lost your Admin user, here are some solutions.

If it is a single-server test tree or a tree that can easily be recreated, you can use the following steps to re-create a new Admin user:

1. Remove DS by loading the NWConfig or Install NLM with the `-DSREMOVE` command-line switch. (For example, `LOAD NWCONFIG -DSREMOVE`.)

2. Select Directory Options.

3. Select Remove Directory Services from the server.

4. Press Enter after reading the warning message.

5. Select Yes to the Remove Directory Services? prompt.

6. Press Esc when prompted for the Admin user and password.

7. Select Yes to the Remove the Directory without logging in recommended? prompt.

8. After DS has been removed, exit NWConfig and reload NWConfig without the -DSREMOVE switch.

9. Use the Directory Options to reinstall DS. You'll be asked to create the Admin user.

The steps described *will* destroy your current DS tree! The file system data will not be touched, however.

Another solution is to open an incident with Novell Technical Support. NTS can help you to create a user with Supervisor rights to [Root] and, thus, admin rights to your tree, via remote access.

Yet another option is to use the MakeSU ("Make SuperUser") NLM from DreamLAN Networking Consulting. This can create a DS User object that has Supervisor rights to [Root]. Visit www.dreamlan.com/makesu.htm for more information.

Unlike the first option, the last two options will create an Admin user in a nondestructive manner.

There are a couple of other NLMs available on the Internet that can create a lost Admin user. MakeSU, however, is the only YES-certified solution (YES Bulletin #44435) that runs on NetWare 4.10 and higher and works with all versions of NDS and eDirectory.

Detecting and Gaining Access to IRF-Blocked Objects

Similar to NetWare file system's Inherited Rights Filters (IRFs), DS administrators can apply IRFs to DS objects so they are not accessible by other users except those that have trustee assignments. The one main difference between file system IRFs and DS IRFs is that you can use IRF to block Supervisor access to DS objects while you can't do this in file systems. Therefore, it is not uncommon for security-conscious DS administrators to protect administrative accounts, such as Admin and admin-equivalent user objects, using IRFs. For details on how to protect DS objects, especially Admin-type user objects, from tampering, see Chapter 15. The following section deals with what to do if you need access to IRF-blocked objects.

IRF-blocked objects can be categorized into three types: visible but unmanageable (you can't delete or modify them), invisible but manageable, and invisible and unmanageable. The invisible objects are generally referred to as *stealth* objects. You can't see stealth objects easily using the standard management utilities, such as ConsoleOne, because the IRF blocked the Browse right to the object. They can be detected, however, using certain techniques (if they leave a "footprint" via ACL assignments, for example) and using specialized utilities. You'll find a discussion of one of the utilities, Hidden Object Locator, in Chapter 15.

NOTE   Another stealth object detector is the NDSTree utility, available from DreamLAN Network Consulting. For more information, see www.dreamlan.com/ndstree.htm.

Once the unmanageable object names are determined, you can regain access to them using one of the following methods:

▶ Open an incident call with Novell Technical Support.

▶ Use the MakeSU NLM to create a DS User object or grant an existing user object full DS right to the stealth or unmanageable object.

Write Your Own Utility

Although there are a large number of utilities available to assist you in data recovery, every network is unique, and you may have specific requirements that the available utilities do not address. If you have some programming background or have access to a programmer, coding your own recovery utility is an option.

A wide variety of tools that interface with network services and NDS/eDirectory are available for your choosing. You're not limited to using the C programming language, as was the case in the past when programming for NetWare and other operating systems. Novell and third-party vendors offer class libraries, JavaBeans, scripting languages (such as Visual Basic, JavaScript and Perl), and C/C++ APIs to support the widest range of developer participation and opportunity. Chapter 10 offers some examples on how you can "roll your own" data recovery utilities.

Summary

This chapter covered a number of tools that can help you in protecting and recovering lost NDS/eDirectory information and help you re-create a lost Admin user. The following topics were discussed:

- ▶ Backing up and restoring DS with Storage Management Services (SMS) and using eDirectory Management Tool Box (eMBox)

- ▶ NDS/eDirectory recovery using Server Specific Information (SSI) data after a server crash

- ▶ Recovering lost passwords and lost Admin user accounts

- ▶ Detecting and gaining objects that are blocked by Inherited Rights Filters (IRFs)

The next chapter shows how to combine the various tools discussed up to this point to maximize their capability.

Diagnosis and Recovery Techniques

Previous chapters discuss the different tools available and the information necessary to diagnose problems with an NDS/eDirectory tree. This chapter looks at some different ways of using that information.

This chapter examines some techniques for combining the different tools available to maximize your ability to resolve tree-related issues. The various tools that are available enhance your ability to diagnose problems and resolve them.

Before you jump into solving a directory services (DS) problem with both feet, though, you need to first establish a plan of attack.

Look Before You Leap

Chapter 1, "The Four Basics of eDirectory Troubleshooting," mentions that a typical troubleshooting process is comprised of five steps:

1. Gather information.
2. Develop a plan of attack.
3. Execute the plan.
4. Evaluate the results. Go back to step 1 if necessary.
5. Document the solution.

When faced with a DS problem, it is important that you follow a *consistent* set of troubleshooting procedures—that you use *every* time—to solve and resolve the problem. The following sections examine each of these five troubleshooting steps as well as some other parts of the troubleshooting process.

Identifying the Problem and Its Scope

Before you attempt to deal with a problem, you need to first determine what the problem is and what the scope of the problem is. You need to know what you are getting yourself into so you can properly allocate time and resources for the task.

NDS/eDirectory problems can manifest in a number of ways. They can appear directly in the form of error or warning messages in utilities or on the server console. They can also show up indirectly as part of an error message when you attempt to perform a DS operation. Sometimes a DS error shows up as a side effect of other system or network problems. For instance, a -625 error is a DS error that indicates communication failure. However, the cause of this error is not DS itself but has to do with the subsystem that is responsible for data communication—which DS has no control over. Therefore, you need to be able to differentiate between the symptoms and the problem.

TIP

Two key points to keep in mind at this initial phase of the troubleshooting process are to keep an open mind about the possible causes of the error and to consider the whole system—not just the DS portion—as a unit. Not all error messages you see indicate situations that you need to deal with right away or concurrently. Often, error conditions snowball: One initial error can result in dozens of other warning and error messages that may or may not point back to the initial error condition.

NOTE

I once saw a Cobol program compilation error listing that was over 15 pages long (the program itself was only 3 pages long). It all resulted from a single missing period starting about the fifth line from the beginning!

Users tend to cry wolf fairly easily. Therefore, before jumping to any conclusions, you should not panic; rather, you should confirm the error condition by either looking for concrete evidence of a problem or try to duplicate the problem. When you have established that there is indeed a problem, you must determine the extent of that problem.

You need to determine two facets of the problem. First, you need to determine the size of impact, such as how many people the error is affecting (including whether the CEO is one of the affected users) and the potential dollar cost of the error to the company. You also need to determine in which subcomponent the error condition happens. You can use these two facets to help prioritize your work schedule and troubleshooting efforts.

Our experience indicates that most of the time the DS errors you are mostly likely to encounter fall into the following three categories:

▶ Communication

▶ Time synchronization

▶ Replica synchronization

During the discovery process, you should check each of these areas in the order listed. You should make note of the following information, as it will help you determine the likely cause of the error:

▶ The symptom or steps required to reproduce the problem

▶ The exact error code and text of the error message

▶ Whether the error is seen on only one server or happens on others; if the error shows up on other servers, is there anything common between these servers, such as being in the same replica ring?

▶ The version of NDS/eDirectory running on the server(s) that reported the error

▶ The version of the operating system and patch level of the affected server(s)

It is important to quickly ascertain whether the error condition is occurring at the server, partition, replica, or object level. For instance, assume that the error code you receive is -601 when you're trying to read the `Title` attribute of a `User` object from Server A. Do you get the same error when you try to access the `Title` attribute from another server in the replica ring? If you do not get the error when you're trying to access this attribute from another server, the likely source of the problem is Server A itself. Otherwise, all the servers in the replica ring may be suspect.

Determining the Cause of the Problem

eDirectory reports problems or generates errors if a certain condition within the network prevents one or more eDirectory background processes from starting or completing. In most cases, your only indication of a DS error is in the form of an error code, which you see only when you perform a health check or enable the DSTrace screen. The following is a list of common DS errors:

▶ Physical communication problems between servers or between servers and client workstations

▶ Time synchronization problems

▶ NDS/eDirectory version incompatibility

▶ Replica inconsistency

▶ Improperly moved or removed servers

▶ An improperly changed server network address

▶ Synchronization problems (perhaps due to schema mismatch)

▶ Performance issues (such as low memory)

▶ Human error

To determine or narrow down the cause of the problem, you need to first ascertain whether it is an actual eDirectory problem or some other type of error that is manifesting itself as an eDirectory issue. When you are certain that the problem is indeed an eDirectory problem, you need to analyze the information you have gathered about the error condition and narrow it down to the particular background process that caused it. Then, using the various resources at your disposal, such as online error code listings that show possible causes and the Novell Knowledge Base, you should try to gain a handle on the real cause of the problem.

Formulating Possible Solutions to the Problem

You can almost always use more than one method or tool to fix a given eDirectory problem. When you search the TIDs for a possible solution to a particular problem, you shouldn't be surprised to find multiple documents that suggest different ways to resolve the problem. However, before you implement any of the solutions, you should do the following:

▶ List all the possible solutions

▶ List the possible consequences of each action (such as doing X will take 2 hours to complete, and doing Y will only take 45 minutes but involves shutting down seven servers)

▶ Check the latest available NDS/eDirectory updates and operating system patches to see whether the problem is one of the addressed issues

When installing a patch, you should *always* select to back up files that will be replaced when the installer prompts you. If the installer does not offer such an option, you should abort the update process, perform a backup of your system files (including those on the DOS partition, in the case of NetWare servers), and then restart the patch update. Furthermore, it is always good practice to keep a library of older patches that you have installed in case the new patch doesn't fix your problem or causes more problems; this way, you can roll back to an older patch that you know to work.

TIP

One of the possible solutions that you should *always* consider is *doing nothing*. NDS/eDirectory is designed to self-heal in many instances. Often, an error you encounter occurs when you try to perform some major operation as soon as a change (such as adding a replica) is made. Generally, the rule of thumb is to give DS an hour or two to "settle down" after such a change, and the error you see will resolve itself. Of course, you don't always have the luxury of letting DS sit for a few hours to see whether the problem goes away—especially when there are a score of people standing around (and one of them is the CEO), asking, "What's happening?" (Refer to Chapter 4, "Don't Panic," for a discussion on how to deal with such situations.) Nonetheless, you should not easily discount the value of the DS self-healing process.

WARNING

Depending on the DS error in question, some of the recommended fixes can be quite drastic. For instance, a TID may recommend that you forcefully remove a replica or even DS from the server as one of the steps to resolve object renames. You need to appreciate the *full* consequence of each step taken in your error-resolving process before taking it, and you need to have a back-out plan in place. If you are uncomfortable with any of the steps, you should consult with someone who is more experienced or open an incident with Novell so you have someone to back you up.

Ranking the Solutions

When you have a list of possible solutions to the problem you're experiencing, you then need to rank them based the following criteria:

▶ The odds that the action will resolve the error condition

▶ The risks associated with the corrective action (for example, if the action fails, it could make the problem worse or result in additional complications, such as extended system downtime)

▶ Additional fixes that may be required as a result of the action (For instance, if the fix calls for you to remove the server from the tree and then add it back in, file system trustee rights may be lost, and you might need to allow extra time to restore the trustee assignments.)

▶ The ease with which the fix can be applied (that is, how long will it take?)

▶ How the users will be further affected during the time when the corrective action is taking place (for example, will the users lose access to resources they now have access to?)

There is a medium to high degree of risk that if a corrective action does not work, it may lead to more harm to the system, and a sign-off from upper management is often warranted. You should present to management the rational for selecting the action but also lay out for them the possible consequences and rollback options.

> **TIP**
>
> If some of your solutions seem to contradict each other, you should consult with a knowledgeable co-worker or a friend. You should also make use of the expertise available to you, free of charge, at various online newsgroups, especially the Novell-sponsored ones available at `http://support-forums.novell.com`.

> **TIP**
>
> It is usually a good idea to solve a problem yourself so you can learn from the experience. Novell Support provides access to certain tools that are not available to the general public, and using these tools could save you hours of work. When you compare the cost of your downtime with the cost of an incident call, you see that there are circumstances when it is more expedient and cost-effective to open an incident with Novell and have Novell dial in to your system to perform the fix. You can always monitor Novell's progress and learn more about DS troubleshooting at the same time.

If at all possible, you should test solutions in a lab environment before attempting them on a production network. At the very least, you should always have a test server available so you can dry-run a procedure before attempting it on a production server.

Implementing a Solution

When you have decided on a course of action and received the necessary management approval, you need to make a backup of the Directory Information Base (DIB) files on the affected servers before implementing the fix. This will provide you with a back-out option in case something goes wrong.

You can find information on how to do this in the "Backing Up a Server's DS Database" section of Chapter 13, "eDirectory Health Checks."

If you are running eDirectory 8.7 or higher, you can use either the hot backup or the cold backup feature of eDirectory Backup eMTool, as discussed in Chapter 8, "eDirectory Data Recovery Tools," to take a snapshot of the current view of the replicas on the servers that you will be working with.

Before you perform any replica ring–related repairs, it is best to first do a local database repair. This ensures that the data in the local DIB is in good order before it is allowed to be replicated to other servers.

The effects of your corrective actions may not show up immediately. You should allow some time for the various eDirectory background processes to perform their tasks. For example, assume that you were unable to merge two partitions because of stuck obituaries. After implementing your fix, you might not be able to merge the partitions right away because you need to allow the obit processes to advance the flags through the different stages and clear out the dead objects. Because this generally involves communication between a couple servers, at least a few minutes will be required before the stuck obits are cleared out. After that, you can perform the partition merge.

Depending on the scope of impact of the DS error, you should keep your user community, especially upper management, informed of what is happening and your progress. This way, they can arrange their work and get a few things accomplished while waiting for access to the tree to be restored.

Verifying the Solution to the Problem

After the eDirectory processes report "All processed = YES" (and you might want to wait until you see this being reported a couple times to be on the safe side), you should verify that the problem has indeed been resolved. You can accomplish this in one of two ways:

▶ Attempt the initial action that caused the error to surface and see whether you can now perform it successfully

▶ Perform an abbreviated DS health check (as outlined in Chapter 13) to ensure that no more errors are being reported

If the problem persists, you should return to your list of possible solutions and consider taking another action. You might need to go back and reexamine and reconsider the possible causes of the problem to ensure that you are on the correct track.

Documenting the Steps in the Solution

You should keep a logbook that contains information about your servers, network configuration, and any special NDS/eDirectory information (such as any special naming convention used for designating administrative users or ACL assignments made to protect admin users). This logbook should also contain maintenance data about your servers and network, such as what operating system or NDS/eDirectory patch was applied and when. This allows you to determine whether the DS or other error condition may be a result of one of these updates. It is also a good idea to keep a copy of the patches installed as part of the logbook so you have ready access to older patches in case you need to roll back an update.

> **TIP**
>
> As the saying goes, "If you didn't write it down, it didn't happen." This is why keeping the logbook is so critical.

In your logbook, you should also document the DS errors that have occurred, their causes, and the solutions you have identified. Even if an error was not resolved by a given solution, you should note it for future reference and label it as an "unlikely" solution. Whatever you do, you shouldn't totally discount it from consideration the next time around because the same or a similar error condition could show up again. Even if a solution didn't work the first time around, it might very well work the next time because the condition that causes the same or similar error message or code might be different the next time around.

Depending on the type of error, you are likely to encounter it again sometime down the road. For instance, no matter how careful you are about your tree, stuck obits will continue to surface from time to time. Having the steps on error resolution clearly documented helps to ensure that if you need to solve a given problem, you have a "play book" that you can follow.

Avoiding Repeating the Problem

It is estimated that more than 90% of the software-related problems you encounter are due to human error. They can be caused by unintentional actions taken by an inexperienced administrator or procedures not being properly followed. They can also be due to a number of other causes. For example, someone might simply turn off the server and remove it from the network instead of first removing DS from the server before removing it from the network.

Once you have identified the source of a DS problem, you should review existing published procedures to ensure that any oversights or omissions that resulted in the error are promptly amended, and you should be sure that the information is passed on to your co-workers.

TIP

New support staff should be adequately trained before being permitted to have physical access to the servers where most harm may occur. At the very least, you should have each new staff member pair up with an experienced member of your staff when performing certain tasks the first couple times.

At the end of a problem-resolution session, depending on the scope of the error involved, you should hold a meeting with your support staff to go over lessons learned and discuss how the problem can be avoided in the future. You should *not*, however, use such a meeting to assign blame of any sort.

Troubleshooting Tools

As discussed in Chapter 7, "Diagnostic and Repair Tools," there are a number of Novell-supplied tools that you can use to diagnose and troubleshoot NDS/eDirectory error conditions. In many cases, these tools may not be the most convenient to use, but the server-based utilities are often the most effective because frequently the error is confined to a given server in a replica ring. In addition, server-centric information is useful, and you simply cannot obtain it by using a workstation-based tool.

The following sections discuss using the Novell server-based tools to diagnose and troubleshoot DS errors.

Use NDS iMonitor to Diagnose and Monitor

NDS iMonitor first shipped with eDirectory 8.5 and is available for all supported operating system platforms. It provides a Web-based portal for accessing server-centric eDirectory information, using a Web browser from any workstation on the network.

NOTE

NDS iMonitor is installed automatically as part of the eDirectory installation process.

You don't need to hunt through a number of different screens in DSRepair and DSBrowse for the necessary information because NDS iMonitor presents you with the easy-to-locate data about a partition, a replica, or a server. Figure 9.1 shows the synchronization status for a partition; you can obtain the server-centric replica status (see Figure 9.2) by clicking the Replica Synchronization link to the right of the partition name. By clicking the NCP server object name in the Replica Status screen, you can retrieve information about the server.

Click here to retrieve replica information

FIGURE 9.1
The partition synchronization status screen.

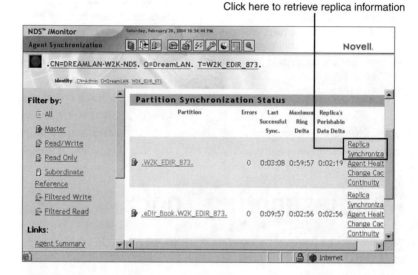

FIGURE 9.2
The Replica Status screen.

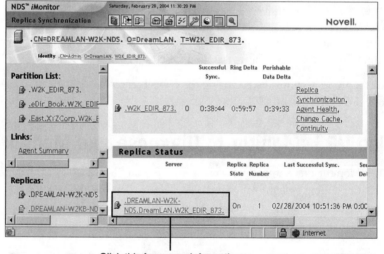

Click this for server information

When diagnosing a DS problem, you generally make use of the Partition Synchronization and Replica Synchronization screens in NDS iMonitor. You start by looking at the big picture at the partition level. When you notice a partition showing a nonzero error count, you can drill down to the replica level. From there, you can examine each of the servers in the replica ring that are reporting DS errors. Depending on your screen resolution, you might need to scroll to the far right of the entry in order to see the error code. Then you click the error code listed to see its meaning, possible causes, and possible actions to take. You can also enable DSTrace with various filter settings to gather additional diagnostic information (see Figure 9.3).

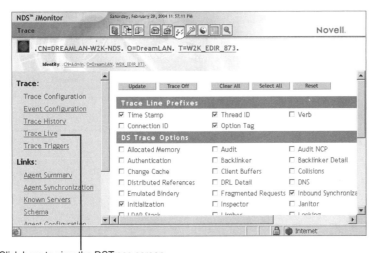

FIGURE 9.3
The DSTrace configuration screen.

Click here to view the DSTrace screen

NOTE

The number of features (such as DSTrace) and amount of information you can see in NDS iMonitor depend on the DS username (thus access rights you have in the tree) you used to access the application. Some options (such as DIB caching information) may not be available, depending on the version of the NDS/eDirectory agent you are monitoring.

When trace is enabled, you can use the additional Live Trace link to view the DSTrace messages in real-time, as shown in Figure 9.4. You can adjust how often the screen is updated; the default is every 15 seconds.

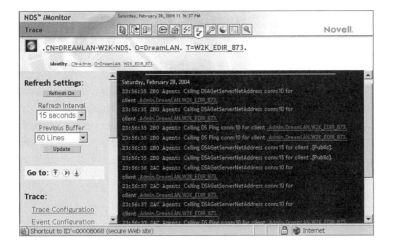

FIGURE 9.4
Live DSTrace messages.

NOTE When working with an NDS/eDirectory server in NDS iMonitor's proxy mode, you will not be able to access the DSTrace, DSRepair, and Background Process Schedule options. For more information about the proxy mode, refer to Chapter 7.

You can also use the Agent Health link and its sublinks to get a quick overview of the status of the partitions and local replicas. Figure 9.5 shows the overall health status of the local DS agent (DSA).

FIGURE 9.5
DSA health status.

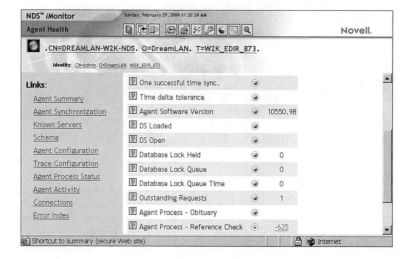

If you do not have time to perform health checks on a regular basis, you can use NDS iMonitor to periodically check the agent and replica/partition health status and run health reports on each server. Refer to Chapter 13 for more information about performing DS health checks.

Using iManager to Diagnose and Repair Problems

Similar to NDS iMonitor, iManager is a Web-based management utility from Novell. It, too, first shipped with eDirectory 8.5 and is available for all supported operating system platforms. Designed to be a replacement for ConsoleOne and NetWare Administrator, iManager does *not* require a Novell Client to be installed on the workstation—all its functions are performed through Tomcat servlets that are running on the server.

Because of the dependency on other applications, such as a working Apache Web server and LDAP server, sometimes you might need to troubleshoot the troubleshooter—your iManager setup—before you can troubleshoot eDirectory problems. You can find some tips on troubleshooting and setting up iManager in Chapter 7.

iManager provides a functionality called role-based services (RBS) that uses the concepts of roles (what the job functions are) and tasks (responsibilities associated with the job) such that members of the role will see only the tools necessary for their assigned roles. Two predefined DS management-related roles are included with iManager:

▶ eDirectory Maintenance

▶ Partition and Replicas

The tasks associated with these roles are identical to many of the DSRepair and DSMerge functions, and you can access them through simple wizards. As you can see in Figure 9.6, you have access to the same repair functions in iManager as you do in DSRepair—tasks such as single object repair and local database repair. You also have access to advanced repair functions such as schema maintenance and replica ring repair. Also available are other functions, such as tree merge (a function otherwise provided by the DSMerge utility).

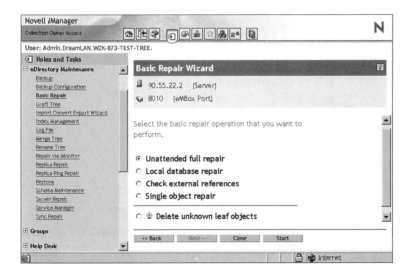

FIGURE 9.6
iManager's basic repair options.

By using the View Partition Information task (see Figure 9.7) and Sync Repair task (see Figure 9.8), you can easily get a quick, overall view of your tree's health. The wizards offer some advanced options in DSRepair but do not allow you to use any of the special command-line options, such as -XK2. However, you can pop over to NDS iMonitor easily via the Repair option under the iMonitor task, and you can use DSRepair command-line switches there.

FIGURE 9.7
Viewing partition synchronization status.

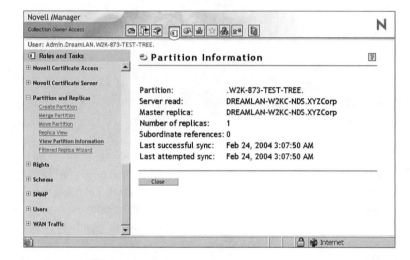

FIGURE 9.8
Viewing server synchronization status.

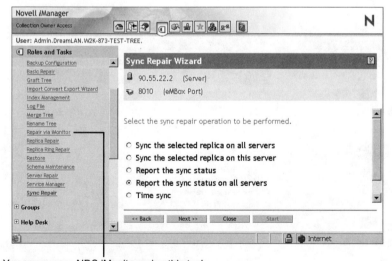

You can access NDS iMonitor using this task

The server must be running eDirectory 8.7 or higher in order for you to use the repair functions in iManager against it. This is because these functions are dependent on the eMBox utility, which ships only with eDirectory 8.7 and above.

Use eMBox and Legacy Tools to Diagnose and Repair Problems

Instead of using Tomcat servlets, iManager accesses the eDirectory database via the eDirectory Management Tool Box (eMBox) utility. This means that if you have the proper DS rights, you can perform all the RBS-based eDirectory Maintenance and Partition and Replicas tasks without using iManager by using the eMBox client instead. Because the eMBox client is Java based, you can run it from a server or workstation and perform tasks for a number of servers (as long as they are running the eMBox server, which is part of eDirectory 8.7 and above).

Refer to Chapter 7 for details about configuring and using the eMBox Java client.

You can perform a large number of repair tasks by using the eMBox client. When you're performing DS troubleshooting and repair procedures, it is easiest—and best—to run it in the graphical mode, as illustrated in Figure 9.9. You don't want to use the command-line text mode and enter a wrong option mistakenly or leave out a necessary flag and have some crucial information not be reported.

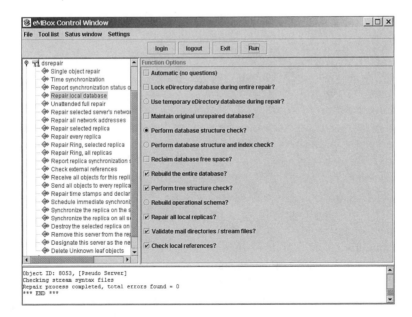

FIGURE 9.9
Performing a local database repair by using the eMBox client.

The one drawback of using the eMBox client instead of iManager or other tools (such as DSRepair) is the inability to browse for an object. You need to know in advance the distinguished name (DN) of the object/partition or the object's ID for certain operations and enter that manually (see Figure 9.10). This can be a dangerous limitation when you are in a rush or are under pressure to expedite a fix.

FIGURE 9.10
Manually entering information in the eMBox client.

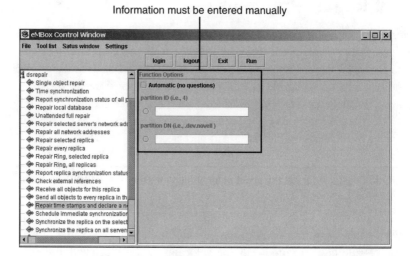

Information must be entered manually

Web-based tools such as NDS iMonitor and iManager are great when you are working from a remote location. However, sometimes, network security policies (such as firewall configuration) or communication disruptions force you to work directly at the server console, where using a Web-based tool becomes unpractical. Therefore, you should also be familiar with using the server-based "legacy" tools: DSRepair, DSTrace, and so on.

The other advantage of these server-based tools (with the exception of Windows versions) is that they are generally "processor efficient" because they are text based. As a result, these tools are generally fast in nature, and most of the processor cycles they consume go directly to collecting and reporting DS information. Note that the Windows versions of these server-based tools are also not overly processor unfriendly. The graphics (dialog boxes and so on) use standard Microsoft Foundation Class APIs and are fairly processor efficient. When compared with text-based applications, however, the GUI-oriented ones always seem to be not as efficient. The tradeoff is in the data representation: It is a lot easier to gain an overall picture of the situation from a graphical view than by having to wade through lines of messages for the necessary information.

When you use server-based tools for troubleshooting DS issues, you should generally start with DSTrace because it is non-intrusive (that is, it doesn't modify the DIB files in any way) and can point to the general problematic area where you should focus your attention. From there, you can move on to using DSRepair to get a closer view of partition and replica status. The following sections cover how you can get the most information out of the available tools by using a number of them so you can see the problem from different angles.

Combining Diagnostic Tools

Being able to combine information from multiple diagnostic tools can give you a better idea of what is really happening. As discussed previously in this book, having as much information as possible available increases your chances for correctly identifying the source of a problem, and correctly identifying the source of a problem is as important as resolving the problem.

Chapter 7 examines a number of different Novell tools for diagnosing problems:

- ▶ DSRepair
- ▶ DSTrace
- ▶ DSView, DSBrowse, and DSDiag
- ▶ NDS iMonitor and iManager
- ▶ NetWare Administrator and ConsoleOne
- ▶ Schema Manager

Chapter 7 also examines four tools for looking up and providing general DS information and information on the tree:

- ▶ LogicSource for eDirectory
- ▶ Online and CD-ROM–based knowledge bases
- ▶ Help files
- ▶ NList

Individually, these tools provide a number of useful functions, but when combined, their usefulness increases significantly.

One combination that you are probably already familiar with is using a diagnostic tool to determine an error condition followed by using an information tool to define an error message. For example, you have probably used DSRepair to determine that there was an error -625 in the NDS synchronization process and then used the help files, knowledge bases, LogicSource for eDirectory, or this book to look up what an error -625 was and possible causes and resolutions. This is a very simple example, but it is intuitive and something you probably do on a day-to-day basis.

Combining different tools needs to become as second nature to you as using an information resource to look up an error code. When you are attempting to determine whether a problem exists, it is important to look at the problem from multiple angles—and that frequently involves using multiple tools.

The diagnostic tools listed previously are good at specific things; in cases where functions and features of two tools overlap—for example, both NDS iMonitor and DSRepair can report replica synchronization status—using both tools to validate a problem is recommended. Doing this enables you to see two different views of the same problem—even to the extent of giving you different views of the same error conditions.

> **NOTE**
>
> Using different tools to examine a problem is highly recommended, especially if the problem is something you have not encountered before or if the symptoms are confusing or inconsistent. This is similar to your being ill with a not-so-common sickness; it may be a good idea to ask for additional opinions from a second doctor so you are presented with a different viewpoint.

Suppose that during a routine health check using NDS iMonitor, you find a partition reporting synchronization errors. You can use the features in NDS iMonitor to isolate the server that is having the problem and isolate the error code itself. The data presented with the Agent Synchronization link (refer to Figure 9.1) is server-centric. To gain a "ringwide" view of the situation, you could switch to either the Replica Synchronization view or the Continuity view (see Figure 9.11) by clicking the appropriate link to the right of the entry. This shows you which server(s) in the replica ring is reporting what error; sometimes two servers in the same replica ring may not report the same error condition because one server is the sender and the other server is the receiver.

Depending on the view you use (Replica Synchronization versus Continuity, in this example), you can get different error codes for the same error condition. In this particular example, two servers are in the replica ring, and one of the servers is taken offline. The Continuity view (refer to Figure 9.11) reports a -626 error when you try to query the downed server for the status flag. A -626 error means "all referrals failed"—that is, the local agent knows about the server but cannot connect to it over the network. The online help for the error code lists a number of causes. You can either try each of those suggested actions or try to narrow down the possibilities.

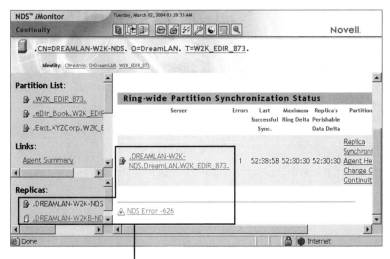

FIGURE 9.11
Replica ring
Continuity view.

There are two servers in this replica ring,
but a -626 error is reported when
trying to access the second server

If you checked the Replica Synchronization view, it would immediately become clear that there is a communication problem because the view shows a -625 error. Simply by looking at different views of the same issue, you can quickly narrow down the possibilities and save yourself from needlessly looking down the wrong alley.

Generally, the synchronization status is based on reading the status flag from the partition root object of only *one* server in each replica ring. Therefore, a utility such as NDS iMonitor may show that everything is running okay, but it does not necessarily mean that synchronization is running correctly across *all* servers. You should treat this option as a quick-check diagnostic and not a definitive one.

Now, suppose the error is something more complex than a -625 error—for example, a -694 error (`ERR_ENTRY_LOST`). At this point, in order to isolate the object that the -694 error is being reported on, you need to switch to a different tool. For instance, you can use DSTrace to watch the synchronization take place and observe the error.

This combination of using diagnostic tools and viewing the error from different perspectives is frequently necessary to completely diagnose a problem. Remember that the better you diagnose a problem, the better your chances are for resolving the issue and returning to normal operation.

Combining Recovery Tools

After you diagnose a problem, you need to work toward resolving the problem. Sometimes, though, complete recovery involves the use of multiple recovery tools because a single tool does not have the complete capability you need to resolve the issue.

Chapter 8 examines a number of different recovery tools, including the following:

- ▶ UImport and NDS Import Convert Export (ICE)
- ▶ SMS Backup and Restore
- ▶ eMBox

In addition to using these tools, you can use a number of the diagnostic tools previously discussed for recovery as well:

- ▶ DSRepair
- ▶ DSDiag and DSBrowse
- ▶ NetWare Administrator and ConsoleOne
- ▶ NDS iMonitor and iManager

You might have noticed that the functions of the recovery tools overlap significantly with those of the management tools, and this is not accidental. You should try to work with all these tools on a day-to-day basis so that you are familiar enough with them to understand how they can help you during a data recovery situation. It is usually difficult to have to use a separate set of tools during data recovery, especially if you don't need to use them frequently; part of your time spent on recovery will be wasted in refamiliarizing yourself with this separate set of tools.

Chapter 11, "Examples from the Real World," provides examples in which combining recovery tools results in a faster solution than using a single recovery tool. Remember that in a disaster-recovery situation, when you have a diagnosis, you need to work as quickly as possible to resolve the problem.

Working with a combination of recovery tools requires a good knowledge of the tools themselves. If you do not know for certain what a tool does or how it can help in resolving a problem, you might end up using a tool that will get you most of the way to a complete resolution but not let you finish the job. Let's continue with the previous example of a -694 error in synchronization. DSTrace showed the object name that was causing synchronization problems, and now you need to work to resolve the issue.

The first thing you should do is to verify that the object on the server that holds the Master replica is good; if it is, you can recover the object without deleting it. You can use DSBrowse (or DSView) to examine the attribute values of this object on the Master replica to make sure they are what you expected.

At the time of this writing, DSBrowse is not available on Unix/Linux. Instead, you can use LDAP to export an object's attribute values for examination. Examples of using LDAP to export (and import) object data from a tree can be found in the section "LDAP Import Convert Export Utility" in Chapter 12, "eDirectory Management Tools."

NOTE

If, on examination, the object appears to be fine, you can run DSRepair on the server that is reporting that it lost the entry. You can select either an unattended full repair of the database or a repair of the local database from the advanced options menu. You do this to ensure that the database is consistent locally. Then you force a replica synchronization with the Master replica.

The best way to proceed is to force a synchronization of all objects within the replica. You can do this most effectively by using the Receive All Objects option in DSRepair, as illustrated in Figure 9.12. This option essentially deletes the partition from the server that is reporting the error (by changing the replica state to New) and re-creating it by using the information received from the Master replica.

This is the least destructive of all fixes because only the replica on the problem server is affected, and the synchronization traffic is between the Master replica and the affected replica. If you use the Send All option instead, all non-Master replicas in the replica ring are set to the New state and are re-created. If the involved partition is large in size, a high volume of network traffic can result between the servers.

FIGURE 9.12
Resolving data
inconsistency
between replicas.

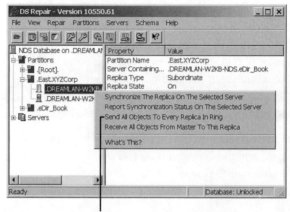

This option generates the least traffic and least overall impact

You could also use the advanced mode in DSBrowse to send a single object from the Master replica to the other replicas in the ring (see Figures 9.13 and 9.14). The one drawback of this is that DSBrowse is not available on Unix/Linux, where you need to use the DSRepair solution described previously.

Sends to all replica in the ring

FIGURE 9.13
Sending the
selected object
by using
DSBrowse in
Windows.

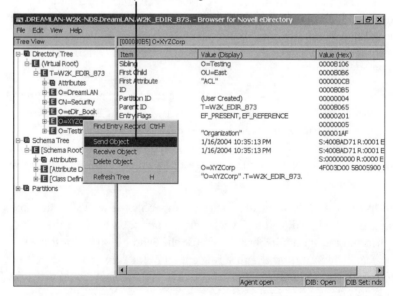

Load DSBrowse with the -A command-line option to get these additional featurers

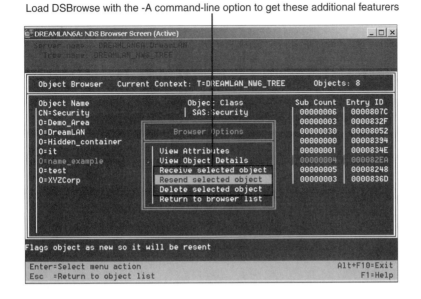

FIGURE 9.14
Sending a select-
ed object by
using DSBrowse
on a NetWare 6
server.

Using Diagnostic Tools with Recovery Tools

The previous section discusses using diagnostic tools with recovery tools in order to resolve an issue with a -694 error in synchronization. The technique for combining diagnostic tools and recovery tools is really no different from the process of combining any of the other tools.

Using diagnostic tools and recovery tools together in the recovery phase of the troubleshooting process provides more flexibility than categorizing each of the tools and using them only during specific phases of the process. Troubleshooting is an iterative process that sometimes involves many trips through the process of examining the problem, making a change, looking at the result, and reexamining the problem to see whether it has been resolved.

As with other combinations of tools, knowing the features and functionality of each tool is critical. If you are using tools that produce output or take input, knowing what the formats are and how to convert them is also a significant part of getting the tools to work together. Chapter 11 examines a situation that calls for the combination of NList and UImport to recover lost group membership information.

This idea of combining tools is central to resolving critical DS issues. If you don't effectively use the tools you have at hand, your troubleshooting approach is more likely to be disorganized and take longer than necessary to resolve the issue.

Bridging Gaps Between Tools

In discussing how to combine tools, we have not yet touched on how to bridge the functional gaps between tools. The preceding section mentions an example that combines NList and UImport to resolve an issue with lost group memberships. These two tools may not appear to have much in common that can be used to resolve problems. On the one hand, NList is a utility that is very powerful but clumsy to use because it has a complex command-line interface but has output that is intended to be human readable. On the other hand, UImport is a utility that is designed to take machine-readable input and update attribute values for existing User objects or to create a new object from the data.

> **NOTE**
>
> The same technique discussed for combining NList and UImport works equally well if you prefer to use ICE instead of NList and UImport because ICE supports the use of .csv files for input. You can find more details in Chapter 12.

There are a few ways to bridge, or "link" utilities together—that is, to take the output from one and turn it into a format that the other can use. For instance, you could take the output from one, import it into a spreadsheet, and use some complex formulas to extract the information you need. If the information is limited in scope, you could even use the Notepad utility and its primitive search-and-replace capability to remove excess information.

However you choose to manipulate the data, the key in bridging the different utilities is to learn how to manipulate data by using whatever tools you are comfortable with. If you are not a programmer, you can pick up an introductory programming book and learn how to program. Which programming language you use doesn't matter; it's the programming skills that are important. For instance, the "Group Membership Recovery" section in Chapter 11 shows that the combination of programming skills along with network administration is a very strong combination that can make your life a lot easier.

Diagnosing Performance Issues

Troubleshooting system performance bottlenecks is not an easy topic to address because you need to check many components. The Agent Activity page in NDS iMonitor provides you with some useful information about eDirectory performance.

Figure 9.15 shows a sample DSA verb/process statistics report. It provides the traffic pattern—in terms of how many hits over a given time period— broken down by type. For instance, since the time the counters were reset, there have been almost 2,000 requests to read entry info but only 3 modify- entry requests. This suggests that this server is read-intensive. In the event of a performance problem with this server, you should check things such as the DS cache allocation, operating system cache availability, and anything else that could affect read functions.

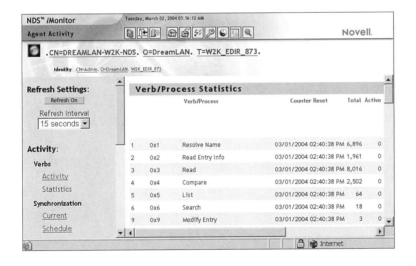

FIGURE 9.15
DSA verb statistics.

Chapter 16, "Tuning eDirectory," covers the details of how you can tune NDS/eDirectory for better performance by setting up indexes and proper DIB cache allocations. It also includes discussions that are operating system specific.

Summary

This chapter looks at a number of techniques for combining tools for troubleshooting purposes. By using various combinations of diagnostic tools and recovery tools, you can effectively handle many critical situations that may arise in your DS implementation. Chapter 10, "Programming for eDirectory," introduces some programming concepts that can help you in data-recovery situations.

Programming for eDirectory

In previous chapters, you've learned how to use a number of Novell-supplied and third-party directory services (DS) data recovery applications. Because every network environment is unique in its own way, however, you might not be able to find one off-the-shelf utility that totally fulfills your requirements. This chapter offers you an overview on how you can use a basic programming background to develop some complex data recovery tools for your own network. Please note, however, that this chapter does not discuss programming in detail and expects you to already have that knowledge.

> **NOTE**
>
> If you are interested in NDS/eDirectory and/or Lightweight Directory Access Protocol (LDAP) programming, we suggest that you take a look at, respectively, *Novell's NDS Developer's Guide* (Novell Press) and *Novell's LDAP Developer's Guide* (Novell Press).

Using awk

Programming for NDS disaster recovery need not always involve the Novell Developer Kit (NDK) or any form of NDS or the NetWare application programming interface (API) set. Some of the most effective programming techniques available are nothing more than text file manipulations. This type of manipulation is good for data conversions such as converting NLIST output to a format suitable for UImport or ICE to use for input.

Several programming languages include text (or *string*) manipulation. BASIC, C, Pascal, Perl, and even assembly language include interfaces and libraries for performing string manipulation. One of the best languages for this sort of work, however, is a programming language called *awk*.

The awk language was developed in 1977 by Alfred Aho, Brian Kernighan, and Peter Weinberger at AT&T Bell Labs; the name of the language comes from the last-name initials of the three authors. The original development of awk was done in a Unix environment, and because of this, many of the concepts are familiar if you have had exposure to utilities such as grep or sed. grep is very similar to the Windows find utility because it searches one or more input files for lines containing a match to a specified pattern. By default, grep prints the matching lines. sed (stream editor) is a non-interactive editor that works from a command line; it's not a GUI Windows application. sed changes blocks of text on-the-fly, without requiring you to open a screen, push a cursor around, and press Delete, Insert, Enter, or function keys.

awk is an interpreted scripting language; this means that there is no compiler or other means to turn an awk program into a self-sufficient executable program as you would a C or Pascal program.

NOTE   The examples in this book are all interpreted using the GNU version of awk (called gawk), available from the Free Software Foundation. (GNU is a recursive acronym for "GNU's Not Unix"; it is pronounced "guh-noo.") The discussion presented in this section is based on version 3.0.3, but newer versions are available for DOS, Windows 32-bit operating systems, Unix/Linux, and other operating system platforms. An updated list of sites that maintain awk source code and binaries is available from the comp.lang.awk **FAQ** at ftp://rtfm.mit.edu/pub/usenet/comp.lang.awk/faq.

Why awk?

You might be wondering why we recommend awk for string manipulation.

There are several reasons awk might be a better choice than other languages for the sort of rapid development that may be necessary in a disaster situation:

▶ awk interpreters are available for many operating system platforms, including DOS, Windows 32-bit operating systems, and Linux.

▶ awk interpreters do not require any sort of special memory manager. Many Intel-platform Perl interpreters require DOS extenders of different sorts.

▶ awk is not a compiled language; therefore, you can readily read and modify its script.

▶ The awk interpreter is very small (typically around 30KB or so), and it can be put on a disk along with a number of standard scripts for disaster recovery purposes.

▶ Unlike C or C++, awk does not require that you understand pointers when manipulating strings.

▶ The awk user interface is very straightforward. If you are recovering from a very serious disaster, a minimal workstation configuration can be used—DOS 6.22 with a Novell Client installed is sufficient to start parsing NList outputs.

▶ awk's regular expression parsing capabilities exceed the capabilities of many of the traditional programming languages, such as C and Pascal.

How Does awk Work?

An awk program takes input a line at a time, parses and processes the input, and produces an output file. This is usually done through command-line *pipes* or *redirection*. Normally, this process involves the use of three files: an awk script, an input file, and an output file.

The awk script itself is a set of rules for processing lines of text from the input file. These rules are written using a pattern-matching technique that is common in the Unix world, called a *regular expression* (*regex*). Regex pattern matching enables you to specify the format of a line of text in the input file; if a line matches the regex, the text is processed in a manner described by that portion of the script.

Regex pattern matching uses this basic format:

/pattern/

where *pattern* is replaced by a string that represents an input format. Table 10.1 shows special sequences of characters that can be used in the pattern.

TABLE 10.1 **Sample Regular Expressions**

REGULAR EXPRESSION	MEANING	EXAMPLES OF MATCHES
/User:/	Match lines containing the case-sensitive string User:	User: Jim
/L* Name:/	Match lines containing a string with L, any other characters, and the string Name:	Last Name: Henderson
/[JK][iu][mo]/	Match lines containing the letter J or K, then the letter i or u, and then the letter m or o	Jim, Kuo, Juo, Kim, Jio
/[Jj][Ii][Mm]/	Match lines containing J or j, I or i, and M or m.	Jim, jIm, JIm, jIM
/^Jim[0-9][0-9]/	Match lines starting with Jim followed by a two-digit number	Jim00, Jim01, Jim90, Jim42
/Jim$/	Match lines ending with Jim.	Hi, Jim
/^$/	Match blank lines	

For example, if you execute this command:

```
NLIST USER SHOW Name /S /R /C > OUTPUT.TXT
```

and use the file OUTPUT.TXT as the input file to the script:

```
/User:/ { print "Found a user ID" }
```

awk searches the input file for the case-sensitive string User:, and if this text is found, it prints the string "Found a user ID."

awk supports two special commands: BEGIN and END. These are not really patterns but are used to include special instructions—such as variable initialization and final output options—in the script. Here's an example:

```
BEGIN { count = 0 }
    /User:/ { count++ }
END { printf("Total users found:  %d\n", count) }
```

NOTE

If you are familiar with the C/C++, Perl, or Java programming languages, resist the urge to put a semicolon (;) at the end of each statement line as it is *not* required by awk!

This script searches for instances of the case-sensitive string User: (as in the previous example), but rather than print a string, it increments the variable count, and when it finishes that, it prints a total count of the user objects listed in the input file.

An awk script parses the input line based on a field separator. By default, the field separator is whitespace. Whitespace includes any number of spaces or tabs between the data. The line is then split out into internal variables based on the field separator found.

For example, this line consists of a total of four fields:

```
Full Name:    Jim Henderson
```

These fields are referred to by the names $1, $2, $3, and $4, with these values:

Field	Value
$1	Full
$2	Name:
$3	Jim
$4	Henderson

The entire line of text is referred to by the variable $0. This variable always represents the entire line up to the *record separator*, which is typically a carriage return.

TIP

Another special value is the NF **value. This value reports the number of fields in the line. If you are uncertain about the number of fields but need the last value from the line, you can reference this as** $NF. **In the preceding example,** $4 **has the value** Henderson, **as does** $NF; **therefore,** NF **would have the value** 4.

You can change the defaults for the various separators, such as field separator and record separator. For example, if you have a tab-delimited file, you would want the field separator (FS) to be the tab character rather than a space. You typically make this change in the beginning of the script, in the BEGIN segment:

```
BEGIN { FS = "\t" }
```

> **NOTE**
>
> As with C, C++, and other programming languages, awk uses escaped characters for nonprintable characters. The \t sequence refers to the tab character, the \n sequence refers to the newline character, and so on.

The output field separator (OFS) denotes the character used to separate the fields when **awk** prints them. The default is a blank or space character. To output a comma-separated variable (CSV) formatted file, you can change the OFS to a comma as follows:

```
BEGIN { OFS = "," }
```

You can also change the record separator (RS) by using the **RS** variable:

```
BEGIN { RS = "\t" }
```

Typically, you do not want to change this, but at times it might make sense to do so.

awk also has a number of string manipulation functions. Table 10.2 shows some of the commonly used functions and what they can be used for.

TABLE 10.2 awk **String Manipulation Functions**

FUNCTION	USE	RETURN VALUE
gsub (*SearchFor*, *Replace*)	Replace all occurrences of *SearchFor* with *Replace* in $0 (the input line).	The number of replacements made.
gsub (*SearchFor*,) *Replace*, *SearchIn*	Replace all occurrences of *SearchFor* with *Replace* in *SearchIn*.	The number of replacements made.
index (*String*, *Text*)	Locate the first occurrence of *String* in *Text*.	The offset in the string where the occurrence is; if not found, returns 0.
length (*String*)	Determine the length (in characters) of *String*.	The number of characters in String.
match (*String*, *Text*)	Locate the first occurrence of *String* in *Text* (case-sensitive).	The offset in the string where the occurrence is; if not found, returns 0. This function also sets the variables RStart and RLength, which are the start index and length of the substring.

Table 10.2   Continued

FUNCTION	USE	RETURN VALUE
split (*String*, *Array*)	Breaks *String* into the array *Array* on the default field separator (specified by FS).	The number of fields. Values in the array can be referred to with a subscript; if the array name is A, the first element is A[1], the second is A[2], and so on.
split (*String*, *Array*, *FieldSeparator*)	Breaks *String* into the array *Array* on the specified field separator, *FieldSeparator*.	The number of fields.
sprintf (*Format*, *Expression list*)	Prints output using a specified output format. This is similar to the C function sprintf(), except that the output is on the left side of the equals sign instead of inside the parentheses.	The formatted string.
sub (*Replace*, *String*)	Substitutes the first instance of *Replace* with *String* in $0.	The number of replacements made (should always be 1).
sub (*Replace*, *String*, *Input*)	Substitutes the first instance of *Replace* with *String* in the input *Input*.	The number of replacements made (should always be 1).
substr (*String*, *Position*)	Returns the suffix of the string *String*, starting at position *Position*.	A string value with the result.
substr (*String*, *Position*, *Length*)	Returns the suffix of *String*, starting at *Position* of *Length*.	A string value with the result.

In addition to doing string manipulation, you can also use awk for numeric manipulation. This type of manipulation of data is done in the same manner as C/C++ numeric manipulation. If you need to manipulate a number with an initial value, you can initialize it in the BEGIN section of the script.

When you're scanning a line and breaking it into the initial subcomponents ($1 through $NF), or when you're breaking it down using the split() function, if a numeric value is found, it is automatically treated as a number.

However, if you need to perform string manipulations on it, you are also able to do this. In this respect, **awk** provides greater flexibility than most other programming languages.

awk also supports the use of several other statements and structures. Table 10.3 lists the most common of these.

TABLE 10.3   awk **Language Actions**

ACTION	EXAMPLE/FUNCTION
Assignment	`x = 25`
Print	`print "The user name is  user-name"`
printf (*format, expression list*)	`printf ("The user name is %s\n", username)`
if (*expression*) *statement*	`if (username == "Jim") print "Found Jim!"`
if (*expression*) *statement* else *statement*	`if (username == "Jim") print "Found Jim!" else print "Found someone else"`
while (*expression*) *statement*	`while (NF > 10) printf("Too many fields, line %d, %d fields\n", NR, NF)`
for (*initialization*; while *expression*; *initialization variable modification*) statement	`for (x=0;x<10;x++) printf("x=%d\n", x)`
Exit	Exits the interpreter
Break	Breaks out of the current for...while...do loop

> **TIP**
>
> awk **uses the pound sign (#) to indicate the start of a comment. Anything after a # will be ignored. Therefore, you can include inline comments anywhere within your script.**

> **NOTE**
>
> awk **resources and documentation are available on the Internet, and the following are two examples of good Web sites for this type of information:**
> www.ling.ed.ac.uk/facilities/help/gawk/gawk_13.html#SEC97 **and**
> www.sunsite.ualberta.ca/Documentation/Gnu/gawk-3.1.0/
> html_chapter/gawk_10.html.

An additional feature of the awk language that is occasionally useful is the capability to create specialized functions for repeated operations. If you are coding an involved script, you can package the code so as to minimize your coding time. However, in disaster recovery situations, you will generally find that the scripts you write will perform very specific manipulations, and as a general rule, you do not need to reuse code within such scripts.

Creating functions within awk is a simple matter. For example, the following would be a function to return the minimum value of two passed-in parameters:

```
function min(a, b){
  if (a < b)
    return a
  else
    return b
}
```

Because awk supports the abbreviated if structure that C provides, the preceding can also be coded as follows:

```
function min(a, b){
  return a < b ? a : b
}
```

This code sample provides the same functionality as the previous sample.

After you have written awk script, you need to give it an input file. When you're using the gawk interpreter, you do this by using a command in the following format:

```
gawk awkfile.awk < inputfile [> outputfile]
```

This tells gawk to use *awkfile.awk* as the script and to pipe the contents of *inputfile* into the script. The input file can be left out, but if it is, you must type the input file by hand. The output file contains the results of the script; if an output file is not specified, the output is written to the screen.

TIP

Writing the output to the screen can be very useful during the development process. By exiting the script with the exit command after processing the first line of text, you can get an idea as to whether the program is working the way you want it to work without processing the entire input file.

In a disaster-recovery situation, it is *not* absolutely necessary that the script work completely correctly when you finish it. Using **awk** with a combination of other tools may get you to the end you need more quickly. Consider this example. Say you have an **awk** script that outputs a UImport file with group membership information in it. It is missing a few of the members because of an extra embedded space for those entries. Instead of trying to perfect the script to handle that small number of exceptions, you can use your favorite text editor to either remove those entries from the file or to make the correction using a search-and-replace function. Remember that during disaster recovery, it doesn't matter if your script is elegant or pretty; it just matters that you get the job done quickly and correctly.

Creating a UImport Data File by Using awk

The example in this section shows a full **awk** program designed to convert the output from the **NLIST** command into a format suitable for importing into a spreadsheet or database program. For simplicity, the scope of this example is limited to a single context. (Chapter 11, "Examples from the Real World," examines a case study that builds a UImport file based on information from the entire tree.)

For this example, the input file is generated by using the following command:

```
NLIST USER SHOW SURNAME, "FULL NAME", "GIVEN NAME" > USERS.TXT
```

The output file **USERS.TXT** contains the same information you would normally see on the screen. The contents of the file in this example are as follows:

```
Object Class: User
Current context: east.xyzcorp
User: JimH
    Last Name: Henderson
    Full Name: Jim Henderson
    Given Name: Jim
User: PeterK
    Last Name: Kuo
    Full Name: Peter Kuo
    Given Name: Peter
User: PKuo
    Last Name: Kuo
    Full Name: Peter Kuo
    Given Name: Peter
```

```
User: JHenderson
   Full Name: Jim Henderson
   Given Name: Jim
   Last Name: Henderson
A total of 4 User objects was found in this context.

A total of 4 User objects was found.
```

From this information, we want to generate a comma-delimited file with the fields User ID, Context, First Name, Last Name, and Full Name. The output file also contains a header line with the field names in it.

This **awk** script performs the conversion to a comma-delimited file:

```
BEGIN { flag = 0
        printf("\"User ID\",\"Context\",\"First Name\",
                \"Last Name\",\"Full Name\"\n")
}


/User:/ {
  if (flag == 1) {
    printf("\"%s\",\"%s\",\"%s\",\"%s\",\"%s\"\n",
           user, context, gn, ln, fn)
    gn = ""
    ln = ""
    fn = ""
  }
  user = $2
  gsub(" ", "", user)
  flag = 1
}


/Full Name:/ { gsub(/Full Name: /,"")
               gsub(/\t/, "")
               fn = $0

               # Cleans up leading blanks (ONLY)
               # from the full name
               nfn = length(fn)
               for (i=1;i<nfn;i++) {
                   if ( match(fn, " ") == 1 )
                       sub(" ", "", fn)
                   else
                       break
               }
}
```

```
/Last Name:/ { gsub(/Last Name: /,"")
               gsub(/\t/, "")
               ln = $0
               gsub(" ", "", ln)
}

/Given Name:/ { gsub(/Given Name: /,"")
                gsub(/\t/, "")
                gn = $0
                gsub(" ", "", gn)
}

/Current context:/ { gsub(/Current context: /, "")
                     context = $0
                     gsub(" ", "", context)
}

END { printf("\"%s\",\"%s\",\"%s\",\"%s\",\"%s\"\n",
             user, context, gn, ln, fn)
}
```

The script starts with the **BEGIN** statement. It executes before any lines of the input file **USERS.TXT** are read. It sets a flag value to **0** in order to avoid printing a blank first line. The field headers are then printed to the output device.

Next, the first line is read. This line contains the object class information. Each line in the script that performs a pattern match on the data file is evaluated, in order. First, the line is checked for the presence of the **User:** string. This line, however, does not contain that specific string, so the next pattern is evaluated. That line also does not contain the other specified strings (**Full Name:**, **Last Name:**, **Given Name:**, or **Current context:**). As a result, the line is not processed and is not sent to output.

The second line contains the string **Current context:**, so the code written to handle that is used to process the line. The first line of code (the **gsub** line) replaces the string **Current context:** with nothing, effectively removing it from the **$0** variable. The variable **context** is then assigned to the string contained in the line, which contains the actual context. This variable is preserved from one line to the next and is printed each time a new user is read in and at the end of the script.

After that line is processed, the next line is processed similarly. It contains a user ID and assigns the value. It also sets the flag variable to **1**, but because the variable was **0** when the script started, the information gathered is not printed out. As soon as the flag is set to **1**, each subsequent time a user ID is

found, the previous user information is printed, and all variables except
`context` are reset to empty strings.

After the last line of the file is read, the last user's information is printed.
The reason for using a `BEGIN/END` block is because `NLIST` may return the
attributes in arbitrary order; therefore, you should not print out the results
until the script has encountered the next `User:` data block.

The result of this script, using the output from the earlier `NLIST` command,
is as follows:

```
"User ID","Context","First Name","Last Name","Full Name"
"JimH","east.xyzcorp","Jim","Henderson","Jim Henderson"
"PeterK","east.xyzcorp","Peter","Kuo","Peter Kuo"
"PKuo","east.xyzcorp","Peter","Kuo","Peter Kuo"
"JHenderson","east.xyzcorp","Jim","Henderson","Jim Henderson"
```

Using C or C++

The C programming language has been, and still is, the programming language of choice for systems programming. It is, therefore, not a surprise that
Novell's initial Software Developer Kit (SDK; now known as the NDK) efforts
were placed in C libraries. Even today, the NetWare Loadable Module (NLM)
libraries are still C based, and workstation application developers now have
more options in their choice of programming language (see the "Other
Programming and Scripting Languages" section, later in this chapter).

NOTE

From a performance viewpoint, NLMs work better than workstation-based applications because in many cases, NLMs do not generate network traffic as they run on
the servers. However, because of the error exception handling routines used by
C++ compilers, C++ generally is not suitable for NLM development. If you want to
use C++ for NLMs, consider using the Metrowerks CodeWarrior compiler. Visit
`http://developer.novell.com/ndk/cwpdk.htm` for more information.

When you're programming for NDS, there are a number of operations that
your application must perform locally when accessing DS information. The
operations include the following:

- Working with naming conventions
- Maintaining directory context data
- Initializing Unicode tables
- Managing local buffers

As mentioned previously, a DS object may be referenced in multiple ways: using its relative distinguished name (RDN) or its distinguished name (DN) in typeful or typeless naming syntax. DS operates on *canonical names* only— that is, names that include full naming paths, with a type specification for each naming component (typeful DNs). Because it's not always convenient or practical to store or use canonical names, APIs enable you to use partial names and enable the underlying library routines to handle the conversion.

Most DS API calls that involve character data or interact with the NDS/eDirectory tree require additional information to be supplied. This is to indicate the default context and whether the character data should be translated to Unicode. This information is collectively held in a structure called the *directory context* and is used to pass the following details:

- ▶ The default context
- ▶ Whether alias objects should be dereferenced
- ▶ Whether character data should be translated to and from Unicode
- ▶ Whether object names should be given in canonical form
- ▶ Whether object names should be given in typeless form

When a directory context (which is essentially a memory pointer) is created, the default context is the same as the workstation's current context, and the four operations listed previously are performed. The directory context should be freed when it is no longer needed (normally when the application terminates).

You can read and modify the information in a directory context. You need to be careful when changing the default context. You can set it to an arbitrary string, unlike with the CX command-line utility, which does not set the default context to an illegal value. If the default context is set to an illegal value, any API calls that rely on the directory context will fail.

The same object-naming conventions apply to the NDS API calls as to the NetWare command-line utilities. That is, leading and trailing periods can be used to modify the default context, and the type qualifiers, such as C=, can be inserted into the name to override the default typing.

The Unicode conversion tables have to be loaded before a workstation application can access NDS (this is not necessary for NLMs), and they should be released prior to an application's terminating. These tables are used to convert character data between the general Unicode format used by the NDS and the local format used by the application. You load the Unicode tables by executing the Unicode API `NWInitUnicodeTables()` and specifying the local code page. You can obtain the local code page by executing the Internationalization Services APIs `NWLsetlocale()` and `NWLlocaleconv()`.

DS API functions use buffers for sending and receiving data between the application and NDS/eDirectory. For example, a typical sequence in reading an object's attribute values would be to initialize an input buffer, load the buffer with the list of desired attributes, execute the read object command, and unload the attribute values from an output buffer. Given that the output buffer is finite, it is sometimes necessary to call the read function repeatedly to get subsequent values. This protocol of using input and output buffers provides a general interface for transferring data.

Memory for directory buffers is allocated using an DS API call. The suggested amount of memory to allocate is given by the constant `DEFAULT_MESSAGE_LEN` that is set to 4096 bytes. This value is normally more than sufficient for a typical DS application. The only exception under normal circumstances would be when there is a single attribute value (such as a stream file) that will not fit in the buffer (thus resulting in a -119 error [buffer too small]). If you are unsure, you can consider using `MAX_MESSAGE_LEN`, which has a 63KB value, or using your own setting. Directory buffers should be freed when they are no longer needed (normally when the application terminates); otherwise, memory leaks result.

The directory buffer management tasks make DS-aware applications more complex than bindery-based programs; don't let that discourage you from developing DS utilities, however, because it only looks harder than it is.

The following is an example of C source code that enables you to change a user's telephone attribute from a command line. Error checking has been removed to simplify the example:

```c
#include <stdio.h>
#include <stdlib.h>
#include <string.h>

#define N_PLAT_DOS
#include <nwcalls.h>
#include <nwnet.h>
#include <nwlocale.h>


void main (int argc, char *argv[])
{
    NWDSContextHandle    Cx;
```

```
        NWDS_BUFFER              *inBuf;
        LCONV                    lconvInfo;


        if ( argc < 4 ) {
            printf ("Usage: ");
            printf ("Newnumber objectname oldTnum newTnum\n");
            exit (1);
        }

// Needed for workstation-based APIs only.
        NWCallsInit (NULL, NULL);

// Unicode table must be loaded in order to use DS calls.
        NWLlocaleconv (&lconvInfo);
        NWInitUnicodeTables (lconvInfo.country_id,
                            lconvInfo.code_page);

// Create directory context
        Cx = NWDSCreateContext ();

// Allocate local buffers
        NWDSAllocBuf (DEFAULT_MESSAGE_LEN, &inBuf);
        NWDSInitBuf (Cx, DSV_MODIFY_ENTRY, inBuf);

// First delete the old value and then add the new one
// (Can not use DS_OVERWRITE_VALUE because Telephone Number
//   is multi-valued and the API would not know which value
//   to overwrite, if there is more than one)
// The two actions can be combined into the same "buffer"
        NWDSPutChange (Cx, inBuf, DS_REMOVE_VALUE,
                        "Telephone Number");
        NWDSPutAttrVal (Cx, inBuf, SYN_CI_STRING, argv[2]);

        NWDSPutChange (Cx, inBuf, DS_ADD_VALUE,
                        "Telephone Number");
        NWDSPutAttrVal (Cx, inBuf, SYN_CI_STRING, argv[3]);

        if ( NWDSModifyObject (Cx, argv[1], NULL, (NWFLAGS)0,
                                inBuf) == 0 ) {
            printf ("%s's old telephone number [%s] has been\n",
                    argv[1], argv[2]);
            printf ("replaced by a new number [%s]\n", argv[3]);
        }
```

```
        else
                printf ("Unable to change telephone number.\n");

// Free allocated resources.
        NWDSFreeBuf (inBuf);
        NWDSFreeContext (Cx);
        NWFreeUnicodeTables ();

        exit(0);
}
```

If you have an external database that contains up-to-date user information, you can use a modified version of this example to read the telephone number (or other attribute values) from this database and repopulate the user objects with the information when needed.

You might be interested in knowing that when you modify eDirectory data via LDAP, you do not need to deal with allocating buffers, directory context, and so on (as is the case when using DS calls). You do, however, have to set up the necessary code to connect and bind to the LDAP server (where a workstation-based DS utility would not require but an NLM would require additional code to authenticate to NDS prior to changes being made). The following is a sample C code snippet (based on Novell's **modattrs.c** example) that changes the telephone number:

```
#include <stdio.h>
#include <stdlib.h>
#include <ldap.h>

int main( int argc, char **argv)
{
        int             version, ldapPort, rc;
        char            *ldapHost, *loginDN, *password, *modifyDN;
        char            *phoneValues[2];
        LDAP            *ld;
        LDAPMod         modPhone, *modify[2];
        // 10-second connection timeout
        struct timeval timeOut = {10,0};


        if (argc != 6) {
                printf( "\n Usage:   modattrs <host name> ");
                printf ("<port number> <login dn> <password>\n");
                printf ("\n\t <modify dn>\n");
                printf ("\n Example: modattrs acme.com 389 ");
```

```
            printf ("cn=admin,o=acme secret\n");
            printf ("\n\t cn=admin,ou=demo,o=testing\n");
            return(1);
        }


// Set up connection and binding info
    ldapHost    =   argv[1];
    ldapPort    =   atoi(argv[2]);
    loginDN     =   argv[3];
    password    =   argv[4];
    modifyDN    =   argv[5];

// Set LDAP version to 3 and set connection timeout
    version = LDAP_VERSION3;
    ldap_set_option ( NULL, LDAP_OPT_PROTOCOL_VERSION,
                        &version);
    ldap_set_option ( NULL, LDAP_OPT_NETWORK_TIMEOUT,
                        &timeOut);

// Initialize the LDAP session
    if (( ld = ldap_init ( ldapHost, ldapPort )) == NULL) {
        printf ( "\n\tLDAP session initialization
➥failed\n");
        return( 1 );
    }
    printf ("\n\tLDAP session initialized\n");

// Bind to the server
    rc = ldap_simple_bind_s( ld, loginDN, password );
    if (rc != LDAP_SUCCESS ) {
        printf ("ldap_simple_bind_s: %s\n",
                    ldap_err2string( rc ));
        ldap_unbind_s ( ld );
        return( 1 );
    }
    printf ("\n\tBind successful\n");

/*
    * To modify the attributes of an entry
    *    1  Specify the modify actions
    *    2. Specify the attribute name to be modified
    *    3. Specify the value of the attribute
    *    4. Add to an array of LDAPMod structures
    *    5. Call ldap_modify_ext_s
    */
```

```
// LDAP_MOD_REPLACE succeeds whether the value
// already exists or not
    modPhone.mod_op = LDAP_MOD_REPLACE
    modPhone.mod_type = "telephoneNumber";
    phoneValues[0] = "1 234 567 8910";
    phoneValues[1] = NULL;
    modPhone.mod_values = phoneValues;

// If you have more than one modifications to make, increase
// the array size of modify[] and add more "&mod*" entries
    modify[0] = &modPhone;
    modify[1] = NULL;

// Modify the attributes
    rc= ldap_modify_ext_s (ld,          // LDAP session handle
                           modifyDN,    // the object to
                                        // modify
                           modify,      // array of LDAPMod
                                        // structures
                           NULL,        // server controls
                           NULL);       // client controls

    if ( rc != LDAP_SUCCESS ) {
        printf ("ldap_modify_ext_s: %s\n",
                ldap_err2string( rc ));
        ldap_unbind_s( ld );
        return(1);
    }
    printf ("\n\t%s modified successfully.\n", modifyDN);

    ldap_unbind_s( ld );

    return( 0 );
}
```

As you can see, although the LDAP code is longer than the DS-based code presented earlier in this chapter, about half of it actually has to deal with connecting and binding to the LDAP server. The actual code necessary for updating the attribute value is less than 10 lines, and most of it is just setup code.

Although the amount of work involved in using DS calls instead of LDAP calls seem about the same, the big advantage of using LDAP is that your application will also work with directories other than NDS. If you have to update a number of different directories with the same data and they all support LDAP, using LDAP calls would be the better way to go.

Other Programming and Scripting Languages

To help you quickly develop applications for NDS and NetWare without having to fully understand the underlying complexity, Novell Developer Support has several tools available. For example, you can build successful network-ready applications and utilities by using your favorite rapid application development (RAD) Windows programming tool, such as Visual Basic.

Visual Basic Libraries for Novell Services gives programmers full access to all the low-level NetWare APIs that have traditionally been available only to C programmers. The libraries are provided in the form of a single text file and a set of helper functions in a **.BAS** file. The text file (**NETWARE.BAS**) contains declarations for most of the NetWare APIs. (The libraries are for the 32-bit Novell Client DLLs and do not support the old 16-bit library.) All the constants, types, and function declarations are in **NETWARE.BAS** to make it easier to include them in a project. The following is a Visual Basic code snippet that illustrates how to remove an attribute value whose syntax type is **SYN_CI_STRING**:

```
Private objName As String
Private attrName As String
Private objType As Integer

Private Sub RemoveValueFromAttribute(objName As String,
                                     attrName As String,
                                     attrValue As String)
Dim inBuf As Long
Dim byteName(127) As Byte
    retCode = NWDSAllocBuf(DEFAULT_MESSAGE_LEN, inBuf)
    If retCode Then
        MsgBox "NWDSAllocBug returned E=" + Str(retCode),
                vbCritical
        Exit Sub
    End If
    retCode = NWDSInitBuf(contextHandle, DSV_MODIFY_ENTRY,
                          inBuf)
    If retCode Then
        MsgBox "NWDSInitBuf returned E=" + Str(retCode),
                vbCritical
        GoTo exit1
    End If
```

```
'defined in NETWARE.BAS
Call StringToByteArray(byteName, attrValue + Chr(0))
retCode = NWDSPutChangeAndVal(contextHandle, inBuf,
                              DS_REMOVE_VALUE,
                              attrName + Chr(0),
                              SYN_CI_STRING,
                              VarPtr(byteName(0)))
retCode = NWDSModifyObject(contextHandle,
                           objName + Chr(0),
                           -1, 0, inBuf)
exit1:
    retCode = NWDSFreeBuf(inBuf)
End Sub
```

Alternately, you can use ActiveX Controls for Novell Services, which supports full access to NDS, as well as administration capabilities for NetWare
servers, print queues, and volumes. All this functionality is packaged so it
can be used quickly and easily in a Windows visual builder and other development tools, such as Visual Basic, Delphi (see Figure 10.1), PowerBuilder,
Active Server Pages for Internet Information Server (IIS), Windows Scripting
Host, and the Internet Explorer Web browser. ActiveX Controls for Novell
Services contains controls that are divided into the following three categories:

▶ Novell Directory Access Protocol (NDAP; that is, NCP-based) controls:

   ▶ Application Administration (NWAppA)

   ▶ Browser (NWBrowse)

   ▶ Directory (NWDir)

   ▶ Directory Administration (NWDirA)

   ▶ Directory Authenticator (NWDirAuth)

   ▶ Directory Query (NWDirQ)

   ▶ NDPS Printer Administration (NWDPPrtA)

   ▶ NDS Corporate Edition Domain (NDSDomain)

   ▶ Network Selector (NWSelect)

   ▶ SecretStore (NWSecStr)

   ▶ Server Administration (NWSrvA)

   ▶ Session Management (NWSess)

   ▶ User Group (NWUsrGrp)

   ▶ Volume Administration (NWVolA)

▶ LDAP controls (to access NDS/eDirectory or any LDAP-complaint directory via LDAP):

   ▶ Internet Directory (`NWIDir`)

   ▶ Internet Directory Authenticator (`NWIDirAuth`)

   ▶ Internet Directory Entries (`NWIDirE`)

   ▶ Internet Directory Query (`NWIDirQ`)

   ▶ Internet Directory Schema (`NWIDirS`)

▶ Socket controls (to develop applications that communicate by using either TCP or SPX protocols):

   ▶ Client and Server Socket (`NWCliSkt` and `NWSvrSkt`)

   ▶ Peer Socket (`NWPrSkt`)

FIGURE 10.1
A Novell sample Delphi application.

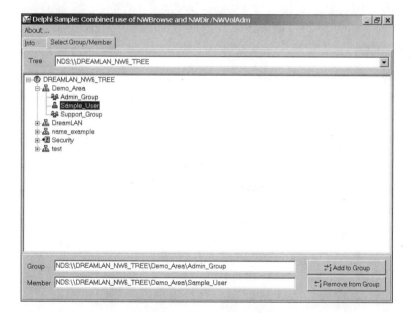

TIP

After installing the core components for ActiveX Controls for Novell Services, you need to also install the necessary **LDAP/NDAP/Socket component** to get the necessary controls. These controls use the `.DLL` extension and not the `.OCX` extension that you expect for ActiveX controls.

NOTE

Although ActiveX Controls for Novell Services provides broad coverage of the most popular features of the NetWare C APIs, the controls do *not* wrap 100% of the available API set.

If you are a Delphi developer, you can use Delphi Libraries for Novell Services, which includes the DCU and PAS files needed to call the NetWare APIs from Delphi, instead of using ActiveX Controls for Novell Services.

Java fans will be glad to know that Novell has classes for Java and Java Naming and Directory Interface (JNDI) providers, as well as JavaBeans, available to use. Java applications can access NDS through the JNDI APIs, with or without Novell client software installed. If you're more comfortable with scripting languages, such as VBScript, you'll be happy to hear that Novell has support for them, too. For example, using the Novell Script for NetWare (NSN), which is a VBScript-compatible language for script automation and Web development on the Netscape FastTrack Server for NetWare platform, you can use Novell Script's prebuilt components to access NetWare and integrate eDirectory, Oracle, Microsoft Access, MySQL, and Pervasive (previously Btrieve) databases into your Web applications.

NOTE

You install and configure Novell Script for NetWare when you install a NetWare 5.1 or later server. You can find the latest at `http://developer.novell.com/ndk/nscript.htm`**.**

More traditional Web page designers can use Perl 5 for NetWare with the Apache Web Server for NetWare or the NetWare Enterprise Web Server. Perl 5 support enables you to enhance and continue your investment in Perl scripts and Perl applications. At the time of this writing, Perl 5 for NetWare is at Perl 5.8 and provides system administration and common gateway interface (CGI) scripting functionality. You can use the `Perl_LDAP` modules to access NDS/eDirectory. However, the standard `Perl_LDAP` modules available from Comprehensive Perl Archive Network (CPAN; `www.cpan.org`) do not support eDirectory-specific extensions such as those related to partition operations. However, the version from Novell, which can be found at `http://developer.novell.com/ndk/perl5.htm`, includes a set of functions for performing extended operations (such as `ChangeReplicaType`) on eDirectory.

With the release of NetWare 6.5, Novell introduced PHP scripting support (used in conjunction with Apache Web Server) to NetWare 6.x servers. (PHP is a recursive acronym for PHP: Hypertext Preprocesser.) PHP for NetWare is based on open-source PHP (`www.php.net`). On NetWare, PHP supports standard extensions and extensions for LDAP, XML, and MySQL. It also has a UCS extension (PHP2UCS) that can be used to access various Novell services, such as eDirectory, file I/O, server management, and volume administration. Through UCS, PHP can use UCX components, JavaBeans and classes, and remote ActiveX controls.

> **NOTE**
>
> **For information on how to set up a NetWare 6 server to take advantage of Apache, MySQL, and PHP/Perl scripting—generally referred to as AMP—see the white paper about NetWare AMP at** `http://developer.novell.com/ndk/ whitepapers/namp.htm.`

Obtaining the NDK

Full access to eDirectory and other NetWare services is available through the use of APIs published in the NDK. You can obtain the NDK by signing up with Novell's DeveloperNet program. There are four levels in the program:

- ▶ **Online or electronic level**—You can sign up at this level at no charge. At this level, you can download the necessary NDK components from the DeveloperNet Web site and have access to all online documentation and Web-based training courses.

- ▶ **Professional level**—In addition to getting all the benefits of the electronic level, at the professional level, you also receive one set of Novell Software Evaluation and Development Library (SEDL; formally known as the Software Evaluation Library [SEL]) CDs or DVDs, which also includes the NDK. In addition, you get two free Developer support incidents as part of this package. The cost of the professional level is $395 per year.

- ▶ **Advantage and premier levels**—Subscriptions to these two levels are by contract only. These levels are generally for companies that require direct hands-on support from Novell engineering. Advantage and premier memberships were designed with corporate developers, independent software vendors, independent hardware vendors, value-added resellers, and consultants in mind. The benefits of these two levels include everything available at the professional level plus more, as determined by the contract.

NOTE

For more information about SEDL, visit `http://support.novell.com/`
`subscriptions/index.html`.

TIP

Unless you have specific needs, the electronic level is probably sufficient for you.
By signing up as an electronic-level member of DeveloperNet, you get no-charge,
Web-based access to the NDK, DeveloperNet resources, DeveloperNet support
forums (`http://developer-forums.novell.com`), and co-marketing opportuni-
ties. Visit `http://developer.novell.com` for more information about the
DeveloperNet program.

Summary

This chapter provides a quick overview of how you can develop your own
NDS disaster recovery and reporting utilities, using various programming
and scripting languages, such as awk, C, and Perl.

In Chapter 11, you'll learn how to apply the various troubleshooting techniques and utilities discussed so far to some commonly encountered real-
world scenarios.

CHAPTER 11

Examples from the Real World

This chapter brings together the concepts and various utilities that are discussed in previous chapters and applies them to some specific examples. The following topics are examined:

- Bindery Services–related issues
- Security issues
- Schema problems
- Data inconsistencies
- Synthetic time
- Server and data recovery

Bindery Services–related Issues

Although NDS and eDirectory are backward-compatible with the bindery, you need to be aware of a number of common issues when dealing with bindery-based applications in a DS environment. NetWare bindery information is server-centric; therefore, when you use Bindery Services in a DS environment, the bindery data that you see is also server-centric. From our experience, there are four general areas of concern when using Bindery Services:

- The (bindery) Supervisor user
- Mail directories and bindery-based queues

▶ Bindery clients

▶ Performance

You can use the procedures outlined in Table 11.1 to verify whether you have Bindery Services enabled.

TABLE 11.1	**Verifying That Bindery Services Is Enabled**
OPERATING SYSTEM	**PROCEDURE**
NetWare	On the server console, enter either the command SET BINDERY CONTEXT or CONFIG. Alternatively, check the SYS:\SYSTEM\AUTOEXEC.NCF file for the line SET BINDERY CONTEXT= (which is generally located near the beginning of the file). If a bindery context is set, the default is to set it to the container where the NCP Server object is located.
Windows	From NDSCon, highlight ds.dlm, click the Configure button, and then select the Bindery Emulation tab. By default, no bindery context is set.
Linux/Unix	Examine the /etc/nds.conf file and look for the n4u.nds.bindery-context= line. If the line is not present or the value is 0, Bindery Services is not enabled. By default, no bindery context is set.

The Bindery Supervisor User

The bindery Supervisor user is an odd creature. It is both a DS object and a non-object. It is a bindery object in that it exists on each and every NetWare 4 and higher server and on non-NetWare eDirectory servers, regardless of whether Bindery Services is enabled on that server or not. Similarly to the [Public] pseudo object, the bindery Supervisor User object doesn't physically show up when you browse the DS tree using standard management tools such as ConsoleOne or iManager, but it is recognized and acted upon by DS servers. You should be aware of the issues discussed in the following paragraphs.

The bindery Supervisor is created as a pseudo-DS object whose rights are restricted to a specific bindery context and *only* to that context. Supervisor does not have Admin-like rights in the whole DS tree. It does, however, have full rights over the objects that are in the same bindery context and full file system rights to the servers that provide the bindery emulation service. Within the bindery context, Supervisor can perform all administrative operations, such as changing a user's password and creating new users, regardless of DS inheritance right filters.

Although you can't see Supervisor via the traditional management tools—except via bindery-based utilities such as SYSCON.EXE—you can see it using DSBrowse because there is actually an entry record in the Directory Information Base (DIB) for this object. When you use the Windows version of DSBrowse, you need to switch to the DIB view, as shown in Figure 11.1. With DSBROWSE.NLM, you need to use the Object Search option from the main menu and specify an object ID of 1 (see Figure 11.2). Unfortunately, because there is no DSBrowse implementation for Linux/Unix, you cannot readily check this on those platforms.

Entry record for bindery Supervisor object

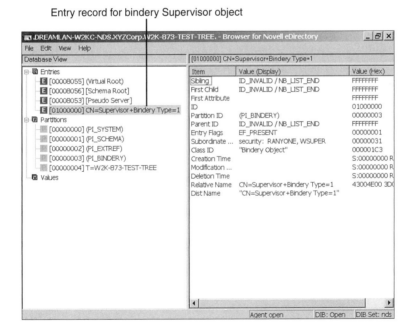

FIGURE 11.1
Database view, showing the bindery Supervisor object.

FIGURE 11.2
Searching for the bindery Supervisor object.

Use an ID of 1 to search for bindery Supervisor

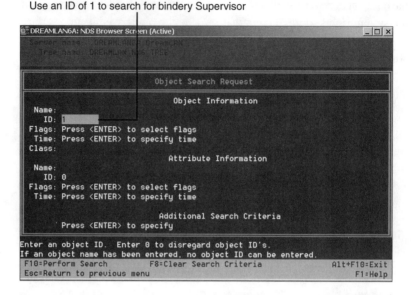

Depending on how you migrated the user information from a bindery server into NDS/eDirectory, you might have a security backdoor that you're not readily aware of. Any user who was security equivalent (SE) to Supervisor in the bindery will be made SE to the NCP Server object (and thus will have full rights to all volumes associated with that server object) on the server that was used to import the bindery data. This means that all users who were SE to bindery Supervisor on the old server now have full rights to the new server.

One of the most confusing issues associated with Supervisor is its password. The initial Supervisor password is the same as that of Admin or that of the user used to authenticate the installation utility. When you install the first server into the DS tree, the passwords of Admin and the bindery Supervisor user are set to be the same. Subsequent changes of the Admin password in NDS/eDirectory are *not* synchronized with the bindery Supervisor password and vice versa.

To change the Supervisor password, you need a bindery utility such as SETPASS.EXE (which is shipped with NetWare 4 and NetWare 5). You can also use SYSCON.EXE, which you can still download from Novell's knowledge base (see TID #1003215) or use third-party bindery tools such as JRB Utilities, from www.jrbsoftware.com, or BinPass, from ftp://ftp.dreamlan.com/Freeware/binpass.zip. It is important to keep in mind that the Supervisor password is *not* synchronized between servers; therefore, when you change the Supervisor password, the change applies only to the one server you are logged in to at the moment of change.

WARNING

NDS 8 and eDirectory handle Supervisor differently than do the legacy versions of NDS. Under eDirectory, you are able to log in as Supervisor but are unable to see the user by using any of the bindery-based tools, even with SYSCON. Figure 11.3 shows that although SYSCON reports that one is logged in as Supervisor, the user list does not indicate that Supervisor exists.

This situation leads to a potential security risk if Bindery Services is enabled because you cannot change Supervisor's password (because the utilities cannot "see" it). Anyone who knows that original password can log in to the server as Supervisor and has full file system access.

This potential security issue is partially addressed in eDirectory 8.7.3, where bindery Supervisor is explicitly prevented from logging in, even though there exists an entry record for it in the DIB, as shown in Figure 11.1.

Logged in as bindery Supervisor

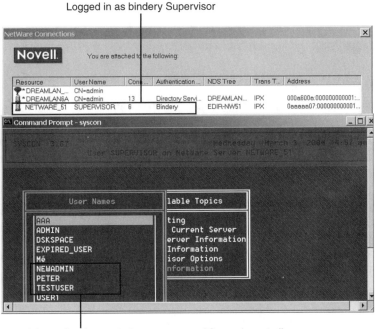

FIGURE 11.3
SYSCON, not showing that Supervisor exists.

But user information does not show presence of Supervisor at all

In NetWare 5 and higher, the screen saver and console-locking function have been removed from `MONITOR.NLM` and placed into a separate NetWare Loadable Module (NLM), `SCRSAVER.NLM`. In addition, DS `User` objects are used to unlock the console. For NetWare 4 servers, however, if you don't know the password that was used to lock MONITOR.NLM or if the console was locked by pressing Enter twice at the Lock File Server Console option, you need the bindery Supervisor password to unlock MONITOR.NLM. The Admin password does not work unless it happens to be the same as the Supervisor password.

> **NOTE** There are some alternatives you can try when you encounter this MONITOR.NLM issue for NetWare 4 servers. Two such examples are using SecureConsole from Protocom and using SSLock for NDS from DreamLAN Network Consulting. Both of these products work on NetWare 4 and higher servers. Refer to the "Console Security" section in Chapter 15, "Effectively Setting Up eDirectory Security," for more information about these products.

Mail Directories and Bindery Queues

Mail directories (created under SYS:MAIL) were an integral part of NetWare prior to version 4; however, they are no longer required for use in the DS environment unless there are users who are still running in bindery emulation mode. These bindery users create the need for mail directories to still exist on NetWare 4 and higher servers.

Each mail directory is tied to its user through the user's hexadecimal object ID; the name of the directory (located under the SYS:MAIL directory) is the hexadecimal number. There are times, however—especially during a restoration—when the ID of the user object is changed and thus the link to the mail directory is broken. As a result, bindery users lose access to their personal login scripts, and any email applications that make use of these directories fail to function correctly.

> **TIP** Novell used to have a utility called RENMDR.NLM that was used to restore the link between the users and their mail directories. However, it seems to have been removed from Novell's support Web site. You may still be able to find a copy on the Internet. Alternatively, you can use Lscripts—from JRB Software (see www.jrbsoftware.com)—to accomplish the same task.

Queues suffer the same issue as user mail directories. The directory corresponding to a bindery queue is named using the queue object's hexadecimal ID number. Thus, if the object ID of a bindery queue object is changed, the link to its queue directory is broken. In such a case, you need to delete the queue object and re-create it so the proper link can be made. DS queue objects do not fall under this category.

Bindery Clients

There may be times when you're unable to switch all your client worksta-tions to use DS-aware client software, such as Novell Client for Windows. Or your workstation platform may be such that you're unable to switch—for example, if you have old Macintosh workstations that can't be upgraded to the latest MacOS version in order to use the DS-aware client without great expense. In such a situation, you need to bear in mind the following differences between a Bindery Services connection and a DS connection:

▶ There's the matter of what NetWare Core Protocol (NCP) API calls the client can use. A bindery connection can't use any of the DS NCPs. That means you can't run utilities such as NetWare Administrator or ConsoleOne to perform administration of the tree.

▶ When you log in through Bindery Services, the container and profile login scripts are not read from the tree. The bindery client looks for a NET$LOG.DAT file in the SYS:PUBLIC directory and a login script in the user's mail directory.

NOTE

The Native File Access Pack (NFAP) enables Macintosh, Windows, and Linux/Unix clients to access storage on NetWare 5.1 and NetWare 6 servers without requiring you to install special client software on each workstation. When communicating with NFAP-enabled NetWare servers, the clients use their own native file proto-cols—such as Apple File Protocol for Macintosh (AFP), Network File System (NFS) and Common Internet File System (CIFS)—instead of NCP calls, thus eliminating the need for Bindery Services.

Whereas it is an optional product for NetWare 5.1, NFAP is included as part of NetWare 6.0 and higher. For more information, visit www.novell.com/products/nfa/.

Performance Considerations

Frequently, administrators are not aware that NetWare assigns only one serv-ice process to service all bindery requests, regardless of the number of bindery connections to the server or the number of currently allocated serv-ice processes. Consequently, you'll notice that a server which services many bindery clients (workstations and/or printers) will show a higher CPU uti-lization than ones servicing NDS clients.

As a point of reference, a server servicing 300 bindery connections may show a CPU utilization of 35%, while the same server servicing 300 DS connections (doing the same type of work) may show a CPU utilization of only 10%.

Security Issues

Although there are many different categories of NDS/eDirectory-related security issues, in our experience, the following rank as the top three:

- ▶ Users getting excessive file system rights
- ▶ Maximum concurrent login limit reached
- ▶ Hidden or stealth objects in the tree

Excessive File System Rights

NetWare implements fairly tight file system security. In order for users to access the files and directories on network volumes, they must have the appropriate file system security access rights. The default NetWare file system security is such that users have *no* access to any files and directories on NetWare volumes except to their own home directories (whether those were set up) and to `SYS:PUBLIC` and `SYS:LOGIN`.

A user can receive file system rights in many different ways, such as from direct trustee assignments, groups belonged to, and even DS containers. Therefore, it is not always easy to determine or troubleshoot a scenario in which a user has full file system rights where he or she is not supposed to. The following are the steps you can take in order:

To track down the cause, at the root of the volume where the user has excessive rights, you type `RIGHTS /T` to see whether there was an explicit rights assignment granted to the user or to any group or DS container the user is a member of. If so, revoke that assignment and see whether that resolves the problem.

NOTE   `RIGHTS.EXE` **is a 16-bit DOS application that is shipped with all versions of NetWare, including NetWare 6.5. It is located in the** `SYS:PUBLIC` **directory.**

If no explicit assignment exists, the user has most likely inherited the rights from DS. This means that somewhere in the DS tree, the user, one of the groups the user is a member of, or the container (or one of its parent containers) the `User` object is in has the Supervisor right to the file server's `Object Trustee` (`ACL`) attribute. This can happen through one or more of the following assignments:

▶ Having Supervisor object rights to the NCP Server object

▶ Having Supervisor or Write rights to the ACL attribute of the NCP Server object

▶ Having Supervisor or Write rights to All Properties

One way to figure out which of these assignments took place is by using ConsoleOne. To do so, you select Trustees of This Object for the [Root] object and then select Effective Rights to see what the user's effective rights are. If the user has excessive rights, you can find the object that was granted the excessive rights in the Trustees of This Object list. Then you do the same thing for each container between [Root] and the NCP Server object, including the NCP Server object itself. At some point you should find that the user's effective right is more than the default (only Browse object rights and Read and Compare All Property rights). It is at this level in the tree that the excessive rights assignment was made.

Consider the sample tree shown in Figure 11.4, where Lisa has full rights to the SYS volume, even though she was given an explicit file system trustee assignment of Read and File Scan to the root of SYS. The following steps illustrate how you can use ConsoleOne to track down and fix the problem of Lisa having full rights to the SYS volume:

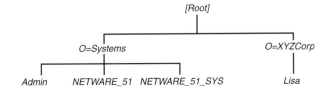

FIGURE 11.4
A sample DS tree for the excessive file system rights example.

1. In ConsoleOne right-click [Root] and select Trustees of This Object. (By default, the only trustees that are here should be [Public] and Admin.)

NDS 7 and later introduced a Tree Root (T=) class to the schema. The T= object's name is the same as the name of the tree. As a result, ConsoleOne does not display the [Root] object for NDS 7 and later trees. Instead, it shows the tree name as the top of the tree. However, in the documentation, the term [Root] is still used.

2. Click the Effective Rights button.

3. Click the Browse icon that is to the right of the For Trustee field. Browse the tree and select the `User` object `Lisa` (located under `O=XYZCorp`).

4. Highlight each of `[All Attribute Rights]`, `[Entry Rights]`, and `ACL` in turn to see what the rights are. Normally a user has only Browse entry rights (see Figure 11.5) and no assigned `[All Attribute Rights]` and `ACL` rights.

Browser button

FIGURE 11.5
Only Browse object rights to `[Root]` exist for Lisa.

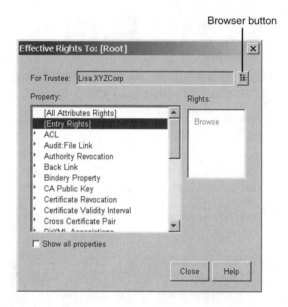

5. Close the dialog boxes because Lisa didn't gain her rights here.

6. Repeat steps 1–4 for `O=Systems`. This time, when you select Effective Rights for `Lisa`, you see that she has full rights to *every* attribute listed, including `[Entry Rights]`, as shown in Figure 11.6.

7. Close the Effective Rights dialog box and return to the Properties of Systems dialog.

8. Examine each of the trustee assignments (by first highlighting the entry and then clicking Assigned Rights) that are in some way related to the user `Lisa` (for instance, `O=XYZCorp`, where the `User` object is located, and `O=Systems`, where some of the groups she belongs are). In this case, you find that `O=XYZCorp` was granted Supervisor rights to `[Entry Rights]` (see Figure 11.7). This is the source of `Lisa`'s excessive rights.

Need to examine rights assigned to these objects

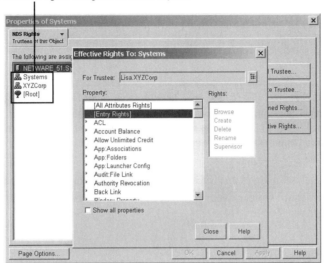

FIGURE 11.6
Lisa has full rights.

FIGURE 11.7
O=XYZCorp with Supervisor object rights to O=Systems.

9. Uncheck the Supervisor rights assignment from [Entry Rights] and click OK to save the change.

10. Check the effective rights again and verify that Lisa does not have excessive rights to the file system anymore.

11. Have Lisa log in to the network and verify that she no longer has excessive effective rights.

In this example, you can stop at this point because Lisa no longer has full rights to the SYS volume. If you didn't find anything at O=Systems, however, you would also need to check the other trustee assignments (such as the NCP Server object) in case the User object was made SE to one of those objects.

TIP

When checking objects that have been granted rights, you need to follow the rules for acquiring rights. You should check all containers above the User object, [Root], [Public], all groups the user is a member of, and any objects the user is SE to (which includes any organizational roles).

The following are some questions you can ask to help determine the location within DS where the user's excessive rights may come from:

- ▶ Is the user SE to Admin?

- ▶ Is the user a trustee or a member of a group that is a trustee with Supervisor rights to the Write right to the ACL attribute of the NCP Server object?

- ▶ Is the user a trustee or a member of a group that is a trustee of a container above the NCP Server object with Supervisor rights to the Write right to the ACL attribute of the object?

- ▶ Is the user a trustee or a member of a group that is a trustee of [Root] with Supervisor rights to the NCP Server object?

- ▶ Is the user under a container that is a trustee with Supervisor rights to the [Root] object?

- ▶ Is [Root] a trustee with Supervisor rights to a container that is over the NCP Server object?

- ▶ Has [Public] been added as a trustee with Supervisor rights to a container that is over the NCP Server object or to the NCP Server object itself?

Maximum Concurrent Logins Limit Reached

One of the most common problems encountered since the initial release of NDS in 1993 is a problem involving maximum concurrent logins. The first instance of this problem you'll probably hear of involves a user calling you or your help desk and saying that he or she is receiving a message indicating that the maximum concurrent logins have been reached but that he or she is not logged in on any other computer on the network.

When a user logs in to the network, the login process compares the current number of values in the `Network Address` attribute of the `User` object to the value of the `Login Maximum Simultaneous` attribute. If the number of network addresses is less than the maximum logins allowed, the login is allowed to proceed; otherwise, the server returns the error code -217 (`ERR_MAXIMUM_LOGINS_EXCEEDED`) to the client, which then displays the appropriate error message to the user.

The issue here is that there are circumstances in which old network addresses are never removed from the `Network Address` property for the user. This most commonly occurs when a workstation the user is logged on to ends its session with the server abnormally. In a NetWare 3.x environment, this is not a problem because the `User` object has separate authentication credentials for each server. In a NetWare 4 or higher environment, however, the credentials are valid for all servers the client is connected to, and the servers do not communicate with each other a loss of communication with the client. During a normal shutdown, the client logout results in the address being properly cleaned up because the client disconnects from all servers. In an abnormal shutdown, however, none of the servers is told that the disconnect occurred—each uses the watchdog process to clear connections that are terminated abnormally.

You can clean up this type of problem in a few different ways:

- ▶ Increase the maximum concurrent logins allowed

- ▶ Remove the concurrent login restriction

- ▶ Use DSRepair to expire network addresses on the `User` objects that are no longer valid

The first two of these options are easy to implement but may not be desirable for security reasons. If the first two options are not viable for your environment, you will have to use the DSRepair option.

DSRepair automatically purges `Network Address` attribute values that are older than 60 days (based on the Creation TimeStamp [CTS] value) during an unattended repair or during repair of the local database from the Advanced Options menu. However, you can control the time period in which to purge unused network address values by using the `-N` switch for DSRepair. To do this on a NetWare server, you load DSRepair as follows:

```
LOAD DSREPAIR -N<number of days>
```

After DSRepair is loaded, you execute either an unattended repair or a repair on the local database. During the repair, the value *<number of days>* is used instead of 60. The main drawback to this solution is that it requires a database repair be run. Running the repair locks the database on the server the repair is being run on. This may not be a desirable side effect (because a locked DIB prevents users from authenticating to that server) for correcting a problem that some administrators consider to be nothing more than a nuisance.

> **TIP**
>
> **You can schedule DSRepair to automatically run during off-hours. For example, you can use the CRON.NLM file that is shipped with NetWare and have it execute the following command every night to clear out all network address values at a predetermined time:**
>
>   LOAD DSREPAIR -N0 -U

The DSRepair option clears out the `Network Address` attributes for all users who are in the partitions hosted by the server. Novell offers a utility called `REMADDR.EXE` that can also remove `Network Address` attribute values for a specific user in IPX environments. Refer to TID #2950374 for details.

> **TIP**
>
> **The DSRepair option works only on NetWare because the other implementations do no support the `-N` option. A more flexible, but workstation-based, option is Deladdr from JRB Software (see `www.jrbsoftware.com`). It works in both IP and IPX environments.**

Dealing with Stealth Objects

Chapter 8, "eDirectory Data Recovery Tools," discusses how you can handle hidden objects. This section describes another possible solution that uses existing tools—DSView on NetWare 4.x servers and DSBrowse on later servers—that you can readily obtain for free without having to call Novell or use a third-party utility.

In a distributed management environment, a network administrator may lock out a branch of a DS tree from administration by other network administrators. This is done by granting one or more users Supervisor object rights to the topmost container of the tree branch and revoking the inheritance of rights from higher in the tree by using inherited rights filters (IRFs). This branch of the DS tree becomes invisible or unmanageable if none of the trustees of the container are available at a later time or have forgotten their passwords.

As long as the users know their User object names and the contexts, they can still log in, even if they cannot browse the tree to see the objects.

NOTE

In such a situation, where there are trustees to the topmost container, you can make use of Bindery Services to change the password of one of the administrators. Here are the steps to accomplish this:

1. Find a user who has explicit rights to the container in question. If you don't know what containers are invisible or hidden, the Hidden Object Locator NLM (see Chapters 8 and 13, "eDirectory Health Checks") can assist you in locating them in a NetWare environment; otherwise, you can use DSBrowse as described next. If the users having rights to the containers in question are also unknown, you can use DSBrowse:

   1. Run DSBrowse on a server that has a replica of the partition containing the blocked container.

   2. Browse the tree until you locate the blocked container object.

   3. Browse through the values of this object's **ACL** attribute until you find a **User** object that has Supervisor object rights. Figure 11.8 shows that a user called **NewAdmin** has full rights to the hidden container.

   4. Although the **User** object's context is not shown in the data, you can use its object ID to locate the object in the tree. In this example, the object ID is 0x00008172. With **DSBROWSE.NLM**, simply enter the value into the ID field (you can leave out any leading zeros) in the Object Search menu and then press F10. With the Windows version, switch DSBrowse into DIB Browser mode, highlight Entries, and right-click. Then select the Go to Record ID option from the context menu and enter the ID value (again, you can leave out any leading zeros). The resulting screen looks similar to what is shown in Figure 11.9. This provides you with the context information of the **User** object.

This user has Supervisor rights to the hidden container

FIGURE 11.8
Locating a user
who has
Supervisor rights.

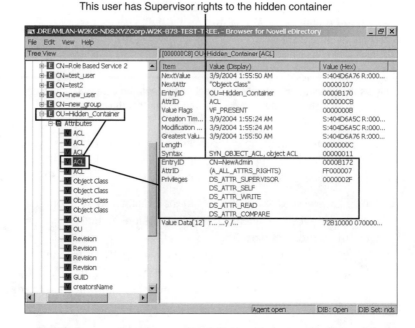

FIGURE 11.9
Locating the user
NewAdmin in the
tree.

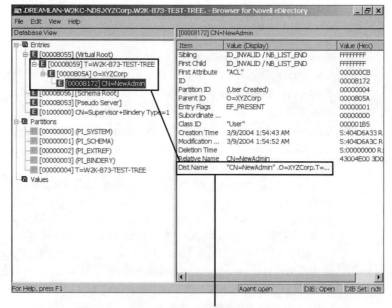

This is the user with Supervisor rights to the hidden container

You cannot use NDS iMonitor or iManager for this step because what these utilities can see in the DIB are based on the rights of the authenticated user.

2. After you locate a user who has Supervisor rights to the blocked container, on a server that holds a writable replica (Master or Read/Write) of the partition, set the server's bindery context to the location of the user who has rights.

3. Log in to the server from step 2 as Supervisor (in Bindery mode). If that server is running eDirectory 8.7.3 or higher, you need to also include the partition where Admin is in the bindery context and log in as Admin instead.

4. Change the password of the administrator user (`NewAdmin` in this example) by using SYSCON.

5. Log in with the revived user and either grant other users rights or remove the IRFs from the container so that it can be administered again.

You can apply this same procedure to blocked objects.

This procedure assumes that there is at least one trustee with Supervisor rights to the blocked object. If there are no trustees or if the amount of time to track down a trustee is long, you should consider trying the solutions outlined in Chapter 8.

Schema Problems

Schema problems are not very common in an NDS/eDirectory tree. However, they do pop up once in a while, just to keep things interesting. The most common source of schema issues is schema synchronization problems between servers. The other has to do with trying to merge two DS trees into one. The following sections look at each of these problems.

Schema Synchronization Problems

Before discussing schema issues, let's first review what a DS schema is and how it may affect the network. The *directory schema* is the rules that define how the directory tree is constructed. The schema defines specific types of information that dictate the way information is stored in the DS database. The following is some of the information defined by the schema:

▶ **Attribute information**—Describes what type of additional information an object can or must have associated with it. Attribute types are defined within the schema by specific constraints and specific syntaxes for their values.

▶ **Inheritance**—Determines which objects inherit the properties and rights of other objects.

▶ **Naming**—Determines the structure of the NDS tree, thus identifying and showing an object's reference name within DS.

▶ **Subordination**—Determines the location of objects in the directory tree, thus identifying and showing an object's location in the directory tree.

The foundation for all entries in a DS database is a set of defined object classes referred to as the *base schema*. Object classes such as `NCP Server`, `User`, and `Print Server` are some of the base object classes defined by the base schema. For a complete list of the base object classes and attribute definitions, see Appendix C, "eDirectory Classes, Objects, and Attributes."

The DS schema can be modified and expanded to suit the specific needs of an organization. Object class definitions can be added to and modified for the existing base schema. Such additions are called *schema extensions*.

There are generally two types of problems associated with a schema: those that are DS rights related and those that are timing related (such as needing to wait for schema synchronization to complete between servers). DS rights-related problems are easy to understand and address. In order to extend the DS schema, you must have Supervisor rights to the `[Root]` object; without Supervisor rights, you are unable to make the changes. The timing-related problem requires some explaining. In large trees where schema extensions can take extended periods of time to be propagated to all servers, the very first installation attempt of an application, such as GroupWise, that requires schema extension may fail a number of times before a successful installation takes place.

As an example, let's assume that one application creates two custom DS objects during the installation process. During the first installation attempt, the application's installation routine attempts to create a new DS object by using an extended class. DS reports that this object class and the needed attributes do not exist in the schema, and the setup program adds them to the schema by using the server that is hosting the Master replica of `[Root]`. The installation then fails because the extension has not yet reached the server on which the object is to be created. Later (possibly 15 minutes or more in very large trees), the administrator attempts to install again. This time the installation finds the first needed object class but not the second one; therefore, the schema is once more extended, but the setup program fails again because the second class extension is not found on the target server. Later, a third installation is successful because all the necessary class extensions are already in the schema.

NOTE

A DS schema is global. Each server stores a replica of the schema in its entirety. The schema data is stored separately from the partitions that contain directory objects. (See Chapter 2, "eDirectory Basics," for more information about replica types.) You can perform modifications to the schema only through a server that stores the Master replica of [Root]. You need to have Supervisor rights to the [Root] object in order to modify the schema.

If it becomes apparent that DS had not yet propagated the schema extensions to the other servers in the tree, you can help speed up the process. From the console of the server that is holding the Master replica of [Root], you issue the following commands:

```
SET DSTRACE = ON
SET DSTRACE = +SCHEMA
SET DSTRACE = *SSA
SET DSTRACE = *H
```

(On Windows servers, the equivalent of using SET DSTRACE=*SSA is clicking the Schema Sync button on the Triggers tab located in the DS.DLM configuration screen.)

TIP

You can use the Schema Compare feature in NDS iMonitor to check whether the schema extension has propagated to the server on which you are installing the application. In NDS iMonitor, you select the Schema link, select to view the base class definitions, and then select the two servers whose schemas you want to compare (see Figure 11.10). Then you repeat the procedure to check the attribute definitions.

Setting DSTrace in this way forces the server to immediately start an outbound schema synchronization process. You need to switch to the DSTrace screen and wait for the message SCHEMA: All Processed = Yes; this may take several minutes, depending on the number of servers in the network and link speeds. If DSTrace says SCHEMA: All Processed = No, there are most likely other issues preventing the synchronization from completing.

FIGURE 11.10
Comparing
schemas between
two servers.

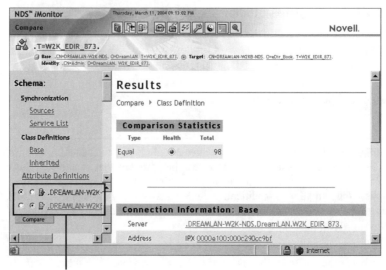

Select the servers for schema comparison

If the setup program crashed in the middle of extending the schema, you
might need to start over with a clean installation. The only way to verify a
clean installation and extension on the DS base schema is to completely
remove all extended class objects (related to the application you're trying to
install) and re-extend the schema. You can use the following procedure to
accomplish this:

1. Log out of all servers except the one you are installing the application
   onto.

2. Delete all related extended schema objects by using ConsoleOne and
   then remove all related file directories from the server volumes.

3. Use Schema Manager to delete all related extended schema class
   objects. If they do not all delete, verify that you are logged in to only
   one server.

4. Reinstall the application. During the installation, the application
   should notice that the schema is not properly extended and reextend
   the schema.

NOTE

There are some known schema synchronization issues that occur in mixed
NetWare 5/6 and NetWare 4.x environments if the DS.NLM on the NetWare 4.x
servers are not fully up-to-date. Refer to TID #10015538 for details. The latest
DS.NLM for NetWare 4.x can be found at Novell's support Web site.

Schema Mismatch During a Tree Merge

With the increasing number of applications that leverage NDS/eDirectory for user authentication and storage of global configuration information, it is not uncommon to encounter schema mismatch errors when you're trying to merge two trees into one. In order to merge two NDS/eDirectory trees, the schema definitions used by both trees must be identical, down to every attribute definition—including any flags (such as `Immediate Sync`) and value bounds associated with an attribute.

The typical cause of schema mismatch is that different DS-aware applications are installed on the two trees. For instance, one tree might have GroupWise and ZENworks installed but the other tree has only GroupWise. Therefore, the second tree does not have the schema extension for ZENworks, and a tree merge fails as a result of this mismatch. There are two ways you can make the schema on the two trees identical. The first method is to simply extend the schema of the tree that is missing the necessary schema information by installing the required applications. This approach is generally successful in 90% of cases.

However, there are instances in which the software license may prohibit you from installing the second copy on a separate tree, even if you are not going to be running the application at all. There can also be situations in which you are unsure what application made which schema extension or in which there are a large number of applications involved. This is where importing schema information by using DSRepair comes in handy. The following steps outline the procedure for doing this:

1. Ensure that you are running the latest DS and the latest DSRepair modules.

2. Load DSRepair on the server that holds the Master replica of `[Root]`.

3. Select the Post NetWare 5 Schema Updates operation from the Advanced Options menu and then select Optional Schema Enhancements (see Figure 11.11). Both of these options are located under Global Schema Operations). In Linux/Unix, use `ndsrepair -S -Ad`; in Windows, select the Schema menu.

4. Select Import Remote Schema from the menu (in the Linux/Unix platform, the option is called Import Schema from Tree) and select the desired tree to import the schema from. This process imports any schema definitions found in the remote tree that are not defined locally. Figure 11.12 shows a DSRepair log file of the import results.

FIGURE 11.11
Global schema
options.

FIGURE 11.12
DirXML and other
schema defini-
tions being
imported from
the remote tree.

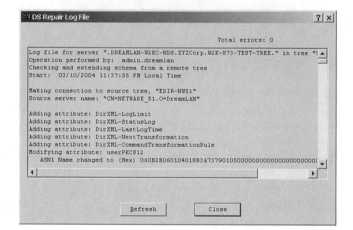

TIP

To verify that a schema is the same between both trees, you should perform the schema import three times—first from source to target, second from target to source, and finally, from source to target—or until no modifications are being made during the schema imports.

If you encounter "Error: -699 An unrecoverable error has occurred and the operation cannot be completed," chances are good that the syntax for one or more attribute definitions in the source tree and the target tree are different. For example, the old NetWare Web Server product creates an attribute called **photo** (to be associated with **User** objects) and uses **SYN_STREAM** as the value syntax. However, NetWare 6 and higher change this attribute to **SYN_OCTET_STRING**. Therefore, when you try to synchronize schemas between a NetWare 5 tree that was extended with the NetWare Web Server product and a NetWare 6.5 tree, you will encounter this -699 error. You can use one of the schema compare methods discussed later in this section to see whether this -699 error is due to the `photo`, `pager`, or `rbsPageMembership` attributes. If it is, you should refer to TID #10066345 for possible solutions. Otherwise, a call to Novell is warranted.

There may be rare cases in which a merge still fails with a schema mismatch error after you synchronize a schema between two trees. This could be a result of some class or attribute definitions in one tree not being the same as those found in the other tree. For instance, in one tree the attribute `cellPhone` may be defined with the `DS_SYNC_IMMEDIATE_ATTR` flag, but in the other tree the same attribute may not include this flag. You need to get Novell involved to have one of these definitions changed before you can merge the trees. However, it would be nice to know how many classes and attributes are involved before you open an incident.

If a merge still fails with a schema mismatch error after you synchronize a schema between two trees, you cannot use the Schema Compare feature in NDS iMonitor because it does not work across trees. You could, however, export the schema information to a file by using LDAP:

```
ldapsearch -h host -D admin_id -w password -b cn=schema
➥ -s base objectclass=subschema > filename
```

and then use a text-compare utility to compare the two files for differences. Alternatively, you could use the two utilities mentioned in Appendix C, `ReadClass32.EXE` and `ReadAttr32.EXE`, to export the class and attribute definitions and then compare the output files for differences. However, the easiest method is to use Novell's Schema Compare utility, Schcmp (see `www.novell.com/coolsolutions/tools/1509.html`).

To use Schcmp to compare schemas between two trees, you first authenticate to both trees and then use the following command to create a text file that you can later examine by using a text editor:

```
schcmp server_in_tree1 server_in_tree2 > schema.txt
```

Although it is not a requirement, it is best if you select the servers holding the Master of [Root] for the schema comparison. The following is an excerpt from Schcmp's output:

```
Comparing NETWARE_51 with DREAMLAN6A...

Classes unique to NETWARE_51
    3x Computer System Policy
    95 Client Config Policy
    ...
Classes unique to DREAMLAN6A
```

```
        bhGadget
        bhPortal
        ...
Attributes unique to NETWARE_51
        App:Administrator Notes
        App:Alt Back Link
        ...
Attributes unique to DREAMLAN6A
        bhArguments
        bhClassName
        ...
Syntaxes unique to NETWARE_51
        NONE

Syntaxes unique to DREAMLAN6A
        NONE

Definition differences for NETWARE_51

Class Definitions
Country
        Optional Attributes
                App:Associations
                App:Launcher Config
                ...
Definition differences for DREAMLAN6A

Class Definitions
domain
        Super Class
                ndsContainerLoginProperties
                ndsLoginProperties
                ...
```

Data Inconsistencies

Missing or lost essential attribute values can lead to data inconsistencies. Sometimes missing or lost values are due to human error (deleting a value or an object when not supposed to), but they can also be a result of system failure (such as time synchronization error or communication issues). The following sections examine the causes and possible solutions to the following situations:

▶ Unknown objects

▶ Renamed objects

▶ Replica ring inconsistency

▶ Replica inconsistency

▶ Stuck obituaries

Unknown Objects

Novell management tools such as ConsoleOne use two different icons to represent unknown objects in DS: a yellow circled question mark and a cube with a black question mark beside it, as illustrated in Figure 11.13.

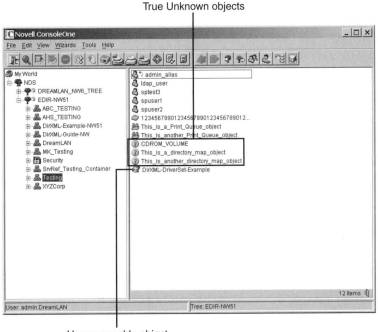

True Unknown objects

Unmanageable object

FIGURE 11.13
The two different types of unknown objects in ConsoleOne.

The cause for the white cubed question mark is completely different from that of the yellow circled question mark. The white cubed question mark means that ConsoleOne could not find the correct snap-in to associate the object with the necessary icon. Essentially, it is saying that the object is perfectly legitimate in DS, but the configuration of ConsoleOne is not correct; consequently, the object is "unmanageable." On the other hand, the yellow circled question mark is usually bad news.

The yellow circled question mark generally means that one or more of the mandatory attributes of the object are missing. When a mandatory attribute is missing from an object, NDS/eDirectory automatically changes the object's class to `Unknown` but leaves the name unchanged.

There are two conditions under which the presence of `Unknown` objects is normal and transitory. The first situation, which is related to timing, happens during replica synchronization. A new replica being added to a server when objects are still being updated from one replica to another can cause `Unknown` objects. Some objects may start as `Unknown` objects (when viewed from ConsoleOne, if the timing is right), but when the synchronization process is complete, they are updated with all the information they need and are turned into real objects. Depending on what you are doing, timing can sometimes make `Unknown` objects go away.

The other situation under which `Unknown` objects appear is during a DS restore. Because the objects are restored in the order in which they are backed up, some objects (such as a `Volume` object) may be restored before the objects (such as the `NCP Server` object) that define their mandatory attributes (`Host Server`, in the case of `Volume` objects) are restored. However, when all the objects are restored, the `Unknown` objects should turn into known objects. For example, if a group is restored but all its members (`User` objects) do not yet exist in the tree, placeholder (`Unknown`) objects are created until the `User` objects are restored. At that time, the placeholder objects become real `User` objects, and the `User` and `Group` objects are fully functional.

If you have not done any of the previously mentioned operations and you have an `Unknown` object, you can delete it and then re-create if it is replaceable. Before you do that, however, you should be familiar with the following repercussions:

- ▶ When the `Unknown` object is a volume, deleting the object causes any user who has a `Home Directory` attribute pointing to that volume to lose its mapping—that is, the `Home Directory` attribute value is cleared.

- ▶ When the `Unknown` object is a user, deleting the object results in the user losing his or her specific trustee assignments (both file system and DS assignments).

▶ When the `Unknown` object is a server, deleting the object causes the server to be deleted from the tree, and all DS references to that specific server are lost. This type of `Unknown` object should not be deleted casually because such deletion can also lead to inconsistent replica rings.

In most cases, however, an `Unknown` object can be deleted and re-created. Anytime an `NCP Server` object or something of importance (such as the `Admin User` object or a `Volume` object) is turned into an `Unknown` object, however, you should consider the consequences of your actions before proceeding.

Before you delete an `Unknown` object and re-create the real object, you need to check whether other replicas have good copies of the `Unknown` object. If they do, you can rescue this object without having to re-create it. You can easily accomplish this by using a combination of NDS iMonitor and DSBrowse or DSRepair.

You can use NDS iMonitor to browse for the object. You'll notice that after you select an object and are viewing its entry information, a Replica frame is shown in the bottom-left corner of the window. This frame shows a list of all servers in the replica ring for this object. The server name that is not hyperlinked is the server you are reading the object's information from. If you want to read the same object from a different server's perspective, you click the hyperlink for that server. After you have determined that there is a good copy of the object in at least one replica of the replica ring, you can proceed. On the server that has `Unknown` objects in its DIB, you load DSRepair with the `-P` switch and perform a repair of the local DS database, leaving all settings at the defaults—but you need to make sure that the Rebuild Operational Schema option is set to `YES` (in Linux/Unix, you use `ndsrepair -R -Ad -P`). Following that, you use one of the following procedures to rectify the issue:

▶ Reload DSRepair without any switches. (However, `-A` may be required for older versions of `DSREPAIR.NLM`.) For NetWare, select Advanced Options, Replica and Partition Operations, View Replica Ring. Then select the server that has the good objects and press Enter. Finally, select Send All Objects to Every Replica in the Ring. For Windows, expand the Partitions list, right-click the server that has the good objects, and select Send All Objects to Every Replica in the Ring. For Linux/Unix, start `ndsrepair` with the `-P` option, select the replica in question, and then select Replica Options, View Replica Ring. Next, select the server that has the good objects and select Server Options, Send All Objects to Every Replica in the Ring.

▶ Instead of using DSRepair to send *all* objects in the replica, as outlined in the previous procedure, you can use DSBrowse instead because it has an option to re-send a *single* selected object. For NetWare, load DSBrowse with -A to get this option. Load DSBrowse on the server that has a good copy of the object, browse to the object, press F3, and choose Resend Selected Object. This changes the object from `Present` (`Flags=1`) to `Present New Entry` (`Flags=801`) on the sending server. DSBrowse also timestamps the object with a newer timestamp, which should send updates to the offending servers, provided that the bad object on those servers has its `flags` value set to `201` (`Present Reference`). For Windows, launch DSBrowse (-A is not required) on a server that has a good copy of the object, browse to the object, right-click, and select Send Object. This procedure cannot be used on Linux/Unix platforms because DSBrowse is not available; however, you can use NDS iMonitor instead, as described in the next procedure.

▶ Instead of using DSRepair to send *all* objects in the replica, as outlined in the first procedure, you can use NDS iMonitor instead because it has an option to send a *single* selected object. NDS iMonitor is especially suited for Linux/Unix platforms because DSBrowse isn't available there. Use NDS iMonitor to locate a server that has a good copy of the object and then click the Send Entry to All Replicas link (see Figure 11.14).

NOTE   The DSRepair -P procedure marks all Unknown **objects in the local DIB as** Present Reference (Flags=201)**. With this flag set, the server is ready to receive the object. In a Reference state, the** Unknown **objects are overwritten if a valid object is sent to that server, and the server will not synchronize the** Unknown **object to other servers in the replica ring.**

Your choice on which of these procedures to use depends mostly on how many Unknown objects there are in the replica. If there are only one or two Unknown objects, the DSBrowse and NDS iMonitor options are the better choice because they generate only small amounts of traffic. However, if there are a fair number of Unknown objects, DSRepair may be more time-efficient, but at the cost of higher network traffic (depending on the number of objects in the replica).

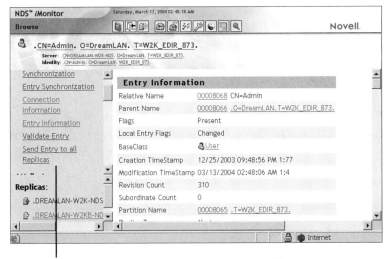

FIGURE 11.14
Sending selected object information to other replicas.

This is equivalent to the Resend Selected Object option in DSBrowse

It has been observed that sometimes `Directory Map` and `Print Server` objects spontaneously mutate into `Unknown` objects for no apparent reason. This can be caused by one of three events:

▶ The server hosting the volume the `Directory Map` object was pointing to at the creation time of the `Directory Map` object has been deleted.

▶ The server hosting the `Print Server` object it was pointing to at the creation time of the `Print Server` object has been deleted.

▶ The `Volume` object the `Directory Map` object is pointing to has been deleted.

The last situation is easy to understand; however, the first two are not. They are due to a bug in the version of NWAdmin that shipped with NetWare 4 that appears when you're dealing with `Directory Map` and `Print Server` objects. (The same bug is also in the version of NetWare Administrator shipped with NetWare 5 and above and carried over into ConsoleOne.)

When a DM object is created, its `Host Server` attribute (which is not visible in NWAdmin but which you can determine by looking in the Others tab in ConsoleOne) points to the server that hosts the volume referred to by the `Directory Map` object. If you change the `Directory Map` object to point to a volume on a different server, the `Host Server` attribute is not updated; it remains pointing to the old server. If the old server object referenced in the `Host Server` attribute gets deleted, DS automatically removes the attribute, and the `Directory Map` object turns into an `Unknown` object because it loses its mandatory `Host Server` attribute. For example, when you create a `Directory Map` object called `TEST_DM` and point it to `NETWARE65-A_VOL1:HOME`, the `Host Server` attribute points to `NETWARE65-A` (or whatever your current default server is). If you later change the `Directory Map` object to point to `NETWARE65-B_SYS:DATA`, the `Host Server` attribute of the `Directory Map` object remains pointing to `NETWARE65-A`. So if at a later time you remove `NETWARE65-A` from the network, `TEST_DM` becomes an `Unknown` object. A similar problem exists with the `Host Device` attribute of `Print Server` objects.

NOTE In the case of `Print Server` **objects, the** `Host Device` **attribute identifies where the** `Print Server` **object's log file is to be kept. When the** `Print Server` **object is brought up, a licensed connection is made to the server identified by the** `Host Device` **attribute, even if the log file option is not enabled. This can also cause performance issues or prevent the** `Print Server` **object from being loaded if the referenced server happens to be across a WAN link or if the (remote) server or the link to it is down.**

Although NWAdmin doesn't show the `Host Server` and `Host Device` attributes, you can easily look them up by using ConsoleOne, NDS iMonitor, or NList. The following NList command shows the `Host Device` settings of all `Print Server` objects in the current context:

```
Nlist "print server" show "host device"
```

The output would look something like this:

```
Current context: test.xyzcorp
Print Server: PS-test
        Host Device: NETWARE5-A.toronto.
--------------------------------------------------------------

One Print Server object was found in this context.

One Print Server object was found.
```

To address these problems, Novell has available the following (unsupported) solutions:

► Novell's developer support Web site, at `developer.novell.com/support/sample.htm`, makes available a sample application called Mapobjch that is contained in a file called `D3MAPOBJ.EXE`. Mapobjch includes a browser to select what container you want to search and automatically changes the host server to that of the volume object's, if they are not the same.

▶ An Appware utility called Hstdev enables you to change the host device of a `Print Server` object. You can locate this program by searching for `HSTDEV.EXE`, using the file finder at Novell's support Web site.

If you are looking for a supported product, you might try HostEditor (see `www.dreamlan.com/hostedit.htm`**). Besides working with** `Directory Map` **and** `Print Server` **objects, HostEditor also works with** `Print Queue` **and** `Volume` **objects.**

NOTE

There is one situation in which the presence of `Unknown` objects is valid. As discussed in Chapter 6, "Understanding Common eDirectory Processes," in a replica ring that consists of servers running eDirectory and legacy NDS versions, objects containing auxiliary class extensions appear as `Unknown` objects on pre-NDS 8 servers because those earlier versions of NDS do not know how to handle auxiliary classes. In such a case, you should not be concerned with these `Unknown` objects and not attempt to delete them unless you have a good reason for so doing.

Renamed Objects

Generally, when a normal object turns `Unknown`, the object name is unchanged (only its object class is changed to `Unknown`). If instead your normal objects have their names changed to names such as `1_2`, `2_1`, and `13_5` (that is, `#_#`) when you didn't name them that way—and they keep coming back after you've renamed or deleted them—you have a synchronization problem.

You should not casually delete these renamed objects when you first detect them. They could be important objects, such as `NCP Server` **objects, that got renamed. Deleting such objects could lead to dire synchronization errors or data inconsistency consequences if you are not careful.**

WARNING

These objects are called *renames*. Renames are caused by name collisions during synchronization. A collision occurs when the same object is found with different CTSs. The name collision problem happens mostly in a mixed

NetWare 4.0x and NetWare 4.10 environment, which is a rare combination these days. It can also occur with the newer versions of NDS/eDirectory on a LAN/WAN where communication is not stable.

You might also observe multiple renamed objects in the **SLP Scope** container when you have multiple Service Location Protocol (SLP) directory agents (DAs) servicing the same scope and writing the information into DS. This is because each DA is attempting to write the same service information it detected into DS, but at a slightly different time. To remedy this, you need to ensure that you are running the latest version of the SLP module for your operating system platform because it contains an option to not store SLP service information in DS but to keep it in the DA cache instead.

TIP When using multiple DAs for the same scope, you should configure only one of the DAs to write service information to DS while keeping the other DAs to use the cache.

The following steps can help you resolve name collision problems:

1. Ensure that the time is in sync on the network and that each server in the replica ring is running the same or the latest compatible version of the DS module. (All the servers in the tree should be running the latest version of DS.) Use the Time Synchronization option from DSRepair's main menu to check whether time is in sync on the network and the versions of the DS modules.

2. Make sure that all the replicas for the partition in question are in the On state. Also make sure that the partition has a Master replica and that the server holding that replica is accessible by the other servers. You can check them by performing a synchronization status report by using DSRepair, NDS iMonitor, or iManager. You should do this on the server that holds the Master replica of the partition.

3. Compare the replica ring information between the related servers in the ring. Resolve any conflicts or inconsistencies if any are found.

4. Use DSBrowse or NDS iMonitor to examine each replica in the replica ring to determine how many servers have been affected by the rename problem. There should be at least one server that shows the original name of the renamed object.

5. From the server that contains the Master replica of the partition, issue
   the following DSTrace commands:

   ```
   set dstrace=on
   set dstrace=+sync
   set dstrace=*h
   ```

   (or the equivalent, using NDSCon on Windows servers) and see
   whether the partition in question is synchronizing successfully.

If DSTrace reports `All Processed = Yes`, you should first try to rename
the objects back to their original names before trying to delete the renamed
objects. They should either keep the name change or be removed from the
tree without reappearing. If they persist, you need to perform a DS health
check to ensure that everything is in order. If nothing obvious shows up and
renames keep happening, you should consider opening a call with Novell
Support and have them dial in for a look at the underlying problem that is
causing the renames to reoccur.

TIP

**There is one more option you can try before calling Novell to deal with renamed
objects. If at least one server in the replica ring is showing the original object
name, you can move the Master replica to a server that shows the correct name.
Then, one by one, you can remove the replicas from the other servers in the replica ring and then slowly add the replicas back again, waiting for each replica to
be added before you go to the next server.**

If the renamed object is an `NCP Server` object, refer to TID #10013224 for
instructions on how to remove the affected server from DS and reinstall it
into the tree. The TID was written for NetWare 4.11, but its concept is
equally applicable to all versions of NetWare and non-NetWare DS servers.

Replica Ring Inconsistency

Although they are not very common, replica ring inconsistencies can reflect
serious problems in a DS tree. A *replica ring inconsistency* is present when
two or more servers holding a replica of a partition do not agree on what
the replica rings look like.

The most common cause of this problem is a change in the replica ring
while a server in the ring is down combined with a timestamp problem
where the server that is down has a future timestamp on its replica information. When this occurs, the replica on the server that was down does not

change its replica list to reflect the recent change. This can result in a number of odd situations: multiple servers holding the Master replica, inconsistent views for Subordinate Reference (SubRef) replicas, or servers missing from the replica ring.

> **NOTE**
>
> **Multiple Master replicas can be a result of the disaster recovery process. If the server holding the Master replica is down for an extended period of time, another server in the replica ring could be designated the Master. When the downed server is brought back online, there would be two Master replicas.**

One of the easiest ways to diagnose an inconsistent ring is to use NDS iMonitor to check continuity. You do this by selecting the Agent Synchronization link and then selecting Continuity for each replica hosted on the server. As discussed in Chapter 7, "Diagnostic and Repair Tools," this method provides a view of the DS partition from each server's perspective. By querying the continuity information from different servers in the ring, you can quickly determine whether there is an inconsistency in the replica ring. Figure 11.15 shows what this might look like for a two-server replica ring. One server sees two servers in the ring (as shown in the Replicas frame) but obtains status for only one server; there is no -625 or -626 error to indicate that there is a communication problem in contacting the other server; there simply wasn't any status information to be reported.

FIGURE 11.15
NDS iMonitor, suggesting that the replica ring for the [Root] partition is inconsistent.

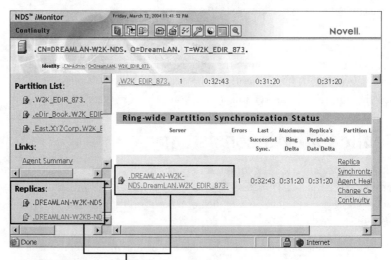

This server sees two servers in th4e replica ring,
but can only obtain status for one server

NOTE

As discussed in Chapter 9, "Diagnosis and Recovery Techniques," you should not rely on a single tool to do your diagnosis. After you have narrowed down which servers are having an inconsistent view of the replica ring, you should use DSRepair to obtain a confirmation before formulating a repair plan.

There are a number of ways to resolve an inconsistent replica ring that has inconsistent views. The first and most advisable is to contact Novell Support to examine the replica list information on the servers, using Novell's diagnostic tools, and repair the database manually. This is the most common resolution we recommend because there are a number of different sets of circumstances that can lead to this sort of situation. If you are comfortable with using DSRepair, however, and are reasonably sure that there are no additional but yet-undetected causes of the inconsistent replica ring problem, you might be able to correct the problem without involving Novell.

WARNING

It is important to realize that an inconsistent replica ring problem is one of the types of problems for which proceeding without Novell's direct assistance may result in both DS and file system trustee data lost.

To start working with an inconsistent replica ring problem, the first thing to do is determine which server has the inconsistent view. If you have more than two servers in the replica ring, the most consistent view is the one you want to work with. The server with the view that does not match the others is the one you want to correct in most circumstances. If there is more than one server with an inconsistent view, you should start with the one that is most inconsistent.

The best way to correct the problem is to uninstall DS from the server in question and reinstall it. This ensures that the timestamps on the affected server are correct. The procedure for this is as follows:

1. Remove DS from that server by using either `INSTALL.NLM` for NetWare 4.x, `NWCONFIG.NLM` for NetWare 5.x and higher, the Add/Remove Programs applet for Windows, or `nds-uninstall` for Linux/Unix platforms.

NOTE

When running eDirectory 8.7 or higher, with the roll-forward log (RFL) enabled, you need to back up the logs before removing DS. This is because the RFL files are also removed by the uninstallation process.

2. Wait a few minutes. How long you wait depends on the speed of any WAN links involved and the number of replicas the change needs to replicate to.

3. Use NDS iMonitor or DSRepair to confirm that the replica lists on all servers in the ring show that the offending server is gone.

4. If NDS iMonitor still thinks the server is in the replica ring, there may be an additional problem with the server remote ID list. If this happens, use DSRepair on each server that is left to verify the remote ID for each server.

5. If the server *still* appears in the replica ring, run DSRepair with the `-A` switch (in Linux/Unix, run `ndsrepair -P -Ad`) on the server that holds the Master replica to manually remove the server from the replica ring. For NetWare, select Advanced Options, Replica and Partition Operations, View Replica Ring. Then select the server you want to remove and press Enter. Finally, select Remove This Server from the Replica Ring. For Windows, expand the Partitions list and select the server that is to be removed. Then select Partitions, Replica Rings, Remove Server from Ring. For Linux/Unix, run `ndsrepair -P -Ad`, select the replica in question, and then select Replica Options, View Replica Ring. Select the server that is to be removed and select Server Options, Remove This Server from Replica Ring. (This step is only necessary on the server with the Master because the rest of the servers receive the update from the server with the Master replica, and the list should appear consistently in NDS iMonitor after this change has propagated. However, if the offending server holds the Master, you need to first designate another server to become the Master before performing this step.)

6. When DS has finished synchronizing the changes to the replica ring, reinstall the server that was removed back into the tree and replace the replicas on that server. This also places SubRef replicas on servers where they are required.

> **NOTE** With eDirectory 8.7 or higher, if the RFL had been enabled previously, don't forget to reenable the RFL files. Refer to the "Configuring and Maintaining Roll-Forward Logs" section in Chapter 8 for details.

There are many different variations to this problem, so it is important to examine the entire situation carefully before proceeding with a plan of action. Remember: Doing something just for the sake of doing something can make a situation much worse.

It is easiest to fix a replica ring that has more than one Master replica. If there are more than two servers in the replica ring, you should run DSRepair on one of the servers that do *not* have the Master replica and designate that server to be the Master. The procedures for doing this are outlined in Table 11.2.

Procedures for Fixing a Replica Ring **TABLE 11.2**

OPERATING SYSTEM	PROCEDURE
NetWare	From the main menu, select Advanced Options, Replica and Partition Operations. From the list of replicas, select the desired partition and press Enter. Select Replica Options, Designate This Server as the New Master Replica (see Figure 11.16). You might need to load DSREPAIR.NLM with the -A option in order to see the Designate This Server as the New Master Replica Option.
Windows	Start dsrepair.dlm from NDSCon. Expand the Partitions view and highlight the desired partition. Right-click and then select Designate This Server as the New Master Replica.
Linux/Unix	Run ndsrepair -P, select the desired partition, and then select Replica Options, Designate This Server as the New Master Replica Option.

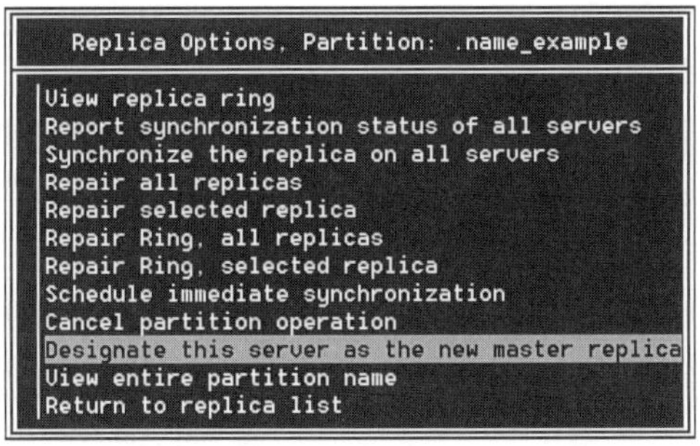

FIGURE 11.16
Using DSRepair to make the current server the Master replica server.

The two servers holding the Master should automatically be demoted to Read/Write replicas. You can then redesignate the original Master server as Master. This procedure must be carried out by using DSRepair and not one of the other management tools, such as ConsoleOne. This is because the other tools will first perform mini-health checks before changing the replica types and will abort when they see that there is more than one Master replica.

NOTE　If there are only two servers in the replica ring (and both are indicating that they are the Master), redesignating one of them as Master by using DSRepair will resolve the conflict.

Replica Inconsistency

Besides inconsistent views of servers in a replica ring, there can also be inconsistency in the number of objects between replicas. This could be due to time-related issues that lead to some servers holding some, but not all, of the objects in the replica rings. Depending on what objects are missing, the problem may go undetected for some time. The issue generally comes to light when users start complaining that they are having intermittent login trouble; they can log in fine when they are attached to one server but not when they are attached to a different server.

WARNING　Before you perform the following procedure, make sure there are no Unknown or renamed objects present. If there are any, refer to the earlier sections in this chapter to resolve them before proceeding.

The following procedure will help ensure that all servers in your replica ring hold the same number of objects. First, you need to use NDS iMonitor or DSBrowse to determine which server has the most accurate replica in the ring. Depending on your finding, you should then exercise one of these options:

- ▶ If the Master has all the data and only a few servers in the ring have incomplete replicas, use DSRepair to perform a "receive all objects from Master to this replica" operation on the servers that have incomplete replicas.

- ▶ If the Master is the only replica that has the complete replica, use DSRepair to perform a "send all objects to every replica in the ring" operation on the Master server.

▶ If none of the replicas have complete information but each replica has some objects that other replicas are lacking, use DSRepair to perform a "send all objects to every replica in the ring" on *each* server in the ring.

Table 11.3 lists the detailed steps for accomplishing these options within each operating system.

DSRepair Procedure to Synchronize Replicas **TABLE 11.3**

OPERATING SYSTEM	PROCEDURE
NetWare	To send from the (Master) replica to all servers in the ring: Select Advanced Options, Replica and Partition Operations, View Replica Ring. Select the (Master replica) local server and press Enter. Select Send All Objects to Every Replica in the Ring. To receive data from the Master replica: Select Advanced Options, Replica and Partition Operations, View Replica Ring. Select the local server and press Enter. Select Receive All Objects for This Replica. (For older versions of `DSREPAIR.NLM`, you might need to load it with the `-A` switch.)
Windows	To send from the (Master) replica to all servers in the ring: Expand the Partitions list, right-click the (Master replica) local server, and select Send All Objects to Every Replica in the Ring. To receive data from the Master replica: Expand the Partitions list, right-click the local server, and select Receive All Objects from Master to This Replica.
Linux/Unix	(Run `ndsrepair` with the `-P` option.) To send from the (Master) replica to all servers in the ring: Select the replica in question and then select Replica Options, View Replica Ring. Select the (Master replica) local server and then select Server Options, Send All Objects to Every Replica in the Ring. To receive data from the Master replica: Select the replica in question and then select Replica Options, View Replica Ring. Select the local server and then select Server Options, Receive All Objects from the Master to This Replica.

WARNING The Send All Objects to Every Replica in the Ring option does exactly what it says: It sends every single object on that server's replica to every other server in the replica ring. Each receiving server will either discard the received information because it already has the object, add the object to the receiving server's DIB because it did not previously have it, or overwrite an Unknown object with a valid object it just received. This process could generate a lot of network traffic, depending on the size of the replica. Therefore, it is advisable that you perform this "send all" operation after-hours and wait for it to complete on each server before starting it on the next server.

Stuck Obituaries

As described in Chapter 6, DS makes extensive use of obituary notifications for object management, and obituary flags are eventually cleared out when an object is removed. There are times, however, when an obituary gets stuck so that DS can't finish the cleanup process. Most obituaries get stuck because a server was not notified that a change to objects has taken place. To see whether you have any stuck obituaries, you should use the latest available version of DSRepair and select Advanced Options, Check External References on the Master replica of each partition. (You need to load DSRepair with the -A command-line switch.) This generates a list of all obituaries on the server. Then you need to review this list, searching for any line with a Flags=0 value. The server listed (that is, the last entry on the Backlink process line) below this value has not been contacted. The following is a sample DSRepair log that shows obituaries:

```
/****************************************************************/
NetWare 6.00 Directory Services Repair 10515.37, DS 10510.64
Log file for server "NETWARE65-B.Test.DreamLAN" in tree
➥ "NETWARE65-TEST"
External Reference Check
Start: Thursday, March 3, 2004 2:14:25 pm Local Time

 Found obituary for: EID: 11000FE8, DN: CN=User3.OU=Test.
➥O=XYZCorp.NETWARE65-TEST
-Value CTS : 01/16/2004 10:36:42 PM  R = 0001  E = 0003
-Value MTS = 01/16/2004 10:36:42 PM  R = 0001  E = 0003,
➥  Type = 0001 DEAD,
-Flags = 0000
-RDN: CN=User3
```

```
 Found obituary for: EID: 11000FE8, CN=User3.OU=Test.
➥O=XYZCorp.NETWARE65-TEST
-Value CTS : 01/16/2004 10:36:42 PM  R = 0001  E = 0004
-Value MTS = 01/16/2004 10:36:42 PM  R = 0001  E = 0004,
➥  Type = 0006 BACKLINK,
-Flags = 0000
-Backlink: Type = 00000005 NEW_RDN, RemoteID = ffffffff,
 ServerID = 010000BD, CN=TEST-FS1.OU=Test.O=XYZCorp.
➥NETWARE65-TEST

 Found obituary for: EID: 11000FE8, CN=User3.OU=Test.
➥O=XYZCorp.NETWARE65-TEST
-Value CTS : 01/16/2004 10:36:42 PM  R = 0001  E = 0004
-Value MTS = 01/16/2004 10:36:42 PM  R = 0001  E = 0004,
➥  Type = 0006 BACKLINK,
-Flags = 0000
-Backlink: Type = 00000005 NEW_RDN, RemoteID = ffffffff,
 ServerID = 030010C3, CN=TEST-FS2.OU=Test.O=XYZCorp.
➥NETWARE65-TEST

 Found obituary for: EID: 11000FE8, CN=User3.OU=Test.
➥O=XYZCorp.NETWARE65-TEST
-Value CTS : 01/16/2004 10:36:42 PM  R = 0001  E = 0004
-Value MTS = 01/16/2004 10:36:42 PM  R = 0001  E = 0004,
➥  Type = 0006 BACKLINK,
-Flags = 0000
-Backlink: Type = 00000005 NEW_RDN, RemoteID = ffffffff,
 ServerID = 03001101, CN=TEST-FS3.OU=Test.O=XYZCorp.
➥NETWARE65-TEST


Checked 0 external references
Found: 4 total obituaries in this dib,
    4 Unprocessed obits, 0 Purgeable obits,
    0 OK_To_Purge obits, 0 Notified obits

*** END ***
```

The information presented in the this DSRepair log is interpreted as follows:

▶ EID stands for entry ID. This is a record number in the **0.NDS** file (or
  ENTRY.NDS file in NetWare 4) that specifies the object that has the
  Obituary attribute assigned.

▶ CTS and MTS are timestamps. They denote when the Obituary attribute was created and modified, respectively.

▶ `Type` indicates both a number and a text description. There are three
categories of types: primary, secondary, and tracking. A primary obituary indicates an action on an object. A secondary obituary indicates
the servers that must be contacted and informed of the primary obituary action. A tracking obituary is associated with certain primary obituaries. The following are the valid obituary types:

     ▶ Primary obituaries are `0000 Restored`, `0001 Dead`, `0002 Moved`,
`0005 NEW_RDN` (New Relative Distinguished Name [RDN]), `0008`
`Tree_NEW_RDN` (Tree New RDN—this does not specify an DS tree
name but rather a partition root name), and `0009 Purge All`.

     ▶ Secondary obituaries are `0006 Backlink` (specifies a target serv-
er that needs to be contacted regarding an obituary) and `0010`
`Move Tree` (this obituary is similar to the Backlink obituary).
There is one move tree obituary for every server that needs to be
contacted regarding a `Tree_NEW_RDN` operation.

     ▶ Tracking obituaries are `0003 Inhibit Move`, `0004 OLD_RDN`
(Old RDN), and `0007 Tree_OLD_RDN` (Tree Old RDN—this does
not specify an DS tree name but rather a partition root name).

▶ `Flags` indicate the level or stage to which the obituary is processed.
The following are the valid flag values:

     ▶ **0000 (Issued)**—This flag indicates that the obituary has been
issued and is ready for processing.

     ▶ **0001 (Notified)**—This flag indicates that the obituary is at the
notify stage, which essentially means that the servers identified
in the backlink or tree move obituaries have been contacted and
notified of the operation or action on an object.

     ▶ **0002 (OK-to-Purge)**—This flag indicates that the obituary is
being cleaned up on the local database of each server identified
in the backlink or tree move obituaries. This cleanup includes
resolving all objects that reference the object with the obituary
and informing them of the change (for example, deletion or
move).

     ▶ **0004 (Purgeable)**—This flag indicates that the obituary is ready
to be purged. The purge process essentially recovers the value to
the free chain and enables it to be reused.

Using this information, you can readily determine that the DSRepair log reports that `User3.Test.XYZCorp` has been deleted but the obituary is temporarily stuck because server `NETWARE65-B` (the server on which this DSRepair was run) is waiting to pass that information to servers `TEST-FS1`, `TEST-FS2`, and `TEST-FS3`.

Armed with the necessary information provided by DSRepair, you can then begin to find the problem with that server. It could be that Transaction Tracking System (TTS) is disabled, the server is down, SAP/RIP filtering may be causing a problem, or the server may not even exist anymore but the server object is still in the tree. By checking these issues, you can resolve almost all obituary problems. With NDS 5.95 and higher, you can use a `SET DSTRACE=*ST` command, and it will report back information in the DSTrace screen on what servers are having the problems with obituaries.

One of the most commonly reported obituary-related DS error is -637 (0xFFFFFD83), which is a "previous move in progress" error. You may encounter this error when trying to do any kind of partition operation, such as adding or moving a replica or even adding a user (after a container move). In many cases with the newer versions of DS, especially with eDirectory, the -637 error can be resolved without the intervention of Novell Support. In some cases, however, Novell will need to dial in to your network to edit the DS database in order to remove the stuck obituary that's causing the problem.

For example, if the case is a server not able to communicate with one or more servers referencing the object being moved, you should be able to resolve the error without involving Novell. If a server referencing the object has actually been removed from the tree and the object move has still not completed, however, you may need to contact Novell for additional help.

The actual -637 error is caused by the `Type=0003` (Inhibit Move) obituary. This obituary is placed on the object that has been moved and on the container it has been moved to, to prevent another move from taking place on this object until the previous move has completed. In some cases, two other obituary types may be involved as the cause to the -637 error: `Type=0002` (Moved) obituary and `Type=0006` (Backlink) obituary. The Moved obit is attached to the (original) object that has been moved from this container. The Backlink obit is attached to the object to point to another server holding an exref of the object, which must be notified when the object is modified (for example, deleted, renamed, moved). The Backlink obit can also be caused by an exref, where a server must hold information about an object in a partition that the server does not hold a replica of. DS stores this information in the server's database as an exref, which is a placeholder that contains information about the object that the server does not hold in a local replica. Exrefs are updated periodically by servers holding replicas of the object via the Backlink process that point to the object on the server holding the exref.

The following three steps can help you resolve most -637 errors without involving outside assistance:

1. Locate the object with the Inhibit Moved obituary because that is the culprit of the error. Go to the server holding the Master replica of the partition reporting the -637 error and use DSRepair (with the `-A` switch) to perform an exref check. Look for lines similar to this:

   ```
   Found obituary for ...
   EID... RN CN=Objectname.OU=Container.O=Container ...
   -Value MTS= ... Type=0003 Inhibit_move
   -Flags=0000
   ```

   This is the object causing a -637 error to be reported. Take note of the object's full name and context.

2. Locate the corresponding Moved obituary. It is placed on the object that was moved from another container to the one with the Inhibit Move obituary. You need to find where this object was moved from. A server holding a replica of the partition where the object was moved from gives you this information. If you are lucky, the same server holding the Inhibit Move obituary also holds a replica of the partition where the object was moved from. If you are not lucky, you will have to run DSRepair (with the `-A` switch) on *every* server in the tree that holds a Master replica of a partition and look for the following error when checking exrefs:

```
Found obituary for ...
EID ... CN=name.OU=ou_name.O=o_name ...
-Value MTS= ... Type=0002 Moved
-Flags=0000
```

You are looking for the same CN name as the Inhibit Move obituary, only in a *different* container (remember that the -637 error is caused by moving objects). A Moved obituary is placed on the object that has been moved until the move is completed. In the same **DSREPAIR.LOG** file, also look for lines similar to the following:

```
Found obituary for ...
EID ... CN=name.OU=ou_name.O=o_name ...
-Value MTS= ... Type=0006 Backlink
-Flags=0000
```

Look for the same object as the Moved obituary object. This object has exrefs, held on other servers in the tree, that must be notified of the move. A Backlink obituary points to the server holding the exref, and **Flags=0000** tells you that the server holding the exref has not yet been notified of the move.

TIP

If all Type=0006 **Backlink** obituaries are at Flags=0000, **you should verify that you have a Master replica of each partition in the tree; the Master replica is responsible for forwarding obituary states.**

3. Find out the status of the server(s) holding the exref(s). To find out which servers have exrefs to the moved object, use DSBrowse. On the server reporting the Moved and Backlink obituaries, use DSBrowse to locate the object and examine the value(s) of its **Obituary** attribute. You should see information similar to this:

```
-Flags = 0000
-Backlink: Type = 00000005 NEW_RDN, RemoteID = ffffffff,
 ServerID = ##, CN=Servername
```

When you find such entries, you have the names of the servers that are holding up the process.

When you have the server names, you need to determine whether the servers are up. Are they communicating properly (that is, no -625 errors)? Do the servers still exist? If the servers are simply down (say, for maintenance), you need to get them back up and running and communicating as soon as possible. If they no longer exist, you need to delete the `NCP Server` objects from DS by using the Partition view in ConsoleOne, and any exrefs they were holding should clean up after the server objects are deleted. If the servers are up and communicating, you can try the following on each of those servers:

1. Load DSRepair with the `-XK3` switch (which kills all exrefs in the local DIB). Select Advanced Options, Repair Local DS Database. Set Check Local References to Yes; set the other options to No.

2. Perform the repair, save the repaired database, and exit DSRepair.

3. At the server console, enable the Backlink trace message and force the Backlink process to run:
   ```
   SET DSTRACE = +BLINK      (+BLNK on Linux/Unix)
   SET DSTRACE = *B
   SET DSTRACE = *H
   ```

4. Toggle to the DSTrace screen and watch for the line `BACKLINK: Finished checking backlinks successfully`. If the screen scrolls too fast for you to catch the message, enter the following commands:
   ```
   SET TTF = ON
   SET DSTRACE = *R
   SET DSTRACE = +BLINK      (+BLNK on Linux/Unix)
   SET DSTRACE = *B
   SET DSTRACE = *H
   SET TTF' = OFF
   ```

   Then use `EDIT.NLM`, `VIEW.NLM`, or a text editor to examine the resulting `SYS:SYSTEM\DSTRACE.DBG` file. (Use `/var/nds/ndstrace.log` on Linux/Unix platforms.)

The Backlink obituary should now have purged, which in turn enables the Moved and then the Inhibit Move obituaries to process. You can check the flags of the obituaries by using either DSBrowse or DSRepair, as described previously.

TIP

You should always allow NDS/eDirectory some time for its various background processes to do their jobs. You should wait at least 15 to 45 minutes. It may take a while for an Inhibit Move obituary to purge, depending on how many replicas and objects are in the partition.

If this procedure doesn't work, there is a trick you can try before having to call Novell. Recall from Chapter 6 that the Master replica initiates most of the obituary processing; the exception to this involves the processing of a Used By obit that is started by the replica that actually modified the object. The trick is to simply move the Master replica around in the replica ring. This forces each replica to process any obituaries in its local database and synchronize the changes to the other servers in the replica ring.

You may actually consider using the move-Master-around procedure before using the -XK3 **option because the move trick is a lot less intrusive.**

If your replica ring consists of mixed NDS/eDirectory versions, putting the Master replica on eDirectory helps to reduce the occurrence of Inhibit Move obits. If the replica ring has one or more NetWare 6 servers, putting the Master replica on one of them is also desirable.

On the other hand, if the server referenced by the obits no longer exists in the tree and the server object has been deleted from NDS, you need to call Novell Support for assistance.

NOTE

In some cases, there may be no corresponding moved obituary because the DS obituary process was (somehow) abnormally interrupted. In such situations, you must contact Novell Support for assistance in cleaning up the orphaned Inhibit Move obituaries.

To prevent orphaned obituaries from occurring, you should perform exrefs for any obituaries that have not completed processing (that is, not at Flags=0004 **[Purgeable])** *before* **bringing down a server permanently or performing any other operation that may prevent communication to a server or its replica.**

Synthetic Time

The synthetic time problem is one the Novell Product Support forums see more often than any other problem. Unfortunately, in many cases, the advice given to users does not include the first few steps necessary to determine whether simply waiting is a viable option for the problem to resolve itself. This is a case where waiting is the best alternative.

Synthetic time occurs when the modification timestamp (MTS) on at least one object in the partition is set to a time that is in the future, according to the real-time clock on the server reporting the problem. Because a single object can cause the error, it is important that you find out how far ahead the MTS is and base your solution on that information.

DSRepair can tell you this when you run either an unattended full repair or a local database repair. Objects with future MTSs are reported in the log file as shown here:

```
ERROR: Illegal timestamps were found in this replica.
You may need to run the advanced option:
   'Repair timestamps and declare new epoch'
Value: 4054e3cb, ID: 00008059, DN: T=W2K-873-TEST-TREE
03/14/2010 05:59:23 PM; rep # = 0001; event = 0001
```

The last line here shows the MTS to be many years in the future.

The way this problem is corrected depends on how far ahead the MTS is. If it is measurable in days, you can simply wait for the time to catch up. *Synthetic time* ensures that the future MTS and the current real-time converge. This convergence typically takes half the time of the difference between the future timestamp and the current time. So if the MTS is reported to be an hour into the future, it should take about 30 minutes for the problem to resolve itself.

If, however, the time differential is measurable in months or years (as the preceding example shows), we recommend that you repair the timestamps. Table 11.4 outlines the procedure that must be repeated for *each* replica stored on the server that has one or more objects with a future MTS.

TABLE 11.4   Procedures for Repairing Each Timestamp

OPERATING SYSTEM	PROCEDURE
NetWare	Load DSREPAIR.NLM with the -A switch. Select Advanced Options, Replica and Partition Operations. Highlight a replica and press Enter. Select Repair Time Stamps and Declare a New Epoch (see Figure 11.17).
Windows	Start dsrepair.dlm with the -A switch. Expand the Partitions list, right-click a replica, and select Repair Time Stamps and Declare a New Epoch (see Figure 11.17).
Linux/Unix	Run ndsrepair -P -Ad. Select a replica and then select Replica Options, Repair Time Stamps and Declare a New Epoch.

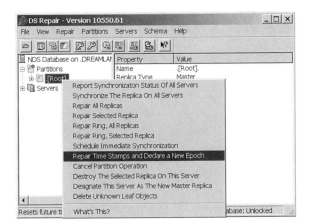

FIGURE 11.17
The Repair Time Stamps and Declare a New Epoch option in DSRepair.

When the Repair Time Stamps and Declare a New Epoch option is selected, you are prompted for a user login and password. The login ID you use here must have Supervisor rights to the portion of the tree where the timestamp repair is taking place.

WARNING

Repairing timestamps is a very traffic-intensive operation because all non-Master replicas of the partition are essentially destroyed and re-created. This can cause loss of services that require bindery contexts for the duration of the repair. Depending on the number of replicas and their sizes, this operation can take hours to complete. You should make sure to schedule time off-hours to perform this operation if it is necessary.

When this operation is initiated, you must wait for it to complete before issuing a second timestamp repair. If the server has multiple replicas with future timestamps, you need to wait for each repair to complete before starting the next one; if you don't, you might flood other servers on the network with too much traffic and introduce further problems. Because this operation destroys replicas on non-Master replica servers, you need to make sure you minimize the number of changes taking place from one repair to the next. You should run the first repair and verify that it has completed (all replicas should show an On state in DSRepair or NDS iMonitor when the repair is complete) before initiating another—even if the other is in a different part of the tree.

Server and Data Recovery

Hardware and human-caused errors are unavoidable. There may be occasions when you need to recover lost DS data, such as group membership information or user **Home Directory** attribute values. There may be other times when the hard drive hosting NDS/eDirectory fails and you need to recover as fast and as completely as possible. The following sections cover the following scenarios:

- ▶ Group membership recovery
- ▶ **Home Directory** attribute recovery
- ▶ Recovering from a server crash
- ▶ Loss of all replicas except for subrefs in a replica ring

Group Membership Recovery

One situation that we have seen occur is that an administrator accidentally deleted group memberships from a large number of users. In this circumstance, the administrator was attempting to add a number of users to a group by using the UImport utility. Unfortunately for the site in question, the administrator used a control file that specified **REPLACE VALUE=Y**, resulting in the new group membership being added but original group memberships being deleted. Because these group memberships were used to assign rights in the file system and determine which applications are available to each user, this became a big problem very quickly.

Fortunately, the change was made off-hours, so the immediate impact was minimal. Of even more importance was the backup of the DS tree that had been made several weeks earlier. Although it is true that in many cases backups of DS are not of much use, in this case, the backup did contain a large percentage of the users in the tree and the information necessary to rebuild the majority of the users' group memberships.

The following tools were used for this recovery:

- ▶ The backup of DS made several weeks earlier
- ▶ A server not connected to the production network
- ▶ NList
- ▶ UImport
- ▶ Two **awk** scripts

The first step in this recovery was the restoration of the old DS group information. The backup product used was only capable of restoring to a server named the same as the server the backup was taken from. In order to accommodate this limitation, we took a lab server from our isolated network and renamed it. Next, the DS tree was restored to that server. To ensure that the dependencies for group memberships were restored properly, we restored the data twice.

While the DS tree was being restored on the isolated network, two awk scripts were developed. The first script was designed to create a batch file to list the group memberships for each user listed in the original UImport data file. Because the number of users affected was about 100 out of 5,000, it did not make sense to restore group membership information for all users. Instead, a text file with the desired list of users and their contexts was created, using the following format:

```
.UserID1.Context1
.UserID2.Context1
.UserID3.Context2
```

The following awk script was used to parse the preceding information into a batch file:

```
BEGIN { print "del grpinfo.txt" }
{
     count = split($0, object, ".")
     printf("cx ")
     for (x=3; x<= count; x++)
          printf(".%s", object[x])
     printf("\n")
     printf("nlist user = " object[2])
     printf(" show \"group membership\" >> grpinfo.txt\n")
}
```

The resulting batch file looks like this:

```
del grpinfo.txt
cx .Context1
nlist user = UserID1 show "group membership" >> grpinfo.txt
cx .Context1
nlist user = UserID2 show "group membership" >> grpinfo.txt
cx .Context2
nlist user = UserID3 show "group membership" >> grpinfo.txt
```

When the DS restore finished, the batch file was run to generate a file called `GRPINFO.TXT`, showing all group memberships for the user objects in question. This `GRPINFO.TXT` file was in the following format:

```
Object Class: User
Current context: Context1
User: userID1
        Group Membership: Group1.Admin.Groups.Admin...
        Group Membership: Group2.XYZCorp
One User object was found in this context

One User object was found.
Object Class: User
Current context: Context1
User: userID2
        Group Membership: Group3.Admin.Groups.Admin...
        Group Membership: Group4.XYZCorp
One User object was found in this context

One User object was found.
Object Class: User
Current context: context2
User: userID3
        Group Membership: Group1.Admin.Groups.Admin...
        Group Membership: Group2.XYZCorp
One User object was found in this context
```

This file was then parsed, using a second **awk** script, to create the final data file used for the new run of UImport. This data file is in a format that is usable by UImport:

```
".userID1.context1",".Group1.Admin.Groups.Admin"
".userID1.context1",".Group2.XYZCorp"
".userID2.context1",".Group3.Admin.Groups.Admin"
".userID2.context1",".Group4.XYZCorp"
".userID3.context2",".Group1.Admin.Groups.Admin"
".userID3.context2",".Group2.XYZCorp"
```

You should note a couple things about the data file created. First, the user ID contains a leading dot. This is done so the script can be run from any context and so the input is valid. The second thing you should notice is that there are multiple entries for a given user ID, but UImport handles these entries just fine.

The challenge is in parsing the trailing dots on the group memberships in
GRPINFO.TXT and coming up with a script that works reliably to perform the
conversion. The following is the awk script that does this:

```
/Current context:/ { cx = $3 }
/User:/ {cn = $2}
/Group Membership:/ {
     printf("\".%s.%s\",", cn, cx)
     gsub(/\tGroup Membership: /, "")
     grptmp = $0
     num = split(cx, tmpcx, ".")
     counter = 1
     while (substr(grptmp, length(grptmp)) == ".")
     {
          counter++
          sub(/\.$/,"",grptmp)
     }
     printf("\".%s", grptmp)
     for (y=counter;y<=num;y++)
     {
          printf(".%s", tmpcx[y])
     }
     printf("\"\n")
}
```

This script counts the number of trailing dots and compares that to the
number of parts in the current context. It then removes the leading portions
of the current context until it runs out of dots at the end of the group name.
Next, it concatenates the group name to the remaining portion of the context, which results in the correct context for the group.

When the new data file is created, we created a control file that uses two
fields: one for the user login ID and one for the group membership being
processed. Upon watching the run of UImport, we were able to determine
which user IDs had been moved or deleted. Even though not all the users
were covered in this fix, there were sufficient users fixed to prevent a major
outage the following day. In total, out of 100 users, only about 10 had to be
modified.

NOTE

This example serves as a reminder that a disaster recovery solution need not be a
100% solution; if you can automate a large portion of the work in a reasonable
amount of time, any remnants can be handled by hand or on a case-by-case basis.

REAL WORLD

Programmatically Adding a User to a Group

If instead of using an existing application such as UImport to add users to a group, you are developing your own application, you should be aware of a few things. The action of adding a user to a group involves a total of four major changes in DS:

- ▶ Add the user's DN to the group's Member attribute.
- ▶ Add the user's DN to the group's Equivalent to Me attribute.
- ▶ Add the group's DN to the user's Group Membership attribute.
- ▶ Add the group's DN to the user's Security Equals attribute.

The current DS module does not automatically make these four changes happen simultaneously. Therefore, if you are writing a program to accomplish this task, you must make all four of these changes in your program's code. If you use the NWUsrGrp ActiveX control in the Novell Developer Kit (NDK), it performs the four necessary steps for you when it adds a user to a group or deletes a user from a group. However, if you use the NWDir or NWIDir controls, you need to code the four steps as part of your program logic.

Home Directory Attribute Recovery

It is a fairly common occurrence that upon fixing certain DS-related issues, the Home Directory attributes of User objects are lost. As discussed earlier in this chapter, in the "Unknown Objects" section, when an object that is referenced by any DS attribute is removed from the tree, that DS attribute's value is automatically cleared. Because Home Directory is a single-valued attribute, clearing its value means deleting the attribute.

TIP

The procedures discussed here can also be used to update existing Home Directory values when you physically move the folders from one volume or server to another.

The Home Directory attribute uses the SYN_PATH syntax and references a Volume object in its value. If, for any reason, that Volume object is removed from the tree, the Home Directory attribute is cleared. You can repopulate this value fairly easily by using one of the following methods:

▶ Generate a text file that contains the username and home directory information and then use UImport to update the **User** objects. The text file would look something like this:

```
".userID.context", ".volume_object.context:\path"
```

▶ Generate a text file that contains the username and home directory information and then use Import Convert Export (ICE) to update the **User** objects via LDAP. The LDIF file would look something like this:

```
version: 1
dn: cn=username,ou=context,o=context
changetype: modify
ndshomedirectory:

cn=vol_object,ou=context,o=context#0#\users
```

▶ The preceding two solutions require you to create a separate record for each user because the path of the home directory is unique for every user. An easy alternative is to use Homes (**www.novell.com/coolsolutions/tools/1568.html**), with which you can simply select a starting context and set the **Home Directory** attribute for all users inside a container (see Figure 11.18).

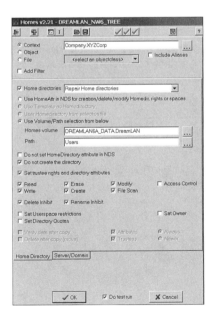

FIGURE 11.18
Setting home directory information by using Homes.

Recovering a Crashed SYS Volume or Server

One of the most-asked questions in any network is, "How do I correctly recover from a crashed server?" For those of you who have worked with NetWare 3, you know it's quite straightforward: Install a new server, restore the bindery from a backup, and restore your file system. In the case of a single-server NDS/eDirectory network, the process is pretty much the same as that with NetWare 3: Install a new server, restore DS from a backup, and then restore your file system. Because of the distributed nature of DS, however, things are a little more interesting when you have a multiserver NDS/eDirectory network.

To successfully recover from a lost server in a multiserver environment, it is essential that you maintain a regular backup of the server-specific information (SSI) files for all the DS servers on your network. (Chapter 8 discusses the situation for eDirectory.) It would also be helpful if you have up-to-date documentation about your DS tree, such as where `NCP Server` and `Volume` objects are located. You should also have a record of the partitions and a list of servers where the Master and various other replicas are stored. Finally, you should have the correct license file(s) for the crashed server.

NOTE   **The process for recovering from a crashed hard drive where NDS/eDirectory resides (such as the SYS volume on NetWare) is the same as having a dead server because your DS is gone.**

NOTE   **For more information about SSI files and their purposes, see Chapter 8.**

The following are the steps you need to take to restore a crashed server or a SYS volume in a multiserver DS environment when you *don't* have a current set of SSI data available:

1. Don't panic!

2. Reconfigure time synchronization configuration in the tree, if necessary.

3. Create a `Computer` object in the tree to act as a placeholder for server references.

4. Use SrvRef (see `ftp://ftp.dreamlan.com/srvref.zip`) to replace server references in the tree (see Figure 11.19).

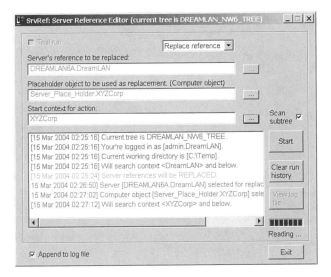

FIGURE 11.19
Replacing server
references.

5. Delete from the tree the old **NCP Server** object for the failed server.
   Do not delete the associated **Volume** objects, however. Leave them
   intact to preserve references that other objects (such as **Directory
   Map** objects) may have to these objects as well as any DS trustee
   assignments made.

6. If the failed server held a Master replica of any partition, go to another
   server in the replica ring that has either a Read/Write or Read-Only
   replica and use DSRepair to promote that replica to a Master. Repeat
   this step for every master replica stored on the failed server. Then
   clean up the replica rings to remove the downed server from the lists.
   (See the "Replica Ring Inconsistency" section, earlier in this chapter,
   for details.)

TIP

After your replica ring cleanup, you should spot-check the DSTrace output on a
number of servers to see whether the replica rings are okay and that everything is
synchronizing correctly. You *do not* want to install a server into a tree that's not
fully synchronized.

7. Rebuild the crashed server by using existing documentation. Ensure
   that the same server name, volume names, IPX/IP addresses, and so
   on are used. Install the server into a separate temporary tree.

8. If you are just recovering a lost **SYS** volume, load **DSREPAIR.NLM** with
   the **-XK6** switch (which deletes all volume trustees) and then perform

a Check Volume Objects and Trustees operation. When prompted to make the change on the **SYS** volume, answer No; for all other volumes, answer Yes. See TID #10013535 for details on this step. (This is Step 22 in TID #10013535.)

9. Remove NDS from the rebuilt server.

10. Reconfigure the time synchronization setting on the rebuilt server, if necessary.

11. Install the rebuilt server back into the production tree, using the same context the original server was installed in.

12. Use SrvRef to restore server references in the tree.

13. Restore data and trustee information to the server. You should be careful when restoring the **SYS** volume data so that you don't overwrite any new support pack files with older ones. If you've made modifications to your **AUTOEXEC.NCF** file, you should ensure that the older copy from your backup does not overwrite it.

14. Reestablish replica information by using ConsoleOne. (You might want to wait until after-hours and after the data restoration has completed.)

15. Reinstall licenses, if necessary.

16. Reinstall any server-based applications, such as BorderManager.

17. Reissue any SSL certificates for the recovered server, as necessary.

18. Delete the temporary **Computer** placeholder object from the tree.

When restoring files to a volume that was nearly full during the backup, you might run into insufficient disk space issues. This is especially true when volume compression is used. Although SMS-compliant backup software can back up and restore a compressed file in its compressed format, that's not the default in most backup software; therefore, chances are good that you'll restore previously compressed files in their uncompressed format. And because compression is a background operating system process, files are not compressed until the compression start time is reached. You can, however, flag files as immediate compress, but that's an extra manual step you have to take. And afterward, you have to remember to undo the flag or else the files will always be compressed again after access, causing unnecessarily high server utilization.

Another volume-related issue that you can get caught with during a restoration is suballocation. Again, because it is a background process, files are not suballocated as they are restored; therefore, if you're restoring many (small) files, you can run out of disk space before the complete restoration is done.

To work around these two disk space problems, it is best that you try to maintain at least 15% to 20% free disk space on each volume. Even better, you should make certain that the replacement drive capacity is larger.

After the restoration of the file system is complete, you should restart the server yet one more time to ensure that the restoration didn't overwrite any important system files. Then you should perform a spot-check on some of the restored directories and files to check for correct trustee assignments, file ownerships, and so on. You should also spot-check DS objects to ensure that you don't have any Unknown or renamed objects.

Subordinate References Only in the Replica Ring

The steps discussed in the section "Recovering a Crashed SYS Volume or Server" work well when you have replicas on other servers to recover DS information from; however, there is also the (very) unlikely situation where you lose one partition within the tree and, for some reason, no replica of that partition exists. What can you do? First of all, take a deep breath and don't panic! Depending on the partition location within the tree structure, all may not be lost.

Consider the sample DS tree shown in Figure 11.20. Two of the servers in this tree contain the following replicas:

Server FS1	Server FS2
Master of [Root]	
Master of B	
SubRef of C	Master of C
Read/Write of E	Master of E

NOTE

Because Server FS1 has a copy of B (the parent) but not C (the child), DS automatically placed a SubRef replica of C on server FS1.

FIGURE 11.20
If FS2 is lost, a hole exists in the DS tree between OU=B and OU=E.

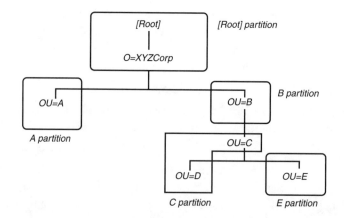

If Server **FS2** is lost due to hardware failure and no other servers hold a replica of C, you lose the only full replica of the C partition. (SubRef replicas are not full replicas, and they contain only enough information to locate other replicas and track synchronization.) When this happens, you have a hole in the DS tree between **OU=B** and **OU=E**. You can't use any of the procedures discussed earlier in this chapter to recover the C partition because no other full replicas exists.

In this scenario, where a SubRef replica of the lost partition exists, it is possible to rebuild the links to the lost portion of the DS tree and then perhaps restore the objects from a recent backup. The following procedure explains how you may recover from the loss of a single partition in a multipartition tree and have no full replicas of that partition:

> **WARNING**   The following procedure may not work for all cases and, therefore, you should consider acquiring the assistance of Novell Support to rebuild the links to the missing partition in your tree. At the very least, you should test the procedure in a lab environment before ever using it in a production environment.

1. Don't panic! Don't attempt any DS recovery or repair procedures.

2. Follow the steps outlined in the section "Replica Ring Inconsistency," earlier in this chapter, to clean up the replica rings for other partitions that have replicas on this crashed server, and make sure your other partitions are synchronizing without errors.

3. If more than one server has a SubRef replica of the lost partition, choose one to work with. The best choice would be a server that has the least number of replicas on it.

4. On the server chosen in step 3, load DSRepair with the -A command-line switch and promote the SubRef replica to a Master by using the steps outlined earlier in this chapter, in the "Replica Ring Inconsistency" section. This changes the SubRef replica into a real replica; however, because a SubRef replica doesn't contain any object information, the recovered replica will be empty.

Depending on your replica placement of this lost partition, SubRef replicas of this partition on other servers may be upgraded to Read/Write replicas.

5. Use DSTrace to check that this partition is synchronizing correctly. If it is not, you should consider opening an incident with Novell for further assistance.

6. When the replica ring is synchronizing, use your most recent backup to perform a selective restoration of the DS objects that were in the lost partition. Take note of any objects in other parts of the tree that may have turned into **Unknown** objects due to loss of their mandatory attributes. You may need to do a selective restoration on those objects or re-create them.

Re-create any bindery objects and DS objects (such as print queues) that depend on object IDs. Reassign DS object trustee assignments, if necessary.

If you don't have a SubRef replica to work with, you need to first make sure no one attempts *any* repair operations because they could make a bad situation worse. Then you should open a call with Novell Support for assistance.

Summary

In this chapter, you learned how the concepts and various tools that have been discussed in previous chapters can be applied to specific NDS/eDirectory issues. The following topics were examined:

- ▶ Bindery Services–related issues
- ▶ Security issues
- ▶ Schema problems
- ▶ Data inconsistencies
- ▶ Synthetic time
- ▶ Server and data recovery

In the chapters that follow, you'll find out how to proactively manage DS to prevent these issues from developing.

PART IV

Managing eDirectory to Prevent Problems

PART IV

eDirectory Management Tools

A key component of avoiding directory services (DS) problems is understanding how to manage the tree effectively and efficiently. Novell provides several good tools for accomplishing standard administrative tasks, but in many cases tools other than those that Novell provides can make the job simpler. This chapter takes a look at the tools supplied with NetWare and eDirectory as well as selected tools available from third-party vendors.

Many of the Novell-supplied tools, such as NDS iMonitor, have already been discussed in Chapters 7, "Diagnostic and Repair Tools," and 8, "eDirectory Data Recovery Tools." This chapter takes a look at them from a management point of view instead of using them purely as diagnostic or repair tools.

NOTE

The tools discussed in this chapter can safely be used against legacy versions of NDS and are not restricted to eDirectory. There are some restrictions, however, when some of the new eDirectory-specific tools are used against older versions of NDS. For instance, when you use NDS iMonitor against an NDS 7 server, you will not be able to obtain as much statistical information about the various NDS processes as you would when running it against an eDirectory 8.7.3 server.

NetWare Administrator

Novell's NetWare Administrator utility has been around as long as NetWare 4 has been shipping. It has been the primary interface most administrators are familiar with for administering DS trees. NetWare Administrator provides the following functionality:

- ▶ A graphical view of the DS tree
- ▶ The capability to view and modify DS object attributes
- ▶ The capability to hide objects from view based on object class
- ▶ The capability to manage DS and file system rights from a single interface
- ▶ Snap-in capabilities to manage extensions to DS
- ▶ The capability to manage multiple trees from the same session
- ▶ The capability to make attribute value changes to multiple User objects simultaneously
- ▶ The capability to search the tree for objects based on a single criterion (for example, find all User objects whose Given Name attribute is equal to Peter).

Over the years, Novell has shipped different versions of the NetWare Administrator tool for different platforms, and the tool has evolved considerably. Table 12.1 outlines some of the differences between the various versions.

TABLE 12.1   **Releases of NetWare Administrator and Their Features**

UTILITY NAME	SHIPPED WITH	FEATURES/LIMITATIONS
NWADMIN.EXE	NetWare 4.0x	16-bit for Windows 3.x, extendable through snap-in development
NWADMN3X.EXE	NetWare 4.10 and NetWare 4.11	16-bit for Windows 3.x, extendable through snap-in development
NWADMN95.EXE	NetWare 4.11	32-bit version for Windows 95/98; snap-in information stored in registry; extendable through snap-in development
NWADMNNT.EXE	NetWare 4.11	32-bit version for Windows NT; snap-in information stored in registry; extendable through snap-in development
NWADMN32.EXE	NetWare 5.0 and higher	Snap-in information not stored in registry—snap-ins loaded from the snap-ins directory on the server; same 32-bit executable for Windows 95 and higher; extendable through snap-in development

This section focuses on NWADMN32.EXE—generally referred to as NetWare Administrator—the version that Novell ships with NetWare 5 and higher. NetWare Administrator is not included with eDirectory but can be used to manage eDirectory.

NOTE

Snap-in DLLs written for older implementations of NetWare Administrator may not work with newer versions of the utility. If you are currently using an older version of NetWare Administrator and find that the newer version does not support the snap-ins you need, you should contact the manufacturer of the product the snap-in is written for to get an update.

You can extend NetWare Administrator through the use of snap-ins. There are two types of snap-ins that can be set up for the utility:

- ▶ **Snap-in object DLLs**—These DLLs enable you to administer additional object classes with NetWare Administrator. A snap-in object DLL handles object creation and modification and is used to define the property pages shown by NetWare Administrator.

- ▶ **Snap-in viewer DLLs**—These DLLs enable you to look at objects in DS differently than through the tree view. These viewer DLLs add items to the Tools menu. Several Novell products add snap-in viewer DLLs; GroupWise is one such product that includes this type of snap-in DLL.

Installing these snap-in DLLs is very easy. In the SYS:PUBLIC\WIN32 directory on the server is a subdirectory called SNAPINS; you simply copy the DLLs into that directory. When NetWare Administrator starts, it checks for and uses the DLLs located in that directory.

Some snap-ins are compiled only for use on Windows 95/98 or Windows NT. When you move DLLs from older versions of NetWare Administrator, some features may only be supported by one operating system or another. The latest version of NetWare Administrator takes this into account by adding subdirectories underneath the snap-ins directory—one for Windows NT–only snap-ins (NTONLY) and one for Windows 95/98 snap-ins (950NLY). If you find that a snap-in doesn't work with one operating system or the other, you can copy it into the respective directory and prevent error messages from appearing in the unsupported operating system.

Snap-ins are created using Novell's Software Developer Kit (SDK), which is available for free through Novell's DeveloperNet Web site (http://developer.novell.com). Development of snap-ins is beyond the scope of this book; for more information on this topic, visit the Novell DeveloperNet support Web site.

NOTE   NetWare Administrator does not allow you to view the properties of an object if it doesn't have a snap-in to handle that class of object. You can only delete, rename, or move such an unmanageable object. ConsoleOne, on the other hand, allows you to examine the object's properties even if it doesn't have a snap-in for it; you can use the Others tab to examine the information.

TIP   If you are not a programmer but have a need for custom NetWare Administrator snap-ins, you might want to look into the ScheMax product discussed later in this chapter.

The primary function NetWare Administrator is typically used for is managing users. Figure 12.1 shows the NetWare Administrator Identification page. This page, shown by default when you open the User object's properties, includes information used to identify the user; none of this information is used by the workstation, the server, or DS. On the right-hand side is a list of tabs that allow you to modify other information associated with a User object, including password limitations, login restrictions, and the personal login script.

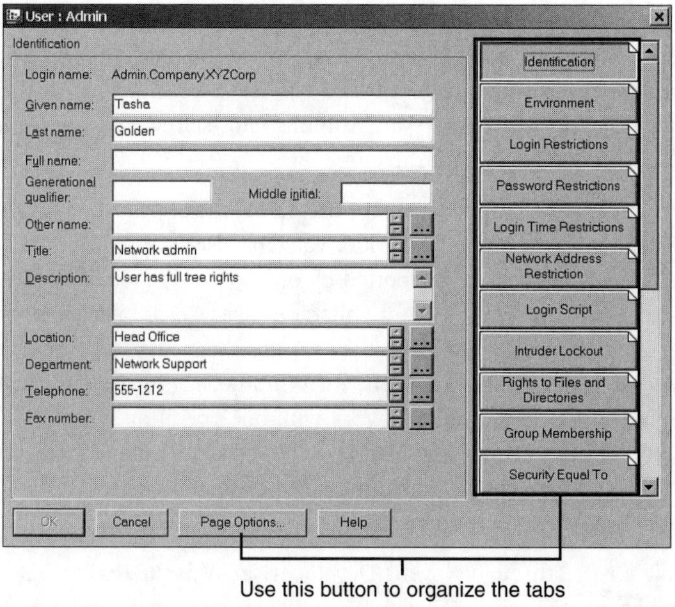

FIGURE 12.1
The Identification page in NetWare Administrator.

Use this button to organize the tabs

You can arrange the order of the tabs such that the most frequently used ones are grouped together and placed near the top. You can also hide any tabs that you do not use. To change the order of the tabs, you can click the Page Options button to open the Page Options dialog, which is shown in Figure 12.2. When a tab is moved to the Available Pages pane, it is no longer listed in the main dialog.

Changes visibility of tabs

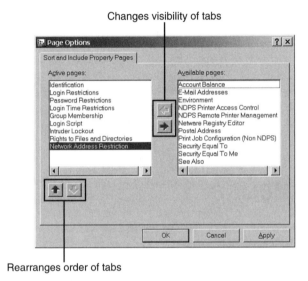

Rearranges order of tabs

FIGURE 12.2
Configuring page options.

Each object class has its own set of pages. Therefore, changes made in the Page Options dialog are specific to the object class and are not global.

TIP

To configure what object classes are displayed and their display order in the browser windows, you select the View drop-down menu and then select Sort and Include (see Figure 12.3).

You will become very familiar with NetWare Administrator because user administration tends to be the most time-consuming task for an administrator. After the network is established, the users are the most dynamic part of the network and require the most attention. Therefore, we will move on from this topic to administration of the other standard class objects in this chapter. Chapter 14, "eDirectory Management Techniques," describes tips and tricks that make administration simpler and covers more information on user creation and administration.

FIGURE 12.3
Configuring
browser display
options.

Changes visibility of object types

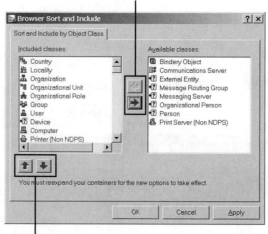

Rearranges display order by object class

ConsoleOne

With the introduction of NetWare 5, Novell started to change direction in
how administration of NetWare and NDS/eDirectory services is performed.
The ConsoleOne utility is a Java application designed to ultimately replace
the 32-bit NetWare Administrator utility. As you will soon learn, however,
ConsoleOne is slowly being phased out in favor of Web-based tools.

The one driving force behind ConsoleOne is cross-platform support because
Java applications can run on other operating system platforms wherever a
compatible Java Runtime Environment (JRE) is available. Today, ConsoleOne
runs on Windows, NetWare 5 and higher server consoles, Macintosh, and
on any Unix/Linux that eDirectory supports.

Figure 12.4 shows the main ConsoleOne screen, as it appears on a Windows
2000 workstation. Similarly to NetWare Administrator, ConsoleOne is capable of managing multiple trees concurrently. As a matter of fact, ConsoleOne
has all the features of NetWare Administrator and many more; the following
are some of the additional enhancements:

▶ Effecting attribute value changes to multiple objects (not limited to
just User objects) simultaneously.

▶ Integrated DS partition and replica management tools.

- ► Wizards to simplify import and export of DS data via LDAP and to configure filters for Filtered replicas. Additional wizards are easily added via snap-ins.

- ► Built-in schema manager (accessed via the Tools pull-down menu).

- ► Advanced search features where multiple criteria may be specified.

Change the width of the display column by right-clicking the "edge" of the column and dragging ti to your desired location

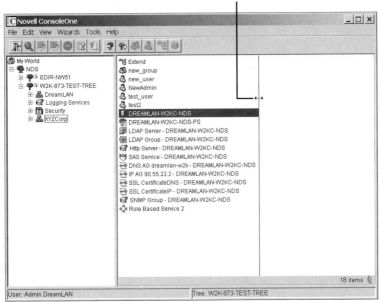

FIGURE 12.4
A Windows 2000 display of the Java-based ConsoleOne utility.

As mentioned in Chapter 7, aside from being an NDS/eDirectory object management tool, ConsoleOne also allows you to manage DS partitions and replicas. Through the View pull-down menu, you can switch between the Console view and Partition and Replica view (see Figure 12.5). There is also a GroupWise view if the GroupWise snap-in is installed.

Similarly to NetWare Administrator, ConsoleOne also supports the use of snap-ins as a way of extending its functionality to support new object types and additional features. You can use ConsoleOne to find out what snap-ins are loaded by selecting the Help, About Snapins.

This symbol indicates this container is a partiion root object

FIGURE 12.5
Managing partitions and replicas by using ConsoleOne.

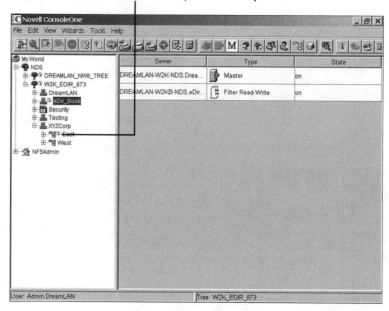

NOTE Because of the difference in architecture between NetWare Administrator and ConsoleOne, their snap-ins are not compatible with each other. Therefore, before you replace NetWare Administrator with ConsoleOne, you should first ensure that all needed snap-ins are available for ConsoleOne.

On a Windows workstation, ConsoleOne uses the privileges of the logged-in user to access the tree. When you're administrating DS from the NetWare server console or from another operating system, however, a login is required. The Novell Client must be installed on Windows workstations in order for ConsoleOne to function. ConsoleOne implementations for non-Windows platforms (such as Unix), on the other hand, do not require the presence of Novell Client software—and there is not a client available.

In many cases, you can use ConsoleOne instead of NetWare Administrator to manage your DS and NetWare servers. Certain management functions, however (such as creation of legacy queue-based printing related objects and management of Novell Distributed Print Services [NDPS]), must still be performed by using NetWare Administrator as a snap-in because queue-based printing is not available for ConsoleOne. Consequently, you must evaluate the environment before switching entirely to ConsoleOne. Often, you will find that you need to use both NetWare Administrator and

ConsoleOne to address your total network management tasks. From the DS management point of view, ConsoleOne can do everything NetWare Administrator can do and more.

A small potential drawback of ConsoleOne is its dependency on a compatible JRE. Therefore, before you upgrade your management workstation's JRE to a newer version, make certain it is compatible with ConsoleOne.

iManager and NDS iMonitor

As discussed in Chapter 7, iManager and NDS iMonitor are two Web-based DS management applications that ship with eDirectory. They were developed as part of the effort to make management tools truly platform independent. They do not require additional software to be installed on the management workstation—unlike ConsoleOne, which requires a compatible JRE.

Although iManager and NDS iMonitor are intended for eDirectory, they can also be used to manage a network where there are servers running both NDS and eDirectory. All you need is *one* eDirectory server in the tree, and information on a non-eDirectory server can be accessed via the proxy mode. Because NDS supports a smaller feature set than eDirectory, not all functions in NDS iMonitor are available when accessing servers running NDS. Similarly, the eDirectory Administration plug-ins for iManager require an eDirectory Management Tool Box (eMBox) utility to be installed. eMBox only ships with eDirectory 8.7 and later.

NDS iMonitor lets you look at the eDirectory environment in depth, on a partition, replica, or server basis. You can also examine what tasks are taking place, when they are happening, what their results are, and how long they are taking. Through NDS iMonitor, you have access to the same information that normally required traditional server-based eDirectory tools—such as DSBrowse, DSTrace, and the diagnostic features available in DSRepair—all from within a Web browser. Therefore, iMonitor's features are primarily server focused, meaning that they focus on the health of individual eDirectory agents rather than on the entire eDirectory tree. The following are some of the features provided by NDS iMonitor 2.x:

▶ eDirectory health checks and health summary reporting

▶ Partition and replica synchronization information

▶ Agent configuration

▶ Agent activity and verb statistics

▶ Agent information and status

▶ Online error code information

▶ Browsing and searching capabilities for objects

▶ A schema browser

▶ DirXML monitoring

▶ Background process scheduling

▶ DSRepair functions

▶ Hyperlinked DSTrace information

Figure 12.6 shows the eDirectory agent summary, which shows the synchronization status, the number of servers known in the Directory Information Base (DIB), and the agent's process status.

FIGURE 12.6
The agent summary screen of NDS iMonitor.

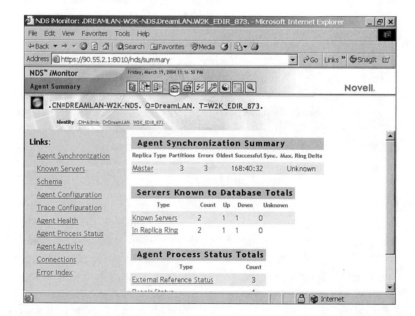

The amount of information you can view in NDS iMonitor is based the following factors:

▶ **The identity you used to log in to NDS iMonitor**—Your identity's eDirectory rights are applied to every request you make in NDS iMonitor. For example, you must log in as the Admin of the server or have Console Operator rights to the server where you are trying to access the DSRepair page.

▶ **The version of eDirectory agent being monitored**—Newer versions of NDS and eDirectory have features and options that older versions do not. For example, you cannot get any DIB caching information from servers running NDS 7.

The status and statistics information you view in NDS iMonitor is real-time data that shows what is happening on your server at that particular time.

NOTE

iManager gives you the ability to assign specific responsibilities to users and to present the users with only the tools necessary to perform those sets of responsibilities. This functionality is called *role-based services* (RBS). RBS allow you to focus the user on a specified set of functions, called *tasks*. One or more tasks are grouped into *roles*. As a result, when users log in to iManager, what tools they have access to from within iManager is based on their role assignments in eDirectory (see Figure 12.7). The users do not need to browse the tree to find an object to administer; the iManager plug-in for that task presents the necessary tools and interface to perform the task.

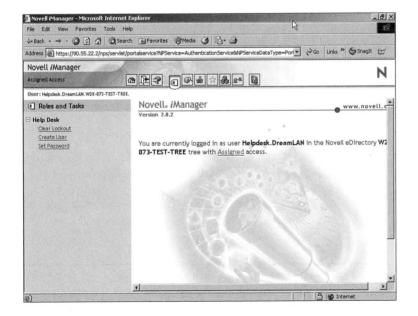

FIGURE 12.7
Users have access to only the roles and tasks assigned to them.

> **WARNING**   Novell documentation suggests that when using RBS, iManager presents the user with only the tools and their accompanying rights necessary to perform the assigned tasks. However, we present evidence in the "Setting Up eDirectory Security for a Help Desk" section in Chapter 15, "Effectively Setting Up eDirectory Security," that the rights are granted to the users even when they are not using iManager.

NDS iMonitor implements its own HTTP stack and does not depend on other components, such as a Web server. iManager, on the other hand, depends on a number of variables, including the following:

- Correctly installed and configured RBS.

- A working Web server, such as an Apache server.

- A working Tomcat servlet engine. (*Servlets* are protocol- and platform-independent server-side components, or programs, that are used to extend the server's functionality. They are the server-side counterpart to applets, which are software that adds functionality to a client.)

- A functioning Java installation.

- A working LDAP server (which Tomcat uses, such as for user authentication and dynamic group management).

- A working SSL/TSL certificate.

If any *one* of these components required by iManager fails, iManager will stop functioning. Therefore, you should not rely on iManager as your sole management platform. You and your staff should also be familiar with using other tools, such as ConsoleOne and NetWare Administrator.

The UImport Utility

The UImport utility is one of the most powerful—and underused—utilities included with NetWare 5. (Alas, it is not included with NetWare 6.) The history of this 16-bit command-line utility dates back to NetWare 4, but its roots can be traced all the way back to the `MAKEUSER.EXE` utility introduced just before NetWare 2.15 started shipping.

> **NOTE**   On NetWare 5.x servers, UImport is installed only if you are running NDS 7. If you upgraded the server or initially installed the server with NDS 8, the utility is removed. However, you can reinstate it and use it against all versions of NDS and eDirectory.

TIP

If you have access to a NetWare 5.x operating system CD, you can copy the following files to the directory of your choice, and you will have a working copy of the UImport utility:

```
SCHEMA.XLT
TEXTUTIL.HEP
TEXTUTIL.MSG
UIMPORT.EXE
UIMPORT.MSG
```

Because UImport is a DOS-based application, you need to ensure that you have a search path to the necessary Unicode files.

The idea behind UImport is very simple: Provide a batch-mode process to enable mass user creation and modification. In pre-NetWare 4 environments, the Makeuser utility provided this functionality; because the bindery definition for a user was fixed, it was a very simple utility to use. UImport is a somewhat more complex utility in comparison to Makeuser because it has to handle the different attribute syntaxes that NDS/eDirectory uses.

UImport uses two data files: a control file and a data file. The file format for these files is easy to understand—they both can be created in any text editor. The control file contains two sections: an Import Control section and a Fields section. Each of these sections is prefaced by the section name. Table 12.2 provides examples for the Import Control section of the file.

UImport Import Control Field Definitions　　　　　　　**TABLE 12.2**

FIELD	DEFINITION	SAMPLE
Create Home Directory	A Boolean value (Y/N) that tells UImport whether to create a home directory in the file system for the user being created.	CREATE HOME DIRECTORY=N
Delete Mailbox Dirs	A Boolean value used to determine whether the mail directory (used for bindery services) for the user should be deleted.	DELETE MAILBOX DIRS=Y

Table 12.2 Continued

FIELD	DEFINITION	SAMPLE
Delete Property	A field that is used to specify a special value for UImport to search for in the data file that means the field should be deleted.	`DELETE PROPERTY= #DEL`
Home Directory Path	The path for the parent directory where the home directory is to be created.	`HOME DIRECTORY PATH=USERS`
Home Directory Volume	The distinguished name (DN) of the `Volume` object the home directory will be created on.	`HOME DIRECTORY= NETWARE65_ USERS. East.XYZCorp`
Import Mode	A field that can have one of the following values: C (create) U (update) B (both create and update) R (remove).	`IMPORT MODE=U`
Maximum Directory Retries	The number of attempts to assign the user as a trustee to the home directory. This is necessary because of synchronization delays if the user is created on a server that the home directory is not on.	`MAXIMUM DIRECTORY RETRIES=5`
Name Context	The default context to use for the UImport operation. If not specified, the current context of the work-station is used.	`NAME CONTEXT= .East.XYZCorp`

Table 12.2   Continued

FIELD	DEFINITION	SAMPLE
Quote	A character that represents a quotation mark. This allows values to have embedded spaces, and it can be changed in order to enable quotation characters to be embedded in property values. The default is the double-quote character.	QUOTE="
Replace Value	With multivalued fields, an option that enables you to overwrite the existing value (when set to Y) or add a new value to the attribute (when set to N).	REPLACE VALUE=Y
Separator	A character that is used to delimit fields within a record. The default is a comma.	Separator=,
User Template	A Boolean value used to designate whether UImport uses the User Template user in the context being used for creation as a template for new user objects.	USER TEMPLATE=Y

The following are some important notes about some of the fields that you need to keep in mind when working with UImport:

▶ The Delete Property field is used to specify a special value to be included in the data file. If you set this value to #DEL and you want to delete the Given Name property for a group of users, you put #DEL in the field of the data file that represents the Given Name attribute.

▶ The Delete Property field also has a few fields it does not affect: the Volume Restrictions field, the Password field, and the Home Directory field. You delete the Volume Restrictions field by specifying that field and putting a space restriction of -1 in it. To delete the Password field, you specify it in the fields section and put a blank value in the data file. For the Home Directory field, you must manually delete the field by using NetWare Administrator, ConsoleOne, or some other DS management tools.

▶ The Replace Value field can be very dangerous if it is not used properly. For example, if you are adding groups to a large number of users and you specify `REPLACE VALUE=Y` in the control file, you need to delete all previous group memberships and explicitly add the memberships specified in the data file.

▶ The User Template `field` used by UImport is a `User` object and *not* a `Template` object that is used by NetWare Administrator or ConsoleOne. If you use this type of template, the following list of fields is copied from the `User Template` object: Account Balance, Account Has Expiration Date, Allow Unlimited Credit, Allow User to Change Password, City, Days Between Forced Changes, Default Server, Department, Description, Fax Number, Foreign Email Address, Foreign Email Alias, Full Name, Generational Qualifier, Given Name, Grace Logins Allowed, Group Membership, Home Directory, Language, Location, Login Allowed Time, Login Script, Low Balance Limit, Mailbox Location, Mailing Label Information, Maximum Connections, Minimum Password Length, Network Address Restriction, Postal (ZIP) Code, Postal Office Box, Profile, Remaining Grace Logins, Require a Password, Require Unique Passwords, Security Equal To, See Also, State Or Province, Street Address, Telephone, and Title.

The absolute minimum number of fields needed in the Import Control section depends on the operation being performed. Table 12.3 shows the fields needed for each operation. The Name field refers to the `CN` attribute of the object and is what UImport uses to designate this attribute.

TABLE 12.3

Minimum Fields Required for the Various Import Modes

IMPORT MODE	MINIMUM FIELDS REQUIRED
C (create)	Name, Surname
U (update)	Name, another field to modify
B (both create and update)	Name, Surname
R (remove)	Name

The Update mode requires only the Name field. Specifying only the Name field would not be useful, however; you also need to specify another field to update. The B mode (both create and update) requires both the Name and Surname fields because users are created if they do not exist, and the Surname field is a mandatory attribute for the User class.

When the Import Control section is completed, you need to define the Fields section. This section starts with the line Fields and then lists the DS attribute names the data file contains, one per line.

TIP

If you don't know the name of a particular DS attribute you want to use, you can use DSBrowse or NDS iMonitor to get the attribute name. Besides the Name field, the other fields use the NDS/eDirectory attribute name as defined in the schema. For a list of all Import Control section field names and supported Fields section names, you use UIMPORT /? ALL.

Determining the syntax of some of the fields can be tricky. For example, if you look at the definition for the Volume Space Restrictions attribute, you will find that there are multiple parts to the attribute. To specify the different parts of the value, you separate them with colons. For example, if you wanted to specify that the user is limited to 100MB (102,400KB) of disk space on server Rigel's DATA: volume, you would specify .RIGEL_DATA.EAST.XYZCorp:102400 in the field used in your data file to represent the desired space restriction.

A sample control file might look like this:

```
IMPORT CONTROL
    Import Mode=U
    User Template=N
    Name Context=.East.XYZCorp
    Delete Property=#Del
```

```
FIELDS
        Name
        Given Name
        Surname
        Full Name
        Telephone Number
```

This control file, named **UPDATE.CTL** (you can call the file anything you want), specifies the following options:

- ▶ Update existing users; do not create new ones.
- ▶ Do not apply the **User Template** object's values for these users.
- ▶ The context the users exist in is **East.XYZCorp**.
- ▶ Fields filled in with **#DEL** should be deleted.
- ▶ Values in the data field are delimited by a comma (which is the default separator).
- ▶ The data file contains the fields Name, Given Name, Surname, Full Name, and Telephone Number.

The data file must then be constructed. To do this, you can use a database program that outputs comma-delimited files (sometimes referred to as comma-separated variable [CSV] text files) or you can create the file by using your favorite text editor.

The fields need to appear in the order specified and need to all be present. The file can contain as many records as you need to update, although with larger files it may be desirable to break the operation into smaller pieces.

For the discussion here, the data file is named **UPDATE.DAT** and contains the following records:

```
"JHenderson","Jim","Henderson","Jim Henderson","801-555-1234"
"PKuo","Peter","Kuo","Peter Kuo","907-555-5678"
"TestUser","Test","User","Temporary Test User","#DEL"
"JimH","Jim","Henderson","Jim Henderson (Admin)","801-555-1234"
"PeterK","Peter","Kuo","Peter Kuo (Admin)","907-555-5678"
```

When you are ready to invoke Uimport, use the following command:

```
UIMPORT UPDATE.CTL UPDATE.DAT /C
```

The **/C** parameter tells UImport not to pause on every screen of information.

TIP

You can use UImport to manipulate users in multiple contexts. The easiest way to do this is to specify the full DN of the user with a leading period in the Name field (for example, `.JimH.Admin.XYZCorp`**).**

Given that it is a legacy utility, UImport has a number of limitations, including the following:

▶ It does not support schema extensions (such as GroupWise) made to User objects, including auxiliary classes.

▶ The password it sets is only the DS password. Other password types, such as simple password, GroupWise password, or Universal Password, are not supported.

▶ Home directory names are limited to the 8.3 DOS format.

TIP

You can work around some of UImport's limitations by using the Import Conversion Export (ICE) utility instead (see the section "The LDAP ICE Utility," later in this chapter). However, an excellent replacement is JRBImprt, which is part of the JRB utilities (see the "JRB Utilities" section, later in this chapter).

The next section looks at the second-most-underutilized tool included with NetWare: NList. Chapter 10, "Programming for eDirectory," offers some advanced techniques for building a data file by using output from NList.

The NList Utility

The 16-bit NList command-line utility provided with NetWare 4 and above is an extremely powerful tool for examining information in a DS tree. Its power, however, is masked by a fairly complex command-line interface. As with UImport, the NList utility is not used by many administrators because it takes time to learn, and the output can take a significant amount of time to interpret.

The NList command line consists of three parts:

▶ The object class to list, with an optional value to look for

▶ An optional "where" component, used to filter requests

▶ An optional "show" component, used to select fields to display

In addition to these components, several switches are used to modify the output of the NList command. The first of these components is the object class component. Whenever you use NList, you must specify a single class to find information on. The classname used is the name found in the DS schema; you can look it up by using DSBrowse, NDS iMonitor, or the Schema Manager component of ConsoleOne.

You can also limit the object class component by specifying that the name be equal to a single value. The value can include wildcards. For example, to look for only users starting with *J*, this would be the format of the NLIST command:

```
NLIST USER = J*
```

This would provide a list of all users whose login name starts with the letter *J*. Because DS object names are not case-sensitive, specifying *J** as the value is the same as specifying *j**.

TIP

If you don't know the name of the class, you can list all classes by specifying the * wildcard character in place of a classname. This shows you all objects, regardless of class. You can limit NList when using it in this way by specifying an object name, in the format NLIST * = *objectname*. This produces a listing showing the object and its class.

The second piece of the NList command line, the optional where component, lets you limit the scope based on an attribute value defined for the object. If the attribute does not fit the values searched for by the where component, the object will not be displayed.

NOTE

Some values, particularly date and time values, are difficult to perform numeric comparisons against. If you want to limit the scope based on a date, you may need to experiment a bit with the value. In cases such as this, it might make more sense to use techniques described in Chapter 7 (such as using the ODBC driver for eDirectory) to build a data file and then use an external program, such as Microsoft Excel, to filter the data more effectively.

If you wanted to list all users whose login name starts with the letter *J*, but only if the last name starts with *H*, you would use the following command:

```
NLIST USER = J* WHERE SURNAME = H*
```

There must be a space after the attribute name (SURNAME**, in this example), or NList will display a syntax error message.**

As with the object class scope, wildcard characters are supported in the where component of the command.

If the classname or attribute name includes one or more spaces, you need to enclose the name in quotation marks. For example, if you are looking for a print queue, you need to use NLIST "PRINT QUEUE" **and not** NLIST PRINT QUEUE.

A number of comparison operators can be used in the where component of the query. Table 12.4 lists them.

Comparison Operators for the Where Component of an NList Command

TABLE 12.4

COMPARISON OPERATOR DEFINITION

EQ	Equal to; can use = instead
NE	Not equal to
LT	Less than
LE	Less than or equal to
GT	Greater than
GE	Greater than or equal to
EXISTS	Exists (that is, a value is present)
NEXISTS	Does not exist (that is, a value is not present)

The only comparison that can use a numeric equivalent is testing for equality. The greater than (>) and less than (<) operators are used by the operating system to pipe information either from a file or to a file in a command prompt session.

NOTE

When you're testing numeric values, the use of comparisons is very straight-forward; however, when you're comparing other values, such as dates or string values, the comparison becomes a bit more difficult to determine. For example, if you execute this command:

```
NLIST USER SHOW "Last Login Time"
```

the information presented includes a date and time in the format *hh:mm:ss* [*am¦pm*] *mm-dd-yyyy*. However, using this format in a where clause results in the error message "NLIST-4.22-130: Dates prior to 1980 are invalid". After a bit of experimentation, you find that performing a comparison on this attribute requires just a date value—a time value will not be accepted. Thus the following command:

```
NLIST USER WHERE "Last Login Time" GE "8:00:00 am 2-5-1999"
```

results in an error message, but this command:

```
NLIST USER WHERE "Last Login Time" GE "2-5-1999"
```

generates a listing of desired users. You can obtain the last login times of these users by appending the show component to the command, as illustrated here:

```
f:\>nlist user where "last login time" ge "1-1-2004"
➥ show "last login time"
Object Class: User
Current context: Admin.XYZCorp
User: admin
        Last Login Time: 01:55:08 am 03/28/04
One User object was found in this context.

One User object was found.
```

Conversely, string comparisons cannot use the **LT**, **LE**, **GE**, or **GE** comparison operators. Strings can only be checked for existence (**EXISTS**) or nonexistence (**NEXISTS**) and for equality (**EQ**) or inequality (**NEQ**).

Thus this command:

```
NLIST USER WHERE SURNAME GE HE
```

is invalid, but this command:

```
NLIST USER WHERE SURNAME EQ H*
```

returns a list of all users where the surname attribute starts with the letter *H*.

The last of the primary sections of the NList command line is the show section. This section determines which attribute values should be displayed in the output. This section is optional, and if it is omitted, the listing will include the object name and other general field values, depending on the class of object being listed.

If a show directive appears on the NList command line, the list of attributes following the directive is displayed in the output. The list can be comma delimited or not, but any attribute that includes a space must be enclosed in quotation marks.

TIP

The help displayed with the command NLIST /? D **shows that commas are required; however, if you have a long list of attributes to display, including the quotes can create problems with the length of the command. Omitting commas may free up enough space to include additional information you want to include.**

After the three main NList command line sections are entered, you might want to use a few command-line switches. The first is the /S switch, which is used to search the entire subtree. This is useful if you want to include information on all users from a particular context down.

The /C parameter tells NList not to pause output at the screen boundaries and wait for user intervention. This is useful if you want to just scan the information visually and pause the output or if you want to use your own paging program—such as MORE.COM. When you're redirecting the output to a file, this parameter is not needed.

The /CO parameter enables you to specify a start context; when it is used in conjunction with the /S parameter, it enables you to search any subtree. The /R switch is similar to the /CO switch, except that it starts at the [Root] of the tree.

TIP

By default, NList uses the current workstation context. Rather than use the /CO **switch, you can set the context with the** CX **command. This saves you space on the command line and has the same effect as specifying the** /CO **switch in NList.**

The /A switch is used to show active connection or server information. If you want to view just information about users who are currently logged in to the tree, for example, you can specify the /A switch to limit the scope of your query to the users who are logged in.

The /B switch is used to display bindery information. The typical use for this is to display users currently logged in to a particular server. The command NLIST USER /A /B results in the same output as the NetWare 3.x utility USERLIST.EXE. Similarly, the command NLIST SERVER /A /B results in the same type of output as the NetWare 3.x SLIST.EXE program.

The /Tree parameter enables you to list the trees available and optionally select a tree to run the command against. The command **NLIST /TREE** shows all trees available to the workstation.

> **TIP**
>
> As with the /CO switch, you can bypass the /Tree switch by setting the workstation's current tree from Network Neighborhood's NetWare Connections option (in Windows). This is recommended rather than using the /Tree switch to set the current tree because it saves space on the command line for the scope and display parameters.

Specifying /D on the command line displays detailed information about the object; it lists *all* the attributes defined for the object. This can be a useful way of obtaining attribute values for a number of attributes when the command line might otherwise be too long.

Using /N on the command line instructs NList to display just the object name. This is a more minimalist option than specifying no show fields and can speed up output if all you want is a list of the object names.

NList is an extremely powerful utility for reporting on DS information. As demonstrated in Chapter 14, the output from this program is designed to be human-readable but can be easily manipulated into a machine-readable format. After it is converted, it can then be reported on, using various database and spreadsheet programs, and it can be converted into a format that is usable by UImport.

> **TIP**
>
> If you like a GUI-based alternative to NList, refer to the "Wolfgang's Tools" section, later in this chapter, for a discussion about DSReport.

The LDAP ICE Utility

When Novell introduced an LDAP server for NetWare 4.1, a server-based utility called **BULKLOAD.NLM** was included. The function of Bulkload is similar to that of UImport: It allows you to mass-import objects into NDS/eDirectory from a data file that follows that LDAP Data Interchange Format (LDIF) standard. However, Bulkload is a lot more flexible than UImport because it works with all object classes supported by the NDS/eDirectory schema—not just **User** objects, as is the case with UImport.

NOTE

LDIF is defined in RFC 2849 (see `ietf.org/rfc/rfc2849.txt`**).**

As its name implies, Bulkload can only import data into DS and not extract information from the tree. When eDirectory 8.5 was introduced, Bulkload was renamed NDS ICE. This updated implementation allows for exporting data from the tree and migrating data between LDAP servers. The following are some of the features supported by ICE:

▶ Importing data from LDIF files to an LDAP directory

▶ Exporting data from the LDAP directory to an LDIF file

▶ Migrating data between LDAP servers

▶ Performing a schema comparison and update

▶ Loading information into NDS/eDirectory by using a template

▶ Importing schema from `.SCH` files to an LDAP directory

ICE is installed as part of the eDirectory installation. The Unix version is included in the NOVLice package.

ICE manages a collection of *handlers* (that is, special subroutines) that read or write data in a variety of formats. *Source handlers* read data; *destination handlers* write data. A single executable module can be both a source and a destination handler. The engine receives data from a source handler, processes the data, and then passes the data to a destination handler. Table 12.5 shows the supported data format handlers for ICE.

Supported Data Handlers for ICE   **TABLE 12.5**

SOURCE HANDLER	DESTINATION HANDLER
LDIF	LDIF
LDAP	LDAP
DELIM	DELIM
SCH	—
LOAD	—

The **DELIM** source handler is for dealing with comma-delimited files, commonly known as CSV files; **DELIM** can also handle tab-separated data records. The **SCH** handler is used for importing schema files (`*.SCH`) into the tree. The **LOAD** handler is used to generate eDirectory information based on commands in a template file; therefore, the **LOAD** handler is also referred to as the Dirload (directory load) handler in some Novell documentation; ICE uses **LOAD** as the handler name.

SCH and **LOAD** cannot be used as destination handlers.

You can combine different types of source and destination handlers to suit your needs. For instance, if you want to import object information into a tree by using data stored in a CSV file, you can specify the **DELIM** handler as the source handler and the LDAP handler as the destination handler (see Figure 12.8).

FIGURE 12.8
Specifying the source handler.

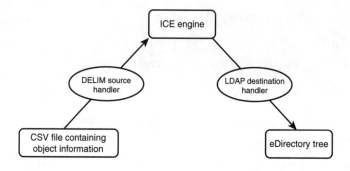

TIP   You cannot use ICE by itself to create user home directories when you're importing user information into the eDirectory tree. However, you can use File System Factory in conjunction with ICE to automatically create home directories.

You can run the ICE utility from the command line, from a snap-in to ConsoleOne, or from the ICE Wizard in Novell iManager. The **DELIM**, **SCH**, and **LOAD** handlers are only available in the command-line version of the utility and in Novell iManager; the ConsoleOne snap-in wizard does not support these options.

NOTE   iManager 2.02 and earlier versions is not able to import a schema file by using the SCH handler; it generates the wrong command-line syntax by including a spurious -a option that is not supported by the SCH handler. The workaround is to use the command-line version of ICE. This defect should be fixed in iManager 2.10 and later.

The following steps illustrate how you can use the ICE Wizard in ConsoleOne to export object information from an eDirectory tree to an LDIF file. This example illustrates the steps of exporting all **User** objects and their associated attributes by using the ICE Wizard, with LDAP as the source data handler and LDIF as the destination data handler:

1. Select NDS Import/Export from the Wizards pull-down menu.

2. Select Export LDIF File and click Next.

3. In the Select Source LDAP Server dialog that appears, fill in the necessary information, such as the IP address of the server and the user's DN and password that will be used for authentication (see Figure 12.9). If you set LDAP to use the default ports (389 and 686), you can leave the Port text box blank. Click Next to continue.

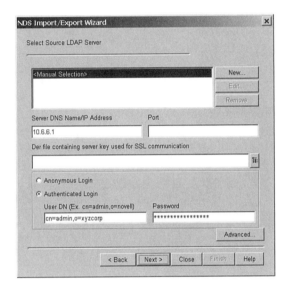

FIGURE 12.9
Providing the necessary information to authenticate to the source LDAP server.

4. In the Set Search Criteria dialog that appears, enter the container from which you want the search to start and select the search scope. If you leave the base DN blank, it will be to [Root]. You can also select the object class to export by using the Filter tab (for instance, to export User objects, you set the filter to objectlcass=user) and select what information about an object is to be exported (see Figure 12.10). Click Next to continue.

5. Enter the LDIF filename, with a path (such as F:\LDIF_FILES\ myfile.ldif) if you like, to be created. You can also use the browse button on the right to select the folder in which the file will be placed. If you don't specify a path, the file will be created in the same directory in which the ICE Wizard module is installed. Click Next to continue.

FIGURE 12.10
Selecting what information about an object is to be exported.

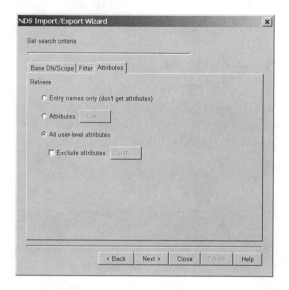

6. Verify the information displayed. If it is correct, click Finish to start processing. Otherwise, click Back and make any necessary changes. A dialog is displayed, showing the processing results (see Figure 12.11).

FIGURE 12.11
The ICE processing summary screen.

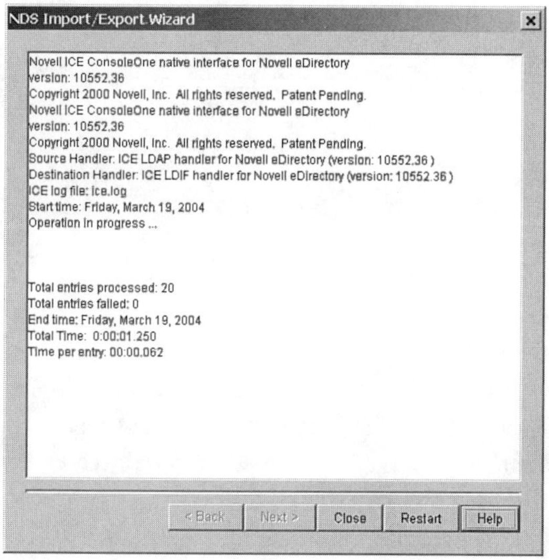

The following is an excerpt from the LDIF file created by using the preceding procedure:

```
#This LDIF file was generated by Novell's ICE and the
#LDIF destination handler.
version: 1


dn: o=XYZCorp
changetype: add
auditFileLink: cn=AFO0_XYZCorp,o=XYZCorp
o: XYZCorp
objectClass: organization
objectClass: ndsLoginProperties
objectClass: ndsContainerLoginProperties
objectClass: top
ACL: 2#entry#o=XYZCorp#loginScript
ACL: 2#entry#o=XYZCorp#printJobConfiguration
ACL: 31#subtree#cn=Admin,ou=IS_Admins,o=XYZCorp#[Entry Rights]
ACL: 47#subtree#cn=Admin,ou=IS_Admins,o=XYZCorp#
➥[All Attributes Rights]
ACL: 1#subtree#cn=Password_Admins,ou=Tree_Admins,ou=Groups,
➥ou=IS_Admins,o=XYZCorp#[Entry Rights]
ACL: 3#subtree#cn=Password_Admins,ou=Tree_Admins,ou=Groups,
➥ou=IS_Admins,o=XYZCorp#[All Attributes Rights]
ACL: 2#entry#o=XYZCorp#auditFileLink


dn: ou=IS_Admins,o=XYZCorp
changetype: add
ou: IS_Admins
objectClass: organizationalUnit
objectClass: ndsLoginProperties
objectClass: ndsContainerLoginProperties
objectClass: top
ACL: 2#entry#ou=IS_Admins,o=XYZCorp#loginScript
ACL: 2#entry#ou=IS_Admins,o=XYZCorp#printJobConfiguration


dn: cn=RootAdmins,ou=Groups,ou=IS_Admins,o=XYZCorp
changetype: add
equivalentToMe: cn=Admin,ou=IS_Admins,o=XYZCorp
objectClass: groupOfNames
objectClass: top
uniqueMember: cn=Admin,ou=IS_Admins,o=XYZCorp
cn: RootAdmins
ACL: 2#entry#[Root]#uniqueMember
```

WARNING   ICE automatically wraps long output lines at 79 characters (which is known as *folding*). The starting position of the second line is indented by one character. This means that if you are to parse the output file for information by using a non–LDIF-aware utility, you need to know about the possible wrapping. When you're using the same LDIF file to import information back into the tree, no editing will be required of these wrapped lines. When the LDIF parser encounters a space at the beginning of a line, it knows to concatenate the rest of the data on that line with the data on the previous line. The leading space is then discarded. This behavior occurs according to RFC 2849, "The LDAP Data Interchange Format (LDIF) - Technical Specification" (see `www.faqs.org/rfcs/rfc2849.html`).

TIP   Some versions of `ldapsearch.exe`, a command-line utility, have a flag that allows long lines to be exported without wrapping. One such implementation can be found in the Mozilla Directory (LDAP) SDK, which you can download for free from `www.mozilla.org/directory`.

To perform the preceding example from a command line, you use the following syntax:

```
ice -S LDAP -s 10.6.6.1 -d cn=admin,o=org -w password
➥ -F objectclass=user -a * -c sub -D LDIF
➥ -f c:\output.ldif
```

NOTE   If you are just importing data from or exporting information to LDIF files, you can also use one of the LDAP tools (such as `ldapadd`, `ldapmodify`, and `ldapsearch`) included with eDirectory instead of using ICE. These tools are installed as part of ConsoleOne. For example, on a NetWare server they can be found in the `SYS:PUBLIC\mgmt\ConsoleOne\1.2\bin` directory.

The Dirload handler is a very powerful tool that you can use when you need to create a test tree and populate it with a large number of objects and for each object to have certain attributes filled in with values. Dirload reads from a source file whose format is very similar to that of LDIF. In the source file, you define the number of objects to create, how the objects should be named, what attributes are to be populated, and how the attribute values will be derived. In essence, the Dirload handler is an LDIF generator that works by using a template file. The following is an example of a Dirload template file:

```
# Comment lines begin with "#" =================================
# Dirload example 1.00
#=============================================================
```

```
# Lines beginning with "!" are control settings:
#  - set the starting value of unique counter value at 300
#  - generate 2 objects using the template
!COUNTER=300
!OBJECTCOUNT=2
#-------------------------------------------------------------
# ATTRIBUTE TEMPLATE
# -------------------------------------------------------------
objectclass: inetorgperson
#
# Pick a randomly select string value from
# the file called "first" and assign it as the given name.
givenname: $R(first)
#
# Pick a randomly select string value from
# the file called "initial" and assign it as the initials.
initials: $R(initial)
#
# Pick a randomly select string value from
# the file called "last" and assign it as the sn.
sn: $R(lastnames)
#
# The cn is derived using the value in givenname plus
#   the first character of the value in initials plus
#   the value in sn
# The context portion of the dn is derived using
#   a randomly selected string value from the file "ou" plus
#   the static string of "ou=test,o=XYZCorp".
#   the file called "first" and assign it as the given name.
#
# CAUTION: DO NOT USE STRING FORMATTING IN $A() FOR ICE
#          INCLUDED WITH EDIR BEFORE 8.7.3. THERE IS A
#          BUG IN THE DIRLOAD HANDLER AND WILL CAUSE
#          SERVER ABENDS!!!
#dn: cn=$A(givenname)$A(initials,%.1s)$A(sn),ou=$R(ou),
➥ou=test,o=XYZCorp
dn: cn=$A(givenname)$A(initials)$A(sn),ou=$R(ou),
➥ou=test,o=XYZCorp
#
# The telephone number is derived using
#   the static string of "1-800-" plus
#   a random three-digit number whose value is between
#   1 and 999 plus a static string of "-" plus
#   a 4-digit number based on the COUNTER control setting
#   (this counter value is incremented every time after
```

```
#   it is used)
telephonenumber: 1-800-$N(1-999,%03d)-$C(%04d)
#
# Pick a randomly select string value from
# the file called "titles" and assign it as the title.
title: $R(titles)
```

WARNING　The $A() option allows you to optionally specify a C-style formatting string to control the string data output. There is a bug in the Dirload handler for all versions of ICE from pre-eDirectory 8.7.3; when the optional formatting string is used, it results in server abends.

The files `first`, `initials`, `last`, `ou`, and `titles` must be located in the same directory as the template file. If those files are located elsewhere, you can specify the path as part of the filename in the `$R()` specification. Here's an example:

```
sn: $R(f:\data_files\lastnames)
```

NOTE　A set of sample `first`, `initials`, **and so on files can be found in ConsoleOne's** `\bin\ice\tables` **directory.**

Each record in the file must be terminated with a line-feed character.

You can process the template file by using this command:

```
ice -S LOAD -f template_filename -D LDIF -f new.ldif
```

(The username and password are not required because you are going from an input file to an output file.) This results in the generation of an LDIF file called `new.ldif` that looks like this:

```
version: 1

dn: cn=JimAHenderson,ou=ds,ou=test,o=XYCorp
changetype: add
objectclass: inetorgperson
givenname: Jim
initials: A
sn: Henderson
telephonenumber: 1-800-123-0300
title: Don't do much
```

```
dn: cn=PeterBKuo,ou=dev,ou=test,o=XYZCorp
changetype: add
objectclass: inetorgperson
givenname: Peter
initials: B
sn: Kuo
telephonenumber: 1-800-015-0301
title: Does nothing either
```

After you verify the data for accuracy, you can use ICE again to import the LDIF file into the tree, using the following command syntax:

```
ice -S LDIF -f new.ldif -D LDAP -s hostname_or_ip
➡-d cn=admin,o=org -w password
```

You can also directly import the data generated by Dirload into the tree without first creating an LDIF file:

```
ice -S LOAD -f template_filename -D LDAP -s hostname_or_ip
➡-d cn=admin,o=org -w password
```

NOTE

Instead of using ICE, you can use NDS iManager by selecting Load File as the file type to be imported. From the eDirectory Maintenance task, you select Import Convert Export Wizard, Next (to import the file on disk), File Type.

You can find an in-depth description of the various command-line options for the different handlers and how the attribute specification works in the Dirload template file in the "Novell Import Conversion Export Utility" section of the eDirectory documentation.

A number of eDirectory management tasks can be performed only by using LDAP-based tools, such as ICE, but not through ConsoleOne or NetWare Administrator. For example, to create and manage dynamic groups and to manage the special [This] and [Self] ACL assignments, you must use an LDAP-based tool.

NOTE

You can use iManager to manage dynamic groups and the two special ACL assignments because iManager uses LDAP functions behind the scenes for these tasks.

Managing Dynamic Groups

Dynamic groups were introduced with eDirectory 8.6.1. Traditionally, a `Group` object's membership is static. That means every time a new member needs to be added or an existing member is removed, you have to manually handle the change. Therefore, these traditional groups are also known as *static groups*. A dynamic group, on the other hand, uses an LDAP URL to populate its `Member` attribute at the time the attribute is accessed. This LDAP URL is a search filter that assigns all objects, not just users, matching the search criteria to its membership list.

> **NOTE** The format of the LDAP URL is specified in RFC 2255 (see www.ietf.org/rfc/rfc2255.txt). The search filter used within the URL is described in RFC 2254 (see www.ietf.org/rfc/rfc2254.txt).

For example, you can create a dynamic group that automatically includes any object whose `OU` attribute (`Department`, as shown in ConsoleOne or NetWare Administrator) value is `Sales`. If you apply a search filter for `OU=Sales`, the search returns a group that includes all object DNs containing the attribute value `OU=Sales`. Any object added to the tree that matches the `OU=Sales` criterion is automatically added to the group. Any object whose `OU` attribute value is changed from `Sales` to another value (or is removed from the tree) is automatically removed from the group.

> **TIP** Generally speaking, group members are `User` objects, but because any object matching the LDAP URL search criterion becomes a member of the dynamic group, you need to take care when constructing the search filter. You should either select an attribute that is populated only for `User` objects or take note when filling in values for attributes that are common to both `User` objects and other object classes. Alternatively, you can use the `excludedMember` attribute of the dynamic group object to block undesired objects from showing up in the membership listing. Note that `excludedMember` applies only to dynamic members.

> **NOTE** If a container (such as an OU) becomes a dynamic member of a dynamic group, *none* of its subordinate objects (including any `User` objects) will gain any rights associated with the dynamic group. The same is true for `Group` objects and their members.

At a glance, it seems that one should convert all static groups to dynamic groups because they offer low management overhead, especially for sites that have many `Group` objects in the tree. Although there are many advantages of dynamic groups, there are also limitations, and there is merit in carefully weighing which type to use. The advantages of dynamic groups can be summarized as follows:

▶ **Object references**—You can create or delete `User` objects without having to touch all the groups that the object is a member of. This is particularly useful in the case of nonlocal members, where the overhead of external references, backlinks, and so on can be avoided. Groups can be created before the objects specified by the membership criterion are created.

▶ **Smaller DIB size**—Because the dynamic members are not stored in the DIB (because they are "calculated" every time the group object is queried), dynamic groups consume less storage when large member lists are involved.

▶ **Faster synchronization**—During synchronization, only the search filter—rather than all the individual members—needs to be transferred.

▶ **Centralized query**—Often, client applications perform a "canned," or predefined, query to obtain a list of objects. But what happens if that query ever needs to be changed? Rather than updating and distributing new client applications, a dynamic group can be employed. The client applications can use the dynamic group as the query; thus you can change it frequently without having to touch the client software.

The following are some of the disadvantages of dynamic groups:

▶ **Referential integrity**—The search filter holds the DN of the base of the search. Currently, this DN is not protected by referential integrity. Thus, moving, deleting, or renaming such an object can stop the dynamic groups using it from working.

▶ **Performance**—Because a query must take place every time, dynamic group operations occur more slowly than static group operations. Be aware that reading the membership list will cause a full search to occur, whereas comparing a specific DN to the membership list will only compare that object to the filter.

▶ **Lack of security-related attributes**—As discussed in the "Group Membership Recovery" section of Chapter 11, "Examples from the Real World," four changes in the DS are made when a user is added to a static group. The `Group` object's `Member` and `Equivalent to Me` attributes are populated with the User object's DN, and the User object's Group Membership and Security Equals properties are populated with the Group object's DN. Dynamic members do *not* have these assignments. As a result, the NetWare file systems and bindery are not aware of dynamic group members and thus do not recognize dynamic members when calculating access control information.

▶ **Application support**—Not all applications are dynamic group aware, and thus you need to maintain static groups for certain applications.

▶ **LDAP-only administration**—Due to lack of a snap-in at the time of this writing, ConsoleOne and NetWare Administrator are not aware of dynamic groups; therefore, dynamic group objects cannot be managed by using these tools.

TIP

If you plan to implement dynamic groups, it is best to upgrade your eDirectory to version 8.7 or higher and use the latest version of iManager. eDirectory 8.7 has optimized the "is member of" functionality. In eDirectory 8.7, the value in the GUID attribute of the entry that is being used in the search is attached to the search criteria. This is an indexed value, and it results in a significantly faster search when you're doing an "is member of" or ACL search. On the other hand, if the dynamic group is performing a member list query, the search will not be much faster.

At the time of this writing, there is no ConsoleOne or NetWare Administrator snap-in for dynamic groups. Therefore, dynamic group objects show up as unmanageable objects in ConsoleOne and NetWare Administrator. Although you can view the dynamic group membership list by using ConsoleOne (but not by using NetWare Administrator), you must create or update the membership information via LDAP. These are the general steps you need to take to create and configure a dynamic group:

1. Create the dynamic group object.

2. Populate the memberQuery attribute of the dynamic group object. (This is a required step.)

3. Populate the dgIdentity attribute of the dynamic group. Ensure that the object specified has Read and Compare rights to the attributes specified in memberQuery. If a dgIdentity attribute is not specified, ensure that [Public] has Read and Compare rights to the attributes specified in memberQuery.

4. Assign a special ACL attribute with LDAP to each of the resources being managed. Because unlike static groups, dynamic members are not security equivalent to a dynamic group, you need to add a special flag to any ACL that points to a dynamic group. This way, when a user tries to perform some privileged operation on the resource object, eDirectory will know that it must check to see whether the user is a member of the dynamic group as opposed to checking the user's security equivalences. This "special flag plus standard ACL" combination is known as *dynamic ACL*.

NOTE

You can also convert an existing static group to a dynamic group. The procedure to do so is described later in this section.

Before we present two examples, one on creating a dynamic group and one on converting a static group to a dynamic group, we need to first cover some of the LDIF attribute syntaxes and properties required to create and manage dynamic group objects. The search criterion for the members is specified by the attribute memberQuery. Other optional attributes that are used by the dynamic group object are excludedMember, dgIdentity, dgAllowUnknown, dgTimeout, and dgAllowDuplicates (see Figure 12.12). To see these attributes on a Windows server, you can use DSBrowse. You select Tree View, Schema Tree, Schema Root, Class Definitions, Dynamic Group, Attributes.

NOTE

Much of the Novell documentation uses the attribute name memberQueryURL. What the documentation does not tell you is that this is the LDAP attribute name and not the eDirectory attribute name. The eDirectory schema name for this attribute is memberQuery. Therefore, when you're looking for this attribute using NDS iMonitor or DSBrowse, for instance, you should look for memberQuery and not memberQueryURL.

The dgAllowDuplicates attribute indicates whether or not duplicates will be found in the member list. Duplicates may occur if an object is found in the search result of the memberQuery attribute, as well as the Member attribute. If dgAllowDuplicates is FALSE (which is the default setting), the server will eliminate the duplicates from the listing. By allowing duplicates, you can reduce the load on the server while listing dynamic group members, at the cost of having to deal with possible redundant data in the result.

This allows the dynamic group object to have a password

FIGURE 12.12
The schema defi-
nition of the
`dynamicGroup`
class.

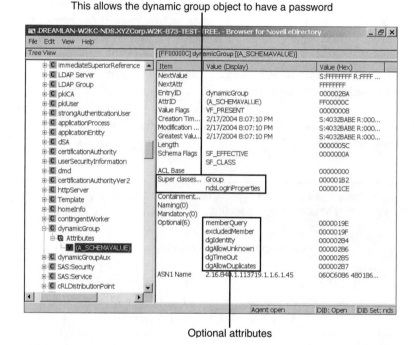

Optional attributes

The `dgAllowUnknown` attribute is a Boolean attribute that determines the behavior when the dynamic group members are not fully expandable for some reason. It determines the inclusion or exclusion of members in the dynamic group when the membership cannot be correctly ascertained. For example, if the search specified by `memberQuery` cannot fully complete because one of the replicas is not accessible, if `dgAllowUnknown` is set to `TRUE`, the object in question will be considered to be a member of the dynamic group. This is also true for dynamic ACL rights computations, and it therefore must be used carefully. In short, unless the implications of setting `dgAllowUnknown` to `TRUE` are fully understood, you should always leave it unset or set it to `FALSE` (which is the default).

The `dgIdentity` attribute holds the DN of the object that the dynamic group will use for authentication while searching. The server decides the identity to be used for a dynamic group object as follows:

▶ If there is a `dgIdentity` attribute set on the dynamic group object, the DN specified in the `dgIdentity` attribute will be used as the identity for the dynamic member search.

▶ If the `dgIdentity` attribute is not present but the dynamic group object has a password, the dynamic group itself will be used as the identity for dynamic member search.

▶ If neither the `dgIdentity` attribute nor the password is present, the search for dynamic members will be done as [`Public`] (the anonymous user).

TIP

You can set a password for the dynamic group object by using an LDIF file similar to the following example:

```
version: 1

dn: cn=dynamic_group,ou=org_unit,o=org
changetype: add
userpassword: 12345
```

Or you can use `setpword` **from JRButils to set the password (see the "JRB Utilities" section, later in this chapter).**

The object specified by `dgIdentity` should have the necessary rights to do the search specified in the `memberQuery` attribute. For example, if the `memberQuery` value is `ldap:///o=XYZCorp??sub?(title=*)`, the object specified by `dgIdentity`, the dynamic group object itself, or [`Public`] should have Read and Compare rights on the attribute `Title` below the container O=XYZCorp. If you are to use [`Public`], you should ensure that you have granted Read and Compare rights to the attribute(s) used in the search filter.

In order for the dynamic member evaluation to work correctly, the object specified by the `dgIdentity` attribute must be present on the same partition as the dynamic group object. The `dgIdentity` attribute has the schema flag `DS_WRITE_MANAGED` set. This means that you can specify an object as the `dgIdentity` attribute of a dynamic group only if it has administrative rights on that object.

The `dgTimeout` attribute is an integer that specifies the maximum duration a server can take, in seconds, to read or compare a member attribute before it times out. When the server exceeds this `dgTimeout` value, the search is terminated and any members found before the search is terminated are included in the list. At the same time, the -6016 error (`ERR_RETURNING_PARTIAL_RESULTS`) is returned, to indicate that the list may be incomplete. The default is zero, meaning that the search can take as long as is required.

The `excludedMember` attribute holds the DNs that are specifically excluded from the membership list of the dynamic group. You can use this information to construct exclusion lists for dynamic groups. `excludedMember` can only be used to exclude DNs from being dynamic members of a dynamic group. Thus, a DN is a dynamic member of a dynamic group only if it is selected by the member criteria specified by `memberQuery` and is not listed in `excludedMember` or explicitly added to the `Member` attribute.

The `Member` attribute of a dynamic group object lists—but does not store—all objects in the group; the exception is if a DN is explicitly added to the `Member` attribute. Rights assignments made to the `Group` object apply to all members of that group. Adding values to the `Member` attribute of a dynamic group adds them as static members. You can do this for specific inclusion of members.

> **NOTE**
>
> The LDAP server maps both the `member` and the `uniqueMember` **LDAP attribute names to the** `Member` **attribute in eDirectory.**

> **NOTE**
>
> Static members added via LDAP do *not* have their `Group Membership` **and** `Security Equal To` **attributes populated. If static members are added via one of the standard management tools, such as ConsoleOne, the dynamic group object's** `Member` **and** `Equivalent To Me` **attributes are populated with the** `User` **object's DN, and the** `User` **object's** `Group Membership` **and** `Security Equals` **properties are populated with the dynamic group object's DN.**

There are a number of ways to determine what are the static members in a dynamic group. You can use NDS iMonitor to view the `Member` attribute of the dynamic group object and the DNs that have a timestamp associated with static members (see Figure 12.13). Another method is to use DSBrowse to examine the values of the `Member` attribute of the dynamic group object. `Member` is a multivalued attribute, and each static member's DN is stored as a value; you will also find a value that is "`(** Unknown)`" (see Figure 12.14), and its `Creation Time Stamp` attribute is the same as that of the dynamic group object's. This value is a placeholder for dynamic members.

If you have extended your schema by using the `dgstatic.sch` schema file, you will have an additional optional attribute for the dynamic group: `staticMember`. As the name implies, the `staticMember` attribute keeps track of the static members of a dynamic group.

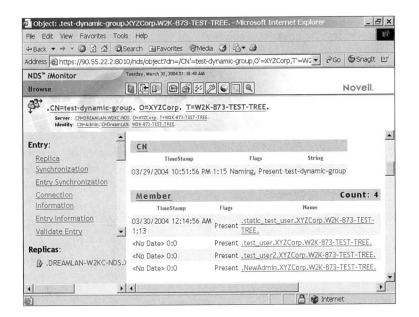

FIGURE 12.13
Static members'
timestamps,
which indicates
when they were
added.

Other Member values contain static members

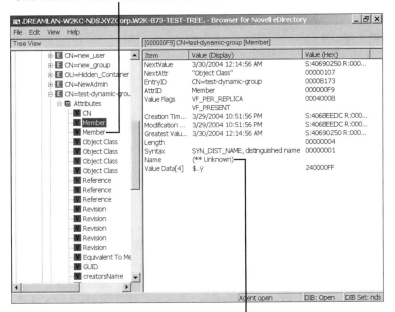

FIGURE 12.14
Checking for
static members
by using
DSBrowse.

Placeholder for dynamic members

The `staticMember` attribute is *not* populated statically. Rather, its value is dynamic and is determined when you query it via LDAP. This means that if you look at the dynamic group object by using ConsoleOne or DSBrowse, there is no `staticMember` attribute listed. When querying via LDAP, you have to ask for it explicitly—that is, query for all attributes (that is, using * for attributes will *not* show `staticMember`)—as illustrated here:

```
ldapsearch -h hostname_or_ip -b o=xyzcorp -D cn=admin,o=xyzcorp
➥ -w password cn=test-dynamic-group-2 staticmember

dn: cn=test-dynamic-group-2,o=XYZCorp
staticmember: cn=static_test_user2,o=XYZCorp
```

The `memberQuery` attribute defines the set of rules that match the group members' attributes. The rules are specified in the form of an LDAP URL format, as specified in RFC 2255, and consist of the following components:

```
ldap://hostname:port/<baseDN>?<attrlist>?<scope>
➥?<search filter>[?<extensions>]
```

hostname, *port*, and *attrlist* have no effect on dynamic groups because the query runs on the local server and the search is based on the search filter. Hence, the general format of the `memberQuery` attribute is as follows:

```
ldap:///<base dn>??<scope>?<search filter>[?x-chain]
```

<base dn> specifies the starting context for the search. If it is not specified, [Root] is assumed. *<scope>* indicates how the search will be performed and can be one of three values: *base* (only search the base DN), *one* (search the direct subordinates of the base DN—the base DN itself is not searched), and *sub* (search the base DN and all objects in the subtree below). The default value is *base*. *<search filter>* is described in RFC 2254, and the default value is `objectclass=*`. At the time of this writing, x-chain is the only

supported extension. If this option is specified, the search for dynamic members will chain across multiple servers. Otherwise, the search will be limited to what is in the local DIB. Depending on your network configuration and tree structure, chaining across servers can be a lengthy process; thus, the default is not to x-chain.

If a dynamic group object does not have a `memberQuery` **attribute, the group will not have any dynamic members.**

WARNING

Although `memberQuery` is a multivalued attribute according to its schema definition, eDirectory 8.6.1 through 8.7.2 servers use only the first value of `memberQuery`. For example, if there are two `memberQuery` values:

```
ldap:///o=org1??sub?cn=*
ldap:///o=org2??sub?cn=*
```

eDirectory 8.6.1 through 8.7.2 servers will only use `ldap:///` `o=org1??sub?cn=*` to compute the members of the group. They will accept more than one value, but they act on only the first query. This limitation is overcome in eDirectory 8.7.3, which computes the members based on all the `memberQuery` values, and the set of members is the union of the members computed using each of the `memberQuery` values. For the preceding example, an eDirectory 8.7.3 server will show all entries under **O=org1** and **O=org2** that have **CN** values as dynamic members.

Because the search filter in the `memberQuery` attribute is the same as that described in RFC 2254, the search criteria can be based on a number of different attributes that are AND'ed or OR'ed together. For instance, the filter (¦(title=manager)(L=Utah)) specifies that any object that has a **Title** attribute value of **manager** or an **L** (location) attribute value of **Utah** will be considered a possible dynamic member (subject to any restriction posed by `excludedMember`). The type of attributes you can use in the search filter, however, is limited based on the attributes' value syntaxes. The following are the syntax types that are allowed in the search filter:

SYN_BOOLEAN	SYN_CE_STRING
SYN_CI_LIST	SYN_CI_STRING
SYN_CLASS_NAME	SYN_COUNTER
SYN_DIST_NAME	SYN_EMAIL_ADDRESS
SYN_FAX_NUMBER	SYN_INTEGER
SYN_INTERVAL	SYN_NU_STRING

```
SYN_PO_ADDRESS          SYN_PR_STRING

SYN_TEL_NUMBER          SYN_TIME
```

For eDirectory 8.7.3 and above, three additional syntax types are supported: `SYN_PATH`, `SYN_TIMESTAMP`, and `SYN_TYPED_NAME`.

TIP

If you are unsure of the syntax used by the attribute you want to use in the search filter, refer to Table C.2 in Appendix C, "eDirectory Classes, Objects, and Attributes." For a discussion about the various syntax types, refer to Table 2.2 in Chapter 2, "eDirectory Basics."

NOTE

Case-sensitivity of the search filter values depends on the attributes used. The syntax may be `SYN_CI_STRING` **(which is not case-sensitive) or** `SYN_CE_STRING` **(which is case-sensitive).**

The following example illustrates the steps necessary to create a dynamic group called `CN=DynamicGroup.OU=ISstaff.O=XYZCorp`. This group will consist of one static member, `CN=Tasha.OU=ISstaff.O=XYZCorp`, and all users in the `OU=ISstaff.O=XYZCorp` container that have `Sales Support` as their `Title` attribute value. The dynamic group will perform the LDAP queries as the Admin user. The dynamic group will be granted rights to the `OU=Sales.O=XYZCorp` container:

1. Create an LDIF file to add a dynamic group to the tree, and call it `dyngrp.ldif`. It should look as follows:

   ```
   version: 1

   dn: cn=DynamicGroup,ou=ISstaff,o=XYZCorp
   changetype: add
   cn: DynamicGroup
   objectclass: dynamicGroup
   memberQueryURL: ldap:///ou=ISstaff,o=XYZCorp??sub
   ➥?(title=Sales Support)
   member: cn=tasha,ou=ISstaff,o=XYZCorp
   dgIdentity: cn=admin,o=XYZCorp
   ```

2. Use ICE or one of the other LDAP tools, such as `ldapadd`, to import the contents of the LDIF file into the tree:

   ```
   ice -S LDIF -f dyngrp.ldif -D LDAP -s hostname_or_ip
   ➥ -d cn=admin,o=org -w password
   ```

3. After the dynamic group is created, add a special ACL to the resource(s) the dynamic group is going to manage. In this example, **DynamicGroup** and the static member **Tasha** will be granted rights to the **OU=Sales.O=XYZCorp** container. To accomplish this, you need to add a dynamic ACL to the attributes that are to be managed. The following LDIF file, called **addacl.ldif**, will grant **CN=DynamicGroup,OU=ISstaff,O=XYZCorp** Browse rights to **[Entry Rights]** and Read and Compare rights to **[All Attributes Rights]** of the **OU=Sales.O=XYZCorp** container:

```
version: 1

dn: ou=Sales,o=XYZCorp
changetype: modify
add: acl
acl: 536870913#entry#cn=DynamicGroup,ou=ISstaff,o=XYZCorp
➥#[Entry Rights]
acl: 536870915#entry#cn=DynamicGroup,ou=ISstaff,o=XYZCorp
➥#[All Attributes Rights]
```

See the "Dynamic ACL Rights Calculation" sidebar for information on how the values in the ACL entries are derived.

4. Use ICE or one of the other LDAP tools, such as **ldapmodify**, to update the tree with the content of the LDIF file:

```
ice -S LDIF -f addacl.ldif -D LDAP -s hostname_or_ip
➥ -d cn=admin,o=org -w password
```

You can combine the contents of the two LDIF files into one LDIF file and import it into the tree in one step if you want.

Dynamic ACL Rights Calculation

REAL WORLD

The dynamic ACL is calculated by setting the privilege bit 0x20000000 along with the value with the other privileges being set. This is done by bit-wise OR'ing (or adding) 536870912 (which is 0x20000000) to the numeric value of the other privileges. For instance, to grant a dynamic ACL of Read and Compare, the value is determined as follows:

```
Attribute privileges required = Read + Compare = 2 + 1 = 3
Dynamic ACL value = 536870912
Dynamic attribute privileges = 3 + 536870912 = 536870915
```

The following table shows which privilege bits are used to specify each privilege for a dynamic ACL:

REQUIRED RIGHT	NORMAL ACL PERMISSION	DYNAMIC ACL PERMISSION
ENTRY RIGHTS		
Browse	1 (0x1)	536870913 (0x20000001)
Add	2 (0x2)	536870914 (0x20000002)
Delete	4 (0x4)	536870916 (0x20000004)
Rename	8 (0x8)	536870920 (0x20000008)
Supervisor	16 (0x10)	536870928 (0x20000010)
ATTRIBUTES RIGHTS		
Compare	1 (0x1)	536870913 (0x20000001)
Read	2 (0x2)	536870914 (0x20000002)
Write	4 (0x4)	536870916 (0x20000004)
Add Self	8 (0x8)	536870920 (0x20000008)
Supervisor	32 (0x20)	536870944 (0x20000020)

If you assign a dynamic group as a trustee and don't add the dynamic ACL bit setting, only the static members of the dynamic group that are added by non-LDAP means will be able to inherit those privileges due to the Security Equals relationship.

You can also use the Create Dynamic Group task under the Dynamic Group role in iManager. To do this, you specify Dynamic Group, Create Dynamic Group and then specify the group name and its context. Then you click OK and then select Modify to specify the additional attributes. If you are using the dynamic group object itself for the `dgIdentity` attribute value, you can set its password by using the Set Password task under the Help Desk role.

The procedure to upgrade existing static groups to dynamic groups is similar to the process for creating a dynamic group detailed earlier. Two main differences are that you need to add an auxiliary class to the static group and you need to upgrade the existing ACL assignments to include the dynamic ACL bit setting. The following are the steps to upgrade an existing static group to a dynamic group:

1. Add the `dynamicGroupAux` object class and any required dynamic group object attributes (such as `dgIdentity` and `memberQuery`) to the existing `Group` object.

2. Populate the `memberQuery` attribute of the dynamic group object. (This is a required step.)

3. Populate the `dgIdentity` attribute of the dynamic group. Ensure that the object specified has Read and Compare rights to the attributes specified in `memberQuery`. If a `dgIdentity` attribute is not specified, ensure that `[Public]` has Read and Compare rights to the attributes specified in `memberQuery`.

4. Update the existing ACL assignments by adding the special ACL flag to each assignment with LDAP.

The following example illustrates the steps necessary to convert a static group called `CN=StaticGroup.OU=ISstaff.O=XYZCorp` to a dynamic group. This group consists of all users in the `OU=ISstaff.O=XYZCorp` container that have `Sales Support` as their `Title` attribute value. The dynamic group will perform the LDAP queries as the Admin user:

1. Create an LDIF file, called `upgrade2dyngrp.ldif`, to add the `dynamicGroupAux` class to the static `Group` object. It should look as follows:

```
version: 1

dn: cn=StaticGroup,ou=ISstaff,o=XYZCorp
changetype: modify
add: objectclass
objectclass: dynamicGroup
-
add: memberQueryURL
memberQueryURL: ldap:///ou=ISstaff,o=XYZCorp??sub
➡?(title=Sales Support)
-
addd:dgIdentity
dgIdentity: cn=admin,o=XYZCorp
```

2. Use ICE or one of the other LDAP tools, such as `ldapmodify`, to import the contents of the LDIF file into the tree:

```
ice -S LDIF -f upgrade2dyngrp.ldif -D LDAP -s
hostname_or_ip
➡ -d cn=admin,o=org -w password
```

NOTE   **You can use ConsoleOne to add the** `dynamicGroupAux` **auxiliary class to the existing** `Group` **object by right-clicking the object, selecting Extensions of This Object, and clicking Add Extension. However, you still have to use LDAP to add the other attributes.**

3. After the static group has been upgraded, update the existing ACL assignments with the dynamic ACL flag. Use ICE or `ldapsearch` to export the object's ACL assignment:

```
ldapsearch -h hostname_or_ip -D cn=admin,o=org -w password
➥ -s base -b ou=org_unit,o=org objectclass=* acl
➥ > acl.ldif
```

or

```
ice -S LDAP -s hostname_or_ip -d cn=admin,o=org -w
password
➥ -c base -b ou=org_unit,o=org -F "objectclass=*"
➥ -a acl -D LDIF -f acl.ldif
```

This example assumes that the ACLs of interest are in the specified container only.

4. Add the dynamic ACL flag value to the existing ACL values (using the information listed in the "Dynamic ACL Rights Calculation" sidebar) to get the new dynamic ACL values. Update `acl.ldif` with these new values.

5. Use ICE or one of the other LDAP tools, such as `ldapmodify`, to update the tree with the content of the modified LDIF file, `acl.ldif`:

```
ice -S LDIF -f acl.ldif -D LDAP -s hostname_or_ip
➥ -d cn=admin,o=org -w password
```

You can also accomplish this task by using the Create Extended Object task under the Dynamic Group role in iManager (see Figure 12.15). To do this, you select Dynamic Group, Create Extended Object and then specify the object you want to add the `dynamicGroupAux` auxiliary class to. Then you click OK and select Modify to specify the additional attributes. If you are using the dynamic group object itself for the `dgIdentity` attribute value, you can set its password by using the Set Password task under the Help Desk role.

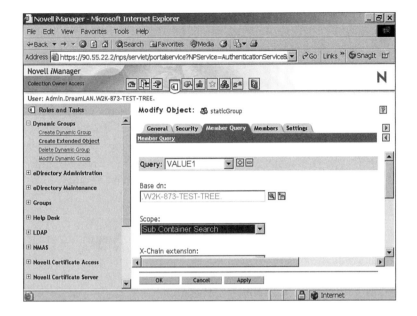

FIGURE 12.15
Upgrading a static group by using iManager.

Managing Special ACL Assignments

One of the features most often asked about by NDS/eDirectory administrators is the option to quickly and easily give users the ability to modify certain attributes in their own user objects. For instance, instead of having to have the administrator or the help desk update a user's `Telephone Number` attribute in DS, they want to grant the users the ability to manage that information. To address this need, eDirectory 8.6 and higher introduced two new special ACL "trustees": `[Self]` and `[This]`.

NOTE

A product called eGuide is included with eDirectory. This is a Web-based application that allows users to look up other users' information, such as telephone number, and to manage their own information (for the attributes that you have granted them rights to). The eGuide product can be found on the eDirectory Web Applications CD or, in the case of NetWare, it is located on the Products CD. You can also download eGuide from `http://download.novell.com`.

As an example, you can grant Read, Compare, and Write rights for each user to that user's own `Telephone Number` attribute. When you have many `User` objects in the tree, however, this becomes a very tedious process. Also, you need to remember to do this for each new `User` object created. You could instead use an LDIF file similar to the following Read, Compare, and Write rights to the `Telephone Number` attribute:

```
version: 1

dn: cn=user1,ou=department1,o=XYZCorp
changetype: modify
add: ACL
ACL: 7#entry#cn=user1,ou=department1,o=XYZCorp#telephoneNumber
```

If you have a lot of users to modify, it might be easier to first generate a list
of users by using NList and then use a script to parse the output and generate the necessary LDIF file. Listing 12.1 shows a sample of NList output,
and Listing 12.2 is a sample awk script that converts the NList data to an
LDIF file, which is shown in Listing 12.3.

Listing 12.1   An NList Listing of All Users in a Specific Context

```
F:\>nlist user
Object Class: User
Current context: Department1.XYXCorp
User name=The name of the user
Dis      =Login disabled
Log exp  =The login expiration date, 0 if no expiration date
Pwd      =Yes if passwords are required
Pwd exp  =The password expiration date, 0 if no expiration date
Uni      =Yes if unique passwords are required
Min      =The minimum password length, 0 if no minimum


User Name                  Dis  Log Exp Pwd  Pwd Exp Uni Min
- - - - - - - - - - - - - - - - - - - - - - - - - - - - - - -
admin                      No   00/00/00 No  00/00/00 No   0
Peter                      No   00/00/00 No  00/00/00 No   0
test_user                  No   00/00/00 No  00/00/00 No   0
Proxy_user                 No   00/00/00 No  00/00/00 No   0
A total of 4 User objects was found in this context.

A total of 4 User objects was found.
```

Listing 12.2   An awk Script That Converts the NList User Listing from Listing 12.1 to an LDIF File

```
BEGIN { flag = 0
        printf("version: 1\n\n");
}
```

```
/Current context:/ { cx = $0
                     gsub("Current context:", "", cx)
                     gsub(" ", "", cx)
}


# No more user information, unset flag to stop further
# printing
/A total of / { flag = 0
}


{if (flag == 1) {
    printf("dn: cn=%s", $1)
    # assumes each level of tree is OU and topmost
    # level is O.
    count = split(cx, levels, ".")
    for (x=1; x< count; x++) {
        printf(",ou=%s", levels[x])
    }
    printf(",o=%s\n", levels[count])
    printf("changetype: modify\n")
    printf("add: ACL\n")
    printf("ACL: 7#entry#")
    printf("cn=%s", $1)
    for (x=1; x< count; x++) {
        printf(",ou=%s", levels[x])
    }
    printf(",o=%s", levels[count])
    printf("#telephoneNumber\n\n");
}}


# The user info starts after a line of dashes, set flag
# This test must be performed here else the line of
# dashes is considered as user info
/---------------/ { flag = 1
}
END {}
```

Listing 12.3   An LDIF File Generated by the awk Script in Listing 12.2

```
version: 1

dn: cn=admin,ou=Department1,o=XYXCorp
changetype: modify
add: ACL
```

```
ACL: 7#entry#cn=admin,ou=Department1,o=XYXCorp#telephoneNumber

dn: cn=Peter,ou=Department1,o=XYXCorp
changetype: modify
add: ACL
ACL: 7#entry#cn=Peter,ou=Department1,o=XYXCorp#telephoneNumber

dn: cn=test_user,ou=Department1,o=XYXCorp
changetype: modify
add: ACL
ACL: 7#entry#cn=test_user,ou=Department1,o=XYXCorp
➡#telephoneNumber

dn: cn=Proxy_user,ou=Department1,o=XYXCorp
changetype: modify
add: ACL
ACL: 7#entry#cn=Proxy_user,ou=Department1,o=XYXCorp
➡#telephoneNumber
```

You can make your script a little simpler by using the special [Self] ACL, as shown in Listing 12.4. The [Self] ACL is essentially a macro that refers to the object itself. Rather than using the DN of the object in the ACL, you can simply reference [Self], and eDirectory will automatically convert that to the object's DN. The resulting LDIF file is shown in Listing 12.5.

Listing 12.4   An awk **Script That Uses the** [Self] **ACL**

```
BEGIN { flag = 0
        printf("version: 1\n\n");
}


/Current context:/ { cx = $0
                      gsub("Current context:", "", cx)
                      gsub(" ", "", cx)
}


# No more user information, unset flag to stop further
# printing
/A total of / { flag = 0
}


{if (flag == 1) {
    printf("dn: cn=%s", $1)
    # assumes each level of tree is OU and topmost
    # level is O.
```

```
    count = split(cx, levels, ".")
    for (x=1; x< count; x++) {
        printf(",ou=%s", levels[x])
    }
    printf(",o=%s\n", levels[count])
    printf("changetype: modify\n")
    printf("add: ACL\n")
    # We eliminated one set of for-loop here
    printf("ACL: 7#entry#[self]#telephoneNumber\n\n");
}}

# The user info starts after a line of dashes, set flag
# This test must be performed here else the line of
# dashes is considered as user info
/----------------/ { flag = 1
}
END {}
```

Listing 12.5 An LDIF File Generated by the awk Script in Listing 12.4

```
version: 1

dn: cn=admin,ou=Department1,o=XYXCorp
changetype: modify
add: ACL
ACL: 7#entry#[self]#telephoneNumber

dn: cn=Peter,ou=Department1,o=XYXCorp
changetype: modify
add: ACL
ACL: 7#entry#[self]#telephoneNumber

dn: cn=test_user,ou=Department1,o=XYXCorp
changetype: modify
add: ACL
ACL: 7#entry#[self]#telephoneNumber

dn: cn=Proxy_user,ou=Department1,o=XYXCorp
changetype: modify
add: ACL
ACL: 7#entry#[self]#telephoneNumber
```

The LDIF files shown in Listings 12.3 and 12.5 both do the same thing, and the end result is the same. If you are generating LDIF files by using scripts, it is perhaps easier (in terms of formatting the output lines) to do it with [Self] rather than by referencing the full DN of the object.

The method shown in Listing 12.4 is not very efficient, however, because each User object will have an ACL entry added. Depending on the number of users, this can dramatically increase the size of the DIB. As mentioned earlier, any time a new user is added to the tree, this ACL needs to be manually added (or needs to be added as part of the object creation script). If you need to change the ACL setting, you need to update *every* User object in the tree; again, this is a very tedious and time-consuming process.

A much easier way is to grant the necessary rights somewhere high up in the tree (such as at the O= level) and let each user inherit the rights to modify this attribute in his or her own object. Prior to eDirectory 8.6, the only way to let subordinate objects inherit rights from their parent containers is to make such a container a trustee of itself, assign the necessary attribute rights, and flag the containers as **Inheritable**. The problem in this case is that everyone in the container and its subtree can change everyone else's **Telephone Number** attribute. This is where the [This] ACL comes in.

What [This] can do is allow you to set the ACL at, say, O=XYZCorp and have it inherit down so that you only modify a single ACL. However, this ACL does *not* grant rights to the **Organization** level and thereby grant rights for every user to change every other users' objects. Rather, it transparently grants each user rights to his or her own object. Here is what this would look like in LDIF syntax:

```
dn: o=XYXCorp
changetype: modify
add: ACL
ACL: 7#subtree#[this]#telephoneNumber
```

Figure 12.16 shows the result of importing the preceding LDIF information into the tree. You can verify the working of the [This] ACL by looking up the effective rights of a User object to its own **Telephone Number** attribute (which should show Read, Compare, Write, and Add Self rights—the Add Self right is a result of having the Write right). Then you can look up the effective rights of one User object to another User object's **Telephone Number** attribute (which should show only Read and Compare rights—this is a result of O=XYZCorp having Read, Compare, Write, and Add Self effective rights to itself due to the [This] ACL assignment).

This special trustee can only be assigned via an LDAP-based tool

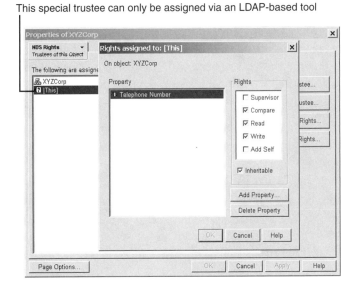

FIGURE 12.16
Using [This] to grant users self-management capabilities.

Because the rights are inherited from a superior container, new **User** objects are granted those rights automatically. This method works well if all users in the same tree branch are to be granted the rights. If there are exceptions, you need to place an Inherited Rights Filter (IRF) on the attribute for each of those **User** objects.

Third-Party Tools

Many excellent third-party tools are available to enhance management of NDS/eDirectory. The following sections briefly discuss a number of the tools we have looked at and use frequently in production networks: JRB utilities, tools by Wolfgang Schreiber, Novell's ScheMax tool, and DS Expert and DS Analyzer from NetPro.

NOTE

Appendix D, "eDirectory Resources," lists links to additional NDS/eDirectory resources and third-party tools.

JRB Utilities

The JRB software is a collection of more than 120 programs and NetWare Loadable Module (NLMs). The majority of the programs are provided in both 32-bit and 16-bit versions. Generally known as *JRButils*, the set of utilities covers almost every aspect of managing NetWare 3.11 through 6.5.

The utilities are mostly command-line based, and they provide considerably greater flexibility than the tools shipped with NetWare. They are particularly suited to managing large numbers of users. At the time of this writing, JRButils version 10.0 is divided into six parts:

- ▶ Part 1 is comprised of 32-bit console (character-mode) utilities for use from Windows 95/98/Me and NT/2000/XP/2003 clients. There are 121 programs in this part.

- ▶ Part 2 is comprised of 101 32-bit utilities that are command-line based but produce graphical output. These utilities are a subset of those in Part 1, excluding those that typically perform small tasks without output. They can also be run without opening a window, allowing them to run "silently" from batch files and scripts.

- ▶ Part 3 is comprised of 22 utilities that have full graphical interfaces for both input and output. With the exception of jrbpass and spacemon, which are provided only as full graphical programs, these programs are from Part 1.

- ▶ Part 4 is comprised of 16-bit DS-aware programs for use from DOS or from a Windows command prompt. There are 93 programs in this section.

- ▶ Part 5 is comprised of 78 bindery utilities plus David Harris's home and sethome programs. These are 16-bit DOS programs for use on NetWare 3.x, and most of them can be used against NDS/eDirectory servers, provided that the appropriate bindery contexts are defined.

- ▶ Part 6 is comprised of two NLMs for running on NetWare servers. They are `OPENFILE.NLM` and `MAKEHOME.NLM`.

NOTE   The 16-bit bindery-based programs of JRButils can be freely downloaded from www.jrbsoftware.com. To obtain copies of individual utilities for evaluation, you can send a request to support@jrbsoftware.com.

The following are some of the tools in the JRButils collection that are on our top-five list:

- ▶ **jrbimprt**—This tool is for mass user creation, deletion, and updating. It supports creation of GroupWise users, creation of GroupWise mailing lists, and setting of NetWare, GroupWise, Simple, and NDS for

Windows NT passwords. It is an excellent replacement for Novell's UImport utility.

▶ **Jrbpass**—This tool is a GUI password changer that supports NetWare, GroupWise, Simple, NDS for NT, and NT domain passwords (see Figure 12.17).

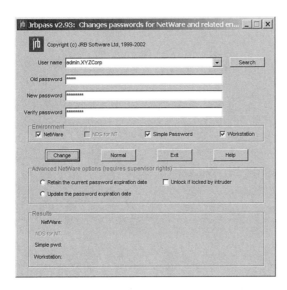

FIGURE 12.17
Jrbpass, a GUI password changer.

▶ **sethome2**—This tool sets the User object's Home Directory attribute en masse and can create home directories. It also sets the file system trustee rights at the same time.

▶ **Setpword**—This tool sets NDS/eDirectory and other types of password (such as GroupWise) for multiple objects. It can also set passwords for non-User objects, as long as the object has ndsLoginProperties as one of its object classes (see Figure 12.18).

▶ **JBLookup**—This GUI user lookup utility allows any attributes to be displayed (see Figure 12.19).

For up-to-date information about the current release of JRButils, visit www.jrbsoftware.com and refer to the Release Notes and Enhancements links.

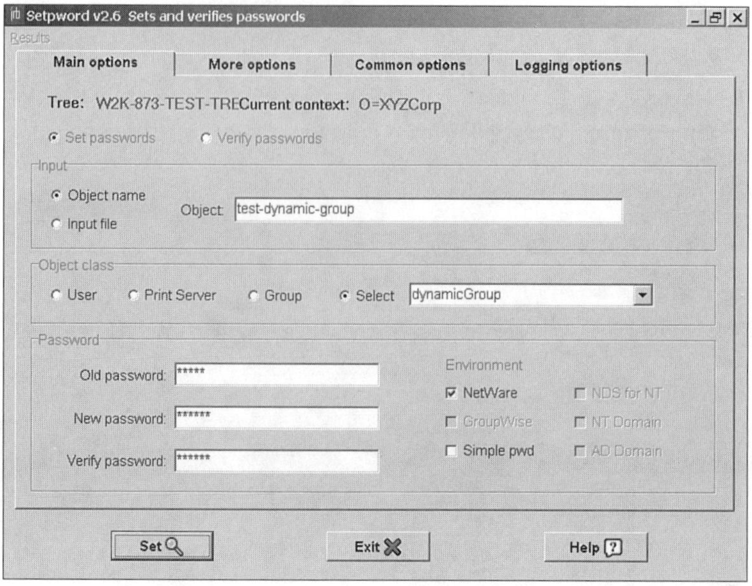

FIGURE 12.18
Using Setpword
to change a
dynamic group
object's pass-
word.

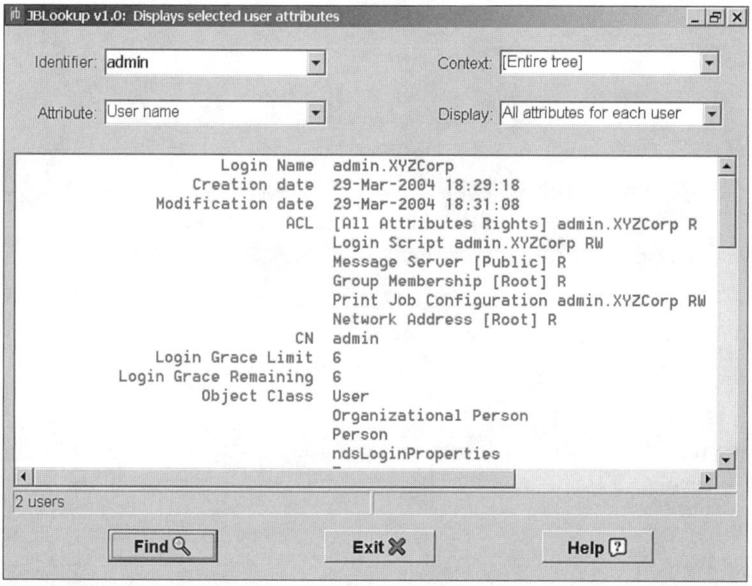

FIGURE 12.19
JBLookup, a GUI
user information
lookup utility.

Wolfgang's Tools

Similarly to the JRB utilities, the tools developed by Dr. Wolfgang Schreiber
(Wolfgang's Tools, as they are normally called) are a collection of standalone
utilities that consultants and network administrators should not do without.

DSReport and Quick for NDS are the most popular and most useful tools in
the collection.

A large majority of Wolfgang's Tools, including DSReport (but not Quick for NDS),
are public domain. You can download the latest version of the tools from
www.wolfgangschreiber.de.

DSReport allows you to run reports on any attribute of any object in an
NDS/eDirectory tree (see Figure 12.20). The resulting data can be exported
into comma-separated, comma- and tab-separated files, Excel files, Quattro
Pro files, HTML files, or XML files, or even into the Windows Clipboard.

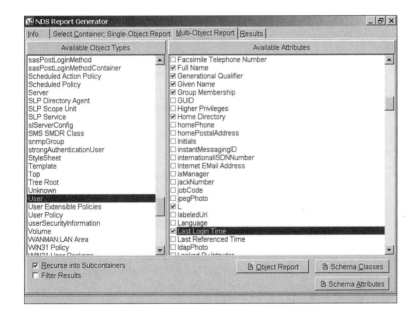

FIGURE 12.20
Selecting specific User attributes
for reporting.

Quick for NDS is a command-line utility that you use to access NDS from
the command prompt or from a batch file. Although NetWare Administrator
and other tools from Novell are great tools for NDS/eDirectory administration, they have some severe limitations, especially if you need automation.
The main purpose of Quick for NDS is to fill these gaps.

Quick for NDS allows you to specify the objects that you want to see or
modify with object types and/or wildcards, so you work with exactly the
objects that you select. You may operate on any specified container, or you
may add an option to operate on all matching objects in the whole
(sub)tree.

Quick for NDS can save you hours of time and reduce errors by automating standard administrative tasks. You can store your standard tasks as batch jobs and run them at your convenience. This can be an alternative for having to develop scripts using awk or Perl for some of your procedures.

The following are some examples of uses of Quick for NDS:

▶ To modify the login scripts of all your OU containers:
```
QUICK LoginScript "organizational unit"=* replace "MAP X:"
➥ "MAP Y:"
```

▶ To change the passwords of all students in a given container:
```
QUICK password user=* newpassword /cont=.grade10.highSchool
```

▶ To set the Password Required flag to TRUE for all users in the tree:
```
QUICK restrict user=* pwdReq true /cont=[root] /sub
```

▶ To list the ACL attribute values for all the objects in the O=XYZCorp container:
```
QUICK ForSet .XYZCorp ACL "echo $value$" /qu
```

The output looks like this:

```
[ R    ] O=XYZCorp. / "Login Script"
[ R    ] O=XYZCorp. / "Print Job Configuration"
[    A ]DEMO-W2KC-NDS.O=XYZCorp./"[All Attributes Rights]"
[    S ] DEMO-W2KC-NDS.O=XYZCorp. / "[Entry Rights]"
[ RW  I] pco.OU=Extend.O=XYZCorp. / "ACL"
[ RW  I] pco.OU=Extend.O=XYZCorp. / "Object Class"
[ RW  I] pco.OU=Extend.O=XYZCorp. / "bhObjectGUID"
[ R   I] publicUser.OU=Extend.O=XYZCorp. / "CN"
[ RW  I] pco.OU=Extend.O=XYZCorp. / "bhCmAcceptList"
[ RW  I] pco.OU=Extend.O=XYZCorp. / "bhCmApprovedList"
[ RW  I] pco.OU=Extend.O=XYZCorp. / "bhCmAssignList"
[ RW  I] pco.OU=Extend.O=XYZCorp. / "bhCmDeniedList"
[ RW  I] pco.OU=Extend.O=XYZCorp. / "bhCmInviteList"
```

ScheMax

Originally developed by Netoria in Australia, ScheMax is now a discontinued Novell product. ScheMax (pronounced "schema-x") is a utility that allows you to create new schema classes and attributes and to create custom snap-ins for NetWare Administrator to manage the schema extensions. It consists of three components: Schema Administrator, Snapin Builder, and ScheMax Viewer.

Because ScheMax is now discontinued and no longer supported, Novell has made it freely available for download from its Cool Solutions Web site, at www. novell.com/coolsolutions/tools/1214.html.

Schema Administrator

The Schema Administrator component of ScheMax is accessible through the Tools menu of NetWare Administrator. When activated, it displays a graphical browser that shows the schema class inheritance tree (see Figure 12.21).

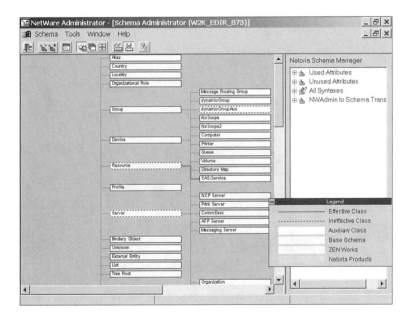

FIGURE 12.21
ScheMax Schema Administrator.

As with the Schema Manager in ConsoleOne, you can use Schema Administrator to add classes and attributes to the DS schema. The real power in ScheMax's Schema Administrator is the presentation. The graphical overview of the schema tree enables you to determine where your new object class appears in the schema tree and gives you greater precision in locating the proper place to put your schema extension.

Snapin Builder

ScheMax doesn't stop where Schema Manager does; through an ingenious twist, rather than create snap-in DLLs with a development tool, ScheMax includes facilities to build pages for NetWare Administrator and associate them with DS objects. The end result is that you can create schema extensions and build pages right into NetWare Administrator. The pages built with ScheMax are stored directly in NDS/eDirectory, so installation of the snap-in is as easy as associating a `Container`, `Group`, or `User` object with the snap-in object.

NOTE

Because ScheMax's snap-ins are stored in the DS, you must ensure that ScheMax's schema extension has been applied to the tree. You can manually extend the schema by selecting Tools, Schema Extensions in NetWare Administrator after ScheMax has been installed.

To create a snap-in, you first select the context in which the snap-in object will be created, by selecting Object, Create and then selecting the ScheMax `Snapin` class. Figure 12.22 shows a sample snap-in page in development. This page includes several standard attributes that are spread through normal administration pages.

FIGURE 12.22
The ScheMax graphical snap-in designer.

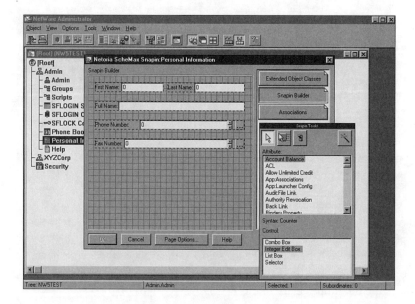

The finalized new attribute page is shown in Figure 12.23. As you can see, the page is accessible directly through the standard NetWare Administrator interface; it appears just the way it would if you spent hours or days developing a snap-in DLL, but using ScheMax takes only a few minutes.

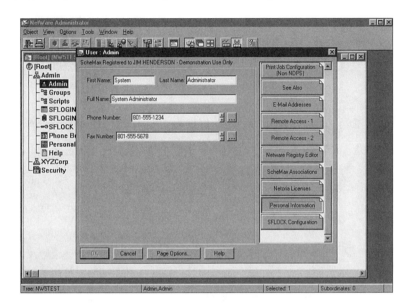

FIGURE 12.23
A ScheMax-built snap-in, added to the User class.

ScheMax Viewer

The final component of ScheMax is ScheMax Viewer. In many cases, it would be easiest if users could populate the data in the DS database themselves. ScheMax Viewer can be used for this. The initial view, shown in Figure 12.24, lets the user pick a view to be displayed.

When the view is selected, the user can display information for a particular subtree or for objects in a specific context. Administration of information is just a double-click away; selecting a record from the view brings up associated snap-ins created for the view. The same snap-ins created for NetWare Administrator are available in ScheMax Viewer.

The view is also stored in DS and is created with NetWare Administrator. As when you create a ScheMax snap-in, you create a view by selecting the context in which the snap-in object will be created; to do this, you select Object, Create and then select the ScheMax **View** class. Figure 12.25 shows how the new view looks.

FIGURE 12.24
The ScheMax
Viewer view
selection screen.

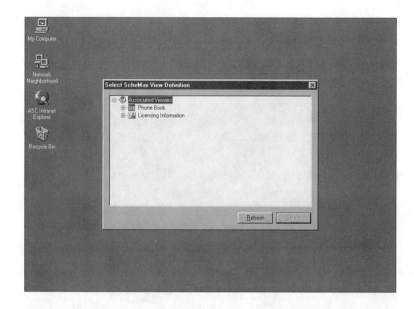

FIGURE 12.25
Creating a view
for use with
ScheMax Viewer.

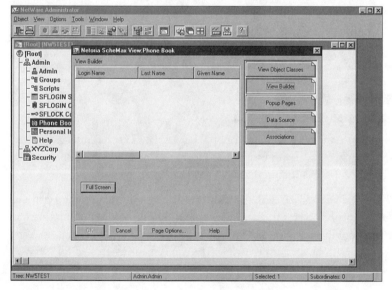

To add the capability to edit data fields, you simply associate a ScheMax snap-in object with the view, as shown in Figure 12.26.

A number of other options are available with ScheMax Viewer. For example, you can force ScheMax Viewer to run for the specific **User** object logged in and require the ScheMax Viewer fields to be updated before the program can be exited. This is one way you could update a telephone list with current employee information.

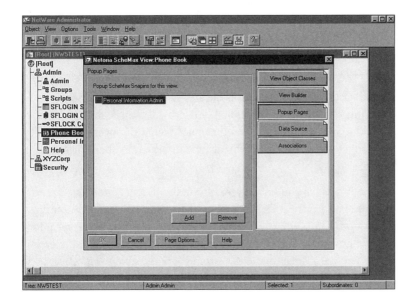

FIGURE 12.26
Associating a
snap-in with a
view to enable
editing of DS
attributes from
the viewer.

Another option is the capability to pass a specific view directly into the executable. This prevents the selection screen shown in Figure 12.24 from appearing and launches the desired view directly.

DS Expert and DS Analyzer

NetPro Computing, Inc. (www.netpro.com) is one of the leading developers of NDS/eDirectory management tools. Its DS Expert and DS Analyzer products can help you monitor and optimize your DS performance and troubleshoot DS problems.

The DS Expert product is for monitoring the overall health of an NDS/eDirectory tree. It monitors the directory for replication processes, time synchronization, and directory background processes, such as obituaries and backlinks—conditions that are vital to the health of the directory. It keeps constant tabs on directory conditions, watching for replication latency issues and synchronization errors that can affect the integrity of the directory and prevent user access to critical services. From stuck obituaries and time sync issues to replica and partition synchronization problems, DS Expert ensures the health of NDS/eDirectory all the time, and it snaps in to whatever management framework you are using.

There are two components to the DS Expert product: a server agent and a workstation-based tool to gather and view the information from the agents loaded on the servers. The latest version also allows you to access the agents by using a Web browser. DS Expert has the capability to send SNMP alerts to any standard SNMP management console and react based on user-defined thresholds.

A unique feature of DS Expert is its capability to provide multiserver DSTrace functionality. This functionality is provided through the workstation-based management console and enables you to discover more about how DS functions as well as view real-time information about problems in the DS tree.

DS Analyzer enables you to analyze, troubleshoot, and tune NDS/eDirectory for optimal performance. DS Analyzer gathers directory traffic and utilization data from across the entire network and displays it in a graphical format, allowing you to quickly trend and analyze the directory traffic on a network. Reports display traffic data from every possible perspective, including servers, partitions, containers, clients, objects, and NDS/eDirectory background processes. With DS Analyzer, you can quickly identify problem areas and drill all the way down to the client level to pinpoint the root causes of directory issues.

One of the unique features in DS Analyzer that sets it apart from other DS troubleshooting tools is its integrated knowledge base. This knowledge base provides you with interpretations of directory traffic and recommendations for problem resolution and directory design suggestions.

Summary

This chapter examines a number of different tools used to manage NDS/eDirectory and looks at how to use these tools to better manage your tree. By having a good understanding of the use of Novell-supplied tools such as NetWare Administrator, ConsoleOne, NList, UImport, iManager, NDS iMonitor, and ICE, as well as third-party administration tools, it is easy to prevent many problems from occurring and manage your trees much more easily. Some of the ways in which you can use these tools more effectively are presented in Chapter 14.

Chapter 13, "eDirectory Health Checks," takes an in-depth look at eDirectory health check procedures.

eDirectory Health Checks

For the best performance, all complex machinery and software requires frequent monitoring. For eDirectory to perform optimally, you should maintain the directory by performing routine health check procedures and upgrading or replacing hardware when necessary. This chapter describes how to perform health checks on your eDirectory tree.

Why, When, and How Often Should You Do Health Checks?

Do you keep tabs on the noises that your car makes and notes what is normal and what is not? Do you change the oil regularly, check the various fluid levels, and monitor the tires for wear and tear? Of course you do. You know you must take good care of your car, or problems can (and do) happen. If not detected early, these problems can be very expensive to repair in terms of both time and money. Your directory services (DS) tree is no different from your car in this regard.

A network administrator's role is to ensure a healthy and working environment so all users can access shared resources quickly when they need them. Unfortunately, users generally only retain memories of the times when the network is unavailable and not of the times the network is running flawlessly. Therefore, it is your responsibility to make sure your network runs like clockwork, and you should perform regular DS health checks to ensure this.

Depending on the environment, the frequency of health checks varies between perhaps once per week to once per quarter. The frequency of health checks depends on whether you the tree is static or dynamic. To determine whether you have a dynamic tree or static tree, consider the following definitions:

▶ **Static DS tree**—A static tree has minimal routine changes. For example, you only make simple changes such as adding or deleting user objects, or you create a partition or add a server every couple months. Because you make fewer changes to a static DS tree than to a dynamic one, you only need to perform DS health checks infrequently.

▶ **Dynamic DS tree**—A dynamic tree sees frequent nonroutine changes. For example, you create a partition or add a server weekly, or you are in the process of developing the tree.

If you have a dynamic DS tree, you should perform a DS health check once per week or whenever a major change is about to be made. However, as the pace of change decreases and the DS tree becomes more static, you can relax a little and perform DS health checks less frequently. Table 13.1 shows some general guidelines for the frequency of performing a DS tree health check tasks.

TABLE 13.1 **Recommended NDS/eDirectory Health Check Task Frequency**

DS HEALTH CHECK TASK	FREQUENCY
DS versions check	Monthly or quarterly
Time synchronization check	Monthly or every two months
DS (server-to-server) synchronization status check	Monthly
Replica synchronization (partition continuity) check	Monthly
Backlink/external references check	Monthly
Obituaries check	Monthly
Replica state check	Monthly or quarterly
Replica ring consistency check	Monthly or quarterly
Schema sync status check	Quarterly
Partition size check	Quarterly
Renamed and unknown object check	Monthly or quarterly
Schema consistency check	Quarterly or after a schema extension operation
Duplicate tree name check	Monthly or quarterly
DS tunable parameter check	Quarterly
eDirectory cache statistics check	Monthly or bimonthly

The first four tasks in Table 13.1 are considered *basic* DS tree health check steps. If you do not perform the full health check, these are the minimal checks that should be performed.

Not only should you perform regular health checks as preventive measures, but you should perform a health check on the DS tree *before* you execute a major DS operation such as moving or deleting large numbers of objects, performing a partition operation, or adding or deleting servers.   **TIP**

Health Check Prerequisites

Before you start a health check, you first need to have a baseline so you know what's already in place in terms of the environment. For instance, suppose your health check results show that there are three Unknown objects in the Users partition; is this an indication of a problem? Generally, Unknown objects are indicative of DS issues. However, if you know that this tree has a mix of NetWare 4.2 servers running NDS 6 and NetWare 5.1 servers running eDirectory 8.7.3 and that auxiliary classes are being used, the presence of Unknown objects could be considered normal (when viewed on a NetWare 4.2 server).

Refer to the "Auxiliary Class Object Handling" section in Chapter 6, "Understanding Common eDirectory Processes," to see why Unknown **objects may be normal in an environment where there are mixed versions of NDS and eDirectory.**   **TIP**

The following is a list of some of the information you should gather before analyzing the health of a DS tree:

- ▶ The number of DS trees on the network.
- ▶ The versions of NDS/eDirectory that are running.
- ▶ The versions and types of operating systems running (such as NetWare and Linux).
- ▶ The service pack level of each operating system.
- ▶ Communication protocols used between DS servers.
- ▶ The network addresses of the DS servers, including internal network addresses of NetWare servers.
- ▶ A drawing of the current tree design.

▶ The current replica matrix, showing the number of replicas (including types) and servers holding them.

▶ The time server infrastructure, including placement of time provider groups and any custom time synchronization configuration used.

▶ WAN link information (number of links, speed, reliability, and so on).

▶ Router hardware information, such as model and firmware level.

▶ The number of objects in the tree. This does not necessarily need to be an accurate count, which can change, but it should be within 5% to 10% of the actual count.

▶ A list of DS-aware applications, both from Novell and third parties. This provides you with information about possible schema extensions and use of auxiliary classes.

▶ The server hardware configuration, such as the amount of total disk space, free disk space, and RAM. For NetWare servers, you should also note the size and free space on the boot partition.

▶ The NetWare server software configuration—in particular, Transaction Tracking System (TTS) settings.

You should be certain to have as much of this information as possible before attempting to analyze the health of a DS tree.

Recommended Health Check Procedures

The health check process involves a detailed list of tasks for ensuring and maintaining a healthy DS tree. We break down these tasks into three sections:

▶ **"Tree Health Check Procedures"**—This section provides information on how to determine the overall health of the tree. These steps should be performed on a fairly regular basis, perhaps monthly.

▶ **"Partition Health Check Procedures"**—This section provides information on procedures that should be performed before you do any major partition operations.

▶ **"Server Health Check Procedures"**—This section describes the steps necessary to identify the health of replicas on a server.

The concepts and procedures discussed in this chapter are applicable equally to all operating system platforms supported by eDirectory: NetWare, Windows, Sun Solaris, and other Unix/Linux platforms.

NOTE

Although NDS iMonitor makes health checking an easier task, we feel it is important to understand the underlying fundamental steps necessary for a health check. Therefore, the procedures given in the following sections are in the "long format," using traditional tools such as DSRepair and DSTrace, instead of NDS iMonitor. Furthermore, sometimes it is simply much more efficient or convenient (say, when you are standing right in front of the server console) to use non-HTTP–based tools.

Tree Health Check Procedures

The following sections discuss the 13 major health check steps for the NDS/eDirectory tree. You don't need to perform all 13 of these steps at all times. You should perform the following 7 of these health check procedures on a regular basis:

- ▶ Verifying DS versions
- ▶ Checking time synchronization
- ▶ Checking server-to-server synchronization
- ▶ Checking replica synchronization
- ▶ Checking external references (exrefs)
- ▶ Checking replica states
- ▶ Checking schema synchronization

TIP

For a proper and complete health check, the tasks listed in this section need to be performed on *every* server in the tree that holds a replica. However, this is not practical for large trees or when there are a large number of partitions and servers. Therefore, although it is advisable to perform all tasks on every server, for an abbreviated version, you can perform the steps on the servers that hold the Master replica for each partition. You should start with the server hosting the Master of [Root] and work down the tree.

The DS Version Check

Ideally, you should run the same version of the DS module throughout a tree. However, this is not always possible, especially if you have mixed versions of NetWare and other operating system platforms running eDirectory. Therefore, the second best thing you can do is ensure that all

NDS/eDirectory versions are at the latest version on their respective operating system platforms. In Unix/Linux and Windows environments you can verify all DS versions that exist in a tree by using the DSRepair utility to perform the following checks:

OPERATING SYSTEM	PROCEDURE
NetWare	Load `DSREPAIR.NLM` at the server console and select the Time Synchronization option.
Windows	Start `dsrepair.dlm` from within NDSCons and select the Time Synchronization option from the Repair menu.
Unix/Linux	Execute `ndsrepair -T`, where the time synchronization report also shows the DS version on all the servers in the tree. If not all servers in the tree are displayed, you have to run this command on those servers separately. On individual servers, you can also execute `ndsrepair -E`, and the DS version is shown at the beginning of the replica synchronization information; or you can execute `ndsstat` on those servers to see the version of eDirectory.

NOTE NDS-aware CD servers are exceptions to this requirement because the version of DS running on them generally cannot easily be updated unless the servers allow flash updates.

This check should be performed on a server holding a replica of [Root]—not necessarily the Master—because that server knows about all the servers in the tree. If it is not run on such a server, the report may be incomplete.

The Time Synchronization Check

Correct time synchronization is important because NDS/eDirectory partitions are replicated and need to be concurrent with one another. Each event that occurs in DS is marked with a timestamp. The timestamps are used to order the processing of events or changes that occur on multiple servers. Time-stamping of events keeps all DS changes in proper order. A time synchronization check must be done regularly to ensure that DS functions correctly. For example, if time is out of synchronization when you perform a change replica type partition operation, the operation will become stuck and not complete.

It is not critical that the servers show a correct local time, but all servers within the tree *must* be time synchronized to each other.

The time synchronization check is performed using the DSRepair utility and should be performed on a server that holds a replica of [Root]—not necessarily the Master—because such a server knows about all the servers in the tree. Otherwise, the report may be incomplete. Here's how you complete this check:

OPERATING SYSTEM	PROCEDURE
NetWare	Load DSREPAIR.NLM at the server console and select the Time Synchronization option.
Windows	Start dsrepair.dlm from within NDSCons and select the Time Synchronization option from the Repair menu.
Unix/Linux	Execute ndsrepair -T, which reports time synchronization status on all the servers in the tree. If not all servers in the tree are displayed, you have to run this command separately on the servers.

All non-NetWare servers will report a time server type of Secondary. Therefore, it would be normal for a pure-Linux eDirectory tree, for instance, to list all servers as secondary time servers and show no single-reference time servers as being present (see Figure 13.1).

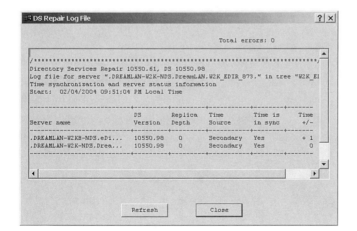

FIGURE 13.1
Timeservers in pure Windows are secondary time servers.

WARNING

NetWare 5 and higher tend to report that time is in sync even when it is not. Therefore, when you run this check on a NetWare 5 or higher server, you should pay special attention to the Time +/- column. If any of the numbers in this column is greater than 2, you are most likely outside the default synchronization radius (which is 2 seconds).

REAL WORLD

Replica Depth?

The output from the time synchronization check includes a field called Replica Depth. The replica depth is an indicator of what replica is on the server. It is reported as -1 if no replicas are stored on the server, 0 if the server contains a replica of the [Root] partition, or a positive integer that indicates how many (container) objects away from [Root] the first replica is on the reporting server. For instance, if the server holds a replica whose partition root object is OU=Test.O=XYZCorp, the reported replica depth is 2.

There is a cosmetic bug in DSRepair for some versions of eDirectory 8.7.x (such as 8.7.1) that reports an erroneous replica depth value (for example, a value of 2 where a [Root] replica exists). This bug is fixed in eDirectory 8.7.3.

The DS (Server-to-Server) Synchronization Status Check

The DS (server-to-server) synchronization status check ensures that the servers within a given replica ring are communicating correctly. However, it does not necessarily guarantee that the replicas are synchronized—a partition continuity check is required to verify replica synchronization status, as discussed later in this section. The check can be performed using the DSTrace facility, as follows:

OPERATING SYSTEM	PRO	
NetWare	At the server console, issue the following commands:	
	SET TTF=ON	Sends the DSTrace screen output to DSTRACE.DBG
	SET DSTRACE=*R	Resets the file to 0 bytes
	SET DSTRACE=ON	Activates the DSTrace screen
	SET DSTRACE=NODEBUG	Turns off all preset filters
	SET DSTRACE=+S	Enables synchronization messages
	SET DSTRACE=*H	Initiates a heartbeat
	After you have collected sufficient information, enter **SET TTF=OFF** to close the DSTRACE.DBG file and then enter **SET DSTRACE=OFF** to stop further display.	

OPERATING SYSTEM	PRO
Windows	Start `dstrace.dlm` from within NDSCons, select Edit, Options, and then clear all settings by clicking Clear All. Check the Partition, Inbound Sync Detail, and Outbound Sync Detail boxes and click OK.
	Select `ds.dlm` from the main NDSCons screen and click Configure. Select the Triggers tab and then click the Replica Sync button. This forces partition synchronization with other servers.
	You can view the synchronization activity by going to the eDirectory Server Trace Utility screen and scrolling through the synchronization process. You can also copy and paste the information from the Trace screen to a text file to make it easier to search for error codes.
Unix/Linux	Run `ndstrace` and from within the `ndstrace` utility enter the following:

`set dstrace=on`	Enables tracing
`set dstrace=nodebug`	Turns off all preset filters
`set dstrace=+sklk`	Enables synchronization messages
`set dstrace=+sync`	Enables inbound sync messages
`set dstrace=*h`	Initiates a heartbeat

The displayed information is saved automatically in the `/var/nds/ndstrace.log` file, which can be viewed through a text editor.

The server must have at least one replica in order to display any DSTrace information. **NOTE**

You can examine the DSTrace log file by using a text editor and search for **-6** and **-7** to find any DS errors encountered during synchronization (such as -625 or -746). Or you can search for **YES** or **Process succeeded** (see Figure 13.2), which reflect successful synchronization for a partition. You need to perform this procedure on *each* server that holds a replica.

FIGURE 13.2
DSTrace, showing
a successful
replica sync.

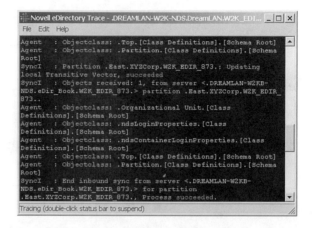

> **TIP** **-625 is a Transport error and -746 is a Zero Creation Time error. NDS 7 and later do not allow an object to have a zero creation timestamp, but earlier versions of** DS.NLM **do.**

The Replica Synchronization (Partition Continuity) Check

The replica synchronization (partition continuity) check operation helps you identify whether any of a partition's replicas are experiencing synchronization errors. This check displays the time of the last successful synchronization to all servers, along with any errors that have occurred since the last synchronization. This operation is also known as "walking the replica ring."

DSRepair can report replica synchronization status for every partition that has a replica on the current server. It reads the `Synchronization Status` attribute from the `Replica Root` object on each server that holds replicas of the partitions. It then displays the time of the last successful synchronization to all servers (see Figure 13.3) and any errors that have occurred since the last synchronization. DSRepair will display a `WARNING` message if synchronization has not completed within a 12-hour timeframe.

Here's how you perform a replica synchronization (partition continuity) check:

OPERATING SYSTEM	PROCEDURE
NetWare	Load `DSREPAIR.NLM` at the server console and select the Report Synchronization Status option.
Windows	Start `dsrepair.dlm` from within NDSCons and select the Report Synchronization Status option from the Repair menu.
Unix/Linux	Execute `ndsrepair -E` at the command line.

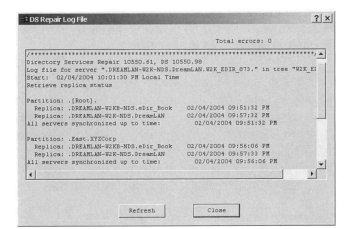

FIGURE 13.3
DSRepair, show-
ing no replica
synchronization
errors.

TIP

You can also perform this check by using NDS Manager.

The External References, Backlink, and Obituaries Check

When a server references an object that it does not have locally, an exref to
that object is created, and the object will have a backlink to the server that
holds its exref (with eDirectory, the backlink is replaced by a distributed reference link [DRL]). It is a good idea to know how many exrefs a server
holds. If there are many, the server should often hold a copy of the replica.
This check will also display obituaries and show you the states of all servers
in the backlink list for the obituaries.

Here's how you perform an exref, backlink, and obituaries check:

OPERATING SYSTEM	PROCEDURE
NetWare	Load DSREPAIR.NLM at the server console and select Advanced Options, Check External References. (Specify the -A command-line option to include obits reporting.)
Windows	Start dsrepair.dlm from within NDSCons and select Repair, Check External References. (Specify the -A command-line option to include obits reporting.)
Unix/Linux	Execute ndsrepair -C at the command line. (Specify the -Ad command-line option to include obits reporting.)

NOTE   **If the server is having problems walking the tree, it will display errors such as -626 (All Referrals Failed) and -634 (No Referrals).**

After you run this option, the log file shows exrefs that are backlinked (see Figure 13.4) and lists any backlinked obituaries that have not yet completed. Of primary concern are the obituaries that have not completed. For example, problems can emerge if the obituary flag remains in the same state and is never purged. This condition indicates a possible communication problem between servers or that a server may have been removed improperly (because servers in the tree still reference the removed server).

FIGURE 13.4
DSRepair, showing that the server has one exref but no stuck obits.

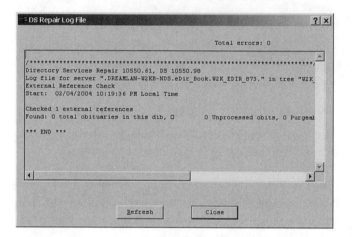

TIP   **The Janitor process is in charge of obituary cleanup and will not run until the setting `All processed = YES` occurs. However, you can try to force Janitor to run by forcing Flat Cleaner to run, using the `*F` switch in DSTrace.**

You can also check for backlink, exref, and obit problems by using DSTrace, as follows:

OPERATING SYSTEM	PROCEDURE	
NetWare	At the server console, issue the following commands:	
	`SET TTF=ON`	Sends the DSTrace screen output to `DSTRACE.DBG`
	`SET DSTRACE=*R`	Resets the file to 0 bytes
	`SET DSTRACE=ON`	Activates the DSTrace screen
	`SET DSTRACE=NODEBUG`	Turns off all preset filters

OPERATING SYSTEM	PROCEDURE
	SET DSTRACE=+BLINK — Enables backlink messages
	SET DSTRACE=+J — Enables Janitor messages
	SET DSTRACE=*B — Forces Backlink to run
	SET DSTRACE=*F — Forces Flat Cleaner to run
	When you have collected sufficient information, enter **SET TTF=OFF** to close the DSTRACE.DBG file and then enter **SET DSTRACE=OFF** to stop further display.
Windows	Start dstrace.dlm from within NDSCons, select the Edit menu, and clear all settings by clicking Clear All. Check the Partition, Inbound Synchronization, Outbound Synchronization, and Sync Detail boxes and click OK.
	Select ds.dlm from the main NDSCons screen and click Configure. Select the Triggers tab and then click the Replica Sync button. This will force partition synchronization with other servers.
	You can view the synchronization activity by going to the eDirectory Server Trace Utility screen and scrolling through the synchronization process. You can also copy and paste the information from the Trace screen to a text file to make it easier to search for error codes.
Unix/Linux	Run ndstrace and from within the ndstrace utility enter the following:
	set dstrace=on — Enables tracing
	set dstrace=nodebug — Turns off all preset filters
	set dstrace=+blnk — Enables backlink messages
	set dstrace=+bldt — Enables detailed backlink messages
	set dstrace=+jntr — Enables Janitor messages
	set dstrace=*b — Forces Backlink to run
	set dstrace=*f — Forces Flat Cleaner to run
	The displayed information is saved automatically in the /var/nds/ndstrace.log file, which can be viewed through a text editor.

> **TIP**
>
> **You should perform the Backlink and Janitor checks as two separate runs so their messages are not intermixed in the same log file.**

You can examine the DSTrace log file by using any text editor and search for the error messages.

The Replica State Check

The replica state check lists partitions and the states of the replicas stored in the current server's Directory Information Base (DIB). Although not likely to happen "spontaneously," it is a good idea to periodically check to ensure that the replica states have not suddenly changed from On to some other undesirable states, such as Dying. Here's how you complete this check:

OPERATING SYSTEM	PROCEDURE
NetWare	Load `DSREPAIR.NLM` at the server console and select Advanced Options, Replica and Partition Operations.
Windows	Start `dsrepair.dlm` from within NDSCons and expand the Partitions tree in the left pane to list each of the partitions. Highlight each partition to see the states of the replicas, which are shown in the right window (see Figure 13.5).
Unix/Linux	Execute `ndsrepair -P` at the command line. Select each partition in turn and check its synchronization status (option 6 in the menu).

Replica type and state of [Root]

FIGURE 13.5
The Master replica of [Root], in the On state.

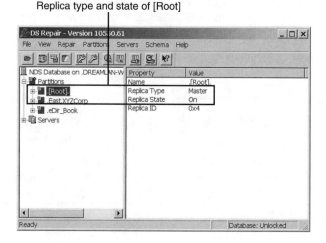

The Replica Ring Consistency Check

You should occasionally check that each partition's replica ring is consistent; that is, the replica ring list on every server holding the same partition should be the same. For example, say that the partition TEST is replicated onto three servers, A, B, and C. The replica ring list for partition TEST on Server A should show Servers A, B, and C; the same should be true for Servers B and C.

To check for replica ring consistency, you first run DSRepair on the server holding the Master replica of each partition. Then you run DSRepair on the other servers in the replica ring to check for possible mismatches. Here's how:

OPERATING SYSTEM	PROCEDURE
NetWare	Load DSREPAIR.NLM at the server console and select the Advanced Options menu. From the Replica and Partition Operations option, highlight each partition in turn, press Return, and then select View Replica Ring.
Windows	Start dsrepair.dlm from within NDSCons and expand the Partitions tree in the left pane to list each of the partitions. For each partition, further expand its listing to reveal the list of servers in the replica ring (see Figure 13.6).
Unix/Linux	Execute ndsrepair -P at the command line. Select each partition in turn and view its replica ring (option 10 in the menu).

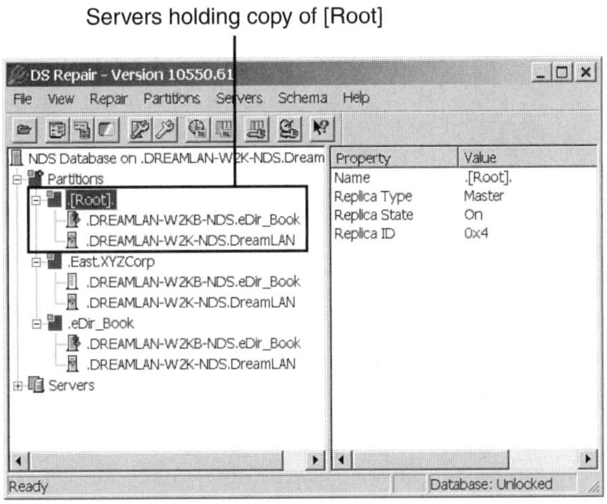

Servers holding copy of [Root]

FIGURE 13.6
The [Root] partition, replicated to two servers.

From the listings, you need to cross-check that the servers holding replicas of that partition are consistent.

The Schema Synchronization and Status Check

Every server in the NDS/eDirectory tree has a copy of the schema, even if the server does not hold any replicas. The schema information on all servers *must* be identical. When schema changes are made to the tree, they are first applied on the server holding the Master of [Root]. From there, the updates are propagated from one server to another, in a trickle-down manner, based on the NCP Server object's location within the tree. Because the NDS schema synchronization process is event driven, changes are scheduled to be synchronized 10 seconds after a schema change is made.

You use DSTrace to check whether the schemas in a tree are in synchronization:

OPERATING SYSTEM	PROCEDURE
NetWare	At the server console, issue the following commands:
	SET TTF=ON — Sends the DSTrace screen output to DSTRACE.DBG
	SET DSTRACE=*R — Resets the file to 0 bytes
	SET DSTRACE=ON — Activates the DSTrace screen
	SET DSTRACE=NODEBUG — Turns off all preset filters
	SET DSTRACE=+SCHEMA — Enables schema messages
	SET DSTRACE=*SS — Forces Schema Sync to run
	When you have collected sufficient information, enter **SET TTF=OFF** to close the DSTRACE.DBG file and then enter **SET DSTRACE=OFF** to stop further display.
Windows	Start dstrace.dlm from within NDSCons and select Edit, Options. Clear all settings by clicking Clear All. Check the Schema box and click OK.
	Select ds.dlm from the main NDSCons screen and click Configure. Select the Triggers tab and then click the Schema Sync button. This will force schema synchronization with other servers.
	You can view the synchronization activity by going to the eDirectory Server Trace Utility screen and scrolling through the synchronization process. You can also copy and paste the information from the Trace screen to a text file to make it easier to search for error codes.

OPERATING SYSTEM	PROCEDURE
Unix/Linux	Run ndstrace and from within the ndstrace utility enter the following:

set dstrace=on	Enables tracing
set dstrace=nodebug	Turns off all preset filters
set dstrace=+scma	Enables schema sync messages
set dstrace=+scmd	Enables detail schema messages
set dstrace=*ss	Forces Schema Sync to run

The displayed information is saved automatically in the /var/nds/ndstrace.log file, which can be viewed through a text editor.

You need to check for the message SCHEMA: All Processed = YES in the log file (see Figure 13.7).

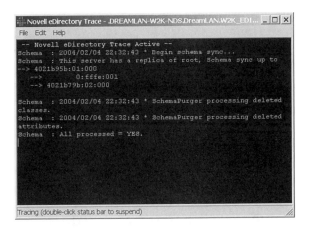

FIGURE 13.7
The schemas being synchronized without error.

WARNING

The DSTrace commands only indicate whether the schema is being synchronized between the servers. They do not provide information that verifies whether the servers indeed have identical schema. A good check would be to compare the schema information between the server holding the Master replica of [Root] and one of the servers that is located lower in the tree structure, using Novell's SCHCMP.EXE utility (see TID #2931699).

The Partition Size and Special Object Check

The partition size and special object check provides you with information about the number of objects in each partition and in the whole tree. This check is useful in determining whether the DS tree is within Novell's recommended partitioning guidelines.

For NDS 6 and 7, Novell recommends that for best performance, partitions should not exceed 2,000 objects each. Of course, this is simply a guideline and not a hard limit. The key question is "Is DS access performance satisfactory?"

You can obtain object counts by using a number of different utilities. Here are some examples:

▶ **SCANTREE.EXE**—This utility is from Novell Research. (Refer to "Understanding **SCANTREE.EXE**'s Statistics," Novell AppNotes, March 1996, for more information; `http://developer.novell.com/ research/appnotes/1996/march/06/index.htm`). You can find a copy of **SCANTREE.EXE** at `ftp.dreamlan.com/Freeware/scands.zip`.

▶ **NDSCount**—For information on this utility, see `www.dreamlan.com/ ndscount.htm`. With this utility, you can report object counts based on container or partition. In addition, you can selectively report based on object type.

▶ **NLIST.EXE**—This utility is included with NetWare. The following command lists all objects in the tree and provides a total count at the end of the output: `NLIST * /R /S /C`.

You should also check for the existence of two special types of objects in the tree:

▶ **Unknown objects**—These objects have lost one or more of their mandatory attributes. For example, a **Volume** object will become **Unknown** if it loses the **Host Server** attribute value.

▶ **Rename objects**—These objects have been renamed due to "name collisions" within NDS/eDirectory. Name collisions occur during the synchronization when the same object is found on different servers, with different creation timestamps. **Rename** objects take on names such as **1_1**, **22_4**, and so on.

REAL
WORLD

Tuned Name

We have discussed the importance of time synchronization to DS in a number of chapters previously. We have also talked about how timestamps are used to identify DS events. Among the various timestamps, creation timestamps (CTS) are of particular importance. The CTS is a component in the tuned name, which is composed of the object's FDN (cn.ou.o) as well as the CTS for each level of the DN (cn CTS, ou CTS, o CTS). DS uses the tuned name in the process of resolving names to identify more completely an object in the DS tree. If the tuned name does not match from replica to replica of a particular partition, the object is identified as a unique object, and an object rename (for example, 1_1, 22_4) will occur. This happens regardless of whether the DN or the CTS is mismatched.

If you use Scantree or NDSCount to report on object counts, any Unknown objects in the tree are revealed. Otherwise, you can check for Unknown objects by using NList, NetWare Administrator, ConsoleOne, or similar management tools:

▶ From a workstation command prompt, execute the following and then review the resulting file:

```
NLIST unknown /S /C /R > unknown.txt
```

▶ Using NetWare Administrator or ConsoleOne, turn off the display of all other object types except for containers and Unknown and then browse the tree.

TIP

As discussed in the "Time Synchronization" section in Chapter 2, "eDirectory Basics," objects having auxiliary class attributes will show up as Unknown objects on servers running NDS 6 and NDS 7 due to these servers' inability to recognize the auxiliary class attributes. Therefore, if you discover the presence of Unknown objects, you should check whether these objects also exist on servers running NDS 8 or higher before raising an alarm.

Finding renamed objects can be quite complex. This is because renamed objects are valid objects with names that take the form #_#. If your object naming convention also includes that format, the determination of collision-renamed objects will require you to inspect each such object manually. You can use NList to generate a list of renamed objects and then review the resulting file:

```
NLIST * = *_* /S /C /R > n_n.txt
```

The Duplicate Tree Name Check

In a properly managed and controlled NDS environment, duplicate tree names should not be an issue. However, if they ever do occur, keep in mind that symptoms of duplicate tree names include -672 errors during a replica synchronization, a sudden appearance of renamed objects, and users losing rights for no apparent reason.

A duplicate tree name can confuse the Backlink process and, thus, lead to DS data corruption or synchronization errors. The Backlink process runs every 13 hours to check on data consistency. During the check, the process resolves exrefs to make sure there is a real entry, and for real entries, the process makes sure that the exrefs are still valid. To accomplish this, the Backlink process uses the resolve name process to walk the tree. Walking the tree involves finding the physical location of an entry ID and obtaining that object's (entry) ID. However, the name/address resolution process does not know what is being requested (trees, servers, or objects); all it knows is a name or an address—there is no context information with it. Duplicate tree names can cause backlinks to be partly resolved to a server in the wrong tree. As a result, exrefs may be wrongfully expired or created, attribute information may be retrieved from the wrong object, or wrong objects may be modified or deleted.

The Backlink process may cross-associate backlinks/DRLs with objects in different trees, and this can result in replica ring confusion, where a server in one tree will try to synchronize with a server in a different tree. But because the RSA key pairs on the NCP Server objects are different, you will encounter -672 errors during replica synchronization and will be unable to authenticate the replicas with each other. In addition, the cross-association may lead DS to think that the tree has two identically named objects that have different CTS values. This results in objects being renamed.

Duplicate tree names can also cause DS rights to become corrupted. When a resolve name operation takes place to determine rights and the desired object does not exist, the object making the query will remove the rights because the object it was supposed to inherit from is nonexistent. Furthermore, this breaks objects that have links to and from other objects.

To illustrate, assume that a Group object has an attribute—Members—that links the Group object to the User objects. In return, a User object has a Group Membership attribute that links the groups the user belongs to. When duplicate tree names occur, these two-way links often become one-way links, resulting in the users losing rights intermittently.

In summary, trees created with the same name as an existing production tree will *not* be given rights to the production tree, nor will they create security holes. However, duplicate tree names can cause significant havoc to otherwise healthy trees.

Duplicate tree names are easier to identify in an IPX environment than in other environments because you can use the DSDiag NLM. However, in an IP environment, unless there are also duplicate IP addresses, the existence of duplicates may not be readily apparent. To check for duplicate tree names by using DSDiag, you do the following:

1. Load `DSDIAG.NLM` from the console prompt on a server that receives the 0x0278 SAP packets for the tree name being checked.

2. From the main menu, select Generate Report.

3. Select Check NDS Versions.

4. From the General Options screen change Retrieve Server List Using from NDS (the default) to SAP. This will allow the following settings to be made:
   ```
   SAP Type:    Change from Bindery (default) to Directory
   Name Filter: treename
   Report File: Enabled
   ```

5. Press F8 to access the Display Options screen. Change the following display settings:
   ```
   Server's Tree SAP Name: Off (default) to On
   Server's Tree Name:     Off (default) to On
   ```

6. Press F10 to create the report.

Using the report generated from `DSDIAG.NLM` (the default report name is `SYS:SYSTEM\DVERS000.RPT`), you can check each server listed to verify that it has the correct server's NDS name. If one or more server NDS names do not belong to the selected tree, a duplicate tree name exists.

> **TIP**
>
> Although not publicized, the DSDiag NLM is shipped with NetWare 5 and higher, including NetWare 6.0. If you do not have it, you can download DSDiag from Novell's Web site (it is included in the NetWare support packs). Refer to TID #2944552 for details on its options.
>
> However, be aware that DSDiag is no longer supported by Novell, which suggests that you instead use NDS iMonitor.

> **NOTE**
>
> You can use the DSMerge utility to rename any identified duplicate trees.

The best, but also the most time intensive, way to determine whether you have duplicate tree names is to compare the CTS values of the [Root] objects on all servers and see whether they were created at the same time. You can use DSVIEW.NLM, DSBrowse, or NDS iMonitor for this purpose; you cannot use the standard management tools such as ConsoleOne for this because CTS is not stored in an object attribute. However, because DSBrowse does not exist for the Unix/Linux platforms, NDS iMonitor would be the best tool to use for cross-platform applicability. Here's how you use it:

1. Access NDS iMonitor's Summary screen.

2. Browse to the T= ([Root]) object.

3. Select the Entry Information link.

4. Note the Creation TimeStamp information that is displayed (see Figure 13.8).

FIGURE 13.8
Creation
TimeStamp
information.

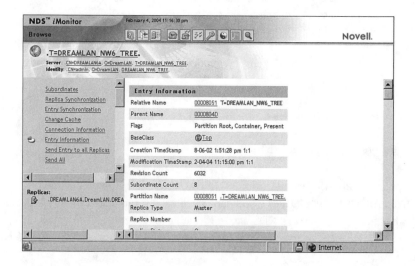

If there is a server whose CTS for [Root] does not match within a few minutes with the CTS found on other servers, you most likely have a duplicate tree.

WARNING

When you detect duplicate tree names and locate the servers hosting the duplicate trees, you need to remove them from the production environment *as soon as possible* in order to prevent (further) DS data corruption. The replica rings (and potentially other corrupt data) have to be cleaned up. You might need assistance from Novell Technical Support.

REAL WORLD

Unique Tree, Server, and Organization Object Names

Other than the facts that all your DS tree names should be unique, you also need to keep server and Organization object names unique.

As previously discussed, the name/address resolution process does not know whether it is resolving a tree name or a server name because there is no context information associated. For example, say that a client attempts to resolve the server name, but the resolution process resolves a tree name instead. When the client uses that entry ID to request server information, such as a list of mounted volumes, tree information or an error is returned instead.

In older DS environments, the tree name could technically be the same as the Organization object name. However, the newer DS modules, especially those of eDirectory, and management tools (such as ConsoleOne) do not tolerate this combination well. Also, such combinations can cause problems with digital certificates.

As a general rule, you should do the following:

- ▶ Ensure that all tree names in the network are unique
- ▶ Ensure that all server names (regardless of operating system platform) are unique
- ▶ Ensure that no DS trees and servers share the same name
- ▶ Ensure that the top-level O= names are not the same as the names of the trees they are in

The DS Tunable Parameter Check

You can change a number of tunable DS performance-related parameters by using the DSTrace command; for Windows servers, this is done via `ds.dlm`'s configuration tabs. You should leave these parameters at the default values unless you are instructed by Novell Technical Support to address a specific issue.

NOTE

Note that Novell's DSTrace output uses the spelling TUNEABLE instead of TUNABLE.

The NDS tunable parameter check is useful to verify that a server's parameters have not been changed or have not be changed to different values than you set for them previously. This is a *server-specific* check, requiring each server in the tree to be checked. On a NetWare server, some of these parameters can be changed through Novell's Servman (NetWare 4.x) or Monitor NLM (NetWare 5.0 and above) utility; others can be changed only with SET DSTRACE commands.

To check the current DS tunable parameter settings, you run DSTrace as follows on the server:

OPERATING SYSTEM	PROCEDURE
NetWare	At the server console, issue the following commands:
	SET TTF=ON Sends the DSTrace screen output to DSTRACE.DBG
	SET DSTRACE=*R Resets the file to 0 bytes
	SET DSTRACE=ON Activates the DSTRACE screen
	SET DSTRACE=*P Displays the parameters
	When you have collected sufficient information, enter SET TTF=OFF to close the DSTRACE.DBG file and then enter SET DSTRACE=OFF to stop further display.
Windows	Select ds.dlm from the main NDSCons screen and click Configure. The different settings can be found under the Intervals, Directory Client, and Server States tabs (see Figures 13.9 through 13.11).
	You can determine the inbound and outbound synchronization status by clicking the Tuneables button on the Trace tab. This sends the status information to the DSTrace screen.
Unix /Linux	Run ndstrace and from within the ndstrace utility enter the following:
	set dstrace=on Enables tracing
	set dstrace=*p Displays the parameters
	The displayed information is saved automatically in the /var/nds/ndstrace.log file, which can be viewed through a text editor.

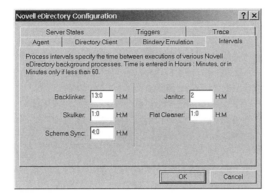

FIGURE 13.9
The Intervals tab, which contains settings for the background processes.

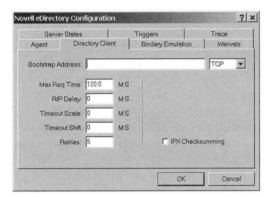

FIGURE 13.10
The Directory Client tab, which contains communications-related settings.

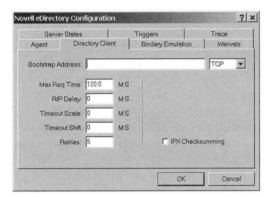

FIGURE 13.11
The Server States tab, which contains the Server "Up" Threshold setting.

The following are the default tunable parameter values for the different types of DS servers:

DS SERVER PLATFORM	PARAMETER VALUE
NetWare 4	ServerStateUpThreshold = 30 minutes External Reference Life Span = 192 hours JanitorInterval = 2 minutes FlatCleaningInterval = 60 minutes BacklinkInterval = 780 minutes Heartbeat Data = 30 minutes Heartbeat Schema = 240 minutes Requests In Progress threshold = 1000 Request IPX checksums = DISABLED IPX:RIPDelay = 20 ticks IPX:Retries = 3 IPX:TimeOutScaleFactor = 2 IPX:TimeOutShiftFactor = 4 Disk accesses before yield = 10 Connection Expiration Timeout = 135 minutes NDS Packet CRC checking = ENABLED Maximum Sockets Threshold = 75% Outbound Synchronization = ENABLED Inbound Synchronization = ENABLED Schema Outbound Synchronization = ENABLED Schema Inbound Synchronization = ENABLED Ensure All Servers available (during partition operations) = Disabled
NetWare 5 and later	ServerStateUpThreshold = 30 minutes External Reference Life Span = 192 hours JanitorInterval = 2 minutes FlatCleaningInterval = 720 minutes BacklinkInterval = 780 minutes Heartbeat Data = 60 minutes Heartbeat Schema = 240 minutes Schema synchronization enabled = 1 SMI Max Cache = 8388608 (Alloced = 1433480, Blks In Use = 0) SMI Entries Cached Per Thread = 50 cached: 23, ~= 52992 bytes) SMI Attr Recs Cached Per Thread = 20 (Cached: 6, ~= 24576 bytes) SMI Partitions Cached Per Thread = 20 (Cached: 13) SMI Force Checkpoint Interval = 180 (cannot change)

DS SERVER PLATFORM	PARAMETER VALUE
	SMI Maximum Read Transaction Seconds = 2400 (cannot change) SMI Maximum Read Transaction Inactive Seconds = 30 (cannot change)
Windows	See Figures 13.9 through 13.11
Unix/Linux	ServerStateUpThreshold = 30 minutes External Reference Life Span = 192 hours JanitorInterval = 2 minutes FlatCleaningInterval = 60 minutes BacklinkInterval = 780 minutes Heartbeat Data = 60 minutes Heartbeat Schema = 240 minutes Max DIB Cache Size = 59498487 bytes Outbound Synchronization = 1 Inbound Synchronization = 1 SMI Max Cache = 59498487 (Alloced = 4855296, Blks In Use = 0) SMI Entries Cached Per Thread = 50 (Cached: 42, ~= 96768 bytes) SMI Attr Recs Cached Per Thread = 20 (Cached: 13, ~= 53248 bytes) SMI Partitions Cached Per Thread = 20 (Cached: 8) SMI Force Checkpoint Interval = 180 (cannot change) SMI Maximum Read Transaction Seconds = 2400 (cannot change) SMI Maximum Read Transaction Inactive Seconds = 30 (cannot change)

NOTE

The tunable parameters output from NetWare 5 and later servers does not include status of inbound and outbound synchronization.

NOTE

The default cache and threads settings are different from server to server because these values depend on the version of DS and the amount of RAM available to DS after all other services are loaded.

The SMI Max Cache value reflects the upper limit of RAM to be allocated for NDS caching.

The eDirectory Cache Statistics Check

Although eDirectory cache statistics do not directly reflect or even impact the health of a tree, they do provide some indication of where the problem lies in the case of slow DS response. For example, imagine that one day you find that searching DS for a list of User objects is taking twice as long as it did the day before. Is this due to a DS problem (such as the local replica not being available and you are searching across a WAN link)? Or did some server RAM configuration change and DS is "disk thrashing," which has resulted in the slow response?

It is easy to check on the statistics by using NDS iMonitor. Refer to the section "Monitoring the Cache Statistics" in Chapter 16, "Tuning eDirectory," for more information.

Periodic review of cache statistics and settings helps to keep your eDirectory at peak performance.

> **TIP**
>
> By keeping tabs on the DIB size (available in NDS iMonitor) you can get some indication of a tree's health. For instance, a sudden increase in DIB size may be normal (due to addition of new objects), but it may also be due to DIB file corruption resulting from (gradual) hardware failure—in which case corrupted DS data will be replicated to other servers in the tree.

The eDirectory Agent Statistics Check

The last, but not least important, tree health check procedure is the eDirectory agent statistics check. Similar to eDirectory cache statistics, the agent usage statistics can act as good indicators of where a problem may be in the case of slow DS response. NDS iMonitor's Verb Statistics page provides information about what types of request the eDirectory agent has been processing.

The Agent Verbs Activity page (see Figure 13.12) provides information that can help you analyze system usage and gauge potential performance bottlenecks. It provides two pieces of data simultaneously. The upper table (DIB Writer Info) shows any process or request currently being written to the DIB or that is waiting to be written (up to five writers may be in a waiting state) and how long they have been in each state. Because any writer must wait until a (DIB) lock is available in order to write to the database, consistently large numbers of concurrent writers with long wait times can signal a performance bottleneck—perhaps in the disk I/O channel.

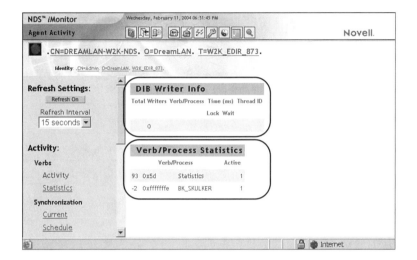

FIGURE 13.12
eDirectory agent
statistics.

The second table on the page (Verb/Process Statistics) shows all processes or requests—whether they are writers or not—that are currently being handled by the DS agent (DSA). Although eDirectory is designed to handle large workloads, large amounts of agent activity at what should be quieter periods could signal an unnecessarily taxed system that needs to be adjusted to properly distribute the workload or an application that is improperly configured or is a resource hog.

Consider this scenario: You have two identically configured servers holding replicas of the same partitions, but one is shown to be consistently busier than the other server. Because the Master replica is responsible for certain background processes, such as obituary processing, distributing the Master replicas more evenly between the servers may help to spread the load. You can also track down the source of any extra traffic and see whether load-balancing it between the servers helps to achieve more optimal system performance, especially for user-interactive applications.

NOTE

Even if the DSA is not processing any requests when you access the Verb Statistics page, the Statistics verb will still show up as active because the Statistics verb is one of the requests that NDS iMonitor uses to generate the displayed data.

Like the Agent Activity page, the agent Verbs Statistics page (see Figure 13.13) helps you analyze system usage and profile the performance of requests made to the DSA. Older versions of NDS simply show a cumulative count of all the requests for all verbs that have been processed since the specified DSA was last initialized. eDirectory 8.5 and later versions also show, in milliseconds, the minimum, maximum, and exponential averages (that is, last 10ms, last 100ms, and so on) that eDirectory requires to process each type of request. This page and the Agent Activity page track background process, bindery, and standard eDirectory requests. You can use this information to find the busier DSAs and attempt to better load-balance between the servers.

FIGURE 13.13
eDirectory verb/
process statis-
tics.

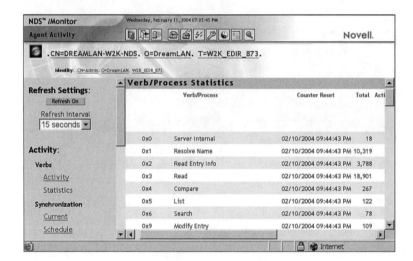

Also available from the Agent Activity page are activity and statistics information for inbound/outbound synchronization processes and various events, such as Add Value and Rename Entry. The event statistics can provide you with data on whether the DS traffic load on the server is read intensive or write intensive. Using this information, you can further tune the cache or disk I/O settings for optimal performance.

Partition Health Check Procedures

As part of DS tree management, various partition operations are performed as needed. In order for the operations to be error free, you should perform some checks before starting any partition-related processes. The following sections outline what checks you should perform, before and after a partition operation, to ensure your tree's health. However, before we look at the various partition operations, we should look at TTS settings in case you are running NDS 6 or NDS 7.

TTS Considerations

Novell's TTS is required for NDS 6 and 7 to function correctly. A NetWare server experiencing a TTS shutdown (a -621 error) indicates that the operating system is not able to track and write the transactions at the maximum transaction level set on the server. This problem may be a temporary problem related to a partition operation that generates a large number of transactions. Or the server might be unable to handle the peak transaction requests generated on a regular basis.

As discussed in Chapter 3, "The Directory Information Base," NDS 6 and 7 use a record-oriented database called Record Manager (RECMAN) that requires TTS to provide transaction protection. NDS 8 and higher, however, use Flexible Adaptive Information Manager (FLAIM) and do not require TTS; FLAIM has it own transaction tracking and rollback mechanism. **NOTE**

Some NDS partition operations, such as removing a replica from the server, require the server to track and write a large number of transactions. When the operating system is unable to manage these requests, errors such as "Growing TTS memory tables" are generated at the console. This particular error indicates that the TTS file will not accept any new transactions, and this usually results in TTS shutdown—which stops NDS from functioning.

Reducing the `Maximum Transactions` parameter can help the server track and write TTS transactions without overburdening the server. You can set this parameter through the Servman (NetWare 4.x) or Monitor (NetWare 5.x and higher) NLM utility. To change the `Maximum Transactions` setting, you do the following:

1. Load the Servman or Monitor NLM at the server console.

2. Select Server Parameters.

3. Select the Transaction Tracking category; on NetWare 6 and higher, select the Common File System category instead.

4. The default setting for `Maximum Transactions` is `10,000`. If TTS shutdown has occurred, try reducing the maximum number of transactions to half that value, `5,000`.

5. If the shutdown condition persists, reduce the setting to `1,000` to resolve most TTS problems.

6. If TTS shutdown continues to occur with changes made to the `Maximum Transactions` parameter, reduce the `TTS UnWritten Cache Wait Time` parameter from its default setting of `1 Min 5.9` sec to `11 sec`.

TIP

When you are removing a *large* replica, setting Maximum Transactions to 1,000 and TTS UnWritten Cache Wait Time to 11 sec can help prevent TTS shutdown for this partition operation.

Backing Up a Server's DS Database

Before you perform any major DS partitioning operation, it is generally a good idea to first make a backup of the DIB on the servers that will be affected by the operation. The DIB backup provides you with a point in time to which you can backtrack.

NOTE

The method discussed here works for all versions of NDS and eDirectory. However, for an eDirectory-only tree, you can also use the eDirectory Backup eMTool utility, which is discussed in Chapter 8, "eDirectory Data Recovery Tools."

Current backup software only backs up objects in the tree. It does not back up partition boundaries. A feature of DSRepair (for NetWare and Windows) allows for backup of the NDS database on a server into a single file, known as the (DIB) "dump file." This file is a snapshot of all the replicas on that server at that moment in time. This information provides for disaster recovery at the server level.

Depending on your server's operating system, you can use one of the following methods to make a backup of the DIB:

OPERATING SYSTEM	PROCEDURE
NetWare	At the server console, enter **LOAD DSREPAIR -RC**. No dialog box will be displayed. DSREPAIR.NLM will create a DIB dump file, silently, and then exit. For NDS 6 and NDS 7, the file is named DSREPAIR.DIB and is located in the SYS:SYSTEM directory. For NDS 8 and higher, the file is located in SYS:SYSTEM\DSR_DIB and is called *xxxxxxxx*.$DU where *xxxxxxxx* is a hex value for the file. The first 100MB of the DIB is copied to 00000000.$DU, the next 100MB is copied to 00000001.$DU, and so on.
Windows	Shut down eDirectory by using NDSCons. Make a copy of all files in *drive*:\Novell\NDS\DIBFiles and its subdirectories.
Unix/Linux	Shut down eDirectory by using ndsd stop. Make a copy of all files in /var/nds/dib and its subdirectories.

You can use DSREPAIR -RC **on Windows servers. If you do that,** dsrepair.dlm
will *not* **display its dialog box after you click Start. Instead, it will quietly create
the DIB dump file,** xxxxxxxx.$DU, **in** drive:\Novell\NDS\DIBFiles, **and then
exit.**

**For NetWare servers, you can use tools such as Novell's Tool Box NLM to make a
copy of the files from the** SYS:_NETWARE **directory. However, Novell does not support this method if you require assistance in restoring the files.**

You will require assistance (via remote dial-in) from Novell Support to
restore a dump file created using DSREPAIR -RC because it is in a compressed format. In the case of Windows and Unix servers, however, you can
restore to the previous state by first shutting down eDirectory and then
overwriting the current DIB, using files from your backup.

Do not **casually restore your current DIB set with a backup copy because that
could result in data loss.**

Adding a Replica

If the partition where the target server will receive a replica has child partitions, you should always run a synchronization and continuity check of the
partition *and* its child partitions before starting the Add Replica operation. If
you do not, then when all servers in the replica ring reply to the Master
server update request, the replica state cannot advance. All servers involved
in this partition operation must be in the Up state until the operation completes.

To verify that the partition operation has completed successfully, you need
to repeat the synchronization (All processed = YES) and replica ring continuity checks on the parent partition and all its child partitions.

Removing a Replica

You should not use DSRepair to remove replicas from servers unless all
other "safer" methods have failed. Instead, you should use NDS Manager,
ConsoleOne, or the Install/NWConfig NLM (which removes servers from
the tree). Before you begin, you should check the synchronization status of
the replica to be deleted and all replicas of its child partitions. You should
verify the synchronization (All processed = YES). You should also check
the partition continuity status and verify that the replica ring is consistent
on all servers in the partition.

To verify that the operation has completed successfully, you should repeat the synchronization (`All processed = YES`) and replica ring continuity checks.

Changing Replica Type

The replica type change sequence is usually where problems occur in the partition health check process. You should be sure to run a continuity check to verify that the process has completed correctly.

Before starting the replica type change process, you should check the time synchronization of the tree. (This is the only partition operation that requires the target server time to be in sync with the network.) You should check the synchronization of the partition where the replica type change is being made and all its child partitions. You should verify the synchronization (`All processed = YES`), and you should also check the replica ring consistency of the replica.

To verify that the partition operation has completed successfully, you should repeat the synchronization (`All processed = YES`) and replica ring continuity checks.

> **NOTE**   If the Master replica is not available, this operation cannot be performed. You need to first use DSRepair to promote a Read/Write or Read-Only replica to Master.

> **WARNING**   Never promote a Subordinate Reference (SubRef) or a Filtered replica—unless for the purpose of disaster recovery and only then as a last resort—to Master because SubRef and Filtered replicas are not full replicas and such an operation would lead to data loss.

Splitting a Partition

Before you begin splitting a partition, you should check the synchronization of the partition involved and verify the synchronization (`All processed = YES`). You should also check the replica ring continuity for the partition.

To verify that the partition operation has completed successfully, you should repeat the synchronization and continuity checks. You should check the status of the parent *and* the new child partition involved in the operation and verify the synchronization (`All processed = YES`). You should also check the partition continuity of the parent and new child partition. Finally, you need to verify that the replica ring list is correct on all servers in the partition.

Joining Two Partitions

Before you make any modifications to the replica ring, you need to make sure the partitions involved are synchronized and that continuity is correct. The Master servers of the parent partition and child partition being joined are responsible for the operation and, thus, must be available for the operation to succeed.

Before you begin joining two partitions, check the partition synchronization of the parent and child partitions. Verify the synchronization (`All processed = YES`) and also check the continuity of the partitions. You should also verify that the replica ring is consistent on all servers in the partition.

To verify that the partition operation has completed successfully, you need to repeat the synchronization (`All processed = YES`) and replica ring continuity checks.

Moving a Subtree

For a move partition operation to complete correctly, the original parent partition, the subtree partition, *and* the new parent partition must be synchronized, and replica rings must be correct on all servers. Before you perform the operation, you need to check the partition synchronization status of each partition involved in the operation (original parent partition, source partition, and destination partition). You need to verify the synchronization (`All processed = YES`) and also check the continuity status of each partition involved in the operation (original parent partition, source partition, and destination partition). Finally, you need to verify that the replica ring is correct on all servers in each partition.

WARNING

This particular partition operation can generate a lot of network traffic, depending on the number of entries in the partition and the parent partition servers involved. This partition operation requires obituary functions to complete their tasks. (Refer to the section "The Move Partition Operation" in Chapter 6, "Understanding Common eDirectory Processes," for details.) If there is a problem with obituaries not cleaning up in the partition, the operation may not complete. Alternatively, if this operation completes but leaves `OBIT_MOVE_INHIBIT` obituaries, the next partition operation involving these partitions will not start.

TIP

It is recommended that before you start the actual partition operation, you first add replicas of the new parent partition to the servers that hold replicas of the partition being moved. The servers that hold replicas of the (old) subtree will still hold replicas after the operation completes. The servers in the parent partition where the subtree will be moved will have subordinate replicas added, and servers in the original parent partition will have their replicas demoted to subordinate replicas.

To verify that the operation has completed successfully, you need to repeat the synchronization (`All processed = YES`) and replica ring continuity checks on each partition involved in the operation.

Server Health Check Procedures

The following sections provide systematic instructions for DS health checks that should be performed when servers are being installed into or removed from a DS tree. When servers are introduced into or removed from the DS tree, replica rings may be modified due to automatic addition or removal of replicas to these servers. Therefore, it is essential that you ensure that the tree is healthy before you add or remove servers from the tree.

Reintroducing a Server into a DS Tree

The following is the recommended procedure for reintroducing a server into the tree; similar health check steps should be taken when installing a new server into the tree:

- ▶ Make sure time is synchronized within the DS tree.

- ▶ Check the DS synchronization and continuity status of the partition where the server will be added. Resolve any errors before proceeding.

The installation process will install DS on the server. If there are fewer than three replicas of the partition into which the `NCP Server` object is being added, a Read/Write replica will automatically be created on the server. If there are child partitions, the necessary SubRef replicas will also be added to the server.

NOTE

If the partition into which the `NCP Server` object is being added is large, it can take some time to put a copy of the replica on it and advance the replica state to On.

> **WARNING** When you install a NetWare 5 or later server into a partition and if this is the first NetWare 5 or NetWare 6 server in the replica ring, a replica may be *automatically* placed on it, even if three or more replicas of the partition exist. This may also happen if the new server runs NDS 8/eDirectory while the servers in the replica ring are not running this version.

Permanently Removing a Server from the DS Tree

There are number of methods for removing a server from a DS tree. The cleanest and preferred method of removing a server is to use the Novell-supplied tools, such as the NWConfig NLM in NetWare, `ndsconfig` in Unix/Linux, or the Install DLM in Windows.

> **NOTE** If you have difficulties uninstalling eDirectory from a Windows server, refer to TID #10058219. For Unix servers, see TID #10080511.

When you uninstall, or remove a server from the tree, the utility you use does the following:

- ▶ Checks for the presence of Master replicas stored on the server being removed. If any are found, you are prompted about whether you want to reassign them to another server manually or automatically. If this is the only replica that currently exists, a replica will be created on another server.

- ▶ Checks all stored replicas to make sure they are all in the On state and that all servers in the replica rings are up.

- ▶ Checks all stored replicas for the `NCP Server` object that is being removed to ensure that it exists either as an actual object or as a back-linked externally referenced object on every server in the replica ring.

- ▶ (NetWare only) Creates a "switch file" (named `SYS:_NETWARE\ UNINSTAL.DS` for NetWare 4.x; NetWare 5 and higher create `SYS:_NETWARE\UNINSTAL.INS` and `SYS:_NETWARE\VOLUME.INS`). This file contains a matrix consisting of the entry ID, entry type, and entry name (DN) for every real object and exref.

- ▶ (NetWare only) Checks for `Volume` objects associated with the `NCP Server` object and deletes them (that is, uses the volume ID stored in the root entry of the directory entry table).

- ▶ Deletes the `NCP Server` object from every replica it can attach to.

- ▶ Clears inbound connections.

- ▶ Removes DS by deleting the DS database files.

Although this procedure is used to remove a server from the tree permanently, it also allows for reinstallation of the NCP Server object by retaining all NetWare file system trustee assignments (using the information stored in the switch file). However, if the server is reinstalled at a later time, replica information will not be restored, nor will references to the NCP Server object. Objects that had referred to the NCP Server object through values such as Default Server, Home Directory, or Print Queues, or through objects such as Directory Maps and Print Servers, will *not* reestablish the reference to the new NCP Server object if it is reinstalled. If the server is to be re-introduced into the tree later, you should see the next section, "Temporarily Removing a Server from the DS Tree," for details.

You follow these steps to remove a server from an DS tree permanently:

1. Make sure time is synchronized within the DS tree.

2. Check the DS synchronization and continuity status of the partition in which the NCP Server object exists. If any errors are found, resolve them before proceeding.

3. Uninstall DS from the server by using the Install or NWConfig NLM in NetWare, the Install DLM in Windows, or ndsconfig in Unix systems.

4. Set the following DSTrace parameters on the server that holds the Master replica of the partition from which the NCP Server object is being deleted:

OPERATING SYSTEM	PROCEDURE
NetWare	At the server console, issue the following commands:

SET TTF=ON	Sends the DSTrace screen output to DSTRACE.DBG
SET DSTRACE=*R	Resets the file to 0 bytes
SET DSTRACE=ON	Activates the DSTrace screen
SET DSTRACE=NODEBUG	Turns off all preset filters
SET DSTRACE=+LIMBER	Enables Limber messages
SET DSTRACE=*L	Forces the Limber process to run

When you have collected sufficient information, enter **SET TTF=OFF** to close the **DSTRACE.DBG** file and then enter **SET DSTRACE=OFF** to stop further display.

OPERATING SYSTEM	PROCEDURE
Windows	Start `dstrace.dlm` from within NDSCons and select Edit, Options. Clear all settings by clicking Clear All. Check the Limber box and click OK.
	Select `ds.dlm` from the main NDSCons screen and click Configure. Select the Triggers tab and then click the Limber button. This will force the Limber process to run.
	You can view the activity by going to the eDirectory Server Trace Utility screen and scrolling through the Limber process. You can also copy and paste the information from the Trace screen to a text file to make it easier to search for error codes.
Unix/Linux	Run `ndstrace` and from within the `ndstrace` utility enter the following:

`set dstrace=on`	Enables tracing
`set dstrace=nodebug`	Turns off all preset filters
`set dstrace=+lmbr`	Enables schema sync messages
`set dstrace=*l`	Forces Schema Sync to run

The displayed information is saved automatically in the `/var/nds/ndstrace.log` file, which can be viewed through a text editor.

NOTE

The Limber process will show the server being removed from the replicas of each server in the replica ring.

5. When all partitions on the server have completed the synchronization process, turn off DSTrace and examine the log file for errors.

6. Use ConsoleOne to verify that the NCP Server object has been removed from the tree and that the server has been removed from all replica rings it previously belonged to.

Temporarily Removing a Server from the DS Tree

There are situations when it is necessary to uninstall or remove a server from the DS tree only for a brief period of time. For example, in the case of an NCP Server authentication key becoming corrupted, it is necessary to bring the server down and reinstall DS on the server (or you will need a dial-in from Novell) to fix it.

During the uninstallation process, the `NCP Server` object is removed from the DS tree. When the `NCP Server` object is removed, objects that reference that server in their mandatory attributes can become `Unknown` objects, and other objects that reference that server in their optional attributes (such as `Home Directory`) will have the attribute values deleted because they are no longer valid.

For NetWare 4, Novell provides the `DSMAINT.NLM` utility to help you avoid the formation of `Unknown` objects and maintain data references during a server uninstallation. DSMaint replaces references to the server with references to another object that you create or that already exists in the tree. After you install DS on the server again, you can use DSMaint to restore the changed references back to the server in other objects' `Host Server`, `Host Device`, or `Message (Default) Server` attributes.

The DSMaint function of server reference replacement is built into the NWConfig NLM for NetWare 5 and later, but it is not implemented for eDirectory on non-NetWare platforms. However, you can use the following steps to remove a server from an NDS/eDirectory tree temporarily and use SrvRef to maintain server references even for non-NetWare platforms:

1. Make sure time is synchronized within the DS tree.

2. Check the DS synchronization and continuity status of the partition in which the `NCP Server` object exists. Resolve any errors before proceeding.

3. Create a `Computer` object to act as the placeholder for the server that will be removed.

4. Download a copy of SrvRef from `ftp://ftp.dreamlan.com/srvref.zip`.

> **NOTE**   By design, SrvRef uses a `Computer` object as the placeholder object because it does not contain any references to servers or server-related objects.

5. Run SrvRef on a Windows workstation (see Figure 13.14).

6. Select Replace Reference from the drop-down list.

7. Select the `NCP Server` object to be replaced.

8. Select the placeholder object.

9. Select the context from which to start the search.

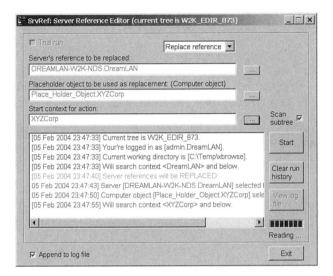

FIGURE 13.14
Using SrvRef to replace and restore server references.

10. Check the Scan Subtree check box.

11. Click Start.

12. Remove the server from the tree by using the appropriate utility: the Install or NWConfig NLM in NetWare, the Install DLM in Windows, or `ndsconfig` in Unix.

13. Use DSTrace to force the Limber process to run (see the previous section).

14. When you are ready to reintroduce the server into the tree, use the appropriate tool to install the server.

15. When DS is operational on the server, repeat steps 4 through 10 but select Restore Reference in step 6 instead.

16. Use ConsoleOne to perform some random checks on objects to ensure that the restoration was successful.

17. Use DSTrace to ensure that the replicas are synchronizing without error.

18. Use ConsoleOne to reestablish any replicas that existed previously on the server, if needed.

19. When everything is done, delete the placeholder `Computer` object.

Novell has available an NDS XBrowse utility (see TID #2960653) that can replace server references. However, it does *not* restore server references. Therefore, it is useful only when NetWare servers are involved (because the option to restore server references is only found in the DSMaint and NWConfig NLMs).
NOTE

Automating Health Checks

Many of the health check procedures described in this chapter can be automated so they are performed periodically, without manual intervention. Novell provides two free NLM utilities (see `http://support.novell.com/produpdate/patchlist.html#tools`) that you can use:

- ▶ **CRON.NLM**—This utility schedules commands to be executed on a NetWare server at specified dates and times. (This utility is included with NetWare 5 and higher, so you may already have it in your **SYS:SYSTEM** directory.)

- ▶ **STUFFKEY.NLM**—This utility allows you to send keystrokes to any NLM screen, giving you the ability to automate processes that require user input.

You can use a text editor to create a Stuffkey script that outlines the keystrokes to be sent. To use the script, you simply supply the filename as a command-line parameter (for example, **LOAD STUFFKEY** *script.txt*). The following is an example of a Stuffkey script file for collecting time synchronization and DS version information using the DSRepair NLM:

```
 # Collect Timesync and DS version info
<screen=System Console>
cls<cr>
load dsrepair<cr>
<waitfor screen=DSRepair Status Screen>
Advanced Options<cr>
Log File And Login Configuration<cr>
<dn>Yes<cr>
SYS:/SYSTEM/COLLECT.TIM<cr>
Overwrite existing file<cr>
<esc>
<esc>
Time<cr>
<waitfor text=Exit the editor>
<esc>
<esc>
<cr>
```

TIP

If you require a better and more powerful scripting facility than what Stuffkey can offer, two excellent options are TaskMaster and TaskMaster Lite from avanti technology, inc. (see www.avanti-tech.com). You can find a sample DS Health Check task script called DSHEALTH.TSK at avanti's Web site; this script not only automatically generates DSTrace and DSRepair logs but also parses them for errors into a formatted final report, eliminating the need to check the various logs manually. When you couple this with an SMTP NLM agent (such as SMTPMAIL.NLM, found at ftp://ftp.dreamlan.com/Freeware/smtp.zip), you can have the final report automatically emailed to you daily.

When you run eDirectory, especially on non-NetWare platforms, NDS iMonitor can help you with health checks. You can use the following steps to set up automated reports:

1. Access NDS iMonitor.

2. Click the Reports icon at the top of the screen.

3. Click the Report Config link.

4. A Runable Report List screen appears (see Figure 13.15). The number of reports varies, depending on the version of eDirectory running on the server.

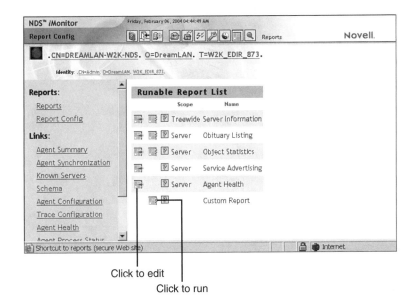

FIGURE 13.15
Available DS health reports.

Click to edit
Click to run

5. Click the Configure Report icon for your desired server information.

6. A Server Information Report screen appears. Use this report to select the desired options. (The options in this screen are eDirectory

version-dependent. For example, eDirectory 8.5 does not have the Health Sub-report option that is shown in Figure 13.16.)

FIGURE 13.16
Report options.

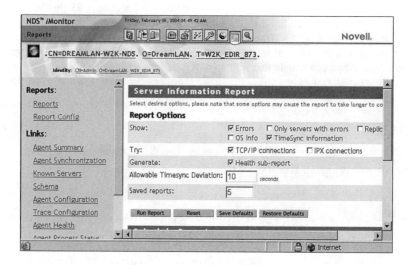

7. To run the report at specified intervals, select the desired options in the Schedule Report section of the Data frame (see Figure 13.17).

FIGURE 13.17
Report scheduling options.

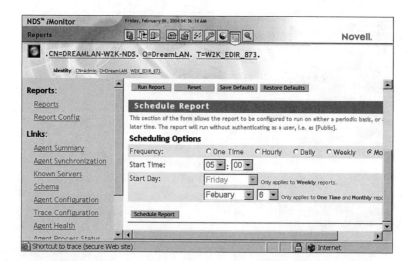

WARNING

If you run a scheduled report, it will run as [Public] and might not be able to gather as much information as it would if you ran it as an authenticated user, such as Admin.

Health Monitoring Using SNMP

The best way to monitor the health of eDirectory (and other networked resources) is to be proactive. One way to be proactive is to be automatically notified of a potential problem before you get phone calls from users. One way to accomplish this is to use the industry-standard Simple Network Management Protocol (SNMP) tools.

SNMP is the standard operations and maintenance protocol of the Internet for exchanging management information between the management console applications and managed devices. Management console applications are applications such as HP OpenView, Novell ManageWise/ZENworks, IBM NetView, and Sun Net Manager. The managed devices can include hosts, routers, bridges, switches, and hubs, as well as network applications such as eDirectory. In order to be able to monitor a device via SNMP, you simply need to install a device- or an application-specific SNMP agent (known as "instrumenting" the device or application, in SNMP parlance) on it. An SNMP agent is included with eDirectory 8.7 and higher.

TIP

Visit the following Web sites for more information about SNMP:

▶ net-snmp.sourceforge.net

▶ www.faqs.org/faqs/snmp-faq/part1/

▶ www.ietf.org/rfc/rfc1157.txt

▶ www.snmplink.org

▶ www.snmpinfo.com

▶ www.wtcs.org/snmp4tpc/snmp_rfc.htm

▶ www.ietf.org/rfc/rfc2605.txt

▶ www.novell.com/coolsolution/nds/features/
a_snmp_faq_edir.html

Of particular interest is RFC 2605, which is about directory monitoring using SNMP.

The eDirectory SNMP agent allows you to do the following:

▶ Real-time monitoring for eDirectory server events (via SNMP traps), such as object creation or deletion and partitioning operations

- ▶ Monitoring of eDirectory from any third-party SNMP MIB browser (by using SNMP `Get` and `GetNext` requests) and management consoles (by receiving SNMP traps)

- ▶ Tracking the status of eDirectory to verify normal operations such as the start and end of various background processes

- ▶ Spotting and reacting to potential problems when they are detected, such as intruder lockout on `User` objects

- ▶ Collecting trends on the access of eDirectory, such as the number of logins over a given time interval

- ▶ Storing and analyzing historical data that has been obtained through SNMP `Get` and `GetNext` request support for statistics

NOTE

The eDirectory Management Information Base (MIB) defines statistics and traps to monitor eDirectory and is assigned the following object ID:
```
iso(1).org(3).dod(6).internet(1).private(4).enterprise(1).
↪novell(23).mibDoc(2).ndsMIB(98)
```

The eDirectory MIB file is called `edir.mib` **and is located in the following directories:**

Platform	Directory
NetWare	`SYS:ETC`
Windows	*drive*`:\Novell\NDS\snmp`
Unix	`/etc/ndssnmp`

The eDirectory MIB is divided into four distinct tables of managed objects:

- ▶ The Cache Database Statistics table, `ndsDbCacheTable`, contains a description of the eDirectory servers as well as summary statistics on the entries cached by these servers.

- ▶ The Config Database Statistics table, `ndsDbConfigTable`, contains a description of the eDirectory servers as well as summary statistics on the entries configured by these servers.

- ▶ The Protocol Statistics table, `ndsProtoIfOpsTable`, provides summary statistics on the accesses, operations, and errors for each application protocol interface of an eDirectory server.

- ▶ The Interaction Statistics table, `ndsServerIntTable`, keeps track of the last *N* eDirectory server with which the monitored directory has interacted or attempted to interact (where *N* is a locally defined constant).

For detailed information on setting up and configuring SNMP for eDirectory, refer to the section "SNMP Support for eDirectory" in the eDirectory documentation.

Summary

This chapter covers, in some detail, the procedures for performing routine eDirectory/NDS health checks, along with information on how to monitor the health status of eDirectory/NDS. Chapter 14, "eDirectory Management Techniques," examines some eDirectory management tips and tricks.

CHAPTER 14

eDirectory Management Techniques

Knowing how to properly use the eDirectory management tools is the first step toward understanding strategies for preventing problems. Understanding effective techniques for using these tools is as important as—if not more important than—understanding how the tools themselves work.

This chapter takes a look at some effective techniques for managing single and multiple objects, using the Novell tools described in Chapter 12, "eDirectory Management Tools," and a few additional tools available from third-party vendors. After looking at basic techniques for single- and multiple-object modification, this chapter delves into advanced techniques of combining tools. These techniques overlap with some of the techniques presented for recovery in Chapter 10, "Programming for eDirectory," because good techniques are effective in both reactive maintenance and preventive maintenance.

Strategies for Managing eDirectory

The specific strategies used for managing eDirectory may vary from environment to environment; however, any strategy for good management is based on three principles:

- ▶ Planning ahead
- ▶ Saving time
- ▶ Knowing your tools

Planning Ahead

Planning ahead can be a difficult task for many administrators—partly because most work reactively rather than proactively. When reacting to situations on a continual basis, you have a constant drain on your time. This drain results in not spending the time to figure out a better way of doing things. Reacting to different situations on a constant basis also frequently results in having to spend time figuring out how to do the same task each time you do it because you cannot remember how you did it the last time, which may have been six months ago.

A good way to start planning ahead is to spend a little extra time documenting solutions to problems as you go along. Finding the time for documentation is not always an easy task when you're moving from crisis to crisis. Remind yourself—and your management—that documenting your solutions ultimately saves you time and saves the company money.

NOTE   Many companies have policies that any network disruption that lasts more than a specified time (often 30 minutes) needs to have the "lesson learned"—the cause, resolution, and recommendation on how the same issue may be prevented in the future—documented *and* shared with affected company divisions.

Start small when documenting solutions: Take some notes along the way and refer back to them. When dealing with problems, one of the most critical phases of evaluating the solution is reviewing the situation and what happened between the time the problem was discovered and the time it was resolved.

TIP   It is often difficult during a crisis to find the time for taking good, detailed, notes that can be used for documentation at a later time. You might find it more convenient to voice-record your thoughts, observations, and actions with a tape recorder and transcribe them later.

Documenting changes as they are made is also a good way to save time during the troubleshooting process. By having a record of recent changes made, you may stand a better chance of solving the problem quickly. By documenting changes, you can also start to lay down a framework for standard ways of doing things. Having standards is a good way to meet the second strategy for managing eDirectory: saving time.

Saving Time

By spending a little extra time looking at how certain repetitive tasks are done, you might find ways to reduce the amount of time spent doing them. By shaving a little bit of time off each iteration, you can make yourself more productive—and in many environments, being productive is a key to promotion or to working on other projects.

Let's take a simple example: starting ConsoleOne. On a 2GHz Celeron-based machine running Windows 2000, when launched locally on the workstation ConsoleOne takes about 45 seconds to start, depending on the number of snap-ins to be loaded and the other applications running on the system. If you need to add a user to a group, that operation can take a minute or two—significantly more time than the startup of the utility.

TIP

Whenever possible, install a copy of your frequently used administration tools, such as ConsoleOne and NetWare Administrator, locally on your workstation.

With the popularity of USB flash drives, you can easily put a copy of your favorite tools (including ConsoleOne, NetWare Administrator, and so on) on one and keep it handy on your key chain.

If you shut down ConsoleOne and have to restart it later to perform another administrative task, you face another repeat of the startup delay. While 45 seconds may not seem like much, it adds up quickly. If you start ConsoleOne an average of 10 times a day, that's over 35 minutes' worth of *your* time just waiting for the utility to start up over the course of a week. That may not seem like much at first, but if you can find a number of places where you can make small changes, the time adds up. Reducing the time you spend performing repetitive—and frequently boring—tasks gives you time to work on projects you want to be working on.

TIP

You may be tempted to leave ConsoleOne running at all times in order to save on its launch time. However, there have been some memory leak issues (depending on the versions of ConsoleOne and the workstation's Java Runtime Environment [JRE]) that can result in degraded performance as time progresses. Instead, it can often be more productive to "save up" a number of changes and do them together. Some companies have polices that certain types of changes (such as updating the employee phone numbers stored in directory services [DS]) are done once a week, on a Monday morning, for instance.

Coming up with standard ways of doing tasks also makes it possible to train others to do repetitive tasks. If you are a programmer, knowing when you can save time by writing a program—as opposed to using standard tools to complete the task at hand—is important. If you know your programming skills can make shorter work of a repetitive task, spend a little extra time writing the program. Using automated tools—even home-grown tools—can help ensure consistency in how tasks are performed and make your network easier to administer.

Knowing Your Tools

There is nothing worse for a new administrator than the overwhelming task of learning how to effectively use all the tools available. To know when to use ICE instead of ConsoleOne, for example, you need to know the features of both utilities and be able to ascertain when one utility is better than the other.

You should spend time with the different utilities to learn the strengths and weaknesses of each one. What works for you may not work for someone else, but knowledge always works to your advantage, particularly when you're trying to save time.

You should look at older tools if they are available. Novell does not provide the DOS-based NETADMIN utility with NetWare 5 and higher, but a NetWare 4.x server on your network would have a copy of it. NETADMIN has its own features that can prove useful in making lots of changes when ICE or UImport cannot be easily applied (for example, when you're updating console operators on multiple servers or making a quick change to a login script). One limitation of NETADMIN to be aware of is that it does not support extended schema classes and attributes, not to mention some of the newer classes introduced in NetWare 5 and higher, and it definitely does not support auxiliary classes.

You should also spend time with third-party tools. If your company spends money on a management tool, the best return it can get on the investment is realized only if the tool is used effectively.

If possible, you should reuse parts of tools. For example, Chapter 13, "eDirectory Health Checks," talks about the product bv-Control for NDS eDirectory from BindView Corporation. bv-Control is an extremely powerful tool, but using it fully involves reusing reports that you have created or that are part of the standard reports included with the product. Not having to re-create reports that already exist—or modifying existing reports that almost contain the information you need—saves you time. The only way you can do this, though, is by knowing what comes with the product and organizing your reports so you can find them for reuse later.

Similarly, if you create a data file for a mass user modification with ICE or UImport, you should save the control and data files as well as the tools and scripts you used to create the data files. You never know when they might come in handy—particularly in a disaster-recovery situation.

Knowing your tools also involves knowing shortcuts for certain functions. For instance, when using NetWare Administrator, why would you use the mouse to open the Object menu and select Move when you could simply select the object and press the F7 key to accomplish the same task more quickly? Train yourself to use the shortcut keystrokes instead of using the mouse.

A Secret Fourth Strategy: Multitasking

No, we are not talking about the capabilities in your operating system of choice to run more than one program, although we are talking conceptually of a similar way of doing things. Desktop operating systems typically do not do true multitasking; they do what is called *task switching*. Task switching between multiple computers is what you need to do as an administrator.

Task switching is particularly effective if you use a tool such as bv-Control that can tie up a machine for a significant amount of time (hours to days sometimes, when you're generating complex reports). Having a separate machine to perform tasks like this can save you time and enable you to work on multiple tasks.

Many administrators benefit from having more than one computer at their disposal. It takes some time to get used to the idea of working on more than one project at a time, and it takes a bit of practice to keep from getting lost. If you can master the skill of task switching, though, you'll find your job a whole lot easier.

TIP

You will find having access to multiple systems, placed side-by-side, very handy during DS partitioning and replication operations. For instance, you can have DSTrace displaying the replica synchronization status on one system; another workstation running some network management software showing you the status of servers, available disk space, and network utilization; and a third machine running ConsoleOne to issue the partitioning and replication commands.

Designing for Fault Tolerance

We are all familiar with the Novell recommendation of having at least three replicas for a given partition for the sake of fault tolerance. This is relatively easy to implement in mid- and large-size installations where there are multiple servers. However, how can you provide a similar level of fault tolerance to single-server sites?

In the past, the solution has been to install a low-end NetWare server and put a two-user or a runtime license on it. This provides the customer with two replicas, which is better than having just one. However, there are two major drawbacks. One is that the customer will have to purchase a second server license. The other is the added administrative overhead resulting from the users attaching to this second server and not getting the correct drive mappings, for instance. With the introduction of eDirectory, which runs on multiple operating system platforms, we have a couple more options to choose from.

Although not officially supported nor endorsed by Novell, one could easily install eDirectory on a Windows NT 4.0 Workstation machine (with Service Pack 3 or higher) and use it to host a second copy of the replica. Windows NT workstations are relatively easy to come by, and the hardware requirement is generally lower than that of a NetWare server. On the other hand, with the popularity and availability of freely downloadable Linux today, you can use a SuSE or Red Hat Linux system to host additional replicas. The drawback here is that you need to learn some Linux if you don't already know it. The benefit is that you don't need to pay for the operating system, and the associated hardware costs less than a standard Windows system.

TIP

If you have remote sites that have single servers at those locations, you can consider using a Windows or Linux system to host a second replica at each of those remote sites. In case the main server is unavailable, the users can still authenticate to eDirectory and access other DS-based services without having to cross the WAN.

Single-Object Management

At first, it may seem obvious to use a tool such as ConsoleOne or NetWare Administrator for administering single objects: The interface is intuitive and easy to use for making single-object changes. Several techniques, however, can be applied to single-object administration. In addition, there are instances where using NetWare Administrator is possible, but a repetitive change made to users one by one (for example, during an office move) may make more sense to automate.

Through simple automation of single-object changes, it is possible to reduce the time spent performing administrative tasks. Despite everything that ConsoleOne and NetWare Administrator do well, they do not excel at automated tasks. This is a key place where using UImport (for user objects) or JRBImprt from JRB Software makes more sense and can save you a lot of time. Generally, mass object modification (for example, setting a common password policy for all users in a given container) is something that can save some time because single-object modifications (where the change for each object is different) can take a lot of your time. A single change doesn't seem to be much, but compounded over time, these tasks added together can take more time than any other task you work on.

Let's start by looking at techniques in ConsoleOne.

The ConsoleOne template technique discussed in the following section can be applied using NetWare Administrator, unless otherwise indicated.   **NOTE**

ConsoleOne

One single-object trick is to create users by using ConsoleOne. As an administrator, you undoubtedly often get requests from managers to create new users that look exactly like other users: "We have a new Accounts Payable clerk named Carl who will be working alongside Jane and needs to access the same information Jane does." Normally, the administrator creates a new user ID for Carl and then spends time examining the group memberships and security equivalences and looking through the file system to make sure that Carl has the same rights as Jane.

With ConsoleOne's support for templates, you have a quick way to accomplish this task through the use of a template. To use this shortcut, you start by creating a template object, as shown in Figure 14.1.

As you can see in Figure 14.1, you select to create the template with the Use Template or User option checked. This option enables you to create the template based on the values in another template object or in a user object. You simply create the template based on Jane's user ID.

FIGURE 14.1
Creating a template object.

Create a template based on
settings of an existing User

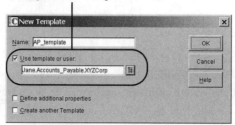

Once the template is created, we can then create Carl's ID using the new template object (`AP_template`), and we will have granted Carl the same (DS) rights that Jane has without having to take any extra steps.

> **NOTE**
> This technique does not create a security equivalence to Jane. Rather, it creates a user with the same security equivalences and group memberships that Jane has. This particular method does *not* duplicate rights in the file system, but if you assigned file system rights by using group objects, Carl would automatically receive many of the required file system rights through group memberships. As part of your management strategy, it is recommended that you keep explicit trustee assignments to a minimum and grant rights through a group or container membership whenever possible.

NETADMIN and Other DOS-Based Tools

Earlier in this chapter, we discussed the use of the NetWare 4.x NETADMIN utility, which is not included with NetWare 5 and higher. The NETADMIN utility and the other DOS-based utilities included with some versions of NetWare are some of the most valuable tools for managing an eDirectory tree. The primary reasons these tools are so valuable are the time you save in launching them and the quick access they offer to various standard attributes used in the base class objects in the tree.

> **NOTE**
> A number of third-party vendors have developed Windows 32-bit operating system console-mode replacements for some of the DOS-based utilities supplied by Novell—with more powerful features in some cases. An example is the suite of JRB utilities (see www.jrbsoftware.com).

> **TIP**
> You can use NETADMIN and the DOS utilities that come with NetWare against an eDirectory tree running on non-NetWare platforms.

Chapter 10 discusses the use of NList and UImport for disaster recovery and building UImport data files using information extracted from DS with NList to rapidly recover from large-scale mistakes. Administration on a large scale is just as effective as disaster recovery. UImport can actually serve as a tool for fast single-object modification as well.

Many people know how to write quick programs in C/C++ or Visual Basic, or even how to use Perl scripts to create and manipulate text files. Rather than learn the NetWare API so you can create or modify users, you can cut a lot of time just by writing a script (using awk, for example) or develop a program to create the data file and use UImport (or ICE or JRBImprt) to make the changes for you. You can even create a single user very rapidly by using UImport, if you have a tool to create a standardized data file for the object creation.

TIP

Using a scripted object creation/modification process provides another means of disaster recovery. You should save the data files once you have finished with them; you never know when they might come in handy. The same data files can serve as a base for your network standards documentation.

Suppose you have a need to make a quick change to your own personal login script. You could start NETADMIN, locate your object, and maneuver through the different tabs to find the login script. If you followed the advice earlier in this chapter, you probably already have NETADMIN or one of your preferred management utilities running, so you've saved some time. You might even have the context your user is in open or use the built-in search feature.

For many people, using the keyboard is more natural and faster than using the mouse. Zipping out to a DOS prompt, using the CX utility (shipped with NetWare) to change to the context your user object is contained in, and starting NETADMIN to make that script change will still be faster than mousing around using a GUI-based application such as NetWare Administrator or ConsoleOne, particularly if you can type quickly.

TIP

Some people have reported that some of the menu-driven DOS-based NetWare utilities do not work with NetWare 5 or higher. Specifically, the problems relate to using the utilities in a pure IP environment because some of the utilities may be hard-coded to use SAP to locate a service that is IPX dependent. When they do not work, you receive error messages that you would not expect. Try the utilities and see what works and what doesn't work. The better you know the limitations of each utility, the better able you will be to decide which tool is the best for the job in your environment.

For most administrators, management of single objects takes more time than any other task they perform. This is the best place to start with trying to find ways to save time by standardizing how you do things. After you standardize single-object management, you can apply the same techniques to multiple-object management.

Multiple-Object Management

Many of the techniques discussed in the previous section apply to multiple-object manipulation as well as to single-object manipulation.

As with single-object manipulation, use of standardized programs in multiple-object manipulation to create scripts for utilities such as UImport, ICE, and JRBImprt can be a tremendous time saver. In the extreme case of a university environment—where you may be creating thousands of users each term—there really is no other approach to mass management than using batch tools.

In this type of environment, the ability to manipulate data is the key. Suppose you receive a list of students from the university administration or the enrollment department. You need to be able to extract the information from the data provided in order to create user objects with standardized names and information. With a project of this scale, standardization is the key to success.

The logical starting place for standardization is the user account names. This is particularly important if you have multiple systems where you want to use the same login identifier for the users. You need to take into consideration several factors when coming up with a standardized naming convention:

- ▸ Standardizing the maximum login name length on all systems
- ▸ Resolving naming clashes
- ▸ Identifying multiple accounts for the same user
- ▸ Updating multiple objects

The following sections talk about each of these in a little more detail.

Standardizing the Maximum Login Name Length

Unlike other systems, NDS and eDirectory allow for a fairly long name length: The login ID has a maximum distinguished name (DN) length of 256 characters. This means the username and all contexts back to the [Root] context must be fewer than 256 characters. This should be more than adequate for any environment; if it is not adequate for your environment, you need to rethink your naming conventions.

However, in some systems, you or another department might use login names that have different limitations. The AS/400 platform running OS/400, for example, has a maximum login name length of only nine characters. Many Unix/Linux limit you to eight characters. In situations where you want to use the same login ID across platforms—even if the user information is not shared—you want to keep the maximum login name lengths in mind for all operating system platforms concerned.

NOTE

When considering what sort of maximum login name length should be used, remember that in NDS, the username the user typically needs to know is his or her object's common name (CN). Thus, if you create the user ID HendersJ in a Unix environment, the DN for that username may end up being something like HendersJ.East.XYZCorp; the CN portion of the full DN is the part that should match between platforms.

Resolving Naming Clashes

The next challenge in multiple-object management is to determine a way to handle name clashes. A naming clash occurs when the following occur:

- ▶ Your standard dictates a way to generate login IDs.
- ▶ Two or more users end up with the same generated login ID.

For example, suppose you opt for an eight-character naming convention that uses up to the first seven characters of the last name and the first initial. This would result in the name Jim Henderson generating the login name HendersJ. The name John Henderson, however, would also result in the login name HendersJ.

Resolving this type of name clash ahead of time in your naming convention—particularly if you're using an automated system—can be difficult. Some companies using this naming convention have opted to use the first six characters of the last name and the first and middle initials. If no middle initial is present, they replace the initial with an uncommon letter—say the letter X. So, Jim Henderson would now become HenderJS, and John Henderson might become HenderJX. If your organization is small enough, this sort of change in the convention might be sufficient.

For larger environments—such as the university environment described earlier in this chapter—the naming scheme just described might not be sufficient. You may want to use some other unique identifier in conjunction with part of the user's name—for example, the user's initials and the last four digits of his or her student number; thus, John Henderson's login ID could end up being JXH1234. In an environment where thousands of users are being created at a time, you do not want to tie the user's name to an arbitrary value. Such a value could be referred to as an "instance number"—the first user being JXH01, the second being JXH02, and so on. Automating the creation of accounts in this manner can become quite complex fairly quickly, depending on the type of constraints you face. The idea is to use the data provided to create a unique key to be used as the user login name.

In smaller environments, it may be sufficient to use first name and last initial or the user's first name or nickname.

Choosing a way to resolve name clashes very much depends on your environment and the politics involved. Whatever method you choose to handle it, you should always keep in mind that you may run into a clash, so you should decide ahead of time how you want to handle it.

Identifying Multiple Accounts for the Same User

Chapter 15, "Effectively Setting Up eDirectory Security," discusses the need to keep administrative accounts separate from non-administrative accounts. Administrative accounts, by their very nature, have the capability to make changes that you may not want to a network during normal operation. For example, an administrative user might be able to make changes to default templates used by the Microsoft Office product suite or, worse, could accidentally delete part of a critical application.

The best solution to this is to create a separate non-administrative account for each user who has administrative authority. That way, these users can perform normal operational tasks such as preparing status reports and project plans by using the non-administrative account, without any risk to the software installations. Their administrative IDs should be used only for administrative tasks, such as creating users. This also gives you the ability to restrict a user's rights if he or she leaves your information systems department (or at least leaves the role where he or she performed administrative tasks). You can simply disable the administrative account and modify the user's non-administrative account to fit his or her new job role.

TIP
One added benefit of having separate IDs for system administration is accountability. If everyone shares the same administrator account, it may be difficult to determine who used the ID last and changed your VP's password.

Using a separate non-administrative account for each user who has administrative authority works very well if the administrative staff has more than one computer to work on.

Administrative accounts should be named such that they are easy to identify at a glance—possibly as obviously as using a user's regular user ID with a special modifier to show the administrative account. Such an identifier could be something obvious, such as the suffix _Admin (making John Henderson's administrative account JXH1234_Admin), but something a little subtler might be called for if your environment is likely to have people attempting to hack into the system. Making the administrative accounts easy for anyone to identify removes a barrier to someone attempting to break into your system.

One variation of using a suffix on the account is to use a different middle initial—say Q—for the user. Searching for administrative accounts that are logged in then becomes a simple matter of searching for all accounts with a middle initial Q.

One other variation is to create two non-admin users and two admin users (other than Admin) and scatter them throughout the tree. This might seem like overkill, but if someone either tries to hack the tree or mistakenly creates a destructive policy with ZENworks, for instance, you always have at least one admin and one non-admin user that you can call on to copy a profile from or to log in without using a script, in order to bypass any issues.

NOTE
Consider keeping at least one hidden admin-type user hidden by placing an Inherited Rights Filter on it. That way, should someone nose around your tree, the person will not be able to come across the administrative username without some efforts. Refer to the section "Protecting Administrative Accounts" in Chapter 15 for more information.

Updating Multiple Objects

ConsoleOne (and NetWare Administrator, too) has the capability to perform modifications on multiple User objects; the newer versions of ConsoleOne can also modify multiple non-user objects. To use this feature, you select multiple user objects while holding down the Ctrl key. Then you select either Object, Properties of Multiple Objects (it is called Details of Multiple Users in NetWare Administrator) or right-click the selected objects and then select Properties of Multiple Objects from the context menu. This brings up the dialog box shown in Figure 14.2.

FIGURE 14.2
Viewing password restriction details about multiple users.

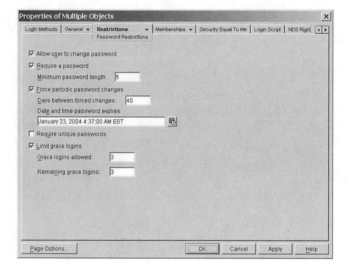

As you can see in Figure 14.2, the dialog box looks nearly identical to the dialog box for a single-object modification. The primary difference is that in this case, you have the ability to set the values for multiple users or to leave values alone.

TIP

You can use the Search function in ConsoleOne or NetWare Administrator to locate the desired User objects in a tree and then use the Properties of Multiple Objects function to view or change that user's settings. For example, to check the password restriction settings on all Sales users (which are located in different containers in a tree), you can start at the [Root] of the tree, select the Search Subtree option, and search for users whose Department attribute has the value Sales. Then from the resulting search window, you can highlight all these users and select Properties of Multiple Objects.

This particular method of changing multiple users is easy to use, but it can also create problems if it is not used properly. For example, if you change user group memberships on a large scale, the result is that the user group membership lists are the same, rather than just having the desired group memberships being added. A better approach in this case is to add multiple users to the group from the group perspective or to use UImport, ICE, or JRBImprt to make this type of mass change.

Administration Tips and Tricks

You can apply a number of tips and tricks to administrating your system. The following sections cover three different classes of tips and tricks: following guidelines and procedures, establishing standards, and considering disk space for DS replication and partitioning operations.

Following eDirectory Management Guidelines and Procedures

There are two types of guidelines you should follow when managing eDirectory. The first type of guideline, of course, is the eDirectory implementation guidelines published by Novell (for instance, the amount of disk space and RAM required for the server as well as the number of objects per container or partition). The hardware guidelines are there to help you to establish the *minimum* requirement, which means you should not only meet them but also exceed them.

Prior to NDS 8, the Novell-recommended number of objects per partition was a good rule of thumb to follow. However, with the advent of eDirectory, the limitation on the number of objects has practically been removed. The constraint now is mostly posed by the management utilities, such as ConsoleOne: The amount of time the utility will take to read and display the objects from a given container becomes a governing factor on how many objects you put in a container. Therefore, depending on your particular application requirement and your own patience (and this goes back to the earlier discussion in this chapter about saving time), you have to make a judgment call on the number of objects per container/partition, but you should use the Novell numbers as a guideline.

The second type of guideline you should follow when managing eDirectory has to do with procedures. You need to have a written set of rules and checklists for performing management tasks. The rules help identify how certain tasks should be done. For instance, there should be a rule that when a user calls the help desk to have his or her password reset, additional confirmation needs to be asked of and verified from the user. Otherwise, it would be easy for someone to impersonate a user, call the help desk to have the password changed, and gain unauthorized access to sensitive company information.

NOTE **We have actually come across some companies where if a user has intruder-locked his or her account, a note from the department manager is required for the help desk to reset the account.**

You should have step-by-step checklists and data forms for performing non-trivial management tasks. For example, you should have a list of steps to take when creating a new user account. The data form may look like this:

User ID requested:	
First name:	
Last name:	
Middle initial:	
Department:	
Telephone number:	
Default/home server:	
Additional groups to be member of:	
Date ID expires:	
Name of manager/Signature:	

Having a form like this helps to ensure that all the required information is associated with the user object and that the required file system rights are properly assigned (through association of group memberships, for example). The most important items are the ID expiration date (in case the user is a seasonal appointment, such as a summer student) and the authorization signature of the user's manager.

TIP **We recommend that you create checklists and data forms for eDirectory partitioning and replication tasks. These checklists and data forms do not need to contain step-by-step instructions on *how* to create a partition or add a new replica but should include *what* steps or tasks need to be performed before and after the creation of a partition/replica. Here are some examples:**

- ▶ **Perform time sync check**
- ▶ **Check replica sync status**
- ▶ **Check obit processing status**
- ▶ **Check amount of free disk space available to DS on servers involved with the operation**
- ▶ **Create replica**
- ▶ **Check replica sync status**
- ▶ **Check amount of free disk space left after operation**

You should refer to the list *every* time you have to work with partitions and replicas and cross off each step as it is done so you don't miss anything. If you have other people helping you with the checklist or data form, have each person initial the steps they performed so you know who to ask questions of, if needed, at a later time.

Every company (and even different divisions within the same company) works differently. Having written rules and procedures helps new staff members to quickly learn what is expected of them and can dramatically reduce the learning curve. Also, having these rules and procedures in writing makes it easier to spot errors and to make improvements.

Establishing eDirectory Management Standards

When creating data files for a mass import, regardless of whether you are using the files for a single object or multiple objects, you should have a standardized way of mapping fields from one file to another. For example, if the new user information you receive contains the full name (consisting of the first and last name of each user), middle initial, employee number, and telephone extension for each user, you should ensure that the data is always presented in a consistent way in the data file. For instance, the fields should always appear in the same order in the data file, perhaps in the same order as the information that you are provided with, to make cross-checking between the two lists easier.

Also, you should ensure that your data conversion program performs the conversions in a consistent manner. Regardless of the programming language you use—or if you use something like Excel to generate the data from another spreadsheet—you need to ensure that the conversion process handles exceptions such as commas in the data fields and the use of special characters.

When using UImport (or ICE or JRBImprt) to create new user objects, you have the option of setting the initial password for the user. The initial password should be fairly easy to remember but should also have a requirement to be changed when the user first logs in. Creating long initial passwords can be difficult to manage; you have to remember that not all platforms support long passwords the way DS does. Whereas DS's password algorithm enables a maximum password length of 128 characters, Windows platforms typically enable 15 characters.

Another standard to consider is the default rights given to the user for his or her home directory. Depending on which utility is used for creating the accounts, you will have different rights granted to the home directory.

If you use a batch procedure to create the accounts, you can use the `RIGHTS.EXE` program (shipped with NetWare) to set the default rights to what you want them to be. Many administrators prefer that users not be able to grant rights to other users for their home directory; unfortunately, creation with many utilities grants the user Access Control rights for the user to his or her home directory, thus allowing the user to grant trustee rights to other users.

> **TIP**
>
> **JRBImprt allows you to specify the file system rights that will be granted to the user's home directory.**

In addition, disk space management is also important: If your environment permits, you should set space restrictions on the home directories and shared data directories. This will save you problems down the road when space starts to get a little thin.

Considering Disk Space for DS Replication and Partitioning

As a rule of thumb, you should create user home directories on a volume other than the `SYS:` volume. On NetWare, DS uses the `SYS:` volume exclusively, and if that volume fills up and you have home directories on it, you will run into synchronization problems that will be compounded by not being able to attach to the server to delete unnecessary files from the volume.

> **TIP**
>
> **On non-NetWare platforms, you should install eDirectory to a dedicated disk whenever possible. For instance, on Windows servers, the default install location is `C:\Novell`. However, the `C:` drive is generally where the Windows operating system files and user applications are located. It would be best to have a separate disk (or volume) for your eDirectory installation to prevent the disk from being filled up too quickly.**

When partitioning a DS tree, you need to use common sense and try to keep partitions from crossing multiple WAN links. Part of the reason for partitioning a tree is to cut down on traffic over the WAN. If you have only two sites, however, partitioning does not make a lot of sense because you still want to maintain three to five copies of each partition in an ideal fault-tolerance setup. If you have only two servers, you should leave just a single partition and keep two copies of the DS replicas.

When removing replicas from a NetWare server, you might receive the following error message:

```
TTS Disabled because of an error growing the TTS memory tables.
```

The way to fix this problem is to decrease the maximum number of transactions by using the `SET MAXIMUM TRANSACTIONS` console parameter. The default for this parameter is 10,000, but for systems with smaller amounts of memory, this can cause a problem. Decreasing the maximum number of transactions causes the Transaction Tracking System (TTS) backout file to grow more because the transactions are queued, but the server will not run out of memory while trying to process the transactions.

When deleting a replica from a server, always ensure that you have plenty of disk space on the volume where DS resides.   **TIP**

With regard to your `SYS:` volume's free space on a NetWare server, there are frequently several categories of files on the `SYS:` volume that you can delete to free up space. These include the following:

▶ Extra language support for utilities. These files include Unicode files and multiple language support at the server. If you use only one language at the server, there is no need to keep the other languages on the server. These files are generally found under `SYS:SYSTEM\NLS`, `SYS:PUBLIC\NLS`, and `SYS:LOGIN\NLS`.

▶ Utilities that you do not use or that you intend to use on a restricted basis (such as `AUDITCON.EXE`).

▶ Any backup files created by support pack installation. These files are generally found in `SYS:SYSTEM\BACKUP.SPx`.

▶ Obsolete `SYS:MAIL` directories, especially the `*.QDR` folders in `SYS:SYSTEM` if the server was upgraded from previous versions of NetWare.

▶ Obsolete `QUEUE` directories (on all volumes).

▶ LAN and DSK/HAM drivers in the `SYS:SYSTEM` directory that are not used at all.

By deleting these files, you can get by with a smaller SYS: volume or at least free up space for larger NDS partitioning and replication operations where the extra disk space would be of use.

Summary

This chapter looks at a number of different techniques for administration of single objects as well as multiple objects. By understanding the four strategies, for eDirectory data management, such as knowing the limitation of the software tools, you can more efficiently provide consistency between objects in the tree. Furthermore, by replicating your DS tree to systems running Linux or Windows, you can achieve additional level of replica fault tolerance for single-server trees.

Chapter 15 examines how to implement DS security in a way that provides flexibility and prevents self-inflicted problems.

Effectively Setting Up eDirectory Security

Management tools and techniques are very important to effectively prevent NDS/eDirectory problems, but they do not address a serious issue facing modern network administrative staff: securing resources from unauthorized access. Experience has shown that the danger of unauthorized access often comes from an internal source (employees, disgruntled or not) rather than from sources outside the organization (hackers).

Another reason to provide security on your network is to prevent the accidental destruction of data. Security is an effective means to limiting the scope of potential damage done by people who do not fully understand how to administer the system or how to properly use administrative tools. Security can prevent non-administrative users from inadvertently causing problems because they deleted something they should have been unable to delete or moved a directory that should not have been moved.

REAL WORLD

Hackers: Good or Evil?
The term *hack* was originally used by electrical engineers to describe clever ways of repairing and improving computer systems. Later, the term was extended to include innovative tricks and algorithms used in designing computer software. The term *hacker*, therefore, generally refers to people who solve computer-related problems quickly, efficiently, and often enthusiastically. You can find additional information about hackers and interesting links at http://fusionanomaly.net/hackers.html.

Unfortunately, Hollywood popularized the term, and *hacker* is now often used to describe a malicious or inquisitive meddler who tries to discover information by poking around—or one who develops and deploys computer viruses and worms. So while good ones do exist, the hackers we refer to in this chapter are of the second variety: the "bad guys."

Effectively securing your system—whether from a deliberate attack or from unintentional error—needs to start with the basic premise that your system is not secure. A good security policy puts enough barriers in the way that the cost of obtaining information is higher than the value of the information to the would-be attacker. These barriers, however, have to be balanced against usability of the system.

This chapter takes an in-depth look at the features of eDirectory security and how to effectively implement security policies so the system is secure and usable.

Physical Security

Before addressing directory services (DS) security, we need to touch on the need for physical security on the servers holding DS replicas. If at all possible, you should take the following measures:

- ▶ Lock the server room

- ▶ Limit access to that room

- ▶ Use an access method that includes a mechanism to trace access to the room

If these measures are not possible, you should find a way to physically secure the system. If someone breaks in and steals the server, no matter how good your security policy is, that person has all the access needed and more than enough time to break into the data.

TIP

It often escapes administrators' attention, but you also need to secure all your backup media. Having access to the data on your system backup is as good as having access to the data on your server.

TIP

If you have a small server that needs to be secured, one option may be Kanguru Solution's Kanguru Encryptor (www.kanguru.com/encryptor.html). It is a real-time data encryption/decryption device and is hardware based. Even if the server is stolen, the data stored on the hard drive is useless to anyone without the correct access key.

Almost all companies have firewalls to protect their data from external attacks across WAN/Internet links. Often overlooked, however, is another aspect of physical security—the various LAN access points located within a network. As with your server room, you should restrict access to network switch rooms where someone can easily plug in a laptop computer running a packet sniffer and gather information that would otherwise require a privileged user ID and password to obtain.

With the popularity of wireless networking, many companies have wireless access points that are interconnected with the LAN infrastructure. It is prudent to enable Wired Equivalent Privacy (WEP) encryption, but even 128-bit WEP is not as secure as you might think, but it's better than not using any security. It is a good idea to change the passphrase or secret key frequently.   **NOTE**

Console Security

Ensuring console security is the next important task in securing the server. If someone can obtain access to your file server's console, that person can copy the DS database files to a publicly accessible directory and take those files offsite for an offline attack (because in DS you do not store the actual password but its public/private key pair). Although the DS database files only yield the password hash, knowing the user ID and length of the password are enough to provide a starting point for a brute-force attack to determine the password.

Unfortunately, when you use RConsole, XConsole, AConsole, and RConag6, passwords may be transmitted in clear text (XConsole) or you might be using an easily reversible encryption scheme (RConsole, AConsole, and RConag6). These problems can open you up to attacks on the console remotely. They provide enough access to obtain the Directory Information Base (DIB) files for such an offline attack. Evaluations of remote console security have turned up problems with using `RConsole`, even when using encrypted passwords (for example, using the `REMOTE ENCRYPT` console command and storing the password in `LDREMOTE.NCF`).

Several services that can be installed on the server grant access to the `SYS:ETC` directory, where the network configuration information is stored if you configure your system with `INETCFG NLM`. If you configure remote access to your system and use Unix Print Services, NFS, or FTP services, the possibility exists that access to your `SYS:ETC` directory is open.

If you set up remote access with RConsole through `INETCFG.NLM` and if unauthorized users have read access to the `SYS:ETC\NETINFO.CFG` file, your console is not secure because the RConsole password is stored in that file in plain text.

> **WARNING**
>
> **We will not go into the details here, but suffice it to say that from a packet capture of an RConsole session, one can easily determine the password, even when it is encrypted.**

Unfortunately, the best policy for remote access is the one that is least feasible: Do not use it. Many system administrators depend on having remote console access to the server for various administrative tasks.

A potentially better solution is to not load the remote console modules until you need them. It is possible to remotely load and unload NetWare Loadable Modules (NLMs) on the server console by using a tool such as Wolfgang's `Remote` utility (`www.geocities.com/wstools`). Setting up RConsole in this manner provides a little more control over who has access to the console and when.

> **NOTE**
>
> **Using remote load/unload commands requires Console Operator privileges on the server you want to execute the command on.**

> **TIP**
>
> **If you are running NetWare 6 and higher, you can use the RconJ module, which supports secured connection via Secure Sockets Layer (SSL). Using that module helps keep your remote access password from being sniffed, but it does not address the problem of finding the password from configuration files that store it in clear-text format.**

Good security for the console is not easy to achieve, but it can be done. You can start by "locking" the console screen, using a password-protected screensaver, or "blanker" (so that the monitor screen does not get burned in). Many people rely on the security of MONITOR NLM's console lock (in NetWare 4.2 and earlier) and the screensaver SCRSAVER NLM in NetWare 5 and higher.

The MONITOR console lock is based on either an entered password or the bindery Supervisor password for the server—even if a bindery context is not present. MONITOR does not, unfortunately, prevent someone from unlocking the console through the NetWare kernel debugger. A password entered at the MONITOR console lock prompt is stored in memory in clear text. If you know where to look, you can read the password directly from memory, continue the server's execution with the G debugger command, and then work from the server console by entering the password discovered in memory.

If you press Enter at the MONITOR lock option, however, the *only* password that unlocks the console is the Supervisor password, and it is stored like any other DS password—after being passed through a one-way hash. Unfortunately, there is a problem with this as well: It is possible, through the NetWare kernel debugger, to completely bypass the security checks in MONITOR and cause MONITOR to think you entered the correct password when you did not. Someone who knows what he or she is doing can do this quickly enough that services hosted by the server are not interrupted. This demonstrates how dangerous it can be to have access to the kernel debugger.

Breaking into the kernel debugger is a simple task: You simply press the left and right Shift keys, one of the two Alt keys, and the Esc key simultaneously—the so-called four-finger salute.

WARNING

Do *not* attempt the four-finger salute on a production system. Breaking into the kernel debugger causes the system to stop responding to client requests. You can restart it with the G debugger command, but it is not recommended that you experiment with production systems.

NetWare 5 and higher remove the screensaver (affectionately referred to as "the snake"—on servers with multiple CPUs, you get multiple snakes, one for each CPU) and console lock components from the MONITOR utility and put them in a separate NLM called SCRSAVER. SCRSAVER, however, requires that the person accessing the console have Supervisor rights to the NCP Server object in the NDS tree. This may not be practical in all cases, and the SCRSAVER NLM does not restrict access to the kernel debugger.

TIP

SCRSAVER **depends on DS to verify and authenticate the user to unlock the screensaver. If the DS is locked (such as when DSRepair is running) when** SCRSAVER **activates, authentication for the admin user cannot take place, resulting in the screensaver hanging in activation mode. However, you can load** SCRSAVER **with the NO PASSWORD option, and it will allow you to unlock the screensaver with no password required when eDirectory is not available.**

For better or stronger console security, you need to look at some third-party solutions. SSLock for NDS (see www.dreamlan.com/sslock.htm), runs on NetWare 4.11 and higher and is an alternative to SCRSAVER and MONITOR's keyboard locking function. The following are some of the features that SSLock v6 offers:

- ▶ Sending of console status change alerts via SMTP email. For instance, when the console is locked or unlocked.

- ▶ Sending of intruder detection warnings via SMTP email.

- ▶ Disabling of access to kernel debugger via the four-finger salute.

▶ Requirement of a valid DS user login ID and password.

▶ Emergency access in case the DS database is locked or corrupted.

▶ Remote status information of **SSLock** and unlocking of the console via a Windows 32-bit operating system GUI client.

▶ Displaying of legal information and requirement of acceptance before the user is allowed to unlock the console.

As with **SCRSAVER**, users who have Supervisor object rights to the **NCP Server** object can unlock and unload SSLock. In addition, you can define users to be members of a group (**SS_UNLOCK**) in order to unlock the console (but *not* unload the NLM). To unload the NLM (that is, to turn it off), the user needs to be a member of a different group (**UNLOAD_SS**). Therefore, when you use SSLock, the users no longer need to be given Supervisor object rights in order to access the server console. Figure 15.1 shows the login screen for SSLock.

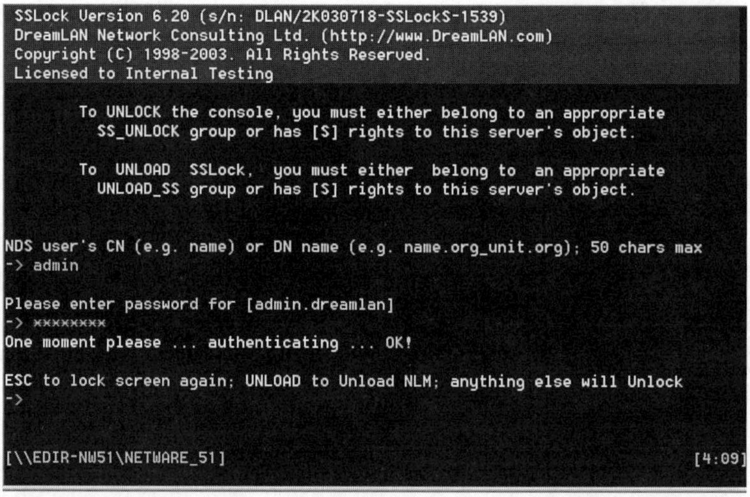

FIGURE 15.1
The SSLock login screen.

```
SSLock Version 6.20 (s/n: DLAN/2K030718-SSLockS-1539)
DreamLAN Network Consulting Ltd. (http://www.DreamLAN.com)
Copyright (C) 1998-2003. All Rights Reserved.
Licensed to Internal Testing

        To UNLOCK the console, you must either belong to an appropriate
          SS_UNLOCK group or has [S] rights to this server's object.

        To  UNLOAD  SSLock,  you must either  belong to  an appropriate
          UNLOAD_SS group or has [S] rights to this server's object.

NDS user's CN (e.g. name) or DN name (e.g. name.org_unit.org); 50 chars max
-> admin

Please enter password for [admin.dreamlan]
-> ********
One moment please ... authenticating ... OK!

ESC to lock screen again; UNLOAD to Unload NLM; anything else will Unlock
->

[\\EDIR-NW51\NETWARE_51]                                          [4:09]
```

If you need something more comprehensive than SSLock, you might try SecureConsole (**www.protocom.com/html/secureconsole.html**), which addresses many needs for console security and provides a high degree of console security. Among other things, SecureConsole does the following:

▶ Requires a valid NDS user login ID and password.

▶ Requires that the login ID be granted explicit access to the server's console. Having Supervisor rights to the server is not sufficient (much like having Supervisor rights is not sufficient to perform print queue operator functions).

- ▶ Is capable of creating an audit trail of all console commands.

- ▶ Has the capability to restrict console commands and access to special console functions, such as the NetWare kernel debugger and the fast restart key sequence introduced in NetWare 4.11.

- ▶ Has a configurable login screen.

- ▶ Can have multiple emergency users (non-DS users) in case the DS database is locked or corrupted.

- ▶ Provides encrypted remote access via IP or IPX.

- ▶ Supports the use of passwords that are available for a specified amount of time for emergency user accounts.

In addition, SecureConsole can be configured through NetWare Administrator, ConsoleOne, or Protocom's server-based administration utility, `SCADMIN.NLM`. Figure 15.2 shows the login screen for SecureConsole.

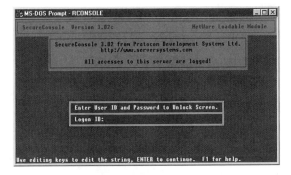

FIGURE 15.2
The Secure-Console login screen.

Security Policies

A well-written data security policy is like a good disaster recovery policy: Everybody says and knows it's important, but only a few people actually implement it. Part of the reason people may be reluctant to write an official security policy is that they hope they never need it—just like they hope they never need a disaster recovery policy. Most people realize they need it only after a problem has been discovered.

A security policy does not need to be very complicated. It should establish the following:

- ▶ Procedures for users requesting access to resources

- ▶ Procedures for granting users access to resources after the request is approved

- ▶ Consequences for accessing unauthorized resources

In addition, if your Information Systems department has multiple levels of administrative authority, the security policy documentation should outline which groups have responsibility for which aspects of the network. In many organizations that implement such a written policy, the policy can be added to the Human Resources manuals or documentation.

It is also recommended that competency testing be implemented. This enables you to verify that people who have a certain level of administrative access know how to properly use their access to perform their job functions. Granting administrative authority of any kind to a resource on the network should be done only if you (or management) have confidence in the people assigned those tasks.

Now that we have covered the physical aspects of security, we can talk about logical, or software-based, security—the security that is inherent in NDS.

Principles of Good Security

There are many for good logical security. Many of the easiest ones to implement are often overlooked because they are not completely obvious. Because many attacks on a network's security system come from inside the organization and can come from people who have help-desk–level authority (that is, authority to change passwords), it is important to protect against that sort of attack.

Figure 15.3 shows a basic structure for granting administrative rights that is used throughout the rest of this chapter. The idea behind this particular architecture is to remove the security administration from the main part of the tree and lock it away where only a few people can make changes—that way, you increase your accountability without compromising flexibility.

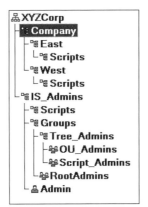

FIGURE 15.3
An administrative container structure.

There are many other ways to structure security, but experience has shown that the model discussed here provides a high degree of flexibility and security because the groups used to assign rights are contained in a separate container (tree branch) that only a few people have access to.

As shown in Figure 15.3, the Admin ID is located in the security administration container. We recommended that you make this branch not browsable by [Public]. You can accomplish this by granting [Public] an explicit object right of "nothing." This helps to limit not-logged-in stations from being able to browse for Admin.

Do not use the Admin ID for daily administrative tasks; use it for emergency situations only. By not using it for daily administrative tasks, you increase accountability for various changes made to the tree.

Another good idea is to generate a long password for the Admin account and store it in a safe, secure place. In one production environment we have worked with, the Admin account is protected with a 40-character randomly generated password. Only two people in the organization—an organization of over 100,000 people—know where that password is stored. Note that if this organization did not implement proper physical security access controls, it would be only a matter of time before that password was compromised.

When creating additional tree administrators, it is generally considered good practice to assign these users explicit rights to the [Root] object in the tree rather than grant them security equivalence to Admin. If something should happen to the Admin account that results in object corruption or deletion, any accounts that are the security equivalent to Admin will lose their rights to the tree.

Protecting Administrative Accounts

The first level of providing good logical security is to protect administrative accounts. This might seem fairly obvious as a need, but the how-to aspect is something that many administrators do not give thought to.

Protecting administrative accounts is quite easy to do. First, you should try to limit the number of partitions that contain administrative accounts and make sure the replicas that hold those objects are on servers that have an extra degree of physical and console security. As discussed earlier in this chapter, if someone can gain access to a server console, he or she can grab the DIB files and attack them offline.

Second, containers where there are administrative accounts should have intruder detection turned on. You can turn this on in NetWare Administrator, for example, by selecting the details of the container and then selecting the Intruder Detection tab. By default, this feature is turned off, and when it's turned off, someone trying to break into your system can try as many passwords as he or she wants in an online brute-force attack. Figure 15.4 shows how to set up this feature.

FIGURE 15.4
Enabling intruder detection through NetWare Administrator.

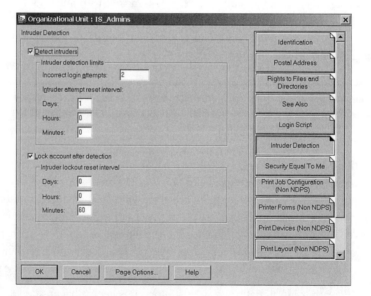

TIP

If you use ConsoleOne to configure intruder detection, the setting is under the General tab and not under the Restrictions tab, as you might expect.

Third, you want to limit the number of workstations the administrative accounts can log in at simultaneously. You may elect to enable administrators to only log in from certain workstations; you can also do this by using a network address restriction. As shown in Figure 15.5, you can enable network address restrictions based on IPX or IP addresses. Although Figure 15.5 also show a number of other address types—Ethernet/Token Ring, AppleTalk, and so on, these entries may be used by custom-developed applications, but they are not used by the Novell Client software to restrict user logins.

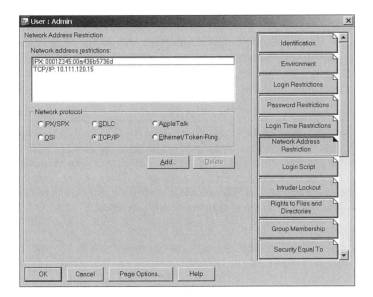

FIGURE 15.5
Specifying network address restrictions.

You can set an address range for the network address restriction instead of entering each node into the list. For instance, to restrict a user to any node on a given IPX segment, you can specify 12 *F*'s for the node address.

For IP, on the other hand, the trick is to set the host address to 0. For example, if you have an IP subnet with an address range from 192.168.1.1 through 192.168.1.254 (a Class C subnet mask of 255.255.255.0), you enter 192.168.1.0 as the address restriction. If you have a nondefault subnet mask (say, 255.255.255.192), you enter the address 192.168.1.64 because IP address restriction will allow login from all computers (192.168.1.64 through 192.168.1.127) in the subnet.

Refer to TID #10065373 for additional information about network address restrictions.

Novell Client software prefers to use IP instead of IPX to connect to NetWare 5.x or higher servers. Therefore, if you have an address restriction set only for IPX, it will not allow the IP connectivity, and this results in the user not being able to log in.

NOTE Enabling some of the additional security options, such as concurrent login restriction and network address restriction, may require you to limit administrators' access to modify their own accounts. If you choose to restrict the number of simultaneous workstations the administrator can use, you might want to prevent administrators from changing that value on their own.

In DS, it is possible to block Supervisor rights to an object or a branch of the tree. The only caveat is that Supervisor rights must be explicitly assigned to at least one user object that is being protected with an Inherited Rights Filter (IRF). Otherwise, you will end up with an unmanageable object.

WARNING Checks are performed by Novell-supplied management utilities, such as NetWare Administrator and ConsoleOne, to validate that at least one user has Supervisor access to a container before an IRF is set. The safety checks are not performed by DS, therefore, when you're using a third-party utility. Therefore, you need to take care when assigning IRFs as NDS may not perform such checks, and you could lock yourself out of a container or from managing an object.

Figure 15.6 shows the Inherited Rights Filter dialog box in its default state. To block a particular right, you simply uncheck it. The arrow next to the check box reflects the state of the filter; when blocked, the arrow icon changes to indicate that a right is blocked. For protecting an administrative account, we recommend blocking all object rights except Browse rights and all property rights except Read and Compare. This prevents someone from deleting the account and re-creating it without the IRF, and it also prevents people from making other changes to the account.

NOTE ConsoleOne shows only the attributes that have an IRF set, which makes checking for IRFs a little easier in ConsoleOne than in NetWare Administrator.

NOTE You access the Inherited Rights Filter dialog box through the Trustees of this Object context menu option.

#### CHAPTER 15

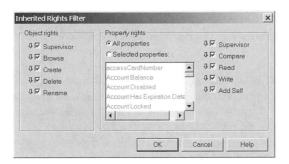

FIGURE 15.6
The Inherited Rights Filter dialog box in NetWare Administrator.

With the Property Rights portion of the Inherited Rights Filter dialog box, you can block rights to specific attributes, such as password management, or to all attributes. The default is to set up the IRF for all properties. By selecting a specific attribute, though, you can be very granular in what you revoke rights to, just as you can when granting rights.

When you're protecting an administrative account, we recommend that in addition to giving a user explicit Supervisor rights to his or her own object, you give another user or group of users rights as well. For example, in Figure 15.3 we have a group called **RootAdmins** located in the **Groups.IS_Admins** container that would be ideal for this type of role. The idea behind doing this is that if an administrative user gets locked out of his or her account, somebody else should be able to unlock the account or change the password. Remember that by applying an IRF to an object, you remove some degree of administrative access to that object.

You might wonder why a special group called **RootAdmins** exists in this example. After all, Admin has explicit rights to **[Root]**, and the discussion thus far has suggested granting explicit rights to **[Root]** for objects that need Admin equivalence. In a large environment, it might make sense to use a group to house administrative accounts other than Admin and possibly one other account; that way, at least one person can get back in if something happens to both the Admin user and the **RootAdmins** group. Using a group membership is somewhat easier to manage if you have a few people with that level of access.

It is also strongly recommended that administrative users change their passwords on a regular basis (perhaps more frequently than the typical end users); it is very easy for administrators to make exceptions for themselves with their own administrative accounts and remove otherwise standard password restrictions and length limitations. If anything, administrative accounts should have their passwords changed more frequently, have longer minimum password lengths than standard user accounts, and be used only for performing administrative tasks. Any other work the administrator does should be performed through a separate account set up as a typical user account.

TIP

Administrative accounts should have strong passwords. A *strong password* is a password with at least a certain number of numeric digits and alphabet characters so that it is not a word that can be found in a dictionary.

You can add strong password support to NetWare 6 by purchasing NMAS, Enterprise Edition. NetWare 4 and 5, on the other hand, do not ship with an option for strong passwords. However, there are third-party solutions available that work with all versions of NDS and eDirectory and do not rely on NetWare servers. One example is Password Policy Manager (PPM) for NDS, from Connectotel Ltd. (www.connectotel.com/ppm**). For more information, refer to the Novell August 2002 AppNote at** http://developer.novell.com/research/appnotes/2000/august/02/a000802.htm.

Also suggested in our tree structure example is a special group called OU_Admins. As the name implies, this group is used for granting rights to all organizational unit (OU) objects and all objects under those containers. The only exception to this is the IS_Admins container itself; only Admin and members of RootAdmins should have rights to the IS_Admins container because these users determine what administrative groups should exist, what rights these groups should have within the tree, and who the group members are.

Protecting the Schema

Having Supervisor rights to the [Root] object grants you another special right: the capability to make changes in the schema partition on all servers. Extending the schema is one of the things that make NDS and eDirectory so versatile. At the same time, you need to control changes to the schema, or you might run into problems due to schema definition clashes. This is a real danger if you have programmers who write programs using the Novell Developer Kit for eDirectory. In most cases, extensions added to the schema can be very difficult to remove, and in some cases, they cannot be removed after they're added.

ConsoleOne includes the Schema Manager (accessed from the Tools pull-down menu; see Figure 15.7) that has the capability of adding extensions to a schema. Administrators who are learning may have a tendency to play with this feature and create new object classes and attribute definitions. If you or another part of the administrative staff want to experiment with this functionality, it is best to test it on a nonproduction tree. For this reason, we recommend using a group for rights at [Root] (the RootAdmins group in the preceding example) and a second group that has rights to all objects under [Root] (the OU_Admins group).

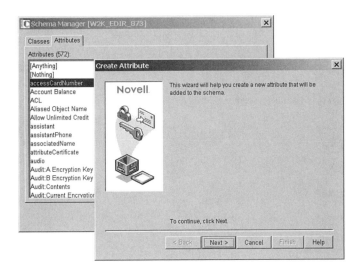

FIGURE 15.7
Creating new class and attribute definitions with Schema Manager.

Limiting the access to [Root] also limits the possibility of someone who is trying to break into your system causing damage. If the administrative accounts are few and are relatively difficult to locate, and if the accounts that are found do not have rights to [Root], the ability for a would-be hacker to extend the schema and create a special class object to be a backdoor into the system is limited.

Protecting Login Scripts

Another aspect of DS that should be closely controlled is the capability to modify login scripts. Refer to Figure 15.3, where another special group is called Script_Admins. The idea behind the Script_Admins group is that only members of the Script_Admins group can change the majority of login scripts.

One large company has implemented this on a rather large scale. Each of the OUs in the tree contains a subcontainer called Scripts. The Scripts container contains profile objects that make up the login scripts for that container. The container script itself contains only one line:

```
INCLUDE ".Main.Scripts.East.Company.XYZCorp"
```

The main script indicated in the INCLUDE statement contains all the standard script components—validation of network address for dial-up accounts (to abort the script and not run programs in the script over a dial-up connection) and execution of an operating system–specific login script.

The operating system–specific script is called with the following line:

```
INCLUDE ".%OS.Scripts.East.Company.XYZCorp"
```

The client performing the login request fills in the %OS portion of the command with the name of the operating system. The Scripts container then contains the following scripts to be included:

- MSDOS
- PCDOS
- DRDOS
- WIN95
- WIN98
- WINNT

These are all created as profile objects and contain commands specific to the operating system in question. The reason this is done is because as the Novell Client has evolved, its login script interpreter has come to include capabilities that are not supported in the old LOGIN.EXE DOS program.

REAL WORLD

Checking for Operating System Type in a Login Script

Depending on the version of Windows and the login script variable you use, you might not be able to tell the difference between a Windows XP workstation and a Windows Server 2003 workstation. You can use the following table to determine what is the best login script variable to use when you need to determine the operating system version of the Windows system:

OPERATING SYSTEM VERSION	PLATFORM	OPERATING SYSTEM	OS_VERSION	WINVER
DOS/ Windows 3.11	WIN	MSDOS (or PCDOS or DRDOS)	6.22 (depends on version of DOS used)	N/A
Windows 95	W95	WIN95	V4.00	4.00.950x
Windows 98	W98	WIN98	V4.10	4.10.1998

OPERATING SYSTEM VERSION	PLATFORM	OPERATING SYSTEM	OS_VERSION	WINVER
Windows NT	WNT	WINNT	V3.51/V4.00	4.0.1381 Service Pack *x*
Windows Me	W98	WIN98	V4.90	4.90.3000
Windows 2000	WNT	WINNT	V5.00	5.0.2195
Windows 2000 SP*x*	WNT	WINNT	V5.00	5.0.2195 Service Pack *x*
Windows XP	WNT	WINNT	V5.01	5.1.2600
Windows codename Longhorn (values subject to change)	WNT	WINNT	6.*x*	6.0.4051

The OS_VERSION **variable returns a value of** V5.01 **instead of the** V5.10 **you would expect for Windows XP. The value returned by Windows XP in binary is** 5.01**, but it is formatted differently in ASCII.**

On 32-bit Windows platforms, the @ command executes an external program and immediately continues the script. It is very similar to the # command (which these interpreters also support), except for the fact that it does not wait for the program that was run to return control back to the interpreter.

Unfortunately, the **LOGIN.EXE** script interpreter does not understand the @ command, and even if you attempt to check for the operating system in the login script as shown here, the script interpreter still interprets the line and returns an error:

```
IF "%OS" = "WINNT" BEGIN
    @NALEXPLD
END
```

You might notice that the list of different script names includes three DOS names and both **WIN95** and **WIN98**. This is because the **%OS** variable actually returns these values, depending on the workstation's operating system. In the case of DOS workstations, however, the scripts for **MSDOS**, **PCDOS**, and

DRDOS are really the same. Rather than copy the script and have to maintain three copies, you can simply work with one (MSDOS is what we use) and then include that script in the others, using the login script INCLUDE command. The same holds true for Windows 98, which is frequently considered by software to be an upgraded Windows 95—the client is the same, the environment is the same, so the script probably should be the same as well.

Protecting login scripts really serves two purposes:

▶ It prevents accidental errors (such as deleting the wrong file from the workstations) in login scripts from causing widespread problems.

▶ It prevents a hacker from inserting commands in the login script to capture passwords or other information or to cause harm to workstations.

When a script change is made and causes problems, it can be difficult to determine what change was made and who made the change. By limiting editing access to the login scripts, you reduce the number of people who might have caused the problem. A good side effect of this is that you can more easily create an environment where script changes are thought out and discussed before implementation.

To limit access to edit the scripts, you need to secure the container. First, you grant Admin and the Script_Admins group explicit Supervisor rights to the Scripts container, as shown in Figure 15.8.

FIGURE 15.8
Granting Supervisor rights to the Scripts container.

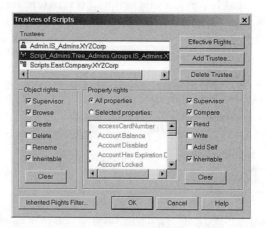

Next, you block all rights to the container except for Browse object rights and Read and Compare rights to all properties.

In addition to the container rights, the users need to have Read rights assigned to the Login Script property of the profile objects; otherwise, the users will not be able to read the scripts in order to run them when they log in.

Protecting Logical Portions of the Tree

In some environments where tree administration is decentralized, it may be necessary to set up regional administration—possibly even site-level administration. If you have administrative groups in Salt Lake City and Toronto, for example, you may not want the administrative group in Toronto to be able to make changes to the users in the Salt Lake City container.

Setting up administrative authority to do this is easy. Using the base model shown in Figure 15.3, you add two groups to the `Groups.Admin` container—one called TorontoAdmins and another called SaltLakeAdmins. For the high-level container in the tree for Salt Lake City, you grant the `SaltLakeAdmins` group Supervisor object rights. Similarly, for the Toronto high-level container, you grant the `TorontoAdmins` group Supervisor object rights.

If multiple sites within a location have their own administration, you can take this a step further. In Salt Lake City, you may have a regional office but also several branch offices with their own IT staff, in Murray, Provo, and Logan. Assuming that these containers are listed under Salt Lake City's container, you would create a container in `Groups.Admin` called `Salt Lake City` and under that container create the groups `MurrayAdmins`, `ProvoAdmins`, and `LoganAdmins`.

The reason for this setup is that you might want to design a hierarchy for adding people to these groups. Putting the branch office administrators in a container named after the region means that you can grant the regional `Admins` groups Supervisor rights to the container. The regional `Admins` groups can add people to those groups, but without having the capability to add people to the regional group.

This type of design is very scalable and easy to manage, and at the same time, it provides a foundation for smaller organizations that will not have to change as the organization grows.

Evaluating Security Equivalences

You should do security equivalence checks from time to time. It never hurts to make sure security is set up the way you think it is.

The first thing you need to understand is how security equivalence works. Figure 15.9 shows three users—AmyP, JimH, and PeterK—and how security equivalence works.

FIGURE 15.9
Security equivalences between three users.

In this figure, JimH is assigned a security equivalence to PeterK, and AmyP is assigned a security equivalence to JimH. In some environments, the result might be that AmyP receives security equivalence to PeterK, but in DS or the bindery, that is *not* the case. Security equivalences are not transitive—they are evaluated only to a single level. This makes the evaluation of security equivalence much simpler.

NetWare 5 introduced a new feature called an Inheritable Access Control List value. As you will see in the section "Setting Up eDirectory Security Access for a Help Desk," later in this chapter, the capability to set this up simplifies administration greatly, but it introduces an additional complexity to evaluating security equivalence—also commonly referred to as the *effective rights* of an object.

Fortunately, NetWare Administrator and ConsoleOne have the capability to perform the evaluation for you, even with the changes that became effective with NetWare 5. Figure 15.10 shows the Effective Rights window in NetWare Administrator.

The evaluation of one object's effective rights to another object's attributes includes several checks:

▸ The trustees of the object being examined (the target object)

▸ Rights granted to parent containers for the target object

▸ Security equivalences of the source object

▸ Rights flagged as Inheritable for the parent container objects to the target object

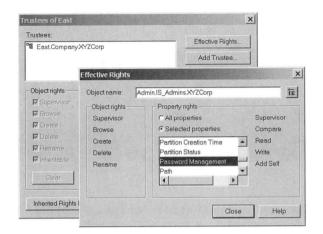

FIGURE 15.10
Using NetWare Administrator to evaluate effective rights.

You might notice that group membership is not one of the things tested. Group membership itself does not grant rights to another object. However, because members of a `Group` object are also security equivalents to the `Group` object, each member will have whatever rights the `Group` object has.

Accountability and Auditing

Starting with the release of NetWare 4, Novell has included a feature for providing an audit trail. The original auditing in NetWare 4.0, and even as late as NetWare 4.10, was not very easy to use. The utility used for manipulating auditing, `AUDITCON.EXE`, was fairly cryptic, and its reports contained too much information to determine who was doing what. In short, it was difficult to find specific information you might look for because the reports were so difficult to read.

In NetWare 4.11, the Auditcon utility became more robust. Gone were the auditing passwords, and in their place was an object placed in the tree to control access to various features of auditing. Auditing in NetWare 5.x is still handled through Auditcon, shown in Figure 15.11. The utility still maintains its somewhat cryptic interface, but the tool has been greatly improved. Because this is a largely unfamiliar utility for administrators, we examine it in some detail. A brief discussion about Novell Nsure Audit (NNA) is presented after the discussion of Auditcon.

FIGURE 15.11
The Auditcon
main menu.

> **NOTE**   Although NetWare 6 no longer ships with Auditcon—NetWare 6.0 ships with
> Novell Advanced Audit Service (NAAS) and NetWare 6.5 ships with NNA—you can
> still use Auditcon against eDirectory running on NetWare 5.1 platforms to perform
> some basic tracking. However, Auditcon only works in a NetWare environment.

Using Auditcon

Auditcon is capable of auditing a large number of events—both file system
and DS events. The following are the audited DS events:

Abort join partitions	Clear NDS statistics
Abort partition	Close bindery
Add attribute to schema	Close stream
Add class to schema	Compare attribute value
Add entry	Create backlink
Add member to group property	Create bindery property
Add partition	Disable user account
Add replica	Enable user account
Add subordinate reference to partition	End replica update
	End schema update
Backup entry	Inspect entry
Change ACL	Intruder lockout change
Change bindery object security	Join partitions
Change bindery property security	List containable classes
Change password	List partitions
Change replica type	List subordinates
Change security also equals	Login user
Change security equivalence	Logout user
Change station restriction	Merge entries

Merge trees

Modify class definition

Modify entry

Move entry

Move tree

Mutate entry

New schema epoch

Open bindery

Open stream

Read entry

Read references

Receive replica update

Reload NDS software

Remove attribute from schema

Remove backlink

Remove bindery property

Remove class from schema

Remove entry

Remove entry directory

Remove member from group property

Remove partition

Remove replica

Rename object

Rename tree

Repair time stamps

Resend entry

Restore entry

Send replica update

Send/receive NDS fragmented request/reply

Split partition

Start partition join

Start replica update

Start schema update

Synchronize partitions

Synchronize schema

Update replica

Update schema

User locked

User unlocked

Verify console operator

Verify password

Auditing is a good way to keep track of what changes are made on a network and who makes them. Auditing can be a very powerful tool, but if it is overused, Auditcon data can become burdensome to maintain and evaluate. Auditing all events is generally not a good idea because of the space needed on all servers and because of the amount of information returned. As you can see, there are many events that can be audited, and many of those events happen very frequently.

You should use auditing when you want to figure out why something is happening. For example, you might want to audit the container objects, but you only see changes in the access control list; this would indicate that someone is granting rights or removing rights in a way that you do not want them to. You might also want to audit changes to passwords or resets of intruder lockouts. In conjunction with a help-desk setup, this is a way to provide checks to verify that only the people you want to be able to make the changes are actually the ones making the changes.

Another use for auditing is to record changes in the DS partitioning and replication scheme. In the Directory Services Auditing dialog box events, there are items to audit partition split/join operations as well as replica additions, deletions, and changes of replica types.

Because an object in the DS tree controls auditing, you can block access to even see the object, thus making the auditing operation transparent to the users and other administrators on the system.

When you have Auditcon running, you can select Audit Directory Services and then select a container to audit by pressing F10. If the container does not have auditing enabled, you see a menu like the one in Figure 15.12.

FIGURE 15.12
Enabling container auditing with Auditcon.

When auditing is enabled, the menu in Figure 15.13 is displayed.

FIGURE 15.13
Menu choices that are available when container auditing is enabled.

The first option in the menu, Change Replica, enables you to select the replica you want to view. DS auditing is stored along with the directory itself and is a part of the partition. Therefore, its information is replicated along with the rest of the partition.

WARNING

Because DS auditing is replicated with the rest of the information in DS, you need to ensure that you have sufficient space on the SYS: volume for the servers that hold replicas of audited containers. If there is insufficient space, you will encounter problems with server utilization and potentially have issues with DS corruption due to insufficient space.

When you're setting up auditing, the menu item you want next is Auditing Configuration. The menu that appears when you select this item, shown in Figure 15.14, is where you select what you want to audit and which objects in the tree you want auditing enabled for.

FIGURE 15.14
The Auditing Configuration menu in Auditcon.

The first item on this menu, Audit by DS Events, enables you to toggle specific events by highlighting the event and pressing F10 (see Figure 15.15). When you have auditing enabled and have selected the events and users you want to audit, you can extract the auditing information from the audit logs. Selecting the Auditing Reports option from the Available Audit Options menu shown in Figure 15.13 brings up the Auditing Reports menu, shown in Figure 15.16.

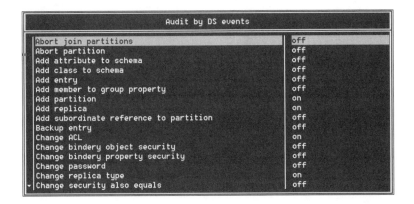

FIGURE 15.15
Selecting which DS events to audit.

FIGURE 15.16
The Auditing
Reports menu.

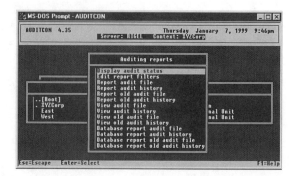

There are several options in the Auditing Reports menu; these options create a readable file that can be browsed offline. If you have few events enabled, browsing offline can be a fast way to see what has been happening on the system. The second type of report is viewed onscreen; this is similar to the report options, except that the information is displayed directly to the screen.

> **NOTE**   Each audit record has an event number and a short description associated with it, as in the following example:
>
> ```
> 23:48:34 Active connection, event 58,
> ➥address 0000E100:0001803750E2, status 0
>              user .CN=admin.O=XYZCorp, replica 1
> ```
>
> If the description text is absent, you can refer to TID #10054493, where many of the event numbers are defined.

The most useful of the different reporting methods is the database report. This creates a comma-delimited file that can be imported into a database or spreadsheet for more detailed analysis. This file format does not lend itself to easy visual examination, but if you are attempting to keep a history of old audit files to establish trends in certain events, this is the best format to use.

The Auditing Reports menu contains the option Edit Report Filters. You can edit these filters either from the menu or after selecting a reporting method. Figure 15.17 shows the options available for creating reporting filters.

In addition to performing DS auditing, you can audit a number of other services. By returning to the main Auditcon menu and enabling volume auditing, you can select the other types of events that can be audited. The information recorded for all the volume-specific auditing events is stored on the volume being audited in the _NETWARE directory on that volume.

FIGURE 15.17
Edit Report Filter
menu options.

All the different types of auditing include the capability to control the configuration of auditing. We mentioned earlier in this chapter that auditing can cause disk space problems if you are not careful with how you use it. The Audit Configuration menu, shown in Figure 15.18, enables you to limit the use of disk space and define what should happen when the audit log is full.

FIGURE 15.18
Audit
Configuration
menu options.

The Audit Configuration menu options are set on a per-volume or per-container basis. Another configuration option is the capability to audit not-logged-in users or to enable auditing of specified users as opposed to all users. The User Restriction menu options are shown in Figure 15.19.

FIGURE 15.19
Special user
restriction config-
uration options.

The other option on the User Restriction menu, also called User restriction, allows you to specify whether all users are audited (value set to NO) or just the specified users selected from the Audit Configuration menu (value set to YES). This is useful if you have containers with a large number of users in them and do not want to have to enable auditing for every user manually or figure out when users are created so you can enable auditing for them.

> **TIP**
>
> The user interface to Auditcon is not one of the friendliest around. If you work for an educational-type establishment, you will probably have to create a number of OUs for new students every semester and then start up Auditcon, enable auditing, and get all the settings right.
>
> A utility called SETAUD.EXE (see www.caledonia.net/setaud.html) may be of help to you. First, you create a template file with the events to audit, and then you simply invoke SETAUD, directly or from an automated procedure that creates the users, to enable and configure the necessary auditing settings. As an added bonus, SETAUD can also disable auditing and clear out the log files before you delete an OU. It can export the auditing logs in a format suitable for importing into Excel for further reporting and analysis.

> **NOTE**
>
> Auditcon works with IPX only. If your NetWare servers are IP only, you need to use the SETAUD utility to enable, disable, and configure auditing.

Because managing auditing requires a fair amount of time and energy, you should not turn on auditing frivolously. Rather, you should use it as a preventive tool. There are two differing philosophies when using auditing:

▶ Let people know you are using an auditing tool.

▶ Do not let people know you are using an auditing tool.

There are advantages to both options. With the first option, people know you are watching what is happening on the network and know that they will be held accountable for the changes they make. This tends to make people think more before they make a change because they know you will find out if something goes wrong.

On the other hand, by not telling people you are using auditing, they do not feel that Big Brother is watching everything they do. Used in this way, auditing can be a tool for helping you learn what shortcomings other administrators have in their education, and you can teach them how to properly do things.

With the second option, if you are not careful, people will find out that you are watching every move they make. It is important when dealing with people that they be at ease and not fearful that you are going to make life difficult for them when they make mistakes. A big part of successfully implementing auditing without letting people know you are auditing them is making sure they cannot see the `Audit:File` objects in the DS tree. If those objects are not blocked, people will likely know that something is up, particularly if they are familiar with how auditing works.

While no method is completely effective for keeping people from knowing auditing is going on, it is possible to make it more difficult to detect. Using an IRF to block rights to the object is a starting place.

NNA

NetWare 6.0 shipped with NAAS, but NAAS is no longer supported as of January 1, 2004. NNA, included with NetWare 6.5, supercedes NAAS. NNA is a centralized, cross-platform, client/server-based auditing service. It can collect event data from multiple applications across multiple platforms; it writes the data to a single data store, using a common data structure; and it includes tools for reporting the logged data. It also provides real-time event information for notification and monitoring.

NNA's installation extends the eDirectory schema and includes Novell iManager 2.0 plug-ins for administration and management. You can configure and manage the various NNA components—including Logging Applications but not Platform Agents—by using Novell iManager or, in environments where eDirectory is not present, by using Novell WebAdmin (see Figure 15.20).

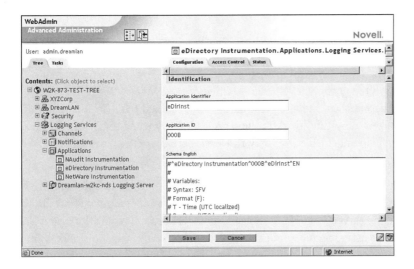

FIGURE 15.20
Managing NNA components using WebAdmin.

NNA is composed of four primary components (see Figure 15.21):

- ▶ Logging applications
- ▶ Platform agents
- ▶ Secure logging server
- ▶ Data store

FIGURE 15.21
NNA architecture
overview.

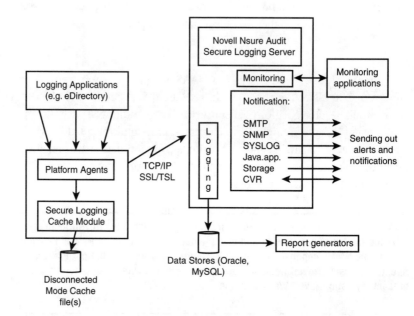

Logging applications, also called reporting applications, are software that reports events to platform agents, using the NNA SDK. Novell has already instrumented many of its systems to log to NNA, including all currently supported versions of NDS and eDirectory; NetWare 4.2, 5.1, and 6.x; BorderManager 3.8; and NetMail 3.5. You can add the instrumentation (that is, event reporting) to your own applications by using the NNA SDK that is freely downloadable from Novell DeveloperNet (`http://developer.novell.com`).

A platform agent is a shared library that collects events from all logging applications on the platform on which it runs and forwards the data to the logging server. One platform agent must reside on every platform that has one or more logging applications. When the platform agent cannot communicate with a secure logging server—due to a downed link, for instance—the collected events are sent to the secure logging cache module, which stores them in a local disconnected mode cache file(s). When the link is reestablished, the contents of these files are transmitted. Similarly, if the platform agent receives a flood of events that might cause network congestion if immediately transmitted, it buffers the events in the secure logging module and trickles the data flow until the traffic lightens.

Unlike other components in NNA, platform agents are not configured through eDirectory. Instead, they use a simple, plain-text configuration file. This makes platform agents small and self-contained and permits them to run on platforms that do not have eDirectory installed.

The communication links between platform agents and the secure logging server can be encrypted using SSL/TLS to ensure the privacy of the events. In addition, platform agents employ two methods—event signing and event chaining—to ensure that the logged events are not otherwise modified by any intervening third parties. In *event signing*, the platform agent (or the logging application, in some cases) embeds a digital signature to each event before the platform agent forwards the event data to the secure logging server. This signature enables the secure logging server to verify the integrity of the event data it receives, ensuring that the data has not been modified.

In *event chaining*, the platform agent establishes a sequential, tamper-evident link of all events. The platform agent (or the logging application, in some cases) includes with each new event from a given logging application a hash of the previous event from the same logging application. The platform agent signs the hash, along with the data from the current event, before sending it on to the secure logging server. The hash enables you to inspect logs to ensure that all events that have occurred are contained in the log in the sequence in which they occurred and that no events are missing.

The secure logging server is a centralized and secure server that aggregates the logging entries received from the various platform agents that it serves. The secure logging server event manager receives the data and forwards it immediately to the logging, notification, and monitoring services provided by the secure logging server. The logging service records the events in the data store. The notification service alerts the appropriate people or systems of particular events or absence of events via one or more of the defined means, such as SNMP and SMTP. The monitoring service sends values in realtime to monitoring applications.

> **TIP**
>
> The Critical Value Reset (CVR) channel in the notification service allows you to *automatically and immediately* reset particular eDirectory attributes' values—but eDirectory attributes only—in the event that those attributes are changed. For instance, say you have a policy that dictates that no user can be the security equivalent to Admin. To enforce this policy, you can create a notification filter object that routes notifications to the CVR handler through a CVR channel object each time a user object is granted security equivalency to Admin. In the CVR channel object, you define a rule that the CVR handler should delete the Security Equals entry by setting the value to NULL.

The secure logging server records all events in a centralized data store, using a format that is similar to the `syslog` packet format. The data store can be kept in a number of different database formats, such as MySQL or Oracle, depending on your selection during NNA installation; if MySQL or Oracle is not already installed, a flat-file database is used instead. NNA is also capable of creating filtered data stores. Based on criteria you define, NNA captures specific types of events and writes those events to secondary data stores. You can query the data stores by using included custom reports and log drivers that support MySQL database, Oracle database, flat-file database, and `syslog`. Novell has planned support for other databases, including DB2 and Sybase. You can also develop your own custom log drivers by using the NNA SDK.

> **NOTE**
>
> Originally developed for Unix systems, the `syslog` protocol, now an Internet standard (see RFC 3164), provides a transport to allow a machine to send event notification messages across IP networks (using UDP with a destination port of 514) to event message collectors—known as `syslog` servers. Because each process, application, and operating system was written somewhat independently, there is little uniformity to the content of `syslog` messages. For this reason, no assumption is made upon the formatting or contents of the messages. The protocol is simply designed to transport these event messages. In all cases, there is one device that originates the message. The `syslog` process on that machine may send the message to a collector. No acknowledgement of the receipt is made.

The NDS/eDirectory Instrumentation application (or *agent*) for NNA, called `auditDS`, allows NNA to log eDirectory events. To log replicated eDirectory events (such as object creation and deletion) on NetWare, Windows, and Linux/Unix systems, `auditDS` should be loaded on one server per DS replica. To log nonreplicated events (such as those associated with DirXML), it must be installed on each individual server for which you want to log nonreplicated events.

> **NOTE**
>
> When `auditDS` **is loaded on more than one server per DS replica, duplicate entries for replicated events will be recorded in the data stores.**

> **NOTE**
>
> **You can find a list of NDS/eDirectory events that can be logged by NNA at** www.novell.com/documentation/lg/nsureaudit/html/ edirectory_events.htm.

The following are two excerpts from the NNA eDirectory event log (in flat-file format)—with the timestamps removed—showing the events associated with Admin logging in and the creation of a new Group object:

```
[eDirInst\Object]: User .Admin.XYZCorp has been allowed to
➥login (Flags: 0)
    by .[Public].
[eDirInst\Object]: User .Admin.XYZCorp (using null password:
➥No)
    logged in (NDS Login: 1).
[eDirInst\Attribute]: A value has been removed by .VEGA-W2KC-
➥NDS.XYZCorp
    from the attribute Last Login Time on the object
➥.Admin.XYZCorp
[eDirInst\Attribute]: A value has been added by .VEGA-W2KC-
➥NDS.XYZCorp
    to the attribute Last Login Time on the object
➥.Admin.XYZCorp
[eDirInst\Attribute]: A value has been removed by .VEGA-W2KC-
➥NDS.XYZCorp
    from the attribute Login Time on the object .Admin.XYZCorp
[eDirInst\Attribute]: A value has been added by .VEGA-W2KC-
➥NDS.XYZCorp
    to the attribute Login Time on the object .Admin.XYZCorp
[eDirInst\Attribute]: A value has been added by .VEGA-W2KC-
➥NDS.XYZCorp
    to the attribute Network Address on the object
➥.Admin.XYZCorp
[eDirInst\Attribute]: A value has been added by .VEGA-W2KC-
➥NDS.XYZCorp
    to the attribute monitoredConnection on the object
[eDirInst\Attribute]: Attribute Object Class was added on
➥object
    .new_group.XYZCorp by .Admin.XYZCorp
[eDirInst\Object]: A new eDirectory object called
➥.new_group.XYZCorp
    (Class: ) was created by .Admin.XYZCorp
[eDirInst\Attribute]: A value has been added by .Admin.XYZCorp
➥to the
```

```
     attribute Object Class on the object .new_group.XYZCorp
[eDirInst\Attribute]: A value has been added by .Admin.XYZCorp
➥to the
     attribute modifiersName on the object .new_group.XYZCorp
[eDirInst\Attribute]: A value has been added by .Admin.XYZCorp
➥to the
     attribute creatorsName on the object .new_group.XYZCorp
[eDirInst\Attribute]: A value has been added by .Admin.XYZCorp
➥to the
     attribute Object Class on the object .new_group.XYZCorp
[eDirInst\Attribute]: A value has been added by .Admin.XYZCorp
➥to the
     attribute CN on the object .new_group.XYZCorp
[eDirInst\Attribute]: A value has been added by .Admin.XYZCorp
➥to the
     attribute GUID on the object .new_group.XYZCorp
[eDirInst\Meta]: Access Control List modified on object
➥.new_group.XYZCorp
     by .Admin.XYZCorp
[eDirInst\Attribute]: A value has been added by .Admin.XYZCorp
➥to the
     attribute ACL on the object .new_group.XYZCorp
[eDirInst\Attribute]: A value has been removed by
➥.Admin.XYZCorp from
     the attribute modifiersName on the object
➥.new_group.XYZCorp
[eDirInst\Attribute]: A value has been added by .Admin.XYZCorp
➥to the
     attribute modifiersName on the object .new_group.XYZCorp
```

As you can see, each event generates a fair number of entries in the log.
Therefore, you need to spend some time considering, deciding, and selecting the types of events to track.

NOTE

The version of NNA that is included with NetWare 6.5 is the NNA Starter Pack. The
Starter Pack allows you to run one logging server (with limited functionality) and
one platform agent; the agent must be on the NetWare 6.5 server. In order to monitor
other non-NetWare 6.5 servers, you must purchase additional platform agents. For
more information about NNA, visit www.novell.com/products/nsureaudit.

TIP

Those of you who have tried to set up NAAS and NNA may have found that these
products are not straightforward in their configuration or that they do too much
(as they provide full-blown event auditing services). Blue Lance, Inc.
(www.bluelance.com) has been a vendor of NetWare auditing applications since
NetWare 3 was introduced. Its new LT Auditor+ suite of applications, which identify eDirectory/NDS vulnerabilities, among other features, may be of interest to you.

Keeping Hackers Out

The majority of the discussion so far in this chapter has been about guarding against internal threats to your NDS tree and servers. External threats can present themselves, as well, and it is therefore necessary to take steps to limit the possibility of someone outside your organization breaking in. The easiest way to accomplish this is to not enable external access to your production network. However, not being connected to outside networks is simply not an option today, due to the need for external email and Internet connectivity.

Because the default protocol for NetWare 5 and higher is TCP/IP, external hackers can become more of a threat if you do not protect your network adequately by using a firewall (if connected directly to the Internet). Using IPX on your LAN puts a distinct barrier into your system—it becomes impossible for you to connect to IPX resources without some sort of IPX-to-IP translation gateway.

There are several things you can do to address this issue:

▶ Use a TCP/IP Network Address Translation (NAT) gateway.

▶ Use a software-based firewall product, such as Novell's BorderManager, or a hardware security appliance, such as Cisco's PIX 535 Firewall, to provide a demilitarized zone (DMZ) between the Internet and your intranet. At the very least, you should put a firewall at your point of presence on the Internet.

▶ Perform your own tests and try to break in to your network from outside your network.

A problem as serious as the threat of someone breaking into your network is the threat of a denial-of-service (DoS) attack. This is an attack on a service hosted on one of your systems that denies users access to the service. Several DoS attacks have surfaced recently, but the concept of DoS attacks has been around for a long time (although it has not always been known by that name).

There are not many DoS attack methods that can be used directly against NetWare, but because many NetWare servers run LDAP and Web-based services, your NetWare servers can easily fall victim to DoS attacks via LDAP and Web ports.

No matter what vendor's firewall product you use at your connection to the outside world, you should be certain you are current with any patches the vendor makes available—especially patches that address security and DoS attacks. DoS can take many forms, from flooding a network interface on a router or server with garbage traffic to intentionally crashing a system that hosts critical services.

Another recommendation is that you keep up on security issues. There are several newsgroups on Usenet as well as mailing lists that discuss security issues. You might also want to search the Internet for sites that specialize in hacking networks. The hackers out there use the information on those sites to learn how to break into other people's systems. You should search those sites and be familiar with the tools of the trade. If you are familiar with those tools, you are better equipped to defend against them.

WARNING   If you decide to experiment with hacking or cracking tools, we *strongly* suggest that you test on an *isolated* nonproduction system. Many of the hacker-programmers out there do not take precautions that professional programmers would take, and it is not worth taking a risk with your production network. If you choose to work with these types of tools, it might be wise to let others in your organization know what you are doing and why; otherwise, when they find out what you are doing, they might not understand your motivations.

Hidden Objects

Earlier in this chapter, we discussed the use of IRFs to block access to certain objects in your tree. Using IRFs in your tree can be beneficial if done properly, but it can be disastrous if the only user object with Supervisor rights to a container or an object is deleted. In addition, you might find that an ex-administrator created a backdoor account in the system and hid the object. Locating hidden objects with excessive authority is not very difficult; the ones that are difficult to find are the ones that are hidden and have no special rights. This type of object is referred to as a *zero-footprint* hidden object.

Tracking down hidden objects with excessive rights is a relatively simple task; however, it can be very repetitive and time-consuming in a large tree. If you have a large network, you might want to look at some of the NDS reporting tools or spend more time learning how to combine NList with awk scripts, as discussed in Chapter 10, "Programming for eDirectory."

Locating hidden objects with excessive rights involves looking at the following:

- ▶ Objects with administrative rights at [Root]

- ▶ Objects with administrative rights at all container levels

- ▶ Objects with administrative rights to Admin and related objects

- ▶ Objects that are listed in the Security Equals attribute for administrative objects

You should also look for objects with administrative rights (specifically, Supervisor rights to [All Entry Rights]) to NCP server objects. These rights grant the user full file system Supervisor rights on all volumes associated with that server.

After you have looked in these places, you will have a list of objects that potentially have Supervisor access to your tree. You can then search your tree for each of the objects you have found to have administrative rights.

Objects that do not have administrative rights but exist in the tree can be a nuisance. For example, if you are attempting to reorganize your tree and need to delete a container, a hidden object or container makes this impossible.

Novell Consulting Services created a utility that is capable of locating hidden objects in the tree. You can find the Hidden Object Locator NLM utility (HOBJLOC.NLM) at www.novell.com/coolsolutions/tools/1098.html. This tool can be extremely useful when you're trying to determine the cause of problems when attempting to delete a container object. For instance, if NetWare Administrator indicates that a container could not be deleted because there are still subordinate objects, there are two possibilities:

- ▶ There are obituaries for objects that used to be in the container that have not purged yet.

- ▶ There are one or more hidden objects in the container.

NOTE

HOBJLOC.NLM **stores its log files, created every time the NLM is run, in the** SYS:SYSTEM\HOBJLOC **directory.**

It is easy to use the Hidden Object Locator utility to rule out the second option as the cause of the problems. If the Hidden Object Locator finds an object (see Figure 15.22), there are at least two options:

▶ Call Novell and ask it to correct the problem.

▶ Visit the DreamLAN Consulting Web site and obtain the MakeSU NLM (www.dreamlan.com/makesu.htm) utility.

FIGURE 15.22
Finding hidden objects in your tree by using HOBJLOC.NLM.

NOTE   At this time, all third-party solutions that deal with IRF-blocked objects are NLM based. That means they require a NetWare server to host the writable replica in which the stealth object resides. If you have a pure-Windows or Unix environment, you need to call Novell.

TIP   Refer to the "Dealing with Stealth Objects" section in Chapter 11, "Examples from the Real World," for additional information on tracking down hidden objects using Novell-supplied tools such as DSBrowse.

Setting Up eDirectory Security Access for a Help Desk

Ever since NetWare 4.0 was first released, administrators have suggested to Novell that it would be nice to be able to set up password administration in NDS without having to grant rights that enable modification of other parts of the User object or tree. Many solutions have been created to solve this need. For example, Novell's own Developer Support group developed a sample utility, called Change Password Service (developer.novell.com/

support/sample/tids/chpasswd/chpasswd.htm), that involved setting up an NLM on the server and building a custom snap-in for NetWare Administrator that communicated the password change to the server.

In order to change a user's password without knowing the current password, you needed to have Write rights to the User object's ACL attribute. As a result, many companies resorted to granting help desk Write access to the ACL attribute of every single User object in the tree—a very long and tedious process. The idea behind using this method was that the password administrators could damage users only if they knew that they could grant themselves additional rights to the User object. This sort of security through obscurity works, but it is dangerous because it leaves the door wide open for those who know what they are doing.

The Danger of Having Write Access to the ACL Attribute

REAL WORLD

Someone having Write access to another object's ACL attribute is equivalent to having Supervisor rights over the target object. The ACL attribute is where the object trustee information is stored. If you can write to it, you can add a trustee entry, granting yourself Supervisor rights to the object. Therefore, many companies have opted not to grant Write access to users' ACL attributes simply for password management purposes. Instead, they use a third-party solution that employs a proxy user. This limits the risk exposure of the help desk making erroneous modifications.

However, in order to achieve the desired goal without purchasing an additional product, this method of granting rights was the only way to solve the problem—until NetWare 5 shipped. With the release of NetWare 5, Novell introduced two features to make setting up help desks a simpler task. The first feature is pseudo-attributes that can be used to grant rights to change passwords and reset intruder lockouts. The second feature is one we have already discussed—the capability to set rights on a container and make those rights inheritable through the tree. By using these two new features, it is now possible to set up password administration for the entire tree with just a few mouse clicks in NetWare Administrator.

To set this up in a tree, you can create a group called `Password_Admins`. This group is going to be granted rights to set passwords and reset intruder lockouts on accounts through the tree. As Figure 15.23 shows, you start by adding this group to the trustees list.

FIGURE 15.23
Granting the
Password_Admin
s group rights to
change pass-
words in the tree.

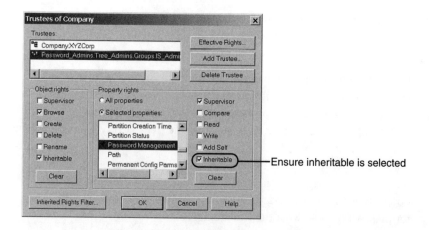

Ensure inheritable is selected

You need to select the Selected Properties item and scroll down to the
`Password Management` attribute. Next, you grant Supervisor rights and
check the Inheritable box. Then you find the `Reset Intruder Lockout`
attribute. Next, you check the Supervisor and Inheritable boxes, just as you
did with the `Password Management` attribute. When this is set up, all you
need to do is add your help desk staff to the `Password_Admins` group, and
they will be able to change passwords and reset intruder detection.

TIP

**For most help desk administration tasks, rights should be granted to the following
attributes:**

`Locked by Intruder`	`Password Allow Change`
`Login Grace Remaining`	`Password Expiration Time`
`Login Grace Limit`	`Password Minimum Length`
`Login Intruder Attempts`	`Password Required`
`Login Intruder Address`	`Password Unique Required`
`Login Intruder Reset Time`	`Password Management`
`Password Expiration Interval`	

**You might want to ensure that the following attributes are not under the control of
the help desk because these settings should be part of your standard security policy and should not be changeable by non-administrators:**

`Intruder Attempt Reset Interval`

`Intruder Lockout Reset Interval`

`Lockout After Detection`

**Refer to the following TIDs for the minimum DS rights required for specific help
desk–related tasks:**

▶ **TID #10051803—NDS for NT user passwords and login settings**

▶ **TID #10084860—Novell Account Management (NAM) 2.1 for Windows 2000**

▶ TID #10016467—Remote control of a workstation in ZENworks

▶ TID #10057330—Managing group memberships

▶ TID #2949136—Reset intruder lockouts

▶ TID #10011322—Minimum rights for a GroupWise administrator

▶ TID #10015319—Password management in NetWare 5 and higher

▶ TID #10068330—Check file system effective rights

▶ TID #10067797—Reset grace logins

NOTE

The password administration feature was first introduced in NetWare 5. In order for it to function correctly, all servers in the tree must be running NetWare 5 and higher. NetWare 4.11 servers running DS.NLM 5.99a or later and NetWare 4.10 servers running DS.NLM 5.12 or later will pass the Inheritable attributes on but do not evaluate, and therefore act on, the security properly for rights flagged as Inheritable. Therefore, if your tree still has NetWare 4 servers, the password administrator's workstation must be attached to a non-NetWare 4 server as its primary connection.

Earlier in this chapter, we talked about protecting administrative accounts. Part of that process was not enabling users with less administrative authority than an account to change administrative account passwords. With this setup, how do you accomplish this?

To start with, the Password_Admins group rights should be granted at the organizational level and not at the [Root] level. This prevents the Password_Admins group from automatically being able to change the Admin user's password. This works well if the administrative accounts are all located in other organizations in the tree (as is the case in this example). If they are mixed in with the typical user accounts, though, this is not going to work.

Let's look at what happens if we set up an IRF on the Admin account that specifically blocks rights to the Password Management attribute. The default right users have to other objects is Browse object rights, and you only granted the Password_Admins group Supervisor rights to the attribute, so all you need to do is block the Supervisor right to the attribute on the Admin user.

TIP

To place an IRF on pseudo-attributes such as Password Management, you need to use ConsoleOne instead of NetWare Administrator.

A quick check of the `Password_Admins` group's effective rights to the Admin user reveals the results in Figure 15.24. As you can see in this figure, with the IRF in place, `Password_Admins` can no longer modify the Admin password.

FIGURE 15.24

The results of checking the `Password_Admins` group's effective rights to the Admin user's Password Management attribute after setting up the IRF.

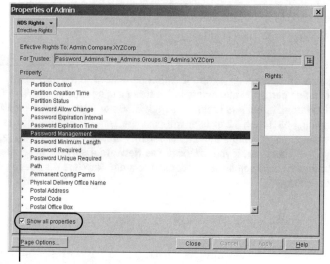

You need to check this box in order to
see the Password Management attribute

When users want call a help desk for assistance with logging in, there might be a second item that they need the help desk to fix: the number of grace logins. Intruder detection can lock an account out, but so can using up all your grace logins. Help desk staff should be able change the number of grace logins. To set this up, all you need to do is set the Write rights to the `Remaining Grace Logins` attribute. When you also check the Inheritable option, this item only needs to be set at the container level, and the rights will be inherited for all objects not explicitly blocked with an IRF.

As mentioned at the beginning of this section, many password-management solutions use a proxy user. This simplifies rights assignment. In addition, these third-party solutions generally provide a GUI front-end that is a lot easier to use than NetWare Administrator or ConsoleOne—and loads much faster, too. Many of these applications also provide options to protect certain users' passwords from being changed. Figure 15.25 shows one such example, NDS Admin want (`www.dreamlan.com/ndsadmin.htm`).

You can place users on an exclusion list
so they cannot be managed by the application

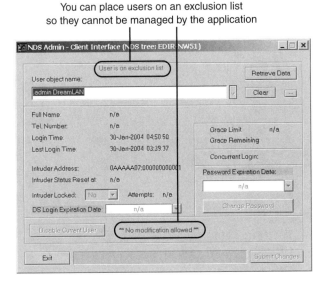

FIGURE 15.25
Excluding Admin and selected users from being managed by the help desk.

Using RBS

You may be wondering why you need to bother with the manual process of setting up security when you can simply use Role-Based Services (RBS). Let's quickly overview RBS. With the introduction of iManager as the direction for a Web-based management tool, a functionality called RBS was introduced. The concept behind RBS is that you have the ability to assign specific responsibilities to users (say, your help desk) and to present them with *only* the tools (and the accompanying DS rights) necessary to perform those sets of responsibilities and those sets only. For instance, the Help Desk role allows the user to only reset intruder lockouts, create users, reset passwords, and nothing more.

RBS allows you to focus the user on a specified set of functions (such as reset intruder lockouts and reset passwords), called *tasks*. One or more tasks can be grouped together and form a *role* (such as Help Desk). What a user sees then when he or she accesses iManager is based on his or her role assignments stored in eDirectory. Only the tasks assigned to that user are displayed (see Figures 15.26 and 15.27). The iManager plug-in for that task presents the necessary tools and interface to perform the task. You can assign multiple roles to a single user. You can also assign the same role to multiple users.

FIGURE 15.26
Giving Admin
access to all
roles and tasks.

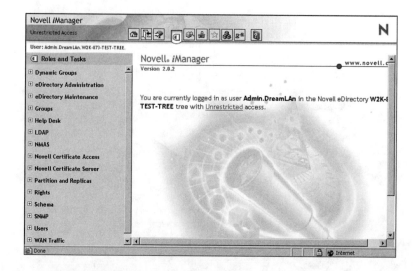

FIGURE 15.27
Giving Users
access to only
the roles and
tasks you have
assigned to
them.

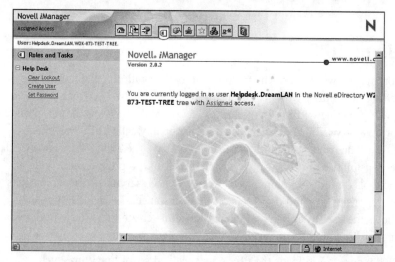

You can either use the existing roles or define additional custom RBS roles
based on your organization's needs. After you have created the desired roles,
you can assign members to each role. In doing so, you also specify the *scope*
(the starting NDS container or context) in which each member can exercise
the functions of the role. A user can be assigned to a role in one or more of
the following ways:

▶ By direct association.

▶ Through group and dynamic group assignments. If a user is a member
of a group or a dynamic group that is assigned to a role, the user has
access to the role.

▶ Through organizational role assignments. If a user is an occupant of an organizational role that is assigned a role, the user has access to the role.

▶ Through container assignment. A User object has access to all the roles to which its parent container is assigned. This could also include other containers, up to the root of the tree.

Therefore, instead of having to go through the steps presented earlier to assign individual rights necessary for a user to perform a specific task, you just use the following simple steps to accomplish the same result by creating role associations and scope assignments:

1. In iManager, click the Configure button (see Figure 15.28).

2. Click Modify iManager Roles under Role Configuration.

3. Click the Modify Members button to the left of the role you want to modify.

4. To add an association to the role, specify the full distinguished name of the object (which can be a user, a group, an organizational role, or a container) in the Name field; you can use the Browse button to the right of the field to locate the object. Fill in the Scope field with a container name; you can also use the Browse button for this.

5. Click Add and then click OK.

Click to display a list
of Roles for selection

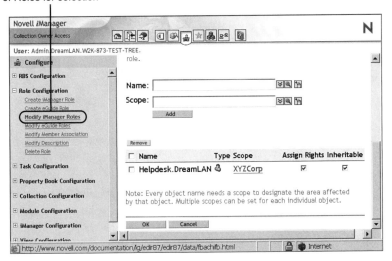

FIGURE 15.28
Modifying
iManager role
assignments.

To remove a role association, you check the box to the left of the listed name(s), click Remove, and then click OK.

NOTE   For more information about setting up and configuring RBS, refer to the "Managing Objects" section in the eDirectory Administration Guide.

TIP   The URL for iManager is `https://ip_address_or_hostname/nps/iManager.html`, and the login requires you to use the LDAP syntax (that is, cn=*username*,ou=*org_unit*,o=*org*) and not the NDS FDN syntax.

On the surface, RBS seems to be the ultimate solution to a security nightmare—giving help desk users only what they need and not too much, with just a few simple clicks. By defining custom roles and tasks, you can present the exact list of tasks for your help desk users to utilize. However, there is a security loophole that is often overlooked.

When you associate a user to a RBS role, the user is granted the necessary DS rights to perform the tasks even when he or she is *not* logged in to iManager! Here is what happens when you add a user to an RBS role, using the example shown in Figure 15.28:

▶ User `Helpdesk.DreamLAN` is added to the Help Desk role with the scope set to `O=XYZCorp`.

▶ An `rbsScope2` object called `XYZCorp` is created under the `Help Desk Management.Role Based Service 2` container.

▶ The `rbsScope2` object is made a trustee of the scope container (`O=XZYCorp` in this case) and granted the necessary rights for the various tasks defined for the Help Desk role (see Figure 15.29).

▶ The user `Helpdesk.DreamLAN` is made an `rbsMember` object of the `rbsScope2` object and is made the security equivalent to the `rbsScope2` object.

All this happens at the eDirectory level, and the assignments are static. This means that `Helpdesk.DreamLAN` has all these DS rights, even when not using iManager. Therefore, the user can use other management utilities, such as ConsoleOne, to perform additional tasks that are allowed by his or her DS rights but not when using iManager—not because he or she doesn't have the necessary rights but because iManager didn't have these additional capabilities listed as available tasks.

This is an rbsScope2 object that functions similarly to a Group object

User will have same rights outside of IManager

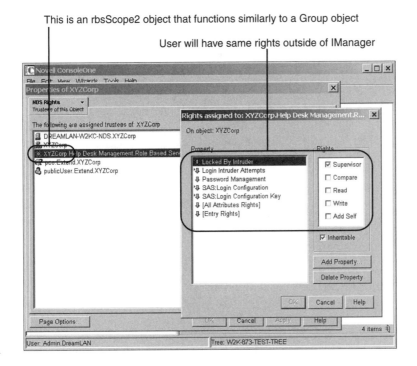

FIGURE 15.29
DS rights
assigned by the
Help Desk RBS
role.

Consider this scenario: The default Help Desk RBS role allows the associated users to create users but not delete users. However, as you recall from the discussion about default ACL templates in Chapter 2, "eDirectory Basics," because of the default ACL template defined for the **Top** class, the object that creates another object has full control (Supervisor rights) over the created object. This means that although the Help Desk role users will not be able to delete users they created using iManager (because it does not give them the option), they *can* delete these **User** objects by using another tool, such as ConsoleOne. Consequently, you must take care when using RBS roles to delegate network management responsibilities.

WARNING

Many administrators took RBS at its face value: "If iManager doesn't allow a certain task for a role, then it can't be performed by members of that role—at all. Therefore, it locks down security assignments." You've seen from the preceding discussion that this perception is inaccurate. Therefore, it is important for you to understand what goes on behind the scene of RBS, especially in regard to the DS rights that are assigned for the different roles.

TIP

You should use some form of auditing (such as NNA, discussed earlier in this chapter), even just for a short period of time, to ensure that there are no unexpected security weaknesses while using RBS roles.

Because RBS role assignments are based on scopes (DS contexts), you should place your administrative users in containers that are not managed by your typical help desk roles to ensure that these users do not get modified accidentally. You should take the precautions and steps outlined earlier to protect your administrative users.

RBS is an excellent tool when used with the right expectation and maintenance. Because it is a Web-based application, its performance and functioning are heavily dependent on a number of factors:

▶ A working Web server, such as Apache.

▶ A working Tomcat servlet engine. (*Servlets* are protocol- and platform-independent server-side components, or programs, that are used to extend the server's functionality. They are the server-side counterparts to *applets*, which are software that adds functionality to a client.)

▶ A functioning Java installation.

▶ A working LDAP server (which Tomcat uses), such as for authentication purposes.

▶ A working SSL/TSL certificate.

If any *one* of these components required by iManager fails, iManager will stop functioning. Therefore, you should not rely on iManager as your sole management platform, and you should have your staff also trained in using other tools, such as ConsoleOne.

Setting Up a Proxy User for LDAP

The final topic this chapter covers is setting up a proxy user for LDAP services (which in turn provides access to eDirectory). At discussed in Chapter 2, when a user performs an anonymous bind (that is, doesn't specify a password), the level of access is based on the rights of the pseudo-object [Public]. By default, [Public] can browse the entire tree hierarchy and read a limited number of attributes on entries. The attributes that [Public] can read are those that are flagged as Public Read.

NOTE

You can find a list of attributes defined in eDirectory 8.7.3, along with their flags, in Appendix C, "eDirectory Classes, Objects, and Attributes."

The default list of attributes accessible by [`Public`] is generally inadequate (for example, searching for `CN` is required for contextless login to function, but `CN` is not one of the `Public Read` attributes). There are two possible solutions to this issue: grant more rights to [`Public`] or use a proxy user that has the required rights.

Some administrators are hesitant to grant additional rights to [`Public`] because every user in the tree is implicitly the security equivalent to [`Public`]. The additional rights may be undesirable. Consequently, most sites opt instead to use a proxy user authentication for LDAP anonymous binds.

Because the proxy user is a real `User` object in the tree, you can easily restrict the types of objects and attributes that anonymous users can access by setting the appropriate DS rights the proxy user has in the tree. However, the proxy user *must* have a blank password (that is, an empty string) in order to work correctly. This is very different from having *no* password. If any user has no password, that user does not have a public/private key pair to compare against when attempting login. A blank password, however, generates a public/private key pair, although the actual string for the password is empty.

TIP

If you allow anonymous binds to your LDAP server, you should use a proxy user instead of [`Public`]. You should grant only the minimum necessary rights (such as Browse and Compare attribute rights) to selected attributes; you should not select the All Properties shortcut unless you have a good reason to.

To discourage someone from logging in from a workstation by using this User object, you should ensure that it has no file system rights anywhere and has network address and concurrent login restrictions.

There may be situations in which you want or need to disallow LDAP anonymous binds, perhaps for the security reason that you don't want just anyone to be able to query your LDAP server. The easiest way to accomplish this is to simply upgrade to eDirectory 8.7 patched to 8.7.0.3 or higher. A new attribute called `ldapBindRestrictions` was introduced in these patches to control the availability of anonymous bind.

WARNING

Keep in mind that the ability for an LDAP server to accept anonymous binds is an RFC requirement. Disallowing anonymous binds may cause some LDAP-compliant applications to fail as they may first perform anonymous binds to do lookups before binding with the actual user credentials.

You perform the following steps to set the LDAP server to *not* accept anonymous binds:

1. Start ConsoleOne and browse to locate your LDAP server object.
2. Right-click the object and select Properties from the context menu.
3. Select the Restrictions tab.
4. Change the Bind Restrictions setting to Disallow Anonymous Simple Bind (see Figure 15.30).
5. Click OK to save the change.

You need to restart the LDAP server for the change to take effect.

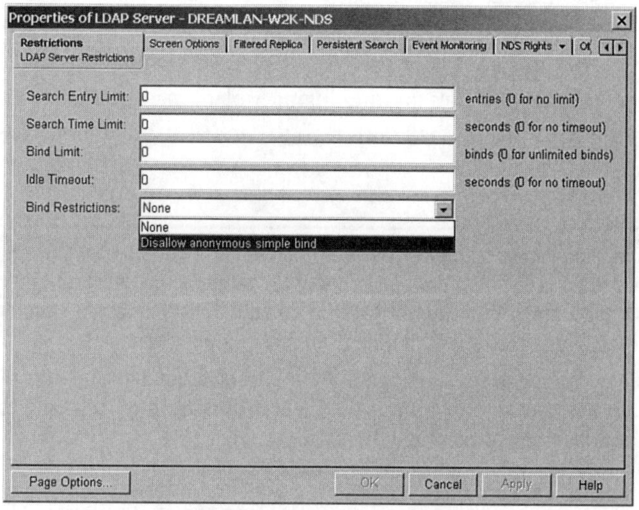

FIGURE 15.30
Disallowing anonymous simple binds.

TIP

Older versions of the LDAP snap-in for ConsoleOne do not have the Bind Restrictions setting. If you're using such a version, you need to use the Other tab to modify the value of the `ldapBindRestrictions` attribute. (If the `ldapBindRestrictions` attribute is not listed, click the Add button, select the `ldapBindRestrictions` attribute, and click OK.) To disable anonymous binds, put the value 1 in the Attribute Value field. Use the value 0 to allow such connections.

If you are running eDirectory 8.7.0.3 or later, if `ldapBindRestrictions` is not one of the available attributes that you can add in the Other tab, or if there is no Bind Restrictions setting under Restrictions, your schema may not have been properly extended for this new attribute. Refer to TID #10077872 for corrective measures.

If you are unable to upgrade to eDirectory 8.7.0.3 or higher, you will have to change the rights of [Public] and those of the proxy user if you are using one so that anonymous bind connections will not be able to browse the tree. You can't prevent users from connecting via anonymous binds, but you can limit what they can see. The reason you need to change the rights of [Public] is that, by default, it has object Browse rights to [Root], which means even if the proxy user has no explicit rights to the tree, the proxy user will still have object Browse rights. You need to take the following measures to make sure the proxy user sees nothing in the tree:

▶ Make the proxy user a trustee of [Root] and grant it no rights of any type.

▶ Remove the object Browse rights of [Public] from the [Root] object.

After you implement these two measures, the proxy user—and thus, anonymous bind connections—will be unable to browse the tree.

Summary

This chapter looks at a number of techniques that can be used to secure NDS/eDirectory in order to proactively prevent administrator-created problems through either accidental or intentional misuse of the management tools. It also discusses different ways of protecting your network from external hackers and describes how to set up security access for help desk personnel in order to perform common tasks such as changing passwords and resetting grace logins. This chapter also covers the pros and cons of using RBS for help desk tasks. Finally, this chapter discusses the use of proxy user to secure LDAP access.

CHAPTER 16

Tuning eDirectory

Other than running eDirectory on a fast CPU, using lots of RAM, using fast disk drives in RAID configuration, and so on, there are also a few noteworthy tricks you can perform from a software perspective to enhance eDirectory's performance without spending additional money. Because Novell's LDAP server uses eDirectory as the back-end database, its performance can be affected by eDirectory's (for example, memory management [cache settings], indexes, replica placement, and search limits).

Certain portions of eDirectory are already configured to take advantage of the presence of multiple processors in the operating environments. The core directory, security, encryption, and LDAP modules are multiprocessor enabled. The following sections discuss the cache settings and indexes in depth. But first, this chapter takes a brief look at replication latency.

Reducing Replication Latency

eDirectory uses a slow-but-sure convergence algorithm to replicate changes from a replica server to its peers in a replication ring. A replica server can manage only a single Directory Information Base (DIB), but a DIB may contain replicas of multiple partitions. Replication uses a batch update mechanism. The period for which changes are accumulated in a replica server is adjustable, from only a few seconds to a few hours, but it defaults to 30 minutes for NDS 6 and 60 minutes for NDS 7 and higher; this is known as the "heartbeat" interval.

Changes to attributes (such as **password**) that are flagged Sync Immediate will be scheduled for immediate synchronization. A background thread that would yield or postpone its operation if a request for a Create, Modify, or Delete operation were received handles synchronization operations. This causes a delay, or latency, in replication. Fortunately, in many instances, partitioning can minimize this delay.

You can partition a tree such that update operations are spread across multiple partitions. Placing these volatile partitions on different servers helps to minimize the peak update load because the partitions are now distributed. For example, if a tree has three containers that are volatile (whose subordinate objects undergo modifications frequently), you should isolate each container into a partition and place the partitions on separate servers. The larger the peak update rate, the smaller the replica ring; but bear in mind that a ring should be designed with at least two servers (three is recommended) for fault tolerance reasons. If the entire server farm is front-ended by a load-balancing switch, you should configure the switch to direct all requests to the primary servers (ones holding the Master replicas) and fail over to the secondary.

> **NOTE**
>
> The By Server synchronization method (discussed in the "Multithreaded Synchronization" section in Chapter 6, "Understanding Common eDirectory Processes") may also help reduce the replication latency by outbounding multiple partitions to multiple unique servers at one time.

Cache Memory Considerations for NDS 7

In versions of directory services (DS) prior to 7.55, any caching done was mainly based on NetWare's caching of the various database files (for example, `*.NDS` files). However, DS 7.55 and later versions of `DS.NLM` included the ability of caching DS objects in memory, which increases performance.

Versions 7.55 and greater of `DS.NLM` will, upon loading, calculate the cache limit based on the amount of free memory (cache buffers) that the server currently has. In these versions, DS determines three values: `MaxMemory`, which is the amount of free memory at the time; `MemoryLimit`, which is equal to 20% of `MaxMemory`; and `BackoffPoint`, which is 80% of `MemoryLimit`. For instance, on a server with 200MB of available memory at `DS.NLM` load time, `MemoryLimit` is set to 40MB (20% of 200MB) and `BackoffPoint` is 32MB (80% of 40MB).

As objects are being referenced, they are cached in memory. When the cache size reaches the `BackoffPoint` value, `DS.NLM` replaces the oldest objects in the cache with new objects that are coming in. Also, a cache cleaning service is scheduled to actually free up the memory within the cache that represents the oldest objects. If memory cannot be allocated for the cache, `DS.NLM` immediately schedules the cache cleaning service.

REAL WORLD

How Much Can DS Cache?
A typical DS object is about 4KB in size. Therefore, with a 32MB cache, `DS.NLM` can cache around 8,000 objects.

When required, you can manually configure `DS.NLM` for a lower or higher value for `MemoryLimit`; the `BackoffPoint` value cannot be changed and will always be 20% of whatever value you set `MemoryLimit` to be. You use the `SET DSTRACE` command to set the limit, as follows:

```
SET DSTRACE=!Mvalue_in_MB
```

NOTE

You do not need to restart the server for the `MemoryLimit` setting to take effect.

For example, `SET DSTRACE=!M64` will permanently configure `DS.NLM` (the value is stored in the database and so is persistent between server restarts) to set the `MemoryLimit` to 64MB instead of the 20% of `MaxMemory` value. Therefore, the value for `BackoffPoint` will be 80% of 64MB, or 51MB. This will give you enough cache for approximately 13,000 objects.

TIP

Do not be concerned if there are 100,000 objects in the tree but your server can only cache 13,000 objects. Remember that the cached objects represent the number of objects being accessed within the same time period (meaning that Objects A and B are both being used within seconds of each other). A good estimate to target for would be to cache 5% of the total objects in the tree.

Novell recommends that no more than 40% of available memory be used for DS caching if the server is an application server. However, if the server is used for DS exclusively, up to 80% may be used.

Cache Memory Considerations for NDS Version 8

Instead of caching the whole NDS object, NDS 8 employed block caching from the beginning. The *block* (or *page*) *cache* is used to increase the performance of reading a block of data from the DS database. Before accessing a block from the database, NDS/eDirectory searches the block cache stored in memory for the requested block of data. If it is found, a cache hit occurs, and the data can be retrieved from memory rather than from disk. If the data is not found in the block cache, a cache fault occurs, and the record must be retrieved from disk. The record is then added to the block cache to prevent subsequent cache faults on the same block of data.

NOTE

The default database block size is 4KB. However, at times you might find that the block size is 5KB on Windows servers. You can check the block size on your server by selecting Agent Configuration, Database Cache in NDS iMonitor. You can see how to change the database block size in the "Changing Database Block Size" section, later in this chapter.

You can specify an upper block cache limit to regulate the amount of memory that eDirectory uses for the cache. The default block cache limit is 8MB of RAM. Using the SET DSTRACE command on the NetWare server console can change the hard limit of this cache size. For example, the following command permanently increases the database cache limit to 80MB:

```
SET DSTRACE=!MB83886080
```

WARNING

You can also use SET DSTRACE=!M*KB_in_hex* to increase the database cache limit. As discussed in the previous section, in NDS 7, the value for the SET DSTRACE command is in megabytes. In NDS 8, however, the expected value is in kilobytes and in hexadecimal notation. Consequently, administrators who are familiar with NDS 7 frequently make the error of entering the wrong value in NDS 8 and higher environments. For example, when trying to specify a cache limit of 64MB, an administrator might wrongly use the command SET DSTRACE=!M64, which allocates only 100KB of memory for eDirectory caching. (The correct command is SET DSTRACE=!M10000.) Because of this easy confusion, we suggest that you always use the !MB option instead of the !M one.

Instead of using the DSTRACE command, you can manually create a text file named _NDSDB.INI in the SYS:_NETWARE directory and put in a line like the following:

```
cache=83886080
```

> **WARNING**
>
> Be careful that you don't put any whitespace around the = sign. Whitespace prevents the value from being set.

To maximize the amount of memory available for DS, Novell suggests using the following formula to calculate the maximum amount of memory needed:

$$\text{MemoryForDSDIB} = (\text{SizeOfDIBSet} + (\text{SizeOfDIBSet} \times 4))$$

where SizeOfDIBSet equals the number of megabytes for *all* NDS.* files found in the DIB directory; this excludes any of the stream files, such as login scripts.

You should check the calculated amount of memory the database might need to see whether it exceeds the Novell-recommended 40% limit (for an application server; 80% for a dedicated DS server) by dividing MemoryForDSDIB by the total server memory and multiplying that amount by 100. If the result does exceed the limit, you might want to adjust the multiplier of 4 down to 2 (do not go below 2 on this multiplier). If you still exceed the limit, you should either get more memory or you can expect some performance degradation to occur.

Cache Memory Considerations for eDirectory

Entry caching was added starting with NDS 8.73 and for eDirectory 8.5 and later. The *entry* (or *record*) *cache* contains logical entries in the eDirectory tree rather than physical blocks of records from the eDirectory database. While traversing the database, eDirectory searches the entry cache stored in memory for the next requested entry. If the entry is found, a cache hit occurs, and the data can be retrieved from memory rather than from disk. If the data is not found in the entry cache, a cache fault occurs, and the entry record must be retrieved from the block cache (and from disk, if the required block is not in the block cache). The record is then added to the entry cache to prevent subsequent cache faults on the same entry record.

Although there is some redundancy between the block and entry caches, each cache is designed to boost performance for different operations. The block cache is most useful for update operations, whereas the entry cache is most useful for operations that browse the eDirectory tree by reading through entries, such as name resolution operations. Both the block and entry caches are useful in improving query performance. The block cache speeds up index searching, and the entry cache speeds up the retrieval of entries referenced from an index. (eDirectory indexes are discussed later in this chapter.)

NOTE

eDirectory caches information for the entire block—which may be more than that asked for in the block cache. However, it will cache only the entry information asked for in entry cache. Stream files (such as login scripts) are only cached on demand and are cached in the file system cache and not in the eDirectory cache.

For instance, if eDirectory is asked for an octet attribute that is only 4 bytes in size, it will cache the entire block, usually 4KB, in the block cache. However, only the entry husk (which includes the entry's ID), not the entire entry, and attribute asked for are placed in the entry cache. (An entry husk is similar to a pointer in that it carries only enough information to link it to the real object.)

Distributing Memory Between the Entry and Block Caches

With an entry cache and a block cache, the total available memory for caching is shared between the two caches. The default is an equal division (50% each). To maintain the amount of block cache available in versions of NDS prior to 8.73, you need to double the total cache size for eDirectory (because of the entry cache you now have). If you use the cache to boost LDIF-import performance, for example, you can either double the total cache size or change the default cache settings (as discussed later in this chapter).

The more blocks and entries that can be cached, the better the overall performance will be. The ideal configuration is to cache the entire database in both the entry and block caches. However, this is usually not possible especially when you have extremely large databases. Generally, the rule of thumb is to try to get as close to a 1:1 ratio of block cache to DIB set size as possible. For the entry cache, you should try to get close to a 1:2 or 1:4 ratio. For the best performance, you should exceed these ratios where possible.

Calculating the Cache Limits

eDirectory provides two methods for controlling cache memory consumption: a dynamically adjusting limit (Dynamic Adjust mode) and a hard memory limit (Hard Limit mode). The Hard Limit mode is the method that versions of eDirectory prior to 8.5 use to regulate memory consumption. You set a hard memory limit by specifying one of the following:

▶ A fixed number of bytes

▶ A percentage of total physical memory

▶ A percentage of available physical memory

When a hard memory limit is specified in percentages, it is translated to a fixed number of bytes based on the amount of memory at the time the setting is made.

The hard memory limit size is for the block and entry caches combined. **NOTE**

The Dynamic Adjust mode causes eDirectory to periodically adjust its memory consumption in response to the change in memory usage by other processes. You specify the limit as a percentage of available physical memory. Using this percentage, eDirectory recalculates a new memory limit at fixed intervals. The new memory limit will be the percentage of physical memory available at the time.

Along with this percentage, you can set maximum and minimum thresholds. Such a threshold is the number of bytes that eDirectory will adjust to. It can be set as either the number of bytes to use or the number of bytes to leave available. The minimum threshold default is 16MB, and the maximum threshold default is 4GB.

If the minimum and maximum threshold limits are not compatible with one another, the minimum threshold limit is followed. For example, suppose you specified the following settings:

▶ Minimum threshold: 8MB

▶ Percentage of available physical memory to use: 75%

▶ Maximum threshold: Keep 10MB available

When eDirectory adjusts its cache limit, there is 16MB of available physical memory. eDirectory calculates a new limit of 12MB (75% of 16MB). eDirectory then checks to see whether the new limit falls within the range of the minimum and maximum thresholds. In this example, the maximum threshold requires that 10MB remain available, so eDirectory lowers the limit to 6MB (leaving 10MB available). However, the minimum threshold is 8MB, so eDirectory resets the final limit to 8MB.

> **NOTE**
>
> Remember: Whenever there is a conflict resulting from the specified settings, the minimum threshold value gets priority over the maximum value.

Setting the Cache Limits

You can specify upper limits for the block cache and the entry cache separately. If no previously permanent cache settings are found when the DS agent (DSA) starts up, the cache defaults to a hard limit of 16MB for the first 10 minutes. Because the DSA usually loads when a server is restarted, this default behavior allows other applications to load and request system resources first. After 10 minutes, the behavior (by default) switches to Dynamic Adjust mode, based on the amount of available memory.

With the dynamically adjusting limit, you can also specify the interval length at which the memory limit is recalculated. The default interval is 15 seconds.

> **NOTE**
>
> The shorter the recalculation interval, the more the memory consumption is based on current conditions. However, shorter intervals are not necessarily better because the percentage recalculation will create more memory allocation and freeing.

> **REAL WORLD**
>
> ### The Cache Cleaner
>
> Because of the multithreading nature of the DS module, NDS 8.73 and later create multiple versions of blocks and entries in the cache for transaction integrity purposes. For instance, if one thread is performing a read transaction while another is doing an update to the DIB, old versions of blocks changed by the writing thread are maintained on behalf of the reading thread. This occurs so that the reading thread will have a consistent view of the data during the lifetime of its transaction, even though modifications are taking place during that time.
>
> Prior to eDirectory 8.5, this cached data did not get removed when it was no longer needed. eDirectory 8.5 and later add a background process that

> periodically browses the cache and cleans out older versions. This helps to min-
> imize cache memory consumption. The default checking interval is 15 seconds
> and is configurable.
>
> Do not confuse this cache cleaner background process—for maintaining caching
> performance—with the Flat Cleaner background process, which is used for DS
> database maintenance.

If the server does not have a replica, and no dynamic adjustments are specified, a hard memory limit of 16MB (with 8MB for the block cache and 8MB
for the entry cache) is used. On the other hand, if the server contains one or
more replicas, the default Dynamic Adjust mode uses a limit of 51% of
available memory, with a minimum threshold of 8MB and a maximum
threshold of keeping 24MB available to the operating system (that is, total
available memory minus 24MB).

WARNING

> Novell's tuning guides recommend very large caches (four times the DIB size). On
> machines with gigabytes of RAM, this is likely to lead to instability if it is not
> capped to 2GB. At the time of this writing, eDirectory is a 32-bit process that has
> a 4GB limit in its virtual address space. If you set the cache to 2GB or more, dur-
> ing peaks of high activity, the address space may exceed the operating system
> limits for a 32-bit process and lead to its abrupt termination (and result in core
> dumps or abends). On Linux 2.4 kernels, the process may run out of virtual
> address map entries and freeze.
>
> When you're working on high-end tree deployments, you should set the cache to
> an absolute figure of 1.5GB or less. You should not use dynamic or hard settings.

You can use either the Hard Limit mode or the Dynamic Adjust mode, but
you can only use one at a time because the two are mutually exclusive. The
last method selected will always replace any prior settings. As discussed in
the following sections, there are three ways you can set the cache limits:

- ► By using the `_NDSDB.INI` file
- ► By using the `SET DSTRACE` command
- ► By using NDS iMonitor

Setting Cache Configuration via _NDSDB.INI

At startup, eDirectory looks for the `_NDSDB.INI` file in the directory where
DIB files are stored. This file is a simple text file that can be created or modified with any text editor.

NOTE The _NDSDB.INI file is read only when eDirectory starts up. Therefore, any changes made after eDirectory is running will not take effect until the eDirectory module has been restarted. On the other hand, no restart is necessary if the changes were made via DSTrace or NDS iMonitor.

Cache settings made via DSTrace and NDS iMonitor will automatically be populated in the _NDSDB.INI file.

The following is the syntax for cache memory settings for eDirectory:

```
cache=option1,option2,option3,...
```

WARNING Do not include any whitespace on either side of the = sign or between the options. Whitespace prevents the value from being set.

NOTE None of the commands and options in _NDSDB.INI are case-sensitive, and they can be specified in any order.

This command sets a hard memory limit or dynamically adjusting limit. Multiple (optional) options may be specified, in any order, separated by commas. These are the allowable options:

- **DYN or HARD**—This option specifies to use a dynamically adjusting limit or a hard limit.

- **cache_in_bytes**—If just a number is specified, it is taken as the upper cache limit for the Hard Limit mode.

- **%:percentage**—This option specifies the percentage of available or physical memory to use for cache. (The default is 51%.)

- **AVAIL or TOTAL**—This option indicates whether the specified percentage value is based on the available physical memory or on total physical memory. (The default is **AVAIL**.)

- **MIN:bytes**—This option specifies the minimum number of bytes to use. (The default is 8388608, or 8MB.)

- **MAX:bytes**—This option specifies the maximum number of bytes to use.

- **LEAVE:bytes**—This option specifies the minimum number of bytes to leave. (The default is 25165824, or 24MB.)

The MIN, MAX, and LEAVE **values are ignored for a dynamically adjusting limit. Dynamic Adjust mode always bases its calculation on the available physical memory.**

The following example sets a dynamically adjusting cache limit of 60% of available memory, with a minimum of 16MB:

```
cache=DYN,%:60,MIN:16711680
```

The following example sets a hard memory limit of 75% of available physical memory, with a minimum of 32MB:

```
cache=HARD,%:75,MIN:33423360,AVAIL
```

The following example sets a hard memory limit of 24MB:

```
cache=25165824
```

In addition to the cache settings, there are two settings that control the dynamic adjust interval and the interval at which the cache cleaner background process runs:

- ▶ **CacheAdjustInterval=*seconds***—The default is 15 seconds.
- ▶ **CacheCleanupInterval=*seconds***—The default is 15 seconds.

The final setting allows you to control the percentage split between the entry and block caches:

- ▶ **BlockCachePercent=*percent***—The *percent* value indicates how much of the cache will be used for block caching. This needs to be between 0 and 100 (inclusive). A value of 70 means that 70% of cache memory will be used for the block cache, and the remaining 30% for the entry cache. The Default value is 50.

***Never* set the** BlockCachePercent **value to zero because that would seriously degrade eDirectory performance. Novell also recommends that no more than 75% of the cache memory should be allocated to either the entry cache or the block cache for typical day-to-day operations.**

Novell recommends setting the BlockCachePercent **value to between 70% and 90%, depending on the proportion of updates in the total operations. And you should set it to 90% for operations such as bulk creations or deletions; you should set it to 50% if you do not expect too many update bursts.**

eDirectory 8.7 introduced a new method for specifying the maximum dirty cache (`MaxDirtyCache`) and the low dirty cache (`LowDirtyCache`) for the eDirectory cache. By default, the value of `MaxDirtyCache` is unlimited (that is, using all of the available eDirectory cache; flush the dirty cache when this limit is reached) and the `LowDirtyCache` value is set to zero (that is, don't flush the dirty cache if it is less than this value). Setting the amount of dirty cache at any given instant below a particular value helps to even out the disk writing instead of burdening the checkpoint thread in the forced mode, which essentially writes the whole cache to the disk, thereby creating an I/O bottleneck.

NOTE   A checkpoint occurs when *all* dirty cache buffers are used and eDirectory must flush them to disk.

Normally, you don't have to set the `MaxDirtyCache` and `LowDirtyCache` values. However, if you are bulk-loading to populate, depopulate, or modify the DS objects, you should set them in the `_NDSDB.INI` file, as follows:

```
MaxDirtyCache=value_in_bytes
LowDirtyCache=value_in_bytes
```

Then you should restart the DSA in order for the settings to take effect. You should make sure to take them out after your bulk-load operation.

WARNING   Novell's testing suggests that for platforms other than HP/UX, setting `MaxDirtyCache` and `LowDirtyCache` is useful only for bulk-loading for less than 1.5 million objects. For higher values, there might be performance degradation if these values are changed from the defaults.

NOTE   There is no "hard value" recommended for the dirty cache settings because they very much depend on the server hardware. On most systems, the `MaxDirtyCache` value is between 1MB and 10MB, while 20MB may be used for fiber channel storage area networks. On HP/UX, setting `MaxDirtyCache` to 340MB and `LowDirtyCache` to 335MB worked well for all scenarios tested.

You can use the following procedure to determine what the `MaxDirtyCache` setting for your server may be. First, measure the random I/O write speed to the disk. Set the `MaxDirtyCache` value such that all modified buffers in a 3-minute interval can be flushed to the DIB volume in 10 seconds (10,000 ms) or less. Set the value of `LowDirtyCache` to about half that of `MaxDirtyCache`. For example, if the random write speed is 10 ms per block (4KB), you set `MaxDirtyCache` to (10,000ms × 4KB/10), or 4,000KB. Alternatively, you can use a simple trial-and-error method: You can set the `MaxDirtyCache` value to 5MB and observe the max update response time during a burst of updates. Then you can adjust this value upward until the response time is acceptable.

Setting Cache Usage via DSTrace

The syntax for setting eDirectory cache by using DSTrace is very similar to that used in the _NDSDB.INI file:

```
SET DSTRACE=!Moption1,option2,option3,...
```

DSTrace also uses the same list of options as used in _NDSDB.INI, with two exceptions and one addition:

- ► !MB*cache_in_bytes* specifies the upper cache limit for the Hard Limit mode.

- ► You cannot adjust CacheAdjustInterval, CacheCleanupInterval, BlockCachePercent, or any of the dirty cache parameters via DSTrace. They need to be specified using the _NDSDB.INI file.

- ► By default, cache settings made using DSTrace are automatically written to the _NDSDB.INI file. The NOSAVE option prevents that. When this option is not specified, the settings are saved.

The following example sets a dynamically adjusting cache limit of 60% of available memory and a minimum of 16MB, and it saves the settings to _NDSDB.INI (because NOSAVE is *not* specified):

```
SET DSTRACE=!MDYN,%:60,MIN:16711680
```

The following example sets a hard memory limit of 75% of available physical memory and a minimum of 32MB, and it does not save the settings to _NDSDB.INI:

```
SET DSTRACE=!MHARD,%:75,MIN:33423360,AVAIL,NOSAVE
```

For instance, if the available system cache memory is 100MB, this command will allocate 75MB of that as a hard memory limit.

The following example sets a hard memory limit of 24MB:

```
SET DSTRACE=!MB25165824
```

Configuring cache usage via DSTrace does not require a reset of DS or the server. Changes are effective immediately.   **NOTE**

Setting Cache Usage via NDS iMonitor

An easier and more user-friendly, but not necessarily the fastest, method to configure cache settings is to use NDS iMonitor. The appropriate settings are made from the Database Cache Configuration page in NDS iMonitor (see Figure 16.1), which is accessed via the Database Cache link under Agent Configuration.

FIGURE 16.1
eDirectory database cache settings.

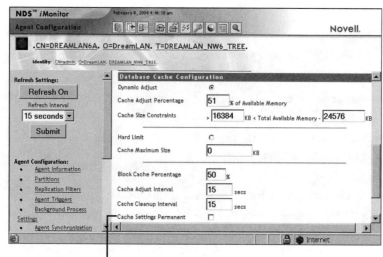

Check to save settings to _NDSDB.INI file

Monitoring the Cache Statistics

Periodically, you should check the eDirectory cache statistics to ensure that the settings used are effective. You can easily determine the various cache hits and misses (which are generally referred to as *cache faults*) by looking at the Database Cache statistics information from the Database Cache link under Agent Configuration in NDS iMonitor (see Figure 16.2).

FIGURE 16.2
eDirectory database cache information.

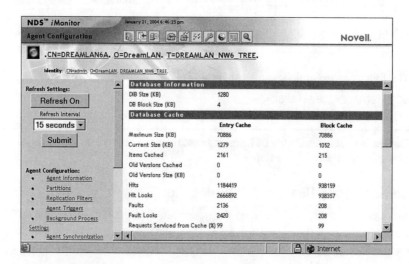

Of particular interest in the cache statistics is the percentage listed next to Requests Serviced from Cache. This number reflects the cache efficiency. The percentage is calculated as (Total Hits) / (Total Hits + Total Faults), where Total Hits is the total for both the block and entry caches. Typically you want to keep this number somewhere in the 90s for best cache efficiency. If this number is below 90%, you might want to look at how much available memory you have in your server and perhaps change the way your cache is allocated (for example, change the percentage of block cache versus entry cache).

By comparing the reported DIB size to the summed maximum size of entry cache and block cache, you can determine how much of the DIB can be cached. The example shown in Figure 16.2 suggests that all of the DIB can be cached because the DIB size is a little over 1MB in size (1,280KB), while the summed maximum cache size is almost 14MB. In this case, you could safely reduce the amount of maximum cache limit and free up the extra RAM for other server processes.

Refer to TID #10082323 for a detailed description about the items on the Database Cache page in NDS iMonitor.	**NOTE**

To ensure optimal performance, you should configure your system based on cache hit and cache fault indicators, database size, and memory available. You should not expect to cache the entire database unless you have a small DIB set. You should not expect to see zero cache faults, and you shouldn't expect the faults to be at zero to have optimal performance in eDirectory.	**TIP**

eDirectory Indexes and Predicate Stats

Versions of NDS prior to NDS 8 relied on a flat-file data store known as Record Manager (RECMAN), which has no real indexing. Anyone with some database experience knows that indexes are essential for efficient and fast database searches. To address this shortcoming, NDS and eDirectory switched away from using a flat-file structure for the data store and now use Flexible Adaptive Information Manager (FLAIM) instead; FLAIM is far more scalable than RECMAN. As a result, NDS 8 and higher allow significantly more information to be held on a single server, without requiring you to partition DS. In addition, database indexes have been introduced to increase performance of any client (including LDAP) accessing the database, especially during attribute value searching.

eDirectory supports the following four types of indexes:

▶ **Operational**—Operational indexes are required for the proper operation of eDirectory (much like the operational schema definitions) and cannot be modified, suspended, or deleted by administrators. Examples of operational indexes include `GUID` and `Obituary`.

▶ **System**—System indexes are required for the proper operation of eDirectory at the database level and cannot be modified, suspended, or deleted by administrators. Examples of system indexes include `Member` and `Reference`.

▶ **Auto Added**—Auto Added indexes are predefined indexes that are added to the database by eDirectory during the database creation phase. Auto Added indexes are indexes for attributes that are frequently used in queries by applications that access eDirectory. `CN` is an example of an Auto-added index. In eDirectory 8.7 and above, if any object in the tree has an attribute that has more than 25 values, an Auto Added index for the attribute will be automatically added by the system.

▶ **User Defined**—User Defined indexes are indexes that have been manually created by the system administrator and are generally used in conjunction with predicate stats for performance-tuning purposes. These indexes can be created, suspended, and deleted as needed.

TIP

Due to the underlying structure of the eDirectory database, System indexes have faster access times than User indexes.

User-added indexes still increase the performance of LDAP queries, for instance, if the attribute does not meet the criteria to be automatically added. You can use predicate stats (discussed later in this chapter, in the "What Attribute Needs to Be Indexed?" section) to determine which attribute can benefit from a User index.

The indexes are defined on a server-by-server basis and are stored in the `indexDefinition` attribute (syntax type `SYN_CI_LIST`) of the `NCP Server` object (see Figure 16.3). Each index on a server applies to the data stored on that server only. Index definitions are *not* replicated to other servers, but by using ConsoleOne or iManager, you can easily copy an index definition from one server to another server.

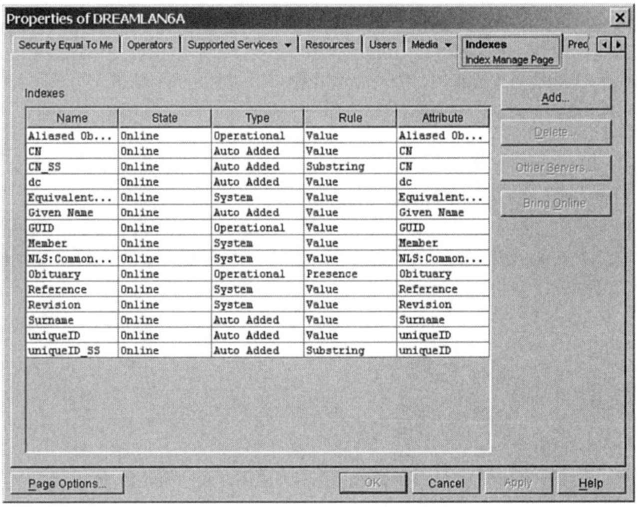
Properties of DREAMLAN6A
Security Equal To Me
Operators
Supported Services
Resources
Users
Media
Indexes
Index Manage Page
Pred
Indexes
Name
State
Type
Rule
Attribute
Aliased Ob... Online Operational Value Aliased Ob...
CN Online Auto Added Value CN
CN_SS Online Auto Added Substring CN
dc Online Auto Added Value dc
Equivalent... Online System Value Equivalent...
Given Name Online Auto Added Value Given Name
GUID Online Operational Value GUID
Member Online System Value Member
NLS:Common... Online System Value NLS:Common...
Obituary Online Operational Presence Obituary
Reference Online System Value Reference
Revision Online System Value Revision
Surname Online Auto Added Value Surname
uniqueID Online Auto Added Value uniqueID
uniqueID_SS Online Auto Added Substring uniqueID
Add...
Delete...
Other Servers...
Bring Online
Page Options...
OK
Cancel
Apply
Help

FIGURE 16.3
Default eDirectory indexes.

Each index is based on one of three types of index matching rules that determine how the index will be matched:

- **Presence**—An index based on the Presence rule simply provides a Boolean value of `True` or `False`, depending on whether the desired attribute exists. A Presence index optimizes queries with criteria that only involve the presence of an attribute. An example of this type of query is to find all entries with a `Login Script` attribute.
- **Value**—An index based on the Value rule provides an ordered list of objects based on the value of the specified attributes. A Value index helps with queries in which the criteria involve the entire value or the first part of the value. For example, a Value index helps on both a query to find all entries with a `Surname` attribute value that is equal to `Jensen` and a query to find all entries with a `Surname` attribute value that begins with `Jen`.
- **Substring**—A Substring index allows for complex searches on characters within the attribute data. A Substring index can be used to optimize queries with criteria that are a subset of a `String` value. For example, a query to find all entries with a `Surname` attribute value that contains `der` would benefit from this index. The query in this example would return matches for (among others) `Derington`, `Anderson`, and `Lauder`.

  Given the large number of possible combinations of attribute data, Substring indexes are costly to create and can require large amounts of resources to keep updated. Therefore, you should keep Substring indexes to a minimum. Indexes based on the Substring rule are by far the most costly index type in eDirectory.

TIP

If your LDAP search performance doesn't improve after adding a Presence index, you should try using a Value index instead for the same attribute. LDAP will use this index when doing a Presence search.

REAL WORLD

Inside the indexDefinition Attribute

The `indexDefinition` attribute on the `NCP Server` object is defined using the `SYN_CI_LIST` syntax. It is a multivalued attribute. Each value of the attribute holds the following information fields:

▶ Index Version—This field is reserved for future use and has a value of 0.

▶ User-defined Index Name—This field is used to identify the index on the Index tab of ConsoleOne. You can define any name that best describes the index (for example, "Group membership" or "Zip code value"). The index name should not contain the $ character because it is used as the delimiter between the data fields within the attribute value. If you use the $ character in the name, you must escape it when working with the indexes via LDAP.

▶ Index State—Possible field values are 0 (Suspended), 1 (Bringing Online), 2 (Online), and 3 (Pending Creation). When an index is in the Suspended state, it is not used in queries and is not updated. The Bringing Online state indicates that an index is in the process of being created. The Online state means that the index is up and working. A Pending Creation state means that the index has been defined and is waiting for the background process to begin its operation.

When you're defining an index using LDAP, you should set this field to 2. The background process automatically changes the state when index building has begun.

▶ Index Rule—Possible field values are 0 (Value Matching), 1 (Presence Matching), and 2 (Substring Matching).

▶ Index Type—This field indicates whether the index is User-Defined (0), Auto Added (1)—that is, added on attribute creation—Operational (2)—that is, required for operation—or a System index (3). When you're defining an index using LDAP, this value should always be set to 0; ConsoleOne automatically sets this field to 0.

▶ Index Value State—eDirectory uses this field to identify the source of the index. Possible values are 0 (Uninitialized), 1 (Added from Server), 2 (Added from Local DIB), 3 (Deleted from Local DIB), and 4 (Modified from Local DIB). Indexes that are predefined or that were added or modified using ConsoleOne are identified with the 2, 3, or 4 values. An index created using LDAP should have this field set to 1.

▶ Attribute Name—This field contains the name of the DS attribute that is being indexed. In many cases, attributes have both a DS name and an LDAP name mapped to it. You should be sure to use the DS name for the attribute. When you create an index by using ConsoleOne or iManager, this is not an issue because you select from the list of known DS attribute names.

> When you create an index by using LDAP, however, you should make sure to use the appropriate DS attribute name, not the LDAP mapped attribute name. You should be careful to escape any characters that need to be escaped.

When a new index is defined or the state of an existing index is changed, the operation does not happen immediately. A background process that runs every 30 minutes checks the index definition values against the current index status and then starts any necessary processes. As a result, indexes are built in the background while the directory is still working. When the index is completed, its status changes to Online automatically, and at that point, the users should notice the performance improvement.

Managing eDirectory Indexes

You manage eDirectory indexes by using ConsoleOne or iManager. Because these indexes are associated with the server, in ConsoleOne you access them through the Indexes tab on the Properties page of the NCP Server object. When using iManager, you select eDirectory Maintenance, Index Management, *server*. Figure 16.4 shows the Create Index dialog box from ConsoleOne. From the Indexes tab in ConsoleOne, you can also change an index's state between Suspend and Online, delete a User Defined index, or copy an index definition to another server. At the time of this writing, you can use NDS iMonitor only to view the indexes and their states (by selecting Agent Summary, clicking the server name in the Navigator frame, and selecting indexDefinition from the list of attributes), as shown in Figure 16.5.

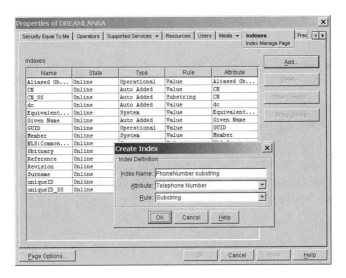

FIGURE 16.4
Adding an eDirectory index.

FIGURE 16.5
eDirectory index
status.

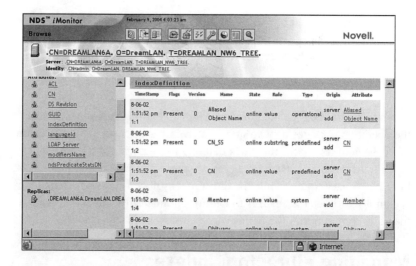

> **NOTE**
> You can also manage the eDirectory indexes by using iManager. In addition, Novell provides a command-line utility called `ndsindex` for managing eDirectory indexes. In Windows, it is found in `\Novell\NDS`, and in Unix, it is in `/usr/ldaptools/bin`. In NetWare, the utility is `NINDEX.NLM`, and it is shipped with NetWare 6.5 and later; you can also get a copy of it by downloading the LDAP NDK from Novell DeveloperNet, installing Service Pack 3 for NetWare 6.0, or installing eDirectory 8.7.3.

Other than by using ConsoleOne and iManager, you can define and manage eDirectory indexes via LDAP. The advantage of using LDAP is that an application can define indexes during the installation process. Index definitions can be part of the same LDIF file that applies the required schema extension for the application. The LDIF file shown in Figure 16.6 creates a Substring index (called `PhoneNumber substring`) for the `Telephone Number` attribute.

> **WARNING**
> Keep in mind the following requirements when creating an eDirectory index via LDAP:
> ▶ If a $ character is present in the field value, it must be escaped. (To make things easiest, it is best not to use the $ character at all.)
> ▶ The Index State field (the third field) value must be set to 2.
> ▶ The Index Value State field (the sixth field) value must be set to 1.
> ▶ The Attribute Name field (the seventh field) value must specify the DS attribute name, not the LDAP mapped name.

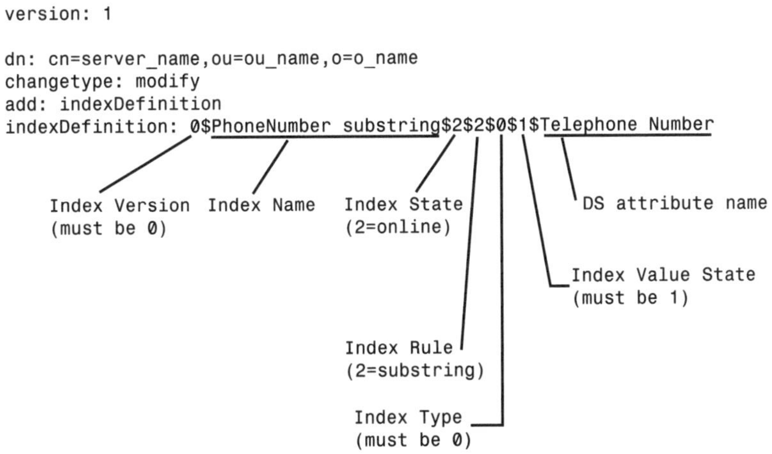

```
version: 1

dn: cn=server_name,ou=ou_name,o=o_name
changetype: modify
add: indexDefinition
indexDefinition: 0$PhoneNumber substring$2$2$0$1$Telephone Number
```

FIGURE 16.6
An LDIF file to add a substring index.

Index Version (must be 0) Index Name Index State (2=online) DS attribute name

Index Value State (must be 1)

Index Rule (2=substring)

Index Type (must be 0)

You can either use ICE (from within ConsoleOne or from a command line) or the `ldapmodify.exe` utility included with eDirectory to process an LDIF file.

You can also use LDAP to programmatically change the state of a defined index. You should first query the NCP Server object's indexDefinition attribute to determine the current Index State value before modifying it. Then you set the Index State field to either 0 to suspend it or 2 to start bringing it online. You should never change the state to either Bringing Online (1) or Pending Creation (3). A background process does this automatically. The following LDIF commands change the state of the PhoneNumber substring index from Online to Suspended:

```
version: 1
dn: cn=server_name,ou=ou_name,o=o_name
changetype: modify
delete: indexDefinition
indexDefinition: 0$PhoneNumber Substring$2$2$0$1$
➥Telephone Number
add: indexDefinition
indexDefinition: 0$PhoneNumber Substring$0$2$0$1$
➥Telephone Number
```

What Attribute Needs to Be Indexed?

Although appropriate indexes can significantly improve performance, you should be aware of the cost associated with each index added to the directory. To start with, each addition, deletion, or modification of an entry in the directory causes *all* indexes affected by the change to be updated. Substring indexes are the most costly (that is, CPU intensive) to create and update, and Presence indexes are the least costly.

The more indexes that exist on a server, the longer the time it takes to perform add, delete, or modify operations. Consequently, indexes should be used judiciously. A secondary side-effect of adding indexes is that each index requires some storage to contain it. Thus, each index adds to the size of the server's DIB.

> **TIP**
>
> Because each object addition or modification requires touching the defined indexes, having all the indexes active may slow down bulk-addition or bulk-modification of data in the directory. To achieve additional speed during bulk operations, you might first want to suspend some or all of the User Defined indexes, especially the Substring ones. After the operation is completed, you can then bring the indexes online. The indexes will (re-)build in the background and become effective when updating is complete.

So, which attributes should you index? To help make that determination, eDirectory provides the capability to capture search predicate statistics data. Predicate statistics data, often called predicate stats data, is a server-specific history of the objects people search for. You can use predicate stats to identify the most frequently searched for objects and then create indexes to improve the speed of future information access.

> **NOTE**
>
> eDirectory 8.7.3 ships with the following set of predefined indexes that provide basic query functionality:

Aliased Object Name

ldapClasssList

CN

Member

Dc

Obituary

Equivalent to Me

Reference

extensionInfo

Revision

Given Name

Surname

GUID

uniqueID

ldapAttributeList

You can look up the index definitions by using ConsoleOne, iManager, or NDS iMonitor, as discussed earlier in this chapter, in the "Managing eDirectory Indexes" section.

eDirectory internally defines a number of Operational and System indexes (for instance, an index for combined class ID and RDN [ClassID_RDN_IX] and an index for combined parent ID and creation time stamp [ParentID+CTS_IX]). They are not documented, but you can see them referenced in DSTrace (see the "Is Your Query Really Using the Indexes?" section, later in this chapter).

When eDirectory is installed, a special **Predicate Stats** object is created. The name of the object is the server name, with -PS appended (for example, NETWARE65-PS or WIN2K-NDS-PS). You can create as many objects of this type as you feel necessary, but typically a single object will suffice.

TIP

Although only one **Predicate Stats** object can be linked with a server at any one time, you can keep multiple **Predicate Stats** objects for testing of multiple scenarios, for instance.

At the time of this writing, only ConsoleOne can be used to view and manage the predicate stats collected by an **NCP Server** object. Figure 16.7 shows an example of the ConsoleOne Predicate Data tab.

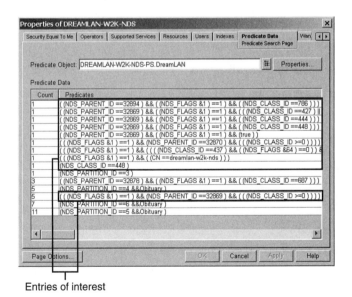

Entries of interest

FIGURE 16.7
eDirectory predicate stats data.

The **Predicate Stats** object itself has no configuration option. All its settings are handled through the Predicate Data tab of the **NCP Server** object.

The following steps describe how to configure the `Predicate Stats` object and its functionality:

1. In ConsoleOne, right-click the `NCP Server` object and select Properties from the context menu.

2. Select the Predicate Data tab.

3. Select the `Predicate Stats` object, using the Browser button if necessary.

4. Click the Properties button to specify the appropriate configuration for the object.

5. Set the update interval, which is the number of seconds to wait before refreshing the data display and writing data to disk. (This updates the `ndsPredicateTimeout` attribute on the `Predicate Stats` object.)

TIP   If the data display does not refresh, you can exit the Properties dialog box and open it again.

6. Click the Advanced button for additional configuration options:

   ▶ **Enable**—This option specifies whether the collection process should run in the background or should be turned off. If you turn off data collection (by unchecking the check box), the most recently collected data will either be released from memory (that is, lost) or, if you've selected Write to Disk, it will be moved to disk. (This updates the `ndsPredicateState` attribute on the `Predicate Stats` object.)

   ▶ **Display Value Text**—This option determines whether the data display will be abbreviated or complete. The abbreviated display provides enough information to determine which predicates are good candidates for indexes. For instance, with Display Value Text selected, the predicate stats data displays one entry for the search `surname=Smith` and another entry for `surname=Jones`. However, if the option is not selected, the prior two queries will be displayed as two instances of the `surname==` predicate. (This updates the `ndsPredicateUseValues` attribute on the `Predicate Stats` object.)

   ▶ **Write to Disk**—This option determines storage location of predicate data, either always in memory or moving from memory to disk—saved to the `ndsPredicate` attribute of the `Predicate Stats` object—as specified in Update Interval. (This updates the `ndsPredicateFlush` attribute on the `Predicate Stats` object.)

7. Click OK to update the `Predicate Stats` object configuration.

For testing purposes, you can shorten the refresh Update Interval setting and perform a few find operations by using ConsoleOne. This will generate some data to populate the Predicate Data tab display.

You can change the settings of the `Predicate Stats` object via its Other Edit tab instead of going through the `NCP Server` object's Predicate Data tab.

WARNING

The in-memory buffer has no upper limit, so if most predicates are unique, it is possible to use up all of a server's available memory.

WARNING

The predicate statistics functionality is not intended to be run all the time that the directory is in operation. Collecting these statistics affects performance of the server, and lengthy accumulation of statistics can result in large databases.

In order to view the predicate statistics from ConsoleOne, the Write to Disk setting must be selected. Each time the internal table is flushed to the `ndsPredicate` attribute of the selected `Predicate Stats` object, the values in the table are compared to the predicates held by the object. If the values are the same, the count is simply updated to reflect the new instance of that predicate. If the internal table holds new predicates, they are added as values to the object.

TIP

If ConsoleOne refuses to display any statistics after you have properly configured the `Predicate Stats` object, you can turn on DSTrace on the server to see whether it is reporting any -649 (Insufficient Buffer) errors when trying to load the predicate statistics table. If it is, then this is the reason you are unable to view the statistics—the server is low on memory.

If you decide to change the statistics display mode by toggling the Display Value Text check box, it is recommended that you first turn statistics collection off, clear out all the old statistics values, change the display mode setting, and then turn statistics collection back on.

TIP

You may have noticed that the Predicate Data tab does not have an option to clear the data from the `Predicate Stats` object. To clear the old values, you can delete the `ndsPredicate` attribute from the `Predicate Stats` object.

Entries in the Predicate Data tab list are sorted by the number of times they have been used. The list may be a little difficult to read because it shows internal search information as well as user query information.

TIP   **Sometimes the full predicate does not fit in the display window. To expand it, you can use a mouse to drag the right column width marker farther to the right. You can then use the horizontal scrollbar to see more of the predicate information.**

Figure 16.8 shows a number of entries that may be helpful in determining what attribute may warrant an index. The following three entries are examples of what to look for when deciding what indexes may be required:

```
(((NDS_FLAG&1)==1)&&((((NDS_CLASS_ID==437)&&
➥((NDS_FLAGS&64)==0)...
(((NDS_FLAG&1)==1)&&((CN==dreamlan-w2k-nds)))
(((NDS_FLAG&1)==1)&&(NDS_PARENT_ID==32869)&&
➥(((NDS_CLASS_ID>=0)))))
```

The first sample entry shows that the query used the filter `NDS_CLASS_ID==437`. This indicates that a search was performed on an object class whose (schema) entry ID value is 437 decimal (1B5 in hex). To find out what object class has an ID of 437, you need to use DSBrowse to perform a find based on the ID. Figure 16.8 shows that the **User** class schema definition has an entry ID of 1B5.

User schema object ID is 0x1B5 (or 437 decimal)

FIGURE 16.8
The entry ID of the **User** class schema definition.

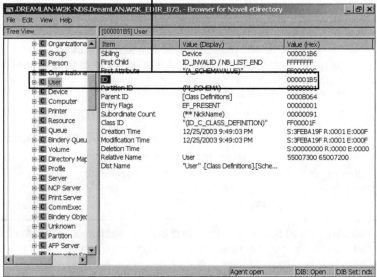

When you have the class ID, it is very easy to locate the classname. In
DSBROWSE.NLM, **you select Object Search, enter the class ID (in hex) into the ID field under Object Information, and press F10 to start the search.**

For DSBrowse in Windows, you switch to the DIB Browser view. Then you right-click [Schema Root] under Entries, Go to Record ID. Next, you enter the class ID in the Record Number field, select Entry for the Record type, and click OK to start the search.

Bear in mind that entry IDs are server specific. Therefore, on a different server, the schema entry ID for the User class will have a different value.

If you are seeing a high count value (meaning many searches using that filter) for NDS_CLASS_ID==437, you should check to see whether the same predicate search includes any attribute names, such as "search in all User objects whose Department attribute value is Sales." If the answer is yes, the specified attribute names are potential candidates for indexing. Otherwise, creating an index for just the Object Class attribute *may* be useful; refer to the "General Guidelines for Using Indexes" section, later in this chapter, for more information.

The second predicate data entry example shows that the search was for a particular CN, an NCP Server object (dreamlan-w2k-nds). In more than 80% of the searches, specific object names (CN) are used. For example, "Show me all values in the ACL attribute for user Chelsea." When you have many objects in the tree, indexing CN is an excellent idea—and that's why CN is one of the predefined indexes. The other 20% of searches would include queries such as "Show me all the objects that have a Location value of New York City," where the CN index is not used.

The third example shows that the filter NDS_PARENT_ID==32869 was used. This indicates that the search is either looking for a DS container (whose parent container's entry ID is 32869 decimal or 0x8065 hexadecimal), objects in this container, or objects in this container and its subordinate containers. However, the parent ID here refers to the entry ID of the partition root object of the partition where the search is targeted. Using DSBrowse or NDS iMonitor, you can determine the name of the container based on the entry ID, thus the partition in question. Although this information does not help you to decide what attribute needs to be indexed, it does suggest whether you should put a replica of that partition on this server.

NOTE   The LDAP server discussion in Chapter 2, "eDirectory Basics," mentions that there would be network traffic implications, depending on whether the LDAP server is configured for chaining or referral. If your predicate stats show that there are many queries—unfortunately, you can't tell whether the searches are made via LDAP—on this server for objects in a partition that it is *not* hosting, you need to consider either placing a replica on it to reduce tree-walking or reconfigure the application to query a different server that does hold a replica of interest.

The following are a few points to keep in mind when working with predicate stats:

▶ Do not leave the predicate statistics function running all the time. Collecting predicate stats affects performance of the server, and lengthy accumulation of statistics can result in a large DIB.

▶ Each object addition or modification requires that the defined indexes be updated. Therefore, having all the indexes active may slow down bulk-addition or bulk-modification of data in the directory. You may first want to suspend all the User Defined indexes. After the operation is completed, you can bring them back online. The indexes will (re-)build in the background and become effective when updating is complete.

▶ Because `Predicate Stats` objects are replicated, you might want to define a partition that exists only on the server being tuned and store the objects there so they are not unnecessarily replicated to other servers.

▶ Not all entries reported in the predicate stats are useful. Many of them are results of background processes running, and you should not let them distract you. You should focus mainly on the entries that include attributes.

▶ Reading and interpreting predicate stats is not straightforward. Before you start using predicate stats in earnest, you should run a few sample queries and examine the resulting predicates. Knowing what the "questions" were makes it easier to understand the data.

General Guidelines for Using Indexes

When the server receives a search request, the query is evaluated and broken into a combination of mini-terms. Each of these mini-terms (or *tokens*, as they are called in text string parsing parlance) becomes a search predicate. One index is selected as being optimal for each predicate. The indexed attribute is used to create the initial result pool for that predicate, and then the other predicate criteria are applied to form the final set. Result sets from the different predicates are then merged to form the final result set.

The complete rules for how an index is selected are complex and generally uninteresting to most people. The following are some simple guidelines to consider when working with eDirectory indexes:

▶ The search predicates that show up in the statistics screen do not necessarily represent the database's optimization of the query. These values are only to be used as *indicators* of the attributes that are most commonly referenced.

▶ Although it is possible, and often tempting, to create an index on the `Object Class` attribute, the effectiveness of the index depends very much on the type of data you are using. For example, if your tree has two million users and five printers defined, an `Object Class` index makes sense when you are searching for printers but would not gain you any performance benefit if you were searching for users.

▶ If the number of objects matching a search filter approaches a high percentage of the number of objects in the tree, query performance may be better if no index is used.

▶ Substring indexes are the most costly type of index to maintain, so the presence of several Substring indexes can severely affect add, delete, and modify performance. You should use Substring indexes sparingly.

▶ Value indexes on large string or octet string attributes may not provide the desired performance improvement. eDirectory truncates indexed string values at 32 bytes and indexed octet string values at 49 bytes. When a query includes a value that is larger than the truncation value (say, a string that is 40 bytes long), the index can only be used to generate a possible result set. Each object in the possible set must then be read and evaluated to make sure it fits the criteria.

▶ Although indexes enhance search performance, each additional index adds to the update time for a new object; this is especially true for Substring indexes. Therefore, for massive bulk-loading operations, you should consider suspending User Defined indexes, especially the Substring indexes, during the operation.

▶ Defining an index for each attribute within a query *rarely* provides performance benefits. Complex search filters are broken down to predicates during the filter evaluation, and eDirectory uses only one index per predicate. The DSA selects one optimal index per complex search and then applies the other filter criteria to the results pulled from the index. Therefore, if you see a predicate searching for four attributes, there is no need to create four indexes—unless they are also used by other predicates.

▶ Queries containing ! in the expression do *not* use indexes. The reason for this is that objects where the attribute is not defined are also returned in the result set.

▶ Queries that contain a greater-than-or-equal-to specification (>=) use an index, but queries containing less-than-or-equal-to (<=) do not. As is the case with ! queries, a <= query assumes that all objects that don't contain the attribute match the query.

▶ If a query includes multiple predicates on the same indexed attribute that are concatenated together, query performance is generally better if the more specific predicate is given before the less specific predicate because eDirectory uses the index attribute on the first predicate only. For example, if you are trying to find users who belongs to both the `GW Support` group and `Support` group, this search filter:

```
((groupMembership=="GW Support")&&
(groupMembership=="Support"))
```

performs better than the following query:

```
((groupMembership=="Support")&&
(groupMembership=="GW Support"))
```

because the first filter has the more specific predicate, `GW Support`, listed first.

Is Your Query Really Using the Indexes?

Indexes are not miracle solutions to all query-based performance bottlenecks. They can greatly help improve search speeds if the applications can take advantage of them, such as by formulating and structuring the search filters to the way eDirectory works. But how can you find out after creating all the necessary indexes whether the still-not-so-speedy search response time is due to the applications or a system bottleneck somewhere else?

DSTrace provides much information to many eDirectory internal processes, and it can help you again in this situation. By setting the Record Manager filter for tracing, you can see which index was picked for a particular query.

NOTE

As discussed in the "Server Tools" section in Chapter 7, "Diagnostic and Repair Tools," there are two implementations of DSTrace on NetWare servers: the built-in SET DSTRACE command and the DSTRACE NLM command. In order to view the RECMAN information, you need to use the NLM implementation.

On Windows servers, the RECMAN filter in DSTrace is called Storage Manager (StrMan) instead.

The following example shows a ConsoleOne query that is looking for the x121Address attribute by doing a find for the attribute. Notice that the boldfaced message indicates that no index was used to perform the query:

```
[02/10/2004 06:24:07.96] StrMan   : Iter #c31e00 query
 ((Flags&1)==1) && ((((x121Address$549A$.Flags&8)==8) &&
 x121Address$549A$.Flags&8)))
[02/10/2004 06:24:07.96] StrMan   : Iter #c31e00 NO INDEX USED
[02/10/2004 06:24:07.96] StrMan   : Iter #c31e00 first
 ( ID_INVALID)
```

NOTE

The ID_INVALID message indicates that the search found no matching objects. Otherwise, an entry ID (EID) value will be displayed.

The following example is a ConsoleOne query for a list of NCP Server objects in the tree. Notice that the highlighted message indicates that the ClassID_RDN_IX index, an internal eDirectory index, was used to perform the query:

```
[02/10/2004 06:23:03.89] StrMan   : Iter #6d74ee0 query
 ((Flags&1)==1) && (((ClassID==448) && ((Flags&64)==0)))
[02/10/2004 06:23:03.89] StrMan   : Iter #6d74ee0
 index = ClassID_RDN_IX
[02/10/2004 06:23:03.89] StrMan   : Iter #6d74ee0 first
 ( eid=32871)
```

Using the information provided by DSTrace along with the predicate stats provides you with some good tools for pinpointing possible bottlenecks in search performance.

Changing Database Block Size

As mentioned earlier in this chapter, the default eDirectory database block size is 4KB. For performance reasons, you might need to change the block size (either larger or smaller) in order to match the physical disk block size. You cannot change the database block size after the DIB files are created, but you can override the default value during eDirectory installation so a different block size is used. You do this by placing a **blocksize** command in the **_NDSDB.INI** file:

```
blocksize=bytes
```

You need to manually create the **_NDSDB.INI** file and place it in the directory where eDirectory expects it:

Platform	Location
NetWare	SYS:_NETWARE_NDSDB.INI
Windows	*drive*:\Novell\NDS\DIBFiles_ndsdb.ini
Unix	/var/nds/dib/_ndsdb.ini

For example, suppose you are installing eDirectory on a Windows 2000 server and want to set the database block size to 10KB. First, you create the **_ndsdb.ini** file with the line **blocksize=10240** in it and put the file in **C:\Novell\NDS\DIBFiles** before you start the eDirectory installation. After eDirectory has been installed, you can verify the database block size by using iMonitor, as shown in Figure 16.9.

FIGURE 16.9
A Windows eDirectory server whose database block size is 10KB.

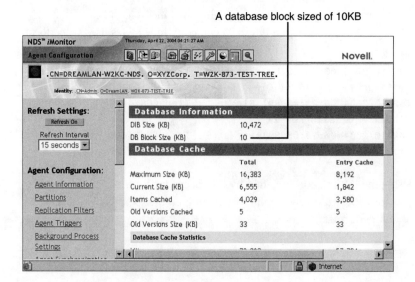

Keep in mind that for best performance, the file system block size should match the size of the database block size or be in multiples thereof.

Unix-Specific Tuning Considerations

Performance tuning of any software application is a complex job. It requires you to have an understanding of various components and subsystems of the software and knowledge of operating system and other system resources, such as file system, memory, storage media, and bandwidth. eDirectory is no exception. Previous sections in this chapter cover many eDirectory-specific tuning tricks. There are also some operating system–specific performance enhancements you can make on Unix systems, and they are covered in the following sections.

TIP

If you are looking for a tool to help you tune a Unix system, SarCheck may be of use to you. It is a Unix performance analysis and tuning tool for most Sun Solaris, HP-UX, AIX, SCO, and Linux (in beta, at the time of this writing) systems that produces recommendations and explanations with supporting graphs and tables. Visit `www.sarcheck.com/index.htm` for more information.

TIP

On high-end Solaris servers with many processors, it is better to create processor sets of not more than four and bind an instance of ndsd to the set. ndsd can then exploit warm on-chip caches to speed up operations.

Rather than go into the details for each supported Unix operating system, which would take a considerable amount of space, we refer you to Novell's eDirectory documentation and its whitepaper on eDirectory performance tuning for Linux and Unix systems (`www.novell.com/products/edirectory/whitepapers.html`) for specifics. The following sections describe the salient points that are common to the supported Unix operating systems.

The Cache Subsystem

eDirectory can dynamically adjust its cache limit to regulate memory consumption in response to the memory demand of other processes. The limit is calculated as a percentage of available physical memory at set intervals. Although this works well for NetWare and Windows servers, it is not recommended for Linux and Unix platforms. Large differences in memory usage patterns and memory allocators do not allow for optimal performance of eDirectory on these operating systems.

On Unix systems (including Linux, unless otherwise specified), the free available memory reported by the operating system will be less than that for other operating systems because of the way the operating system uses free memory for internal caching of file system blocks, frequently run programs, libraries, and so on. In addition to this memory allocation, libraries on Unix normally do not return the freed memory back to the operating system. For these reasons, it is best to employ the Hard Limit mode and allocate a fixed amount of RAM to the eDirectory cache.

NOTE   On Unix/Linux, the operating system tries to cache file system blocks in its internal buffer cache. You should tune the operating system to flush this internal buffer cache as fast as possible—and even bypass it completely, if possible. If bypassing the internal cache is not an option, you should not specify more than 50% to 75% of the total physical memory for the eDirectory cache.

eDirectory Threads

eDirectory uses an internal pool of threads to service client requests and internal operations. This thread pool avoids the overhead of starting or stopping a new thread for every request. Maximum performance is achieved by using the minimum number of threads required to service the requests. The lower the number of threads, the fewer system resources are required to manage them. eDirectory 8.7 and later automatically use a lower number of threads and start or stop threads as needed. This delivers optimum performance in most cases; however, it may need to be tuned to handle sudden heavy client loads.

You can place four parameters in the /etc/nds.conf file to help with tuning the thread requirements:

- ▶ n4u.server.active-interval controls when a new thread is started. A thread is considered busy on another job if it does not return to the thread pool within the time interval (in milliseconds) specified by the parameter. This parameter is scaled based on the number of processors available on the machine and can be increased to its maximum value (25,000) to get the maximum performance.

- ▶ n4u.server.idle-threads specifies the minimum number of threads (regardless of activity) in the thread pool. The value of this parameter should be based on the average client load in order to minimize the time required to produce new threads during normal client activity.

▶ `n4u.server.start-threads` specifies the number of threads that get created and placed in the thread pool when eDirectory starts. The value of this parameter should be based on the average client load in order to minimize the time required to produce new threads during normal client activity.

▶ `n4u.server.max-threads` specifies the maximum number of threads to be created. Each thread uses about 200KB of memory when performing heavy searches. The value of this parameter should be based on the maximum number of simultaneous clients that need to be serviced, along with the following recommendations:

  ▶ eDirectory requires a minimum of 16 threads for its internal operations.

  ▶ There should be one Monitor thread for every 255 LDAP client connections.

  ▶ There should be one Worker thread for every four concurrent clients that need to be serviced.

  ▶ There should be eight threads for every processor configured to service client search requests.

The default value for this parameter is **64**, and a value of **128** is sufficient in most cases, except when the server is serving a very large number of clients concurrently.

File System

As with the case of a disk subsystem and its configuration, the choice of the file system can significantly influence the performance of bulk updates; search performance is less affected because of the rather aggressive caching in eDirectory. One of the great things about Unix systems is the diverse choice of file systems that is available. Each has its own strengths and weaknesses, depending on your requirement. This is also one of the "bad" things about Unix: There are too many different file systems to choose from.

There are complete books, not just chapters, written about Unix/Linux file systems. If you are interested in more information, take a look here: `www.linuxshelf.com/servlet/books?category=filesystem`.

NOTE

If it's available for your Unix operating system, Novell recommends using the VERITAS file system with a block size of 4KB (the eDirectory database block size) because it can give significantly improved performance over "standard" Unix file systems. For HP-UX, Novell recommends that you use the JFS (VxFS) partition for storing the DIB directory. The default database block size of 4,096 bytes provides better performance for HP-UX.

> **NOTE**   The VERITAS file system is a quick-recovery, journaling file system that is similar in some ways to Novell's NSS implementation. You can find more information about the VERITAS file system at `www.veritas.com/products/category/ProductDetail.jhtml?productId=filesystem`.

Summary

This chapter concentrates on performance tuning for an eDirectory tree, using eDirectory indexes and predicate stats data. Some noteworthy tricks are presented that you can use from a software perspective to enhance eDirectory's performance without spending additional money. Performance can be affected by many elements of eDirectory, including memory management (cache settings), indexes, replica placement, and search limits.

PART V

Appendixes

PART V

APPENDIX A

eDirectory Error Codes

This appendix provides an exhaustive listing and explanation of all the published eDirectory error codes. You can use this appendix as a starting point to determine the actual cause of a problem and then formulate a corrective action plan. For each eDirectory error code, the following information is shown, in a tabular format:

- Error code in decimal
- Error code in hexadecimal
- Name of constant, as used in the Novell Developer Kit (NDK), that corresponds to the error code
- Explanation of the error

The error code listings are separated according to their source: the server, client, or directory services agent (DSA).

Table A.1 shows the server operating system–related error codes that are returned through directory services (DS). Many of the errors are generated by bindery-based API calls. To provide backward compatibility with older applications, eDirectory or NDS sometimes returns the positive numeric error code rather than the negative error code normally used by eDirectory or NDS. Therefore, any occurrence of an error code within the range of 1 through 255 should be treated as the same error as its negative equivalent (for example, 3 and -3).

NOTE You will notice that some of the error codes have multiple meanings and multiple sources. For instance, the error code —250 may be reported by the DS module or via the Novell SecureLogin product. Because most of the -001 through -255 errors are really server operating system error codes reported as DS errors, you need to be aware of the context under which the error code is returned in order to correctly interpret the cause of the error.

Table A.2 shows the DS client API library error codes. The eDirectory or NDS client built into the DS module generates these error codes. The eDirectory or NDS client error codes fall in the range of -301 through -399.

Certain eDirectory or NDS background processes or operations require the use or functionality provided by other programs (such as the Unicode module). If any of these modules encounters an error, it can be passed on to the DS module, and the error code is in the range of -400 through -599. This error category is shown in Table A.3.

Table A.4 shows the error codes that are returned by the DSA. These codes are in the ranges -601 through -799 and -6001 through -6999. Error codes -6001 through -6999 are strictly for use by eDirectory 8.7 and higher.

TIP New error codes may be introduced when new versions of eDirectory modules are released. If you don't find the error code you are looking for in any of the tables in this appendix, check Novell's documentation Web site, at www.novell.com/documentation/lg/nwec/nwec_enu/nwec_list_of_all_codes.html or www.novell.com/documentation/lg/nwec/index.html, for updates. Another source for up-to-date error codes is the NWDSERR.H C header file from the NDK. You can find an HTML version of this file by searching for "nwdserr.h" at http://developer.novell.com.

Operating System–Related DS Error Codes

TABLE A.1

DECIMAL	HEXADECIMAL	CONSTANT	DESCRIPTION
-001	0xFFFFFFFF	DSERR_INSUFFICIENT_SPACE	Insufficient space to process an auditing request. This error can also be returned by Authentication Tool Box (ATB)or Secure Authentication Service (SAS).
-002 through -012	0xFFFFFFFE through 0xFFFFFFF4		Used by ATB library or SAS. (ATB errors are hardware-level errors that relate to the physical portion of a server. These are calls that are made during initial startup and after startup of the server.)
-013 through -101	0xFFFFFFF3 through 0xFFFFFF9B		Unused.
-102 through -118	0xFFFFFF9A through 0xFFFFFF8A		Used by the Novell SecureLogin product.
-119	0xFFFFFF89	DSERR_BUFFER_TOO_SMALL	The buffer allocated is too small for the amount of data to be passed back. This error can also suggest that the server has insufficient IPX sockets available. If this is the case, you can increase the maximum number of IPX sockets by using SPXCONFG.NLM.
-120	0xFFFFFF88	DSERR_VOLUME_FLAG_NOT_SET	The service requested is not available on the selected volume.
-121	0xFFFFFF87	DSERR_NO_ITEMS_FOUND	Requesting to identify any accounting changes pending on the specified object and none were found.
-122	0xFFFFFF86	DSERR_CONN_ALREADY_TEMPORARY	Trying to convert a temporary connection to a temporary connection.
-123	0xFFFFFF85	DSERR_CONN_ALREADY_LOGGED_IN	The connection is already authenticated.
-124	0xFFFFFF84	DSERR_CONN_NOT_AUTHENTICATED	Trying to perform an operation that requires an authenticated connection using a connection that is not yet authenticated.
-125	0xFFFFFF83	DSERR_CONN_NOT_LOGGED_IN	Trying to log out of a connection that you're not logged in to.
-126	0xFFFFFF82	DSERR_NCP_BOUNDARY_ CHECK_FAILED	The size of NCP data received doesn't match NCP subfunction size. This can be due to faulty LAN drivers or networking hardware. This error can also arise from an improperly formatted auditing request.

Table A.1 Continued

DECIMAL	HEXADECIMAL	CONSTANT	DESCRIPTION
-127	0xFFFFFF81	DSERR_LOCK_WAITING	Timed out while trying to put a lock on a file.
-128	0xFFFFFF80	DSERR_LOCK_FAIL	Attempting to open or create a file that's already opened.
-129	0xFFFFFF7F	DSERR_OUT_OF_HANDLES	The server is out of file handles.
-130	0xFFFFFF7E	DSERR_NO_OPEN_PRIVILEGE	Attempting to open a file without the Open privilege.
-131	0xFFFFFF7D	DSERR_HARD_IO_ERROR	A hard disk I/O error on a NetWare volume; possible bad sector found on disk and could be fatal.
-132	0xFFFFFF7C	DSERR_NO_CREATE_PRIVILEGE	Attempting to create a file without the Create privilege.
-133	0xFFFFFF7B	DSERR_NO_CREATE_DELETE_PRIV	Trying to create an already existing file without the Create/Delete privilege.
-134	0xFFFFFF7A	DSERR_R_O_CREATE_FILE	Cannot create an already existing file with read-only status.
-135	0xFFFFFF79	DSERR_CREATE_FILE_INVALID_NAME	Attempting to create a file by using an ambiguous filename (for example, one that contains wildcard characters).
-136	0xFFFFFF78	DSERR_INVALID_FILE_HANDLE	Attempting to perform an I/O operation on a file with an invalid file handle (for example, trying to write to a file that has been closed).
-137	0xFFFFFF77	DSERR_NO_SEARCH_PRIVILEGE	Trying to search a directory without the Search privilege (File Scan) in that directory.
-138	0xFFFFFF76	DSERR_NO_DELETE_PRIVILEGE	Unable to delete a file without the File Deletion privilege in that file's directory.
-139	0xFFFFFF75	DSERR_NO_RENAME_PRIVILEGE	Unable to rename a file without the Rename privilege in that file's directory.
-140	0xFFFFFF74	DSERR_NO_SET_PRIVILEGE	Cannot set a file's attribute without the Modify privilege in that file's directory.
-141	0xFFFFFF73	DSERR_SOME_FILES_IN_USE	Attempting to delete, rename, or modify file attributes by using a wildcard filename while some of the files matching the filename are in use by another process.
-142	0xFFFFFF72	DSERR_ALL_FILES_IN_USE	Attempting to delete, rename, or modify file attributes by using a wildcard filename while all the files matching the filename are in use by another process.

Table A.1   Continued

DECIMAL	HEXADECIMAL	CONSTANT	DESCRIPTION
-143	0xFFFFFF71	DSERR_SOME_READ_ONLY	Trying to delete, rename, or set file attributes by using a filename when some of the files specified have read-only status.
-144	0xFFFFFF70	DSERR_ALL_READ_ONLY	Cannot delete, rename, or modify file attributes using a wildcard filename while all the files matching the filename are read-only.
-145	0xFFFFFF6F	DSERR_SOME_NAMES_EXIST	Failed to rename files using a wildcard filename when one or more files matching the new filename specification already exist.
-146	0xFFFFFF6E	DSERR_ALL_NAMES_EXIST	Failed to rename files by using a wildcard filename when all the files matching the new filename specification already exist.
-147	0xFFFFFF6D	DSERR_NO_READ_PRIVILEGE	Cannot read from a file without the Read privilege to that file.
-148	0xFFFFFF6C	DSERR_NO_WRITE_PRIVILEGE	Cannot write to a file without the Write privilege to that file, or the specified file is opened as read-only.
-149	0xFFFFFF6B	DSERR_FILE_DETACHED	Caused by an internal auditing error. You need to contact Novell about this error.
-150	0xFFFFFF6A	ERR_INSUFFICIENT_MEMORY	The server does not have sufficient dynamic memory to process the current auditing request. This is the same as operating system error ERR_NO_ALLOC_SPACE (0x96).
-150	0xFFFFFF6A	DSERR_NO_ALLOC_SPACE	The server failed to allocate memory for the current DS request, process, or operation.
-150	0xFFFFFF6A	DSERR_TARGET_NOT_A_SUBDIR	The target is not a subdirectory.
-151	0xFFFFFF69	DSERR_NO_SPOOL_SPACE	There is insufficient disk space left on the NetWare volume for spool files.
-152	0xFFFFFF68	DSERR_INVALID_VOLUME	A bindery API call was made to retrieve a bindery-emulated object's file system rights, but the specified volume name cannot be found. Perhaps the volume is not mounted.
-153	0xFFFFFF67	DSERR_DIRECTORY_FULL	Cannot write to volume due to being out of directory space.
-154	0xFFFFFF66	DSERR_RENAME_ACROSS_VOLUME	Cannot rename a file and move the renamed file from one volume to another volume; the rename command can only move the file between directories on the same volume.

Table A.1   Continued

DECIMAL	HEXADECIMAL	CONSTANT	DESCRIPTION
-155	0xFFFFFF65	DSERR_BAD_DIR_HANDLE	Trying to use an invalid directory (not file) handle. This could happen if the server were brought down and brought back up without rebooting the client.
-156	0xFFFFFF64	DSERR_INVALID_PATH	A bindery API call was made to create a bindery-emulated queue object. However, the specified (directory/filename) path is invalid or not accessible. This error can also be caused by faulty LAN driver or networking hardware.
-156	0xFFFFFF64	DSERR_NO_SUCH_EXTENSION	No more trustees are listed in the directory entry table.
-157	0xFFFFFF63	DSERR_NO_DIR_HANDLES	The server's directory handle table is full. (Each client is allowed up to 255 directory handles.)
-158	0xFFFFFF62	DSERR_BAD_FILE_NAME	Cannot create a file whose name contains illegal character(s).
-159	0xFFFFFF61	DSERR_DIRECTORY_ACTIVE	Unable to delete a directory that is currently in use by another process.
-160	0xFFFFFF60	DSERR_DIRECTORY_NOT_EMPTY	Cannot delete a directory that contains other directories or files.
-161	0xFFFFFF5F	DSERR_DIRECTORY_IO_ERROR	This nonrecoverable I/O error occurs when trying to access the directory entry table (DET). Both copies of the DET are not accessible, and the error is fatal.
-162	0xFFFFFF5E	DSERR_IO_LOCKED	Attempting to read a file where data is physically locked.
-163	0xFFFFFF5D	DSERR_TRANSACTION_RESTARTED	An aborted TTS transaction has been restarted.
-164	0xFFFFFF5C	DSERR_RENAME_DIR_INVALID	The rename operation specified a directory name that contains one or more invalid characters.
-165	0xFFFFFF5B	DSERR_INVALID_OPENCREATE_MODE	An invalid combination of Open/Create mode option was specified.
-166	0xFFFFFF5A	DSERR_ALREADY_IN_USE	The auditor is trying to access an object that is currently being accessed by another auditor.
-167	0xFFFFFF59	DSERR_INVALID_RESOURCE_TAG	An application is trying to register a DS event by using an invalid resource tag. This is due to faulty applications.

Table A.1   Continued

DECIMAL	HEXADECIMAL	CONSTANT	DESCRIPTION
-168	0xFFFFFF58	DSERR_ACCESS_DENIED	Access to resource has been denied.
-169 through -187	0xFFFFFF57 through 0xFFFFFF45		Unused.
-188	0xFFFFFF44	DSERR_LOGIN_SIGNING_REQUIRED	Packet signing is required for the login process.
-189	0xFFFFFF43	DSERR_LOGIN_ENCRYPT_REQUIRED	Data encryption is required for the login process.
-190	0xFFFFFF42	DSERR_INVALID_DATA_STREAM	The specified data stream is invalid. This is an internal auditing error.
-191	0xFFFFFF41	DSERR_INVALID_NAME_SPACE	The specified namespace is not supported.
-192	0xFFFFFF40	DSERR_NO_ACCOUNTING_PRIVILEGES	Trying to perform an accounting function without the proper privileges.
-193	0xFFFFFF3F	DSERR_NO_ACCOUNT_BALANCE	A bindery login was attempted, but the object has no accounting balance, and the server's accounting is enabled.
-194	0xFFFFFF3E	DSERR_CREDIT_LIMIT_EXCEEDED	Attempting to log in with no credit available or attempting to perform an operation that will exceed its accounting credit limit.
-195	0xFFFFFF3D	DSERR_TOO_MANY_HOLDS	Too many accounting transactions on hold.
-196	0xFFFFFF3C	DSERR_ACCOUNTING_DISABLED	Trying to perform an accounting function when the server's accounting is disabled.
-197	0xFFFFFF3B	DSERR_LOGIN_LOCKOUT	Attempting to log in after the system has locked the account due to intruder detection.
-198	0xFFFFFF3A	DSERR_NO_CONSOLE_RIGHTS	Attempting to perform console functions (such as changing the server's time) without operator privileges.
-199 through -207	0xFFFFFF39 through 0xFFFFFF31		Unused.
-208	0xFFFFFF30	DSERR_Q_IO_FAILURE	An I/O error occurs when you try to access the queue.
-209	0xFFFFFF2F	DSERR_NO_QUEUE	Queue directory not found.
-210	0xFFFFFF2E	DSERR_NO_Q_SERVER	No queue server associated with the queue.
-211	0xFFFFFF2D	DSERR_NO_Q_RIGHTS	Insufficient rights to service the queue.
-212	0xFFFFFF2C	DSERR_Q_FULL	Queue is full. A QMS-based queue can hold up to 250 jobs.

Table A.1   Continued

DECIMAL	HEXADECIMAL	CONSTANT	DESCRIPTION
-213	0xFFFFFF2B	DSERR_NO_Q_JOB	There is no serviceable job in the queue.
-214	0xFFFFFF2A	DSERR_NO_Q_JOB_RIGHTS	Cannot assume the rights of a queue job's submitter in order to service that queue job. (This is controlled by the Allow Change to Client Rights SET command.)
-214	0xFFFFFF2A	DSERR_UNENCRYPTED_NOT_ALLOWED	A bindery API call was made, using an unencrypted password when the server does not permit it. (This is controlled by the Allow Unencrypted Passwords SET command.)
-215	0xFFFFFF29	DSERR_Q_IN_SERVICE	The queue server is already servicing the specified queue.
-215	0xFFFFFF29	DSERR_DUPLICATE_PASSWORD	Attempting to change the NDS or bindery password to a previously used password when the unique password requirement is specified for the account.
-216	0xFFFFFF28	DSERR_Q_NOT_ACTIVE	Trying to service a queue that does not allow queue servers to service jobs in the queue.
-216	0xFFFFFF28	DSERR_PASSWORD_TOO_SHORT	The new NDS or bindery password has fewer characters than the required minimum specified for the account.
-217	0xFFFFFF27	DSERR_Q_STN_NOT_SERVER	The station making the queue service request is not logged in as a queue server.
-217	0xFFFFFF27	DSERR_MAXIMUM_LOGINS_EXCEEDED	Attempting to log in using an NDS or bindery account that has limits on the number of concurrent connections and that number has been reached.
-218	0xFFFFFF26	DSERR_Q_HALTED	Trying to place a job into a queue that does not allow new jobs to be added.
-218	0xFFFFFF26	DSERR_BAD_LOGIN_TIME	Attempting to log in during an unauthorized time of day, as specified in the Login Time Restriction for the NDS or bindery user account.
-219	0xFFFFFF25	DSERR_Q_MAX_SERVERS	The queue already has its maximum number of queue servers attached. Each QMS-based queue can be serviced by up to 16 queue servers.

Table A.1　Continued

DECIMAL	HEXADECIMAL	CONSTANT	DESCRIPTION
-219	0xFFFFFF25	DSERR_NODE_ADDRESS_VIOLATION	Attempting to log in from an unauthorized station using an NDS or bindery account with limits to a specific network and/or node.
-220	0xFFFFFF24	DSERR_LOG_ACCOUNT_EXPIRED	Trying to log in using an NDS or bindery account that has expired or has been disabled.
-222	0xFFFFFF22	DSERR_BAD_PASSWORD	Attempting to log in using an NDS or bindery account whose password has expired and all grace logins have been used up.
-223	0xFFFFFF21	DSERR_PASSWORD_EXPIRED	Trying to log in using an expired DS or bindery password and the login was allowed because the account had a grace login.
-224	0xFFFFFF20	DSERR_NO_LOGIN_CONN_AVAILABLE	The server is out of connections and rejected the login request.
-225 through -231	0xFFFFFF1F through 0xFFFFFF19		Unused.
-232	0xFFFFFF18	DSERR_WRITE_TO_GROUP_PROPERTY	Attempting to write a data segment to a group property, using the call to write a property value. Wrong bindery API call used. This error can also be caused by attempting to use an item not associated with this group or an item that has been deleted from this group.
-233	0xFFFFFF17	DSERR_MEMBER_ALREADY_EXISTS	Trying to redundantly add an object to a group.
-234	0xFFFFFF16	DSERR_NO_SUCH_MEMBER	Trying to access an object that is not a member of the specified group.
-235	0xFFFFFF15	DSERR_PROPERTY_NOT_GROUP	Attempting to access data that is not a property of the specified group.
-236	0xFFFFFF14	DSERR_NO_SUCH_VALUE_SET	Attempting to access a nonexistent data set.
-237	0xFFFFFF13	DSERR_PROPERTY_ALREADY_EXISTS	Trying to redundantly add a single-valued property to an object; you need to delete the existing property value before adding the new information.
-238	0xFFFFFF12	DSERR_OBJECT_ALREADY_EXISTS	Trying to create an object that already exists.

Table A.1　Continued

DECIMAL	HEXADECIMAL	CONSTANT	DESCRIPTION
-239	0xFFFFFF11	DSERR_ILLEGAL_NAME	Making a request with an object or property name that contains illegal characters, such as a control character, a comma, a colon, a semicolon, a slash, a backslash, a question mark, an asterisk, or a tilde. This error may also occur if the DS module can't map the supplied name to its Unicode representation. (This is the same as error `ERR_NO_CHARACTER_MAPPING` [-638])
-240	0xFFFFFF10	DSERR_ILLEGAL_WILDCARD	Attempting to use a wildcard character or wild object type in an API call where wildcards are not allowed.
-241	0xFFFFFF0F	DSERR_BINDERY_SECURITY	Trying to assign a security level of a bindery object or property to be higher than the requester's security level. This would make the object or property inaccessible to the requester.
-242	0xFFFFFF0E	DSERR_NO_OBJECT_READ_RIGHTS	A station's attempting to access an object's information or scan the object's properties without the necessary security to access that information.
-243	0xFFFFFF0D	DSERR_NO_OBJECT_RENAME_RIGHTS	Attempting to rename an object without the necessary security. Requires `Supervisor` or `Rename` object rights to rename objects.
-244	0xFFFFFF0C	DSERR_NO_OBJECT_DELETE_RIGHTS	Cannot delete an object without the necessary security. Requires `Supervisor` or `Delete` object rights to delete objects.
-245	0xFFFFFF0B	DSERR_NO_OBJECT_CREATE_RIGHTS	Cannot create or modify an object without the necessary security. Requires `Supervisor` or `Create` object rights to create objects.
-246	0xFFFFFF0A	DSERR_NO_PROPERTY_DELETE_RIGHTS	A client's attempting to delete a property without having the necessary security privilege to delete a property from the given object. Requires `Supervisor` or `Delete` property rights to delete a property.
-247	0xFFFFFF09	DSERR_NO_PROPERTY_CREATE_RIGHTS	A client is unable to add a new property value without having the necessary security privilege to add a property to the given object. Requires `Supervisor` or `Write` property rights to add a property or property value.

Table A.1   Continued

DECIMAL	HEXADECIMAL	CONSTANT	DESCRIPTION
-248	0xFFFFFF08	DSERR_NO_PROPERTY_WRITE_RIGHTS	A client is unable to write to a property without having the necessary security privilege. Requires Supervisor or Write property rights to change the property data.
-249	0xFFFFFF07	DSERR_NO_PROPERTY_READ_RIGHTS	A client's attempting to read a property without having the necessary read security to access the property data. Requires Supervisor or Read property rights to retrieve a property value.
-250	0xFFFFFF06	DSERR_TEMP_REMAP	Attempting to use an unknown or invalid directory path.
-251	0xFFFFFF05	ERR_REQUEST_UNKNOWN	Requesting with an invalid parameter (drive number, path, or flag value) during a set drive path API call.
-251	0xFFFFFF05	DSERR_UNKNOWN_REQUEST	An unknown request was received. This is the same as operating system error ERR_UNKNOWN_REQUEST (0xFB).
-251	0xFFFFFF05	DSERR_NO_SUCH_PROPERTY	Trying to access a property that doesn't exist for the specified object.
-252	0xFFFFFF04	DSERR_MESSAGE_QUEUE_FULL	The message queue (as used by the console BROADCAST command or the NetWare SEND.EXE utility) is full. No new messages can be queued.
-252	0xFFFFFF04	DSERR_TARGET_ALREADY_HAS_MSG	There is already a message waiting in the message queue. No new messages can be added.
-252	0xFFFFFF04	DSERR_NO_SUCH_OBJECT	Attempting to use an object that doesn't exist, or the calling station doesn't have the proper security to access the object. Note that the object name and type must both match for the object to be found. This is the bindery equivalent of error ERR_NO_SUCH_ENTRY (-601).
-253	0xFFFFFF03	DSERR_BAD_STATION_NUMBER	Attempting to use a bad (undefined, unavailable, and so on) station number. For example, the connection was cleared just prior to trying to access that connection.
-254	0xFFFFFF02	DSERR_BINDERY_LOCKED	Trying to access a locked bindery. On DS servers, this can be due to DSRepair being run and the local DS database being temporarily locked.

Table A.1 Continued

DECIMAL	HEXADECIMAL	CONSTANT	DESCRIPTION
-254	0xFFFFFF02	DSERR_DIR_LOCKED	Attempting to access a directory whose data area on the volume is physically locked.
-254	0xFFFFFF02	DSERR_SPOOL_DELETE	Trying to access a spool file that doesn't exist.
-254	0xFFFFFF02	DSERR_TRUSTEE_NOT_FOUND	The specified trustee is not found.
-254	0xFFFFFF02	DSERR_TIMEOUT	The request timed out.
-255	0xFFFFFF01	DSERR_HARD_FAILURE	A bindery-emulation error has occurred. This can be a result of an attempt to verify a bindery object's password while Bindery Services was not enabled on the server or an unsupported bindery API call was used. You can gather additional information by using DSTrace on the source server with the Bindery Emulation flag (EMU) turned on.
-255	0xFFFFFF01	DSERR_FILE_NAME	An illegal filename was specified.
-255	0xFFFFFF01	DSERR_FILE_EXISTS	The specified file already exists. This is an internal auditing error.
-255	0xFFFFFF01	DSERR_CLOSE_FCB	An error occurred in closing the File Control Block (FCB).
-255	0xFFFFFF01	DSERR_IO_BOUND	Attempting to write beyond the end of the file or disk. This is an internal auditing error.
-255	0xFFFFFF01	DSERR_NO_SPOOL_FILE	The specified spool file does not exist.
-255	0xFFFFFF01	DSERR_BAD_SPOOL_PRINTER	Attempting to use a bad (undefined, unavailable, and so on) printer.
-255	0xFFFFFF01	DSERR_BAD_PARAMETER	The API called tried to pass an illegal parameter.
-255	0xFFFFFF01	DSERR_NO_FILES_FOUND	No files matching the search parameter were found.
-255	0xFFFFFF01	DSERR_NO_TRUSTEE_CHANGE_PRIV	Unable to change trustee due to insufficient rights.
-255	0xFFFFFF01	DSERR_TARGET_NOT_LOGGED_IN	Trying to send a message to a user who is not logged in.
-255	0xFFFFFF01	DSERR_TARGET_NOT_ACCEPTING_MSGS	Trying to send a message to a user who has disabled broadcast message reception. (The user has issued a "castoff" command, using SEND /A=N.)

Table A.1   Continued

DECIMAL	HEXADECIMAL	CONSTANT	DESCRIPTION
-255	0xFFFFFF01	DSERR_MUST_FORCE_DOWN	The server cannot be downed gracefully (perhaps due to opened files) when a down-server API (such as NWDownFileServer) is issued.
-255	0xFFFFFF01	ERR_OF_SOME_SORT	An unknown error was encountered. This is the same as operating system error ERR_OF_SOME_SORT (0xFF).

Client API Library Error Codes   **TABLE A.2**

DECIMAL	HEXADECIMAL	CONSTANT	DESCRIPTION
-301	0xFFFFFED3	ERR_NOT_ENOUGH_MEMORY	Unable to allocate memory. The client (workstation) may be low on memory, or the application may have been repeatedly allocating buffers and failed to release them.
-302	0xFFFFFED2	ERR_BAD_KEY	An unknown key value was passed when making a context API (NWDSSetContext or NWDSGetContext) call.
-303	0xFFFFFED1	ERR_BAD_CONTEXT	Trying to pass an invalid context value to a DS API call. The most likely cause of this error is that NWDSCreateContext or NWDSCreateContextHandle was not first called to obtain a valid context value.
-304	0xFFFFFED0	ERR_BUFFER_FULL	The buffer is full when you're trying to add data to an input buffer. The default buffer size is 4KB and the maximum is 63KB.
-305	0xFFFFFECF	ERR_LIST_EMPTY	An empty list (a NULL pointer) was passed to the NWDSPutAttrVal call when using the SYN_CI_LIST or SYN_OCTET_LIST syntax type.
-306	0xFFFFFECE	ERR_BAD_SYNTAX	An invalid syntax ID was passed. This error could be due to an internal auditing error.
-307	0xFFFFFECD	ERR_BUFFER_EMPTY	Attempting to retrieve data from an empty buffer.
-308	0xFFFFFECC	ERR_BAD_VERB	Trying to initialize a buffer, using a verb that is not associated with the API call. For example, a call to NWDSInitBuf may have been made with the DSV_RESOLVE_NAME verb, which is not a valid verb for this API call.

Table A.2   Continued

DECIMAL	HEXADECIMAL	CONSTANT	DESCRIPTION
-309	0xFFFFFECB	ERR_EXPECTED_IDENTIFIER	The DS object name being parsed is not typed.
-310	0xFFFFFECA	ERR_EXPECTED_EQUALS	The expected equal sign in the object name is not found.
-311	0xFFFFFEC9	ERR_ATTR_TYPE_EXPECTED	The name being parsed must be typed.
-312	0xFFFFFEC8	ERR_ATTR_TYPE_NOT_EXPECTED	The name being parsed must *not* be typed.
-313	0xFFFFFEC7	ERR_FILTER_TREE_EMPTY	Trying to delete an empty filter.
-314	0xFFFFFEC6	ERR_INVALID_OBJECT_NAME	The specified object name is invalid. Perhaps the name contained both a leading *and* a trailing period, or perhaps a NULL string was passed.
-315	0xFFFFFEC5	ERR_EXPECTED_RDN_DELIMITER	The specified relative distinguished name (RDN) doesn't have the expected delimiter (a period, .).
-316	0xFFFFFEC4	ERR_TOO_MANY_TOKENS	Too many trailing delimiter dots in the specified name; a maximum of three context levels and four trailing dots are allowed.
-317	0xFFFFFEC3	ERR_INCONSISTENT_MULTIAVA	An error occurred when checking the name field for the specified multivalued attribute. (An attribute value association [AVA] is one of the values in a multivalued attribute, and multiAVA refers to a link in a value's linked list.)
-318	0xFFFFFEC2	ERR_COUNTRY_NAME_TOO_LONG	Too many characters in the specified country name. A country name can be only two characters long.
-319	0xFFFFFEC1	ERR_SYSTEM_ERROR	An internal system error.
-320	0xFFFFFEC0	ERR_CANT_ADD_ROOT	Unable to add or restore an object at [Root].
-321	0xFFFFFEBF	ERR_UNABLE_TO_ATTACH	Unable to attach to the specified server.
-322	0xFFFFFEBE	ERR_INVALID_HANDLE	Invalid iteration handle. Functions such as NWDSList, NWDSRead, and NWDSSearch can retrieve data from the server iteratively. To do this, a valid iteration handle is needed on each API call.
-323	0xFFFFFEBD	ERR_BUFFER_ZERO_LENGTH	An API call to NWDSAllocBuf was made with a zero-length buffer size.

Table A.2   Continued

DECIMAL	HEXADECIMAL	CONSTANT	DESCRIPTION
-324	0xFFFFFEBC	ERR_INVALID_REPLICA_TYPE	The specified replica type is not one of RT_MASTER (Master), RT_SECONDART (Read/Write), RT_READONLY (Read/Only), RT_SPARSE_READ (Read/Only Filtered), or RT_SPARSE_WRITE (Read/Write Filtered); the later two are only valid for eDirectory 8.5 or higher.
-325	0xFFFFFEBB	ERR_INVALID_ATTR_SYNTAX	The specified attribute syntax ID is invalid.
-326	0xFFFFFEBA	ERR_INVALID_FILTER_SYNTAX	The specified filter syntax is invalid.
-327	0xFFFFFFB9		Unused.
-328	0xFFFFFEB8	ERR_CONTEXT_CREATION	Unable to create a context handle. This may be caused by not having called the NWInitUnicodeTables API first.
-329	0xFFFFFEB7	ERR_INVALID_UNION_TAG	The server-returned data does not agree with the data type (attribute name, attribute value, or effective privileges) you specified.
-330	0xFFFFFEB6	ERR_INVALID_SERVER_RESPONSE	The NWDSGetSyntaxID API call is unable to retrieve the syntax ID of the specified attribute.
-331	0xFFFFFEB5	ERR_NULL_POINTER	A NULL pointer was found when a real pointer was expected.
-332	0xFFFFFEB4	ERR_NO_SERVER_FOUND	An attempted connect failed to find any servers responding.
-333	0xFFFFFEB3	ERR_NO_CONNECTION	Attempting to get connection information from a server that's not currently attached.
-334	0xFFFFFEB2	ERR_RDN_TOO_LONG	The specified RDN is longer than 128 bytes.
-335	0xFFFFFEB1	ERR_DUPLICATE_TYPE	Multiple AVAs were specified, and they can't contain the same data. (An AVA is one of the values in a multivalued attribute.)
-336	0xFFFFFEB0	ERR_DATA_STORE_FAILURE	Internal error.
-337	0xFFFFFEAF	ERR_NOT_LOGGED_IN	Internal error. The client is not logged in to any servers.
-338	0xFFFFFEAE	ERR_INVALID_PASSWORD_CHARS	One or more characters specified in the password are invalid.
-339	0xFFFFFEAD	ERR_FAILED_SERVER_AUTHENT	Unable to authenticate to the server using the cached credentials.

Table A.2 Continued

DECIMAL	HEXADECIMAL	CONSTANT	DESCRIPTION
-340	0xFFFFFEAC	ERR_TRANSPORT	Communication fault detected.
-341	0xFFFFFEAB	ERR_NO_SUCH_SYNTAX	The specified syntax is not found.
-342	0xFFFFFEAA	ERR_INVALID_DS_NAME	A NULL or empty string is specified for an object name.
-343	0xFFFFFEA9	ERR_ATTR_NAME_TOO_LONG	The specified attribute name is longer than 32 characters. (A number of Novell documents erroneously indicates 128 characters, but a valid DS class or attribute name cannot be longer than 32 characters.)
-344	0xFFFFFEA8	ERR_INVALID_TDS	Internal (Tagged Data Store) error. The usual cause of this error is that NWDSLogin wasn't first called.
-345	0xFFFFFEA7	ERR_INVALID_DS_VERSION	The version of the DS module is incompatible with the version of the operating system.
-346	0xFFFFFEA6	ERR_UNICODE_TRANSLATION	A Unicode translation error from an NWDSListPartitions, NWDSSyncPartition, or NWDSSyncSchema API call.
-347	0xFFFFFEA5	ERR_SCHEMA_NAME_TOO_LONG	The specified schema name is longer than 32 characters.
-348	0xFFFFFEA4	ERR_UNICODE_FILE_NOT_FOUND	The required Unicode file or files could not be found.
-349	0xFFFFFEA3	ERR_UNICODE_ALREADY_LOADED	The NWInitUnicodeTables call was made more than once.
-350	0xFFFFFEA2	ERR_NOT_CONTEXT_OWNER	The specified context handle doesn't belong to the current DS tree or NLM thread.
-351	0xFFFFFEA1	ERR_ATTEMPT_TO_AUTHENTICATE_0	Internal error.
-352	0xFFFFFEA0	ERR_NO_WRITABLE_REPLICAS	Cannot locate a writeable replica of a partition.
-353	0xFFFFFE9F	ERR_DN_TOO_LONG	The specified distinguished name is longer than 256 characters. (Because DS stores all characters using Unicode representation, the maximum internal object name length is 512 characters.)
-354	0xFFFFFE9E	ERR_RENAME_NOT_ALLOWED	Not permitted to rename the specified object.
-355	0xFFFFFE9D	ERR_NOT_NDS_FOR_NT	The server is not running NDS for NT.
-356	0xFFFFFE9C	ERR_NDS_FOR_NT_NO_DOMAIN	No NDS for NT domain found.

Table A.2   Continued

DECIMAL	HEXADECIMAL	CONSTANT	DESCRIPTION
-357	0xFFFFFE9B	ERR_NDS_FOR_NT_SYNC_DISABLED	Synchronization between NDS for NT and NT PDC is disabled.
-358	0xFFFFFE9A	ERR_ITR_INVALID_HANDLE	An invalid iterator object was passed as a parameter to the NDS Iterator Services API (NWDSItr* calls).
-359	0xFFFFFE99	ERR_ITR_INVALID_POSITION	Trying to position the NDS iterator in a logical position that is not within the 0 to 1,000 range.
-360	0xFFFFFE98	ERR_ITR_INVALID_SEARCH_DATA	The entry data to be searched is in an unexpected format.
-361	0xFFFFFE97	ERR_ITR_INVALID_SCOPE	Subtree search is not supported for the specified iterator object.
-362	0xFFFFFE96	ERR_ITR_INVALID_MAX_COUNT	A limit was specified on the number of entries to count before returning from the API call, and this limit has been reached.
-363 through -399	0xFFFFFF95 through 0xFFFFFE71		Unused.

Server-Based–Specific Client API Library Error Codes   **TABLE A.3**

DECIMAL	HEXADECIMAL	CONSTANT	DESCRIPTION
-400	0xFFFFFE70	ERR_BAD_SERVICE_CONNECTION	An invalid server connection handle was specified.
-401	0xFFFFFE6F	ERR_BAD_NETWORK	The specified network address is unreachable.
-402	0xFFFFFE6E	ERR_BAD_ADDRESS	The specified MAC address is unknown.
-403	0xFFFFFE6D	ERR_SLOT_ALLOCATION	Unable to allocate a server connection slot.
-404	0xFFFFFE6C	ERR_BAD_BROADCAST	An invalid broadcast address was specified.
-405	0xFFFFFE6B	ERR_BAD_SERVER_NAME	There are one or more invalid characters in the specified server name.
-406	0xFFFFFE6A	ERR_BAD_USER_NAME	There are one or more invalid characters in the specified user name.
-407	0xFFFFFE69		Unused.
-408	0xFFFFFE68	ERR_NO_MEMORY	Unable to allocate memory.
-409	0xFFFFFE67		Unused.
-410	0xFFFFFE66	ERR_BAD_SOCKET	Request attempted with an invalid socket number.

Table A.3   Continued

DECIMAL	HEXADECIMAL	CONSTANT	DESCRIPTION
-411	0xFFFFFE65	ERR_TAG_ALLOCATION	Unable to allocate resource tag.
-412	0xFFFFFE64	ERR_CONNECTION_ABORTED	The connection attempt to a server was aborted.
-413	0xFFFFFE63	ERR_TIMEOUT	The request has timed out.
-414	0xFFFFFE62	ERR_CHECKSUM	A CRC checksum error was detected.
-415	0xFFFFFE61	ERR_NO_FRAGMENT_LIST	No request fragment list was found when one was expected. (An NCP request/reply may be split into multiple packets, called fragments, if the information doesn't fit in a single packet.)
-416 through -488	0xFFFFFE60 through 0xFFFFFE18		Unused.
-489	0xFFFFFFE17	UNI_ALREADY_LOADED	A Unicode table is already loaded.
-490	0xFFFFFFE16	UNI_FUTURE_OPCODE	The Unicode table has unimplemented rules.
-491	0xFFFFFFE15	UNI_NO_SUCH_FILE	Trying to load a Unicode file that does not exist, or the directory from which you try to load the Unicode file does not exist.
-492	0xFFFFFFE14	UNI_TOO_MANY_FILES	Too many Unicode files are already open.
-493	0xFFFFFFE13	UNI_NO_PERMISSION	Trying to open a Unicode file that you have no access rights to.
-494	0xFFFFFFE12	UNI_NO_MEMORY	Insufficient memory to load the Unicode files.
-495	0xFFFFFFE11	UNI_LOAD_FAILED	Unable to load the Unicode files.
-496	0xFFFFFFE10	UNI_HANDLE_BAD	The Unicode table in use is invalid. This error is from the Unicode module. This error can prevent the DS database from being initialized and opened because DS data is stored in Unicode representation. If the Unicode module is unable to translate the data for DS, the data can't be used. During server bootup, on NetWare, the Unicode module looks for its Unicode files in the SYS:LOGIN\NLS directory (\winnt\system32\nls on Windows, or /usr/share/nwlocale on Unix/Linux). If any of the required files are missing from this directory, the DS database may not open.

Table A.3 Continued

DECIMAL	HEXADECIMAL	CONSTANT	DESCRIPTION
-497	0xFFFFFE0F	UNI_HANDLE_MISMATCH	The Unicode file is not valid. The file may be missing or corrupted.
-498	0xFFFFFE0E	UNI_RULES_CORRUPT	The Unicode file is not of the correct version or is corrupted.
-499	0xFFFFFE0D	UNI_NO_DEFAULT	The data contained one or more characters that can't be mapped to the corresponding Unicode representation.
-500	0xFFFFFE0C	UNI_INSUFFICIENT_BUFFER	The buffer allocated is not large enough to load the Unicode file.
-501	0xFFFFFE0B	UNI_OPEN_FAILED	The Unicode file cannot be opened, for an unknown reason.
-502	0xFFFFFE0A	UNI_NO_LOAD_DIR	Cannot determine the load directory for the Unicode files.
-503	0xFFFFFE09	UNI_BAD_FILE_HANDLE	The Unicode file handle is bad or invalid.
-504	0xFFFFFE08	UNI_READ_FAILED	Unable to read from the Unicode file.
-505	0xFFFFFE07	UNI_TRANS_CORRUPT	The translator for the Unicode file is corrupt.
-506 through -599	0xFFFFFFE6 through 0xFFFFFDA9		Unused.

DSA Error Codes   **TABLE A.4**

DECIMAL	HEXADECIMAL	CONSTANT	DESCRIPTION
-601	0xFFFFFDA7	ERR_NO_SUCH_ENTRY	The specified object is not found on the server replying to the request. The context could be a factor, or the client doesn't have sufficient rights to the object.
-602	0xFFFFFDA6	ERR_NO_SUCH_VALUE	The requested attribute value is not found on the server replying to the request. The client may not have sufficient rights to the attribute.
-603	0xFFFFFDA5	ERR_NO_SUCH_ATTRIBUTE	The requested attribute is not found on the server replying to the request. The client may not have sufficient rights to the attribute.
-604	0xFFFFFDA4	ERR_NO_SUCH_CLASS	The specified schema class is not found on the server replying to the request.

Table A.4   Continued

DECIMAL	HEXADECIMAL	CONSTANT	DESCRIPTION
-605	0xFFFFFDA3	ERR_NO_SUCH_PARTITION	The specified partition doesn't exist on the server replying to the request. There may be communication problems between servers in the DS tree.
-606	0xFFFFFDA2	ERR_ENTRY_ALREADY_EXISTS	Trying to create, rename, or restore an object when an object with the same name already exists at the same context level of the tree.
-607	0xFFFFFDA1	ERR_NOT_EFFECTIVE_CLASS	Attempting to create an object using a schema class definition that is not an effective class.
-608	0xFFFFFDA0	ERR_ILLEGAL_ATTRIBUTE	Attempting to add an attribute that's not listed as an optional or mandatory attribute in the object's class.
-609	0xFFFFFD9F	ERR_MISSING_MANDATORY	Trying to create an object that's missing one or more mandatory attributes. For example, a User object must have its Surname attribute defined when being created. (You can use Schema Manager to determine which attributes are mandatory for a given schema class; see Chapter 7).
-610	0xFFFFFD9E	ERR_ILLEGAL_DS_NAME	The specified object name is incorrectly formatted or is longer than 256 characters. (Because DS stores all characters using Unicode representation, the maximum internal object name length is 512 characters.)
-611	0xFFFFFD9D	ERR_ILLEGAL_CONTAINMENT	Attempting to add an object that violates the schema's containment rules.
-612	0xFFFFFD9C	ERR_CANT_HAVE_MULTIPLE_VALUES	Attempting to add more than one attribute value to a single-value attribute. If you want to replace the value, you need to either delete the old value first or overwrite it with the new.
-613	0xFFFFFD9B	ERR_SYNTAX_VIOLATION	Trying to modify an attribute by using data that doesn't conform to the syntax specified for the attribute. For example, your API call specified SYN_INTEGER instead of SYN_STRING.

Table A.4   Continued

DECIMAL	HEXADECIMAL	CONSTANT	DESCRIPTION
-614	0xFFFFFD9A	ERR_DUPLICATE_VALUE	Attempting to add the same value-attribute combination to an object. For example, a User object already has a telephone number of 555-1212, and you're trying to add another telephone number whose value is also 555-1212.
-615	0xFFFFFD99	ERR_ATTRIBUTE_ALREADY_EXISTS	Attempting to create a schema attribute that already exists.
-616	0xFFFFFD98	ERR_MAXIMUM_ENTRIES_EXIST	Unable to add a new object to the DS database because the maximum number of entries (16,777,215,) in the object database has been reached. (Applies to DS 6 and DS 7 only.)
-617	0xFFFFFD97	ERR_DATABASE_FORMAT	The record structure of the DS database doesn't match the structure expected by the version of the DS module being used. The database cannot be used. If you ever encounter this error, it will be while the DS module is trying to open the database or when you're attempting to abort a DS operation, such as partitioning.
-618	0xFFFFFD96	ERR_INCONSISTENT_DATABASE	The DS module is unable to open the DS database. This can be due to unexpected data returned from the local database to the DS module or due to a problem with the database. This error may be rectified using DSRepair, by running a local database repair.
-619	0xFFFFFD95	ERR_INVALID_COMPARISON	Attempting to compare two attributes whose syntax is not comparable (for example, one is numeric and the other is text string) or using an invalid compare syntax.
-620	0xFFFFFD94	ERR_COMPARISON_FAILED	The two attribute values specified for comparison are not the same.
-621	0xFFFFFD93	ERR_TRANSACTIONS_DISABLED	No DS request can be processed because the server's TTS has been disabled.
-622	0xFFFFFD92	ERR_INVALID_TRANSPORT	The server does not support the specified type of transport.
-623	0xFFFFFD91	ERR_SYNTAX_INVALID_IN_NAME	The naming attribute specified for the new schema class definition is not of the character string type.

Table A.4 Continued

DECIMAL	HEXADECIMAL	CONSTANT	DESCRIPTION
-624	0xFFFFFD90	ERR_REPLICA_ALREADY_EXISTS	Trying to place a replica on a server that is already holding a (non-subref) replica of the same partition.
-625	0xFFFFFD8F	ERR_TRANSPORT_FAILURE	Unable to communicate with the target server. This error is generally a result of the target server being down, a LAN/WAN outage, or some sort of routing problems.
-626	0xFFFFFD8E	ERR_ALL_REFERRALS_FAILED	The local server has no objects that match the request, and all attempts to tree-walk to other servers to find the objects have failed. This error is not the same as ERR_NO_REFERRALS (-634). This error could be an indirect result of SAP/RIP filtering on the network.
-627	0xFFFFFD8D	ERR_CANT_REMOVE_NAMING_VALUE	Cannot remove the attribute value that's flagged as a naming attribute of an object. You can use Schema Manager to determine the naming attributes of a particular object class.
-628	0xFFFFFD8C	ERR_OBJECT_CLASS_VIOLATION	Trying to create an object without specifying its base class.
-629	0xFFFFFD8B	ERR_ENTRY_IS_NOT_LEAF	Attempting to delete an object containing subordinates, such as an organizational unit (OU) that still has objects in it.
-630	0xFFFFFD8A	ERR_DIFFERENT_TREE	The request was sent to a server that is not located in the current DS tree.
-631	0xFFFFFD89	ERR_ILLEGAL_REPLICA_TYPE	The server responding to the request doesn't have a replica with the required replica type to service the request. For example, the server has a Read/Only replica and not a Read/Write replica. This error is generally due to an application bug.
-632	0xFFFFFD88	ERR_SYSTEM_FAILURE	An unknown and unexpected error. This error can be a result of memory corruption in the server or an inconsistent DS database. Restarting the server or using DSRepair may resolve the problem.
-633	0xFFFFFD87	ERR_INVALID_ENTRY_FOR_ROOT	Trying to restore an object as [Root] but the object's base class is not "Top". Or attempting to assign an object as a partition root object but the object's base class is not of "container class".

Table A.4   Continued

DECIMAL	HEXADECIMAL	CONSTANT	DESCRIPTION
-634	0xFFFFFD86	ERR_NO_REFERRALS	The local server has no objects that match the request and has no referrals on which to search for the object. This error is not the same as ERR_ALL_REFERRALS_FAILED (-626). This error could be an indirect result of SAP/RIP filtering on the network.
-635	0xFFFFFD85	ERR_REMOTE_FAILURE	Unable to connect to another server. Unlike error ERR_TRANSPORT_FAILURE (-625), this is *not* an error due to the network. Rather, it is due to the requester using an invalid server handle or unsupported NCP call, or it is due to the remote server returning an invalid reply. Therefore, this is mostly an application-related error.
-636	0xFFFFFD84	ERR_UNREACHABLE_SERVER	A partition operation can't be performed because one or more of the servers in the replica ring is unreachable due to a ERR_TRANSPORT_FAILURE (-625) error.
-637	0xFFFFFD83	ERR_PREVIOUS_MOVE_IN_PROGRESS	Cannot process the current request because a previous object move operation is still in progress.
-638	0xFFFFFD82	ERR_NO_CHARACTER_MAPPING	Making a request with an object or property name that contains illegal characters, such as a control character, a comma, a colon, a semicolon, a slash, a backslash, a question mark, an asterisk, or a tilde. This error may also be due to the DS module being unable to map the supplied name to its Unicode representation. (This is the same as error DSERR_ILLEGAL_NAME [-239].)
-639	0xFFFFFD81	ERR_INCOMPLETE_AUTHENTICATION	An error happened during the final phase of the DS authentication process. This is generally due to LAN/WAN hardware or software as it is suggestive of packet corruption.
-640	0xFFFFFD80	ERR_INVALID_CERTIFICATE	An invalid security certificate was specified. (Applies to NetWare 5 and higher.)
-641	0xFFFFFD7F	ERR_INVALID_REQUEST	The request was invalid or unsupported by the running version of the DS module.
-642	0xFFFFFD7E	ERR_INVALID_ITERATION	The iteration handle in a message fragment of a DS request is invalid. This could be a result of packet corruption.

Table A.4   Continued

DECIMAL	HEXADECIMAL	CONSTANT	DESCRIPTION
-643	0xFFFFFD7D	ERR_SCHEMA_IS_NONREMOVABLE	Attempting to delete a base schema class flagged as nonremovable.
-644	0xFFFFFD7C	ERR_SCHEMA_IS_IN_USE	Attempting to delete a schema class definition that still contains an object using that definition.
-645	0xFFFFFD7B	ERR_CLASS_ALREADY_EXISTS	Trying to add a schema class definition that already exists in the schema.
-646	0xFFFFFD7A	ERR_BAD_NAMING_ATTRIBUTES	Trying to add a schema class definition whose naming attribute is not a valid attribute for the class.
-647	0xFFFFFD79	ERR_NOT_ROOT_PARTITION	Attempting to perform a partitioning operation on a nonpartition root object.
-648	0xFFFFFD78	ERR_INSUFFICIENT_STACK	Internal error. The server ran out of stack.
-649	0xFFFFFD77	ERR_INSUFFICIENT_BUFFER	The server ran out of memory or the calling application didn't provide sufficient buffer space for the request.
-650	0xFFFFFD76	ERR_AMBIGUOUS_CONTAINMENT	Attempting to create a schema class definition that contained an ambiguous containment rule.
-651	0xFFFFFD75	ERR_AMBIGUOUS_NAMING	Attempting to create a schema class definition that contained an ambiguous containment name.
-652	0xFFFFFD74	ERR_DUPLICATE_MANDATORY	Attempting to create a schema class definition that contained a duplicate mandatory attribute name.
-653	0xFFFFFD73	ERR_DUPLICATE_OPTIONAL	Attempting to create a schema class definition that contained a duplicate optional attribute name.
-654	0xFFFFFD72	ERR_PARTITION_BUSY	Cannot process the request because the specified partition is currently involved in a partition operation or the replica's state is not On.
-655	0xFFFFFD71	ERR_MULTIPLE_REPLICAS	Attempting to add a new replica attribute value to the partition root object that already has a replica attribute with the same value.
-656	0xFFFFFD70	ERR_CRUCIAL_REPLICA	An illegal partition operation was requested (such as trying to add a Read/Write replica to a server holding the Master replica of the same partition).

Table A.4 Continued

DECIMAL	HEXADECIMAL	CONSTANT	DESCRIPTION
-657	0xFFFFFD6F	ERR_SCHEMA_SYNC_IN_PROGRESS	The request can't be processed because the schema sync process is in progress.
-658	0xFFFFFD6E	ERR_SKULK_IN_PROGRESS	The request can't be processed because the skulk process is in progress.
-659	0xFFFFFD6D	ERR_TIME_NOT_SYNCHRONIZED	The time between the source and target server is not synchronized. Consequently, partition operation can't be performed.
-660	0xFFFFFD6C	ERR_RECORD_IN_USE	NDS tried to purge a DS database record that's still in use. Running DSRepair may resolve this error.
-661	0xFFFFFD6B	ERR_DS_VOLUME_NOT_MOUNTED	Internal error. Logically, you should never encounter this error because it is used by the operating system to indicate that the DS module can't be loaded at this time because the SYS volume is not yet mounted.
-662	0xFFFFFD6A	ERR_DS_VOLUME_IO_FAILURE	Internal error. An I/O operation attempted on the SYS volume failed, possibly because the volume is not yet mounted.
-663	0xFFFFFD69	ERR_DS_LOCKED	Can't process request because the DS database is locked (or closed); this is analogous to the bindery being locked. The database may be locked by DSRepair while it is doing a repair or it may be closed because the server's TTS is shut down. In some cases, this error is due to a UNI_HANDLE_MISMATCH (-497) error from the Unicode module.
-664	0xFFFFFD68	ERR_OLD_EPOCH	Trying to modify objects on a server that is using an older epoch of the data. This can happen during either a replica sync process or a schema sync process. This is a transitory error and will disappear when the sync process updates the epoch on the servers. (An *epoch* is an arbitrary time and date that marks the beginning of an event. In the context of DS schema, a schema epoch defines the time at which the schema was last updated or changed.)

Table A.4   Continued

DECIMAL	HEXADECIMAL	CONSTANT	DESCRIPTION
-665	0xFFFFFD67	ERR_NEW_EPOCH	Trying to modify objects on a server that is using a newer epoch of the data. This can happen during either a replica sync process or a schema sync process. This is a transitory error and will disappear when the sync process updates the epoch on the servers.
-666	0xFFFFFD66	ERR_INCOMPATIBLE_DS_VERSION	Unable to synchronize with the target server due to either incompatible DS module versions between the source and target servers or the version of the DS module on the source server being on the target server's restricted version list. On NetWare, you can check a server's restricted DS version list by using the "NDS do not synchronize with" console SET command.
-667	0xFFFFFD65	ERR_PARTITION_ROOT	Attempting to perform a DS operation on a partition root object when it is not allowed. For example, you tried to delete a container root object without first merging it with its parent partition.
-668	0xFFFFFD64	ERR_ENTRY_NOT_CONTAINER	Attempting to perform a partition operation on a leaf object.
-669	0xFFFFFD63	ERR_FAILED_AUTHENTICATION	Using an invalid password to authenticate into DS.
-670	0xFFFFFD62	ERR_INVALID_CONTEXT	Internal error. A request was made using an invalid context handle. The server's task and connection management table may be corrupted. Reloading the DS module may help resolve the problem.
-671	0xFFFFFD61	ERR_NO_SUCH_PARENT	Attempting to modify an object whose parent object cannot be found.
-672	0xFFFFFD60	ERR_NO_ACCESS	The requester doesn't have sufficient rights to the requested information. For example, you're trying to perform a partitioning operation but you don't have the necessary rights to the specified partition root objects.
-673	0xFFFFFD5F	ERR_REPLICA_NOT_ON	Cannot process the request because the specified partition's replica state is not On. You can check the current state of the replica by using DSRepair.

Table A.4 Continued

DECIMAL	HEXADECIMAL	CONSTANT	DESCRIPTION
-674	0xFFFFFD5E	ERR_INVALID_NAME_SERVICE	The specified name service is not available or is not supported.
-675	0xFFFFFD5D	ERR_INVALID_TASK	Internal server error. A request of an NCP connection was made, using a task ID of 0. The server's task and connection management table may be corrupted. Reloading the DS module may help resolve the problem.
-676	0xFFFFFD5C	ERR_INVALID_CONN_HANDLE	Internal server error. A request was made of an NCP connection, using an invalid NCP connection handle or an invalid task ID. The server's task and connection management table may be corruption. Reloading the DS module may help resolve the problem.
-677	0xFFFFFD5B	ERR_INVALID_IDENTITY	Internal DS error. A request was made using an invalid NDS identity. The server's identity tables may be corrupted. Reloading the DS module may help resolve the problem.
-678	0xFFFFFD5A	ERR_DUPLICATE_ACL	Attempt to add an access control list (ACL) attribute value to an object that already has the same ACL attribute value and trustee.
-679	0xFFFFFD59	ERR_PARTITION_ALREADY_EXISTS	Trying to create a partition on a server that already has the specified object as a partition root object.
-680	0xFFFFFD58	ERR_TRANSPORT_MODIFIED	A communication inconsistency occurred when attempting to connect to a remote server. The initial attempt resulted in a -625 error. However, a subsequent retry succeeded by re-negotiating the IPX checksum, IPX packet signatures, or maximum packet size. This error is generally caused by faults in the LAN/WAN hardware or software components.
-681	0xFFFFFD57	ERR_ALIAS_OF_AN_ALIAS	Trying to create an alias of an Alias object.
-682	0xFFFFFD56	ERR_AUDITING_FAILED	Internal error due to DS auditing operations. This error may be a result of an attempt to audit an object that has not been flagged for auditing or a failure to reset the auditing files.

Table A.4   Continued

DECIMAL	HEXADECIMAL	CONSTANT	DESCRIPTION
-683	0xFFFFFD55	ERR_INVALID_API_VERSION	An API call specified a version number that is not supported by the currently running DS module. The application may have been created using an outdated library.
-684	0xFFFFFD54	ERR_SECURE_NCP_VIOLATION	The source server or client attempted to authenticate with a remote server, using IPX packet signatures, but the remote server doesn't support packet signing.
-685	0xFFFFFD53	ERR_MOVE_IN_PROGRESS	The specified object is currently involved in a DS object move operation; the object has either Move Obituary or Inhibit Move Obituary. (For more information about obits, see Chapter 6.)
-686	0xFFFFFD52	ERR_NOT_LEAF_PARTITION	Attempting to perform a move subtree partition operation, but the specified object is not a leaf partition. You must first merge any subordinate partition root object with its parent partition.
-687	0xFFFFFD51	ERR_CANNOT_ABORT	The current partition operation can't be aborted because it has progressed past a specific turnaround state. Typically when a change replica type, split partition, or merge partition operation has gone beyond its initial phase (for example, state RS_CRT_0 or replica state 4 during a change replica type operation), the operation cannot be aborted. The same is true during a move subtree operation when any of the move tree-related obits are changed to Notified, OK To Purge, or Purgeable; the operation can't be aborted.
-688	0xFFFFFD50	ERR_CACHE_OVERFLOW	An internal error from the cache used by the NDS replica synchronization process.
-689	0xFFFFFD4F	ERR_INVALID_SUBORDINATE_COUNT	The subordinate object count in the object's database record doesn't match the number of presently found child objects. A repair local database operation using DSRepair may resolve the error.

Table A.4 Continued

DECIMAL	HEXADECIMAL	CONSTANT	DESCRIPTION
-690	0xFFFFFD4E	ERR_INVALID_RDN	The RDN specified in the object's database record doesn't match the name found in the object's naming attribute. Or the specified object's parent object, as identified by the database record, is invalid. A repair local database operation using DSRepair may resolve the error.
-691	0xFFFFFD4D	ERR_MOD_TIME_NOT_CURRENT	The modification timestamp of an object attribute is newer than the modification timestamp found in the object's database record. A repair local database operation using DSRepair may resolve the error.
-692	0xFFFFFD4C	ERR_INCORRECT_BASE_CLASS	The base class of an object doesn't match the base class specification found in the object's database record. A repair local database operation using DSRepair may resolve the error.
-693	0xFFFFFD4B	ERR_MISSING_REFERENCE	The specified object has an attribute value that references another object in the local database, but the referenced object doesn't have a reference attribute indicating that the specified object references it. A repair local database operation using DSRepair may resolve the error.
-694	0xFFFFFD4A	ERR_LOST_ENTRY	The NDS replica synchronization process tried to update an object on the target server, but the target server has not yet received the object. This is a transitory error because the NDS replica synchronization process will re-send the lost object before trying to update it.
-695	0xFFFFFD49	ERR_AGENT_ALREADY_REGISTERED	Trying to load the DS when another module has already registered with the operating system as an NDS agent.
-696	0xFFFFFD48	ERR_DS_LOADER_BUSY	The DS loader was busy when a request was made to unload and reload the DS module. You should try the operation again at a later time.
-697	0xFFFFFD47	ERR_DS_CANNOT_RELOAD	Trying to unload and reload the DS module when one or more DS-dependent modules (such as DSRepair) are still loaded.

Table A.4 Continued

DECIMAL	HEXADECIMAL	CONSTANT	DESCRIPTION
-698	0xFFFFFD46	`ERR_REPLICA_IN_SKULK`	Attempting to start the NDS replica synchronization process with a target server when the target server is busy synchronizing with another server. This is a transitory error and the NDS replica synchronization process will reschedule.
-699	0xFFFFFD45	`ERR_FATAL`	An internal error. If this happens during normal DS operations, it is generally transitory. However, if the error persists, you can try reloading the DS module or restarting the server. If the standard repair methods (such as performing a local database repair by using DSRepair) do not resolve the error, you need to open a call with Novell.
-700	0xFFFFFD44	`ERR_OBSOLETE_API`	An API request that's no longer supported by the running version of the DS module. This is the opposite of error `ERR_NOT_IMPLEMENTED` (-714).
-701	0xFFFFFD43	`ERR_SYNCHRONIZATION_DISABLED`	The NDS replica synchronization process is unable to sync with the target server as its inbound replica synchronization is disabled using the SET DSTRACE=!D or SET DSTRACE=!DI command. If this is the case, the message "*SKULKER: SYNCHRONIZATION DISABLED" is displayed on the target server's DSTrace screen. You can re-enable the inbound sync by using the SET DSTRACE=!E or SET DSTRACE=!EI command. The error can also be due to the local server's outbound replica synchronization process being disabled. If this is the case, the message "*SYNC: SYNCHRONIZATION DISABLED" is displayed on the local server's DSTrace screen. You can re-enable the outbound sync by using the SET DSTRACE=!E or SET DSTRACE=!EO command. This error may also be a result of the schema synchronization process being disabled. If this is the case, you need to re-enable the schema synchronization by using the SET DSTRACE=!SI1 or SET DSTRACE=!SO1 command.

Table A.4   Continued

DECIMAL	HEXADECIMAL	CONSTANT	DESCRIPTION
-702	0xFFFFFD42	ERR_INVALID_PARAMETER	Attempt to register for an unsupported DS event or to unregister an unregistered event. This error is due to logic faults in NLM applications.
-703	0xFFFFFD41	ERR_DUPLICATE_TEMPLATE	This is an internal error that is expected during schema initialization.
-704	0xFFFFFD40	ERR_NO_MASTER_REPLICA	Unable to locate the Master replica of the partition. The server holding the Master may be unavailable.
-705	0xFFFFFD3F	ERR_DUPLICATE_CONTAINMENT	This is an internal error that is expected during schema initialization.
-706	0xFFFFFD3E	ERR_NOT_SIBLING	The objects specified in a merge entries operation are not siblings to one another. A repair local database operation using DSRepair may resolve the error.
-707	0xFFFFFD3D	ERR_INVALID_SIGNATURE	The packet signature is invalid. This may be due to packet corruption.
-708	0xFFFFFD3C	ERR_INVALID_RESPONSE	The data received by the DS module is invalid or contains unexpected information. This may be due to packet corruption.
-709	0xFFFFFD3B	ERR_INSUFFICIENT_SOCKETS	All available NCP sockets are currently in use. This is a transitory error. However, if the error persists, you can increase the number of sockets by using SPXCONFG.NLM.
-710	0xFFFFFD3A	ERR_DATABASE_READ_FAIL	Unable to read the DS database.
-711	0xFFFFFD39	ERR_INVALID_CODE_PAGE	The currently running DS module does not support the code page used by the operating system.
-712	0xFFFFFD38	ERR_INVALID_ESCAPE_CHAR	The currently running DS module does not support the specified escape character. An escape character tells DS to treat the following character as a regular text character, as opposed to whatever meaning that character might normally have for DS.
-713	0xFFFFFD37	ERR_INVALID_DELIMITERS	The currently running DS module does not support the specified delimiters. (DS uses dots, ., as delimiters in object names.)
-714	0xFFFFFD36	ERR_NOT_IMPLEMENTED	The currently running DS module does not support the requested operation or function. You need to upgrade to a newer version of DS module. This is the opposite of error ERR_OBSOLETE_API (-700).

Table A.4   Continued

DECIMAL	HEXADECIMAL	CONSTANT	DESCRIPTION
-715	0xFFFFFD35	ERR_CHECKSUM_FAILURE	The NDS checksum in the request packet is invalid. This error is generally caused by faults in the LAN/WAN hardware or software components. NDS checksumming is generally not recommended because the current version of the DS module uses a transport-independent CRC checking for all traffic between servers. You can enable NDS checksumming by using the SET DSTRACE=CHECKSUM command or disable it with the SET DSTRACE=NOCHECKSUM command. Note that NDS checksumming is not supported on all frame types, such as Novell's Ethernet 802.3.
-716	0xFFFFFD34	ERR_CHECKSUMMING_NOT_SUPPORTED	Attempting to negotiate an NCP connection with a server that doesn't support NDS checksumming, while the source server has NDS checksumming enabled.
-717	0xFFFFFD33	ERR_CRC_FAILURE	The NDS CRC (different from the NDS checksum) in the request packet is invalid. This error is generally caused by faults in the LAN/WAN hardware or software components.
-718	0xFFFFFD32	ERR_INVALID_ENTRY_HANDLE	The file handle for the object entry database file is invalid.
-719	0xFFFFFD31	ERR_INVALID_VALUE_HANDLE	The file handle for the attribute value database file is invalid.
-720	0xFFFFFD30	ERR_CONNECTION_DENIED	NDS outbound traffic or NCP connection to a remote server is not permitted because of WAN Traffic Manager (WANMan) restriction policies.
-721	0xFFFFFD2F	ERR_NO_SUCH_FEDERATION_LINK	Reserved error code for federated partition implementation.
-722	0xFFFFFD2E	ERR_OP_SCHEMA_MISMATCH	A mismatch in the operational schema was detected.
-723	0xFFFFFD2D	ERR_STREAM_NOT_FOUND	The specified stream file doesn't exist. This could be a result of no database files being found in the DIB directory.
-724	0xFFFFFD2C	ERR_DCLIENT_UNAVAILABLE	The DSA is not running.
-725	0xFFFFFD2B	ERR_MASV_NO_ACCESS	Cannot access Mandatory Access Control Service. (Applies to NetWare 5 and higher.)

Table A.4 Continued

DECIMAL	HEXADECIMAL	CONSTANT	DESCRIPTION
-726	0xFFFFFD2A	ERR_MASV_INVALID_REQUEST	The Mandatory Access Control Service received an invalid request. (Applies to NetWare 5 and higher.)
-727	0xFFFFFD29	ERR_MASV_FAILURE	A failure condition was detected in the Mandatory Access Control Service. (Applies to NetWare 5 and higher.)
-728	0xFFFFFD28	ERR_MASV_ALREADY_EXISTS	The Mandatory Access Control Service is already running. (Applies to NetWare 5 and higher.)
-729	0xFFFFFD27	ERR_MASV_NOT_FOUND	The Mandatory Access Control Service is not running. (Applies to NetWare 5 and higher.)
-730	0xFFFFFD26	ERR_MASV_BAD_RANGE	The Mandatory Access Control Service data is out of range. (Applies to NetWare 5 and higher.)
-731	0xFFFFFD25	ERR_VALUE_DATA	The value received is invalid.
-732	0xFFFFFD24	ERR_DATABASE_LOCKED	The database files are locked.
-733	0xFFFFFD23	ERR_DATABASE_ALREADY_EXIST	Internal error. (Currently unused.)
-734	0xFFFFFD22	ERR_DATABASE_NOT_FOUND	Internal error. (Currently unused.)
-735	0xFFFFFD21	ERR_NOTHING_TO_ABORT	Cannot abort the specified NDS operation because it has already completed or has been aborted.
-736	0xFFFFFD20	ERR_END_OF_STREAM	End-of-file encountered while accessing the stream file.
-737	0xFFFFFD1F	ERR_NO_SUCH_TEMPLATE	The specified user template doesn't exist.
-738	0xFFFFFD1E	ERR_SAS_LOCKED	The SAS database is locked. (Applies to NetWare 5 and higher.)
-739	0xFFFFFD1D	ERR_INVALID_SAS_VERSION	The currently running SAS module does not support the version information in the SAS request. (Applies to NetWare 5 and higher.)
-740	0xFFFFFD1C	ERR_SAS_ALREADY_REGISTERED	The SAS module is already running. (Applies to NetWare 5 and higher.)
-741	0xFFFFFD1B	ERR_NAME_TYPE_NOT_SUPPORTED	The specified object type is not supported.
-742	0xFFFFFD1A	ERR_WRONG_DS_VERSION	The specified DS version is not supported.
-743	0xFFFFFD19	ERR_INVALID_CONTROL_FUNCTION	The specified control function is not supported.
-744	0xFFFFFD18	ERR_INVALID_CONTROL_STATE	The specified control function state is not supported.

Table A.4   Continued

DECIMAL	HEXADECIMAL	CONSTANT	DESCRIPTION
-745	0xFFFFFD17	ERR_CACHE_IN_USE	Trying to use the data cache while it is in use by another process.
-746	0xFFFFFD16	ERR_ZERO_CREATION_TIME	The specified object has a zero creation timestamp. A repair local database operation using DSRepair may resolve the error.
-747	0xFFFFFD15	ERR_WOULD_BLOCK	The specified API call is blocked (that is, control is not returned to the calling client until the execution of the API function is completed).
-748	0xFFFFFD14	ERR_CONN_TIMEOUT	The connection has timed out.
-749	0xFFFFFD13	ERR_TOO_MANY_REFERRALS	The tree-walking process has reached the maximum number of servers that the local server can contact to retrieve an object's information.
-750	0xFFFFFD12	ERR_OPERATION_CANCELLED	The specified DS operation has been (successfully) cancelled.
-751	0xFFFFFD11	ERR_UNKNOWN_TARGET	The specified server is unknown.
-752	0xFFFFFD10	ERR_GUID_FAILURE	The SGUID (set global unique identifier) module can't process the request, or can't find the required GUID. (Applies to NetWare 5 and higher.)
-753	0xFFFFFD0F	ERR_INCOMPATIBLE_OS	The software module can't be loaded on this version of the operating system.
-754	0xFFFFFD0E	ERR_CALLBACK_CANCEL	The execution of the callback routine has been cancelled.
-755	0xFFFFFD0D	ERR_INVALID_SYNCHRONIZATION_DATA	Invalid data was found in the data sent by the NDS replica synchronization process.
-756	0xFFFFFD0C	ERR_STREAM_EXISTS	The specified stream file already exists.
-757	0xFFFFFD0B	ERR_AUXILIARY_HAS_CONTAINMENT	Internal error. (Currently unused.)
-758	0xFFFFFD0A	ERR_AUXILIARY_NOT_CONTAINER	Internal error. (Currently unused.)
-759	0xFFFFFD09	ERR_AUXILIARY_NOT_EFFECTIVE	Internal error. (Currently unused.)
-760	0xFFFFFD08	ERR_AUXILIARY_ON_ALIAS	Internal error. (Currently unused.)
-761	0xFFFFFD07	ERR_HAVE_SEEN_STATE	The server received notification of the state of a partition operation that it is involved in, but it had previously received the same state information. This may occur during normal operation and may be a transitory error.
-762	0xFFFFFD06	ERR_VERB_LOCKED	Internal error. (Currently unused.)

Table A.4   Continued

DECIMAL	HEXADECIMAL	CONSTANT	DESCRIPTION
-763	0xFFFFFD05	ERR_VERB_EXCEEDS_TABLE_LENGTH	Internal error. (Currently unused.)
-764	0xFFFFFD04	ERR_BOF_HIT	Internal error. (Currently unused.)
-765	0xFFFFFD03	ERR_EOF_HIT	Indicates no more data on recursive search. This is not a real error condition.
-766	0xFFFFFD02	ERR_INCOMPATIBLE_REPLICA_VER	Internal error. (Currently unused.)
-767	0xFFFFFD01	ERR_QUERY_TIMEOUT	Internal error. (Currently unused.)
-768	0xFFFFFD00	ERR_QUERY_MAX_COUNT	Internal error. (Currently unused.)
-769	0xFFFFFCFF	ERR_DUPLICATE_NAMING	Internal error. (Currently unused.)
-770	0xFFFFFCFE	ERR_NO_TRANS_ACTIVE	Internal error. The database expected a transaction to be active prior to executing an operation, but the calling code did not start one. You need to report this to Novell.
-771	0xFFFFFCFD	ERR_TRANS_ACTIVE	Internal error. The database did not expect a transaction to be active prior to executing an operation. You need to report this to Novell.
-772	0xFFFFFCFC	ERR_ILLEGAL_TRANS_OP	Internal error. This error is returned when an update operation is attempted against the database within the context of a read-only transaction. You need to report this to Novell.
-773	0xFFFFFCFB	ERR_ITERATOR_SYNTAX	A malformed request was sent to the NDS iterator.
-774	0xFFFFFCFA	ERR_REPAIRING_DIB	A request is rejected because the DIB directory is currently being repaired.
-775	0xFFFFFCF9	ERR_INVALID_OID_FORMAT	Failed object identifier (OID) check during a schema extension operation. If this error is encountered during schema synchronization, you should run DSRepair on the servers involved.
-776	0xFFFFFCF8	ERR_DS_AGENT_CLOSING	A request is rejected because the DIB directory is being closed.
-777	0xFFFFFCF7	ERR_SPARSE_FILTER_VIOLATION	Attempting to add invalid DirXML replication filters. Or attempting to change to attributes of a DS entry that is contained in filtered replicas on that server, but the filtered replicas do not contain these attributes. (Applies to eDirectory 8.5 and above.)
-778	0xFFFFFCF6	ERR_VPVECTOR_CORRELATION_ERR	Internal error. (Not currently used; applies to eDirectory 8.5 and above.)

Table A.4   Continued

DECIMAL	HEXADECIMAL	CONSTANT	DESCRIPTION
-779	OxFFFFFCF5	ERR_CANNOT_GO_REMOTE	A DS request was made but cannot be serviced by any of the local replicas; however, the application cannot connect to any of the referred servers because it is logged in to and authenticated to the local server only. The application must perform a full login to the tree and not just a local login.
-780	OxFFFFFCF4	ERR_REQUEST_NOT_SUPPORTED	The requested action is not supported by the current version of NDS/eDirectory.
-781	OxFFFFFCF3	ERR_ENTRY_NOT_LOCAL	The object is not found in any of the local replicas.
-782	OxFFFFFCF2	ERR_ROOT_UNREACHABLE	Unable to contact [Root] for tree-walking purposes.
-783	OxFFFFFCF1	ERR_VRDIM NOT_INITIALIZED	A driver is requested to start via the ConsoleOne administration snap-in, but the DirXML interface module (VRDIM) is not currently loaded. This error appears only when the VRDIM has been explicitly unloaded.
-784	OxFFFFFCF0	ERR_WAIT_TIMEOUT	This error is returned from a routine when a specified time limit for a timeout value has been exceeded. This is not necessarily an error condition.
-785	OxFFFFFCEF	ERR_DIB_ERROR	An unknown error was encountered in the DIB subsystem.
-786	OxFFFFFCEE	ERR_DIB_IO_FAILURE	An unknown I/O error was encountered in the DIB subsystem.
-787	OxFFFFFCED	ERR_ILLEGAL_SCHEMA ATTRIBUTE	The specified attribute is invalid.
-788	OxFFFFFCEC	ERR_SCHEMA_PARTITION	An unknown error was detected in the schema partition.
-789	OxFFFFFCEB	ERR_INVALID_TEMPLATE	The error is returned when the subjectDN (the object that will be granted a right) in an ACL template is not one of [Self], [Root], [Public], or [Creator]. (An ACL template is the ACL of a class definition that is automatically added to the object of that class when it is created.)
-790	OxFFFFFCEA	ERR_OPENING_FILE	The operating system returns this error to eDirectory when eDirectory made a call to the operating system to open a file. This error may be transitory. Restarting DS or the server may resolve the problem.

Table A.4 Continued

DECIMAL	HEXADECIMAL	CONSTANT	DESCRIPTION
-791	0xFFFFFCE9	ERR_DIRECT_OPENING_FILE	The operating system returns this error to eDirectory when eDirectory made a call to the operating system to open a file in direct I/O mode. This error may be transitory. Restarting DS or the server may resolve the problem.
-792	0xFFFFFCE8	ERR_CREATING_FILE	The operating system returns this error to eDirectory when eDirectory made a call to the operating system to create a file. This error may be transitory. Restarting DS or the server may resolve the problem.
-793	0xFFFFFCE7	ERR_DIRECT_CREATING_FILE	The operating system returns this error to eDirectory when eDirectory made a call to the operating system to create a file in direct I/O mode. This error may be transitory. Restarting DS or the server may resolve the problem.
-794	0xFFFFFCE6	ERR_READING_FILE	The operating system returns this error to eDirectory when eDirectory is reading from a file. This error may be transitory. Restarting DS or the server may resolve the problem.
-795	0xFFFFFCE5	ERR_DIRECT_READING_FILE	The operating system returns this error to eDirectory when eDirectory is reading from a file in direct I/O mode. This error may be transitory. Restarting DS or the server may resolve the problem.
-796	0xFFFFFCE4	ERR_WRITING_FILE	The operating system returns this error to eDirectory when eDirectory is writing to a file. This error may be transitory. Restarting DS or the server may resolve the problem.
-797	0xFFFFFCE3	ERR_DIRECT_WRITING_FILE	The operating system returns this error to eDirectory when eDirectory is writing to a file in direct I/O mode. This error may be transitory. Restarting DS or the server may resolve the problem.
-798	0xFFFFFCE2	ERR_POSITIONING_IN_FILE	The operating system returns this error to eDirectory when eDirectory is positioning within a file. This error may be transitory. Restarting DS or the server may resolve the problem.

Table A.4   Continued

DECIMAL	HEXADECIMAL	CONSTANT	DESCRIPTION
-799	0xFFFFFCE1	ERR_GETTING_FILE_SIZE	The operating system returns this error to eDirectory when eDirectory is getting the file size. This error may be transitory. Restarting DS or the server may resolve the problem.
-800 through -6000	0xFFFFFCE0 through 0xFFFFE890		These are not DS error codes; they are used by other Novell products.
-6001	0xFFFFE88F	ERR_TRUNCATING_FILE	The operating system returns this error to eDirectory when eDirectory is truncating a file. This error may be transitory. Restarting DS or the server may resolve the problem.
-6002	0xFFFFE88E	ERR_PARSING_FILE_NAME	The operating system returns this error to eDirectory when eDirectory is parsing a filename. This error may be transitory. Restarting DS or the server may resolve the problem.
-6003	0xFFFFE88D	ERR_CLOSING_FILE	The operating system returns this error to eDirectory when eDirectory is closing a file. This error may be transitory. Restarting DS or the server may resolve the problem.
-6004	0xFFFFE88C	ERR_GETTING_FILE_INFO	The operating system returns this error to eDirectory when eDirectory is getting file information (such as file attributes). This error may be transitory. Restarting DS or the server may resolve the problem.
-6005	0xFFFFE88B	ERR_EXPANDING_FILE	The operating system returns this error to eDirectory when eDirectory is expanding a file. This error may be transitory. Restarting DS or the server may resolve the problem.
-6006	0xFFFFE88A	ERR_GETTING_FREE_BLOCKS	The operating system returns this error to eDirectory when eDirectory is getting free disk blocks from the file system. This error may be transitory. Restarting DS or the server may resolve the problem.
-6007	0xFFFFE889	ERR_CHECKING_FILE_EXISTENCE	The operating system returns this error to eDirectory when eDirectory is checking to see whether a file exists. This error may be transitory. Restarting DS or the server may resolve the problem.

Table A.4 Continued

DECIMAL	HEXADECIMAL	CONSTANT	DESCRIPTION
-6008	0xFFFFE888	ERR_DELETING_FILE	The operating system returns this error to eDirectory when eDirectory is deleting a file. This error may be transitory. Restarting DS or the server may resolve the problem.
-6009	0xFFFFE887	ERR_RENAMING_FILE	The operating system returns this error to eDirectory when eDirectory is renaming a file. This error may be transitory. Restarting DS or the server may resolve the problem.
-6010	0xFFFFE886	ERR_INITIALIZING_IO_SYSTEM	The operating system returns this error to eDirectory when eDirectory is initializing to perform file I/O operations. This error may be transitory. Restarting DS or the server may resolve the problem.
-6011	0xFFFFE885	ERR_FLUSHING_FILE	The operating system returns this error to eDirectory when eDirectory is flushing data from the system cache to disk. This error may be transitory. Restarting DS or the server may resolve the problem.
-6012	0xFFFFE884	ERR_SETTING_UP_FOR_READ	The operating system returns this error to eDirectory when eDirectory is setting up to perform file read operations. This error may be transitory. Restarting DS or the server may resolve the problem.
-6013	0xFFFFE883	ERR_SETTING_UP_FOR_WRITE	The operating system returns this error to eDirectory when eDirectory is setting up to perform file write operations. This error may be transitory. Restarting DS or the server may resolve the problem.
-6014	0xFFFFE882	ERR_OLD_VIEW	A consistent snapshot of the database could not be maintained for the requested operation. This error could occur if a query has been posed against a very large database and the query results in a scan search. If the search runs for more than 40 minutes, the database aborts the operation and returns this error. It is also possible for transactions that have run for less than 40 minutes to be aborted if the database is in a state where it is trying to reclaim rollback space (for example, if the rollback log file has grown too large). The 40-minute timeout value is not changeable at this time.

Table A.4   Continued

DECIMAL	HEXADECIMAL	CONSTANT	DESCRIPTION
-6015	0xFFFFE881	ERR_SERVER_IN_SKULK	The local server can't send outbound data to another server because the target server is currently receiving inbound data (either from the local server or another server in the same replica ring). This is a transitory error, and the NDS replica synchronization process will resolve it.
-6016	0xFFFFE880	ERR_RETURNING_PARTIAL_RESULTS	An error has occurred during a search or read operation, and the entry being returned as the result contains partial values. This is a nonfatal error. The client might attempt to retrieve and use the partial results that have been returned. This error is specifically returned during a lookup of dynamic group memberships when the search fails for some reason (perhaps due to being unable to contact some servers).
-6017	0xFFFFE87F	ERR_NO_SUCH_SCHEMA	The requested schema definition does not exist. You should check to ensure that the schema synchronization process runs without error.
-6018	0xFFFFE87E	ERR_SERIAL_NUM_MISMATCH	This can happen when an incremental DS backup (of the roll-forward log [RLF] files) is being restored and the serial number of the database stored in the incremental backup's header does not match the serial number of the database. Generally, this means that an attempt is being made to restore an incremental backup from another database.
-6019	0xFFFFE87D	ERR_BAD_RFL_DB_SERIAL_NUM	This can happen when the serial number of the database stored in the header of the RFL file that is being restored does not match the serial number of the database. Generally, this means that an attempt is being made to restore an RFL file from another database.

Table A.4   Continued

DECIMAL	HEXADECIMAL	CONSTANT	DESCRIPTION
-6020	0xFFFFE87C	ERR_BAD_ RFL_SERIAL_NUM	This can happen when the serial number of the database stored in the header of the RFL file that is being restored does not match the serial number of the database or the prior RFL file. Generally, this means that an attempt is being made to restore an RFL file from another database.
-6021	0xFFFFFE7B	ERR_INVALID_FILE_SEQUENCE	This can happen when the sequence number or incremental backup ID of the RFL file that is being restored does not match the expected number stored in the database.
-6022	0xFFFFE87A	ERR_RFL_TRANS_GAP	During recovery (after a server crash) or during a database restore operation, gaps in the transactions recorded in the log were detected due to one or more RFL files having been damaged. Using DSRepair may rectify the problem.
-6023	0xFFFFE879	ERR_BAD_RFL_FILE_NUMBER	The RFL file number desired does not match the file number recorded in the RFL file's header. Specifying the wrong RFL file during a database restore operation causes this error.
-6024	0xFFFFE878	ERR_RFL_FILE_NOT_FOUND	A RFL file required for the database restore could not be found in the NDS.RFL directory. You should use one of the methods described in the "Locating the DIB" section in Chapter 3 to check for the existence of RFL files. You should restore missing files from backup if possible.
-6025	0xFFFFE877	ERR_BACKUP_ACTIVE	The requested action cannot be performed while a database backup is running.
-6026	0xFFFFE876	ERR_RFL_DEVICE_FULL	The disk/volume hosting the RFL files is full.
-6027	0xFFFFE875	ERR_UNSUPPORTED_VERSION	The file format of the backup data set is not supported by the running version of the DS module. This is caused by trying to restore a newer version of the eDirectory database by using an older version of the DS module.

Table A.4   Continued

DECIMAL	HEXADECIMAL	CONSTANT	DESCRIPTION
-6028	0xFFFFE874	ERR_MUST_WAIT_CHECKPOINT	An operation was requested at a time when eDirectory had to force a checkpoint. (A *checkpoint* operation is eDirectory flushing all dirty cache buffers to disk.)
-6029	0xFFFFE873	ERR_ATTR_MAINT_IN_PROGRESS	This transitory error condition is reported when a query is made against one or more attributes that are currently being maintained (that is, reorganized for more optimal storage).
-6030	0xFFFFE872	ERR_ABORT_TRANSACTION	A problem has been encountered during an update operation. Because of the nature of the problem, the active update transaction cannot be committed and has been rolled back.
-6031	0xFFFFE871	ERR_SETTING_FILE_INFO	This error is returned if eDirectory is unable to change a file's attributes. This error is returned on NetWare if the Rename Inhibit flag of a file cannot be cleared. Other platforms do not currently return this error.
-6032	0xFFFFE870	ERR_REPLICA_RING_CHANGED	The local database is unaware of replica ring changes that occurred after the database was restored. This error may be due to some RFL files not being processed during a restore or a server being forcibly removed from the replica ring and the ring being altered while the server is down.
-6033	0xFFFFE86F	ERR_NOT_PARTITION_ROOT	A partition join operation has occurred, and the local database is unaware of it. An object that was once a partition root is no longer a partition root. This error may be due to some RFL files not being processed during a restore or a server being forcibly removed from the replica ring and the ring being altered while the server is down.
-6034	0xFFFFE86E	ERR_SERVER_NOT_UP_TO_DATE	A discrepancy was found when checking the transitive vectors. The restored database is missing data that the other servers in the replica ring expect to be there. This error may be due to some RFL files not being processed during a restore.

Table A.4   Continued

DECIMAL	HEXADECIMAL	CONSTANT	DESCRIPTION
-6035	0xFFFFE86D	ERR_INCONSISTENT_BACKUP	Invalid data has been detected in the backup set during a database restore operation. This is usually the result of a checksum error detected in the backup set during block verification.
-6036	0xFFFFE86C	ERR_NO_SUCH_INDEX	If this error is reported while the database is being upgraded by a new version of eDirectory, it is an informational error. This is because the operationally required indexes are unavailable until the upgrade completes. However, if this error happens under other circumstances, an internal error may have occurred, and if using DSRepair or restarting the server does not resolve the error, it should be reported to Novell.
-6037	0xFFFFE86B	ERR_INDEX_OFFLINE	If this error is reported while the database is being upgraded by a new version of eDirectory, it is an informational error. This is because the operationally required indexes are unavailable until the upgrade completes. However, if this error occurs under other circumstances, an internal error may have occurred, and if using DSRepair or restarting the server does not resolve the error, it should be reported to Novell.
-6038	0xFFFFE86A	ERR_CLOSING_DATABASE	Some other components of the system have the database open, and eDirectory is unable to close it. This is generally a transitory error, but it may take several minutes for all components to relinquish access.
-6039	0xFFFFE869	ERR_OBJECT_OP_DISABLED	The current system configuration prohibits any type of operation (such as changing the DS password) on this object.
-6040	0xFFFFE868	ERR_OP_STARTED	This is more of a status code than an error. It means that the requested operation started as expected.
-6041	0xFFFFE867	ERR_OP_ABORTED	This is more of a status code than an error. It means that the requested operation was successfully cancelled.
-6042	0xFFFFE866	ERR_OP_FAILED	The requested operation failed.
-6043	0xFFFFE865	ERR_OP_IN_PROGRESS	The requested operation is already in progress.

Table A.4   Continued

DECIMAL	HEXADECIMAL	CONSTANT	DESCRIPTION
-6044	0xFFFFE864	ERR_NO_VALUE	A parameter in the FLAIM initialization file (NDSDB.INI) that is supposed to have a value associated with it (such as the cache setting) does not have a value. The default value is used instead.
-6045	0xFFFFE863	ERR_PARAM_NOT_FOUND	A query is made for a certain parameter in the FLAIM initialization file, but that parameter doesn't exist.
-6046	0xFFFFE862	ERR_VALUE_TOO_LARGE	A value passed to eDirectory exceeds the maximum value size that can be stored in the database (64,000 characters).
-6047 through -6999	0xFFFFE861 through 0xFFFFE4F9		Reserved for future DS error codes.

APPENDIX B

DS Verbs

Directory services (DS) verbs are commands or requests. They can be issued by the directory services agent (DSA) on a server or by a client requesting that the server perform some action on DS. Many of the verbs can be observed in the DSTrace screen on a NetWare server by using the following server console command:

```
SET DSTRACE = +DSA
```

This command enables tracing of the DSA on the server and shows all inbound and outbound DSA requests.

NOTE

On Unix/Linux, load `ndstrace` **first and then issue the** `SET DSTRACE=+DSA` **command in the** `ndstrace` **console.**

For Windows servers, go to the Control Panel, select Novell eDirectory Services, highlight `dstrace.dlm`**, and then click the Start button. From the Novell eDirectory Trace screen, select Edit | Options, check the DS Agent box, and click OK.**

The DSTrace screen shows the information in this format:

```
DSA: DSACommonRequest(r) conn:c for client <ObjectName>
```

The request value is shown in decimal format for value *r*. The connection number making the request is value *c*, and the object name (if known) is *ObjectName*.

For example, if `Amy.East.XYZCorp` on connection 42 on the server attempts to read the Last Name attribute of her user object, the DSTrace screen would show this:

```
DSA: DSACommonRequest(3) conn:42 for client <Amy.East.XYZCorp>
```

If you turn on the `BUFFERS` flag as well (`SET DSTRACE=+BUFFER`), you also see the request/reply buffers that go along with this request, and you see the Last Name attribute referenced in the request buffer with the value of the Last Name attribute returned in the reply buffer.

WARNING   DS server-to-server and client-to-server traffic is sent in clear text, so DSTrace may reveal some data that you might deem sensitive. DS passwords, however, are not passed as clear text; as a matter of fact DS passwords are never transmitted on the wire, so there is no danger of them being captured.

Table B.1 lists all the current DSA common request and reply values and their definitions, as used by eDirectory.

TABLE B.1   **DSA Common Request and Reply Values**

DEFINE VALUE	DECIMAL	HEXADECIMAL	DESCRIPTION
DSV_UNUSED_0	0	0x00	Is not used
DSV_RESOLVE_NAME	1	0x01	Performs DS name lookup
DSV_READ_ENTRY_INFO	2	0x02	Reads basic information about an entry
DSV_READ	3	0x03	Reads attribute values in an object
DSV_COMPARE	4	0x04	Performs comparison with an attribute value
DSV_LIST	5	0x05	Lists subordinate objects
DSV_SEARCH	6	0x06	Searches the tree for an object, based on an attribute value
DSV_ADD_ENTRY	7	0x07	Creates an object
DSV_REMOVE_ENTRY	8	0x08	Deletes an object
DSV_MODIFY_ENTRY	9	0x09	Commits changes to an entry's attributes
DSV_MODIFY_RDN	10	0x0A	Moves an object
DSV_DEFINE_ATTR	11	0x0B	Creates a new attribute in the schema
DSV_READ_ATTR_DEF	12	0x0C	Reads the schema definition for an attribute

Table B.1   Continued

DEFINE VALUE	DECIMAL	HEXADECIMAL	DESCRIPTION
DSV_REMOVE_ATTR_DEF	13	0x0D	Deletes the attribute definition from the schema
DSV_DEFINE_CLASS	14	0x0E	Creates a new class in the schema
DSV_READ_CLASS_DEF	15	0x0F	Reads the schema definition for a class
DSV_MODIFY_CLASS_DEF	16	0x10	Changes the schema definition for a class (typically used when adding attributes to a class)
DSV_REMOVE_CLASS_DEF	17	0x11	Deletes the class definition from the schema
DSV_LIST_CONTAINABLE_CLASSES	18	0x12	Lists all classes that are flagged as being container classes
DSV_GET_EFFECTIVE_RIGHTS	19	0x13	Determines the currently logged-in object's effective rights to another object
DSV_ADD_PARTITION	20	0x14	Adds a partition to a replica list
DSV_REMOVE_PARTITION	21	0x15	Removes a partition from a replica list
DSV_LIST_PARTITIONS	22	0x16	Lists partitions in a replica list
DSV_SPLIT_PARTITION	23	0x17	Creates a partition operation
DSV_JOIN_PARTITIONS	24	0x18	Merges a partition operation
DSV_ADD_REPLICA	25	0x19	Creates a replica operation
DSV_REMOVE_REPLICA	26	0x1A	Deletes a replica operation
DSV_OPEN_STREAM	27	0x1B	Opens a stream file (for example, a login script)
DSV_SEARCH_FILTER	28	0x1C	Is used for building a DS server-based search
—	29 through 30	0x1D through 0x1E	Are for DS internal use
DSV_CHANGE_REPLICA_TYPE	31	0x1F	Changes the replica type operation
—	32 through 36	0x20 through 0x24	Are for DS internal use
DSV_UPDATE_REPLICA	37	0x25	Synchronizes a replica
DSV_SYNC_PARTITION	38	0x26	Partitions synchronization
DSV_SYNC_SCHEMA	39	0x27	Performs schema synchronization
DSV_READ_SYNTAXES	40	0x28	Lists all defined syntaxes

Table B.1   Continued

DEFINE VALUE	DECIMAL	HEXADECIMAL	DESCRIPTION
DSV_GET_REPLICA_ROOT_ID	41	0x29	Gets the object ID for the replica root object
DSV_BEGIN_MOVE_ENTRY	42	0x2A	Is issued during an object or partition move
DSV_FINISH_MOVE_ENTRY	43	0x2B	Is issued during an object or partition move
DSV_RELEASE_MOVED_ENTRY	44	0x2C	Is issued during an object or partition move
DSV_BACKUP_ENTRY	45	0x2D	Performs object backup
DSV_RESTORE_ENTRY	46	0x2E	Performs an object restore
—	47 through 49	0x2F through 0x31	Are for DS internal use
DSV_CLOSE_ITERATION	50	0x32	Ends iteration for large operations
DSV_MUTATE_ENTRY	51	0x33	Changes the object type
—	52	0x34	Is for DS internal use
DSV_GET_SERVER_ADDRESS	53	0x35	Gets the referenced server's network address
DSV_SET_KEYS	54	0x36	Generates a public key/private key pair (for example, a set password)
DSV_CHANGE_PASSWORD	55	0x37	Changes the object password
DSV_VERIFY_PASSWORD	56	0x38	Verifies the object password
DSV_BEGIN_LOGIN	57	0x39	Starts login
DSV_FINISH_LOGIN	58	0x3A	Ends login
DSV_BEGIN_AUTHENTICATION	59	0x3B	Starts background authentication
DSV_FINISH_AUTHENTICATION	60	0x3C	Ends background authentication
DSV_LOGOUT	61	0x3D	Logs out
DSV_REPAIR_RING	62	0x3E	Repairs the replica ring
DSV_REPAIR_TIMESTAMPS	63	0x3F	Issues a repair timestamps request
—	64 through 68	0x40 through 0x44	Are for DS internal use
DSV_DESIGNATE_NEW_MASTER	69	0x45	Causes the replica set to become the new master
—	70 through 71	0x46 through 0x47	Are for DS internal use

Table B.1 Continued

DEFINE VALUE	DECIMAL	HEXADECIMAL	DESCRIPTION
DSV_CHECK_LOGIN_RESTRICTIONS	72	0x48	Validates that login can occur
—	73 through 75	0x49 through 0x4B	Are for DS internal use
DSV_ABORT_PARTITION_OPERATION	76	0x4C	Aborts the partition operation
—	77 through 78	0x4D through 0x4E	Are for DS internal use
DSV_READ_REFERENCES	79	0x4F	Reads object reference information
DSV_INSPECT_ENTRY	80	0x50	Inspects entry in ENTRY.NDS (or 0.DSD for DS 7 or NDS.xx for DS 8 or eDirectory)
DSV_GET_REMOTE_ENTRY_ID	81	0x51	Requests the entry ID of a remote object
DSV_CHANGE_SECURITY	82	0x52	Modifies a security setting
DSV_CHECK_CONSOLE_OPERATOR	83	0x53	Checks whether the user is a console operator (which is necessary for some API calls)
—	84	0x54	Is for DS internal use
DSV_MOVE_TREE	85	0x55	Performs a move subtree operation
—	86 through 87	0x56 through 0x57	Are for DS internal use
DSV_CHECK_SEV	88	0x58	Checks security equivalence vectors (SEVs), which are used to calculate security equivalence
—	89 through 90	0x59 through 0x5A	Are for DS internal use
DSV_RESEND_ENTRY	91	0x5B	Requests that an object be re-sent
—	92	0x5C	Is for DS internal use
DSV_STATISTICS	93	0x5D	Returns DS statistics
DSV_PING	94	0x5E	Performs a DS ping, used to check the DS version of a remote server
DSV_GET_BINDERY_CONTEXTS	95	0x5F	Obtains bindery context settings
DSV_MONITOR_CONNECTION	96	0x60	Sets a connection to the "monitored" state (which is authenticated but not licensed); used during the client logon process and by ZENworks

Table B.1 Continued

DEFINE VALUE	DECIMAL	HEXADECIMAL	DESCRIPTION
DSV_GET_DS_STATISTICS	97	0x61	Retrieves DS statistics, such as the number of times name resolution resulted in finding the entry local to this server and the number of DS requests received from a remote client
DSV_RESET_DS_COUNTERS	98	0x62	Resets DS statistics counters
DSV_CONSOLE	99	0x63	Indicates that the user is a console operator
DSV_READ_STREAM	100	0x64	Reads from a stream file
DSV_WRITE_STREAM	101	0x65	Writes to a stream file
DSV_CREATE_ORPHAN_PARTITION	102	0x66	Creates an orphan partition—that is, a partition that does not have a parent; this is to support LDAP extension features
DSV_REMOVE_ORPHAN_PARTITION	103	0x67	Deletes an orphan partition; this is to support LDAP extension features
—	104 through 105	0x68 through 0X69	Are for DS internal use
DSV_GUID_CREATE	106	0x6A	Creates a global unique ID (GUID)
DSV_GUID_INFO	107	0x6B	Returns GUID info
—	108 through 109	0x6C through 0x6D	Are for DS internal use
DSV_ITERATOR	110	0x6E	Is an initial iterator search feature
—	111	0x6F	Is unused
DSV_CLOSE_STREAM	112	0x70	Closes the stream file
—	113	0x71	Is unused
DSV_READ_STATUS	114	0x72	Returns the status of a replica
DSV_PARTITION_SYNC_STATUS	115	0x73	Returns partition sync status info
DSV_READ_REF_DATA	116	0x74	Retrieves referral information
DSV_WRITE_REF_DATA	117	0x75	Writes referral information
DSV_RESOURCE_EVENT	118	0x76	Reports events associated with defined (cluster) resources
—	119 through 121	0x77 through 0x79	Are for DS internal use

Table B.1 Continued

DEFINE VALUE	DECIMAL	HEXADECIMAL	DESCRIPTION
DSV_CHANGE_ATTR_DEF	122	0x7A	Changes the attribute definition (of an auxiliary class)
DSV_SCHEMA_IN_USE	123	0x7B	Indicates that there exists one or more objects in the tree, using a specific attribute or a class; this may happen when you try to remove an auxiliary class without first removing the objects using the class or if you try to remove a schema extension made to a base class

APPENDIX C

eDirectory Classes, Objects, and Attributes

The schema defines what attributes an NDS object class (such as Users, Printers, or Groups) can have. For example, a User object can have login restriction properties associated with it, and a Print Queue object can have attributes identifying the NetWare server where the queue directory is located. The schema also defines which information (attribute) is required or optional at the time that an NDS object is created. Every NDS object has a schema class that has been defined for that type of object.

The schema that originally shipped with NetWare is called the *base schema*. After the base schema has been modified in any way—such as adding a new class or a new attribute—the addition is considered the *extended schema*. eDirectory 8.7.3 ships with 100 class and 572 attribute definitions—not counting any classes or attributes added by NetWare.

TIP

The tables presented in this appendix were generated using output from two utilities, `ReadClass32.EXE` and `ReadAttr32.EXE`. They can be found in `ftp://ftp.dreamlan.com/Freeware/schema.zip`.

NOTE

If you are interested in finding out more about a specific class or attribute definition, click the **NDS Schema Reference** link at `http://developer.novell.com/ndk/doc/ndslib/index.html`.

Class Definitions

Out of the 100 classes defined for eDirectory 8.7.3, there are 72 effective classes that you can use to create NDS objects; Top is an effective class, but you cannot create any objects by using this class. Table C.1 list all 100 object class definitions shipped with eDirectory 8.7.3. The table shows the following information:

▸ **Class name**—The name of the class.

▸ **Class flags**—In addition to basic information such as mandatory and optional attributes and containment, class flags are used to further define a class object. The following are some examples:

Flag	Description
DS_CONTAINER_CLASS	This flag indicates that objects of the class can have subordinates.
DS_EFFECTIVE_CLASS	This flag indicates an effective class.
DS_AUXILIARY_CLASS	This flag indicates an auxiliary class (NDS 8 and higher).
DS_NONREMOVABLE_CLASS	This flag indicates that the class cannot be removed from the schema.
DS_OPERATIONAL_CLASS	This flag is for internal use by NDS 8 and higher to indicate whether this class must be present for NDS to function correctly; it also provides compatibility with LDAP.
DS_AMBIGUOUS_NAMING	This flag indicates that the class cannot be used as a base class. It is set by eDirectory.
DS_AMBIGUOUS_CONTAINMENT	This flag indicates that the class cannot be used as a base class. It is set by eDirectory.

Ambiguous Class Flags

The ambiguous containment and ambiguous naming class flags indicate whether the object class has clearly defined containment classes and naming attributes, respectively.

Ambiguous containment occurs when an object inherits non-identical containment classes from different superclasses. For instance, the Alias class object is one example because it needs to inherit the containment classes of its reference object class. As a general rule, non-effective classes can be created with ambiguous containment, but effective classes *must* have non-ambiguous containment.

Similar to ambiguous containment, ambiguous naming occurs when an object inherits non-identical naming attributes from different superclasses. Again, Alias class objects fall into this category because they need to inherit the naming attributes of their reference object class. As a general rule, non-effective classes can be created with ambiguous naming, but effective classes *must* have non-ambiguous naming.

For most object classes in the base schema, the ambiguous containment and ambiguous naming flags are Off. The classes Top, Alias, and Partition are some examples of classes for which these two flags are On.

▶ **Superclass**—The immediate class from which the current object class inherits.

▶ **Containment**—The object classes under which the current object class can be created, as defined for the current class.

▶ **Named by**—The naming attribute(s) for the class.

▶ **Mandatory attributes**—Mandatory attributes defined for the current class.

▶ **Optional attributes**—Optional attributes defined for the current class.

Using Table C.1, you can easily determine all the properties of a given class, such as a list of all its optional attributes. The following uses the **Directory Map** class as an example:

CLASS	CONTAINMENT	NAMED BY	MANDATORY ATTRIBUTES	OPTIONAL ATTRIBUTES
Directory Map	—	—	Host Server	Path
Resource (superclass to Directory Map)	Organization Organizational Unit Domain	CN	CN	Description Host Resource Name L OU O See Also Uses
Top (superclass to Resource)	—	—	Object Class	CA Public Key CA Private Key Certificate Validity Interval Authority Revocation Last Referenced Time Equivalent To Me ACL Back Link Bindery Property Obituary Reference Revision Cross Certificate Pair Certificate Revocation Used By GUID Other GUID DirXML-Associations creatorsName modifiersName objectVersion auxClassCompatibility Unknown Base Class Unknown Auxiliary Class masvProposedLabel masvDefaultRange masvAuthorizedRange Audit:File Link rbsAssignedRoles rbsOwnedCollections rbsAssignedRoles2 rbsOwnedCollections2

By combining the preceding information, taking into account all the attributes inherited from superclasses, the `Directory Map` class has the following properties:

- ▶ **Containment**—Domain, Organization, Organizational Unit
- ▶ **Class flags**—Effective (`DS_EFFECTIVE_CLASS`), nonremovable (`DS_NONREMOVABLE_CLASS`)
- ▶ **Named by (or naming attribute)** —CN
- ▶ **Mandatory attributes**—CN, Host Server, Object Class
- ▶ **Optional Attributes**—ACL, Audit:File Link, Authority Revocation, auxClassCompatibility, Back Link, Bindery Property, CA Public Key, CA Private Key, Certificate Revocation, Certificate Validity Interval, creatorsName, Cross Certificate Pair, DirXML-Associations, Equivalent To Me, GUID, Host Resource Name, L, Last Referenced Time, masvAuthorizedRange, masvDefaultRange, masvProposedLabel, modifiersName, O, Obituary, objectVersion, Other GUID, OU, Path, rbsAssignedRoles, rbsAssignedRoles2, rbsOwnedCollections, rbsOwnedCollections2, Reference, Revision, See Also, Unknown Auxiliary Class, Unknown Base Class, Used By, Uses

---

NOTE

Because every object class inherits from Top **(directly or indirectly), the mandatory attribute** Object Class **(which indicates that the current definition is for an object class) exists for all class definitions within an NDS tree. In many cases, its presence is implied, and it is not explicitly mentioned in documentation or displayed by utilities.**

TABLE C.1   eDirectory 8.7.3 Object Class Definitions

CLASS NAME	CLASS FLAGS	SUPERCLASS	CONTAINMENT	NAMED BY	MANDATORY ATTRIBUTES	OPTIONAL ATTRIBUTES
[Anything]	DS_CONTAINER_CLASS DS_AMBIGUOUS_NAMING DS_AMBIGUOUS_CONTAINMENT	Top	—	—	—	—
[Nothing]	DS_CONTAINER_CLASS DS_AMBIGUOUS_NAMING DS_AMBIGUOUS_CONTAINMENT	Top	—	—	—	—
AFP Server	DS_EFFECTIVE_CLASS DS_NONREMOVABLE_CLASS	Server	—	—	—	Serial Number Supported Connections
Alias	DS_EFFECTIVE_CLASS DS_NONREMOVABLE_CLASS DS_AMBIGUOUS_NAMING DS_AMBIGUOUS_CONTAINMENT	Top	—	—	Aliased Object Name	—
applicationEntity	DS_CONTAINER_CLASS DS_EFFECTIVE_CLASS	Top	Country Locality Organizational Unit Organization domain	CN	presentation Address CN	supported ApplicationContext See Also OU O L Description
applicationProcess	DS_CONTAINER_CLASS DS_EFFECTIVE_CLASS	Top	Country Locality Organizational Unit Organization domain	CN	CN	See Also OU L Description

Table C.1 Continued

CLASS NAME	CLASS FLAGS	SUPERCLASS	CONTAINMENT	NAMED BY	MANDATORY ATTRIBUTES	OPTIONAL ATTRIBUTES
Audit::File Object	DS_EFFECTIVE_CLASS	Top	Top Country Locality Organization domain Organizational Unit Tree Root	CN	CN Audit:Policy Audit: Contents	Description Audit:Path Audit:Link List Audit:Type Audit:Current Encryption Key Audit:A Encryption Key Audit:B Encryption Key
Bindery Object	DS_EFFECTIVE_CLASS DS_NONREMOVABLE_CLASS	Top	Organization domain Organizational Unit	CN Bindery Type	Bindery Object Restriction Bindery Type CN	—
Bindery Queue	DS_EFFECTIVE_CLASS DS_NONREMOVABLE_CLASS	Queue	—	CN Bindery Type	Bindery Type	—
certification Authority	DS_AMBIGUOUS_NAMING DS_AMBIGUOUS_CONTAINMENT DS_AUXILIARY_CLASS	Top	Top	—	authority RevocationList certificate RevocationList cACertificate	crossCertificatePair Auxiliary Class Flag
certification AuthorityVer2	DS_AMBIGUOUS_NAMING DS_AMBIGUOUS_CONTAINMENT DS_AUXILIARY_CLASS	Top	Top	—	authority RevocationList certificate RevocationList cACertificate	crossCertificatePair deltaRevocationList Auxiliary Class Flag
CommExec	DS_EFFECTIVE_CLASS DS_NONREMOVABLE_CLASS	Server	—	—	—	Network Address Restriction

Table C.1   Continued

CLASS NAME	CLASS FLAGS	SUPERCLASS	CONTAINMENT	NAMED BY	MANDATORY ATTRIBUTES	OPTIONAL ATTRIBUTES
Computer	DS_EFFECTIVE_CLASS DS_NONREMOVABLE_CLASS	Device	—	—	—	Operator Server Status
ContingentWorker	DS_AMBIGUOUS_NAMING DS_AMBIGUOUS_CONTAINMENT DS_AUXILIARY_CLASS	Top	Top	—	—	vendorName vendorAddress vendorPhoneNumber Auxiliary Class Flag
Country	DS_CONTAINER_CLASS DS_EFFECTIVE_CLASS DS_NONREMOVABLE_CLASS	Top	Top Tree Root [Nothing] domain	C	C	Description searchGuide
cRLDistribution Point	DS_EFFECTIVE_CLASS	Top	Country Locality Organizational Unit Organization domain SAS:Security	CN	CN	authorityRevocationList cACertificate certificateRevocation List crossCertificatePair deltaRevocationList
dcObject	DS_NONREMOVABLE_CLASS DS_AMBIGUOUS_CONTAINMENT DS_AUXILIARY_CLASS	Top	Top	dc	dc	Auxiliary Class Flag
Device	DS_EFFECTIVE_CLASS DS_NONREMOVABLE_CLASS	Top	Organization domain Organizational Unit	CN	CN	Description L Network Address OU O Owner See Also Serial Number

Table C.1   Continued

CLASS NAME	CLASS FLAGS	SUPERCLASS	CONTAINMENT	NAMED BY	MANDATORY ATTRIBUTES	OPTIONAL ATTRIBUTES
Directory Map	DS_EFFECTIVE_CLASS DS_NONREMOVABLE_CLASS	Resource	—	—	Host Server	Path
dmd	DS_AMBIGUOUS_NAMING DS_AMBIGUOUS_CONTAINMENT DS_AUXILIARY_CLASS	ndsLogin Properties Top	Top	—	dmdName	searchGuide See Also businessCategory x121Address registeredAddress destinationIndicator preferredDeliveryMethod telexNumber teletexTerminal Identifier Telephone Number internationaliSDNNumber Facsimile Telephone Number SA Postal Office Box Postal Code Postal Address Physical Delivery Office Name L Description Auxiliary Class Flag

PART V Appendixes

Table C.1 Continued

CLASS NAME	CLASS FLAGS	SUPERCLASS	CONTAINMENT	NAMED BY	MANDATORY ATTRIBUTES	OPTIONAL ATTRIBUTES
domain	DS_CONTAINER_CLASS DS_EFFECTIVE_CLASS DS_NONREMOVABLE_CLASS	Top ndsLogin Properties ndsContainer LoginProperties	Top Tree Root Country Locality Organization domain Organizational Unit [Nothing]	dc	dc	searchGuide O See Also businessCategory x121Address registeredAddress destinationIndicator preferredDeliveryMethod telexNumber teletexTerminal Identifier Telephone Number internationaliSDNNumber Facsimile Telephone Number SA Postal Office Box Postal Code Postal Address Physical Delivery Office Name L associatedName Description
dSA	DS_CONTAINER_CLASS DS_EFFECTIVE_CLASS	applicationEntity	Country Locality Organizational Unit Organization domain	—	—	knowledgeInformation

Table C.1   Continued

CLASS NAME	CLASS FLAGS	SUPERCLASS	CONTAINMENT	NAMED BY	MANDATORY ATTRIBUTES	OPTIONAL ATTRIBUTES
dynamicGroup	DS_EFFECTIVE_CLASS	Group ndsLoginProperties	—	—	—	memberQuery excludedMember dgIdentity dgAllowUnknown dgTimeOut dgAllowDuplicates
dynamicGroupAux	DS_AUXILIARY_CLASS	Group ndsLoginProperties Top	Top	—	—	memberQuery excludedMember dgIdentity dgAllowUnknown dgTimeOut dgAllowDuplicates Auxiliary Class Flag
edirSchemaVersion	DS_NONREMOVABLE_CLASS DS_AMBIGUOUS_NAMING DS_AMBIGUOUS_CONTAINMENT	Top	—	—	—	edirSchemaFlagVersion
External Entity	DS_EFFECTIVE_CLASS DS_NONREMOVABLE_CLASS	Top	Organization domain Organizational Unit	CN OU	CN	Description See Also Facsimile Telephone Number L EMail Address OU Physical Delivery Office Name Postal Address Postal Code Postal Office Box

Table C.1   Continued

CLASS NAME	CLASS FLAGS	SUPERCLASS	CONTAINMENT	NAMED BY	MANDATORY ATTRIBUTES	OPTIONAL ATTRIBUTES
						S
						SA
						Title
						External Name
						Mailbox Location
						Mailbox ID
federationBoundary	DS_NONREMOVABLE_CLASS DS_AMBIGUOUS_NAMING DS_AMBIGUOUS_CONTAINMENT DS_AUXILIARY_CLASS	Top		—	federationBoundaryType	federationControl federationDNSName federationSearchPath Auxiliary Class Flag
Group	DS_EFFECTIVE_CLASS DS_NONREMOVABLE_CLASS	Top	Organization domain Organizational Unit	CN	CN	Description L Member OU O Owner See Also GID Full Name EMail Address Mailbox Location Mailbox ID Profile Profile Membership Login Script businessCategory nspmPasswordPolicyDN
homeInfo	DS_AMBIGUOUS_NAMING DS_AMBIGUOUS_CONTAINMENT DS_AUXILIARY_CLASS	Top		—	—	homeCity homeEmailAddress homeFax

Table C.1 **Continued**

CLASS NAME	CLASS FLAGS	SUPERCLASS	CONTAINMENT	NAMED BY	MANDATORY ATTRIBUTES	OPTIONAL ATTRIBUTES
						homePhone homeState homePostalAddress homeZipCode personalMobile spouse children Auxiliary Class Flag
httpServer	DS_EFFECTIVE_CLASS	Top	Country Locality Organizational Unit Organization domain	CN	CN	httpHostServerDN httpThreadsPerCPU httpIOBufferSize httpRequestTimeout httpKeepAliveRequest Timeout httpSessionTimeout httpKeyMaterialObject httpTraceLevel httpAuthRequiresTLS httpDefaultClearPort httpDefaultTLSPort
immediateSuperior Reference	DS_AMBIGUOUS_NAMING DS_AMBIGUOUS_CONTAINMENT DS_AUXILIARY_CLASS	Top	Top	—	—	ref Auxiliary Class Flag
LDAP Group	DS_EFFECTIVE_CLASS	Top	Country Locality Organizational Unit Organization domain	CN	CN	LDAP Referral LDAP Server List LDAP Allow Clear Text Password LDAP Anonymous Identity LDAP Suffix LDAP Attribute Map v11 LDAP Class Map v11

Table C.1   Continued

CLASS NAME	CLASS FLAGS	SUPERCLASS	CONTAINMENT	NAMED BY	MANDATORY ATTRIBUTES	OPTIONAL ATTRIBUTES
						LDAP:searchReferralUsage LDAP:otherReferralUsage transitionGroupDN ldapAttributeList ldapClassList ldapConfigVersion Version ldapDefaultReferral Behavior ldapTransitionBackLink referralIncludeFilter referralExcludeFilter
LDAP Server	DS_EFFECTIVE_CLASS	Top	Country Locality Organizational Unit Organization domain	CN	CN	LDAP Host Server LDAP Group LDAP Screen Level LDAP Server Bind Limit LDAP Server Idle Timeout LDAP UDP Port LDAP Search Size Limit LDAP Search Time Limit LDAP Log Level LDAP Log Filename LDAP Backup Log Filename LDAP Log Size Limit Version searchSizeLimit searchTimeLimit LDAP Enable TCP LDAP TCP Port

Table C.1 Continued

CLASS NAME	CLASS FLAGS	SUPERCLASS	CONTAINMENT	NAMED BY	MANDATORY ATTRIBUTES	OPTIONAL ATTRIBUTES
						LDAP Enable SSL
						LDAP SSL Port
						LDAP:keyMaterialName
						filteredReplicaUsage
						extensionInfo
						nonStdClientSchema
						CompatMode
						sslEnableMutual
						Authentication
						ldapEnablePSearch
						ldapMaximumPSearch
						Operations
						ldapIgnorePSearchLimits
						ForEvents
						ldapTLSTrustedRoot
						Container
						ldapEnableMonitorEvents
						ldapMaximumMonitor
						EventsLoad
						ldapTLSRequired
						ldapTLSVerifyClient
						Certificate
						ldapConfigVersion
						ldapDerefAlias
						ldapNonStdAllUserAttrs
						Mode
						ldapBindRestrictions
						ldapDefaultReferral
						Behavior
						LDAP Referral
						LDAP:searchReferralUsage
						LDAP:otherReferralUsage

Table C.1 Continued

CLASS NAME	CLASS FLAGS	SUPERCLASS	CONTAINMENT	NAMED BY	MANDATORY ATTRIBUTES	OPTIONAL ATTRIBUTES
List	DS_EFFECTIVE_CLASS DS_NONREMOVABLE_CLASS	Top	Organization domain Organizational Unit	CN	CN	Description L Member OU O EMail Address Mailbox Location Mailbox ID Owner See Also Full Name
Locality	DS_CONTAINER_CLASS DS_EFFECTIVE_CLASS DS_NONREMOVABLE_CLASS	Top	Country Organizational Unit Locality Organization domain	L S	—	Description L See Also S SA searchGuide
MASV:Security Policy	DS_EFFECTIVE_CLASS	Top	SAS:Security	CN	CN	Description masvDomainPolicy masvPolicyUpdate masvClearanceNames masvLabelNames masvLabelSecrecyLevel Names masvLabelSecrecyCategory Names masvLabelIntegrityLevel Names masvLabelIntegrity CategoryNames masvNDSAttributeLabels

Table C.1 Continued

CLASS NAME	CLASS FLAGS	SUPERCLASS	CONTAINMENT	NAMED BY	MANDATORY ATTRIBUTES	OPTIONAL ATTRIBUTES
Message Routing Group	DS_EFFECTIVE_CLASS DS_NONREMOVABLE_CLASS	Group	—	—	—	—
Messaging Server	DS_EFFECTIVE_CLASS DS_NONREMOVABLE_CLASS	Server	—	—	—	Messaging Database Location Message Routing Group Postmaster Supported Services Messaging Server Type Supported Gateway
NCP Server	DS_EFFECTIVE_CLASS DS_NONREMOVABLE_CLASS	Server	—	—	—	Operator Supported Services Messaging Server DS Revision Permanent Config Parms ndsPredicateStatsDN languageId indexDefinition LDAP Server httpServerDN emboxConfig SAS:Service DN cACertificate NDSPKI:Public Key NDSPKI:Private Key NDSPKI:Certificate Chain NDSPKI:Parent CA DN NDSPKI:SD Key ID NDSPKI:SD Key Struct snmpGroupDN

Table C.1   Continued

CLASS NAME	CLASS FLAGS	SUPERCLASS	CONTAINMENT	NAMED BY	MANDATORY ATTRIBUTES	OPTIONAL ATTRIBUTES
						slConfigObject
						WANMAN:WAN Policy
						WANMAN:LAN Area
						Membership
						WANMAN:Cost
						WANMAN:Default Cost
ndsContainer LoginProperties	DS_NONREMOVABLE_CLASS DS_AMBIGUOUS_NAMING DS_AMBIGUOUS_CONTAINMENT	Top	—	—	—	Login Intruder Limit
						Intruder Attempt Reset Interval
						Detect Intruder
						Lockout After Detection
						Intruder Lockout Reset Interval
						ndapPasswordMgmt
						nspmPasswordPolicyDN
ndsLoginProperties	DS_NONREMOVABLE_CLASS DS_AMBIGUOUS_NAMING DS_AMBIGUOUS_CONTAINMENT	Top	—	—	—	Group Membership
						Login Allowed Time Map
						Login Disabled
						Login Expiration Time
						Login Grace Limit
						Login Grace Remaining
						Login Intruder Address
						Login Intruder Attempts
						Login Intruder Reset Time
						Login Maximum Simultaneous
						Login Script
						Login Time
						Network Address

Table C.1 Continued

CLASS NAME	CLASS FLAGS	SUPERCLASS	CONTAINMENT	NAMED BY	MANDATORY ATTRIBUTES	OPTIONAL ATTRIBUTES
						Restriction
						Network Address
						Passwords Used
						Password Allow Change
						Password Expiration Interval
						Password Expiration Time
						Password Minimum Length
						Password Required
						Password Unique Required
						Private Key
						Profile
						Public Key
						Security Equals
						Account Balance
						Allow Unlimited Credit
						Minimum Account Balance
						Language
						Locked By Intruder
						Server Holds
						Last Login Time
						Higher Privileges
						Security Flags
						Profile Membership
						Timezone
						loginActivationTime
						SAS:NDS Password Window
						SAS:Login Secret
						SAS:Login Secret Key

Table C.1   Continued

CLASS NAME	CLASS FLAGS	SUPERCLASS	CONTAINMENT	NAMED BY	MANDATORY ATTRIBUTES	OPTIONAL ATTRIBUTES
						SAS:Encryption Type SAS:Login Configuration SAS:Login Configuration Key sasDefaultLoginSequence sasAuthorizedLogin Sequences sasAllowableSubjectNames ndapPasswordMgmt nspmPasswordKey nspmPassword nspmDistributionPassword nspmPasswordHistory nspmAdministratorChange Count nspmPasswordPolicyDN
NDSPKI:Certificate Authority	DS_EFFECTIVE_CLASS	Top	SAS:Security	CN	CN	Host Server NDSPKI:Public Key NDSPKI:Private Key NDSPKI:Public Key Certificate NDSPKI:Certificate Chain NDSPKI:Parent CA NDSPKI:Parent CA DN NDSPKI:Subject Name caCertificate
NDSPKI:Key Material	DS_EFFECTIVE_CLASS	Top	SAS:Security Organization	CN	CN	Host Server NDSPKI:Key File

Table C.1 Continued

CLASS NAME	CLASS FLAGS	SUPERCLASS	CONTAINMENT	NAMED BY	MANDATORY ATTRIBUTES	OPTIONAL ATTRIBUTES
			domain Organizational Unit			NDSPKI:Private Key NDSPKI:Public Key NDSPKI:Public Key Certificate NDSPKI:Certificate Chain NDSPKI:Subject Name NDSPKI:Given Name ndspkiAdditionalRoots
NDSPKI:SD Key Access Partition	DS_CONTAINER_CLASS DS_EFFECTIVE_CLASS	Top	SAS:Security	CN	CN	—
NDSPKI:SD Key List	DS_CONTAINER_CLASS DS_EFFECTIVE_CLASS	Top	NDSPKI:SD Key Access Partition	CN	CN	NDSPKI:SD Key Server DN NDSPKI:SD Key Struct NDSPKI:SD Key Cert
NDSPKI:Trusted Root	DS_CONTAINER_CLASS DS_EFFECTIVE_CLASS	Top	SAS:Security Organization domain Organizational Unit Country Locality	CN	CN	—
NDSPKI:Trusted Root Object	DS_EFFECTIVE_CLASS	Top	NDSPKI:Trusted Root	CN	CN NDSPKI: Trusted Root Certificate	NDSPKI:Subject Name NDSPKI:Not Before NDSPKI:Not After External Name Given Name Surname

Table C.1   Continued

CLASS NAME	CLASS FLAGS	SUPERCLASS	CONTAINMENT	NAMED BY	MANDATORY ATTRIBUTES	OPTIONAL ATTRIBUTES
ndsPredicateStats	DS_EFFECTIVE_CLASS DS_NONREMOVABLE_CLASS	Top	Country Locality Organization domain Organizational Unit	CN Flush	CN ndsPredicate State ndsPredicate	ndsPredicate ndsPredicateTimeout ndsPredicateUseValues
nspmPasswordPolicy	DS_EFFECTIVE_CLASS	Top	nspmPassword PolicyContainer Locality Organization domain Organizational Unit	CN	CN	Description nspmPolicyPrecedence nspmConfigurationOptions nspmChangePassword Message Password Expiration Interval Login Grace Limit nspmMinPasswordLifetime Password Unique Required nspmPasswordHistoryLimit nspmPasswordHistory Expiration Password Allow Change Password Required Password Minimum Length nspmMaximumLength nspmCaseSensitive nspmMinUpperCase Characters nspmMaxUpperCase Characters

Table C.1 Continued

CLASS NAME	CLASS FLAGS	SUPERCLASS	CONTAINMENT	NAMED BY	MANDATORY ATTRIBUTES	OPTIONAL ATTRIBUTES
						nspmMinLowerCase Characters
						nspmMaxLowerCase Characters
						nspmNumericCharacters Allowed
						nspmNumericAsFirst Character
						nspmNumericAsLast Character
						nspmMinNumericCharacters
						nspmMaxNumericCharacters
						nspmSpecialCharacters Allowed
						nspmSpecialAsFirst Character
						nspmSpecialAsLast Character
						nspmMinSpecialCharacters
						nspmMaxSpecialCharacters
						nspmMaxRepeated Characters
						nspmMaxConsecutive Characters
						nspmMinUniqueCharacters
						nspmDisallowedAttribute Values
						nspmExcludeList
						nspmExtendedCharacters Allowed

Table C.1   Continued

CLASS NAME	CLASS FLAGS	SUPERCLASS	CONTAINMENT	NAMED BY	MANDATORY ATTRIBUTES	OPTIONAL ATTRIBUTES
nspmPassword PolicyContainer	DS_CONTAINER_CLASS DS_EFFECTIVE_CLASS	Top	SAS:Security	CN	CN	Description
nspmPolicyAgent	DS_EFFECTIVE_CLASS	Top	nspmPassword PolicyContainer	CN	CN	Description nspmPolicyAgentNetWare nspmPolicyAgentWINNT nspmPolicyAgentSolaris nspmPolicyAgentLinux nspmPolicyAgentAIX nspmPolicyAgentHPUX
Organization	DS_CONTAINER_CLASS DS_EFFECTIVE_CLASS DS_NONREMOVABLE_CLASS	ndsLogin Properties ndsContainer LoginProperties	Top Tree Root Country Locality [Nothing] domain	O	O	Description Facsimile Telephone Number L Login Script EMail Address Physical Delivery Office Name Postal Address Postal Code Postal Office Box Print Job Configuration Printer Control See Also S SA Telephone Number Login Intruder Limit Intruder Attempt Reset Interval Detect Intruder Lockout After Detection

Table C.1 Continued

CLASS NAME	CLASS FLAGS	SUPERCLASS	CONTAINMENT	NAMED BY	MANDATORY ATTRIBUTES	OPTIONAL ATTRIBUTES
						Intruder Lockout Reset Interval
						NNS Domain
						Mailbox Location
						Mailbox ID
						x121Address
						registeredAddress
						destinationIndicator
						preferredDeliveryMethod
						telexNumber
						teletexTerminal Identifier
						internationaliSDNNumber
						businessCategory
						searchGuide
						RADIUS:Attribute Lists
						RADIUS:Default Profile
						RADIUS:Dial Access Group
						RADIUS:Enable Dial Access
						RADIUS:Service List
Organizational Person	DS_EFFECTIVE_CLASS DS_NONREMOVABLE_CLASS	Person	Organization domain Organizational Unit	CN OU uniqueID	—	Facsimile Telephone Number
						L
						EMail Address
						OU
						Physical Delivery Office Name
						Postal Address

Table C.1 Continued

CLASS NAME	CLASS FLAGS	SUPERCLASS	CONTAINMENT	NAMED BY	MANDATORY ATTRIBUTES	OPTIONAL ATTRIBUTES
						Postal Code
						Postal Office Box
						S
						SA
						Title
						Mailbox Location
						Mailbox ID
						uniqueID
						Internet EMail Address
						NSCP:employeeNumber
						destinationIndicator
						internationaliSDNNumber
						preferredDeliveryMethod
						registeredAddress
						teletexTerminal
						Identifier
						telexNumber
						x121Address
						businessCategory
						roomNumber
						x500UniqueIdentifier
Organizational Role	DS_EFFECTIVE_CLASS DS_NONREMOVABLE_CLASS	Top	Organization domain Organizational Unit	CN	CN	Description
						Facsimile Telephone Number
						L
						EMail Address
						OU
						Physical Delivery Office Name
						Postal Address
						Postal Code

Table C.1 Continued

CLASS NAME	CLASS FLAGS	SUPERCLASS	CONTAINMENT	NAMED BY	MANDATORY ATTRIBUTES	OPTIONAL ATTRIBUTES
						Postal Office Box
						Role Occupant
						See Also
						S
						SA
						Telephone Number
						Mailbox Location
						Mailbox ID
						x121Address
						registeredAddress
						destinationIndicator
						preferredDeliveryMethod
						telexNumber
						teletexTerminal
						Identifier
						internationaliSDNNumber
Organizational Unit	DS_CONTAINER_CLASS	ndsLogin Properties	Locality	OU	OU	Description
	DS_EFFECTIVE_CLASS	ndsContainer	Organization			Facsimile Telephone Number
	DS_NONREMOVABLE_CLASS	LoginProperties	domain			L
			Organizational Unit			Login Script
						EMail Address
						Physical Delivery
						Office Name
						Postal Address
						Postal Code
						Postal Office Box
						Print Job Configuration
						Printer Control
						See Also
						S

Table C.1   **Continued**

CLASS NAME	CLASS FLAGS	SUPERCLASS	CONTAINMENT	NAMED BY	MANDATORY ATTRIBUTES	OPTIONAL ATTRIBUTES
						SA
						Telephone Number
						Login Intruder Limit
						Intruder Attempt Reset Interval
						Detect Intruder
						Lockout After Detection
						Intruder Lockout Reset Interval
						NNS Domain
						Mailbox Location
						Mailbox ID
						x121Address
						registeredAddress
						destinationIndicator
						preferredDeliveryMethod
						telexNumber
						teletexTerminal Identifier
						internationaliSDNNumber
						businessCategory
						searchGuide
						RADIUS:Attribute Lists
						RADIUS:Default Profile
						RADIUS:Dial Access Group
						RADIUS:Enable Dial Access
						RADIUS:Service List

Table C.1   Continued

CLASS NAME	CLASS FLAGS	SUPERCLASS	CONTAINMENT	NAMED BY	MANDATORY ATTRIBUTES	OPTIONAL ATTRIBUTES
Partition	DS_NONREMOVABLE_CLASS DS_AMBIGUOUS_NAMING DS_AMBIGUOUS_CONTAINMENT DS_AUXILIARY_CLASS	—	—	—	—	Convergence Partition Creation Time Replica Inherited ACL Low Convergence Sync Interval Received Up To Synchronized Up To Authority Revocation Certificate Revocation CA Private Key CA Public Key Cross Certificate Pair Low Convergence Reset Time High Convergence Sync Interval Partition Control Replica Up To Partition Status Transitive Vector Purge Vector Synchronization Tolerance Obituary Notify Local Received Up To federationControl syncPanePoint syncWindowVector authoritative

Table C.1 Continued

CLASS NAME	CLASS FLAGS	SUPERCLASS	CONTAINMENT	NAMED BY	MANDATORY ATTRIBUTES	OPTIONAL ATTRIBUTES
						SAS:Security DN
						masvLabel
						ndapPartitionPasswordMgmt
Person	DS_EFFECTIVE_CLASS	ndsLogin	Organization	CN	CN	Description
	DS_NONREMOVABLE_CLASS	Properties	domain		uniqueID	Surname See Also
			Organizational			Telephone Number
			Unit			Full Name
						Given Name
						Initials
						Generational Qualifier
						uniqueID
						assistant
						assistantPhone
						city
						S
						company
						co
						directReports
						manager
						mailstop
						mobile
						personalTitle
						pager
						workforceID
						instantMessagingID
						preferredName
						photo
						jobCode
						siteLocation

Table C.1   Continued

CLASS NAME	CLASS FLAGS	SUPERCLASS	CONTAINMENT	NAMED BY	MANDATORY ATTRIBUTES	OPTIONAL ATTRIBUTES
						employeeStatus employeeType costCenter costCenterDescription tollFreePhoneNumber otherPhoneNumber managerWorkforceID roomNumber jackNumber departmentNumber vehicleInformation accessCardNumber isManager
pkiCA	DS_AMBIGUOUS_NAMING DS_AMBIGUOUS_CONTAINMENT DS_AUXILIARY_CLASS	Top	Top	—	—	cACertificate certificateRevocation List authorityRevocationList crossCertificatePair attributeCertificate Public Key Private Key Network Address Login Time Last Login Time Auxiliary Class Flag
pkiUser	DS_AMBIGUOUS_NAMING DS_AMBIGUOUS_CONTAINMENT DS_AUXILIARY_CLASS	Top	Top	—	—	userCertificate Auxiliary Class Flag

Table C.1   Continued

CLASS NAME	CLASS FLAGS	SUPERCLASS	CONTAINMENT	NAMED BY	MANDATORY ATTRIBUTES	OPTIONAL ATTRIBUTES
Print Server	DS_EFFECTIVE_CLASS DS_NONREMOVABLE_CLASS	Server	—	—	—	Operator Printer SAP Name
Printer	DS_EFFECTIVE_CLASS DS_NONREMOVABLE_CLASS	Device	—	—	—	Cartridge Printer Configuration Default Queue Host Device Print Server Memory Network Address Restriction Notify Operator Page Description Language Queue Status Supported Typefaces
Profile	DS_EFFECTIVE_CLASS DS_NONREMOVABLE_CLASS	Top	Organization domain Organizational Unit	CN	CN Login Script	Description L OU O See Also Full Name

Table C.1   Continued

CLASS NAME	CLASS FLAGS	SUPERCLASS	CONTAINMENT	NAMED BY	MANDATORY ATTRIBUTES	OPTIONAL ATTRIBUTES
Queue	DS_EFFECTIVE_CLASS DS_NONREMOVABLE_CLASS	Resource	—	—	Queue Directory	Device Operator Server User Network Address Volume Host Server
RADIUS:Dial Access System	DS_EFFECTIVE_CLASS	Top	Country Locality Organizational Unit Organization	CN	CN	Public Key Private Key RADIUS:Aged Interval RADIUS:Client RADIUS:Common Name Resolution RADIUS:Concurrent Limit RADIUS:DAS Version RADIUS:Enable Common Name Login RADIUS:Enable Dial Access RADIUS:Interim Accting Timeout RADIUS:Lookup Contexts RADIUS:Max DAS History Record RADIUS:Maximum History Record RADIUS:Password Policy RADIUS:Private Key RADIUS:Proxy Context RADIUS:Proxy Domain RADIUS:Proxy Target

Table C.1   Continued

CLASS NAME	CLASS FLAGS	SUPERCLASS	CONTAINMENT	NAMED BY	MANDATORY ATTRIBUTES	OPTIONAL ATTRIBUTES
						RADIUS:Public Key SAS:Login Configuration SAS:Login Configuration Key
RADIUS:Profile	DS_EFFECTIVE_CLASS	Top	Country Locality Organizational Unit Organization	CN	CN	RADIUS:Attribute List
rbsBook rbsPageMembership	DS_EFFECTIVE_CLASS	rbsTask	—	—	—	rbsTargetObjectType
rbsBook2	DS_EFFECTIVE_CLASS	rbsTask2	—	—	—	rbsTargetObjectType rbsPageMembership
rbsCollection	DS_CONTAINER_CLASS DS_EFFECTIVE_CLASS	Top	Country Locality Organizational Unit Organization domain	CN	CN	Owner Description rbsXMLInfo
rbsCollection2	DS_CONTAINER_CLASS DS_EFFECTIVE_CLASS	Top	Country Locality Organizational Unit Organization domain	CN	CN	rbsPortalObject rbsXMLInfo rbsParameters Owner Description

Table C.1 Continued

CLASS NAME	CLASS FLAGS	SUPERCLASS	CONTAINMENT	NAMED BY	MANDATORY ATTRIBUTES	OPTIONAL ATTRIBUTES
rbsExternalScope	—	Top	rbsCollection	CN	CN	rbsURL Description rbsXMLInfo
rbsExternalScope2	—	Top	rbsCollection2	CN	CN	rbsXMLInfo Description
rbsModule	DS_CONTAINER_CLASS DS_EFFECTIVE_CLASS	Top	rbsCollection	CN	CN	rbsURL rbsPath rbsType Description rbsXMLInfo
rbsModule2	DS_CONTAINER_CLASS DS_EFFECTIVE_CLASS	Top	rbsCollection2	CN	CN	rbsXMLInfo rbsPath rbsType Description
rbsRole	DS_CONTAINER_CLASS DS_EFFECTIVE_CLASS	Top	rbsCollection	CN	CN	rbsContent rbsMember rbsTrusteeOf rbsGALabel rbsParameters Description rbsXMLInfo
rbsRole2	DS_CONTAINER_CLASS DS_EFFECTIVE_CLASS	Top	rbsCollection2	CN	CN	rbsXMLInfo rbsContent rbsMember rbsTrusteeOf rbsParameters Description
rbsScope	DS_EFFECTIVE_CLASS	Group	rbsRole	—	—	rbsContext rbsXMLInfo

Table C.1 Continued

CLASS NAME	CLASS FLAGS	SUPERCLASS	CONTAINMENT	NAMED BY	MANDATORY ATTRIBUTES	OPTIONAL ATTRIBUTES
rbsScope2	DS_EFFECTIVE_CLASS	Group	rbsRole2	—	—	rbsContext rbsXMLInfo
rbsTask	DS_EFFECTIVE_CLASS	Top	rbsModule	CN	CN	rbsContentMembership rbsType rbsTaskRights rbsEntryPoint rbsParameters rbsTaskTemplates rbsTaskTemplatesURL Description rbsXMLInfo
rbsTask2	DS_EFFECTIVE_CLASS	Top	rbsModule2	CN	CN	rbsGadget rbsXMLInfo rbsContentMembership rbsType rbsTaskRights rbsEntryPoint rbsParameters Description
Resource	DS_NONREMOVABLE_CLASS	Top	Organization domain Organizational Unit	CN	CN L OU O See Also Uses	Description Host Resource Name

Table C.1   Continued

CLASS NAME	CLASS FLAGS	SUPERCLASS	CONTAINMENT	NAMED BY	MANDATORY ATTRIBUTES	OPTIONAL ATTRIBUTES
SAS:Login Method Container	DS_CONTAINER_CLASS DS_EFFECTIVE_CLASS	Top	SAS:Security Country Locality Organizational Unit Organization	CN	CN	Description
SAS:Login Policy	DS_EFFECTIVE_CLASS	Top	SAS:Security	CN	CN	Description Private Key Public Key SAS:Allow NDS Password Window SAS:Policy Credentials SAS:Policy Methods SAS:Policy Object Version SAS:Policy Service Subtypes SAS:Policy Services SAS:Policy Users SAS:Login Sequence SAS:Login Policy Update sasNMASProductOptions sasPolicyMethods sasPolicyServices sasPolicyUsers sasAllowNDSPassword Window sasLoginFailureDelay nspmPasswordPolicyDN

Table C.1 Continued

CLASS NAME	CLASS FLAGS	SUPERCLASS	CONTAINMENT	NAMED BY	MANDATORY ATTRIBUTES	OPTIONAL ATTRIBUTES
SAS:NMAS Base Login Method	DS_CONTAINER_CLASS	Top	SAS:Login Method Container	CN	CN	Description
						SAS:Login Secret
						SAS:Login Secret Key
						SAS:Encryption Type
						SAS:Login Configuration
						SAS:Login Configuration Key
						SAS:Method Identifier
						SAS:Method Vendor
						SAS:Vendor Support
						SAS:Advisory Method Grade
						SAS:Login Client Method NetWare
						SAS:Login Server Method NetWare
						SAS:Login Client Method WINNT
						SAS:Login Server Method WINNT
						sasCertificateSearch Containers
						sasNMASMethodConfigData
						sasMethodVersion
						SAS:Login Policy Update
						sasLoginClientMethod Solaris
						sasLoginServerMethod Solaris
						sasLoginClientMethod Linux

Table C.1 Continued

CLASS NAME	CLASS FLAGS	SUPERCLASS	CONTAINMENT	NAMED BY	MANDATORY ATTRIBUTES	OPTIONAL ATTRIBUTES
						sasLoginServerMethod Linux sasLoginClientMethod Tru64 sasLoginServerMethod Tru64 sasLoginClientMethodAIX sasLoginServerMethodAIX sasLoginClientMethodHPUX sasLoginServerMethodHPUX sasLoginClientMethods390 sasLoginServerMethods390
SAS:NMAS Login Method	DS_CONTAINER_CLASS DS_EFFECTIVE_CLASS	SAS:NMAS Base Login Method	—	—	—	—
SAS:Security	DS_CONTAINER_CLASS DS_EFFECTIVE_CLASS	Top	Top Tree Root Country Organization domain	CN	CN	NDSPKI:Tree CA DN masvPolicyDN SAS:Login Policy DN SAS:Login Method Container DN sasPostLoginMethod ContainerDN nspmPolicyAgentContainer DN
SAS:Service	DS_EFFECTIVE_CLASS	Resource	—	CN	—	Host Server Private Key Public Key Allow Unlimited Credit Full Name Last Login Time Locked By Intruder

Table C.1   Continued

CLASS NAME	CLASS FLAGS	SUPERCLASS	CONTAINMENT	NAMED BY	MANDATORY ATTRIBUTES	OPTIONAL ATTRIBUTES
						Login Allowed Time Map
						Login Disabled
						Login Expiration Time
						Login Intruder Address
						Login Intruder Attempts
						Login Intruder Reset Time
						Login Maximum Simultaneous
						Login Time
						Network Address
						Network Address Restriction
						Notify
						Operator
						Owner
						Path
						Security Equals
						Security Flags
						Status
						Version
						NDSPKI:Key Material DN
sasPostLoginMethod	DS_CONTAINER_CLASS DS_EFFECTIVE_CLASS	Top	sasPostLogin Method Container	CN	CN	Description
						SAS:Login Secret
						SAS:Login Secret Key
						SAS:Encryption Type
						SAS:Login Configuration
						SAS:Login Configuration Key
						SAS:Method Identifier
						SAS:Method Vendor

Table C.1 Continued

CLASS NAME	CLASS FLAGS	SUPERCLASS	CONTAINMENT	NAMED BY	MANDATORY ATTRIBUTES	OPTIONAL ATTRIBUTES
						SAS:Vendor Support
						SAS:Advisory Method Grade
						SAS:Login Client Method NetWare
						SAS:Login Server Method NetWare
						SAS:Login Client Method WINNT
						SAS:Login Server Method WINNT
						sasMethodVersion
						SAS:Login Policy Update
						sasLoginClientMethod Solaris
						sasLoginServerMethod Solaris
						sasLoginClientMethod Linux
						sasLoginServerMethod Linux
						sasLoginClientMethod Tru64
						sasLoginServerMethod Tru64
						sasLoginClientMethodAIX
						sasLoginServerMethodAIX
						sasLoginClientMethodHPUX
						sasLoginServerMethodHPUX
						sasLoginClientMethods390
						sasLoginServerMethods390

Table C.1 Continued

CLASS NAME	CLASS FLAGS	SUPERCLASS	CONTAINMENT	NAMED BY	MANDATORY ATTRIBUTES	OPTIONAL ATTRIBUTES
sasPostLogin MethodContainer	DS_CONTAINER_CLASS DS_EFFECTIVE_CLASS	Top	SAS:Security	CN	CN	Description
Server	DS_NONREMOVABLE_CLASS	Top	Organization domain Organizational Unit	CN	CN	Description Host Device L OU O Private Key Public Key Resource See Also Status User Version Network Address Account Balance Allow Unlimited Credit Minimum Account Balance Full Name Security Equals Security Flags Timezone ndapClassPasswordMgmt
slServerConfig	DS_AMBIGUOUS_NAMING DS_AMBIGUOUS_CONTAINMENT DS_AUXILIARY_CLASS	Top	Top	—	—	slConfigData slConfiglist Auxiliary Class Flag

Table C.1 Continued

CLASS NAME	CLASS FLAGS	SUPERCLASS	CONTAINMENT	NAMED BY	MANDATORY ATTRIBUTES	OPTIONAL ATTRIBUTES
snmpGroup	DS_EFFECTIVE_CLASS	Top	Country Locality Organization domain Organizational Unit	CN	CN	Version snmpServerList snmpTrapDisable snmpTrapInterval snmpTrapDescription snmpTrapConfig
strong AuthenticationUser	DS_AMBIGUOUS_NAMING DS_AMBIGUOUS_CONTAINMENT DS_AUXILIARY_CLASS	Top	Top	—	—	userCertificate Auxiliary Class Flag
Template	DS_EFFECTIVE_CLASS	Top	Organizational Unit Organization	CN	CN	Trustees Of New Object New Object's DS Rights New Object's FS Rights Setup Script Run Setup Script Members Of Template Volume Space Restrictions Set Password After Create Home Directory Rights Account Balance Allow Unlimited Credit Description EMail Address Facsimile Telephone Number Group Membership Higher Privileges Home Directory L Language

Table C.1 Continued

CLASS NAME	CLASS FLAGS	SUPERCLASS	CONTAINMENT	NAMED BY	MANDATORY ATTRIBUTES	OPTIONAL ATTRIBUTES
						Login Allowed Time Map
						Login Disabled
						Login Expiration Time
						Login Grace Limit
						Login Maximum Simultaneous
						Login Script
						Mailbox ID
						Mailbox Location
						Member
						Message Server
						Minimum Account Balance
						Network Address
						Restriction
						New Object's Self Rights
						OU
						Password Allow Change
						Password Expiration Interval
						Password Expiration Time
						Password Minimum Length
						Password Required
						Password Unique Required
						Physical Delivery Office Name
						Postal Address
						Postal Code
						Postal Office Box

Table C.1 Continued

CLASS NAME	CLASS FLAGS	SUPERCLASS	CONTAINMENT	NAMED BY	MANDATORY ATTRIBUTES	OPTIONAL ATTRIBUTES
						Profile
						S
						SA
						Security Equals
						Security Flags
						See Also
						Telephone Number
						Title
						assistant
						assistantPhone
						city
						company
						co
						manager
						managerWorkforceID
						mailstop
						siteLocation
						employeeType
						costCenter
						costCenterDescription
						tollFreePhoneNumber
						departmentNumber
Top	DS_CONTAINER_CLASS	—	—	—	Object Class	CA Public Key
	DS_EFFECTIVE_CLASS					CA Private Key
	DS_NONREMOVABLE_CLASS					Certificate Validity
	DS_AMBIGUOUS_NAMING					Interval
	DS_AMBIGUOUS_CONTAINMENT					Authority Revocation
						Last Referenced Time
						Equivalent To Me
						ACL
						Back Link

Table C.1 Continued

CLASS NAME	CLASS FLAGS	SUPERCLASS	CONTAINMENT	NAMED BY	MANDATORY ATTRIBUTES	OPTIONAL ATTRIBUTES
						Bindery Property
						Obituary
						Reference
						Revision
						Cross Certificate Pair
						Certificate Revocation
						Used By
						GUID
						Other GUID
						DirXML-Associations
						creatorsName
						modifiersName
						objectVersion
						auxClassCompatibility
						Unknown Base Class
						Unknown Auxiliary Class
						masvProposedLabel
						masvDefaultRange
						masvAuthorizedRange
						Audit:File Link
						rbsAssignedRoles
						rbsOwnedCollections
						rbsAssignedRoles2
						rbsOwnedCollections2
Tree Root	DS_CONTAINER_CLASS DS_EFFECTIVE_CLASS DS_NONREMOVABLE_CLASS	Top	[Nothing]	T	T	—
Unknown	DS_CONTAINER_CLASS DS_EFFECTIVE_CLASS DS_NONREMOVABLE_CLASS	Top	—	—	—	—

Table C.1 Continued

CLASS NAME	CLASS FLAGS	SUPERCLASS	CONTAINMENT	NAMED BY	MANDATORY ATTRIBUTES	OPTIONAL ATTRIBUTES
User	DS_EFFECTIVE_CLASS DS_NONREMOVABLE_CLASS	Organizational Person	—	—	—	Group Membership Home Directory Login Allowed Time Map Login Disabled Login Expiration Time Login Grace Limit Login Grace Remaining Login Intruder Address Login Intruder Attempts Login Intruder Reset Time Login Maximum Simultaneous Login Script Login Time Network Address Restriction Network Address Passwords Used Password Allow Change Password Expiration Interval Password Expiration Time Password Minimum Length Password Required Password Unique Required Print Job Configuration Private Key Profile Public Key

Table C.1   Continued

CLASS NAME	CLASS FLAGS	SUPERCLASS	CONTAINMENT	NAMED BY	MANDATORY ATTRIBUTES	OPTIONAL ATTRIBUTES
						Security Equals
						Account Balance
						Allow Unlimited Credit
						Minimum Account Balance
						Message Server
						Language
						UID
						Locked By Intruder
						Server Holds
						Last Login Time
						Type Creator Map
						Higher Privileges
						Printer Control
						Security Flags
						Profile Membership
						Timezone
						SAS:Service DN
						SAS:SecretStore
						SAS:SecretStore:Key
						SAS:SecretStore:Data
						SAS:PKIStore:Keys
						userCertificate
						NDSPKI:userCertificate Info
						NDSPKI:Keystore
						RADIUS:Active Connections
						RADIUS:Attribute Lists
						RADIUS:Concurrent Limit
						RADIUS:Connection History
						RADIUS:Default Profile

Table C.1 Continued

CLASS NAME	CLASS FLAGS	SUPERCLASS	CONTAINMENT	NAMED BY	MANDATORY ATTRIBUTES	OPTIONAL ATTRIBUTES
						RADIUS:Dial Access Group
						RADIUS:Enable Dial Access
						RADIUS:Password
						RADIUS:Service List
						audio
						businessCategory
						carLicense
						departmentNumber
						NSCP:employeeNumber
						employeeType
						displayName
						Given Name
						homePhone
						homePostalAddress
						Initials
						jpegPhoto
						labeledUri
						Internet EMail Address
						manager
						mobile
						O
						pager
						ldapPhoto
						preferredLanguage
						roomNumber
						secretary
						uniqueID
						userSMIMECertificate
						x500UniqueIdentifier
						userPKCS12

Table C.1 Continued

CLASS NAME	CLASS FLAGS	SUPERCLASS	CONTAINMENT	NAMED BY	MANDATORY ATTRIBUTES	OPTIONAL ATTRIBUTES
userSecurity Information	DS_AMBIGUOUS_NAMING DS_AMBIGUOUS_CONTAINMENT DS_AUXILIARY_CLASS	Top	Top	—	—	supportedAlgorithms Auxiliary Class Flag
Volume	DS_EFFECTIVE_CLASS DS_NONREMOVABLE_CLASS	Resource	—	—	Host Server	Status
WANMAN:LAN Area	DS_EFFECTIVE_CLASS	Top	Country Locality Organization Organizational Unit	CN	CN	Description L Member O OU Owner See Also WANMAN:WAN Policy WANMAN:Cost WANMAN:Default Cost

Base Attributes

Table C.2 lists all 572 attributes defined for eDirectory 8.7.3. For each attribute, its value's range is listed, and any special definition flags used when the attribute is defined (such as if the attribute is single-valued or is nonremovable) are also shown. The following definition flags are used by NDS/eDirectory:

- ▶ **Single Valued (DS_SINGLE_VALUED_ATTR)**—The attribute is single valued. By default, if this flag is not specified, an attribute may contain multiple values.

- ▶ **Sized Attribute (DS_SIZED_ATTR)**—The attribute has length or range limits. For example, the **Postal Code** attribute is limited to 0x28 or 40 bytes in size.

- ▶ **Nonremovable (DS_NONREMOVABLE_ATTR)**—The attribute cannot be deleted. By default, an attribute definition may be removed from the schema.

- ▶ **Read-Only Attribute (DS_READ_ONLY_ATTR)**—Clients cannot write to the attribute but can read its value.

- ▶ **Hidden Attribute (DS_HIDDEN_ATTR)**—Clients can neither read from nor write to the attribute.

- ▶ **String Attribute (DS_STRING_ATTR)**—Attribute syntax is string. An attribute that does not have this flag set cannot be used as a naming attribute.

- ▶ **Sync Immediate (DS_SYNC_IMMEDIATE_ATTR)**—The attribute value is scheduled for immediate synchronization. This is required on some attributes, such as the **Password Required** attribute of an **User** object, to maintain either proper data integrity or security.

- ▶ **Public Read (DS_PUBLIC_READ_ATTR)**—Anyone can read this attribute without needing **Read** privileges to be assigned. You cannot use an Inheritance Rights Filter (IRF) to block access to an attribute flagged as Public Read.

- ▶ **Server Read (DS_SERVER_READ_ATTR)**—**Server** class objects can read the attribute without an inherited or explicit **Read** right for this attribute.

- ▶ **Write Managed (DS_WRITE_MANAGED)**—This flag forces the user to have **Supervisor** rights to the attribute before it can be modified. This flag can only be used on attributes that use **SYN_DIST_NAME** syntax. **Group Membership** is one such example.

▶ **Per Replica (`DS_PER_REPLICA`)**—The information of the attribute is not synchronized with other servers in the replica ring. This flag is mostly used by DirXML-related attributes.

▶ **Sync Never (`DS_SCHEDULE_SYNC_NEVER`)**—The name of this flag is a little misleading. This flag indicates that changes to the attribute's value do not trigger synchronization (immediately). The attribute can wait to propagate the change until the next regularly scheduled synchronization cycle or some other event triggers synchronization.

▶ **Operational (`DS_OPERATIONAL`)**—This flag is used internally by NDS to indicate that the attribute definition must be present for NDS to function correctly. It was introduced in NDS 8 to provide compatibility with LDAP.

TABLE C.2   **eDirectory 8.7.3 Attribute Definitions**

ATTRIBUTE NAME	DEFINITION FLAGS	SYNTAX	LOWER LIMIT	UPPER LIMIT
[Anything]	—	SYN_OCTET_STRING	0x0000	0xFFFF
[Nothing]	—	SYN_OCTET_STRING	0x0000	0xFFFF
accessCardNumber	String Attribute Sync Immediate	SYN_CI_STRING	0x0000	0xFFFF
Account Balance	Single Valued Nonremovable Sync Immediate	SYN_COUNTER	0x0000	0xFFFF
ACL	Nonremovable Sync Immediate	SYN_OBJECT_ACL	0x0000	0xFFFF
Aliased Object Name	Single Valued Nonremovable Sync Immediate	SYN_DIST_NAME	0x0000	0xFFFF
Allow Unlimited Credit	Single Valued Nonremovable Sync Immediate	SYN_BOOLEAN	0x0000	0xFFFF
assistant	Sync Immediate	SYN_DIST_NAME	0x0000	0xFFFF
assistantPhone	String Attribute Sync Immediate	SYN_TEL_NUMBER	0x0000	0xFFFF
associatedName	Sync Immediate	SYN_DIST_NAME	0x0000	0xFFFF
attribute Certificate	Sync Immediate Public Read	SYN_OCTET_STRING	0x0000	0xFFFF
audio	Sync Immediate	SYN_OCTET_STRING	0x0000	0xFFFF

Table 3.2   Continued

ATTRIBUTE NAME	DEFINITION FLAGS	SYNTAX	LOWER LIMIT	UPPER LIMIT
Audit:A Encryption Key	Single Valued Sync Immediate	SYN_OCTET_STRING	0x0000	0xFFFF
Audit:B Encryption Key	Single Valued Sync Immediate	SYN_OCTET_STRING	0x0000	0xFFFF
Audit:Contents	Single Valued Sync Immediate	SYN_INTEGER	0x0000	0xFFFF
Audit:Current Encryption Key	SingleValued Sync Immediate	SYN_OCTET_STRING	0x0000	0xFFFF
Audit:File Link	Single Valued Sync Immediate	SYN_DIST_NAME	0x0000	0xFFFF
Audit:Link List	Sync Immediate	SYN_DIST_NAME	0x0000	0xFFFF
Audit:Path	Single Valued Sync Immediate	SYN_PATH	0x0000	0xFFFF
Audit:Policy	Single Valued Sync Immediate	SYN_OCTET_STRING	0x0000	0xFFFF
Audit:Type	Single Valued Sync Immediate	SYN_INTEGER	0x0000	0xFFFF
authoritative	Single Valued	SYN_INTEGER	0x0000	0xFFFF
Authority Revocation	Single Valued Nonremovable Read-Only Attribute Sync Immediate	SYN_OCTET_STRING	0x0000	0xFFFF
authority RevocationList	Sync Immediate Public Read	SYN_OCTET_STRING	0x0000	0xFFFF
AuxClass Object Class Backup	Nonremovable Read-Only Attribute Sync Immediate Operational	SYN_CLASS_NAME	0x0000	0xFFFF
auxClass Compatibility	Nonremovable Read-Only Attribute Sync Immediate Public Read Operational	SYN_CLASS_NAME	0x0000	0xFFFF
Auxiliary Class Flag	Single Valued Nonremovable Read-Only Attribute Sync Immediate Operational	SYN_UNKNOWN	0x0000	0xFFFF

Table C.2   Continued

ATTRIBUTE NAME	DEFINITION FLAGS	SYNTAX	LOWER LIMIT	UPPER LIMIT
Back Link	Nonremovable Read-Only Attribute Server Read	SYN_BACK_LINK	0x0000	0xFFFF
Bindery Object Restriction	Single Valued Nonremovable Read-Only Attribute	SYN_INTEGER	0x0000	0xFFFF
Bindery Property	Nonremovable Read-Only Attribute	SYN_OCTET_STRING	0x0000	0xFFFF
Bindery Restriction Level	Single Valued Nonremovable Operational	SYN_INTEGER	0x0000	0xFFFF
Bindery Type	Single Valued Nonremovable Read-Only Attribute String Attribute	SYN_NU_STRING	0x0000	0xFFFF
businessCategory	Sized Attribute String Attribute Sync Immediate	SYN_CI_STRING	0x0001	0x0080
c	Single Valued Sized Attribute Nonremovable String Attribute Sync Immediate	SYN_CI_STRING	0x0002	0x0002
CA Private Key	Single Valued Nonremovable Read-Only Attribute Hidden Attribute Sync Immediate	SYN_OCTET_STRING	0x0000	0xFFFF
CA Public Key	Single Valued Nonremovable Read-Only Attribute Sync Immediate Public Read	SYN_OCTET_STRING	0x0000	0xFFFF
cACertificate	Sync Immediate Public Read	SYN_OCTET_STRING	0x0000	0xFFFF
carLicense	String Attribute Sync Immediate	SYN_CI_STRING	0x0000	0xFFFF
Cartridge	Nonremovable String Attribute Sync Immediate	SYN_CI_STRING	0x0000	0xFFFF

Table 3.2   Continued

ATTRIBUTE NAME	DEFINITION FLAGS	SYNTAX	LOWER LIMIT	UPPER LIMIT
Certificate Revocation	Single Valued Nonremovable Read-Only Attribute Sync Immediate	SYN_OCTET_STRING	0x0000	0xFFFF
Certificate Validity Interval	Single Valued Sized Attribute Nonremovable Sync Immediate	SYN_INTERVAL	0x003C	0xFFFF
certificate RevocationList	Sync Immediate Public Read	SYN_OCTET_STRING	0x0000	0xFFFF
children	String Attribute Sync Immediate	SYN_CI_STRING	0x0000	0xFFFF
city	String Attribute Sync Immediate	SYN_CI_STRING	0x0000	0xFFFF
CN	Sized Attribute Nonremovable String Attribute Sync Immediate	SYN_CI_STRING	0x0001	0x0040
co	String Attribute Sync Immediate	SYN_CI_STRING	0x0000	0xFFFF
company	String Attribute Sync Immediate	SYN_CI_STRING	0x0000	0xFFFF
Convergence	Single Valued Sized Attribute Nonremovable Sync Immediate	SYN_INTEGER	0x0000	0x0001
costCenter	String Attribute Sync Immediate	SYN_CI_STRING	0x0000	0xFFFF
costCenter Description	String Attribute Sync Immediate	SYN_CI_STRING	0x0000	0xFFFF
creatorsName	Single Valued Nonremovable Read-Only Attribute String Attribute Sync Immediate Operational	SYN_CI_STRING	0x0000	0xFFFF
Cross Certificate Pair	Nonremovable Sync Immediate	SYN_OCTET_STRING	0x0000	0xFFFF
crossCertificate Pair	Sync Immediate Public Read	SYN_OCTET_STRING	0x0000	0xFFFF

Table C.2   Continued

ATTRIBUTE NAME	DEFINITION FLAGS	SYNTAX	LOWER LIMIT	UPPER LIMIT
dc	Sized Attribute Nonremovable String Attribute Sync Immediate	SYN_CI_STRING	0x0001	0x0040
Default Queue	Single Valued Nonremovable Sync Immediate Server Read	SYN_DIST_NAME	0x0000	0xFFFF
deltaRevocation List	Sync Immediate Public Read	SYN_OCTET_STRING	0x0000	0xFFFF
departmentNumber	String Attribute Sync Immediate	SYN_CI_STRING	0x0000	0xFFFF
Description	Sized Attribute Nonremovable String Attribute Sync Immediate	SYN_CI_STRING	0x0001	0x0400
destination Indicator	Sized Attribute String Attribute Sync Immediate	SYN_PR_STRING	0x0001	0x0080
Detect Intruder	Single Valued Nonremovable Sync Immediate	SYN_BOOLEAN	0x0000	0xFFFF
Device	Nonremovable Sync Immediate	SYN_DIST_NAME	0x0000	0xFFFF
dgAllowDuplicates	Single Valued Sync Immediate	SYN_BOOLEAN	0x0000	0xFFFF
dgAllowUnknown	Single Valued Sync Immediate	SYN_BOOLEAN	0x0000	0xFFFF
dgIdentity	Single Valued Sync Immediate Write Managed	SYN_DIST_NAME	0x0000	0xFFFF
dgTimeOut	Single Valued Sync Immediate	SYN_INTEGER	0x0000	0xFFFF
digitalMeID	Single Valued Sync Immediate	SYN_PATH	0x0000	0xFFFF
directReports	Sync Immediate	SYN_DIST_NAME	0x0000	0xFFFF
DirXML-Associations	Nonremovable Sync Immediate Operational	SYN_PATH	0x0000	0xFFFF

Table 3.2 Continued

ATTRIBUTE NAME	DEFINITION FLAGS	SYNTAX	LOWER LIMIT	UPPER LIMIT
displayName	String Attribute Sync Immediate	SYN_CI_STRING	0x0000	0xFFFF
dmdName	Sized Attribute String Attribute Sync Immediate	SYN_CI_STRING	0x0001	0x8000
dn	Single Valued Sync Immediate	SYN_DIST_NAME	0x0000	0xFFFF
dnQualifier	String Attribute Sync Immediate	SYN_PR_STRING	0x0000	0xFFFF
DS Revision	Single Valued Nonremovable Sync Immediate Public Read	SYN_INTEGER	0x0000	0xFFFF
edirSchemaFlag Version	Single Valued Nonremovable Read-Only Attribute Hidden Attribute Sync Immediate Operational	SYN_UNKNOWN	0x0000	0xFFFF
EMail Address	Nonremovable Sync Immediate Public Read	SYN_EMAIL_ADDRESS	0x0000	0xFFFF
emboxConfig	Single Valued Sync Immediate	SYN_OCTET_STRING	0x0000	0xFFFF
employeeStatus	String Attribute Sync Immediate	SYN_CI_STRING	0x0000	0xFFFF
employeeType	String Attribute Sync Immediate	SYN_CI_STRING	0x0000	0xFFFF
enhancedSearch Guide	Sync Immediate	SYN_OCTET_STRING	0x0000	0xFFFF
Equivalent To Me	Nonremovable Sync Immediate Server Read	SYN_DIST_NAME	0x0000	0xFFFF
excludedMember	Nonremovable Sync Immediate	SYN_DIST_NAME	0x0000	0xFFFF
extensionInfo	Sync Immediate Public Read	SYN_OCTET_STRING	0x0000	0xFFFF
External Name	Single Valued Nonremovable Sync Immediate	SYN_OCTET_STRING	0x0000	0xFFFF

Table C.2 Continued

ATTRIBUTE NAME	DEFINITION FLAGS	SYNTAX	LOWER LIMIT	UPPER LIMIT
External Synchronizer	Nonremovable Sync Immediate	SYN_OCTET_STRING	0x0000	0xFFFF
Facsimile Telephone Number	Nonremovable Sync Immediate	SYN_FAX_NUMBER	0x0000	0xFFFF
federation BoundaryType	Single Valued Nonremovable Read-Only Attribute Sync Immediate Operational	SYN_INTEGER	0x0000	0xFFFF
federationControl	Nonremovable Sync Immediate Operational	SYN_PATH	0x0000	0xFFFF
federationDNSName	Single Valued Nonremovable Sync Immediate Public Read Operational	SYN_DIST_NAME	0x0000	0xFFFF
federation SearchPath	Single Valued Nonremovable Sync Immediate Operational	SYN_CI_LIST	0x0000	0xFFFF
filteredReplica Usage	Single Valued Sync Immediate	SYN_INTEGER	0x0000	0xFFFF
Full Name	Sized Attribute Nonremovable String Attribute Sync Immediate	SYN_CI_STRING	0x0000	0x007F
Generational Qualifier	Single Valued Sized Attribute Nonremovable String Attribute Sync Immediate Public Read	SYN_CI_STRING	0x0001	0x0008
GID	Single Valued Nonremovable Sync Immediate	SYN_INTEGER	0x0000	0xFFFF
Given Name	Sized Attribute Nonremovable String Attribute Sync Immediate Public Read	SYN_CI_STRING	0x0001	0x0020

Table 3.2 Continued

ATTRIBUTE NAME	DEFINITION FLAGS	SYNTAX	LOWER LIMIT	UPPER LIMIT
Group Membership	Nonremovable Sync Immediate Write Managed	SYN_DIST_NAME	0x0000	0xFFFF
GUID	Single Valued Sized Attribute Nonremovable Read-Only Attribute Sync Immediate Public Read Operational	SYN_OCTET_STRING	0x0010	0x0010
High Convergence Sync Interval	Single Valued Nonremovable Sync Immediate	SYN_INTERVAL	0x0000	0xFFFF
Higher Privileges	Nonremovable Sync Immediate Server Read Write Managed	SYN_DIST_NAME	0x0000	0xFFFF
Home Directory	Single Valued Sized Attribute Nonremovable Sync Immediate	SYN_PATH	0x0001	0x00FF
Home Directory Rights	—	SYN_INTEGER	0x0000	0xFFFF
homeCity	String Attribute Sync Immediate	SYN_CI_STRING	0x0000	0xFFFF
homeEmailAddress	String Attribute Sync Immediate	SYN_CI_STRING	0x0000	0xFFFF
homeFax	String Attribute Sync Immediate	SYN_TEL_NUMBER	0x0000	0xFFFF
homePhone	String Attribute Sync Immediate	SYN_TEL_NUMBER	0x0000	0xFFFF
homePostalAddress	Sync Immediate	SYN_PO_ADDRESS	0x0000	0xFFFF
homeState	String Attribute Sync Immediate	SYN_CI_STRING	0x0000	0xFFFF
homeZipCode	String Attribute Sync Immediate	SYN_CI_STRING	0x0000	0xFFFF
Host Device	Single Valued Nonremovable Sync Immediate	SYN_DIST_NAME	0x0000	0xFFFF

Table C.2 Continued

ATTRIBUTE NAME	DEFINITION FLAGS	SYNTAX	LOWER LIMIT	UPPER LIMIT
Host Resource Name	Single Valued Nonremovable String Attribute Sync Immediate	SYN_CI_STRING	0x0000	0xFFFF
Host Server	Single Valued Nonremovable Sync Immediate	SYN_DIST_NAME	0x0000	0xFFFF
houseIdentifier	Sized Attribute String Attribute Sync Immediate	SYN_CI_STRING	0x0001	0x8000
httpAuth RequiresTLS	Single Valued Sync Immediate	SYN_INTEGER	0x0000	0xFFFF
httpDefault ClearPort	Single Valued Sync Immediate	SYN_INTEGER	0x0000	0xFFFF
httpDefaultTLS Port	Single Valued Sync Immediate	SYN_INTEGER	0x0000	0xFFFF
httpHostServerDN	Single Valued Sync Immediate	SYN_DIST_NAME	0x0000	0xFFFF
httpIOBufferSize	Single Valued Sync Immediate	SYN_INTEGER	0x0000	0xFFFF
httpKeepAlive RequestTimeout	Single Valued Sync Immediate	SYN_INTEGER	0x0000	0xFFFF
httpKeyMaterial Object	Single Valued Sync Immediate	SYN_DIST_NAME	0x0000	0xFFFF
httpRequest Timeout	Single Valued Sync Immediate	SYN_INTEGER	0x0000	0xFFFF
httpServerDN	Sync Immediate	SYN_DIST_NAME	0x0000	0xFFFF
httpSession Timeout	Single Valued Sync Immediate	SYN_INTEGER	0x0000	0xFFFF
httpThreadsPerCPU	Single Valued Sync Immediate	SYN_INTEGER	0x0000	0xFFFF
httpTraceLevel	Single Valued Sync Immediate	SYN_INTEGER	0x0000	0xFFFF
indexDefinition	—	SYN_CI_LIST	0x0000	0xFFFF
Inherited ACL	Nonremovable Read-Only Attribute Sync Immediate	SYN_OBJECT_ACL	0x0000	0xFFFF

Table 3.2 Continued

ATTRIBUTE NAME	DEFINITION FLAGS	SYNTAX	LOWER LIMIT	UPPER LIMIT
Initials	Sized Attribute Nonremovable String Attribute Sync Immediate Public Read	SYN_CI_STRING	0x0001	0x0008
instantMessaging ID	String Attribute Sync Immediate	SYN_CI_STRING	0x0000	0xFFFF
international iSDNNumber	Sized Attribute String Attribute Sync Immediate	SYN_NU_STRING	0x0001	0x0010
Internet EMail Address	String Attribute Sync Immediate Public Read	SYN_CI_STRING	0x0000	0xFFFF
Intruder Attempt Reset Interval	Single Valued Nonremovable Sync Immediate	SYN_INTERVAL	0x0000	0xFFFF
Intruder Lockout Reset Interval	Single Valued Nonremovable Sync Immediate	SYN_INTERVAL	0x0000	0xFFFF
isManager	Single Valued Sync Immediate	SYN_BOOLEAN	0x0000	0xFFFF
jackNumber	String Attribute Sync Immediate	SYN_CI_STRING	0x0000	0xFFFF
jobCode	String Attribute Sync Immediate	SYN_CI_STRING	0x0000	0xFFFF
jpegPhoto	Sync Immediate	SYN_OCTET_STRING	0x0000	0xFFFF
knowledge Information	Sized Attribute String Attribute Sync Immediate	SYN_CI_STRING	0x0001	0x8000
L	Sized Attribute Nonremovable String Attribute Sync Immediate	SYN_CI_STRING	0x0001	0x0080
labeledUri	String Attribute Sync Immediate	SYN_CI_STRING	0x0000	0xFFFF
Language	Single Valued Nonremovable Sync Immediate	SYN_CI_LIST	0x0000	0xFFFF

Table C.2 Continued

ATTRIBUTE NAME	DEFINITION FLAGS	SYNTAX	LOWER LIMIT	UPPER LIMIT
languageId	Nonremovable String Attribute Sync Immediate	SYN_CI_STRING	0x0000	0xFFFF
Last Login Time	Single Valued Nonremovable Read-Only Attribute	SYN_TIME	0x0000	0xFFFF
Last Referenced Time	Single Valued Nonremovable Per Replica	SYN_TIMESTAMP	0x0000	0xFFFF
LDAP Allow Clear Text Password	Single Valued Sync Immediate	SYN_BOOLEAN	0x0000	0xFFFF
LDAP Anonymous Identity	Single Valued Sync Immediate	SYN_DIST_NAME	0x0000	0xFFFF
LDAP Attribute Map v11	Single Valued Sync Immediate	SYN_OCTET_STRING	0x0000	0xFFFF
LDAP Backup Log Filename	Single Valued String Attribute Sync Immediate	SYN_CI_STRING	0x0000	0xFFFF
LDAP Class Map v11	Single Valued Sync Immediate	SYN_OCTET_STRING	0x0000	0xFFFF
LDAP Enable SSL	Single Valued Sync Immediate	SYN_BOOLEAN	0x0000	0xFFFF
LDAP Enable TCP	Single Valued Sync Immediate	SYN_BOOLEAN	0x0000	0xFFFF
LDAP Group	Single Valued Sync Immediate	SYN_DIST_NAME	0x0000	0xFFFF
LDAP Host Server	Single Valued Sync Immediate	SYN_DIST_NAME	0x0000	0xFFFF
LDAP Log Filename	Single Valued String Attribute Sync Immediate	SYN_CI_STRING	0x0000	0xFFFF
LDAP Log Level	Single Valued Sized Attribute Sync Immediate	SYN_INTEGER	0x0000	0x8000
LDAP Log Size Limit	Single Valued Sized Attribute Sync Immediate	SYN_INTEGER	0x0800	0xFFFF

Table 3.2   Continued

ATTRIBUTE NAME	DEFINITION FLAGS	SYNTAX	LOWER LIMIT	UPPER LIMIT
LDAP Referral	Single Valued String Attribute Sync Immediate	SYN_CI_STRING	0x0000	0xFFFF
LDAP Screen Level	Single Valued Sized Attribute Sync Immediate	SYN_INTEGER	0x0000	0x8000
LDAP Search Size Limit	Single Valued Sized Attribute Sync Immediate	SYN_INTEGER	0x0001	0xFFFF
LDAP Search Time Limit	Single Valued Sized Attribute Sync Immediate	SYN_INTEGER	0x0001	0xFFFF
LDAP Server Bind Limit	Single Valued Sized Attribute Sync Immediate	SYN_INTEGER	0x0000	0xFFFF
LDAP Server Idle Timeout	Single Valued Sized Attribute Sync Immediate	SYN_INTEGER	0x0000	0xFFFF
LDAP Server	Sync Immediate	SYN_DIST_NAME	0x0000	0xFFFF
LDAP Server List	Sync Immediate	SYN_DIST_NAME	0x0000	0xFFFF
LDAP SSL Port	Single Valued Sized Attribute Sync Immediate	SYN_INTEGER	0x0000	0xFFFF
LDAP Suffix	Sync Immediate	SYN_DIST_NAME	0x0000	0xFFFF
LDAP TCP Port	Single Valued Sized Attribute Sync Immediate	SYN_INTEGER	0x0000	0xFFFF
LDAP UDP Port	Single Valued Sized Attribute Sync Immediate	SYN_INTEGER	0x0000	0xFFFF
LDAP:key MaterialName	Single Valued String Attribute Sync Immediate	SYN_CI_STRING	0x0000	0xFFFF
LDAP:other ReferralUsage	Single Valued Sync Immediate	SYN_INTEGER	0x0000	0xFFFF
LDAP:search ReferralUsage	Single Valued Sync Immediate	SYN_INTEGER	0x0000	0xFFFF
ldapAttributeList	Sync Immediate	SYN_CI_LIST	0x0000	0xFFFF

Table C.2   Continued

ATTRIBUTE NAME	DEFINITION FLAGS	SYNTAX	LOWER LIMIT	UPPER LIMIT
ldapBind Restrictions	Single Valued Sync Immediate	SYN_INTEGER	0x0000	0xFFFF
ldapClassList	Sync Immediate	SYN_CI_LIST	0x0000	0xFFFF
ldapConfigVersion	Single Valued Sync Immediate	SYN_INTEGER	0x0000	0xFFFF
ldapDefault ReferralBehavior	Single Valued Sync Immediate	SYN_INTEGER	0x0000	0xFFFF
ldapDerefAlias	Single Valued Sync Immediate	SYN_BOOLEAN	0x0000	0xFFFF
ldapEnable MonitorEvents	Single Valued Sync Immediate	SYN_BOOLEAN	0x0000	0xFFFF
ldapEnablePSearch	Single Valued Sync Immediate	SYN_BOOLEAN	0x0000	0xFFFF
ldapIgnore PSearchLimits ForEvents	Single Valued Sync Immediate	SYN_BOOLEAN	0x0000	0xFFFF
ldapMaximum MonitorEventsLoad	Single Valued Sync Immediate	SYN_INTEGER	0x0000	0xFFFF
ldapMaximum PSearchOperations	Single Valued Sync Immediate	SYN_INTEGER	0x0000	0xFFFF
ldapNonStdAll UserAttrsMode	Single Valued Sync Immediate	SYN_BOOLEAN	0x0000	0xFFFF
ldapPhoto	Sync Immediate	SYN_OCTET_STRING	0x0000	0xFFFF
ldapTLSRequired	Single Valued Sync Immediate	SYN_BOOLEAN	0x0000	0xFFFF
ldapTLSTrusted RootContainer	Sync Immediate	SYN_DIST_NAME	0x0000	0xFFFF
ldapTLSVerify ClientCertificate	Single Valued Sync Immediate	SYN_INTEGER	0x0000	0xFFFF
ldapTransition BackLink	Single Valued Sync Immediate	SYN_DIST_NAME	0x0000	0xFFFF
Local Received Up To	Nonremovable Read-Only Attribute Public Read Per Replica Operational	SYN_OCTET_STRING	0x0000	0xFFFF
localFederation Boundary	Single Valued Nonremovable Operational	SYN_DIST_NAME	0x0000	0xFFFF

Table 3.2   Continued

ATTRIBUTE NAME	DEFINITION FLAGS	SYNTAX	LOWER LIMIT	UPPER LIMIT
localReferral	Single Valued Nonremovable OperationalF	SYN_OCTET_STRING	0x0000	0xFFF
Lockout After Detection	Single Valued Nonremovable Sync Immediate	SYN_BOOLEAN	0x0000	0xFFFF
Locked By Intruder	Single Valued Nonremovable Sync Immediate	SYN_BOOLEAN	0x0000	0xFFFF
Login Allowed Time Map	Single Valued Sized Attribute Nonremovable Sync Immediate	SYN_OCTET_STRING	0x002A	0x002A
Login Disabled	Single Valued Nonremovable Sync Immediate	SYN_BOOLEAN	0x0000	0xFFFF
Login Expiration Time	Single Valued Nonremovable Sync Immediate	SYN_TIME	0x0000	0xFFFF
Login Grace Limit	Single Valued Nonremovable Sync Immediate	SYN_INTEGER	0x0000	0xFFFF
Login Grace Remaining	Single Valued Nonremovable Sync Immediate	SYN_COUNTER	0x0000	0xFFFF
Login Intruder Address	Single Valued Nonremovable Sync Immediate	SYN_NET_ADDRESS	0x0000	0xFFFF
Login Intruder Attempts	Single Valued Nonremovable Sync Immediate	SYN_COUNTER	0x0000	0xFFFF
Login Intruder Limit	Single Valued Nonremovable Sync Immediate	SYN_INTEGER	0x0000	0xFFFF
Login Intruder Reset Time	Single Valued Nonremovable Sync Immediate	SYN_TIME	0x0000	0xFFFF
Login Maximum Simultaneous	Single Valued Nonremovable Sync Immediate	SYN_INTEGER	0x0000	0xFFFF

Table C.2 Continued

ATTRIBUTE NAME	DEFINITION FLAGS	SYNTAX	LOWER LIMIT	UPPER LIMIT
Login Script	Single Valued Nonremovable Sync Immediate	SYN_STREAM	0x0000	0xFFFF
Login Time	Single Valued Nonremovable	SYN_TIME	0x0000	0xFFFF
loginActivation Time	Single Valued Nonremovable Sync Immediate	SYN_TIME	0x0000	0xFFFF
Low Convergence Reset Time	Single Valued Nonremovable Sync Immediate	SYN_TIME	0x0000	0xFFFF
Low Convergence Sync Interval	Single Valued Nonremovable Sync Immediate	SYN_INTERVAL	0x0000	0xFFFF
Mailbox ID	Single Valued Sized Attribute Nonremovable String Attribute Sync Immediate Public Read	SYN_CI_STRING	0x0001	0x0008
Mailbox Location	Single Valued Nonremovable Sync Immediate Public Read	SYN_DIST_NAME	0x0000	0xFFFF
mailstop	String Attribute Sync Immediate	SYN_CI_STRING	0x0000	0xFFFF
manager	Sync Immediate	SYN_DIST_NAME	0x0000	0xFFFF
managerWork forceID	String Attribute Sync Immediate	SYN_CI_STRING	0x0000	0xFFFF
masvAuthorized Range	Sync Immediate Public Read	SYN_OCTET_STRING	0x0000	0xFFFF
masvClearanceNames	Sync Immediate Public Read	SYN_OCTET_STRING	0x0000	0xFFFF
masvDefaultRange	Single Valued Sync Immediate Public Read	SYN_OCTET_STRING	0x0000	0xFFFF
masvDomainPolicy	Single Valued Sync Immediate Public Read	SYN_OCTET_STRING	0x0000	0xFFFF

Table 3.2   Continued

ATTRIBUTE NAME	DEFINITION FLAGS	SYNTAX	LOWER LIMIT	UPPER LIMIT
masvLabel	Single Valued Sync Immediate Public Read	SYN_OCTET_STRING	0x0000	0xFFFF
masvLabelIntegrity CategoryNames	Sync Immediate Public Read	SYN_OCTET_STRING	0x0000	0xFFFF
masvLabelIntegrity LevelNames	Sync Immediate Public Read	SYN_OCTET_STRING	0x0000	0xFFFF
masvLabelNames	Sync Immediate Public Read	SYN_OCTET_STRING	0x0000	0xFFFF
masvLabelSecrecy CategoryNames	Sync Immediate Public Read	SYN_OCTET_STRING	0x0000	0xFFFF
masvLabelSecrecy LevelNames	Sync Immediate Public Read	SYN_OCTET_STRING	0x0000	0xFFFF
masvNDSAttribute Labels	Sync Immediate Public Read	SYN_OCTET_STRING	0x0000	0xFFFF
masvPolicyDN	Single Valued Public Read	SYN_DIST_NAME	0x0000	0xFFFF
masvPolicyUpdate	Single Valued Public Read	SYN_INTEGER	0x0000	0xFFFF
masvProposedLabel	Single Valued Sync Immediate Public Read	SYN_OCTET_STRING	0x0000	0xFFFF
Member	Nonremovable Sync Immediate	SYN_DIST_NAME	0x0000	0xFFFF
memberQuery	Nonremovable Sync Immediate	SYN_OCTET_STRING	0x0000	0xFFFF
Members Of Template	—	SYN_DIST_NAME	0x0000	0xFFFF
Memory	Single Valued Nonremovable Sync Immediate	SYN_INTEGER	0x0000	0xFFFF
Message Routing Group	Nonremovable Sync Immediate	SYN_DIST_NAME	0x0000	0xFFFF
Message Server	Single Valued Nonremovable Sync Immediate	SYN_DIST_NAME	0x0000	0xFFFF
Messaging Database Location	Single Valued Nonremovable Sync Immediate	SYN_PATH	0x0000	0xFFFF

Table C.2   Continued

ATTRIBUTE NAME	DEFINITION FLAGS	SYNTAX	LOWER LIMIT	UPPER LIMIT
Messaging Server	Nonremovable Sync Immediate	SYN_DIST_NAME	0x0000	0xFFFF
Messaging Server Type	Single Valued Sized Attribute Nonremovable String Attribute Sync Immediate	SYN_CI_STRING	0x0001	0x0020
Minimum Account Balance	Single Valued Nonremovable Sync Immediate	SYN_INTEGER	0x0000	0xFFFF
mobile	String Attribute Sync Immediate	SYN_TEL_NUMBER	0x0000	0xFFFF
modifiedACLEntry	Nonremovable Operational	SYN_DIST_NAME	0x0000	0xFFFF
modifiersName	Single Valued Nonremovable Read-Only Attribute String Attribute Sync Immediate Operational	SYN_CI_STRING	0x0000	0xFFFF
monitored Connection	Nonremovable Operational	SYN_OCTET_STRING	0x0000	0xFFFF
ndapClass PasswordMgmt	—	SYN_UNKNOWN	0x0000	0xFFFF
ndapPartition PasswordMgmt	Single Valued	SYN_INTEGER	0x0000	0xFFFF
ndapPasswordMgmt	Single Valued	SYN_INTEGER	0x0000	0xFFFF
ndsAgentPassword	Single Valued Nonremovable Read-Only Attribute Hidden Attribute Operational	SYN_OCTET_STRING	0x0000	0xFFFF
ndsOperation Checkpoint	Nonremovable Operational	SYN_OCTET_STRING	0x0000	0xFFFF
NDSPKI: CertificateChain	Sync Immediate Public Read	SYN_OCTET_STRING	0x0000	0xFFFF
NDSPKI:Given Name	Single Valued String Attribute Sync Immediate	SYN_CI_STRING	0x0000	0xFFFF

Table 3.2 Continued

ATTRIBUTE NAME	DEFINITION FLAGS	SYNTAX	LOWER LIMIT	UPPER LIMIT
NDSPKI:Key File	Single Valued Sync Immediate	SYN_OCTET_STRING	0x0000	0xFFFF
NDSPKI:Key Material DN	Sync Immediate	SYN_DIST_NAME	0x0000	0xFFFF
NDSPKI:Keystore	Hidden Attribute Sync Immediate	SYN_OCTET_STRING	0x0000	0xFFFF
NDSPKI:Not After	Single Valued String Attribute Sync Immediate Public Read	SYN_CI_STRING	0x0000	0xFFFF
NDSPKI:Not Before	Single Valued String Attribute Sync Immediate Public Read	SYN_CI_STRING	0x0000	0xFFFF
NDSPKI:Parent CA	Single Valued String Attribute Sync Immediate	SYN_CI_STRING	0x0000	0xFFFF
NDSPKI:Parent CA DN	Single Valued Sync Immediate	SYN_DIST_NAME	0x0000	0xFFFF
NDSPKI:Private Key	Single Valued Sync Immediate	SYN_OCTET_STRING	0x0000	0xFFFF
NDSPKI:Public Key	Single Valued Sync Immediate Public Read	SYN_OCTET_STRING	0x0000	0xFFFF
NDSPKI:Public Key Certificate	Single Valued Sync Immediate Public Read	SYN_OCTET_STRING	0x0000	0xFFFF
NDSPKI:SD Key Cert	Single Valued Sync Immediate	SYN_OCTET_STRING	0x0000	0xFFFF
NDSPKI:SD Key ID	Single Valued Sync Immediate	SYN_OCTET_STRING	0x0000	0xFFFF
NDSPKI:SD Key Server DN	Sync Immediate Server Read	SYN_DIST_NAME	0x0000	0xFFFF
NDSPKI:SD Key Struct	Sync Immediate	SYN_OCTET_STRING	0x0000	0xFFFF
NDSPKI:Subject Name	Single Valued String Attribute Sync Immediate	SYN_CI_STRING	0x0000	0xFFFF
NDSPKI:Tree CA DN	Sync Immediate	SYN_DIST_NAME	0x0000	0xFFFF

Table C.2   Continued

ATTRIBUTE NAME	DEFINITION FLAGS	SYNTAX	LOWER LIMIT	UPPER LIMIT
NDSPKI:Trusted Root Certificate	Single Valued Sync Immediate Public Read	SYN_OCTET_STRING	0x0000	0xFFFF
NDSPKI:user CertificateInfo	Sync Immediate	SYN_PATH	0x0000	0xFFFF
ndspkiAdditional Roots	Sync Immediate Public Read	SYN_OCTET_STRING	0x0000	0xFFFF
ndsPredicate	Nonremovable Sync Immediate	SYN_NET_ADDRESS	0x0000	0xFFFF
ndsPredicateFlush	Single Valued Nonremovable Sync Immediate	SYN_BOOLEAN	0x0000	0xFFFF
ndsPredicateState	Single Valued Nonremovable Sync Immediate	SYN_BOOLEAN	0x0000	0xFFFF
ndsPredicate StatsDN	Nonremovable Sync Immediate	SYN_DIST_NAME	0x0000	0xFFFF
ndsPredicate Timeout	Single Valued Sized Attribute Nonremovable Sync Immediate	SYN_INTEGER	0x0000	0xFFFF
ndsPredicate UseValues	Single Valued Nonremovable Sync Immediate	SYN_BOOLEAN	0x0000	0xFFFF
ndsStatusExternal Reference	—	SYN_OCTET_STRING	0x0000	0xFFFF
ndsStatusLimber	—	SYN_OCTET_STRING	0x0000	0xFFFF
ndsStatusObituary	—	SYN_OCTET_STRING	0x0000	0xFFFF
ndsStatusRepair	—	SYN_OCTET_STRING	0x0000	0xFFFF
ndsStatusSchema	—	SYN_OCTET_STRING	0x0000	0xFFFF
Network Address	Nonremovable Sync Immediate	SYN_NET_ADDRESS	0x0000	0xFFFF
Network Address Restriction	Nonremovable Sync Immediate	SYN_NET_ADDRESS	0x0000	0xFFFF
New Object's DS Rights	—	SYN_OBJECT_ACL	0x0000	0xFFFF

Table 3.2   Continued

ATTRIBUTE NAME	DEFINITION FLAGS	SYNTAX	LOWER LIMIT	UPPER LIMIT
New Object's FS Rights	—	SYN_PATH	0x0000	0xFFFF
New Object's Self Rights	—	SYN_OBJECT_ACL	0x0000	0xFFFF
NNS Domain	Sized Attribute Nonremovable String Attribute Sync Immediate	SYN_CI_STRING	0x0001	0x0080
nonStdClient SchemaCompatMode	Single Valued Sync Immediate	SYN_BOOLEAN	0x0000	0xFFFF
Notify	Nonremovable Sync Immediate	SYN_TYPED_NAME	0x0000	0xFFFF
NSCP:employee Number	String Attribute Sync Immediate	SYN_CI_STRING	0x0000	0xFFFF
nspmAdministrator ChangeCount	Single Valued Hidden Attribute Sync Immediate	SYN_COUNTER	0x0000	0xFFFF
nspmCaseSensitive	Single Valued	SYN_BOOLEAN	0x0000	0xFFFF
nspmChange PasswordMessage	Single Valued String Attribute	SYN_CE_STRING	0x0000	0xFFFF
nspmConfiguration Options	Single Valued	SYN_INTEGER	0x0000	0xFFFF
nspmDisallowed AttributeValues	String Attribute	SYN_CE_STRING	0x0000	0xFFFF
nspmDistribution Password	Single Valued Hidden Attribute Sync Immediate	SYN_OCTET_STRING	0x0000	0xFFFF
nspmExcludeList	Single Valued	SYN_STREAM	0x0000	0xFFFF
nspmExtended CharactersAllowed	Single Valued	SYN_BOOLEAN	0x0000	0xFFFF
nspmMaxConsecutive Characters	Single Valued	SYN_INTEGER	0x0000	0xFFFF
nspmMaximumLength	Single Valued	SYN_INTEGER	0x0000	0xFFFF
nspmMaxLowerCase Characters	Single Valued	SYN_INTEGER	0x0000	0xFFFF
nspmMaxNumeric Characters	Single Valued	SYN_INTEGER	0x0000	0xFFFF

Table C.2   Continued

ATTRIBUTE NAME	DEFINITION FLAGS	SYNTAX	LOWER LIMIT	UPPER LIMIT
nspmMaxRepeated Characters	Single Valued	SYN_INTEGER	0x0000	0xFFFF
nspmMaxSpecial Characters	Single Valued	SYN_INTEGER	0x0000	0xFFFF
nspmMaxUpperCase Characters	Single Valued	SYN_INTEGER	0x0000	0xFFFF
nspmMinLowerCase Characters	Single Valued	SYN_INTEGER	0x0000	0xFFFF
nspmMinNumeric Characters	Single Valued	SYN_INTEGER	0x0000	0xFFFF
nspmMinPassword Lifetime	Single Valued	SYN_INTEGER	0x0000	0xFFFF
nspmMinSpecial Characters	Single Valued	SYN_INTEGER	0x0000	0xFFFF
nspmMinUnique Characters	Single Valued	SYN_INTEGER	0x0000	0xFFFF
nspmMinUpperCase Characters	Single Valued	SYN_INTEGER	0x0000	0xFFFF
nspmNumericAs FirstCharacter	Single Valued	SYN_BOOLEAN	0x0000	0xFFFF
nspmNumericAs LastCharacter	Single Valued	SYN_BOOLEAN	0x0000	0xFFFF
nspmNumeric CharactersAllowed	Single Valued	SYN_BOOLEAN	0x0000	0xFFFF
nspmPassword	Single Valued Hidden Attribute Sync Immediate	SYN_OCTET_STRING	0x0000	0xFFFF
nspmPassword History	Hidden Attribute Sync Immediate	SYN_OCTET_STRING	0x0000	0xFFFF
nspmPassword HistoryExpiration	Single Valued	SYN_INTEGER	0x0000	0xFFFF
nspmPassword HistoryLimit	Single Valued	SYN_INTEGER	0x0000	0xFFFF
nspmPasswordKey	Single Valued Hidden Attribute Sync Immediate	SYN_OCTET_STRING	0x0000	0xFFFF
nspmPassword PolicyDN	Single Valued Public Read	SYN_DIST_NAME	0x0000	0xFFFF

Table 3.2 Continued

ATTRIBUTE NAME	DEFINITION FLAGS	SYNTAX	LOWER LIMIT	UPPER LIMIT
nspmPolicyAgentAIX	Single Valued Public Read	SYN_STREAM	0x0000	0xFFFF
nspmPolicyAgent ContainerDN	Single Valued Public Read	SYN_DIST_NAME	0x0000	0xFFFF
nspmPolicy AgentHPUX	Single Valued Public Read	SYN_STREAM	0x0000	0xFFFF
nspmPolicy AgentLinux	Single Valued Public Read	SYN_STREAM	0x0000	0xFFFF
nspmPolicyAgent NetWare	Single Valued Public Read	SYN_STREAM	0x0000	0xFFFF
nspmPolicyAgent Solaris	Single Valued Public Read	SYN_STREAM	0x0000	0xFFFF
nspmPolicyAgent WINNT	Single Valued Public Read	SYN_STREAM	0x0000	0xFFFF
nspmPolicy Precedence	Single Valued	SYN_INTEGER	0x0000	0xFFFF
nspmSpecialAs FirstCharacter	Single Valued	SYN_BOOLEAN	0x0000	0xFFFF
nspmSpecialAs LastCharacter	Single Valued	SYN_BOOLEAN	0x0000	0xFFFF
nspmSpecial CharactersAllowed	Single Valued	SYN_BOOLEAN	0x0000	0xFFFF
O	Sized Attribute Nonremovable String Attribute Sync Immediate	SYN_CI_STRING	0x0001	0x0040
Obituary	Nonremovable Read-Only Attribute Sync Immediate	SYN_OCTET_STRING	0x0000	0xFFFF
Obituary Notify	Nonremovable Read-Only Attribute Sync Immediate	SYN_OCTET_STRING	0x0000	0xFFFF
Object Class	Nonremovable Sync Immediate Public Read	SYN_CLASS_NAME	0x0000	0xFFFF

Table C.2   Continued

ATTRIBUTE NAME	DEFINITION FLAGS	SYNTAX	LOWER LIMIT	UPPER LIMIT
objectVersion	Single Valued Nonremovable Read-Only Attribute Sync Immediate Public Read Operational	SYN_TIMESTAMP	0x0000	0xFFFF
Operator	Nonremovable Sync Immediate Server Read	SYN_DIST_NAME	0x0000	0xFFFF
Other GUID	Sized Attribute Nonremovable Sync Immediate Public Read Operational	SYN_OCTET_STRING	0x0010	0x0010
otherPhoneNumber	String Attribute Sync Immediate	SYN_TEL_NUMBER	0x0000	0xFFFF
OU	Sized Attribute Nonremovable String Attribute Sync Immediate	SYN_CI_STRING	0x0001	0x0040
Owner	Nonremovable Sync Immediate	SYN_DIST_NAME	0x0000	0xFFFF
Page Description Language	Sized Attribute Nonremovable String Attribute Sync Immediate	SYN_PR_STRING	0x0001	0x0040
pager	String Attribute Sync Immediate	SYN_TEL_NUMBER	0x0000	0xFFFF
Partition Control	Nonremovable Read-Only Attribute Sync Immediate Public Read	SYN_TYPED_NAME	0x0000	0xFFFF
Partition Creation Time	Single Valued Nonremovable Read-Only Attribute Sync Immediate Public Read	SYN_TIMESTAMP	0x0000	0xFFFF

Table 3.2   Continued

ATTRIBUTE NAME	DEFINITION FLAGS	SYNTAX	LOWER LIMIT	UPPER LIMIT
Partition Status	Nonremovable Read-Only Attribute Public Read Per Replica Operational	SYN_OCTET_STRING	0x0000	0xFFFF
Password Allow Change	Single Valued Nonremovable Sync Immediate	SYN_BOOLEAN	0x0000	0xFFFF
Password Expiration Interval	Single Valued Nonremovable Sync Immediate	SYN_INTERVAL	0x0000	0xFFFF
Password Expiration Time	Single Valued Nonremovable Sync Immediate	SYN_TIME	0x0000	0xFFFF
Password Management	Single Valued Nonremovable Sync Immediate Operational	SYN_UNKNOWN	0x0000	0xFFFF
Password Minimum Length	Single Valued Nonremovable Sync Immediate	SYN_INTEGER	0x0000	0xFFFF
Password Required	Single Valued Nonremovable Sync Immediate	SYN_BOOLEAN	0x0000	0xFFFF
Password Unique Required	Single Valued Nonremovable Sync Immediate	SYN_BOOLEAN	0x0000	0xFFFF
Passwords Used	Nonremovable Hidden Attribute Sync Immediate	SYN_OCTET_STRING	0x0000	0xFFFF
Path	Nonremovable Sync Immediate	SYN_PATH	0x0000	0xFFFF
Permanent Config Parms	Nonremovable Sync Immediate Public Read Operational	SYN_OCTET_STRING	0x0000	0xFFFF
personalMobile	String Attribute Sync Immediate	SYN_TEL_NUMBER	0x0000	0xFFFF
personalTitle	String Attribute Sync Immediate	SYN_CI_STRING	0x0000	0xFFFF

Table C.2 Continued

ATTRIBUTE NAME	DEFINITION FLAGS	SYNTAX	LOWER LIMIT	UPPER LIMIT
photo	Sync Immediate	SYN_OCTET_STRING	0x0000	0xFFFF
Physical Delivery Office Name	Sized Attribute Nonremovable String Attribute Sync Immediate	SYN_CI_STRING	0x0001	0x0080
Postal Address	Nonremovable Sync Immediate	SYN_PO_ADDRESS	0x0000	0xFFFF
Postal Code	Sized Attribute Nonremovable String Attribute Sync Immediate	SYN_CI_STRING	0x0000	0x0028
Postal Office Box	Sized Attribute Nonremovable String Attribute Sync Immediate	SYN_CI_STRING	0x0000	0x0028
Postmaster	Nonremovable Sync Immediate	SYN_DIST_NAME	0x0000	0xFFFF
preferred DeliveryMethod	Single Valued Sync Immediate	SYN_OCTET_STRING	0x0000	0xFFFF
preferredLanguage	Single Valued String Attribute Sync Immediate	SYN_CI_STRING	0x0000	0xFFFF
preferredName	String Attribute Sync Immediate	SYN_CI_STRING	0x0000	0xFFFF
presentation Address	Single Valued Sync Immediate	SYN_OCTET_STRING	0x0000	0xFFFF
Print Job Configuration	Single Valued Nonremovable Sync Immediate	SYN_STREAM	0x0000	0xFFFF
Print Server	Single Valued Nonremovable Sync Immediate	SYN_TYPED_NAME	0x0000	0xFFFF
Printer	Nonremovable Sync Immediate	SYN_TYPED_NAME	0x0000	0xFFFF
Printer Configuration	Single Valued Nonremovable Sync Immediate	SYN_OCTET_STRING	0x0000	0xFFFF

Table 3.2 Continued

ATTRIBUTE NAME	DEFINITION FLAGS	SYNTAX	LOWER LIMIT	UPPER LIMIT
Printer Control	Single Valued Nonremovable Sync Immediate	SYN_STREAM	0x0000	0xFFFF
Private Key	Single Valued Nonremovable Read-Only Attribute Hidden Attribute Sync Immediate	SYN_OCTET_STRING	0x0000	0xFFFF
Profile	Single Valued Nonremovable Sync Immediate	SYN_DIST_NAME	0x0000	0xFFFF
Profile Membership	Nonremovable Sync Immediate Write Managed	SYN_DIST_NAME	0x0000	0xFFFF
protocol Information	Sync Immediate	SYN_OCTET_STRING	0x0000	0xFFFF
Public Key	Single Valued Nonremovable Read-Only Attribute Sync Immediate Public Read	SYN_OCTET_STRING	0x0000	0xFFFF
Purge Vector	Nonremovable Read-Only Attribute Public Read Per Replica Sync Never Operational	SYN_TIMESTAMP	0x0000	0xFFFF
Queue	Nonremovable Sync Immediate	SYN_TYPED_NAME	0x0000	0xFFFF
Queue Directory	Single Valued Sized Attribute Nonremovable String Attribute Sync Immediate Server Read	SYN_CI_STRING	0x0001	0x00FF
RADIUS:Active Connections	—	SYN_OCTET_STRING	0x0000	0xFFFF
RADIUS:Aged Interval	Single Valued	SYN_INTEGER	0x0000	0xFFFF
RADIUS:Attribute List	Single Valued	SYN_OCTET_STRING	0x0000	0xFFFF

Table C.2   Continued

ATTRIBUTE NAME	DEFINITION FLAGS	SYNTAX	LOWER LIMIT	UPPER LIMIT
RADIUS:Attribute Lists	—	SYN_OCTET_STRING	0x0000	0xFFFF
RADIUS:Client	—	SYN_OCTET_STRING	0x0000	0xFFFF
RADIUS:Common Name Resolution	Single Valued	SYN_INTEGER	0x0000	0xFFFF
RADIUS:Concurrent Limit	Single Valued	SYN_INTEGER	0x0000	0xFFFF
RADIUS:Connection History	—	SYN_OCTET_STRING	0x0000	0xFFFF
RADIUS:DAS Version	Single Valued	SYN_INTEGER	0x0000	0xFFFF
RADIUS:Default Profile	Single Valued String Attribute	SYN_CI_STRING	0x0000	0xFFFF
RADIUS:Dial Access Group	Single Valued	SYN_DIST_NAME	0x0000	0xFFFF
RADIUS:Enable Common Name Login	Single Valued	SYN_BOOLEAN	0x0000	0xFFFF
RADIUS:Enable Dial Access	Single Valued	SYN_BOOLEAN	0x0000	0xFFFF
RADIUS:Interim Accting Timeout	Single Valued	SYN_INTEGER	0x0000	0xFFFF
RADIUS:Lookup Contexts	—	SYN_DIST_NAME	0x0000	0xFFFF
RADIUS:Max DAS History Record	Single Valued	SYN_INTEGER	0x0000	0xFFFF
RADIUS:Maximum History Record	Single Valued	SYN_INTEGER	0x0000	0xFFFF
RADIUS:Password Policy	Single Valued	SYN_INTEGER	0x0000	0xFFFF
RADIUS:Password	Single Valued	SYN_OCTET_STRING	0x0000	0xFFFF
RADIUS:Private Key	Single Valued	SYN_OCTET_STRING	0x0000	0xFFFF
RADIUS:Proxy Context	—	SYN_PATH	0x0000	0xFFFF
RADIUS:Proxy Domain	—	SYN_OCTET_STRING	0x0000	0xFFFF

Table 3.2   Continued

ATTRIBUTE NAME	DEFINITION FLAGS	SYNTAX	LOWER LIMIT	UPPER LIMIT
RADIUS:Proxy Target	—	SYN_OCTET_STRING	0x0000	0xFFFF
RADIUS:Public Key	Single Valued	SYN_OCTET_STRING	0x0000	0xFFFF
RADIUS:Service List	—	SYN_PATH	0x0000	0xFFFF
rbsAssignedRoles	Sync Immediate	SYN_TYPED_NAME	0x0000	0xFFFF
rbsAssignedRoles2	Sync Immediate	SYN_TYPED_NAME	0x0000	0xFFFF
rbsContent	Sync Immediate	SYN_TYPED_NAME	0x0000	0xFFFF
rbsContent Membership	Sync Immediate	SYN_TYPED_NAME	0x0000	0xFFFF
rbsContext	Single Valued Sync Immediate	SYN_DIST_NAME	0x0000	0xFFFF
rbsEntryPoint	Single Valued String Attribute Sync Immediate	SYN_CE_STRING	0x0000	0xFFFF
rbsGadget	Sync Immediate	SYN_DIST_NAME	0x0000	0xFFFF
rbsGALabel	Single Valued Sync Immediate	SYN_OCTET_STRING	0x0000	0xFFFF
rbsMember	Sync Immediate	SYN_TYPED_NAME	0x0000	0xFFFF
rbsOwned Collections	Sync Immediate	SYN_DIST_NAME	0x0000	0xFFFF
rbsOwned Collections2	Sync Immediate	SYN_DIST_NAME	0x0000	0xFFFF
rbsPageMembership	String Attribute Sync Immediate	SYN_CE_STRING	0x0000	0xFFFF
rbsParameters	String Attribute Sync Immediate	SYN_CE_STRING	0x0000	0xFFFF
rbsPath	Sync Immediate	SYN_TYPED_NAME	0x0000	0xFFFF
rbsPortalObject	Sync Immediate	SYN_DIST_NAME	0x0000	0xFFFF
rbsTargetObject Type	String Attribute Sync Immediate	SYN_CI_STRING	0x0000	0xFFFF
rbsTaskRights	Sync Immediate	SYN_OCTET_STRING	0x0000	0xFFFF
rbsTaskTemplates	Sync Immediate	SYN_OCTET_STRING	0x0000	0xFFFF
rbsTaskTemplates URL	Single Valued Sync Immediate	SYN_OCTET_STRING	0x0000	0xFFFF
rbsTrusteeOf	Sync Immediate	SYN_TYPED_NAME	0x0000	0xFFFF

Table C.2   Continued

ATTRIBUTE NAME	DEFINITION FLAGS	SYNTAX	LOWER LIMIT	UPPER LIMIT
rbsType	Single Valued Sized Attribute String Attribute Sync Immediate	SYN_CI_STRING	0x0001	0x0100
rbsURL	Single Valued Sync Immediate	SYN_OCTET_STRING	0x0000	0xFFFF
rbsXMLInfo	Single Valued String Attribute Sync Immediate	SYN_CI_STRING	0x0000	0xFFFF
Received Up To	Nonremovable Read-Only Attribute Sync Immediate Public Read	SYN_TIMESTAMP	0x0000	0xFFFF
ref	String Attribute	SYN_CE_STRING	0x0000	0xFFFF
Reference	Nonremovable Read-Only Attribute Hidden Attribute Per Replica	SYN_DIST_NAME	0x0000	0xFFFF
referralExclude Filter	String Attribute Sync Immediate	SYN_CI_STRING	0x0000	0xFFFF
referralInclude Filter	String Attribute Sync Immediate	SYN_CI_STRING	0x0000	0xFFFF
registeredAddress	String Attribute Sync Immediate	SYN_CI_STRING	0x0000	0xFFFF
Replica	Nonremovable Read-Only Attribute Sync Immediate Public Read	SYN_REPLICA_POINTER	0x0000	0xFFFF
Replica Up To	Nonremovable Read-Only Attribute Public Read Per Replica	SYN_OCTET_STRING	0x0000	0xFFFF
replicationFilter	Single Valued Nonremovable Operational	SYN_OCTET_STRING	0x0000	0xFFFF
Resource	Nonremovable Sync Immediate	SYN_DIST_NAME	0x0000	0xFFFF

Table 3.2   Continued

ATTRIBUTE NAME	DEFINITION FLAGS	SYNTAX	LOWER LIMIT	UPPER LIMIT
Revision	Single Valued Nonremovable Read-Only Attribute Public Read Sync Never Operational	SYN_COUNTER	0x0000	0xFFFF
Role Occupant	Nonremovable Sync Immediate	SYN_DIST_NAME	0x0000	0xFFFF
roomNumber	String Attribute Sync Immediate	SYN_CI_STRING	0x0000	0xFFFF
Run Setup Script	Single Valued	SYN_BOOLEAN	0x0000	0xFFFF
S	Sized Attribute Nonremovable String Attribute Sync Immediate	SYN_CI_STRING	0x0001	0x0080
SA	Sized Attribute Nonremovable String Attribute Sync Immediate	SYN_CI_STRING	0x0001	0x0080
SAP Name	Single Valued Sized Attribute Nonremovable String Attribute Sync Immediate	SYN_CI_STRING	0x0001	0x002F
SAS:Advisory Method Grade	Single Valued String Attribute Public Read	SYN_CI_STRING	0x0000	0xFFFF
SAS:Allow NDS Password Window	Single Valued	SYN_BOOLEAN	0x0000	0xFFFF
SAS:Encryption Type	Single Valued Sync Immediate Server Read	SYN_INTEGER	0x0000	0xFFFF
SAS:Login Client Method NetWare	Single Value Public Read	SYN_STREAM	0x0000	0xFFFFd
SAS:Login Client Method WINNT	Single Valued Public Read	SYN_STREAM	0x0000	0xFFFF
SAS:Login Configuration	Sync Immediate Server Read	SYN_OCTET_STRING	0x0000	0xFFFF
SAS:Login Configuration Key	Sync Immediate Server Read	SYN_OCTET_STRING	0x0000	0xFFFF

Table C.2 Continued

ATTRIBUTE NAME	DEFINITION FLAGS	SYNTAX	LOWER LIMIT	UPPER LIMIT
SAS:Login Method Container DN	Single Valued Public Read	SYN_DIST_NAME	0x0000	0xFFFF
SAS:Login Policy DN	Single Valued Public Read	SYN_DIST_NAME	0x0000	0xFFFF
SAS:Login Policy Update	Single Valued Public Read	SYN_INTEGER	0x0000	0xFFFF
SAS:Login Secret	Sync Immediate Server Read	SYN_OCTET_STRING	0x0000	0xFFFF
SAS:Login Secret Key	Sync Immediate Server Read	SYN_OCTET_STRING	0x0000	0xFFFF
SAS:Login Sequence	String Attribute Public Read	SYN_CI_STRING	0x0000	0xFFFF
SAS:Login Server Method NetWare	Single Valued Public Read	SYN_STREAM	0x0000	0xFFFF
SAS:Login Server Method WINNT	Single Valued Public Read	SYN_STREAM	0x0000	0xFFFF
SAS:Method Identifier	Single Valued Public Read	SYN_OCTET_STRING	0x0000	0xFFFF
SAS:Method Vendor	Single Valued String Attribute Public Read	SYN_CI_STRING	0x0000	0xFFFF
SAS:NDS Password Window	Single Valued	SYN_INTEGER	0x0000	0xFFFF
SAS:PKIStore:Keys	Hidden Attribute Sync Immediate	SYN_OCTET_STRING	0x0000	0xFFFF
SAS:Policy Credentials	Single Valued Server Read	SYN_OCTET_STRING	0x0000	0xFFFF
SAS:Policy Methods	—	SYN_PATH	0x0000	0xFFFF
SAS:Policy Object Version	Single Valued	SYN_INTEGER	0x0000	0xFFFF
SAS:Policy Service Subtypes	—	SYN_PATH	0x0000	0xFFFF
SAS:Policy Services	—	SYN_PATH	0x0000	0xFFFF
SAS:Policy Users	—	SYN_PATH	0x0000	0xFFFF
SAS:SecretStore	Single Valued Sync Immediate	SYN_BOOLEAN	0x0000	0xFFFF

Table 3.2 Continued

ATTRIBUTE NAME	DEFINITION FLAGS	SYNTAX	LOWER LIMIT	UPPER LIMIT
SAS:SecretStore: Data	Hidden Attribute Sync Immediate	SYN_OCTET_STRING	0x0000	0xFFFF
SAS:SecretStore: Key	Single Valued Hidden Attribute Sync Immediate	SYN_OCTET_STRING	0x0000	0xFFFF
SAS:Security DN	Single Valued Sync Immediate Server Read	SYN_DIST_NAME	0x0000	0xFFFF
SAS:Service DN	Single Valued Sync Immediate Server Read	SYN_DIST_NAME	0x0000	0xFFFF
SAS:Vendor Support	Single Valued String Attribute Public Read	SYN_CI_STRING	0x0000	0xFFFF
sasAllowable SubjectNames	String Attribute Sync Immediate Public Read	SYN_CI_STRING	0x0000	0xFFFF
sasAllowNDS PasswordWindow	Single Valued	SYN_BOOLEAN	0x0000	0xFFFF
sasAuthorized LoginSequences	String Attribute Sync Immediate Public Read	SYN_CI_STRING	0x0000	0xFFFF
sasCertificate SearchContainers	Public Read	SYN_DIST_NAME	0x0000	0xFFFF
sasDefaultLogin Sequence	Single Valued String Attribute Sync Immediate Public Read	SYN_CI_STRING	0x0000	0xFFFF
sasLoginClient MethodAIX	Single Valued Public Read	SYN_STREAM	0x0000	0xFFFF
sasLoginClient MethodHPUX	Single Valued Public Read	SYN_STREAM	0x0000	0xFFFF
sasLoginClient MethodLinux	Single Valued Public Read	SYN_STREAM	0x0000	0xFFFF
sasLoginClient Methods390	Single Valued Public Read	SYN_STREAM	0x0000	0xFFFF
sasLoginClient MethodSolaris	Single Valued Public Read	SYN_STREAM	0x0000	0xFFFF

Table C.2   Continued

ATTRIBUTE NAME	DEFINITION FLAGS	SYNTAX	LOWER LIMIT	UPPER LIMIT
sasLoginClient MethodTru64	Single Valued Public Read	SYN_STREAM	0x0000	0xFFFF
sasLoginFailure Delay	Single Valued Sync Immediate Server Read	SYN_INTEGER	0x0000	0xFFFF
sasLoginServer MethodAIX	Single Valued Public Read	SYN_STREAM	0x0000	0xFFFF
sasLoginServer MethodHPUX	Single Valued Public Read	SYN_STREAM	0x0000	0xFFFF
sasLoginServer MethodLinux	Single Valued Public Read	SYN_STREAM	0x0000	0xFFFF
sasLoginServer Methods390	Single Valued Public Read	SYN_STREAM	0x0000	0xFFFF
sasLoginServer MethodSolaris	Single Valued Public Read	SYN_STREAM	0x0000	0xFFFF
sasLoginServer MethodTru64	Single Valued Public Read	SYN_STREAM	0x0000	0xFFFF
sasMethodVersion	Single Valued Sync Immediate Server Read	SYN_INTEGER	0x0000	0xFFFF
sasNDSPassword Window	Single Valued	SYN_INTEGER	0x0000	0xFFFF
sasNMASMethod ConfigData	Single Valued Public Read	SYN_OCTET_STRING	0x0000	0xFFFF
sasNMASProduct Options	Single Valued Sync Immediate Public Read	SYN_OCTET_STRING	0x0000	0xFFFF
sasPolicyMethods	—	SYN_PATH	0x0000	0xFFFF
sasPolicyServices	—	SYN_PATH	0x0000	0xFFFF
sasPolicyUsers	—	SYN_PATH	0x0000	0xFFFF
sasPostLogin MethodContainerDN	Single Valued Public Read	SYN_DIST_NAME	0x0000	0xFFFF
schemaResetLock	Single Valued Nonremovable Operational	SYN_OCTET_STRING	0x0000	0xFFFF
searchGuide	Sync Immediate	SYN_OCTET_STRING	0x0000	0xFFFF

Table 3.2   Continued

ATTRIBUTE NAME	DEFINITION FLAGS	SYNTAX	LOWER LIMIT	UPPER LIMIT
searchSizeLimit	Single Valued Sized Attribute Sync Immediate	SYN_INTEGER	0x0000	0xFFFF
searchTimeLimit	Single Valued Sized Attribute Sync Immediate	SYN_INTEGER	0x0000	0xFFFF
secretary	Sync Immediate	SYN_DIST_NAME	0x0000	0xFFFF
Security Equals	Nonremovable Sync Immediate Server Read Write Managed	SYN_DIST_NAME	0x0000	0xFFFF
Security Flags	Single Valued Nonremovable Sync Immediate	SYN_INTEGER	0x0000	0xFFFF
See Also	Nonremovable Sync Immediate	SYN_DIST_NAME	0x0000	0xFFFF
Serial Number	Sized Attribute Nonremovable String Attribute Sync Immediate	SYN_PR_STRING	0x0001	0x0040
Server	Nonremovable Sync Immediate Server Read	SYN_DIST_NAME	0x0000	0xFFFF
Server Holds	Nonremovable Sync Immediate	SYN_HOLD	0x0000	0xFFFF
Set Password After Create	Single Valued	SYN_BOOLEAN	0x0000	0xFFFF
Setup Script	Single Valued	SYN_STREAM	0x0000	0xFFFF
siteLocation	String Attribute Sync Immediate	SYN_CI_STRING	0x0000	0xFFFF
slConfigData	Single Valued	SYN_STREAM	0x0000	0xFFFF
slConfigList	—	SYN_DIST_NAME	0x0000	0xFFFF
slConfigObject	Single Valued Server Read	SYN_DIST_NAME	0x0000	0xFFFF
snmpGroupDN	Single Valued Sync Immediate	SYN_DIST_NAME	0x0000	0xFFFF
snmpServerList	Sync Immediate	SYN_DIST_NAME	0x0000	0xFFFF
snmpTrapConfig	Single Valued Sync Immediate	SYN_OCTET_STRING	0x0000	0xFFFF

Table C.2   Continued

ATTRIBUTE NAME	DEFINITION FLAGS	SYNTAX	LOWER LIMIT	UPPER LIMIT
snmpTrap Description	Single Valued Sync Immediate	SYN_OCTET_STRING	0x0000	0xFFFF
snmpTrapDisable	Single Valued Sync Immediate	SYN_BOOLEAN	0x0000	0xFFFF
snmpTrapInterval	Single Valued Sync Immediate	SYN_INTEGER	0x0000	0xFFFF
spouse	String Attribute Sync Immediate	SYN_CI_STRING	0x0000	0xFFFF
sslEnableMutual Authentication	Single Valued Sync Immediate	SYN_BOOLEAN	0x0000	0xFFFF
Status	Single Valued Nonremovable Sync Immediate Public Read	SYN_INTEGER	0x0000	0xFFFF
Supported Connections	Single Valued Nonremovable Sync Immediate	SYN_INTEGER	0x0000	0xFFFF
Supported Gateway	Sized Attribute Nonremovable String Attribute Sync Immediate	SYN_CI_STRING	0x0001	0x1000
Supported Services	Sized Attribute Nonremovable String Attribute Sync Immediate	SYN_CI_STRING	0x0001	0x0040
Supported Typefaces	Sized Attribute Nonremovable String Attribute Sync Immediate	SYN_CI_STRING	0x0001	0x0040
supported Algorithms	Sync Immediate	SYN_OCTET_STRING	0x0000	0xFFFF
supported Application Context	String Attribute Sync Immediate	SYN_CI_STRING	0x0000	0xFFFF
Surname	Sized Attribute Nonremovable String Attribute Sync Immediate Public Read	SYN_CI_STRING	0x0001	0x0040

Table 3.2   Continued

ATTRIBUTE NAME	DEFINITION FLAGS	SYNTAX	LOWER LIMIT	UPPER LIMIT
Synchronization Tolerance	Nonremovable Sync Immediate Public Read Operational	SYN_TIMESTAMP	0x0000	0xFFFF
Synchronized Up To	Nonremovable Read-Only Attribute Public Read Per Replica	SYN_TIMESTAMP	0x0000	0xFFFF
syncPanePoint	Single Valued Nonremovable Read-Only Attribute Public Read Per Replica Operational	SYN_OCTET_STRING	0x0000	0xFFFF
syncWindowVector	Single Valued Nonremovable Read-Only Attribute Public Read Per Replica Operational	SYN_OCTET_STRING	0x0000	0xFFFF
T	Sized Attribute Nonremovable String Attribute Sync Immediate Operational	SYN_CI_STRING	0x0001	0x0020
Telephone Number	Nonremovable String Attribute Sync Immediate	SYN_TEL_NUMBER	0x0000	0xFFFF
teletexTerminal Identifier	Sync Immediate	SYN_OCTET_STRING	0x0000	0xFFFF
telexNumber	Sync Immediate	SYN_OCTET_STRING	0x0000	0xFFFF
Timezone	Single Valued Nonremovable Public Read	SYN_OCTET_STRING	0x0000	0xFFFF
Title	Sized Attribute Nonremovable String Attribute Sync Immediate	SYN_CI_STRING	0x0001	0x0040
tollFreePhone Number	String Attribute Sync Immediate	SYN_TEL_NUMBER	0x0000	0xFFFF

Table C.2   Continued

ATTRIBUTE NAME	DEFINITION FLAGS	SYNTAX	LOWER LIMIT	UPPER LIMIT
transitionGroupDN	Single Valued Sync Immediate	SYN_DIST_NAME	0x0000	0xFFFF
Transitive Vector	Nonremovable Read-Only Attribute Sync Immediate Public Read Sync Never Operational	SYN_OCTET_STRING	0x0000	0xFFFF
treeReferral	Nonremovable Operational	SYN_OCTET_STRING	0x0000	0xFFFF
Trustees Of New Object	—	SYN_OBJECT_ACL	0x0000	0xFFFF
Type Creator Map	Single Valued Nonremovable Sync Immediate	SYN_STREAM	0x0000	0xFFFF
UID	Single Valued Nonremovable Sync Immediate	SYN_INTEGER	0x0000	0xFFFF
uniqueID	Sized Attribute Nonremovable String Attribute Sync Immediate Public Read	SYN_CI_STRING	0x0001	0x0040
Unknown	Nonremovable	SYN_UNKNOWN	0x0000	0xFFFF
Unknown Auxiliary Class	Sized Attribute Nonremovable String Attribute	SYN_CI_STRING	0x0001	0x0020
Unknown Base Class	Single Valued Sized Attribute Nonremovable String Attribute	SYN_CI_STRING	0x0001	0x0020
Used By	Nonremovable Read-Only Attribute Sync Immediate Server Read Operational	SYN_PATH	0x0000	0xFFFF
User	Nonremovable Sync Immediate Server Read	SYN_DIST_NAME	0x0000	0xFFFF

Table 3.2   Continued

ATTRIBUTE NAME	DEFINITION FLAGS	SYNTAX	LOWER LIMIT	UPPER LIMIT
userCertificate	Sync Immediate Public Read	SYN_OCTET_STRING	0x0000	0xFFFF
userPKCS12	Sync Immediate	SYN_OCTET_STRING	0x0000	0xFFFF
userSMIME Certificate	Sync Immediate	SYN_OCTET_STRING	0x0000	0xFFFF
Uses	Nonremovable Read-Only Attribute Sync Immediate Server Read Operational	SYN_PATH	0x0000	0xFFFF
vehicleInformation	String Attribute Sync Immediate	SYN_CI_STRING	0x0000	0xFFFF
vendorAddress	String Attribute Sync Immediate	SYN_CI_STRING	0x0000	0xFFFF
vendorName	String Attribute Sync Immediate	SYN_CI_STRING	0x0000	0xFFFF
vendorPhoneNumber	String Attribute Sync Immediate	SYN_TEL_NUMBER	0x0000	0xFFFF
Version	Single Valued Sized Attribute Nonremovable String Attribute Sync Immediate Public Read	SYN_CI_STRING	0x0001	0x0040
Volume	Single Valued Nonremovable Sync Immediate	SYN_DIST_NAME	0x0000	0xFFFF
Volume Space Restrictions	—	SYN_PATH	0x0000	0xFFFF
WANMAN:Cost	—	SYN_OCTET_STRING	0x0000	0xFFFF
WANMAN:Default Cost	Single Valued	SYN_INTEGER	0x0000	0xFFFF
WANMAN:LAN Area Membership	Single Valued	SYN_DIST_NAME	0x0000	0xFFFF
WANMAN:WAN Policy	—	SYN_OCTET_LIST	0x0000	0xFFFF
workforceID	String Attribute Sync Immediate	SYN_CI_STRING	0x0000	0xFFFF

Table C.2 Continued

ATTRIBUTE NAME	DEFINITION FLAGS	SYNTAX	LOWER LIMIT	UPPER LIMIT
x121Address	Sized Attribute String Attribute Sync Immediate	SYN_NU_STRING	0x0001	0x000F
x500Unique Identifier	Sync Immediate	SYN_OCTET_STRING	0x0000	0xFFFF

eDirectory Resources

Throughout this book, we refer to a number of different third-party products and eDirectory resources. This appendix contains additional resource information to help you expand your knowledge of eDirectory. This list is by no means exhaustive, but it provides a good starting point.

Novell Resources

- ▶ "Novell's eDirectory Product Page"—www.novell.com/products/edirectory

- ▶ "Novell's eDirectory Cool Solutions Page" —www.novell.com/coolsolutions/nds

- ▶ "Novell DeveloperNet Program" —http://developer.novell.com

- ▶ "Novell Forge (Open Source Projects) " —http://forge.novell.com

- ▶ "Novell Advanced Technical Training (ATT) " —www.novell.com/training/pep/att/def.html

- ▶ "Novell Connection Magazine" —www.novell.com/connectionmagazine

- ▶ "Novell LogicSource Documents for eDirectory" — http://support.novell.com/subscriptions/subscription_products/list_all_ls.html

- ▶ "Novell Application Notes" —www.novell.com/appnotes

- ▶ "Novell Technical Support (knowledgebase, patches, updates, and so on)"—http://support.novell.com

- ▶ "Novell DeveloperNet Support Forums"—http://developer-forums.novell.com

- "Novell Product Support Forums" —`http://support.novell.com/forums`, `http://support-forums.novell.com`, and `nntp://forums.novell.com`

- "Novell NDS/eDirectory Schema Information" — `http://developer.novell.com/ndk/doc_ndslib.htm`

Third-Party Tools

- bv-Control for NDS eDirectory, Bindview Corporation— `www.bindview.com`

- SecureConsole, Protocom Development Pty Systems— `www.protocom.com`

- eDirectory Performance Pack, NetPro Computing, Inc.— `www.netpro.com`

- GNU awk (gawk), GNU Software—`ftp://ftp.gnu.org/gnu/gawk` (DOS versions of awk are widely available on the Internet. One such repository is `www.simtel.com/pub/pd/51371.html`.)

- NDS ToolKit, DreamLAN Network Consulting, Ltd.— `www.DreamLAN.com` and `ftp://ftp.DreamLAN.com`

- JRBUtils/JRBImprt, JRB Software—`www.jrbsoftware.com`

- LT Auditor+, Blue Lance—`www.bluelance.com`

- Wolfgang's Tools Network, Wolfgang Schreiber— `www.geocities.com/wstools`

- TaskMaster/TaskMaster Lite, avanti technology, inc.— `www.avanti-tech.com`

- Password Policy Manager for NDS/eDirectory, Connectotel Ltd.— `www.connectotel.com`

Third-Party NDS/eDirectory Resources

- "Jim Henderson's NDS information page"—`http://hendersj.dyndns.org`

▶ "Connectotel Ltd's NDS resource page"—
www.connectotel.com/ctres.html

▶ "Novell shareware and freeware collection"—
www.novellshareware.com

▶ "NetWare shareware and freeware files"—www.netwarefiles.com and
www.netwarefiles.de

Books

▶ *Novell's NDS Developer's Guide,* by Chris Andrew, et al., Novell Press,
ISBN 0-7645-4557-4

▶ *Novell's NDS Basics,* by Peter Kuo, Novell Press, ISBN 0-7645-4726-7

▶ *Novell's LDAP Developer's Guide*, by Roger G. Harrison, Jim
Sermersheim, and Steve Trottier, Novell Press, ISBN 0-7645-4720-8

▶ *Novell's Four Principles of NDS Design*, by Jeffrey F. Hughes and Blair W.
Thomas, Novell Press, ISBN 0-7645-4522-1

▶ *Effective eDirectory Design & Proactive Analysis*, by Jeffery F. Hughes,
DirectoryDesign, ISBN 0-9717-4200-6

▶ *The Complete Guide to Novell Directory Services*, by David Kearns and
Brian Iverson, Sybex, ISBN 0-7821-1823-2

▶ *The AWK Programming Language,* by Alfred V. Aho, Brian W.
Kernighan, and Peter J. Weinberger, Addison-Wesley, ISBN 0-201-
07981-X

▶ *Programming PERL*, by Larry Wall, Tom Christiansen, and Jon Orwant,
O'Reilly & Associates, ISBN 0-5960-0027-8

Humor

▶ *The Official Dilbert Website by Scott Adams—Dilbert, Dogbert and
Coworkers! —*www.unitedmedia.com/comics/dilbert

INDEX

J - K